Encyclopedia of
MEDIA VIOLENCE

Editorial Board

Encyclopedia of
MEDIA VIOLENCE

EDITED BY
MATTHEW S. EASTIN
The University of Texas at Austin

⑤SAGE reference

Los Angeles | London | New Delhi
Singapore | Washington DC

Los Angeles | London | New Delhi
Singapore | Washington DC

FOR INFORMATION:

SAGE Publications, Inc.
2455 Teller Road
Thousand Oaks, California 91320
E-mail: order@sagepub.com

SAGE Publications Ltd.
1 Oliver's Yard
55 City Road
London, EC1Y 1SP
United Kingdom

SAGE Publications India Pvt. Ltd.
B 1/I 1 Mohan Cooperative Industrial Area
Mathura Road, New Delhi 110 044
India

SAGE Publications Asia-Pacific Pte. Ltd.
3 Church Street
#10-04 Samsung Hub
Singapore 049483

Acquisitions Editor: Jim Brace-Thompson
Developmental Editor: Carole Maurer
Production Editor: David C. Felts
Reference Systems Manager: Leticia Gutierrez
Reference Systems Coordinators: Laura Notton,
    Anna Villasenor
Copy Editor: Pam Suwinsky
Typesetter: Hurix Systems Pvt. Ltd.
Proofreader: Talia Greenberg
Indexer: Wendy Allex
Cover Designer: Bryan Fishman
Marketing Manager: Carmel Schrire

Printed in the United States of America.

Library of Congress Cataloging-in-Publication Data

Encyclopedia of media violence / edited by Matthew S. Eastin, The University of Texas at Austin.

pages cm
Includes bibliographical references and index.

ISBN 978-1-4129-3685-9

1. Violence in mass media—Encyclopedias.
2. Mass media—Social aspects—Encyclopedias. I. Eastin, Matthew S.

P96.V5E59 2013
303.603—dc23   2013018904

SFI Certified Sourcing
www.sfiprogram.org
SFI-00453

13 14 15 16 17 10 9 8 7 6 5 4 3 2 1

Contents

List of Entries

Reader's Guide

The Reader's Guide is provided to assist readers in locating articles on related topics. It classifies articles into seven general topical categories: general aggression; media content; media effects; media policy; research process; society and media; and theories of media influence. Entries may be listed under more than one topic.

General Aggression

Aggression, Definition and Assessment of
Aggression, Risk Factors for
Aggression and Affect
Aggression and Anger
Aggression and Attachment
Aggression and Brain Functioning
Aggression and Culture
Aggression in Youth
Aggressive Behavior
Aggressive Personality
Bullying, Definition and Laws of
Cognition: Schemas and Scripts
Cognitive Psychology of Violence
Cognitive Script Theory and the Dynamics of Cognitive Scripting
Cyberbullying, Definition and Effects of
Gender and Aggression
Genetics of Aggressive Behavior
Group Aggression
Memory and Violence
Priming Theory
Psychobiology of Violence
Psychopathology and Susceptibility to Violence
Reasons for Consuming Violent Entertainment
Relational Aggression
Trait Aggression

Media Content

Advertising, Violent Content in
Arousal and Aggressive Content, Theory and Psychology of
Character Development Within Violent Content
Competition, Sports, and Video Games
Cultivating Content and Social Representation of Violence
Cyberbullying, Violent Content in
Drench Hypothesis
Fantasy Genre, Violence and Aggression in
Films, Representation of Violence and Its Effects in
Grand Theft Auto
Media Violence, Definitions and Context of
Music Videos and Lyrics, Violent Content in
National Television Violence Study
Pornography, Violent Content in
Realism of Violence Content, Real-World Violence on Television, and Their Effects
Sexualized Aggression
Sports, Violence and Aggression in
Stereotyping in Violent Media Content
Television Violence
Violence, Definition of
Violent Artistic Expression
Virtual Reality, Violent Content in

Media Effects

Attitude, Effects of Media Violence on
Audience Interpretation of Media Violence, Effects of
Bobo Doll Studies
Comedic Violence, Effects of
Demographic Effects
Desensitization Effects on Society
Developmental Effects

Theories of Media Influence

Boundary Testing
Catharsis Theory
Cognitive Script Theory and the Dynamics of
　Cognitive Scripting
Cultivation Theory
Drench Effects From Video Games

Excitation-Transfer Theory
Flow Theory
Forbidden Fruit Hypothesis
Lineation Theory
Presence Theory
Priming Theory
Social Cognitive Theory
Transportation Theory

About the Editor

Matthew S. Eastin (PhD, Michigan State University) is an associate professor in the Department of Advertising and Public Relations at The University of Texas at Austin. His research focuses on media behavior. From this perspective, he investigates message development, information processing, and the social and psychological factors associated with the use and effects of newer technology. In particular, Eastin has focused much of his research on video game engagement, including violence. Eastin has published approximately 70 research manuscripts. The *Encyclopedia of Media Violence* will be his third edited book.

Contributors

Robert Abelman
Cleveland State University

Ellen R. Albertson
Fielding Graduate University

Craig A. Anderson
Iowa State University

Kathryn B. Anderson
Our Lady of the Lake University

Osei Appiah
The Ohio State University

Marios N. Avraamides
University of Cyprus

C. Mo Bahk
California State University, San Bernardino

Albert Bandura
Stanford University

Bruce D. Bartholow
University of Missouri

Elizabeth Behm-Morawitz
University of Missouri

Katharina-Maria Behr
University of California, Santa Barbara

Leonard Berkowitz
University of Wisconsin–Madison (Retired)

Gregory Blackburn
University of Massachusetts Amherst

Nicholas David Bowman
West Virginia University

Cheryl Campanella Bracken
Cleveland State University

Paul F. Brain
Swansea University

Jeffrey E. Brand
Bond University

Laura F. Bright
Texas Christian University

Kevin Browne
University of Nottingham

Julie Cajigas
Cleveland State University

Clay Calvert
University of Florida

Esther Calvete
University of Deusto

David S. Chester
University of Kentucky

Vincent Cicchirillo
The University of Texas at Austin

Jenna L. Clark
University of North Carolina at Chapel Hill

Dov Cohen
University of Illinois

Debra L. Corey
Our Lady of the Lake University

Teresa Correa
Diego Portales University

Juliann Cortese
Florida State University

Sarah M. Coyne
Brigham Young University

Nicole Cunningham
The University of Texas at Austin

Menno D. T. De Jong
University of Twente

Matt DeLisi
Iowa State University

James Denny
Cleveland State University

Thomas F. Denson
The University of New South Wales

C. Nathan DeWall
University of Kentucky

Karen E. Dill-Shackleford
Fielding Graduate University

Edward Donnerstein
The University of Arizona

Mary Elizabeth Dunn
The University of Texas at Austin

Matthew S. Eastin
The University of Texas at Austin

Allison Eden
VU University Amsterdam

Bobbie Eisenstock
California State University

Christopher R. Engelhardt
University of Missouri

Kostas A. Fanti
University of Cyprus

Allan Fenigstein
Kenyon College

Corinne Ferdon
Centers for Disease Control and Prevention

Karin M. Fikkers
University of Amsterdam

Rachel M. Flynn
University of California, Riverside

Catherine E. Goodall
Kent State University

Jordy F. Gosselt
University of Twente

Donald S. Grant
Fielding Graduate University

Melanie C. Green
University of North Carolina at Chapel Hill

Bradley S. Greenberg
Michigan State University

Jennifer L. Gregg
University of Louisville

Robert P. Griffiths
The Ohio State University

Matthew Grizzard
Michigan State University

Christopher Groves
Iowa State University

Gert Martin Hald
University of Copenhagen

Richard Jackson Harris
Kansas State University

Amir Hetsroni
Ariel University

Jay Hmielowski
The University of Arizona

James D. Ivory
Virginia Tech

Seung-A Annie Jin
Boston College

Tim Jones
Memorial University Newfoundland

LeeAnn Kahlor
The University of Texas at Austin

Robin M. Kowalski
Clemson University

Barbara Krahé
Universität Potsdam

Michael Kurtz
Cleveland State University

Robert LaRose
Michigan State University

Lisa LaViers
Emory University

Allison Lazard
The University of Texas at Austin

Seungae Lee
The University of Texas at Austin

Seung-ha Lee
National Youth Policy Institute in South Korea

Anthony F. Lemieux
Georgia State University

Melinda A. Lemke
The University of Texas at Austin

Jason Levitt
Georgia State University

Robert Joel Lewis
The University of Texas at Austin

Susan P. Limber
Clemson University

Jennifer Ruh Linder
Linfield College

Amanda Mabry
The University of Texas at Austin

Chad Mahood
The University of Texas at San Antonio

Galit Marmor-Lavie
The University of Texas at Austin

Dana Mastro
University of California, Santa Barbara

Christopher J. McKinley
Montclair State University

W. James Potter
Knowledge Assets, Inc.

Sara Prot
Iowa State University

Rebekah A. Richert
University of California, Riverside

Karyn Riddle
University of Wisconsin–Madison

Anthony J. Roberto
Arizona State University

Muniba Saleem
University of Michigan-Dearborn

Meghan S. Sanders
Louisiana State University

Kevin W. Saunders
Michigan State University

Joanne Savage
American University

Angela Scarpa
Virginia Tech

Erica Scharrer
University of Massachusetts Amherst

Jaclyn Schildkraut
Texas State University–San Marcos

John L. Sherry
Michigan State University

Paul Skalski
Cleveland State University

Peter K. Smith
Goldsmiths, University of London

Kristin Stewart
The University of Texas at Austin

Carmen Stitt
California State University, Sacramento

Victor C. Strasburger
Mediatrix LLC

Robert Sweeny
Indiana University of Pennsylvania

Ron Tamborini
Michigan State University

Joel Timmer
Texas Christian University

Riva Tukachinsky
Chapman University

Monique Mitchell Turner
The George Washington University

Patti M. Valkenburg
University of Amsterdam

Joris J. van Hoof
University of Twente

Edward T. Vieira Jr.
Simmons School of Management

Zheng Wang
The Ohio State University

Wayne Warburton
Macquarie University

René Weber
University of California, Santa Barbara

Kevin D. Williams
Mississippi State University

Laura C. Wilson
Virginia Tech

Jay Wood
Georgia State University

Paul J. Wright
Indiana University

Mu Wu
Pennsylvania State University

Marjorie Yambor
Western Kentucky University

Melissa M. Yang
Endicott College

Paul Zube
Ferris State University

Introduction

Topic Relevance

There is a rich history of research looking at the relationship between media and violence. From the early experimental research conducted by Albert Bandura in the 1960s to the initial cultivation research by George Gerbner in the 1970s, researchers, politicians, and the press have cautiously sought to understand the relationship between media exposure and violent outcomes, whether they are affective, cognitive, or behavioral. Yet never before has media been under more scrutiny over violent content. Recent tragedies such as the mass shooting at a movie theater in Colorado in July 2012, in which 12 people were killed, and the school shooting at Sandy Hook Elementary School in Connecticut in December 2012, in which 20 children and 6 adults were killed, have kept the topic of media violence in the popular press. From rap music to television to video games, media content (especially violent content) has fallen under great scrutiny as the world tries to make sense of needless violence. Although television research dominated the academic literature and public discourse during the 1970s, 1980s, and 1990s, an increasing literature base investigating video games has been growing since the early 2000s. Video games are thought to increase audience engagement and thus potential effects of content exposure. For instance, although television offers audiences the opportunity to watch acts of violence, video games allow audiences to perform violent acts through their characters. Moreover, with the relatively recent diffusion of technologies such as smartphones, new topics such as cyberbullying have spurred new research agendas.

There has been an overwhelming amount of research, opinions, and perspectives on the topic. In addition to communication research, other disciplines such as sociology, psychology, and media create a diverse interdisciplinary research perspective on the topic of media violence. Recently, research looking at functional magnetic resonance imaging (fMRI) data from violent media exposure has pointed to a more rigorous approach to the research agenda.

Defining the Encyclopedia

Although there have been books and articles related to the subject of media violence, this encyclopedia is the most comprehensive look at the subject. To avoid confusion throughout the encyclopedia, I propose a working definition of *aggression*. For this, I generally speak to Craig Anderson and Brad Bushman's definition of aggression as "any behavior directed toward another individual that is carried out with the proximate (immediate) intent to cause harm. In addition, the perpetrator must believe that the behavior will harm the target, and that the target is motivated to avoid the behavior" (2002, p. 28). By providing readers with a platform definition, I am not trying to exclude other authors' definitions; rather, I hope readers will be able to broadly position their expectations as they read through many of the entries.

To this end, to add a comprehensive perspective, the encyclopedia seeks to help readers broadly understand the topic of violence and media. Unlike other publications that have looked at this topic, this encyclopedia approaches the topic as it relates specifically within each medium as well as more broadly within the fields of psychology, sociology, and communication. Rather than simply pointing out effects from each medium, the encyclopedia allows users to read entries on topics such as the culture of violence, psychobiology of violence, and psychopathology of violence, to name a few. Moreover, with entries on narrative, moral development, memory, methodologies of investigation, and general effect sizes, this encyclopedia allows readers to look beyond current perspectives to a newer media or perhaps a new agenda that will, we hope, provide greater precision in understanding the influence of violent media exposure on the individual audience.

Organization of the Entries

Readers will be able to examine entries that explore theory, research, and debates as related to media violence in relatively jargon-free and balanced perspectives. There are 135 entries listed in alphabetical order from A to Z. Entries are 3,000, 2,000, or 1,000 words in length. Longer entries (3,000 words) are well-developed concepts or ideas and represent a complete coverage of the topic area. Entries that are 2,000 words, while core to the field, are less developed and focus more on the current thinking on the topics. Finally, shorter entries (1,000 words) represent topics that require less depth and more precision for content delivery. Each entry is grounded in a theoretical perspective or core literature.

In addition, the Reader's Guide at the front of the encyclopedia, which classifies entries by general topic category, will assist readers in locating related entries. The Reader's Guide provides seven general topic categories: General Aggression; Media Content; Media Effects; Media Policy; Research Process; Society and Media; and Theories of Media Influence.

Acknowledgments

This encyclopedia was developed over more than one year and required the cooperation of many people. The SAGE group consisting of Jim Brace-Thompson (senior acquisitions editor), Carole Maurer (senior developmental editor), and Leticia Gutierrez (reference systems supervisor) tirelessly worked to develop and keep this project moving forward. In addition to the SAGE group, I thank Pam Suwinsky for her work on the final review of this encyclopedia. I thank each of the editorial board members: Craig Anderson, Vincent Cicchirillo, Bradley Greenberg, Dana Mastro, and Ron Tamborini. Each editorial board member was instrumental in identifying authors and crafting the headword list. They each also contributed entries as experts in their respected fields.

I also thank my wife, Emily Eastin; my son, Johnathan Eastin; and my daughter, Anna Eastin, for dealing with the continual motion of this project. Many holidays and vacations were spent with me working to make sure the encyclopedia was finished. I also thank my mother- and father-in-law, Colleen and Robert Geiger, for their support throughout the editorial process and my career. Finally, and perhaps most important, I thank my dad, Harold Eastin; without his support I would not be where I am today. He has always been a voice of support and inspiration. Although media no doubt has had a socializing influence, there is no better window into who I am than my dad. Thanks, Dad!

Matthew S. Eastin

Reference

Anderson, C. A., & Bushman, B. J. (2002). Human aggression. *Annual Review of Psychology, 53*(1), 27–51.

ADVERTISING, INFLUENCE ON SOCIETY

Public concern about violence in advertising is persistent and increasing, prompting greater scrutiny by authorities responsible for responding to complaints about advertising. This entry examines violent advertising from two perspectives: (1) the use of violent advertisements by advertisers and (2) the possible effects, both positive and negative, of viewer exposure to violent content in advertisements.

The Use of Violence in Advertising—How Much, Why, and How

Research on the frequency of violent content in advertising is surprisingly sparse, particularly given concerns about its possible effects. Researchers tend to study the frequency of violent advertising using content analyses of both broadcast and print media. The use of many different definitions of violence in these studies cause estimates of the prevalence of violence in advertising to vary widely, ranging from about 3% in general programming to 62% in food ads aimed at children.

Violence has also been used in different types of advertising appeals such as fear appeals (e.g., for self-defense products), informational appeals (e.g., for products that have a violent component, such as certain video games), and shock appeals (e.g., some fashion advertisements). Fear appeals attempt to frighten target audience members in order to motivate them to take appropriate precautionary, defensive action. Violent executions have been used to instill fear in viewers; this fear arousal has been found to enhance interest in the ad, create favorable attitude toward the ad, and influence behavioral intentions. The content of informational advertising emphasizes facts, learning, and logical persuasion. In general, informational appeals assume that target audience members are open to the information provided in the advertisement and will then use the information to make a decision about the subject of the advertising. Since some products, services, or ideas have a violent component (e.g., video games, sporting events), the use of violent content in an advertisement can be viewed as an informational appeal. Shock appeals deliberately startle and upset audiences; oftentimes this is accomplished through gratuitous violence. Advertisers use shock appeals for several reasons, including the following: to capture audience attention; to attract media interest that will result in free publicity; to raise awareness; to affect attitudes; to enhance recall; to influence behaviors; and to increase sales and profits.

Only a few studies have examined the effectiveness of advertising with violent content. In a semiotic analysis of three violent fashion advertisements appearing in magazines, Svante Andersson and colleagues found that respondent interpretations of the violent content were different and more negative than advertisers expected. Using experimental methods, Barrie Gunter, Adrian Furnham, and Eleni Pappa found that the violent version of a target advertisement was much better remembered than the nonviolent version when it appeared in a violent film clip. However, Brad J. Bushman and Angelica M. Bonacci showed that violent ads were no more memorable than were neutral ads.

Advertisers seem to use violence for a variety of reasons: to capture attention, raise awareness, provide information, affect attitudes, enhance recall, and influence behavior. It is unclear, though, whether violence in advertising is actually effective, because only a few dependent variables have been tested and the results of the effectiveness studies have been inconsistent.

The Possible Societal Effects of Exposure to Violent Advertising

A debate about the societal consequences of advertising appeared in the *Journal of Marketing* in the mid-1980s. Despite their disagreement on the effects of advertising, Richard Pollay and Morris Holbrook both described advertising as pervasive and environmental, and an important social and cultural force. Holbrook, however, defended advertising as diverse, promoting both positive and negative values; whereas Pollay critiqued advertising as a collective, monolithic force that promoted materialism and greed, degraded people, subverted core values, and desensitized people to negative behaviors such as violence.

Unlike programming that is designed to entertain, advertisements, by their very nature, are designed to be memorable and to persuade. Thus, behaviors depicted in ads are often put forth as something to aspire to or be emulated by a target consumer. Furthermore, associating violence with the sale of products or services may dehumanize and commodify violence while desensitizing consumers toward it. The effects of violent content in advertising, therefore, may be more consequential than violent content in television programming. While violence in advertising has received little attention, studies linking other types of advertising content (e.g., smoking) to harmful attitudes and subsequent behaviors of children and adolescents lead many to hypothesize that violence in advertising may also have negative outcomes.

Although most of the research focuses on the harmful effects of advertising violence, one positive theme has been noted. Some articles in the trade press contend that there are potentially positive societal benefits resulting from advertisements with violent themes. For example, Bennetton advertisements using violent imagery have been acclaimed by some for raising the awareness of such issues as racism, war, and the death penalty while being criticized by others for creating negative personal consequences such as mean world perceptions and acceptance of aggressive behavior.

The paradox of violent advertising lies within the negative effects of exposure to violent content in the media in general. These negative effects include desensitization to violence; increased mean world perceptions; and heightened anxiety. Others point to situations when exposure to violent content has positive effects such as increased processing of prosocial messages; awareness of real-life issues such as war, crime, and delinquency; and/or the reinforcement of societal rules and regulations against violence. There is still much work to be done by researchers to fully understand the effects of exposure to violent content in advertising.

Tim Jones

See also Advertising, Violent Content in; Advertising Laws Regarding Violent and Aggressive Content; Cultivation Theory; Desensitization Effects on Society; Marketing of Violence; Television Violence

Further Readings

Andersson, S., Hedelin, A., Nilsson, A., & Welander, C. (2004). Violent advertising in fashion marketing. *Journal of Fashion Marketing and Management, 8*(1), 96–112.

Bushman, B. J., & Bonacci, A. M. (2002). Violence and sex impair memory for television ads. *Journal of Applied Psychology, 87*(3), 557–564.

Gunter, B., Furnham, A., & Pappa, E. (2005). Effects of television violence on memory for violent and nonviolent advertising. *Journal of Applied Social Psychology, 35*(8), 1680–1697.

Holbrook, M. B. (1987). Mirror, mirror, on the wall, what's unfair in the reflections on advertising? *Journal of Marketing, 51*(3), 95–103.

Kanti, P. V., & Smith, L. J. (1994). Television commercials in violent programming: An experimental evaluation of their effects on children. *Journal of the Academy of Marketing Science, 22*(4), 34–35.

Pollay, R. W. (1986, April). The distorted mirror: Reflections on the unintended consequences of advertising. *Journal of Marketing, 50*, 18–36.

Violence in advertising. (2010, Winter). Special issue. *Journal of Advertising, 39*(4).

ADVERTISING, VIOLENT CONTENT IN

For several decades researchers have been documenting the appearance of violence in the popular media and particularly in television shows and movies, but less attention has been given to the presentation of this material in paid advertisements or commercials. This entry reviews the studies that did delve into this issue and discusses the conclusions that stem from these works.

Why Should We Study the Presentation of Violence in Advertising?

Documenting the frequency with which violence appears in the media and the context in which this material shows up is important because media portrayals help to shape consumers' conceptions of reality (for review, see Comstock & Scharrer, 1999). Although researchers disagree over the size of the effect of media violence and its practical implications on daily life, several meta-analyses have shown that featuring violence in popular media outlets increases, to some extent, aggressive behavior, fearfulness, distrust, desensitization, frustration, and pessimism (see, e.g., Bushman & Anderson, 2001). The appearance of violence in advertising may not lead directly to violent reactions, but it may yield a considerable cultivation effect. As Kim Sheehan (2004) demonstrates, people who are at least partly inoculated to the commercial message itself (by their awareness of the advertiser's intentions) remain more defenseless to internalizing social norms regarding aggression that go beyond the purchase of specific products and services. The fact that advertising—as opposed to television shows, radio interviews, or newspaper articles—constitutes a content sphere to which large publics are exposed regardless of their specific media preferences intensifies the need to know how violence is presented in this channel.

Content Analyses of Violence in Advertising

Research done over decades by George Gerbner, Nancy Signorielli, Bradley S. Greenberg, Barrie Gunter, and others, and confirmed recently in a meta-analysis conducted by Amir Hetsroni, shows that the level of violence in mainstream fictional media outlets has been high for decades, with only limited ebb and flow. Since the late 1990s, the use of gory images in lieu of sterile views of aggression has increased, but violent content in mainstream television programming and feature films is still more often presented in a sanitized manner, with just a limited portrayal of death and a preponderance of successful single-handed assaults of lonesome heroes. Violent scripts rarely place the perpetrators'

actions in meaningful context, nor do they portray the long-term effects of their aggressive behavior. This assists in creating an image of "justified aggression" that appeals favorably to viewers.

Studies that have counted the occurrences of violence in television commercials (at the time of writing, no content analysis of violence in advertisements in other media outlets could be found in the literature) found a low rate. An analysis of U.S. network commercials from the 1996–1997 season detected the presence of violent content in 2.8% of the ads, about half of which took place in a socially appropriate context such as sports (Maguire, Sandage & Weatherby, 2000). Mary Strom Larson (2003) coded U.S. network and non-network commercials that feature children broadcast in the 1997–1998 season and found a slightly higher frequency of physical aggression (4.1%). A European study by Moniek Buijzen and Patti M. Valkenburg (2002), who coded Dutch commercials from the late 1990s that targeted children, teens, and adult viewers, found that more than one-third of the ads were aimed at children, approximately 15% of the ads were aimed at teens, and nearly 5% of the ads that targeted adults included an action-adventure theme, but physical violence appeared in barely one-tenth of these action-adventure ads. Research conducted in 2010 by Hetsroni applied content analysis to over 3,000 U.S. and Israeli commercials from the mid-2000s that were aired during primetime by major mainstream stations. Violence of any type appeared in less than 2.5% of the U.S. ads and in less than 1.5% of the Israeli ads. Minor violence (e.g., physical threat, vandalism, bare-handed assault) was responsible for most of the violent content. Major violence (e.g., rape, act of war, kidnapping) was less common, with the exception of shooting. Most of the violence was presented in a humorous manner, thereby defining the commercial fare as TV-G (suitable for all ages) violence-wise. Furthermore, violence appeared rather infrequently, in approximately 1 out of every 40 ads in the United States and in 1 out of every 65 ads in Israel.

According to these studies, male characters are responsible for three-quarters of the violent acts that are portrayed in advertising. Here, the implied message may reinforce the belief that violence is not for girls; however, such association between gender and violence reflects what popular programming, particularly in the United States, has been portraying for decades and is consistent with the crime statistics of Western countries.

Sexual violence is almost entirely absent from advertising, perhaps because advertisers are afraid that dealing with exceptionally objectionable content may alienate audiences (Hetsroni, 2011). This assumption is in line with a more general framework offered by Maguire and colleagues (2000) to explicate the low rate of violence in mainstream television advertising. First, as proven empirically by James Strong and Khalid Dubas (1993), violence can provoke fear to an extent that becomes counterproductive to the advertiser's objective to glorify the product. Second, placing violent scenes in temporal and spatial proximity to the advertised product can create a negative association between the two and damage the brand's image. Third, advertisers may not push broadcast networks to take risks with ads that contain physical aggression, because in light of the well-publicized campaigns to boycott violent programming they may be afraid of a similar fate to their products.

The relatively minimal presence of violent content in television advertising has not discouraged the U.S. public from agreeing with statements such as "there is too much violence in television advertising" (Dolliver, 1999). Similar opinions were voiced in Israel, despite the even lower frequency of violent advertisements there and even though television viewers are capable of correctly estimating the actual prevalence of violent ads and are not tainted with pluralistic media ignorance—a situation in which public opinion misperceives the true world of popular media content (Hetsroni, 2011). The result—a lack of proportion between the (low) frequency in which violence appears in advertising and the (considerable) concern that it raises—might be explained by the fact that ads that feature atypical depictions of violence are well remembered due to their rarity, as suggested by Greenberg's drench hypothesis. In other words, violent advertising is often protested not because it is common but because it is uncommon. While in most cases violent advertising is not exceptionally effective, unusually violent ads might be beneficial when they promote products and services that are congruent with the visual images (e.g., personal accident insurance).

What We Still Need to Know About Violence in Advertising

Nonscientific observations suggest that violent advertising rarely exists outside television because radio commercials, billboards, and even the Internet are less compatible with sponsored violent messages.

Nonetheless, in the absence of scientific reports, any claim about the lack of violence in nontelevision advertising remains speculative. Studies of violent content in television advertising are also not free of criticism. Because of the lack of large-scale cross-cultural comparisons, conclusions cannot be generalized internationally. A rigid coding scheme, which considers mainly aggressive conduct as an expression of violence, threatens reliability. The repetitive use of this coding scheme, which was developed decades ago by Greenberg and colleagues to study violence in television programming, enables comparisons across time, but it may miss manifestations of nonviolent antisocial behavior (e.g., verbal aggression, hostile looks) that may not be regarded as "violent conduct" in the literal sense, but, nonetheless, some may see them as expressions of "belligerence." Studies that use a more flexible set of definitions for violence may be able to tell us whether the miniscule rate of violence in advertising reflects reality or is partly an artifact of coding.

Amir Hetsroni

See also Advertising, Influence on Society; Advertising Laws Regarding Violent and Aggressive Content; Cultivation Theory; Drench Hypothesis; Marketing of Violence; Priming Theory

Further Readings

Buijzen, M., & Valkenburg, P. M. (2002). Appeals in television advertising: A content analysis of commercials aimed at children and teenagers. *Communications: European Journal of Communication Research, 27*(3), 349–364.

Bushman, B. J., & Anderson, C. A. (2001). Media violence and the American public: Scientific facts versus media misinformation. *American Psychologist, 56*(6–7), 477–489.

Comstock, G., & Scharrer, E. (1999). *Television: What's on, who's watching and what it means.* San Diego, CA: Academic Press.

Dolliver, M. (1999). Is there too much sexual and violent imagery in advertising? *Adweek, 21,* 22.

Hetsroni, A. (2010). Violent content in mainstream TV advertising: A cross cultural comparison. *Communications: The European Journal of Communication Research, 35*(1), 29–45.

Hetsroni, A. (2011). Violence in television advertising: Content analysis and audience attitudes. *Atlantic Journal of Communication, 19*(2), 97–112.

Larson, M. S. (2003). Gender, race and aggression in television commercials that feature children. *Sex Roles, 48*(1/2), 67–75.

Maguire, B., Sandage, D., & Weatherby, G. A. (2000). Violence, morality and television commercials. *Sociological Spectrum, 20,* 121–143.

Sheehan, K. (2004). *Controversies in contemporary advertising.* Thousand Oaks, CA: Sage.

Strong, J., & Dubas, K. (1993). The optimal level for fear-arousal in advertising: An empirical study. *Journal of Current Issues and Research in Advertising, 15,* 93–99.

ADVERTISING LAWS REGARDING VIOLENT AND AGGRESSIVE CONTENT

Concerns about violent and aggressive content in the media appeared as early as the late 1920s, following the Payne Fund studies, which focused on movies and their effects on children. Legislators and government officials were alarmed when research findings pointed to the linkage between media violence and aggressive behavior, especially when vulnerable populations such as children are involved. The Federal Trade Commission (FTC) and the Federal Communications Commission (FCC) are the two government agencies in charge of advertising regulation. Nevertheless, monitoring of violent advertising is mostly conducted by the FTC.

Because advertising is protected by the First Amendment to the U.S. Constitution, governmental regulations and laws concerning advertising content are scant. Accordingly, the function of self-regulation in the advertising industry is pertinent, especially when addressing violent and aggressive content, because it was previously linked to aggressive behavior. The aforementioned legal situation ignites discussions and debates among professionals and scholars, mostly trying to settle between two conflicting values: commercial speech (a term coined by the U.S. Supreme Court to describe any form of for-profit persuasive speech; the practice of advertising falls under this category) and the protection of the public from offensive or harmful advertising content (e.g., violent and aggressive content). This entry discusses government regulation of advertising, industry self-regulation, and criticisms of violent content in advertising research.

Government Regulation of Advertising

Even though the law speaks firmly about freedom of speech in the context of advertising, it is subject to restrictions. The Court has addressed how people are free to print and publish anything as long as they don't infringe on the rights of others; injure others; or publish libels or indecency (e.g., *Near v. Minnesota* [1931]). The FTC is a regulatory body that protects consumers and exercises limitations on commercial speech; it is the most important regulator of the advertising industry. As stated on its website, the FTC is committed to protecting consumers from deceptive, unfair, and anticompetitive business activities. For example, the FTC administers the Telemarketing Sales Rule, which assists consumers to lessen fraudulent telemarketing calls, among other methods, via the National Do Not Call Registry. The FCC is an agency that is responsible for broadcasting regulations and thus is relevant to advertising cases.

These two major regulatory bodies—the FTC and the FCC—focus most of their time on regulating deceptive advertisements and less on content-related issues because of the protection of advertising under the First Amendment. As for the regulation of violent and aggressive content in advertising, the Division of Advertising Practices at the FTC focuses its efforts on the protection of children in relation to advertisement of violent entertainment. The division screens marketing and advertising of violent entertainment to children, including violent movies, electronic games, and music. In 2000, at the request of President Bill Clinton, the FTC prepared and submitted a comprehensive report about marketing violent entertainment for children, while focusing on three industries: motion picture, music, and electronic games (since the 2000 report, a few follow-ups have been submitted by the FTC to government officials). Findings suggest that although the three industries have attempted to adequately label violent content, flaws in the system have demanded additional self-regulations by the industries. For example, one of the major problems that were found is that children under the age of 17 years are continuously approached by these industries, while, at the same time, the content being advertised is labeled or identified as unsuitable for children under 17. Furthermore, the report discusses how easily children can obtain access to products with violent content. For example, children between the ages of 13 and 16 years were able to buy tickets to R-rated films (R means restricted and requires that children under the age of 17 years be accompanied by a parent or a legal guardian). In addition, music recordings that contained violent content were not labeled as such and were advertised in media settings geared toward children under the age of 17 years. Finally, the electronic games industry was found to advertise violent games in magazines and on television shows appropriate for younger audiences. To summarize the report, the FTC recommended the following self-regulation activities: (a) including labels of violent content in advertisements; (b) restricting children's accessibility to products containing violent content; and (c) providing adequate information to parents about labeling and ranking methods of products containing violent content.

Self-Regulation

As discussed earlier, federal agencies encourage the advertising industry to self-regulate its content and commercial practices. Hence, oftentimes the academic and professional discussion has shifted to the realm of ethics. Wallace S. Snyder, a national expert on advertising ethics, stresses that advertising professionals must learn and promote ethical practices when creating and communicating advertising messages, especially when regulatory opportunities are scarce. He also addresses the issue of how advertising ethical practices should come from within, with a heightened sense of responsibility toward the public.

The commercial and legal environments surrounding the advertising industry have led to the development of a few self-regulation programs as well as codes of ethics. For example, the Advertising Self-Regulatory Council (ASRC) consolidates self-regulation efforts for the advertising industry. It sets up policies and is used as an umbrella organization for various self-regulation bodies in the field. It also regulates issues such as children's advertising, online advertising, electronic retailing, and more. For instance, the Children's Advertising Review Unit (CARU) is active under the ASRC framework and is dedicated to self-regulation of children's advertising. Pertaining to violent and aggressive content, the CARU has declared that advertising should not expose children to inappropriate violent content or violent behavior. Moreover, it asserts that advertising should exclude materials that could cause anxiety among children. In the past, CARU has submitted complaints about the advertisement of violent films on inappropriate media channels targeted to children, such as Nicktoons.

The Internet is another medium in which self-regulation can be implemented. For example, advertising networks experience some difficulties managing and controlling online advertising. Advertisers may give specific instructions to advertising networks about where to and not to publish their advertisements online. However, a few instances have been reported where some advertisements with violent content appeared on inappropriate websites because of human mistake or negligence of the advertising network. Subsequently, a number of UK advertising networks have formed a self-regulatory body named Internet Advertising Sales Houses (IASH) to protect brand names and reputations. Generally, the organization promotes fair online advertising practices and scans websites to make sure brands are not advertised next to inappropriate content.

An example of a program that promotes ethics in the field is the Institute for Advertising Ethics, which operates under the structure of the American Advertising Federation (a national advertising association that covers all aspects of the advertising industry). The institute has developed principles and practices for advertising ethics to be used by professionals in the communication field. The institute promotes principles such as truth, personal ethics, transparency, sensitivity to vulnerable populations, and protection of consumers' privacy.

Criticism

Although the investigation of media violence has received a great deal of attention in media research, the exploration of violent content in advertising is relatively scant. That said, it has been found that the use of violence in advertising serves a few different functions: increasing awareness, influencing attitudes and behavior, affecting memory, and providing information. Findings demonstrate an inconsistent pattern as to the representation of violence in commercials. For instance, studies that have focused on violence in television commercials report that results fluctuate from very small percentages in general programming to more than 50% of violence appearance in food advertising targeted to children. Moreover, the effectiveness of violent content in advertising is also debatable; only a few studies have investigated the phenomenon, with each focusing on a different aspect of advertising effects (e.g., interpretation, memory, or behavioral intent). Overall, findings point to some mixed tendencies concerning the influence of violent content in advertising.

Both scholars and professionals have criticized the study approach to violent content in advertising. One major criticism addresses the issue of the definition of violence. Some researchers believe that the inconsistencies found in previous studies are related to the fact that there is no clear, coherent, and comprehensive definition of the term *violence*. Some definitions are broad and thus resulted in findings that suggest high levels of violence in commercials; other definitions of violence are narrow and therefore point at lower levels of violence in advertisements. These scholars claim that in order to receive authentic results, on which regulators and self-regulators can base regulations and policy, it is important to develop a strong theoretical framework for the definition of violence in advertising.

An additional complaint focuses on the analysis used by regulatory bodies, such as the FCC, when reporting to government officials. Some scholars assert that there is too much focus on medium-based analysis (medium is the channel of communication—examples of media are radio, television, the Internet, the phone) and less on content-based analysis. These researchers claim that although it is important to know where, when, and how violence content is published, it is also important to examine what is published.

Another criticism focuses on the topic of violent advertising effectiveness. The effects of violent media content on emotions, thoughts, attitudes, and behavior are well known and established in the literature. However, there is a lack of research and thus understanding of violent content in advertising. Some scholars have argued that there is a need to further develop this area of exploration and to establish research facts about the influence of violent content on various audiences. Additional knowledge can provide accuracy and confidence to the day-to-day administration and policy making of both regulatory and self-regulatory bodies of the advertising industry.

Galit Marmor-Lavie

See also Advertising, Influence on Society; Advertising, Violent Content in; Legislating Media Violence: Law and Policy; Rating Systems, Film; Rating Systems, Video Games; Regulating Systems, Internet

Further Readings

Federal Trade Commission. (2000). Marketing violent entertainment to children: A review of self-regulation and industry practices in the motion picture, music recording and electronic game industries. Washington, DC: Author.

Jones, T., Cunningham, P. H., & Gallagher, K. (2010). Violence in advertising: A multilayered content analysis. *Journal of Advertising, 39*(4), 11–36.

Moore, R. L., Farrar, R. T., & Collins, E. L. (1998). *Advertising and public relations law.* Mahwah, NJ: Erlbaum.

Near v. Minnesota, 283 U.S. 697 (1931).

Nutley, M. (2007, July 26). Ad misplacement exposes flaws in buying processes. *MarketingWeek,* 25.

Snyder, W. S. (2011). *Principles and practices for advertising ethics.* Institute for Advertising Ethics. Retrieved from http://www.aaf.org/default.asp?id=1236

Sparr, F. (2009). *Regulation broadcast violence: Is the medium the message?* Paper presented at the NCA 95th Annual Convention, Chicago.

Timmer, J. (2002). When a commercial is not a commercial: Advertising of violent entertainment and the First Amendment. *Communication Law and Policy, 7*(2), 157–186.

Websites

Advertising Self-Regulatory Council; http://www.asrcreviews.org

Federal Communications Commission; http://www.fcc.gov

Federal Trade Commission; http://www.ftc.gov

AFRICAN AMERICANS IN MEDIA, CHARACTER DEPICTIONS AND SOCIAL REPRESENTATION OF

A growing number of media effects studies have found media to be influential on people's lives, including their self-perceptions, perceptions of others, and their social reality judgments. For people for whom access to a group is limited solely to media exposure, their media-related vicarious experiences take the place of real-life experiences to form their knowledge base. That is, the interactions viewers have and the connections they may form with those represented in the media, although not replacing interpersonal relationships, are similar to their offline counterpart. Because the association between media and society is twofold, impressions of others can be based either on beliefs taught by and held in society or on beliefs taught by the media. What does violent imagery induce in people's perceptions of African Americans and other ethnic groups? Here, media effects research has shown an association between media and society, finding that people's impressions of others may be based on beliefs taught and held in society and/or on beliefs presented in the media. Thus, one area of media effects research has focused on the perceptions of African Americans and other ethnic groups that are induced by violent media content. Many research studies have found that mediated information can influence attitudes and beliefs of individuals who have had little or no direct contact with people belonging to various ethnic and/or social groups in reinforcing stereotypes, and even in influencing feelings on race-based public policy issues. Media experiences can inform viewers' real-life behaviors and attitudes, especially how they react to individuals from historically marginalized groups. This can be detrimental, as research shows that many depictions, especially of marginalized groups, tend to be either one-sided or stereotypical in nature.

Scholars in mass communication, communication studies, psychology, sociology, women's studies, and African American studies have devoted theoretical and empirical research to understanding how media serve as extremely powerful institutions, influencing users' social perceptions, attitudes, beliefs, behaviors, and how they conceive of themselves and others. Research in this area tends to approach the subject from two perspectives: the nature of the content and the effects. By examining the types of portrayals, prevalence of characteristics, and behaviors of a given group, scholars and others hope to gain a sense of when role inequities may exist. Put more simply, to determine the impact stereotypes may have, one must have an idea of how often they are presented and what forms they take. This entry first discusses depictions of African Americans in news and entertainment media and then examines theories regarding the impact such depictions may have on individuals' perceptions.

News Media

Analyses of news content have shown that news media tend to present African Americans, particularly males, as perpetrators of crime, often showing them as violent. Stories about African Americans are also more likely to be accompanied with prejudicial information (e.g., mug shots, being physically held by officers, information on prior arrests) that implies danger and threat. News media also tend to over-represent minority involvement in crime while simultaneously under-representing Whites' involvement. Increasingly, African Americans appear mostly in news stories related to drugs and violent crimes rather than stories that illustrate a serious, beneficial contribution to society at large. As a result, the consistently negative presentations in conjunction with a lack of favorable images contribute to individuals aligning African Americans with criminality.

Heavier viewing of both local and network news content has been connected to an increased likelihood of accessing an African American crime stereotype. Even when a perpetrator's race or ethnicity is not identified in a news story, individuals are more likely to identify the suspect as African American rather than White, incorrectly remember having seen a Black criminal suspect, or misidentify a suspect as having been African American. Viewers also tend to make harsher culpability judgments toward and perceive guilt of African Americans underestimate their income levels and perceive African Americans as intimidating, violent, dangerous, and menacing. The effect extends beyond perceptions of individuals and groups to attitudes toward various public policy issues related to ethnic minorities, such as affirmative action, welfare, and so on.

Content analyses of news have found that backstory, or information that provides context, links the behaviors back to societal structure, and mentions of whether the actions are possibly justifiable or accidental are rarely presented. Instead, crime stories are presented as various episodes that focus only on the actual events, providing decontextualized information. This story-telling convention aids in the development and maintenance of stereotypes, prejudice, and discrimination against African Americans because the recurring images imply that many unrelated members of the African American community are performing violent and illegal acts in large numbers. The only thread connecting these individuals is their race, so audiences may begin to see race as a cause and violence as a characteristic of the group.

Entertainment Media

Although studies have examined detrimental effects of stereotypical representations of African Americans in local and network news, the results regarding portrayals in the entertainment realm have shown both positive and negative portrayals. Donald Bogle's seminal analysis of representations of African Americans in early film found five recurring archetypes of African Americans, including hypersexuality, violence, and submissiveness. Successive studies revealed more expansive portrayals, including over-representations of African Americans as comical, poor, and uneducated. Despite the perceived expansion of roles, many images were still consistent with stereotyped perceptions of African Americans as linked to violence.

In music videos and video games, the range of images is much more limited and negative. Many rap music videos and lyrics, while political, are also radical, suggesting the use of hostility and violence to achieve social equality goals. These same videos, which are often produced by African American artists and depict the African American community, tend to have higher prevalence of talk of drugs, guns, and physical violence than other music genres such as pop and R&B. Exposure to rap music videos can lead to adversarial attitudes toward relationships and acceptance of negative images for both men and women and how they interact with one another. In gaming content, non-Whites, including African Americans, perform the majority of gun violence, which is repeated often and tends to have lethal effects on other characters in the game environment.

Impact on Others

Many theories have suggested ways in which media can affect individuals' perceptions of other social groups. George Gerbner's cultivation theory argues that heavier media consumption of certain kinds of content leads to an expectation that the real world resembles that of the media world. Media viewing, in essence, can lead to distorted perceptions of reality, especially about violence and its connection to African Americans. Priming theories suggest that media can be a powerful agent in activating and strengthening existing stereotypes by presenting stimuli that can bring to mind related thoughts that affect the way new information is processed. In other words, when one aspect of a stereotype is presented, even if the rest of the portrayal is nonstereotypic, that stereotypic element will activate other associated elements in the viewer and cause him or her to interpret the presented individual through a stereotypic lens. Long-term use of such processing and application of stereotypes can lead to prejudice.

According to Gordon Allport, prejudice results from a hasty generalization that is made about a group. This generalization is based on incomplete information. One way to decrease such attitudes is through personal contact with individuals from other groups. Allport's contact hypothesis states that sustained and close contact with members of

"other" groups has the ability to promote more positive attitudes. Support for these arguments has varied, with critics saying that such changes occur only under certain ideal conditions and that not enough evidence in support of the hypothesis is provided from minorities' attitudes about other social groups. For example, interracial friendships have been found to improve Blacks' perceptions of Whites' values and lifestyles, but only if the relationship was a strong one. Casual relationships and contact have little direct influence on perceptions. Direct experience, however, does play a role. When people have to make social reality estimates on issues with which they are highly familiar, firsthand experience is a stronger influencing factor.

Because media, in many instances, can replicate interpersonal contact, they can serve a similar purpose about prejudice—not just in creating it but also in reducing it. Social cognitive theory argues that individuals can learn prosocial behaviors, attitudes, and moral values vicariously through media and others' interpersonal interactions. Media can also serve as such a socializing force, especially when an individual has limited opportunities for direct contact with members of various ethnic and social groups. Media then become important sources of images of how people belonging to these groups live and interact and the characteristics such people may possess. Edward Schiappa, Peter B. Gregg, and Dean E. Hewes refer to this contact as "parasocial contact." By expanding quantitatively and qualitatively to show more equitable and prosocial aspects of individuals and groups, media can provide a form of seemingly direct contact for viewers who have had little or no direct contact with marginalized groups such as Native Americans, African Americans, and gays and lesbians, increasing such viewers' understanding of these groups.

Meghan S. Sanders

See also Attitude, Effects of Media Violence on; Cognition: Schemas and Scripts; Cultivation Theory; Identity, Media Violence and Its Effects on; Priming Theory; Social Cognitive Theory; Violence in Media, Effects on Aggression and Violent Crime

Further Readings

Bogle, D. (1973). Toms, coons, mulattoes, mammies and bucks: An interpretative history of Blacks in films. New York, NY: Viking Press.

Carter, T., & Allen, R. (2004). An examination of mainstream and Black media's influence on the self-concept of African Americans. In G. Meiss & A. Tait (Eds.), *Ethnic media in America: Images, audiences, and transforming forces* (pp. 27–32). Dubuque, IA: Kendall Hunt.

Casas, M. C., & Dixon, T. L. (2003). The impact of stereotypical and counter-stereotypical news on viewer perceptions of Blacks and Latinos: An exploratory study. In A. N. Valdivia (Ed.), *A companion to media studies* (pp. 480–494). Malden, MA: Blackwell.

Entman, R. M., & Rojecki, A. (2000). *The Black image in the White mind.* Chicago: University of Chicago Press.

Mastro, D. E. (2009). Effects of racial and ethnic stereotyping. In J. A. Bryant & M. B. Oliver (Eds.), *Media effects: Advances in theory and research* (pp. 325–341). New York, NY: Routledge.

Oliver, M. B. (2003). Race and crime in the media: Research from a media effects perspective. In A. N. Valdivia (Ed.), *A companion to media studies* (pp. 421–436). Malden, MA: Blackwell.

Sanders, M. S., & Banjo, O. (forthcoming). Mass media and African American identities: Examining Black self-concept and intersectionality. In D. Lasorsa and A. Rodirigue (Eds.), *New agendas: Social identity and communication.* Lanham, MD: Rowman & Littlefield.

Schiappa, E., Gregg, P. B., & Hewes, D. E. (2005). The parasocial contact hypothesis. *Communication Monographs, 72,* 92–115.

Squires, C. (2009). *African Americans and the media.* Cambridge, UK: Polity Press.

AGGRESSION, DEFINITION AND ASSESSMENT OF

There is yet to be universal acceptance of any one definition of *aggression;* however, researchers in the field of psychology have tended to broadly agree that aggression is a behavior (which could be physical, verbal, relational/social, direct, or indirect) performed with the intent to hurt another who does not want to be hurt. Acts of aggression can be assessed in many ways, with laboratory experiments examining the willingness to hurt another in a controlled environment, questionnaire research asking about one's own or another's aggressive behavior, field research taking observational notes of aggression seen in everyday situations, and brain-scanning research examining changes to the brain associated with aggression. Crucially, each form of assessing aggression has unique strengths and weaknesses, leading to controversy about whether aggression has been truly measured in each case. The best evidence that something causes aggression comes from converging evidence from all types of assessment, each of which can overcome the shortcomings of another. This entry first examines how aggression is defined and categorized, and then examines these four types of aggression assessment that are commonly used in media violence research, describing the strengths and weaknesses of each, noting the assessment methods used, and providing examples.

Definitions of Aggression

Although many dictionaries define human aggression in terms of both behavior (e.g., "Hitting someone is an act of aggression") and a frame of mind (e.g., "He was filled with aggression"), behavioral scientists generally differentiate among thoughts, feelings, and behaviors and tend to use the noun *aggression* to describe only behavior, and the adjective *aggressive* to indicate specific types of thoughts and feelings or the nature of an aggressive act. This way, feelings like anger, which may or may not result in aggressive behavior, can be separated from the aggressive act itself. These delineations are often not adhered to, and words like *aggression, violence, anger,* and *hostility* are regularly used interchangeably, particularly by nonspecialists. Some researchers in the field have argued in recent times for clearer definitions along the following general lines: Aggression is any behavior carried out with the intent to harm or hurt another, as long as the other is motivated to avoid that harm or hurt. Violence is an extreme subset of physically aggressive behavior that, if successful, would likely cause severe bodily damage or death. Anger is a strong emotion that is usually coupled with physiological arousal, a combination that sometimes overcomes the thought processes that might inhibit a person's impulse to hurt another and may thus cause the person to act on an aggressive impulse. Hostility is both a personality trait and a set of interconnected aggressive feelings and thoughts that includes feeling resentful, believing that others are antagonistic toward oneself, and holding enmity toward others.

Types of Aggression

Aggression takes many forms, and may be physical, verbal, or relational/social. Acts of *physical aggression* have the potential to physically harm another person or another person's property, and may range from pinching or slapping to acts of extreme violence. *Verbal aggression* is any act of speaking that can hurt another, and may include verbal abuse, attacking another's self-concept, mockery, insults, and a large array of other hostile verbal behaviors. *Relational/social aggression* involves one person hurting another by sabotaging important relationships or undermining the other person's social status. This may be through spreading unkind rumors, excluding the other person from activities, telling a third person not to associate with the person, publicly humiliating the person, or withdrawing attention and friendship.

Further distinctions are also often made. *Direct aggression* involves acts made directly toward a target, whereas *indirect aggression* involves harming a person in his or her absence. *Reactive aggression* (also described as hostile, affective, or angry aggression) is usually fuelled by an angry response to a provocation such as an insult, whereas *instrumental aggression* (i.e., proactive, cold, or thought-through aggression) involves a person deliberately hurting another to obtain a desired goal after having considered the consequences.

Assessing Aggression

Each method of assessing aggressive behavior has specific strengths and weaknesses and a range of measurement tools.

Assessment in the Laboratory

Strengths and Weaknesses

Laboratory experiments are considered to be powerful assessment tools because they theoretically allow researchers to manipulate the experience of participants in one area while ensuring that all other experiences are the same. This enables causality to be strongly implied. For example, in media violence research, every participant may experience the same procedure, with the exception that participants experience exposure to either a violent or a nonviolent media stimulus. If one group differs from another (e.g., if the group that saw the violent media is subsequently more aggressive than the group that did not), then the experimenter can have some confidence that the difference in responses was caused by the experience that was manipulated (in this case, that media violence exposure caused the subsequent aggression). The disadvantage with experiments is that they are artificial environments with strong constraints on

what can be carried out ethically, and findings cannot be automatically generalized to the "real world" with confidence. It is also important to note that laboratory experiments can only measure mild and short-term effects such as a brief increase in the likelihood of aggression after a violent media stimulus.

Assessment Methods

There are a number of ways of experimentally assessing aggression and the psychological changes that can lead to aggression. Aggressive thoughts are typically assessed with tasks that test whether aggression-related words more readily come to mind than others. For example, participants may be asked to complete word stems that can be completed with either aggressive or neutral words (e.g., *ki__* could be completed as *kiss* or *kill*), or to make a fast decision about whether a stimulus is a word or non-word, using aggression-related compared with neutral or non-words. A higher percentage of aggression-word completions or faster decision times to aggression-related words are presumed to indicate that aggression-related words are partially activated in a participant's brain.

Aggressive feelings are generally assessed with self-report questionnaires that present a series of emotion-related adjectives (such as *angry, antagonistic, unfriendly*) and ask participants to rate on a scale the degree to which they feel those emotions at that time. Sometimes, the physiological correlates of emotions are also measured (e.g., heart rate, blood pressure, and facial muscle activity).

Behavioral measures of aggression are the most powerful and most controversial. These typically involve contriving a situation in a laboratory that will allow participants to act in a way they believe will cause harm to another, but within the ethical constraints that others cannot actually be hurt and there must be little risk to the participant's self-image or emotional state. Examples from media violence research include (a) counting observed aggressive acts by children that are a direct imitation of a film-mediated model, (b) measuring the duration and loudness of aversive "noise blasts" delivered to an unseen opponent in a competitive reaction time (CRT) game, (c) measuring the amount of hot chili sauce allocated to an innocent and unseen stranger who is known to dislike hot foods and who will have to eat all of the hot sauce given, and (d) calculating the ratio of hard compared with easy tangram puzzles allocated to an unseen participant who would be unpaid if he or she cannot complete all those tangrams in a specified period.

Such laboratory assessments of aggressive behaviors have been criticized for producing small and temporary effects, not necessarily generalizing to real-world situations, being subject to biases (such as the desire to please the researcher), failing to assess the true motivations of participants, and failing to provide the opportunity for nonaggressive responses. In reply to such criticisms, aggression researchers have pointed out that small effects can have significant social importance, and that temporary changes to behavior can accumulate over time to form more stable patterns of responding. Some also point to a growing body of evidence that (a) although different experimental aggression paradigms have different strengths and weaknesses, they tend to find comparable results, and (b) people who are aggressive in some popular laboratory paradigms (such as the CRT task) tend also to be aggressive outside the laboratory, findings indicative that laboratory measures can generalize to the real world. In addition, well-designed tasks can minimize experimenter bias through careful cover stories and scripts, and some newer paradigms are designed to overcome the shortcomings of earlier methodologies. For example, the tangram task and modern CRT tasks allow nonaggressive alternative responses, and the hot sauce paradigm involves an outcome that would genuinely hurt the target if enacted, implying a clear motive to aggress.

Assessment Through Questionnaire Research

Strengths and Weaknesses

Unlike laboratory experiments, questionnaire research can examine a wide range of real-world phenomena and can look at longer-term effects. For example, researchers may be able to determine whether there is a relationship (i.e., a correlation) between heavy exposure to violent media and more frequent occurrences of aggressive behavior in everyday life. The most powerful forms of questionnaire research are *longitudinal* studies that ask the same or similar questions of people at various time points in their life (usually starting in childhood) and then examine the trends of these relationships over time.

The key weaknesses of correlational studies are that (a) they cannot be used to determine that one thing causes another if data are from a single time point; (b) they cannot take into account every possible factor that might influence the relationships of

interest; and (c) the questionnaires themselves rely on the respondent having good self-awareness, the ability to understand the questions, and the motivation to answer truthfully. In practice, humans are subject to a number of biases, memory limitations, and conflicting motivations that make "true" responses hard to guarantee. In terms of (a), it should be noted that more recent statistical techniques (such as nonrecursive structural equation modeling) make it possible to imply a greater degree of causality from correlational data than has previously been possible, and that longitudinal studies can also imply the direction of causality, because it is logically impossible for a later behavior to influence an earlier one.

Assessment Methods

Assessment methods are quite straightforward. A sample of people from a population of interest is asked to complete questionnaires that measure the factors the researchers are interested in. When it is important to generalize study findings to the wider population of interest, regard should be given to the sample's distribution of ages, gender, ethnicity, and geographic location (an aim that is often difficult to achieve in practice due to high costs and recruitment issues). Data quality depends largely on whether the measures themselves are valid (measure what they are supposed to measure) and reliable (elicit the same responses from a person time after time), characteristics that are best achieved when measures have been thoroughly tested in advance for these properties.

In violent media research, there are a number of well-validated measures for trait aggression, trait anger, hostility, beliefs around the notion that aggression is normal and socially acceptable, and a person's typical level of exposure to violent media content.

Assessment Through Field Observation

Strengths and Weaknesses

Field observations involve watching and recording behaviors in the natural environment of participants (such as watching children's behavior in a playground). Such studies overcome the issues of biased responding and generalization to the outside world that may affect laboratory studies, and also the problems associated with self-awareness, bias, and capacity to respond associated with questionnaire research. Importantly, observed acts of aggression are real and direct rather than implied, and can be observed in populations unsuitable for questionnaire research, such as younger children. The main weakness of this approach is that assessing observed behaviors is notoriously difficult, and the coding and rating of behaviors can be somewhat subjective. In addition, aggressive behavior has a fairly low base rate in most observed social situations, and considerable lengths of observation time might be required to detect a small number of occurrences of aggression. This in turn means that data sets might be based on a fairly small number of observations of aggression.

Assessment Methods

Good field studies require comprehensive guides to coding behaviors, thorough training of those who will do the coding and rating, and clear and easy-to-use instruments on which to record data. Behaviors are often recorded digitally or on film to assist coding and to allow for multiple raters. Data are considered more valid when there is high inter-rater agreement on how each behavioral instance should be coded and/or rated. Researcher observations can be supplemented with the observations and reports of others, such as parents, teachers, and peers, with converging findings offering the strongest evidence.

In media violence field studies, participants (often children) are observed in natural settings (such as a playground or playgroup) after having seen a media stimulus such as a violent or nonviolent movie clip. Behaviors that could be considered aggressive (such as pushing, shoving, hitting, name calling, or swearing at another) are decided in advance, along with thresholds below which behaviors might be considered normal (such as rough-and-tumble play) and above which are clearly intended to hurt another. Then, such occurrences are counted, and sometimes also coded for extent (e.g., as mildly aggressive, somewhat aggressive, quite aggressive, and very aggressive).

Assessment Using Brain-Scanning Techniques

Strengths and Weaknesses

In brain-scanning studies of aggression, participants are given a stimulus for aggression while undergoing a brain scan that can indicate either which parts of the brain are active or which types of brain activity are occurring. Comparisons are made to data before, during, and after the stimulus for each individual, and comparisons may also be made between individuals who experience different

stimuli. Functional magnetic resonance imaging (fMRI) measures changes to blood flow and captures changes to brain activity with reasonable accuracy in location, but less accuracy in terms of the timing of these changes (i.e., to within a few seconds at best). Magnetoencephalography (MEG) measures changes to the patterns of brainwaves across time. Unlike fMRI, MEG detects changes to brain activity to within fractions of a second, but it has the disadvantage of not providing an accurate location where activity occurs. Brain-scanning studies have the advantage that they do not rely on the participant being motivated to help, responding honestly, or being self-aware. In addition, such scans can measure a number of things that are difficult to assess using other methods, in particular desensitization to violence, fear responses, and emotional arousal. Disadvantages of brain-scanning studies include the small sample sizes tested (due to cost constraints) and the difficulties inherent in interpreting the images, which are averaged over time and across participants by complicated software. In addition, many brain areas have multiple functions and interact with other areas, so it is not possible to be sure what psychological processes are occurring when a part of the brain is active.

Assessment Methods

In media violence research, participants are generally scanned before, during, and after exposure to a media source such as a video clip or computer game. Researchers map responses against existing knowledge of brain areas linked with aggressive behavior (and other functions of interest) to see whether the patterns of activation are similar. In addition, participants might be assessed to see whether their levels of emotional activation to a violent stimulus decrease over time, thus demonstrating desensitization to violence over the short term. Additionally, the responses to violent media of frequent players of nonviolent games might be compared to the responses of frequent players of violent games, to ascertain whether a long-term desensitization has occurred in the latter group.

Assessment of Aggression Related to Media Violence

The area of media violence is an important one when examining the issue of assessing aggression, because many studies have been conducted using the different techniques involved. Each technique has its strengths and weaknesses, but, importantly, the four techniques together provide data on short- and long-term effects infer causality, describe relationships between aggression and various factors at one time and across time, provide data from the real world, take into account the effect of other factors that might also cause aggression, and are used with humans female and male, of many races, from children to adults, and with different personalities. Across all the methods, each of which can overcome the deficit of another, the evidence seems to converge to find consistent evidence of a modest but robust impact of media violence exposure on aggression and desensitization to violence.

Wayne Warburton

See also Aggression and Affect; Aggression and Anger; Aggression and Brain Functioning; Aggressive Behavior; Effects From Violent Media, Short- and Long-term; Effects of Media Violence on Relational Aggression; Media Violence, Definitions and Context of; Methodologies for Assessing Effects of Media; Violence, Definition of

Further Readings

Anderson, C. A., & Bushman, B. J. (1997). External validity of "trivial" experiments: The case of laboratory aggression. *Review of General Psychology, 1,* 19–41.

Anderson, C. A., & Bushman, B. J. (2002). Human aggression. *Annual Review of Psychology, 53,* 27–51.

Anderson, C. A., Gentile, D. A., & Buckley, K. E. (2007). *Violent video game effects on children and adolescents: Theory, research, and public policy.* New York, NY: Oxford University Press.

Anderson, C. A., Shibuya, A., Ihori, N., Swing, E. L., Bushman, B. J., Sakamoto, A., et al. (2010). Violent video game effects on aggression, empathy, and prosocial behavior in Eastern and Western countries: A meta-analytic review. *Psychological Bulletin, 136,* 151–173.

Bushman, B. J., & Anderson, C. A. (1998). Methodology in the study of aggression: Integrating experimental and nonexperimental findings. In R. G. Geen & E. Donnerstein (Eds.), *Human aggression: Theories, research and implications for social policy* (pp. 24–48). San Diego, CA: Academic Press.

Huesmann, L. R., & Taylor, L. D. (2003). The case against the case against media violence. In D. A. Gentile (Ed.), *Media violence and children: A complete guide for parents and professionals* (pp. 107–130). Westport, CT: Praeger.

Ritter, D., & Eslea, M. (2005). Hot sauce, toy guns and graffiti: A critical account of current laboratory aggression paradigms. *Aggressive Behavior, 31,* 407–419.

Tedeschi, J. T., & Quigley, B. M. (1996). Limitations of laboratory paradigms for studying aggression. *Aggression and Violent Behavior, 1,* 163–177.

Aggression, Risk Factors of

Researchers have long been interested in the effects of media on behavioral outcomes. Although some forms of media may be educational or entertaining, other forms—especially ones containing violent content—have been shown to be risk factors for increased aggression. Risk factors are considered to be stimuli that have the potential to increase aggressive behavior following exposure to them. This entry reviews evidence suggesting that the effects of some forms of media (violent movies, violent games, and violent song lyrics) on subsequent aggression accumulate across time and can be elicited following acute (short-term) exposure.

Violence in Movies

The first movie to include a depiction of violence was *The Great Train Robbery,* a 1903 black-and-white movie lasting 12 minutes that ended with the main character, Justus Barnes, pointing a pistol at the audience and firing. Early showings of this film resulted in audiences running scared from the theater, a far cry from the typical (non)reaction observed today during movies featuring violent scenes. Indeed, violence in the media has become increasingly common; some estimates suggest that children will be exposed to more than 100,000 acts of violence (e.g., murders) by the time they graduate from elementary school.

As movies included more violence over time, researchers became increasingly interested in whether exposure to such movies made people more aggressive. Several committees and agencies, such as the American Psychological Association and the National Institute of Mental Health, concluded that exposure to media violence may alter both perceptions and attitudes toward real-world violence. Moreover, based on evidence from hundreds of research studies, most researchers now agree that exposure to media violence is associated with and causes increases in aggressive behavior.

Substantial evidence exists suggesting that the amount of time spent watching violent movies is associated with increases in aggressive behaviors in the real world. For example, in a study investigating patterns of hitting, fighting, and other aggressive behaviors, researchers found higher rates of these behaviors in adolescents who viewed more television violence. Other research reported similar findings, such that 12- to 17-year-old males who reported heavy TV violence exposure engaged in 49% more violent acts over the course of six months than a similar group rarely exposed to TV violence.

However, whether exposure to televised violence causes increases in aggression cannot be inferred from these types of studies given their correlational nature. That is, it could be that individuals who are aggressive in general also prefer violent media. Therefore, to address the causality issue, experimenters randomly assign participants to watch various types of media content (nonviolent or violent) and then subsequently measure aggressiveness. Indeed, several experiments have shown that acute exposure to violent movies increases short-term aggressive behavior. For example, in one study 5- to 6-year-old children were assigned to watch a nonviolent or violent film, after which they were observed during a free play period by observers who were unaware of the films they had just watched. Relative to the children who had seen the nonviolent film, children who had seen the violent film engaged in more aggressive behaviors, such as hitting, during the free play period.

Not all studies have shown effects like these. Indeed, some studies observe no relationship between exposure to TV violence and aggressive behavior, which makes it difficult to determine whether TV violence exposure predicts aggression. A meta-analysis essentially combines the information gathered from numerous individual studies to determine the extent to which one variable (TV violence) influences another variable (aggressive behavior), essentially providing a more reliable estimate of specific effects than can be seen in any single study. Several meta-analyses of the televised violence and aggression relation have been conducted, and these analyses have indicated a significant relationship between TV violence exposure and aggression. Thus, the conclusion of the majority of studies on this topic is that exposure to TV violence is not only associated with increased aggression but can also cause it.

Violence in Video Games

Each new technology provides an opportunity for media content to affect media consumers in a new way, and during the past century each such innovation has raised new questions for researchers interested in media effects on behavior. In recent decades, by far the most popular form of media entertainment among young people (and the not-so-young, as well) has been video games. Given their popularity and the fact that video games can be played virtually any time, anywhere, it makes sense that media scholars—not to mention policy makers and the public at large—should want to know whether video game content affects important social behaviors, such as aggression. Given the evidence linking violent TV and movie exposure with aggression, there is reason to think that exposure to violent video games will also increase aggression, and perhaps even more so than other forms of media. Whereas TV and movie exposure is passive, playing video games represents a more active form of engagement in which the player controls the actions of the characters, essentially behaving aggressively in a virtual world. Video games also more directly reinforce aggressive behavior—for example, by awarding points—than do other forms of media.

Consistent with these ideas, numerous studies have documented a relationship between violent video game exposure and aggressive behavior. For example, previous exposure to video game violence is strongly associated with aggressive delinquent behavior. Additionally, chronic exposure to violent games is associated with the likelihood of accepting aggression-related norms, getting into arguments with teachers, and engaging in physical fights. Research has also shown that this relationship holds even after accounting for several variables that might be related to both an increased tendency to play violent video games and to be aggressive, such as sex (being male), trait hostility, aggressive personality, and the total number of hours spent playing video games in general.

Such correlations do not prove a causal relationship, however. To more definitively establish the causal role of violent video games in increasing aggression, researchers typically randomly assign participants to play a violent or nonviolent game and then assess aggressive responding. In the best of such studies, researchers strive to ensure that the violent and nonviolent games are as similar as possible on a number of characteristics other than violent content (e.g., how exciting or frustrating they are). To date, several studies have found that acute exposure to violent games in a lab increases aggressive behavior.

Given the general consensus indicated by the scientific evidence, most researchers now agree that, similar to the effects of violent movies, exposure to violent video games causes increases in aggressive behavior, and that the debate over whether violent video game exposure increases aggressiveness should be put to rest. More recently, researchers have turned their attention to investigating factors that might moderate the association between violent video game play and aggression (i.e., individual differences), as well as factors that might explain *why* violent video games increase aggressiveness (i.e., mediators).

Research on moderating factors has shown that variability in both video game characteristics and trait-like individual differences affect the relationship between video game exposure and aggression. For example, one group of researchers found that participants were especially likely to behave aggressively if they played a violent game and strongly identified with the game character than if they did not strongly identify with the character. In a study examining individual differences, another group of researchers showed that individuals high in dispositional anger respond more aggressively following exposure to violent, but not nonviolent, games than do people low in this trait.

Other studies have focused on understanding the mechanisms that might account for the violent game effects on aggression. For example, researchers found that the link between violent game exposure and increased aggressiveness was driven, in part, by a concomitant increase in aggressive thinking. Other work has found evidence that repeated exposure to violence in video games might lead to a desensitization-like effect in which players become inured to effects of violence in the real world.

More recent research has found experimental evidence that desensitization processes in the brain mediate the relationship between violent game exposure and aggression. That is, when a group of participants with little to no previous exposure to violent games were assigned to play a violent game in the lab, their brains were found to be less responsive to depictions of violence (e.g., a man holding a gun in another man's mouth) during a picture-viewing task following exposure to a violent game. Importantly, this reduction in brain activity during the picture task was also associated with increases in aggressive responding later in the experiment.

In sum, much evidence now points to the conclusion that violent games cause increases in aggressive

behavior. Finally, violent games seem to have their effect through increasing aggressive thoughts and through desensitization to depictions of violence.

Violence in Music Lyrics

Listening to music is a popular activity. In fact, the average American youth spends about 2 hours a day listening to music (not including music videos). Although there are numerous differences among watching violent movies, playing violent video games, and listening to music, in theory listening to music can affect behavior in similar ways. For example, if music contains violent or misogynistic lyrics, exposure to such songs could lead to attitudes more accepting of such behaviors and/or increase the accessibility of aggressive thoughts, in much the same way that violence in other forms of media do, ultimately leading to increases in aggressive tendencies.

Building on basic social cognitive work showing that exposure to aggressive words can facilitate aggressiveness, some studies have shown a link between aggressive song lyrics and increases in aggressive thoughts, feelings, and behaviors. For example, college students who reported preferring heavy metal and rap music showed more hostile attitudes than did participants who preferred alternative and country music.

Beyond such correlational demonstrations, researchers have used experimental designs to test the effects of violent song lyrics on aggressive behavior. For example, in one study participants listened to either a violent song ("Jerk-Off") or nonviolent song ("Four Degrees") from the band Tool. Results from this study showed that participants who listened to the violent song felt more hostile following exposure to the song than did participants who listened to the nonviolent song. Of course, simply feeling more hostile does not necessarily lead to behaving more aggressively. To more directly assess the link between aggressive song lyrics and aggressive behavior, one group of researchers assigned participants to listen to two aggressive songs (related to mistreatment of women) or two neutral songs. Aggression was measured as the amount of hot sauce allocated to another participant who presumably did not enjoy spicy foods. As expected, following exposure to the misogynistic song lyrics in the aggressive songs, not only were men more likely to think aggressively, they were also especially likely to allocate larger amounts of hot sauce to women.

However, not all studies have shown a link between aggressive song lyrics and aggression-related variables. For example, one group of researchers had participants listen to music with different lyric content (homicidal, suicidal, or neutral) and from different genres (rap versus heavy metal). They found that lyric content did not change the mood of participants, such as increase their anger. Non-results such as these could be attributed to the fact that some genres (e.g., heavy metal) make the lyrics difficult to hear and process.

To summarize, although some of the earlier studies investigating the relationship between musical lyrics and aggressive behavior showed little to no effect, more recent work using different methods does implicate such a link, particularly if men listen to lyric content that includes the mistreatment of (or violence against) women.

Conclusion

In sum, several decades of research including hundreds of empirical articles point to a link between exposure to various forms of media (violent movies, violent games, and songs with violent lyrics) and aggressive responding. That is, short- and long-term exposure to a variety of media containing violent content has been shown to reliably predict increases in aggressive behavior.

Christopher R. Engelhardt and
Bruce D. Bartholow

See also Aggression, Definition and Assessment of; Aggression and Anger; Aggression in Youth; Aggressive Behavior; Arousal and Aggressive Content, Theory and Psychology of; Attitude, Effects of Media Violence on

Further Readings

Anderson, C. A., Carnagey, N. L., & Eubanks, J. (2003). Exposure to violent media: The effects of songs with violent lyrics on aggressive thoughts and feelings. *Journal of Personality and Social Psychology, 84,* 960–971.

Anderson, C. A., & Dill, K. E. (2000). Video games and aggressive thoughts, feelings, and behavior in the laboratory and in life. *Journal of Personality and Social Psychology, 78,* 772–790.

Anderson, C. A., Shibuya, A., Ihori, N., Swing, E. L., Bushman, B. J., Sakamoto, A., Rothstein, H. R., et al. (2010). Violent video game effects on aggression, empathy, and prosocial behavior in Eastern and Western countries: A meta-analytic review. *Psychological Bulletin, 136*(2), 151–173.

Bushman, B. J., & Anderson, C. A. (2001). Media violence and the American public: Scientific facts versus media misinformation. *American Psychologist, 56,* 477–489.

Engelhardt, C. R., Bartholow, B. D., Kerr, G. T., & Bushman, B. J. (2011). This is your brain on violent video games: Neural desensitization to violence predicts increased aggression following violent video game exposure. *Journal of Experimental Social Psychology, 47,* 1033–1036.

Engelhardt, C. R., Bartholow, B. D., & Saults, J. S. (2011). Violent and nonviolent video games differentially affect physical aggression for individuals high vs. low in dispositional anger. *Aggressive Behavior, 37*(6), 539–546.

Konijn, E. A., Bijvank, M. N., & Bushman, B. J. (2007). I wish I were a warrior: The role of wishful identification in the effects of violent video games on aggression in adolescent boys. *Developmental Psychology, 43*(4), 1038–1044.

AGGRESSION AND AFFECT

Affect is the result of an animal's or human's exposure to stimuli. Affect has been equated to other feeling states such as mood and emotion in past research; however, in its most basic form, affect represents a neurophysiologic state characterized by valance (pleasure versus displeasure) and strength (high activation versus low activation), and is conceptually and operationally different from other feeling states. Furthermore, scholars continue to conflate core affect by using it interchangeably with the concepts of emotion and mood. However, these three feeling states are different with respect to the level of description they provide for explaining responses to stimuli. For the purposes of this discussion, this entry uses James Russell and Lisa Feldman Barrett's (1999) conceptualization of core affect as an ever-present state marked by fluctuating biological, mental, and physiological responses to the environment or a situation. Core affect represents an objective state onto which subjective attributions and evaluations have not been placed. In contrast, emotion and mood represent as internal subjective states that correlate with core affect but have been attributed and evaluated.

Core affect is a central topic in psychological research; however, it is also very relevant to media effects, and especially to media violence. Media (the physical medium) and content (the information communicated through a medium) are both stimuli that can evoke affective states. Research on core affect addresses topics in human psychology such as cognition, attitudes, and behavior; however, little is known about how affect is related to the aforementioned areas. Nonetheless, one domain in which the association between core affect and human behavior is related is that of aggression. For the purposes of this discussion, Craig Anderson and Brad Bushman's (2002) conceptualization of aggression as a goal-directed behavior toward another individual or group with the immediate purpose of causing harm is used. One's internal state can directly influence the appraisal or decision process preceding aggressive action. These internal states are made up of feelings (affect) and thought (cognition), whereby core affective states of displeasure and high activation combined with thoughts of hostility or resentment may lead to decision processes ending in aggressive action.

Consequently, one can hypothesize that media violence acts as a stimulus that makes accessible or evokes these internal states (both cognitive and affective) that influence aggressive behavior; however, little is known about alternate explanations for the role of affect and aggression. For example, an individual might seek out certain stimuli for the purpose of evoking aggressive affective states. In this case, media violence may not be directly associated with aggressive action. Instead, exposure to media violence may reflect an individual's preexisting preferences, or personality traits, that may ultimately be the cause of aggressive action. Thus, the question of whether media violence begets aggressive behavior is confounded. What is clear, however, is that violent content in the media, which represents a stimulus, evokes affective states that can be, but are not necessarily, associated with aggressive behavior. Consequently, a better understanding of how core affect is influenced, as well as how core affect influences behavior, may clarify effect of media violence on aggression.

Understanding Core Affect

Passion and reason, feeling and thought, affect and cognition have been linked to diverse human responses to stimuli. A 1980 study by Richard Solomon reported multiple studies that demonstrated the presentation of certain stimuli might produce pleasurable or unpleasurable affective states. For example, newborn babies were awakened and given a bottle. They were then allowed to feed for

one minute. After a minute the bottle was removed. After 5 to 10 seconds the babies began to cry for several minutes and then went back to sleep. This is one of the studies that showed differential affective states as well as subsequent behaviors, such as crying and sleeping. Other studies have investigated the association between core affect and behavior: John Pinel, Sunaina Assanand, and Darrin Lehman (2000) linked affect to eating; Leonard Berkowitz (1993) connected affect and aggression, and Abraham Tesser (2000) explained self-esteem maintenance as a function of affect. Affect is prominent in human life and behavior and is therefore a critical area of study in social sciences; however, the mysterious nature of affect, affective states (e.g., mood and emotions), and affective outcomes (e.g., aggression) complicate past and present research.

The Structure of Affect

The neurological structure of core affect is one in which conscious feelings evident in moods and emotions are accessible; however, the mental events of core affect occur subconsciously. Core affect is a neurological process that is physically experienced; however, it is not a cognitive process. Experienced affective states are composed of two separate but integrated dimensions, as seen in Figure 1. The vertical dimension, activation, ranges from extremes of alertness. Consistent with Russell and Barrett's conceptualization of core affect, a stimuli can evoke states that range from low activation (e.g., calm or sedated) to high activation (e.g., alertness or excitement). The horizontal dimension, pleasure to displeasure, ranges from one extreme (e.g., misery) to its opposite extreme (e.g., rapture). These dimensions intersect to create a circumplex in which a pictorial representation of affect is created to imply circular order.

Russell and Barrett have shown that states of core affect influence reflexes, perception, cognition, and behavior. Conversely, core affect is influenced by many factors that exist both internally and externally. Studies using self-reported measures of emotions with regard to past experiences consistently indicate that pleasure and arousal factors are correlated to reported discrete emotions, and affective elements account for a good portion of the variance in the self-reports.

Measuring Core Affect

The aforementioned conceptualization of affect is based on dimensions that describe the nature of the

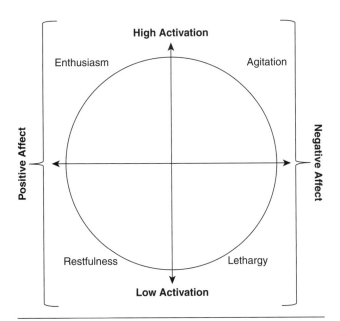

Figure 1   Core Affect Categorized as Positive and Negative

basic feeling state of core affect. However, pleasure is not universal. One individual may experience pleasure running a marathon; another may not. Furthermore, similar levels of pleasure and activation can be described by different words (i.e., *excitement* versus *alertness* versus *elation*). Scales have been created for the purpose of measuring affect; however, little consensus exists regarding correlational versus experimental supremacy. According to David Watson, Lee Anna Clark, and Auke Tellegen (1988), because of the subjective nature of qualitative descriptions of core affect, positive affect and negative affect should be measured through self-report as two distinct dimensions.

Although positive affect and negative affect are negatively correlated, they are linearly independent and have been represented as orthogonal dimensions. In other words, positive affect (feelings of attentiveness or alertness) and negative affect (feelings of hostility or distress) can together predict distinct moods and emotions as independent dimensions. Using the positive and negative affect scale (PANAS), Silvia Knobloch-Westerwick and colleagues (2009) conducted a multilevel analysis of what attracts people to watch sports. Results show that changes in both positive and negative affect cause feelings of suspense for supporters of both teams in a sports competition between two universities. As the sporting event progresses, plays are continually being made that evoke both a hope of winning and a fear of losing in both teams' supporters. The tension that

exists as a result of fluctuating affect states (fear to hope, and hope to fear) heightens a sports-watching experience.

In the aforementioned case, suspense is a complex emotion that could be comprised of multiple basic emotions such as fear, stress, nervousness, or excitement. Suspense is a combination of positive and negative affect, whereby levels of pleasure and arousal fluctuate over the course of an event. This further exemplifies the basic nature of core affect as well as the representation of core affect in more complex affective states. Furthermore, these findings support the hypothesis that positive affect and negative affect are distinct dimensions of affect. Although there is disagreement among emotion scholars regarding the dimensions measured in the PANAS, Russell and Barrett show the similarities between these opposing views through the use of circumplex dimensions.

Causes of Core Affect

Core affect can be deliberately manipulated by administering drugs, such as stimulants or depressants. In addition, core affect can be unintentionally manipulated by the occurrence of a combination of multiple events, such as changes to the temperature of a room or cumulative emerging pressures during a week of school. Causes of affect are at times undetectable by an individual. An example is a high-pitched, low-frequency noise that emanates from an electronic device in a room. A fundamental assumption of core affect is that people oftentimes cannot directly access the actual cause of affect. Furthermore, the process of seeking out the cause of core affect is confounded by other events in the environment. Therefore, humans attribute and interpret possible causes of core affect, although these may not be the actual causes.

From Core Affect to Aggression

The relationship between core affect and behavior is complex, such that a direct link may be overgeneralized. The basic neurophysiological state of core affect is naturally occurring and ever-present; therefore, linking it to behavior through cause and effect is troublesome. The bridge that many scholars use to link these concepts is emotion. Emotion can be less troublesome because it does not naturally occur; rather, it emanates from a human's evaluation of both the experienced affective state and its cause.

The Concept of Emotion

Basic or automatic human responses to the environment or to cues or stimuli are accompanied by affect; however, the psychological nature denotes emotion. For example, when a human perceives a threat in the environment, feelings of fear may transpire. People then instinctually respond to this fear by running away or preparing to fight. At the foundation of this response is an unpleasant activated core affective state that, when paired with cognition, is experienced and expressed as complex emotions (e.g., anger). Whereas anger is a complex affective state or emotion, core affect describes the activated displeasure that is experienced. Consequently, emotion appears to give some clarity to the relationship between affect and aggression.

In accordance with Barrett and Russell, emotion is conceptualized as a functional complex affective state that represents directed, brief responses to changes in the environment or stimuli. There are a number of subcomponents of emotion: (a) cognitive appraisal (e.g., thinking about a situation as exciting), (b) subjective feeling (e.g., feeling aroused), (c) physiological response (e.g., breathing quickens), (d) expression (e.g., the person smiles), (e) action tendency (e.g., the person approaches a stimuli), and (f) regulation (e.g., the person controls his or her breathing). Emotion is functional in individual development across one's life span, both cognitively and emotionally. Additionally, emotion plays a key role in motivating and moderating learning, social behavior, and judgments.

Functions of Emotion

Human Development

Many emotion scholars assume that development across the life span is driven by cognition or the accumulation and processing of information and knowledge. However, other emotion scholars argue that cognitive psychologists discount emotional transactions' role in human development. Emotions enable people to transition through different life stages, achieve certain milestones, and overcome developmental obstacles. Many cognition scholars assume that human development is primarily driven by cognitive attainment. Additionally, emotion is not seen as functional in human development. However, according to Jo Ann Abe and Carroll Izard's differential emotions theory (DET), cognitive development can influence emotional development and vice versa.

Social Behavior

Emotions have been linked with social behavior. Emotions experienced across a person's development can play an important role in a person's ability to engage in social interaction, to understand other people's thoughts and feelings, and to evaluate one's own emotions. Emotions can guide social interactions among individuals. Furthermore, emotions can serve multiple roles in social settings such as work or school. Positive emotions have been linked to low levels of stress, open-mindedness, and flexible decision making. Positive emotions can enable productive group or teamwork. And negative emotions have been associated with anxiety and stress, which may lead to closed-mindedness and poor decision making. In this case, negative emotions can hamper productivity in social settings.

Summary

If core affect represents a mental state marked by feelings of pleasure and arousal, and cognition is multiple complex processes marked by thought, memory, and neurological activation, then emotion is the complex process marked by both objective affect and subjective cognition. Negative emotions, such as anger, connect affective states of activated displeasure to aggression by attributing and contextualizing a source of the affective states toward which aggressive thoughts and actions are directed.

Aggression

There are multiple theories of aggression that explain what aggression is and what causes it. Consensus exists among the theories regarding the nature of aggression. Anderson describes aggression as being an emotionally charged act in which people intend to inflict harm on the target of the behavior. The intent of aggression can vary based on the amount of harm one wishes to cause. In other words, the primary goal of aggression is to cause harm; however, the outcome of aggression may differ based on the ultimate goal, which could be death. Negative feelings can lead to aggressive thoughts, which can lead to aggressive behaviors. However, this relationship can be more accurately described as reciprocal. Aggression research focuses on factors that influence aggressive behavior. These factors can be biological, environmental, psychological, and social. Personal factors (e.g., gender, values, personality) and situational factors (e.g., ingesting drugs or experiencing pain) both cause aggression.

According to cognitive neoassociation theory, aggressive thoughts, feelings, and behaviors are connected in a person's memory and can be evoked by certain situations or cues that resemble past events associated with those memories. For example, if you get in an argument (unpleasant situation), it may trigger memories of past arguments associated with negative emotions and feelings. These may then be expressed as aggression. A person's memories are built from personal interpretations of past events. For example, the interpretation of burning your tongue on hot chocolate when you were young will result in you being careful drinking hot beverages. Certain cues, such as steam, are now stored in memory and guide subsequent behavior. Basic human fight (versus flight) behaviors or tendencies are an example of how memories influence an automatic aggressive response. A fight response is often manifested in aggressive, combative behavior, while a flight response can be manifested in running away, quitting, or submitting.

Social script, social learning, and social interaction theories explain aggression as a result of learning. Accordingly, aggression becomes a learned behavior when it is observed or experienced by a person. The behavior is then adopted and emulated in subsequent situations. Social interaction theory varies from social learning and social script theory based on the role of expectancy outcomes associated with aggressive behavior. These outcomes (e.g., rewards, costs, consequences) motivate aggressive behavior. Although these theories offer a framework for understanding the concept of aggression, they do not provide an explanation of the component parts that make up the construct.

Research by Anderson and colleagues provides an integrative social cognitive framework for understanding aggression, as applied to the context of media exposure. Unlike earlier theories, the general aggression model (GAM) explores the construct of aggression and its influences and antecedents. The GAM integrates multiple microtheories of aggression into a single framework in order to provide a more parsimonious model of aggression. According to the GAM, aggression is transient. In other words, aggression is short lived and passes as the situation passes. Evolutionary psychologists attribute aggression to the perceived threatening of a person's needs. Therefore, when needs are no longer being threatened, aggressive behavior ceases. Psychological and physical pain, for example, reflect a threat to one's need for safety, and therefore they may elicit aggressive behaviors. In media such as video games, although there is no physical pain inflicted on the player during play, a character experiences threatening situations through game play provocation, and pain through combat. If the player is highly identified with the character, in that he or she is empathizing with the character, understanding the character, assuming the character's goals as his or her own, and experiencing absorption within narrative, the player may experience a threat to safety.

Conclusion

Affect acts as an input for aggressive feelings. In other words, negative affect marked by feelings of distress can produce aggressive feelings. Aggressive feelings that persist may lead to aggressive thought. Consider, for example, a child who is playing rough on the playground and pins another child to the ground. If the child is pinned for an extended period of time, he or she may form thoughts of retaliation or fighting back. These thoughts can then influence action. The link between affect and aggression is not direct; however, the relationship can be conceptualized when attributions and context are created. Media violence can evoke negative affective states that act as inputs to aggressive behavior. However, subsequent complex processes determine whether aggressive feelings, thoughts, and actions actually arise. Emotion may explain a process by which affect influences aggression through cognitive appraisal of the situation and the source.

Kristin Stewart and Matthew S. Eastin

See also Aggression and Anger; Aggressive Behavior; Cognitive Psychology of Violence; General Aggression Model; Priming Theory; Social Learning From Media

Further Readings

Abe, J. A. A., & Izard, C. E. (1999). The developmental functions of emotions: An analysis in terms of differential emotions theory. *Cognition & Emotion, 13*(5), 523–549.

Anderson, C. A., & Bushman, B. J. (2002). Human aggression. *Annual Review of Psychology, 53*(1), 27–51.

Berkowitz, L. (1993). Aggression: Its causes, consequences, and control. New York, NY: McGraw Hill.

Knobloch-Westerwick, S., David, P., Eastin, M. S., Tamborini, R., & Greenwood, D. (2009). Sports spectators' suspense: Affect and uncertainty in sports entertainment. *Journal of Communication, 59*(4), 750–767.

Pinel, J. P., Assanand, S., & Lehman, D. R. (2000). Hunger, eating, and ill health. *American Psychologist, 55*(10), 1105.

Randolph, M. E., Pinkerton, S. D., Bogart, L. M., Cecil, H., & Abramson, P. R. (2007). Sexual pleasure and condom use. *Archives of Sexual Behavior, 36*(6), 844–848.

Russell, J. A. (2003). Core affect and the psychological construction of emotion. *Psychological Review, 110*(1), 145.

Russell, J. A., & Barrett, L. F. (1999). Core affect, prototypical emotional episodes, and other things called emotion: Dissecting the elephant. *Journal of Personality and Social Psychology, 76*(5), 805–819.

Solomon, R. L. (1980). The opponent-process theory of acquired motivation: the costs of pleasure and the benefits of pain. *American Psychologist, 35*(8), 691.

Tesser, A. (2000). On the confluence of self-esteem maintenance mechanisms. *Personality and Social Psychology Review, 4*(4), 290–299.

Watson, D., Clark, L. A., & Tellegen, A. (1988). Development and validation of brief measures of positive and negative affect: The PANAS scales. *Journal of Personality and Social Psychology, 54*(6), 1063.

AGGRESSION AND ANGER

Anger is a common emotion that it is often a causal antecedent to aggressive behavior. This entry briefly introduces the concepts of anger and aggression. The entry then discusses how researchers determine the extent to which violent media influences these phenomena. Finally, the entry presents evidence showing that anger and aggression may arise from violent media exposure.

Anger

People report experiencing anger from several times per week to several times per day. However, like many emotions, the definition one adopts depends on one's theoretical perspective. Biological perspectives emphasize that anger may be a remnant of our ancestral past. Anger may have helped our ancestors obtain access to resources and mates and protect their offspring. By contrast, social constructivist theories of emotion suggest that the experience of anger is socioculturally determined. Appraisal theories of emotion suggest that anger arises in response to cognitive interpretations that people make in response to certain situations. Thinking that one has been unjustly harmed is a common anger-inducing appraisal. Other perspectives on anger suggest that

anger can arise in the absence of any particular appraisal or social construction. Two eminent anger scholars recently emphasized the commonalities of the various theoretical perspectives by defining anger as "a syndrome of relatively specific feelings, cognitions, and physiological reactions linked associatively with an urge to injure some target" (Berkowitz & Harmon-Jones, 2004, p. 108).

Aggression

There are many forms of aggression and overlap among the different forms, but aggression induced largely by anger is called *hostile, reactive, impulsive,* or *affective* aggression. This is in contrast to other subtypes of aggression such as *instrumental* aggression or *defensive* aggression. The definition of aggression is sometimes questioned, but scientists generally agree that aggression contains two key features. The first feature is that aggression is behavior enacted toward a target with the intent to harm the target. The second key feature is that the behavior enacted must be aversive and the target must be motivated to avoid the behavior (e.g., being insulted or slapped in the face). For example, shooting one's hunting partner certainly meets the first criterion but would be considered an act of aggression only if the shooting were intentional. The terms *violence* and *aggression* are often used interchangeably, but many scientists define violence as extreme acts of physical aggression.

Examining the Effects of Violent Media on Anger and Aggression

Violent media researchers typically examine films, television, video games, comic books, and music. Most of these forms of media contain a high proportion of aggressive content and are popular among children and adults. Short-term effects are determined through experimental methods, usually within the confines of a research laboratory. In these experiments, some participants are randomly assigned to exposure to media with aggressive content and others are not. Anger and aggressive behavior are then measured. Long-term effects are typically examined by assessing exposure to violent media, anger, and aggression over time in the real world. Researchers can then determine to what extent exposure to violent media may influence anger and aggression at future time points. The best way to determine whether exposure to violent media influences anger or aggression is through meta-analysis. A meta-analysis is a statistical synthesis of many experimental or nonexperimental studies on a topic that share a similar independent variable (e.g., media violence) and similar outcome variable (e.g., aggression). This procedure allows the researcher to estimate the size of the effect of media violence on anger and aggression.

Media Violence and Anger

Violent media exposure can induce anger. A meta-analysis of 50 experimental and nonexperimental studies reported that the effect of violent media on angry feelings was moderate in size. Another meta-analysis that focused specifically on video games found a moderate effect of violent games on anger in laboratory experiments. The long-term effects were much smaller.

Violent media can also indirectly increase anger via physiological arousal and the activation of hostile thoughts. Violent media is often exciting and increases short-term physiological arousal. Classic social psychological research shows that people often look to the social situation to interpret feelings of arousal. In the context of violent media, if someone is provoked after violent media exposure, he or she may misinterpret the heightened physiological arousal as caused by the provoking incident rather than the media. This misattribution of the physiological arousal can cause people to become angry. This phenomenon is known as *excitation transfer*.

Media Violence and Aggression

Social cognitive theories are typically invoked to explain the effects of violent media on aggression. These theories emphasize how individuals develop cognitive scripts for social interaction and learn what behavior is acceptable or not by observing others. Observing repeated acts of media violence is thought to bias the way children and adults think about their social world in a hostile manner. Indeed, two meta-analyses found that the effect of exposure to violent media on aggressive thinking was small to moderate. Consistent with the effects of violent media on anger and aggressive thinking, several meta-analyses have found consistently small-to-moderate effects of violent media on aggressive behavior. The short-term effects are typically larger than the long-term effects. One of these meta-analyses found that the effects of violent media exposure on aggression were greater in adults than children in the short term,

but long-term effects were greater in children than adults. Although men tend to be more aggressive than women, violent media effects on aggression are comparable in men and women. Interestingly, the size of the relationship between violent media exposure and aggressive behavior is larger than many well-known health effects (e.g., exposure to asbestos and cancer). Of the nine health effects examined in one report, only the effect of smoking on lung cancer was greater than the effect of violent media on aggression.

One caveat is in order. Although the majority of published evidence supports the notion that media violence increases anger and aggression, the extent to which media violence increases serious acts of violence (e.g., homicide) still remains debated by some scientists.

Thomas F. Denson

See also Aggression, Definition and Assessment of; Aggression, Risk Factors of; Aggression and Brain Functioning; Aggression and Culture; Aggression in Youth; Aggressive Behavior; Aggressive Personality; Arousal and Aggressive Content, Theory and Psychology of; Bobo Doll Studies; Catharsis Theory; Effect Size in Media Violence, Research and Effects of; Effects From Violent Content, Short- and Long-Term; Gender, Effects of Violent Content on; General Aggression Model; Longitudinal Research Findings on the Effects of Violent Content; Psychobiology of Violence; Realism of Violent Content, Real-World Violence on Television, and Their Effects; Relational Aggression; Trait Aggression; Violence, Definition of

Further Readings

Anderson, C. A., Shibuya, A., Ihori, N., Swing, E. L., Bushman, B. J., Sakamoto, A., Rothstein, H. R., & Saleem, M. (2010). Violent video game effects on aggression, empathy, and prosocial behavior in Eastern and Western countries: A meta-analytic review. *Psychological Bulletin, 136,* 151–173.

Berkowitz, L., & Harmon-Jones, E. (2004). Toward an understanding of the determinants of anger. *Emotion, 4,* 107–130.

Bushman, B. J., & Anderson, C. A. (2001). Media violence and the American public: Scientific fact versus media misinformation. *American Psychologist, 56,* 477–489.

Bushman, B. J., & Huesmann, L. R. (2006). Short-term and long-term effects of violent media on aggression in children and adults. *Archives of Pediatrics & Adolescent Medicine, 160,* 348–352.

Huesmann, L. R. (2007). The impact of electronic media violence: Scientific theory and research. *Journal of Adolescent Health, 41,* S6—S13.

Paik, H., & Comstock, G. (1994). The effects of television violence on antisocial behavior: A meta-analysis. *Communication Research, 21,* 516–546.

AGGRESSION AND ATTACHMENT

Attachment theory, formulated by John Bowlby (1982), was first developed to explain emotional bonding between children and their primary caregivers. The theory has since been expanded to many domains and has become one of the leading frameworks for understanding close relationships, social development, and various interpersonal social behaviors. Recently, scholars have successfully applied attachment theory to the study of interpersonal and intergroup conflict, anger, and aggression. This entry gives an overview of research findings concerning the role of attachment processes in interpersonal and intergroup conflict. Suggestions are also given on how attachment theory may be relevant to understanding media violence effects on aggression, and recommendations are made for future research in this area.

Overview of Attachment Theory

Bowlby posited that children are born with an attachment behavioral system that motivates them to seek proximity to caregivers in times of need. Attachment behaviors serve an evolutionary function. Infants protect themselves and increase their chances of survival by being closely attached to their primary caregivers.

All children are attached to their primary caregivers, but important individual differences exist in attachment styles. These attachment differences are shaped by interactions with attachment figures across the life span, especially in childhood. Interactions with attachment figures who are available and responsive contribute to a dispositional sense of attachment security consisting of positive expectations about others' availability and positive views of the self as competent and valued. When attachment figures are not reliably available and supportive, a sense of insecurity arises. Current scholars describe attachment insecurity in terms of two dimensions. *Attachment anxiety* reflects the degree to which a person worries that the attachment figure

will not be available in times of need and is afraid of being rejected or abandoned. *Attachment avoidance* reflects the extent to which a person distrusts attachment figures' goodwill and strives to maintain behavioral independence and emotional distance from attachment figures. Like other cognitive networks, attachment cognitive models (referred by Bowlby as "internal working models") and their associated responses are automatically activated in relevant situations.

Attachment and Aggression in Childhood

Bowlby viewed anger in children as a functional response to separation that may motivate attachment figures to pay attention and provide care. Aggression may be viewed as an exaggerated version of this otherwise functional behavior. Extreme anger, aggression, and violence are most typical of children who experience repeated separations and are subjected to the threat of being abandoned. Indeed, attachment insecurity has been found to predict fighting and bullying in children (e.g., Renken et al., 1989).

Attachment and Aggression in Adulthood

Beyond childhood, research finds positive associations among attachment insecurities, interpersonal conflict, and aggression. For instance, the experience and expression of anger in adults have been linked to attachment insecurity. Significant differences also exist in secure and insecure individuals' responses to conflict situations. Secure individuals tend to emphasize the challenging aspects of interpersonal conflicts, whereas insecure individuals are likely to appraise interpersonal conflicts in more threatening terms and apply less effective conflict resolution strategies.

Attachment processes have been linked to various aggressive behaviors in adolescence and adulthood. Attachment insecurity, especially anxious attachment, is a risk factor for intimate partner violence (e.g., Mauricio, Tein, & Lopez, 2007). Insecure attachment has been linked to intimate partner violence among men and among women (Dutton, 2011), and in heterosexual and homosexual relationships (Bartholomew, Oram, & Landolt, 2008).

Studies show that insecure attachment is also associated with delinquency and criminality. Although both attachment anxiety and avoidance predict a greater risk of antisocial behavior, anxious and avoidant individuals may engage in such behavior for different reasons. Scholars suggest that whereas anxious individuals sometimes perform criminal acts as a way of crying out for attention and care, avoidant individuals are more likely to do so to distance themselves, demonstrating a lack of concern for others.

Attachment effects on intergroup aggression can be considered an extension of attachment effects on interpersonal conflict. A sense of attachment security can reduce the fear and threat of the unknown, be it settings or people who are different and unfamiliar to us. Outgroup members are often perceived to be different and threatening to ingroup members, leading to intergroup biases and conflict between the two groups. Mario Mikulincer and Phillip Shaver (2001) suggested that attachment insecurities, which are characterized by conflict-management deficiencies, would be associated with destructive responses to intergroup conflict and with more hostility and aggression toward outgroup members. Indeed, self-reported attachment anxiety has been associated with more negative responses to different outgroups (Mikulincer & Shaver, 2001). Furthermore, these scholars find that increasing people's sense of attachment security can reduce hostile responses and decrease aggression toward an outgroup member.

Media Effects, Attachment, and Aggression

Attachment processes may be relevant to media violence effects in several ways. First, trait attachment style differences may act as moderators of media violence effects on aggression. Given the positive effects of attachment security on responses to interpersonal conflict, it is possible that secure attachment acts as a protective factor that mitigates the negative effects of violent media. Attachment may also act as a mediator of media violence effects on aggression. The general aggression model formulated by Craig Anderson and Brad Bushman (2002) posits that media violence exposure increases aggression in the long term by influencing one's stable personality traits. One important personality variable to consider may be a person's predominant attachment style. It is possible that, in addition to causing hostile attribution bias and decreased empathy, habitual exposure to violent media can also cause a person to shift toward a more insecure dispositional attachment style. Links among media violence exposure, aggression, and attachment have not yet been empirically explored. However, the growing research literature concerning attachment and

aggression indicates that attachment style may be an important variable to consider in future research on media violence effects.

Summary

Attachment theory has been successfully applied to the study of interpersonal conflict, anger, and aggression. Attachment processes have been linked to a diverse array of aggressive behaviors in childhood, adolescence, and adulthood. Attachment insecurity, and especially anxious attachment, is characterized by conflict management deficiencies and has been linked to an increased risk of intimate partner violence, antisocial behavior, and intergroup aggression. Conversely, secure attachment has been shown to predict more constructive conflict resolution strategies and a decreased risk of aggression. Future research is needed to shed light on the possible role of attachment processes in media violence effects on aggression.

Muniba Saleem and Sara Prot

See also Aggression, Definition and Assessment of; Aggression, Risk Factors of; Aggression in Youth; Aggressive Behavior

Further Readings

Anderson, C. A., & Bushman, B. J. (2002). Human aggression. *Annual Review of Psychology, 53,* 27–51.

Bartholomew, K., Oram, D., & Landolt, M. A. (2008). Correlates of partner abuse in male same sex relationships. *Violence and Victims, 23,* 348–364.

Bowlby, J. (1982). *Attachment and loss: Vol. 1. Attachment* (2nd ed.). New York, NY: Basic Books.

Dutton, D. (2011). Attachment and violence: An anger born of fear. In P. R. Shaver & M. Mikulincer (Eds.), *Human aggression and violence: Causes, manifestations, and consequences* (pp. 241–257).

Mauricio, A. M., Tein, J. Y., & Lopez, F. G. (2007). Borderline and antisocial personality scores as mediators between attachment and intimate partner violence. *Violence and Victims, 22,* 139–157.

Mikulincer, M., & Shaver, P. R. (2001). Attachment theory and intergroup bias: Evidence that priming the secure base schema attenuates negative reactions to out-groups. *Journal of Personality and Social Psychology, 81,* 97–115.

Renken, B., Egeland, B., Marvinney, D., Mangelsdorf, S., & Sroufe, L. A. (1989). Early childhood antecedents of aggression and passive withdrawal in early elementary school. *Journal of Personality, 57,* 257–281.

AGGRESSION AND BRAIN FUNCTIONING

Originating in the late 19th century and early 20th century with the ideas of Cesare Lombroso and Earnest Hooton, researchers have long taken an interest in understanding violent behaviors in terms of biological factors. These early works had racist overtones and were used to inform some unfortunate policies, including eugenics and euthanasia. Following the fallout from these movements, researchers began to distance themselves from exploring the biological correlates of aggression and instead focused on environmental influences. In the past several decades, however, literature again has begun to showcase studies that provide support for biological risk factors. Because the growing empirical evidence is assumedly free of political agenda and consistently demonstrates support for biological predictors of aggression, biological criminology has reappeared, and the field is growing.

Within the field of biological criminology, numerous factors have been linked to aggression, including neurobiology, psychophysiology, genes, and hormones. Of these influences, neurobiology, specifically brain functioning, is the topic presented in this entry. The importance of brain functioning in understanding aggression is underscored by one of the key researchers in the field, Adrian Raine, when he said, "It is now beyond doubt that brain deficits contribute in some way to antisocial and aggressive behavior" (2002, p. 4). Because of the central role of brain functioning in understanding pathways to aggression, it is apparent that empirical evidence of this nature is relevant when examining media violence. More specifically, media exposure may interact with brain functioning to predict aggressive tendencies. For example, if an individual is exposed to high levels of media violence and has neurobiological risk factors, then he or she may be at greater risk of becoming aggressive. This entry provides a summary of aggression-related constructs, a review of brain-imaging techniques, themes seen in the empirical evidence related to structural and functional factors, and ethical considerations.

Aggression-Related Constructs

There are a number of interrelated constructs that are frequently cited in the aggression and brain functioning literature. Two of the most commonly studied

aggression-related constructs in brain-imaging studies are antisocial personality disorder and psychopathy. Based on the *Diagnostic and Statistical Manual of Mental Disorders IV-TR*, antisocial personality disorder is characterized by a persistent pattern of disregard for societal norms and the rights of other individuals, deceitfulness, aggressiveness, and irritability. Some behaviors of an individual diagnosed with antisocial personality disorder may be aggressive in nature, but this is not a necessary criterion.

Psychopathy, as discussed by Hervey Cleckley, is associated with impulsivity, superficial charm, lack of empathy and remorse, and narcissism. Individuals with psychopathic personality traits often exhibit extreme violent behaviors. Psychopathy is distinct from antisocial personality disorder because a large number of psychopaths meet the criteria for antisocial personality disorder; however, approximately only 25% of individuals with antisocial personality disorder are psychopaths. Psychopaths are convicted of more violent crimes than non-psychopaths.

Because these various terms are relevant, this entry includes empirical evidence related not only to aggression but also to antisocial personality disorder and psychopathy. Furthermore, individuals who are at greater risk of becoming aggressive tend to have many of the features associated with antisocial personality disorder and psychopathy, even if they do not meet full criteria (e.g., lack of concern for others, impulsivity, irritability).

Brain-Imaging Techniques

The field of neuroanatomy dates back as far as the early 18th century and the development of phrenology by Franz Joseph Gall. By studying the shape of the cranial bones, Gall claimed he could make inferences regarding brain functioning. Current brain-imaging techniques allow us to more accurately map both structural aspects of the brain and neural processes that occur during emotional and cognitive tasks. The two main advances that improved our ability to understand brain structure and functioning were computerized axial tomography (CAT) and magnetic resonance imaging (MRI). CAT scans produce a series of X-rays that pass unevenly through tissues that vary in density, which then allows the evaluator to distinguish among fluid, bone, and brain tissue by creating a series of cross-sectional images. MRI scans involve a power magnet that is used to create a magnetic field that orients all hydrogen atoms in the same direction. Radio frequency is then used to alter the alignment of the magnetization, and this signal is used to construct an image. The development of these techniques and subsequent advances (e.g., positron emission tomography, PET; single photon emission computed tomography, SPECT; functional magnetic resonance imaging, fMRI) have enhanced our understanding of the link between brain functioning and aggression.

Structural Differences

Structural techniques have allowed researchers to examine the volume of various parts of the brain, which are called *regions of interest*. Research conducted in the 1990s demonstrated that murderers tended to evidence brain atrophy, or the loss of cells, particularly in the frontotemporal region. More recent research conducted by Raine and colleagues found that antisocial individuals demonstrated an 11% reduction of gray matter in the prefrontal cortex. Follow-up research found that unsuccessful psychopaths (i.e., psychopaths who were criminally convicted at least once) evidenced reduced prefrontal cortical gray matter when compared with both successful psychopaths (i.e., psychopaths who were never convicted of a crime) and noncriminal controls. Therefore, it appears that reduced gray matter in the prefrontal cortex is predictive of a particular type of antisocial tendency (i.e., unsuccessful criminals).

Research conducted in noncriminal samples has also demonstrated the importance of the structure of the frontal cortex for understanding aggression. Specifically, noncriminal individuals who experience damage to the frontal cortex display personality changes that may help us understand risk factors for aggressive tendencies, such as argumentativeness, lack of concern for behavioral consequences, impulsivity, distractibility, emotional lability, and violence. Additional structural deficits that have been demonstrated in individuals with antisocial personality disorder include reductions in the dorsolateral, medial frontal and orbitofrontal cortices, and temporal lobes. Overall, there is some inconsistency in empirical findings, but the most consistently demonstrated finding is that individuals who evidence greater aggressiveness and violence tend to display structural deficits in the prefrontal cortex. Furthermore, results suggest that these brain deficits appear to be particularly relevant in violent offenders who engage in reactive violence, rather than proactive violence (i.e., premeditated, planned), and unsuccessful criminals.

Individuals who exhibit greater aggressive tendencies tend to exhibit psychopathic and antisocial tendencies, regardless of whether these individuals meet criteria for antisocial personality disorder or psychopathy. Therefore, it is not surprising that imaging studies have demonstrated structural differences in the prefrontal cortex in violent individuals, because this area of the brain has been linked to planning, decision making, emotion regulation, empathy, moral judgment, and self-reflection.

Functional Differences

Structural imaging techniques provide information such as the volume of regions of interest, whereas functional techniques examine neural processes in various parts of the brain. Fortunately, the functional differences found in aggressive individuals tend to parallel the results demonstrated using structural imaging techniques. Functional differences provide additional information above and beyond structural differences because researchers can examine minute-to-minute neural changes that occur in response to laboratory tasks.

Numerous studies using PET, a tomographic nuclear medical imaging technique that produces three-dimensional images of the brain, found lower glucose metabolism in the temporal and frontal lobes of violent individuals. Raine and colleagues found that during a continuous performance task, murderers evidenced significantly reduced glucose metabolism in the medial and lateral prefrontal cortex. Lower levels of glucose metabolism in this area of the brain have been linked to impulsive violent offenders and likely provide support for the prefrontal cortex as a key mechanism in stopping emotional drives generated by the limbic system. Upon closer examination, it was demonstrated that murderers who did not experience early psychosocial risk factors evidenced lower levels of glucose metabolism than those who did experience early psychosocial deficits. This finding is in line with the Social Push Hypothesis, which is discussed by many researchers, including Sarnoff Mednick, Peter Venables, and Raine. According to this hypothesis, if an individual is not exposed to psychosocial risk factors that would "push" him or her toward antisocial or aggressive behaviors, then physiological factors will likely better account for his or her antisocial tendencies. This theory has been demonstrated in reference to numerous biological markers of aggression, including resting heart rate. Empirical evidence of this nature suggests that although biological correlates, such as brain functioning, may be consistently linked to a particular behavior, numerous factors influence the development of complex behaviors such as violent tendencies.

An additional area of deficit that has been consistently demonstrated in functional imaging studies of aggression is the limbic system, specifically reduced amygdala activity. Numerous studies have found that psychopathic individuals have reduced amygdala activity during emotional moral decision making. Individuals who exhibit particularly high levels of manipulative and deceitful behaviors show deficits in the entire moral neural circuit (i.e., medial prefrontal cortex, posterior cingulate, angular gyrus). The amygdala has also been linked to fear conditioning, which is another risk factor for aggressiveness. It is thought that individuals who exhibit high levels of violence have weakened fear conditioning and therefore do not adhere to societal norms because they do not learn to distinguish right and wrong. Because psychopathy is characterized by disruptions in moral behavior, emotional processing, and fearlessness, it is not surprising that deficits in the areas of the brain linked to emotional moral decision making have been demonstrated in this population.

Ethical Considerations

Although studies examining brain functioning have made considerable strides in recent years and have significantly contributed to our understanding of pathways to aggression, readers are cautioned about the application of these findings. The empirical evidence presented here should be considered support for risk factors that may increase the likelihood of aggression in particular contexts and in conjunction with additional risk factors (e.g., exposure to media violence). The methodology utilized in brain-imaging studies is relatively new and has limitations. For example, activation in a brain-imaging study may reflect the activation of an inhibitory system. Therefore, research should be dedicated to further expanding and understanding this type of research.

Readers are also cautioned because these types of findings are often misinterpreted as representing unchangeable biological predispositions toward a life of violence. An individual may exhibit one of the neurobiological risk factors presented here and never exhibit aggressive tendencies. Likewise, an aggressive individual may not evidence any brain deficits. These results can only be interpreted at a group level and cannot be considered predictive of aggression in

a particular case. Findings related to neurobiology may help researchers explain why some individuals exposed to high levels of media violence become violent themselves, while others do not. Also, the nervous system is quite malleable and displays a high level of plasticity. Therefore, it is possible for these biological systems to change during development and should be kept in mind when studying the effects of media violence across the life span. Overall, brain-imaging studies have provided important information about aggression; however, this type of information can only be considered a piece of a larger puzzle.

Laura C. Wilson and Angela Scarpa

See also Aggression, Risk Factors of; Aggressive Behavior; Ethical Issues in Researching Media Violence Effects; Psychobiology of Violence

Further Readings

Gao, Y., Glenn, A. L., Schug, R. A., Yang, Y., & Raine, A. (2009). The neurobiology of psychopathy: A neurodevelopmental perspective. *Canadian Psychiatric Association Journal, 54*, 813–823.

Martin, G. N. (2003). *Essential biological psychology.* New York, NY: Oxford University Press.

Nordstrom, B. R., Gao, Y., Glenn, A. L., Peskin, M., Rudo-Hutt, A. S., Schug, R. A., Yang, Y., & Raine, A. (2011). Neurocriminology. In R. Huber, D. L. Bannasch, & P. Brennan (Eds.), *Aggression* (pp. 255–283). San Diego, CA: Academic Press.

Raine, A. (1997). The psychopathology of crime: Criminal behavior as a clinical disorder. San Diego, CA: Academic Press.

Raine, A. (2002). Annotation: The role of prefrontal deficits, low autonomic arousal, and early health factors in the development of antisocial and aggressive behavior in children. *Journal of Child Psychology and Psychiatry, 43*, 417–434.

Volavka, J. (2002). *Neurobiology of violence.* Washington, DC: American Psychiatric Publishing.

Wager, T. D., Hernandez, L., Jonides, J., & Lindquist, M. (2007). Elements of functional neuroimaging. In J. T. Cacioppo, L. G. Tassinary, & G. G. Berntson (Eds.), *Handbook of psychophysiology* (3rd ed., pp. 19–55). Cambridge, UK: Cambridge University Press.

AGGRESSION AND CULTURE

Aggressive behavior is a universal phenomenon through time and space. This entry reviews interpersonal aggression, defined as behavior intentionally targeted to hurt another person, rather than intergroup or societal conflicts such as warfare. All human cultures exhibit a range of aggressive behaviors. This range encompasses physical, verbal, relational, and more recently, cyber types of aggression. However, cultures vary considerably in the incidence of different types of aggression and exhibit gender differences. Various factors help us to understand these differences, including descriptions and definitions of aggression; the encouragement, tolerance, or prohibition of various forms of aggression; and organizational and technological factors.

Behavioral Differences in Aggression in Different Cultures

In many Western cultures (e.g., the United States, the United Kingdom), direct physical assaults, damaging someone's personal belongings, and verbal taunts or insults are the dominant forms of aggression. Physical aggression is evident from early childhood, and is most frequent at around 2 years of age; it tends to decrease in most children, to be replaced by verbal and relational aggression through childhood, but with some increase in bullying and sexual harassment in early adolescence and dating violence in later adolescence. Socialization processes tend to decrease direct aggression in later life, but partner violence, workplace violence, and child abuse remain considerable societal problems.

In other cultures, such as Far East Asian (e.g., South Korea, Japan), verbal or relational aggression are more common than physical forms of aggression, even in middle childhood. In Japan, physical kinds of *ijime* (Japanese bullying) are relatively rare, and social exclusion by classmates is more likely. In South Korea, a common form of aggression in school is *wang-ta,* in which pupils ostracize one person from a group; aggressive behavior is used to reinforce ingroup conformity and belongingness. The emphasis on suppressing physical violence (but being more tolerant of social exclusion) carries through to the workplace.

Comparative surveys sponsored by the World Health Organization, such as those on Health Behavior in School-Aged Children, show variations in behaviors, such as bullying in European and North American countries, by up to 10 times. Country differences often outweigh age and gender differences. Bullying rates tend to decline with age, and perpetrator rates are generally higher in males, but these differences also vary across cultures.

Linguistic Issues and Aggression

All languages have a number of words describing different kinds of aggressive behaviors, such as in English: *aggression, violence, harassment, intimidation, abuse, bullying.* However, the meanings of terms may not be equivalent across languages. This has been most studied in the case of *bullying,* an English term usually defined as repeated physical, verbal, or relational aggression in which an imbalance of power exists. However, many Latin-based languages do not have a term corresponding to *bullying* but do have terms related to violence or intimidation (e.g., *violencia* or *prepotenza* in Italian) that do not necessarily include imbalance of power. The definition of *ijime* in Japan emphasizes group processes and relational aggression more than the definition of *bullying* does.

Words and their meanings also change historically. In Western societies, for many decades *aggression* was used mainly for direct physical or verbal aggression; its extension to indirect and relational aggression came about in the 1980s and 1990s. This broadening of usage came through the work of social scientists but appears to have permeated to the general public. Also, the terms used by laypeople for aggressive behavior can change. For example, different generations of South Korean people use different words; pupils have created a new word, *jjin-ta* (not in any current dictionary), to replace *wang-ta* to indicate a bullied or socially isolated person. Change of terms may reflect changes in aggressive behavior over time, or changes in people's perception for aggressive behavior, or both.

Aggressive Behavior Versus Normative Behavior

Aggressive behavior often brings some kind of sanction, and socialization pressures and such sanctions can affect life-course trends in aggression. However, what is considered aggressive, and deserving of negative sanction, varies by culture. Consider, for example, an older pupil who forces a younger one to carry his bags; English pupils might describe this as bullying, but Japanese pupils do not regard this as *ijime*, because a hierarchical imposition of power in this context is seen as normative. Another example in which historical changes in recent decades is evident is in the physical chastisement of children by parents or caregivers: in some countries this is considered normative but is considered illegal in others.

Psychological Aspects of Culture

Cultures vary in their characteristics in ways that can affect interpersonal relationships. Geert Hofstede proposed five dimensions: power distance, uncertainty avoidance, individualism/collectivism, masculinity, and long/short-term orientation (often overlapped to Confucian values). Power distance may be relevant in understanding the acceptance or lack of acceptance of hierarchically imposed behaviors. Masculinity may be important in understanding gender differences in aggression. The individualism/collectivism dimension can be important for understanding contrasts between many Western and Eastern societies: in individualistic cultures social ties between individuals are loose and cultural values emphasize self-reliance, autonomy, and personal achievement; in collectivistic cultures, people are in strong and cohesive ingroups, and group goals have primary concern over individual goals when there is conflict between them. Thus, for harming someone else, individual attacks may be chosen as most effective in individualistic societies, whereas in collectivist societies social exclusion may be chosen as most effective.

Organizational and Technological Factors

The mass media portray aggressive behaviors with varying degrees of negative sanctioning, neutral representation, or glorification and enjoyment (as in some video and computer games). Societies vary in the penetration of various forms of mass media and in the extent to which aggression and violence are censored or controlled (e.g., regulation of presentation or sales of aggressive or violent content to children). Despite continuing debate on the issue, it is likely that aggression portrayed in the mass media has some influence on real-life behaviors.

Cyber-aggression, using mobile phones and/or the Internet to engage in aggressive behavior, can take a variety of forms, and has become a significant factor in the past decade. The extent of cyber-aggression in part is influenced by the availability and penetration of mobile phones (and especially smartphones) and the Internet in different societies—a rapidly developing and changing pattern in the first decades of the 21st century.

Because negative sanctions are in operation for many kinds of aggressive behavior, its expression is influenced by opportunity factors. For example, violence in schools can be influenced by school and class ethos and school design. Even factors such as the extent of homeroom class teaching, and the length and supervision of playground breaks, vary across societies and can help explain differences in aggression and bullying.

Peter K. Smith and Seung-ha Lee

See also Aggression, Definition and Assessment of; Gender and Aggression; Media as a Reflection of Society; Media Violence, Definitions and Context of; Moral Development, Effects of Media Violence on; Social Cognitive Theory; Social Learning From Media; Socialization of Violence in Media and Its Effects; Television Violence

Further Readings

Anderson, C. A., Shibuya, A., Ihori, N., Swing, E. L., Bushman, B. J., Sakamoto, A., Rothstein, H. R., & Saleem, M. (2010). Violent video game effects on aggression, empathy, and prosocial behavior in Eastern and Western countries: A meta-analytic review. *Psychological Bulletin, 136*, 151–173.

Lee, S., Smith, P. K., & Monks, C. (2011). Perception of bullying-like phenomena in South Korea: A qualitative approach from a lifespan perspective. *Journal of Aggression, Conflict and Peace Research, 3*, 210–221.

Smith, P. K., Cowie, H., Olafsson, R., Liefooghe, A. P. D., & 17 colleagues. (2002). Definitions of bullying: A comparison of terms used, and age and sex differences, in a 14-country international comparison. *Child Development, 73*, 1119–1133.

AGGRESSION IN YOUTH

Although considerable debate may still exist regarding violent media's influence on aggression in adults, there is considerable agreement about its influence on aggression in youth. The arrival of new forms of entertainment media is usually accompanied by concerns and research regarding their antisocial effects on children. Dime novels, comic books, films, radio programs, and television shows have all received their share of criticism by politicians, social advocates, and scholars for their alleged effects on youth aggression.

Scholars define *media violence* as content portraying aggressive or violent behaviors by one character against another. In this context, *aggression* is generally defined as any physical or verbal behavior intended to cause physical or emotional harm to another person, whereas the terms *violence* or *violent behavior* are reserved for more acute forms of aggression, such as those severe enough to produce serious physical harm. Extensive research has examined violent media's influence on violent behaviors as well as its influence on aggressive thoughts, feelings, and physiological reactions that might affect a youth's subsequent aggressive or violent behavior. After defining youth audiences and describing the role of developmental difference in responding to media violence and in the exposure and appeal of media violence, this entry reviews the evidence and theories regarding the role of media violence on youth aggression and discusses ways to moderate its influence.

Defining Youth Audiences

When considering violent media's influence on youth aggression, it is important to recognize that *youth* is not a monolithic term. Developmental scholars often separate youth into stages such as *infancy* (from birth until 12 months), *toddlerhood* (up to the age of 3 years), *early childhood* (to age 5 years), *middle childhood* (to age 10 years), *early adolescence* (to age 13 years), *middle adolescence* (to age 16 years), and *late adolescence* (to age 19 years). Although broader categories may be used such as *childhood* (from the ages of 1 to 10 years) and *adolescence* (from the ages of 11 to 19 years), the guiding principle for separating children into stages relates to developmental differences, which are likely to govern the influence of violent media.

Developmental Differences in Responding to Media Violence

Theories of child development pay close attention to age-related changes in information processing, yet most traditional theories of media effects overlook developmental changes. This is surprising, given that cognitive development has important implications for a child's response to media broadly and to violent media in particular. For example, the ability to distinguish fiction from reality is not present in early childhood. As such, young children are more likely to imitate cartoon characters and fantasy violence than are their older counterparts. Furthermore, prior to middle childhood, children lack the ability to incorporate abstract plot information into judgments. This results in judgments of right and wrong that are based more on perceptual information (i.e., whether a character appears good or bad) than conceptual information (i.e., whether actions were justified or

unjustified). Related middle childhood developments in inferential skills allow children to connect consequences occurring late in a story to earlier events; prior to this, punishments at the story's end for earlier violent behavior may not be understood or function as a learned deterrent to aggression.

Exposure and Appeal

Developmental differences are also important in the appeal of and exposure to violent media among youth audiences. Existing research shows that television viewing and video game play occupy a large part of children's lives: children watch approximately 28 hours of television per week and may spend more than 10 hours playing video games. In both cases, violent content pervades these experiences, with some of the highest occurrences being found in children's Saturday morning cartoons and nearly all video games rated appropriate for teens containing violence. As such, the American Academy of Child Adolescent Psychiatry reports that the average American child will view more than 200,000 acts of media violence and 16,000 murders before graduating from high school.

The sheer prevalence of violence across many forms of media suggests that individuals are drawn to it. Yet the reasons for this appeal are complex, and questions remain unanswered. Many scholars believe that the appeal of violence depends on several contextual factors related to both the violence itself and developmental characteristics. For example, research with both children and adolescents shows that justified violence against a disliked and deserving villain is more appealing than the unjustified punishment of a liked character; sex differences exist in the appeal of violence, with boys being more attracted to violence than girls; and individual differences such as sensation seeking and trait aggression are positively associated with the appeal of violence across several different media. Meanwhile, some researchers distinguish attraction (i.e., being drawn to violent media) from its enjoyment, suggesting that even those drawn to violence do not always enjoy it. Extensive research is needed to explicate how developmental differences and contextual factors shape the exposure to and appeal of violent media for youth.

Evidence of Violent Media's Effects on Aggression

Theory and research suggest that *some* media representations of violent behavior may decrease aggression in viewers. For example, social learning theory suggests that repeated exposure to media content showing that violence has negative consequences for perpetrators and victims alike should inhibit modeling among viewers who learn that violence led to the negative consequences. Yet the necessary conditions for understanding and learning are often absent among youth audiences. In their absence, exposure to any violent media may increase aggression.

Although media are not the sole cause of violent behavior, evidence amassed during 60 years has led scholars to argue conclusively that violent media exposure can be an important contributor to youth aggression. Some think media's influence is rather small, whereas others regard it as substantial, particularly when considering its cumulative effect over years of exposure, or when comparing its influence to other known contributors to youth violence such as lower IQ level, broken homes, abusive parents, and antisocial peers. Yet in either case, the accumulated evidence demonstrates that exposure to violent media can increase aggression in children, adolescents, and young adults. For example, meta-analyses summarizing more than 200 studies on exposure to television violence and aggression revealed a significant average effect size across survey and experimental research. Notably, the average effect seems negatively related to age, with effects found to be largest from infancy through early childhood, smaller for middle childhood, and smallest for early and middle adolescents. Meta-analyses examining the association of violent video games and aggression produced similar findings across a wide range of outcomes, including aggressive thoughts, feelings, and behaviors.

Theory on Violent Media's Influence

Scholars from multiple disciplines have attempted to identify the mechanisms responsible for violent media's influence on aggression, along with factors that moderate this influence. These efforts have revealed several factors that contribute to the complex association between media violence and human aggression. Recent theory distinguishes between temporary and enduring influence, often explaining short-term effects based on activation processes such as priming and arousal, and long-term effects originating from observational learning and desensitization. An overview of these processes is provided by the general aggression model, which identifies media violence as an environmental attribute that

can activate aggressive knowledge structures and influence learning processes to shape both short- and long-term effects.

Short-Term Influence Processes

Scholars have identified several mechanisms associated with violent media's short-term influence on aggression, including *physiological arousal*, which may intensify aggression caused by other sources, and *mimicry*, which is governed by automatic response tendencies among younger children. Research conducted on infants, toddlers, and early childhood viewers shows that young children will automatically copy behaviors immediately after observing them in real life or media. This mechanism was first demonstrated in the well-known Bobo Doll studies by Albert Bandura, who observed that children mimic novel violent behaviors demonstrated in a film.

The most discussed mechanism regarding violent media's temporary influence is *priming*. Research on cognitive priming suggests that exposure to environmental stimuli can elicit or "prime" related thoughts and feelings. Applied here, violent media content can activate aggression-related thoughts. Once activated, these thoughts can bias automatic appraisal and response processes that govern aggressive thoughts, feelings, and motor tendencies. For a short time, activated thoughts and feelings can bias behavior toward aggression, particularly in viewers who were already angered (either habitually or temporarily due to provocation), ready to aggress, or lacking in impulse control (such as children and adolescents). Experimental research shows evidence that violent media "primes" can temporarily activate aggressive thoughts, feelings, and behaviors in people of all ages.

Long-Term Influence Processes

Accounts of violent media's long-term influence on aggression often include learning mechanisms explaining how short-term processes can produce lasting change. Social learning theory discusses these mechanisms in terms of *observational learning*, or acquiring knowledge through examples provided by others. Observational learning distinguishes the mechanism of short-term *mimicry*, in which behaviors are automatically copied, from long-term *imitation*, in which children acquire a set of attitudes, beliefs, and behavioral scripts that govern the likelihood of performing related behaviors in the future.

Long-term processes are also the focus of social information processing, a theory that combines observational learning and priming logic to consider how repeated exposure to media violence (as one of many environmental factors) can influence how aggressive scripts are developed and maintained over time. According to this perspective, each exposure to violent media is another learning trial that can shape the lasting structure and chronic accessibility of aggression-related scripts. Repeated childhood exposure to violence, either in media or real life, can strengthen scripts that promote the use of aggression and increase the likelihood of aggressive behavior into adulthood.

Along with learning mechanisms, desensitization is central to violent media's long-term influence. Desensitization is a form of reduced emotional responsiveness that results from repeated exposure to a stimulus. Existing research suggests that repeated exposure to violent media can reduce arousal responses to real-life aggression and the likelihood that children will intervene to stop real-life aggression. Some scholars hold that the reduced negative response associated with desensitization minimizes sympathy for victims, making people less critical of their own behavior and more likely to aggress themselves.

Moderators of Violent Media's Influence

In addition to explicating the mechanisms of violent media's influence, literature has begun to identify several viewer characteristics and media content factors that moderate this impact. Research on viewer characteristics suggests the importance of several viewer trait variables distinct from developmental differences. Although some of these factors may help mitigate potential aggressive effects, none appear to completely counteract these effects and others may even increase them. For example, gender appears to mitigate effects in certain instances, but prevailing patterns indicate that children of both sexes are affected by exposure. Similarly, though traits such as aggressive disposition and intelligence may strengthen and weaken, respectively, violent media's association with aggression, neither reverses or eliminates the relationship. Last, although factors producing identification are thought to moderate aggressive effects, some argue that all children can find identifiable perpetrators due to the prevalence and diversity of violent media characters. As such, only increased aggressive effects should be expected.

Research on media content also suggests certain factors that may be strong and meaningful moderators of violent media's influence on youth aggression. For example, the positive association between violent media exposure and aggressive response is increased when the perpetrator is attractive, the motive for violence is justified, the act is unpunished or rewarded, or the portrayal is more realistic. By contrast, the association may be weakened, and potentially reversed, when the motive is unjustified, the act is punished, or the victim is shown to suffer. Although the extent to which these moderators alter the influence of violent media is undefined, the importance of these viewer characteristics and media content features has encouraged their study.

Beyond viewer and media content features, research has provided some limited evidence regarding the efficacy of intervention programs designed to counter the influence of violent media on aggression in youths. For example, studies have demonstrated that an in-school antiviolence curriculum can reduce middle school aggression and that a critical viewing program can both decrease aggressive behavior and suppress its association with exposure to violent television.

Future Directions

Although many social and psychological factors combine to affect aggressive behavior, media violence has been shown to be an important contributor to aggression in youths. Indeed, the body of evidence examining media violence has led several professional organizations (e.g., American Academy of Pediatrics, American Medical Association) to make statements cautioning the public about violent media's adverse effects on childhood aggression in particular. Efforts to reduce children's exposure to media violence, whether through government regulation or adult oversight, have been hailed by some scholars as an appropriate measure. Yet additional research is needed to answer questions regarding the best way to minimize violent media's antisocial influence on youth aggression.

Ron Tamborini and Matthew Grizzard

See also Aggression, Definition and Assessment of; Aggression, Risk Factors of; Bobo Doll Studies; Censorship of Violent Content; Cognition: Schemas and Scripts; Desensitization Effects on Society; Ethical Development, Effects on; Forbidden Fruit Hypothesis; National Television Violence Study; Pediatricians and

Media Violence; Peer Influence on Violent Content Effects; Priming Theory; Social Learning From Media; Television Violence

Further Readings

Anderson, C. A., Berkowitz, L., Donnerstein, E., Huesmann, L. R., Johnson, J., Linz, D., et al. (2003). The influence of media violence on youth. *Psychological Science in the Public Interest, 4,* 81–110.

Bushman, B. J., & Huesmann, L. R. (2008). Violence as media content: Effects on children. In W. Donsbach (Ed.), *The International Encyclopedia of Communication* (pp. 5287–5291). Malden, MA: Blackwell.

Kirsh, S. J. (2010). Media and youth: A developmental perspective. Malden, MA: Blackwell.

Strasburger, V. C., Wilson, B. J., & Jordan, A. B. (2009). *Children, adolescents, and the media* (2nd ed.). Thousand Oaks, CA: Sage.

AGGRESSIVE BEHAVIOR

More than 40 years ago, the possibility that television and film violence may have adverse effects on viewers was publicly presented. Repeated exposure to entertainment violence is believed to be a major contributor to aggressive and violent behavior in real life, because media violence can (a) instigate imitation, (b) make real-world violence more acceptable, (c) distort viewers' perceptions of real-world crime and violence, (d) desensitize viewers to the suffering of victims of violence, and (e) increase the accessibility of violent constructs in memory. An increasing number of correlational, experimental, psychophysiological, and longitudinal studies on the effects of violent media have shown that both chronic and brief exposure to violence in films and video games lead to an increase of aggression. Thus, a causal link between media violence and aggression has been established in the literature. This entry begins by defining aggressive behavior and describing its various subtypes. Next, it examines the causal link between media violence and aggression with regard to the general aggression model and individual differences. Last, it suggests future avenues of research.

Definition and Subtypes of Aggressive Behavior

Aggression is defined as a behavior by one person against another that is intended to cause physical or emotional harm when the other person is motivated to avoid or escape this behavior. Aggressive behavior can be distinguished as direct or overt (i.e., physical and verbal) and indirect or covert (i.e., relational aggression; harm is caused through damage to one's social status or relationships). There is also a distinction between reactive and proactive aggression. Reactive aggression is described as a defensive reaction to a perceived threatening stimulus and is accompanied by some visible form of anger. The reactive aggressor is viewed as short tempered and volatile. Proactive aggression is described as unprovoked aversive means of influencing or coercing another person and is more goal directed than is reactive aggression. Proactive aggressors use aggression for social gain and dominance and think of aggression as a positive behavior leading to a desired goal. Researchers investigating the effects of media violence exposure tend to focus on overt forms of aggression, with a number of correlational and experimental studies suggesting changes in physical and verbal aggression after immediate or prolonged exposure to media violence.

However, different types of aggression are portrayed in the media, which raises the possibility that media violence exposure might indeed result in the engagement of multiple forms of aggressive behaviors. Evidence suggests that after viewing indirect aggression, research participants are more likely to engage in indirect forms of aggression, and after viewing instances of overt aggression, research participants are more likely to engage in overt aggressive behaviors. Additionally, individuals exposed to media violence may perceive the violent behavior they view as appropriate, profitable, or even morally justified, which is likely to increase proactive aggressive behaviors. Furthermore, individuals exposed to media violence might be more likely to attribute hostile intent to another person's behavior, which has been associated with reactive aggressive behaviors. Importantly, media violence exposure leads to lower empathetic concern toward the victims of violence, and low empathy has been associated with severe and multiple aggressive behaviors within different settings.

General Aggression Model

Initial exposure to media violence typically produces aversive responses such as fear, increased heart rate, perspiration, discomfort, and disgust, although after prolonged and repeated exposure across a person's lifetime, the psychological impact of media violence reduces or habituates, and the observer becomes emotionally and cognitively desensitized to media violence across time. According to the general aggression model, proposed by Craig A. Anderson and Brad J. Bushman (2002), each exposure to media violence constitutes a learning trial in which aggression-related schemas and scripts in memory are activated. Even brief exposures to media violence affect a person's current internal state as defined by cognitive, affective, and arousal variables. That is, each episode of media violence exposure serves to prime aggressive cognitions, to increase arousal, and to create an aggressive affective state. The repeated activation of these structures leads to changes in five types of knowledge structures, namely, aggressive beliefs and attitudes, aggressive perceptual schemas, aggressive expectation schemas, aggressive behavior scripts, and aggression desensitization. Changes in these knowledge structures may induce an aggressive personality, which may in turn lead to changes in situational variables, (e.g., the person seeks different types of social interactions and peer groups).

Support for the general aggression model has been provided by various studies showing that indeed brief exposure to media violence can alter the present internal state of the individual. For example, playing a violent game made aggressive thoughts more accessible than playing a nonviolent game. In this study, conducted by Craig A. Anderson and Karen E. Dill in 2000, participants played either a violent or a nonviolent game and then were asked to pronounce a list of words. Participants who played the violent game were faster at pronouncing the violent words than those who played the nonviolent game. Furthermore, game violence was found to increase aggressive expectations. In a 1998 study conducted by Steven J. Kirsh, children played a violent or nonviolent game and then listened to stories describing a protagonist in various provocative situations. They were asked to identify themselves with the protagonist and respond to questions regarding their expectations for imminent actions. Children who played the violent game described more aggressive next actions than those who played the nonviolent game. Furthermore, adult participants who played a violent game for 20 minutes and then responded to questions regarding the actions and the feelings of a story protagonist expected the protagonist to feel more angry and aggressive and react more aggressively to the situation.

Evidence also suggests that children's exposure to movie or video game violence results in pro-violence attitudes (cognitive desensitization) and lower empathy or sympathy for the victims of violence (emotional desensitization). For example, children exposed to video game violence tend to show lower responsiveness to real-world violence and are more likely to view violence as pleasurable in comparison with children who are not exposed to this form of media violence. Therefore, it seems that media violence exposure has lasting effects on viewers' attitudes toward violence and viewers' empathy toward the victims of violence through the process of desensitization.

Individual Differences

Although the literature provides a convincing account for the presence of a causal link between violent movies and aggression in both the laboratory and real life, it is of great importance to determine whether this link is mediated by personal characteristics. Thus, researchers also investigated the possibility that there are individual differences that can provide evidence for the association between media violence exposure and aggression. Research on this topic reveals that trait aggressiveness is positively correlated with the desire to watch violent films, and media violence is found to elicit more aggression in high-trait-aggressive individuals than in low-trait-aggressive individuals. Furthermore, research has shown that participants with longer records of antisocial behavior exhibit more aggression after viewing violent films in laboratory-constructed situations. In general, violent movies can give the audience ideas that may then be translated into antisocial behavior, and this behavior is likely to be in accordance with the viewers' interpretations of whether the witnessed action was appropriate, profitable, or morally justified. As a result, a bidirectional relationship in which the violent media have an adverse effect on the viewer's behavior, but in which the viewer brings his or her own interpretation of what he or she perceives may be at work. Thus, it is possible that aggressive individuals enjoy the violence portrayed in the media more and are less concerned for the suffering of victims of violence.

Importantly, among aggressive individuals, those high on callous-unemotional traits (i.e., lack of remorse or empathy; callous use of others; shallow or deficient emotions) engage in a more severe and persistent pattern of aggressive behavior. Furthermore, individuals with callous-unemotional traits are less reactive to threatening and emotionally distressing stimuli, such as media violence. Therefore, individuals with these traits might be more likely to enjoy media violence. Indeed, initial evidence suggests that aggressive individuals with callous-unemotional traits are more likely to be exposed to media violence than those scoring high on aggression with low callous-unemotional traits. Studies investigating desensitization to media violence propose that long-term exposure to media violence is associated with lower empathetic responding, leading to greater aggression, which might explain the association between media violence exposure and callous-unemotional traits. However, it remains to be seen whether media violence exposure is a risk factor leading to the development of callous-unemotional traits, or whether individuals with these characteristics are more prone to watch or interact with this type of media. That individuals high on callous-unemotional traits are more likely to be exposed to media violence might also suggest that they are less likely to be influenced by exposure to negative stimuli, because these individuals show lower responsiveness to negative and distressing stimuli.

Future Directions

Despite the fact that most scientists agree that chronic exposure to media violence may have deleterious effects on personality and influence behavior, it is not yet fully established how these effects come about. The general aggression model offers a theoretical framework on which many studies have been carried out, yet the variables that are involved are so complex that further systematic research is needed before drawing definite conclusions about its validity. One avenue in which research on media violence could move is the examination of how various types of aggressive behaviors may make some people more prone to the effects of either brief or chronic exposure to media violence. For example, proactive aggressors view aggression as a positive behavior, and because of that they have no negative emotions when acting aggressively. These individuals tend also to be characterized by low empathy and high callous-unemotional traits. However, reactive aggressors are characterized in part by feelings of remorse and thought confusion following the aggressive acts. The differences between the two types of aggression suggest that proactive

aggressors might enjoy media violence more and reactive aggressors might sympathize with the victims of violence more.

Moreover, desensitization may arise from different sources of screen-based media, including television, movies, video games, and the Internet. Even though prior research suggested that viewers get desensitized to television, movie, and video game violence, it is not clear how Internet violence is related to desensitization or aggressive behavior. Current work provides evidence for a new form of aggressive behavior: cyberbullying (e.g., sending threatening or harassing e-mails, instant and chat room messages). Evidence suggests that media violence exposure increases cyberbullying behaviors; however, it remains unclear whether exposure to Internet violence is more strongly associated with this new form of Internet aggression compared with other types of media.

In conclusion, children, adolescents, and adults are exposed to high levels of media violence, and evidence suggests that media violence exposure can result in maladaptive behaviors and even abnormal brain functioning. Individuals may get so desensitized to violence that they may start believing that violence is normative. However, of concern to many is not that viewers get desensitized to violence but that aggressive behaviors may result from such desensitization.

Kostas A. Fanti and Marios N. Avraamides

See also Desensitization Effects on Society; General Aggression Model

Further Readings

Anderson, C. A. (2004). An update on the effects of violent video games. *Journal of Adolescence, 27,* 113–122.

Anderson, C. A., & Bushman, B. J. (2002). The effects of media violence on society. *Science, 295,* 2377–2379.

Anderson, C. A., & Dill, K. E. (2000). Video games and aggressive thoughts, feelings, and behavior in the laboratory and in life. *Journal of Personality and Social Psychology, 78,* 772–790.

Bandura, A., Ross, D., & Ross, S. A. (1963). Imitation of film-mediated aggressive models. *Journal of Abnormal and Social Psychology, 66,* 3–11.

Fanti, K. A., & Avraamides, M. N. (2011). Desensitization to media violence. In M. Paludi (Ed.), *The psychology of teen violence and victimization* (pp. 121–133). Santa Barbara, CA: Praeger.

Fanti, K. A., Vanman, E., Henrich, C. C., & Avraamides, M. N. (2009). Desensitization to media violence over a short period of time. *Aggressive Behavior, 35,* 179–187.

Funk, J. B., Bechtoldt-Baldacci, H., Pasold, T., & Baumgartner, J. (2004).Violence exposure in real-life, video games, television, movies, and the Internet: Is there desensitization? *Journal of Adolescence, 27,* 23–39.

Kirsh, S. J. (1998). Seeing the world through *Mortal Kombat*–colored glasses: Violent video games and the development of a short-term hostile attribution bias. *Childhood, 5,* 177–184.

Watt, J. H., & Krull, R. A. (1977). Examination of three models of television viewing and aggression. *Human Communication Research, 3*(2), 99–112.

AGGRESSIVE PERSONALITY

There is no consensus on a precise definition of human state aggression, henceforth referred to as *aggression*. However, aggression may be described by its characteristics. Aggression is immediate and hostile. It is provoked by environmental stimuli and is short lived. It requires the social interaction of at least two individuals. It is intended to harm one or more persons who find the harmful act aversive and are thus motivated to avoid it. Some theorists consider harm to oneself or destruction to one's possessions as forms of aggressive behavior. Aggression can also be verbal and/or physical (violence). Verbal aggression is used to humiliate, reject, or threaten another person. Physical aggression focuses on personal injury or damage to property. Other researchers make a distinction between direct and indirect aggression. Direct aggression occurs when the aggressor is easily identifiable by the victim during the aggressive act. Indirect aggression happens when the victim is not present during the aggressive behavior, such as talking negatively about the victim.

In short, aggression may be defined as some form of short-term, immediate, intentional, and unwelcomed harm from one party that is directed against another party. Furthermore, scholars and researchers continue to debate whether it is nature (i.e., aggressive personality) or nurture (i.e., media violence) that drives human aggression. This entry explores the nature versus nurture debate and examines moderating factors.

The Aggressive Personality: The Role of Nature

From a psycho-evolutionary perspective, all humans possess the potential to aggress. It is a carryover from ancient times, when the ability of humans to dominate through violence was used to continue the genetic line. For instance, scientists study the relationship between testosterone and social aggressive behaviors in men. Some scientists posit that this hormone evolved to assist in the mating process and propagation of genes. Today, evolutionary psychologists believe that testosterone is in part responsible for the desire for status and social power, which are prerequisites for dominance.

Some researchers believe that as much as 50% of personality is derived from biological parents. In a number of studies, correlations were found between aggression and sibling twins, identical and nonidentical. This association was stronger for identical twins, suggesting that more than environmental factors account for the correlation. Similar findings were found among adopted children and their biological parents.

What biological mechanism is responsible for aggression? The limbic system and the cerebral cortex are the two areas of the brain that play important roles in regulating aggression. The limbic system is responsible for the fight-or-flight response. This part of the brain is reactive and can facilitate impulsive aggressive behaviors. The cerebral cortex controls, modulates, and makes sense out of reactive responses from the limbic system so that it can inhibit aggression through the cognitive processing and evaluation of contextual information such as assessing consequences to reacting aggressively and empathizing with others.

Moreover, research has discovered a link among level of aggression and chemical neurotransmitters such as serotonin and dopamine. Low levels of these neurotransmitters in the limbic system and cerebral cortex have been associated with aggression excitation and aggression disinhibition, respectively. Research findings suggest that these neurological relationships are complex and may involve interactions with any of 50 or more neurotransmitters.

Impaired neurological processes can occur in a number of ways. Congenital deficits can cause imbalances in the levels of neurotransmitters, resulting in increased or decreased aggression. Limbic or cortical dysfunction can occur through chromosomal anomalies, disease, or injury. In short, any disruption of normal functioning can cause a rise or decline in aggression regardless of environmental factors.

One functional model increasingly cited as an alternative to the environmental perspective is the catalyst model of violence developed by Christopher Ferguson and colleagues. Proponents of the catalyst model claim that the development of a violent personality is mostly biological, and genetically predisposed, and continues throughout life. Exposure to family and other types of environmental violence reinforce the already aggressive person. However, individuals predisposed to violence can be triggered to aggress when exposed to environmental stressors. The amount of environmental stress required to activate aggression is contingent upon how much of an aggressive personality the person possesses. According to the catalyst model, violent media exposure is viewed as a stylistic catalyst that provides models for specific violent behaviors. Therefore, any propensity to consume media violence is an outcome of a genetically predisposed aggressive personality.

Media Violence as a Cause of Aggression: The Role of Nurture

Craig Anderson and colleagues developed the general aggression model (GAM), which largely incorporates what is known about aggression and is widely used as the theoretical basis for explaining media violence effects. The GAM focuses on situational episodes of violence and is thus well suited to explain state aggression. According to the GAM, people learn aggression in social contexts, many of which occur through media. This mediated social learning process involves thoughts, feelings, and states of arousal that have short-term effects as well as long-term influences through repeated exposure.

The theory holds that individuals learn to be aggressive through observation and through direct experience or modeling of aggressive behaviors. People learn by observing others in the same room, on television, or in video game play. L. Rowell Huesmann (1994) proposed that learning specifically occurs through scripting. *Scripts* are knowledge structures stored in memory that serve as the basis for learning and behaviors, especially so in children. Observed or acted behaviors are compared with existing scripts and knowledge structures. Some scripts are adopted and others are not. Adopted scripts and their associated behaviors become part of humans' choices for future behavior.

Violent behaviors can be automatically activated or triggered without much thought through a *priming* mechanism. Experimental research has found that seeing a picture of a gun or weapon can prime or activate aggressive thoughts. This activation spreads to related concepts as well. For example, consider a child who watches a television program in which a cartoon character hits his friend every time the friend disagrees with him. The child may adapt this aggressive behavior in real life when the child disagrees with friends and may actually encourage others to do the same as well. In the long term, each repeated exposure to such violent behavior, whether taking place in a video game, television, or real life, is like another learning trial. Over time, the activated scripts become more ingrained and more readily accessible with each subsequent exposure. The effects are more salient when connected to real-life experiences, thus contributing to the development of an aggressive personality. Recent research suggests that an aggressive predisposition can increase the influences of media violence on aggression, forming a feedback loop that reinforces aggressive behavior.

Factors That Can Moderate the Relationship Between Media Violence and Aggression

There are a number of environmental factors that can contribute to aggressive behaviors and often operate in tandem with exposure to media violence. Some of the major ones are as follows: frustration, anger, impulsivity, physiological arousal, physical or verbal assaults, uncomfortable heat, unpleasant noises, darkness, poverty, and drugs. Driven by exposure to media violence and other social learning factors, these situational factors can trigger an immediate aggressive episode.

Although many researchers claim that media violence is a key player in aggressive behavior, media content alone may not be the only cause. Where biological bases of aggression are present and can be impulsively activated, environmental influences to aggress work together over time to perpetuate an aggressive personality. It is likely that a convergence of a number of conditions, many of which are discussed in this entry, contribute to aggressive personalities and behaviors.

Edward T. Vieira Jr.

See also Aggressive Personality; Arousal and Aggressive Content, Theory and Psychology of; Cognition: Schemas and Scripts; Cognitive Psychology of Violence; Cognitive Script Theory and the Dynamics of Cognitive Scripting; Excitation-Transfer Theory; Social Learning Theory; Trait Aggression

Further Readings

Anderson, C. A., & Bushman, B. J. (2002). Human aggression. *Annual Review of Psychology, 53*, 27–51.

Coccaro, E. F. (Ed.). (2003). *Aggression psychiatric assessment and treatment.* New, York: Marcel Dekker.

Ferguson, C. J. (2012). Violent video games and the Supreme Court lessons for the scientific community in the wake of *Brown v. Entertainment Merchants Association. American Psychologist.* Retrieved from http://dx.doi.org/10.1037/a0030597

Huesmann, R. L. (Ed.). (1994). *Aggressive behavior: Current perspectives.* New York, NY: Plenum Press.

AROUSAL AND AGGRESSIVE CONTENT, THEORY AND PSYCHOLOGY OF

The focus of this entry is on arousal and its relationship to aggressive media content. First, this entry defines arousal and contextualizes arousal in terms of relevant theories of emotion. Second, it briefly discusses individual differences in the arousal experience. Third, it reviews the relevant literature on arousal and aggression and desensitization to aggressive media material.

What Is Arousal?

Physiological arousal can be caused by distinct forms of media resulting in both a psychological and physiological state of excitation, restlessness, agitation, or alertness that manifests in automatic physical responses as well as emotional responses such as fear, anxiety, joy, and so on. An early definition of arousal is found in W. B. Cannon's fight-or-flight theory. Cannon (1914) argued that when humans are in stressful situations their sympathetic nervous system (generally considered the quick response mechanism of the autonomic nervous system) sends a charge through the body, preparing it for an immediate survival-oriented response: either run away from the threat or prepare to fight. In most modern-day scenarios such extreme responses to acutely stressful situations are often considered an overreaction, so the arousal construct has since been extended to a phenomenon that is conceptualized as a continuum that ranges in both duration (from acute to prolonged) and intensity.

Acute arousal is often measured as a state of reactance to strong emotions and is a state when extreme excitation is considered a short-term, immediate response to stress (e.g., fight or flight). Conversely, prolonged arousal is typically associated with low-level affect related to an individual's mood state. Arousal levels are often measured through one or more autonomic responses (i.e., involuntary physical responses controlled by the autonomic nervous system) such as sweating and skin conductance levels, pupil dilation, heart rate, and blood pressure. In some cases psychological arousal is also assessed through self-reported affect such as fear, disgust, anger, enjoyment, and so on toward a particular stimulus.

Arousal and Emotion

Two-Factor Theory of Emotion

Arousal is widely accepted as a key mechanism in human emotion. Stanley Schachter and Jerome Singer's (1962) two-factor theory of emotion defines arousal as the energizing factor of an emotional experience. In this conceptualization, arousal itself does not have an inherent valence (i.e., positive or negative association); rather, it is an implicit physiological response, the intensity of which contributes to one's perception of the intensity of an emotional episode. The second factor in this theory of emotion is guidance by cognitions, which allows individuals to determine the source of the arousal and comprehend which emotion they are experiencing.

Interestingly, studies measuring autonomic responses to television and film viewing have found that different stimuli can lead to unique physiological manifestations. For example, increases in skin conductance levels have been associated with stressful scenarios, while increases in blood pressure and heart rate have been found to occur more frequently when an individual is exposed to more pleasant arousal.

These findings may be explained by the two-arousal hypothesis that suggests there are actually two arousal systems, the behavioral activation system (BAS) and the behavioral inhibition system (BIS). The BAS is the system that engages quick autonomic responses to stimuli, whereas the BIS is responsible for engaging cognition and is typically activated in scenarios in which arousal is associated with fear. Engaging cognition can help prevent prolonged uncomfortable arousal responses; for example, an individual may consciously think "This isn't real" as a way of regulating his or her physiological response to stressful content. Additionally, physiological arousal responses (e.g., heart rate, pupil dilation) caused by a negative emotional episode can be reversed more quickly through exposure to pleasurable stimuli that induce a positive emotion.

Three-Factor Theory of Emotion

Dolf Zillmann extended the two-factor theory of emotion to include three factors by separating the guidance component into two factors that account for guidance by cognition and the origins of arousal called *disposition* and *experience*, respectively. In this three-factor theory of emotion, the dispositional factor remains the cognitive guidance component that determines the emotion causing arousal based on learned or inherent associations. The experiential factor speaks to one's cognitive assessment of situational factors at play during a given emotional episode. Furthermore, the experiential factor often acts as a monitoring mechanism that ensures an individual's overt responses to a particular scenario are not inappropriate (i.e., suppressing an immediate fight-or-flight reaction to a modern-day non-life-threatening situation in which such a response would be extreme). Arousal can still be intense even when the experiential factor controls for overreaction; various intensity levels are then linked with a particular emotion and help guide future responses. The third factor, arousal (also called the *excitatory component*), is operationalized as the activation of the sympathetic nervous system that prepares the body for response and manifests in autonomic functions.

The three-factor theory of emotion further proposes three key ways in which the components interact. First, when an individual experiences an excitatory reaction without an associated motor response (e.g., a facial expression), he or she will become restless and, upon recognizing the ambiguous state, seek out the source of the heightened arousal. Second, when experience evokes a motor response but does not lead to increases in physiological arousal, it will not be considered an emotional experience. Finally, an emotional experience will most likely occur when both a motor and excitatory response are induced by a particular stimulus. Furthermore, as an individual becomes aware of his or her aroused state, he or she simultaneously assesses his or her reaction and either suppresses inappropriate motor responses or determines the response appropriate and continues unabated. Although motor responses can be immediately controlled in most cases, an elevated level of excitation

(and its associated physiological responses) requires more time to reach homeostasis.

Excitation-Transfer Theory

The tendency for an excitatory reaction to linger is a key component to the excitation transfer theory. The excitation transfer theory suggests arousal caused by an emotional episode takes longer to diminish than do cognitions associated with the episode. As a result, feelings of arousal tend to extend beyond the original event and influence situations immediately following the emotion-provoking experience. Thus, when an unrelated event occurs shortly after an excitatory response has been induced, the lingering arousal from the first event will transfer to the second event. The excitation transfer will lead to more intense and misattributed arousal related to the second event. Arousal caused by the first event may be stimulated by a pleasant or unpleasant stimulus as well as by hedonically neutral stimuli; for instance, arousal induced via strenuous exercise has been found to amplify subsequent emotions such as aggressiveness and anger as well as experiences of sexual arousal.

The theory was originally tested in the context of social interactions, but has since been used extensively in the study of media effects. For example, excitation transfer helps explain why individuals may be entertained by media that create high levels of anxiety, such as suspenseful dramas or horror films. The arousal caused by tense or scary scenarios throughout the film (or television program) intensifies feelings of relief or happiness upon resolution at the end of the show.

Individual Differences in Arousal

Individuals vary in terms of their desire for arousal. Sensation seeking is a personality trait associated with individuals' propensity to seek out more or less intense levels of sensation. High sensation seeking is associated with a desire for new, complex, and stimulating situations and may be associated with risk-taking behaviors. In the context of media effects, a high sensation-seeking individual is more likely to watch content that increases arousal such as scary or violent movies and fast-paced video games.

Some research has even suggested that arousal varies along with the Big Five personality traits (extraversion, agreeableness, conscientiousness, neuroticism, openness to experience). Specifically, neuroticism (i.e., emotional instability) and extraversion describe how individuals contend with anxiety-provoking or emotional stimuli. Neurotics experience more tense arousal—that is, arousal states may be marked by tension and nervousness. Extraverts, though, experience high energetic arousal, which is characterized by energy. J. A. Gray (1972) posited that, relative to introverted individuals, extraverts have a higher sensitivity to reward signals than to punishment signals. Reward signals aim to raise the energy levels. Therefore, extraverts typically have a higher energetic arousal because of their greater response to rewards.

Arousal and Aggression

Exposure to violent media often leads to heightened arousal. Zillmann (1996), in his excitation transfer theory, argues that latent arousal from viewing violent media will lead to an amplification of normally mild emotion educed in subsequent situations, which can exacerbate hostile or aggressive emotions. Congruent with previously discussed conceptualizations, the arousal itself has no inherent hedonic valence, so excitation can be induced in both pleasant and unpleasant emotional episodes, although it has been argued that violence is more conducive to arousal than are other types of mass media experiences.

The effects of excitation transfer are relatively short lived; however, the general aggression model (GAM) proposed that aggressive behaviors are learned over time and multiple intense episodes of aroused hostile emotions contribute to the learning process. In fact, arousal is a key construct in the GAM, which is a framework based on several theories of human aggression that is commonly applied to research on how media violence affects aggressive behavior. In the GAM, arousal, along with cognition and affect, is one of three internal routes that lead to aggressive behavior. One or more of these three internal mechanisms may be influenced by the interaction of existing personal factors (e.g., trait aggression, encoded scripts or schemas) and situational factors (e.g., exposure to a violent movie or video game) to increase one's propensity to aggress.

Concerns regarding the effects of video game violence have become increasingly prevalent as video game consoles become more commonplace in U.S. households and technology continues to advance. Increased arousal has been associated with how much blood and gore is present in a particular game, levels of emotion in the game, feelings of presence (i.e., one's feeling of being engulfed in realistic scenarios during game play) created by a player's involvement in the storyline of a game, and even larger screen sizes. Realism in video games is another area of concern for researchers of media violence effects and has been defined and studied in two ways. First, sensory realism is defined as how accurate images of game characters (human or otherwise), background scenery, weapons, and so on appear because of advances in technology (e.g., more realistic features, less pixilation), as well as the accuracy of audio cues. The second definition of realism pertains to the degree of believability of the violent acts; in other words, could this happen in real life? Extant literature indicates that as technology advances and scenarios become more realistic, arousal levels are more likely to increase during game play; however, additional research is necessary to determine which factors are most associated with arousal.

Desensitization

The GAM has also been extended to help explain how repeated exposure to violent media, particularly in the context of video games, can lead to long-term desensitization, which subsequently influences increased aggressive behaviors. While it is natural for most individuals to experience arousal when viewing violent content, *desensitization* refers to the psychological process that explains violent media viewers' dulled affective responses to the violence. The GAM posits that desensitization occurs when one is exposed repeatedly to violence that is humorous, involves fictionalized characters, is rewarded, and becomes increasingly more intense. Over time, fear and anxiety associated with violence are diminished, leading to decreases in affect and cognitions toward perceived severity of violence and empathy toward victims (among other factors), and ultimately increases in aggressive and decreases in helping behaviors (Carnagey, Anderson, & Bushman, 2007).

In some scenarios, desensitization may be a desirable state, such as with surgeons who must remain steady-handed when performing surgery or soldiers who need to stay calm in the midst of a battle. However, for most humans, desensitization caused by repeated exposure to media violence leads to decreases in their perceptions of negative outcomes associated with "real" violence and results in less empathy for "real" victims. This is particularly concerning because heightened arousal is linked to increased helping behaviors in situations involving real victims of violence.

Desensitization can occur in short-term experimental settings as well as accumulate over time. Autonomic measures of arousal can decrease as quickly, such as during one television show or movie. Studies have found significant decreases in galvanic skin response in individuals between the first violent scenes of a media segment and similarly violent scenes at the end of the same segment, indicating an almost immediate arousal habituation effect (i.e., desensitization). In longer-term studies with children and adolescents, researchers have found that as frequency of exposure to televised violence increases, the intensity of autonomic responses to violent media content decreases (Cline, Croft, & Courrier, 1973). L. Rowell Huesmann and Lucyna Kirwil (2007) further assert that for some individuals, violence may elicit positive affect that would normally be subdued by anxious arousal. Through a process called *sensitization*, individuals who enjoy violent content begin to associate positive arousal with violent media as their exposure to it becomes more frequent.

Generally, mass mediated programs seek to elicit some form of arousal to engage and entertain viewers, but as individuals become habituated or desensitized to violent media, producers are increasing the novelty and intensity of violence or sexual behavior depicted in an effort to produce arousal. The rise of reality television has been cited as one such tactic because the behaviors depicted are presumably real and cannot be ignored as purely fictional.

In sum, arousal is a critical component of human emotion that is susceptible to influence from external stimuli such as mass mediated violence. Excitatory responses related to an aroused state, regardless of hedonic valence, tend to linger beyond one emotional episode, resulting in intensified and misattributed arousal associated with a subsequent event via excitation transfer. Violence may be more conducive to arousal than other types of mass media experiences, and latent arousal can amplify aggressive or hostile emotions. Although excitation transfer theory helps explain the short-term effects of media violence on arousal, the GAM provides a framework for understanding how repeated exposure to violent media may also result in increased aggression, decreases in empathy, and desensitization to fictional and real violence.

Amanda Mabry and Monique Mitchell Turner

See also Desensitization Effects on Society; Excitation-Transfer Theory; General Aggression Model

Further Readings

Cannon, W. B. (1914). The emergency function of the adrenal medulla in pain and the major emotions. *American Journal of Physiology—Legacy Content, 33*(2), 356–372.

Carnagey, N. L., Anderson, C. A., & Bushman, B. J. (2007). The effect of video game violence on physiological desensitization to real-life violence. *Journal of Experimental Social Psychology, 43*(3), 489–496.

Cline, V. B., Croft, R. G., & Courrier, S. (1973). Desensitization of children to television violence. *Journal of Personality and Social Psychology, 27*(3), 360.

Fredrickson, B. L., & Levenson, R. W. (1998). Positive emotions speed recovery from the cardiovascular sequelae of negative emotions. *Cognition & Emotion, 12*(2), 191–220. doi: 10.1080/026999398379718

Gray, J. A. (1972). The psychophysiological basis of introversion-extraversion: A modification of Eysenck's theory. In V. D. Nebylitsyn & J. A. Gray (Eds.), *The biological basis of individual behavior* (pp. 182–205). New York, NY: Academic.

Gray, J. A., & McNaughton, N. (2003). *The neuropsychology of anxiety: An enquiry into the functions of the septo-hippocampal system.* New York, NY: Oxford University Press.

Huesmann, L. R., & Kirwil, L. (2007). Why observing violence increases the risk of violent behavior by the observer. In D. J. Flannery, A. T. Vazsonyi, & I. D. Waldman (Eds.), *The Cambridge handbook of violent behavior and aggression* (pp. 545–570). Cambridge, UK: Cambridge University Press.

Schachter, S., & Singer, J. (1962). Cognitive, social, and physiological determinants of emotional state. *Psychological Review, 69*(5), 379.

Zillmann, D. (1996). Sequential dependencies in emotional experience and behavior. In R. D. Kavanaugh, B. Zimmerberg, & S. Fein (Eds.), *Emotion: Interdisciplinary perspectives* (pp. 243–272). Mahwah, NJ: Erlbaum.

ASIANS IN MEDIA, CHARACTER DEPICTIONS AND SOCIAL REPRESENTATION OF

Research documenting the portrayals of Asians in U.S. media has demonstrated a consistent link between representations of Asians and media violence. Asians have historically been exoticized and villainized in entertainment and news media. The characterization of Asians as villains and terrorists and as less civilized than other characters has tied this ethnic group to images of media violence. The social representation of Asians in U.S. media is of import because media effects research has demonstrated a relationship between viewing media stereotypes and real-world beliefs about racial and ethnic groups. This entry provides an overview of media stereotypes of Asians that are tied to imagery of media violence.

Media Representations of Asians

The continent of Asia includes a diversity of cultures, and Asians as a group are highly heterogeneous. Despite this diversity, the media and many Americans view Asians as a uniform group with few differences in appearance and cultural practices. The diversity of Asian heritage, however, is recognized in media research through examinations of Asians of Eastern (e.g., Chinese), Western or Middle Eastern (e.g., Saudi Arabian), and Southern (e.g., Indian) descent in the media. Regardless of place of origin, it is believed that Asians have distinct racial features that mark them as different from mainstream American culture, and U.S. media have a tendency to depict these differences as potentially dangerous.

Scholarship examining the social representation of Asians in U.S. media has considerable significance in shedding light on the picture, or pictures, of Asians that may be developed from attending to entertainment and news media offerings. Indeed, media effects research demonstrates that the media contribute to our understanding and treatment of groups, particularly cultural groups different from White Americans. Specifically, exposure to racial and ethnic stereotypes in the media has been associated with negative attitudes and feelings toward the stereotyped group, negative attributions about the minority group's behaviors, as well as decreased willingness to help members of the group.

Gordon Allport's contact hypothesis offers a theoretical explanation for understanding the impact of media images of groups (e.g., Asians) with whom a person has little contact in the real world. It is generally hypothesized that increased contact between cultural groups can serve to reduce prejudice. However, in this case, for Americans, "contact" is made with Asians via exposure to often stereotypical representations of Asians in the media. These media stereotypes may serve to reinforce negative attitudes and beliefs rather than increase understanding and accord between racial and ethnic groups.

Scholars who study media representations of race and ethnicity seek to draw conclusions about the frequency and types of depictions of these cultural groups. In other words, both how often a racial or ethnic group appears in the media as well as the nature of portrayal are of significance. Content analysis and textual analysis are two popular methods for examining media content. Content analysis is a quantitative approach that seeks to systematically analyze media content, typically across multiple media offerings (e.g., television shows), in order to make inferences about how a group is represented. Textual analysis takes a qualitative approach to describing and interpreting themes of representation in media content. Additionally, some scholars take a critical approach to describing and discussing the meaning of messages and the potential audience interpretations of Asian media portrayals.

When studying media depictions of Asians, most research relies on textual analysis or critical content analysis. In comparison with other racial and ethnic groups, Asians appear infrequently in U.S. media, making it difficult to study media portrayals of Asians from a quantitative standpoint. The infrequency of appearance of Asians in the media also sometimes necessitates that scholars study Asians in the media as one group, without making distinctions between different Asian cultures. In general, Asians appear in U.S. media in very limited numbers and roles, and they are more likely to appear as secondary or background rather than primary characters. Furthermore, unlike the study of Blacks in U.S. television programming, most of what is known about Asian media representation comes from the study of the portrayal of Asians in American films. More recent research has added to this picture by examining the representation of Asians as terrorists in U.S. news media and as aggressors in video games.

The majority of popular U.S. media characterizations of Asians, particularly those in television news and films, depict Asians as foreign or exotic others rather than as acculturated Americans. This othering of Asians occurs in U.S. media by portraying them as accented, dressed in traditional Asian garb, and generally antithetical or a challenge to the American way of life. Particularly relevant to the present volume of work is the association of violence with these representations.

Asians and Violence in U.S. Media

The stereotype of the Asian villain is one of the more frequent representations of Asians in U.S. films, particularly action-oriented films. Scholars have noted that during times of heightened political tension between the United States and Asian countries, the portrayal of Asians as threatening is resurgent in U.S. media. The depiction of Asian characters as sinister in entertainment media aligns well with propaganda messages about Asian cultures during times of war and strife.

The Asian villain is a character who is devious in nature and exhibits physical prowess, typically martial arts skills. The villain is stereotypically represented as being skilled at swordplay and martial arts such as kung fu and karate. Additionally, as with the model minority stereotype (i.e., the reserved, studious, and successful Asian American), Asian villains may be depicted as intelligent. Though intelligence is a positive trait, when coupled with the devious nature of the villain this characterization serves to represent Asians as cunning, sinister, and a threat.

The Asian villain is a gendered role; it is applied to Asian men and women differentially. The male villain is usually depicted as amoral, violent, and undesirable. This character is often portrayed as asexual or as an unfriendly predator of White women, and as representing a threat to American culture. Historically, the male Asian villain has been depicted as being exceptionally cruel and barbaric in enacting violence. A frequently cited example of the evil Asian male character is Jet Li's role in *Lethal Weapon 4*. The female villain, however, is sexually desirable in addition to being deviant and violent. This characterization of the Asian female has been termed the "Dragon Lady" and serves to exoticize the Asian female. Lucy Liu in *Kill Bill* may be used as an example of this type of character. Liu has publicly commented about the limited options for roles for her in Hollywood, most of which center on the trope of the sexy but deadly Asian female. The Dragon Lady is aggressive both physically and sexually and is an object of mystique and desire. Although this representation is indeed recurrent in U.S. films, most often Asian women have been historically portrayed as passive, coy, and emotional. Asian women are more likely to be depicted in submissive rather than dominant roles such as villains. These submissive but sexualized characterizations of the Asian female have been termed the "China Doll" or "Geisha Girl." Thus, it is the representation of the male Asian villain that is more common in U.S. media.

Central to the Asian villain characterization is media violence. From the devious Siamese cats in *Lady and the Tramp* to Asian foes in the more recent *Rush Hour* movie series, Asians have been depicted in popular films as engaging in aggressive acts toward innocent others. These acts of violence are depicted as sneaky or underhanded in nature and characterize Asians as untrustworthy and unfriendly. Consistent with historical representations of other minorities in the United States, the representation of Asians reflects the stereotypes of the criminal and the gangster. This serves to position the (White) hero as noble, whereas the Asian villain is savage and threatening. Although both the hero and villain are characterized by violence, the hero is justified, whereas the villain is not.

Notably, the image of the West Asian or Middle Eastern terrorist has emerged as a special type of Asian villain characterization. The film *Wanted: Dead or Alive*, for example, presents Arabs as a threat to American safety. Similar to other Asian villain characters, the terrorist is vicious and violent. However, this media violence takes on a political context. To understand the cultural significance of these representations, scholars may wish to simultaneously examine the social, cultural, and political contexts of media portrayals of Asians.

Recent research has demonstrated that the stereotype of the Asian villain is also recurrent in video games. Ninjas and samurais populate fighting and action games. These characters are typically situated within historical contexts of Asian culture, and game play centers on sword fighting and martial arts combat. For example, the *Dynasty Warriors* game series features a host of playable Asian ninja characters, and the game art evokes imagery of ancient Asian cultures. The Asian terrorist stereotype is also present. Here, the terrorist appears in games with a modern-day setting, typically involving game play combat between U.S. military and Arab or Muslim foreigners. *Conflict: Global Terror* is an example of this video game representation of Asians. Content analyses suggest that Asian characters appear more frequently in video games than in U.S. television programming and are depicted in ways similar to film representations of Asians and violence.

In addition to studying entertainment media, scholars have examined how images of media violence are linked to representations of Asians in news media. Most relevant here is the analysis of Middle Easterners in U.S. news media. The repetitive depiction of the Asian male as terrorist in U.S. news media reinforces negative stereotypes and fears about people of Middle Eastern descent. Such news coverage propagates a "yellow peril" discourse that constructs Asians as invaders of American culture and threats to freedom and safety. Current political and world events have arguably heightened such focus on the Asian terrorist in news media. These news characterizations depict Asians as foreigners; little news coverage is devoted to stories about Asian Americans.

Future Outlook

Asians have historically and contemporarily been depicted in limited ways in U.S. media. One dominant theme associated with Asians in the media is violence, in which Asians are depicted as deviants and savages who threaten the American way of life. Although the stereotype of the Asian villain depicts Asians as aggressors, Asians often end up in the roles of victim as they are defeated by the White male hero. These representations have been largely produced by White media industry professionals and have served to propagate stereotypes about Asian Americans and Asian foreigners.

In sharp contrast to these stereotypes associated with media violence, the model minority and buffoon stereotypes of Asians in the media have been documented with frequency in media research. The model minority is arguably a more positive portrayal, although it is still very limiting. Here, Asians are depicted as introverted, studious, intelligent, and successful. The buffoon stereotype, like the villain stereotype, is inherently negative. Although not associated with media violence, the buffoon characterization also serves to represent Asians as different from and inferior to other Americans. Common to all three Asian stereotypes—the villain, model minority, and buffoon—is the social representation of Asians as unacculturated and un-American.

In the future, however, Asian depictions may begin to deviate from these long-standing media stereotypes. Today, with the ability to produce and distribute content via the Internet, communication scholar Kent Ono argues, Asian Americans have new opportunities to play more active roles in controlling the representations of Asians in U.S. media. The changing media environment, characterized by audience fragmentation and increased ability of individuals to come together and produce content with fewer restrictions of traditional media gatekeepers, may result in a greater diversity of Asian voices and representations in new media and traditional media alike.

Elizabeth Behm-Morawitz

See also Character Development Within Violent Content; Cultivating Content and the Social Representation of Violence; Demographic Effects; National Television Violence Study; Social Learning From Media; Stereotyping in Violent Content

Further Readings

Kamalipour, Y. R. (1997). *The U.S. media and the Middle East: Image and perception.* Westport, CT: Praeger.

Ono, K. A., & Pham, V. (2009). *Asian Americans and the media.* Malden, MA: Polity Press.

Ramasubramanian, S. (2005). A content analysis of the portrayal of India in films produced in the West. *Howard Journal of Communications, 16,* 243–265. doi:10.1080/10646170500326533

Shaheen, J. G. (2001). *Reel bad Arabs: How Hollywood vilifies a people.* New York, NY: Olive Branch Press.

Sheridan, P. (2005). *The Asian mystique: Dragon ladies, geisha girls, and our fantasies of the exotic Orient.* New York, NY: Public Affairs.

ATTITUDE, EFFECTS OF MEDIA VIOLENCE ON

Media violence has a known relationship with the behavior of children and adults such that increased exposure can lead to increases in aggressive behaviors. But the relationship between media violence and behavior may be mediated by one's attitudes.

Attitude and Attitude Formation

Attitude is defined as one's propensity to respond more positively or negatively to a particular attitudinal object. Attitude is often conceptualized as the combination of three underlying mechanisms: cognition, affect, and behavioral intention. *Cognition* refers to one's beliefs about an object, whereas *affect* is associated with feelings toward the object. *Behavioral intention* refers to individuals' expressed plans to engage in a particular behavior. Individuals often strive to create coherence between attitudes and behavior in order to avoid internal strife caused by cognitive dissonance (i.e., the feelings of discomfort one experiences when confronted with two disparate thoughts, ideas, or identities).

In addition to this three-component model of attitude, scholars often segment individual attitudes into those that are implicit versus those that are explicit. An *implicit attitude* is one that an individual is unaware he or she holds and may even deny. Research regarding implicit attitudes typically pertains to sensitive or socially unacceptable topics such as stereotypical or disparaging beliefs about racial or ethnic groups. *Explicit attitudes* are those an individual recognizes within himself or herself and can typically verbalize upon introspection. Media violence can affect attitudes that are both implicit (racial prejudice) and explicit (a negative evaluation of a city).

Research indicates that most attitudes, both implicit and explicit, are learned rather than inherent. Media violence, for example, can lead to learned attitudes by pairing a particular attitude object (e.g., a racial group) with a particular emotional act (e.g., violent crime). If the media repeatedly show a particular group engaging in behaviors that are deemed unacceptable and that evoke negative emotions in individuals, over time this may provoke negative attitudes about that racial group.

This outcome can be explained by Ivan Pavlov's classical conditioning theory. In experimental studies of traditional Pavlovian conditioning (also called *signal learning*) a conditioned stimulus (CS) is paired with an unconditioned stimulus (UCS) to determine how an individual's response to the CS changes based on the type of UCS it is paired with, such as a free meal (i.e., a reward) versus a piercing sound (i.e., a punishment). Through repeated exposure to a particular pairing, the CS becomes a signal for the presence of the UCS, and a transfer of a positive or negative association occurs from the UCS to the CS.

Attitude formation is often attributed to a similar process called *evaluative conditioning* (EC). The key difference between traditional Pavlovian conditioning and EC is that the stimulus (i.e., CS) is neutral. In experimental EC studies participants are asked to identify their affect toward a set of objects; those that are labeled as neutral (i.e., the participants report having no positive or negative affect toward the object) are paired with a UCS that has been identified as either positive or negative. Through repeated exposure over time, the valence of one's affect toward the UCS is transferred to the CS.

Although EC and traditional Pavlovian conditioning are similar at a procedural level, the underlying cognitive processes are believed to be fundamentally different in three ways. First, EC has led to effective affect transfer regardless of the contingency between the CS and the UCS. These findings are contrary to much of the data on Pavlovian conditioning that indicate an individual must form a correlation between each stimulus for conditioning

to occur. Furthermore, affect transfer has been effective in situations in which both stimuli are presented simultaneously, when they are presented sequentially, or a combination of both. Second, EC does not require an overt pairing in order for affect transfer to occur from UCS to CS, whereas attitude change associated with traditional Pavlovian conditioning is largely predicated on an individual's awareness that the CS is being presented in conjunction with the UCS. The third, and arguably most significant, difference is that the effects of EC are more resilient to extinction than Pavlovian conditioning; after CS liking or disliking has been formed via pairing with the UCS, the affective valence toward the CS will tend to remain intact even after the UCS is removed.

Media Violence and Attitudes

Media violence, "the overt expression of physical force against others or self, or the compelling of action against one's will on pain of being hurt or killed" (Gerbner, 1972, p. 31), has long been studied because of its potential to cause violent behaviors. Concerns surrounding exposure to mass mediated violence grew as the prevalence of television sets in homes across the country grew, resulting in numerous experimental, cross-sectional, and longitudinal studies assessing the relationship between media violence and aggressive behavior.

An overwhelming number of studies indicated that exposure to media violence increases the likelihood of an individual engaging in aggressive or violent behaviors, both in short-term experimental studies and longer-term (longitudinal) studies. For example, exposure to violent media clips tends to lead to an immediate increase in aggressive thoughts and behaviors, and consistent exposure during childhood and adolescence can lead to increased aggression into adulthood (Anderson et al., 2003). Burgeoning research also indicates violence in video games specifically can negatively influence attitudes toward women as well as cause rape myth acceptance (i.e., various reasons sometimes used to assign blame to the female victim while excusing the male perpetrator's sexual aggressiveness).

Most of this research has focused on children and adolescents because they represent a population that is more susceptible to influence from a developmental perspective and may be exposed to media violence often. The average American child under the age of 18 years spends 28 hours a week watching television, and children's programming, particularly cartoons, contains up to 20 violent acts per hour of programming. Additionally, the majority of video games, regardless of the rating, contain violent content. The context of violence presents additional concerns, particularly in children's programming; content analyses indicate that the violence is frequently committed by likeable characters for justified purposes of resolving a conflict or problem, presented in a comedic manner that does not result in realistic injuries to the victim or punishment to the perpetrator, and often results in rewards to the protagonist or—in the case of video games—earning points and/or accolades for the player.

Media violence can affect aggressive attitudes; repeated exposure to violent content may affect an individual's attitude by increasing his or her hostile expectations of others; such expectations act as a cognitive mediator between media violence—typically via video games—and aggressive behaviors. Attitude is also posited to be a key component in the multi-episode general aggression model. Over time, repeated exposure increases aggressiveness in attitude and beliefs, perceptual schemas, expectation schemas, and behavioral scripts, and leads to arousal desensitization. These five knowledge structures are linked to long-term change in one's personality by increasing aggression as well as one's propensity for violent behavior. Furthermore, presenting violent acts in tandem with positive stimuli, such as humor, acts of justice, or rewards, influences an individual's attitude toward violence via positive affective transfer.

Concerns about the influence of media violence on children led to the development of interventions such as media literacy programs. In general, media literacy programs teach children and adolescents how to think critically about the media they are watching by analyzing its believability, the real meaning of the content, and its effects on themselves and others. Although media literacy programs are relatively novel, they address topics ranging from the sexualization and objectification of women, to stereotyping based on race and class, to violent content. There are relatively few programs pertaining specifically to media violence that have been empirically evaluated. Erica Scharrer developed and implemented a program in 2006 that was geared to change the participants' critical attitude toward media violence by engaging in critical thinking and analysis of several common types of violence seen by children of their age group (sixth grade). The materials used highlighted four types of violence found in children's television programming: rewarded violence, violence that does not result in negative consequences to the perpetrator, violence that does not result in pain, and justified violence.

Media violence can lead to desensitization. Desensitization is a psychological process explaining violent media viewers' affective reactions to the violence. Studies indicate that repeated and continued exposure to media violence can undermine feelings of concern, empathy, or sympathy that viewers might have toward victims (both real and fictional) of actual violence.

Current thinking is that viewers of media violence may become at ease with violence that initially caused negative arousal. Therefore, viewers may end up with a distorted sense of reality, leading them to believe that negative events they view via the media (rape, crime, physical harm to others) were justifiable and that they can enact such a role in real-life situations. Desensitization effects have also been shown with older age groups, suggesting that these effects are not limited to children.

Media violence can lead to risk-related attitudes. In addition to the desensitizing effect that media violence can have on children and adults comes an increased anxiety of risks—regardless of the actual risk probabilities. Research indicates long-term exposure to violence via the mass media can lead to inflated perceptions of real-world violence (e.g., cultivation theory). According to the affect heuristic, vivid images in people's minds (like those caused by violent media) are denoted with varying degrees of affect. Individuals rely on these affect-laden images when they need to make risk judgments. According to Ellen Peters and colleagues (2006), relying on affect may be simpler and more efficient than using deliberative processes, such as weighing the pros and cons of a situation or retrieving relevant examples from memory, especially when the required judgment or decision is complex or mental resources are limited. These research findings help explain why people may overestimate risk.

The research reviewed here indicates that attitude plays a critical role in mediating the relationship between exposure to media violence and aggressive behavior. As such, future research is warranted to further knowledge on this relationship and how influencing attitudes may play a key role in interventions designed to decrease the negative effects of media violence.

Amanda Mabry and Monique Mitchell Turner

See also Aggression, Risk Factors of; Aggressive
Behavior; Developmental Effects; Exposure to Violent
Content, Effect on Child Development; General
Aggression Model; Media Education and Media
Literacy; Social Learning From Media

Further Readings

Anderson, C. A., Berkowitz, L., Donnerstein, E.,
Huesmann, L. R., Johnson, J. D., Linz, D., . . . Wartella,
E. (2003). The influence of media violence on youth.
Psychological Science in the Public Interest, 4(3),
81–110. doi: 10.2307/40059680

De Houwer, J., Thomas, S., & Baeyens, F. (2001).
Association learning of likes and dislikes: A review of
25 years of research on human evaluative conditioning.
Psychological Bulletin, 127(6), 853.

Gerbner, G. (1972). Violence in television drama: Trends
and symbolic functions. In F. A. Comstock &
E. A. Rubenstein (Eds.), *Television and social behavior:
Vol. 1: Media content and control* (pp. 28–187).
Washington, DC: Government Printing Office.

Peters, E., McCaul, K. D., Stefanek, M., & Nelson, W.
(2006). A heuristics approach to understanding cancer
risk perception: Contributions from judgment and
decision-making research. *Annals of Behavioral
Medicine, 31*(1), 45–52.

Scharrer, E. (2006). "I noticed more violence": The Effects
of a media literacy program on critical attitudes toward
media violence. *Journal of Mass Media Ethics, 21*(1),
69–86.

Shanahan, J., & Morgan, M. (1999). *Television and its
viewers: Cultivation theory and research.* Cambridge,
UK: Cambridge University Press.

AUDIENCE INTERPRETATIONS OF MEDIA VIOLENCE, EFFECTS OF

One of the most important variables in understanding the effects of violent media content is how individual audience members interpret said content. As discussed in this entry, audience interpretations can vary based on the cultural environment of a media production, the critical reception of violent content, or the shared schemas that are invoked by the presence of constructed social symbols and activities. Mainly studied in the scholarly tradition of reception studies, audience interpretations of violence have become increasingly important to social scientists. Additionally, understanding how audiences understand violence can aid greatly in the development of media literacy interventions designed to interrupt or even eliminate the potential negative effects of exposure to violent content.

Different Audiences, Different Interpretations

One of the broadest and most general approaches to understanding the effect of audience interpretations of violent content is George Gerbner's cultivation theory. This approach suggests that heavy media consumers tend to make estimates about real-world phenomenon based on what they view in their media programming. One of the most common discussions of cultivation effects is the *mean world effect*, which suggests that audiences who view much violent media content begin to cultivate a shared sense of their social world as a violent place. As this effect is dependent on the amount of time viewers spend with television, the underlying effect may be due to heavy users of television interpreting the violence as more realistic, more likely to happen, and more frightful than do light viewers.

However, cultivation studies focus primarily on media content and exposure patterns rather than the role of the audience in making sense of the content. In contrast, audience interpretation studies revolve around the idea of *meaning making*. Meaning making assumes that individuals interpret symbols based on idiosyncratic meaning codes that allow for individualized experience of mass content. This has special importance for violent media. For example, Sonia Livingstone and colleagues interviewed different generations about their interpretation of violent crime and its representation in current-day media content. Generational differences emerged such that individuals who grew up during the post–Vietnam War period felt that crime dramas should be more escapist and fantasy, whereas younger audiences found crime drama to be most interesting when it was realistic and relevant to their own lives. These differences extended to interpretations of how violence is represented on screen as well. When asked to explain what made a violent act seem more realistic, younger preteen audiences suggested realism to be a feature of moral and narrative complexity, whereas older viewers interpreted realism to mean recognizable characters and an absence of glamorized portrayals. This suggests that when defining types of violent contact, definitional understandings are shaded by audience characteristics.

This type of traditional active audience analysis—in which the audience is participant to and involved with the construction of meaning from a common text—suggests that it is not just the content itself, but also how the audience relates to and understands that context that are important in understanding reactions to violence. Research in the uses and gratifications tradition similarly holds the active audience concept as central to understanding both audience selection of and reactions to violent content. Uses and gratifications theorists saw incorporating audience reception to content as building a bridge between psychological and cultural studies by way of incorporating these *sense-making* activities of audiences within a social constructivist paradigm of social psychology. For example, selective exposure to media content is driven by the gratifications sought from particular media as well as the gratifications obtained. Individuals differ in their needs, and these differing needs lead to disparate selection of and attention to media content in order to meet—or gratify—these needs. Regarding violent media in particular, the need for excitement (sensation seeking), the need for character identification, and the need to manage moods have all been identified in research as predictors of seeking violent media content. In addition, gender and age are consistently noted as significant moderators of attraction to violent content, with younger male audiences demonstrating greater affinity toward and enjoyment of violent content than female audiences. These individual differences in preference for violent content suggest that different psychological processes are active for different individuals when they are exposed to the same violent content. One rationale for this may be found in schema theory, which suggests that viewers use individual schemas or templates to guide their perceptions of the world. Because each individual is equipped with different schemas—based on behavioral exposure, experience, culture, and education— the individual interpretation and reception of, not to mention attraction to, violent content may vary. Gender socialization theory is a particular application of schema theory regarding how gender roles are socialized, often in terms of attraction to violence. It suggests that male and female children are socialized to expect and enjoy different portrayals of and types of violence in toys, books, and media content, and thus may experience media violence in different ways. This is echoed in the mass media presentations of who is committing what types of violence—research suggest that men are more likely to be represented in media as sexually aggressive or dominant, and women as weak, victimized, or

sexually submissive. This may socialize young boys to believe that violence and sexual dominance are important aspects of masculinity as socially normative and desirable traits. Thus, the portrayal of violence by male characters may be particularly potent for young men, and may be used by male and female audiences very differently in making sense of their social worlds.

Violence as Multidimensional

Attempting to better quantify the characteristics of an active audience interpretation particular to violent content reception, James Potter and colleagues demonstrated that audience judgments of the amount and type of violence in different versions of the same television show are at least four times more accurately predicted by studying perceptions of the content than by the amount of violence coded for by "objective" content coding schemes. In other words, it is the subjective interpretation of the content, rather than an objective determination of content via experimental manipulation, that seems to be more meaningful in determining perceptions of violence. Moreover, the perceptions of violence tended to form along specific narrative or content considerations, suggesting that audiences considered different contextual elements of a portrayal in determining it as being more or less violent.

Their research on film audiences, for example, found that individuals tended to focus on the explicitness of violence, the graphicness of violence, the degree of punishment for violent acts, and the extent to which remorse for violence was shown. Further studies in this line have similarly found that perceptions of violent content along three main dimensions of graphicness (the depiction of blood and gore), realism (the possibility for the shown act to be possible in reality), and justification (the narrative justification for the violent act) predicted preference for video games and films differently than predicted by their experimental manipulations. Taken as a whole, this research suggests that not only are audience perceptions of violent content perhaps more important in understanding how much violence might be in popular media than merely counting and summing the number of violent acts on screen, and that a given act is not simply violent or not violent. Rather, perceptions of something as being violent are determined by several contextual elements of the on-screen portrayal—such as how graphic or bloody the act is, whether or not the act could be performed in reality, and the motives of the perpetrator(s) of the act. In addition, more recent research suggests that even the form of a violent portrayal—such as it being interactive or not—can influence the relative importance of these contextual dimensions in assessing the overall violence contained in any given portrayal.

These findings are of particular importance for overarching theories regarding observational learning such as the general aggression model and social cognitive theory—perspectives that are based on viewer perceptions of models as being identifiable, attractive, and realistic. Although these variables are often measured and thus accounted for in experimental work, the inherent variability of individual viewer interpretations of each dimension makes the predictive value of these studies weak when determining which individuals will be affected by what content and in which ways. Thus, subjective interpretations of models and their behaviors may be stronger determinants of media effects than objective quantifications of the same content. For understanding media violence effects, it would be fruitful for researchers to study the interaction between model attractiveness and the relative amount of violence of a given act as interpreted by individual audience members.

The Joy and Pain of Violence

Arguing that feelings of enjoyment and appreciation can also be conceptualized as media effects in themselves as well as moderators of the link between media content and aggressive effects, researchers can examine how audiences come to enjoy and appreciate (or not) different violent media portrayals. In discussing enjoyment—a hedonic and pleasurable experience of temporal positive affect—the aforementioned studies by Potter and his contemporaries suggest that audiences prefer violent media that is less graphic, realistic, and justified. In contrast to enjoyment, appreciation—defined by Art Raney and Mary Beth Oliver as eudaimonic and meaningful experiences—may be argued to decrease negative effects of exposure to violence. For example, current theorizing by media scholars such as Ian Bogost argues that intensely violent media portrayals might actually be useful in preventing and buffering audience members' aggressive outcomes. One example is that of Steven Spielberg's *Schindler's List*—a film that features intensely graphic and realistic violent actions that are not designed to be enjoyed by audiences but rather are meant to force audiences

to interpret actions and events beyond their worldviews. The difference between enjoyment and appreciation in response to viewing violent content may also explain divergent accounts of the role violence plays in selective exposure to violent media; audiences may be strongly *attracted* to specific types of violence without *enjoying* them per se.

Media Literacy: Reinterpreting Violence for Specific Audiences

Media literacy interventions have focused extensively on teaching audience members how to reinterpret violent actions so as to minimize their cognitive, affective, and behavioral effects. Such interventions embrace the notion of studying audience subjective interpretations rather than objective quantifications of media content by suggesting that viewers who are particularly susceptible to negative effects from viewing violent media (particularly children) can be guided in their formation of subjective judgments—usually by a parent or teacher. Indeed, some of these interventions tend to work with vulnerable audiences to reinterpret on-screen action along many of the lines discussed earlier in this entry, such as teaching children that most media violence is unrealistic, overly graphic, and often unjustified or unpunished. This type of intervention hopes to short-circuit the production of schema and reward patterns that would encourage replication of violent or aggressive behaviors in real life; that is, these interventions attempt to make models of violent behaviors appear less attractive. Tailoring these interventions to specific audience members who may systematically vary in their interpretations of violent content may increase their effectiveness and utility in the future.

Allison Eden and Nicholas David Bowman

See also Cultivation Theory; Culture of Violence; Rating Systems, Film; Rating Systems, Video Games; Realism of Violent Content, Real-World Violence on Television, and Their Effects; Sexualized Aggression; Social Learning From Media; Uses and Gratifications Perspective of Media Effects

Further Readings

Bogost, I. (2011). *How to do things with video games.* Minneapolis: University of Minnesota Press.

Goldstein, J. (Ed.). (1998). *Why we watch: The attractions of violent entertainment.* New York, NY: Oxford University Press.

Oliver, M. B., & Raney, A. A. (2011). Entertainment as pleasurable and meaningful: Identifying hedonic and eudaimonic motivations for entertainment consumption. *Journal of Communication, 61*, 984–1004.

Reiner, R., Allen, J., & Livingstone, S. (2001). The audience for crime media 1946–91: A historical approach to reception studies. *Communication Review, 4*(2), 165–193,

Tamborini, R., Weber, R., Bowman, N. D., Eden, A., & Skalski, P. (2013). "Violence is a many-splintered thing": The importance of realism, justification and graphicness in understanding perceptions of and preferences for violent films and video games. *Projections: The Journal for Movies and Mind, 7*(1).

Weaver, A. J. (2011). A meta-analytical review of selective exposure to and the enjoyment of media violence. *Journal of Broadcasting & Electronic Media, 55*(2), 1–19.

BOBO DOLL STUDIES

The Bobo Doll experiments conducted in the United States in the early 1960s were an outgrowth of a program of research designed to explain how people learn by social modeling. The traditional theories of psychology in the mid-20th century focused almost entirely on learning through direct trial-and-error experience, even though, in everyday life, one's attitudes, values, emotional proclivities, and styles of behavior are largely acquired through social modeling. This entry discusses the context, experimental methodology, and outcomes of the Bobo Doll studies.

With the advent of television, viewers began to be exposed to heavy doses of modeled violence within the comfort of their homes day in and day out. There was growing public concern over the effects of heavy exposure to the televised brutality. The prevailing theory contended that vicarious participation in violence is cathartic. By draining aggressive impulses, vicarious participation, it was thought, reduced the likelihood of aggressive behavior. It was in this context, some 50 years ago, that the Bobo Doll experiments were conducted.

Evidence from diverse lines of research revealed that exposure to televised violence has four distinctive effects. First, it teaches aggressive styles of behavior. Second, it weakens restraint over previously learned forms of aggression. This is because television legitimizes, glamorizes, and trivializes human violence and portrays it as the preferred solution to human conflicts. When good triumphs over evil by violent means, violence is sanctioned.

Third, repeated exposure to televised violence desensitizes and habituates viewers to human cruelty. Individuals are no longer upset by or moved to take action against it. Fourth, televised images shape people's views of reality on which they base many of their actions. Because programs with violent plot lines include much scheming and many villainous characters, heavy viewers of televised violence are more distrustful of others and more fearful of becoming crime victims.

Each of these separable media effects requires a different experimental methodology. *Learning effects* are assessed under conditions in which individuals are free to reveal the forms of aggression they have learned. In *performance effects*, individuals are assessed for inflicting harm with the aggressive means they have learned. In *desensitization effects*, individuals are tested for their emotional reactions to displays of violence and their willingness to speak out against them. In the *reality construction effect*, individuals are assessed for their perceptions of the societal norms and sanctions, power relations, and threats to their social environment.

At the time of the experiments, the studies of television effects were mainly descriptions of what viewers were watching and correlational studies relating television viewership to rated aggressiveness. The direction of causation was hotly debated. There were four alternative paths of influence: Violence viewing fosters aggressiveness; aggressive individuals are attracted to televised violence; the influence works bidirectionally; or viewing violent programs and aggressiveness are both co-effects of a third factor, such as socioeconomic status. The Bobo Doll paradigm addressed the issue of causation experimentally. It was designed to test the first effect, the acquisition of novel forms of aggression through symbolic social modeling.

In a simulated televised presentation, nursery school children watched an adult beat up a large inflated clown in novel ways. The model pummeled it with a mallet, kicked it about the room, flung it aggressively into the air, and knocked it down, sat on it, and beat it in the face. This novel pattern of aggression was interspaced with aggressive neologisms. The children's behavior was then recorded over a long session in a room containing not only a Bobo Doll but a wide variety of play materials that provided a host of behavioral options. Attractive alternatives removed social pressure to behave aggressively.

Contrary to catharsis theory, children who were exposed to the aggressive modeling adopted the novel pattern of aggression either in toto or by using various elements of it. Children in the control condition, who had not been not exposed to the aggressive modeling, rarely did so. Interestingly, the aggressive modeling had a generalized disinhibitory effect on other forms of aggression, such as rampant car crashes and fierce fights among animals. In addition, child viewers of aggressive modeling engaged in more gun play than did those who had no exposure to modeled aggression.

A number of control conditions were included to address the claim that the Bobo Doll was meant to be punched. The controls were blocked into levels of aggressiveness and assigned randomly from each block into experimental and control conditions. The experimental focus was not on whether children punched the Bobo Doll, but whether they assaulted it, both physically and verbally, in the novel ways. As noted, children in the control condition rarely did so.

Another experimental condition verified that children did not behave aggressively toward the Bobo Doll simply because the televised program drew attention to it, or that it naturally invites the novel type of aggression. In this condition, the model engaged in some artistic activities but completely ignored the Bobo Doll in the room. Children exposed to the modeled disinterest in the Bobo Doll rarely performed the novel aggressive acts.

There were notable gender differences in the extent to which children patterned their behavior after the aggressive model. Boys displayed a higher level of modeled aggression than did girls. Further research was conducted to determine whether the gender difference was one of learning or performance. To clarify the source of this difference, children observed the model rewarded, punished, or left without consequences for assaulting the Bobo Doll. Seeing modeled aggression rewarded enhanced adoption of the novel behavior; seeing it punished reduced performance of it. Following the performance test, children were offered attractive rewards to enact the model's behavior. The findings showed that girls learned the modeled aggression just about the same as the boys did under all conditions, but they were reluctant to perform it. The performance difference reflected the stronger social sanctions against the use of aggressive means by girls. The findings also showed that punishment of models' aggression does not prevent viewers from learning it.

The strength of the models' influence was partly determined by the perceived gender appropriateness of their behavior. The aggression by the male aggressor was approved and emulated by boys ("Al is a good socker. I want to sock like Al") and by girls ("That man is a strong fighter. He hit Bobo right down and said 'Punch your nose.' He's a good fighter. like Daddy"). The aggression by the female model was firmly disapproved and less emulated by boys ("That's no way for a lady to behave. Ladies are not supposed to act like that") and by girls ("You should've seen what that lady did. I never saw a girl act like that. She was punching and fighting but not swearing").

The Bobo Doll paradigm provided a vehicle for studying experimentally a variety of factors governing the acquisition of styles of aggression through social modeling. Some individuals contend that studies of the effects of media effects on aggression should use human targets. As previously noted, the Bobo Doll studies were designed to clarify the process of observational learning. The methodology for measuring learning effects requires conditions in which viewers feel free to reveal all they have learned. In the case of aggression, it requires simulated targets, not human ones. To use human targets to assess the instructional function of televised influence would be as nonsensical as to require bombardiers to bomb San Francisco or New York to test their level of acquisition of bombing skills.

Albert Bandura

See also Aggression in Youth; Audience Interpretation of Media Violence, Effects of; Catharsis Theory; Effects From Violent Content, Short- and Long-Term; Media

Violence, Definitions and Context of; Social Cognitive Theory; Social Learning From Media; Television Violence

Further Readings

Anderson, C. A., et al. (2003). The influence of media violence on youth. *Psychological Science in the Public Interest, 4*(3), 81–110.

Bandura, A. (2009). Social cognitive theory of mass communications. In J. Bryant & M. B. Oliver (Eds.), *Media effects: Advances in theory and research* (2nd ed.; pp. 94–124). Mahwah, NJ: Erlbaum.

Bandura, A., Ross, D., & Ross, S. A. (1963). Imitation of film-mediated aggressive models. *Journal of Abnormal and Social Psychology, 66,* 3–11.

BOUNDARY TESTING

Boundary testing refers to the power that media users have to explore the limits of social acceptability. Media forms that are based in representation can provide opportunities for the transgression of sociocultural boundaries in a controlled manner, which advocates see as a healthy form of release. Critics of media violence interpret these interactions as harmful to the media user, particularly if the user is a young person. This entry provides a brief overview of boundary testing as related to historical and contemporary media forms, summarizing positions related to liberatory media practices and media violence.

Moral Panic and Boundary Testing

Boundary testing has its historical roots in the various familial and social structures that are found across culture and geographic location. To better understand how boundary testing relates to media violence, it is necessary to explore the notion of moral panic as it relates to media use. *Moral panic* refers to the dangers associated with actions or behaviors that a society deems inappropriate or immoral. It is common to find historical examples of moral panic intertwined with media use; Plato's fear that the printed word would lead to the destruction of memory and the corruption of youth is an early example.

More recently, one can find examples of moral panic in the popular acceptance of comic books in the 1950s, and the concern over violent video games at the end of the 20th century. *Seduction of the Innocents,* published in 1954 by psychologist Frederic Werthem, summarized the fear associated

with the new popular comic book medium, setting into motion U.S. Senate hearings on comic books and juvenile delinquency and spawning the Comics Code Authority. Video games such as the *Grand Theft Auto* series brought the potential dangers of racist, sexist, and violent content to public attention. The ban on the sale of video games that had been labeled as violent was argued in front of the U.S. Supreme Court in 2011. The voluntary labeling system, similar to the Comics Code, was put into place by video game manufacturers. However, the Supreme Court found that video game sellers could not ban the sale of such products because such a ban represented an infringement upon the First Amendment right to free speech. Boundary testing can be seen in the popular acceptance of comic books and video games. As discussed, the acceptance of media forms by young people is often accompanied by controversy.

Age and Boundary Testing

The moral panics of comic books and video games are closely associated with the age of the media user. Boundary testing is a common occurrence in the development of the child. Most theories of child development address the challenges to the early boundaries that children encounter. Swiss psychologist Jean Piaget developed his stage theory based on the actions of the child upon genetic factors and within the milieu of the family structure. The child in stage theory encounters boundaries, in the form of schema, and in the act of engagement creates new knowledge in the process. Russian psychologist Lev Vygotsky developed his theory of child development, known as the *zone of proximal development,* around the idea that young people learn from those who are more experienced. Learning takes place in the situations when young people are challenged to develop novel responses to new experiences.

Boundary testing in child development is seen as a natural occurrence. It is also a necessary one, without which the child cannot develop and mature successfully. The media forms that children encounter often represent schema that the child must assess and accommodate. These media forms can take on the role of a tutor or guide, which assists the young person as he or she develops and learns. As media forms have assumed the role of guide or tutor, they have also been seen as a detrimental force in the development of the child, as evident in the examples of the moral panics of comic books and video games cited earlier. These examples are often considered the most egregious examples of media violence.

Media Violence and Boundary Testing

Media violence is a contentious issue that plays a central role in the dynamic forms of boundary testing discussed previously. As a symbolic form of representation, the direct impact of media violence is hard to ascertain. For the dangers ascribed to literature, rock music, and pornography there are equivalent arguments for the cathartic, artistic, and liberatory qualities of such media forms. In *The Uses of Enchantment*, psychologist Bruno Bettleheim argued that fairy tales were an important guide for young people who were learning how to negotiate the complexities of social expectation and biological development. The dangers of literature are expanded in an age of interactive media, when readers become users of interactive media and players of video games that require active engagement and decision making.

Contemporary video games such as *inFAMOUS* and *Fable* incorporate the decision-making process into the game play, changing the character according to choices that are labeled "good" and "evil." In this manner, we can see that contemporary media accommodate a level of interactivity demonstrated by the ability to choose the actions of the character, further complicating the judgment that such media forms are violent. If such media forms are, indeed, violent, this inevitably reflects back upon the choices made by the user. The boundary testing that contemporary digital media enables is related to the zone of proximal development as discussed previously. Additionally, it is a boundary testing that folds back onto the choices made by the user; the ethical boundaries are those of the media form as well as the individual.

Robert Sweeny

See also Developmental Effects; Moral Development, Effects of Media Violence on; Social Cognitive Theory; Social Learning Theory From Media

Further Readings

Bettleheim, B. (1989). *The uses of enchantment: The meaning and importance of fairy tales.* New York, NY: Vintage.

Piaget, J. (1952). *The origins of intelligence in children.* New York, NY: International University Press.

Vygotsky, L. (1963). *Thought and language.* Cambridge, MA: MIT Press.

Werthem, F. (1996). *Seduction of the innocents.* New York, NY: Main Roads Books. (Originally published 1954)

BULLYING, DEFINITION AND LAWS OF

According to Dan Olweus, one of the foremost experts on bullying and lead designer of the Olweus Bullying Prevention Program, bullying occurs when someone repeatedly and purposely says or does mean or hurtful things to another person who has a hard time defending himself or herself. According to this definition, there are four key components to bullying.

First, bullying includes direct and indirect verbal, physical, and emotional abuse. *Direct bullying* consists of inflicting physical or psychological harm on another person. These are the types of things most people traditionally think of when they hear the word *bullying*. For example, direct verbal aggression includes actions like making fun of someone, calling someone names, or threatening a person, and direct physical aggression consists of actions like hitting, kicking, or shoving someone. *Indirect* or *relational bullying* is seeking to damage another person's relationships. Examples of indirect relational bullying include excluding a person from his or her group of friends, telling lies or spreading false rumors about another person, or trying to make other students dislike him or her. Research suggests that boys are more likely to be bullied via direct aggression, while girls are more likely to be bullied via indirect aggression.

Second, bullying is intentional. A person who bullies wants to harm his or her victim. This component of the definition is designed to distinguish bullying from things like teasing that is done in a friendly or playful way. A bully engages in a behavior to gain power over another person, to put another person down, or to build himself or herself up. What starts out as friendly teasing turns into bullying when it is repeated even though it is clear the target takes offense, gets hurts, no longer wants to be teased, or asks the person to stop and he or she does not stop.

Third, bullying typically consists of a repeated behavior that happens more than just once. For traditional bullying, examples might include making fun of a person or physically hitting or pushing a person over a period of time, or an ongoing campaign to damage the victim's reputation or relationships. However, in the relatively newer context of cyberbullying (which is the use of electronic communication to inflict harm on victims), the term *repeated* often takes on much broader meaning. To illustrate, a cyberbully might create a single website or send or post a single text, picture, or video message to hurt or embarrass his or her intended victim that can then be viewed repeatedly by hundreds of other people.

Finally, bullies are more powerful than their victims in one or more ways (i.e., it is not a fair fight). Typical definitions of bullying include phrases like "It is *not* bullying when two people of about equal strength or power argue or fight," or "It is bullying when it is difficult for the person being bullied to defend himself or herself." Bullies misuse their power by purposefully singling out someone who they know is weaker than they are. For example, bullies might be physically bigger, stronger, smarter, or more popular. Other examples include using knowledge of another's weakness (e.g., learning disability, physical disability) against him or her, or using one's membership in a majority group against a member of a minority group (e.g., racism, sexism, homophobia).

Prevalence and Effects

In the United States, at least 20% of sixth through tenth graders have bullied someone else during the current school term, and at least 17% of this same age group reported being victims of bullying (Nansel et al., 2001). Results suggest that bullying tends to decrease somewhat between junior high and high school. Bullying can lead to both short- and long-term problems such as lower self-esteem, difficulty concentrating, higher absenteeism, and greater depression and anxiety. Research also suggests that victims of bullying are at an increased risk of suicide. Notably, there is evidence that many school shooting perpetrators were victims of bullying.

While bullying is typically considered something that happens between children and adolescents, there is a growing body of research on adult and workplace bullying. In fact, recent research suggests that approximately 10% of U.S. employees experience bullying at work each year, and that up to 40% experience it at some point during their work lives. Workplace bullying has been shown to negatively affect both employee well-being and organizational productivity.

Laws

In 2011 the U.S. Department of Education released a report containing a detailed analysis of state bullying laws. At the time the report was written, 46 states had enacted bullying laws, and the remaining 4 states had pending bills set to address bullying. Furthermore, 36 states had laws addressing cyberbullying. This report identified 11 key components that are often included in state laws. Four of these (scope, prohibited behavior, school district policies, and communication) are included in more than 90% of state bullying prevention laws and are reviewed briefly in the next paragraph. A fifth component, training and prevention, is also reviewed as part of the next section of this entry.

Scope refers to where the legislation applies and when schools have authority over student bullying behavior. Most laws apply and are clearly enforceable when bullying occurs on school grounds, at school-sponsored functions, and on school buses. A number of laws also include off-campus conduct (e.g., at bus stops, adjacent to campus, and cyberbullying) when it is severe or disruptive enough to create a hostile learning environment. *Prohibited behavior* deals with the types of actions that are barred under the law. Here, again, the key focus is often on behaviors that might create a hostile learning environment or disrupt the school setting. Common examples include physical harm, threats of physical harm, or property damage. Some states also prohibit psychological harm and relational aggression. All but one state require that *school district policies* be developed and implemented. Examples of topics that could be included in these policies are how bullying is defined, reported, investigated, and addressed. Finally, *communication* refers to how school districts must publicize their bullying policies to all members of the school community, including students, parents, teachers, and other school personnel. More often than not state laws require that schools publish policies in student handbooks and employee manuals, but in some instances only verbal discussions are required or encouraged.

Prevention

As noted previously, another common component of many bullying laws is bullying prevention. Eighty-five percent of states' laws require or encourage school districts to implement bullying prevention, education, or awareness programs. Many evidence-based bullying prevention programs have been designed, implemented, and evaluated in the past two decades. For example, Olweus Bullying Prevention Program is designed for kindergarten through eighth grade students. Although this program is designed to be implemented by schools, it is a comprehensive program designed to address bullying at the community, school, classroom, and individual levels. This program has been evaluated in at least six large-scale studies involving more than 40,000 students. Results across these studies suggest this program is effective at reducing student bullying behavior (based on self-report, peer, and teacher ratings). A similar program has been developed for cyberbullying, although at the time this entry was written it had not been evaluated. Examples of other evidence-based bullying prevention programs include Steps to Respect: Bullying Prevention for Elementary Schools and Get Real About Violence.

Effective bullying prevention programs share a number of important aspects. First, they tend to be complete curricula administered in class over a period of time. For example, Steps to Respect contains 11 lessons, and Get Real About Violence contains 12 lessons. Most programs include numerous support materials such as posters and videos for students and handouts, worksheets, and discussion topics for both students and parents. Second, they tend to focus on all members of a school or community, and not just students. For example, and in addition to students, they often involve training for teachers, school bus drivers, cafeteria workers, and parents. Third, they typically teach and provide an opportunity (often through role playing) for students to practice new skills such as perspective taking, emotional regulation, assertiveness training, and conflict resolution. Fourth, they often include components that focus on the bullies themselves, victims of bullying, and bystanders who witness bullying. Focusing on bystanders is important because bullying often takes place in front of peers when adults are not present. It is important to remind bystanders not to encourage bullying and to teach them ways to safely respond when they observe bullying. Even walking away can discourage bullying because many bullies like an audience, and it can reinforce the norm that bullying is not acceptable.

Finally, recent research on computer-tailored messages suggests that such messages might also be a useful tool at reducing bullying behavior. Computer-tailored messages are typically created by asking individuals to answer a series of questions and then generating messages that are customized to each individual. In a recent study, researchers designed, implemented, and evaluated a tailored intervention that was delivered over the Internet to reduce a variety of bullying-related behaviors in 25 middle and high schools. Results suggest that the intervention was effective at producing significant reductions in the number of students who bullied, were victims of bullying, or watched bullying.

Anthony J. Roberto

See also Aggression in Youth; Cyberbullying, Definition and Effects of; Cyberbullying, Violent Content in; Cyberbullying Laws

Further Readings

Aluede, O., Adeleke, F., Omoike, D., & Afen-Akpaida, J. (2008). A review of the extent, nature, characteristics and effects of bullying behaviour in schools. *Journal of Instructional Psychology, 35,* 151–158.

Evers, K. E., Prochaska, J. O., Van Marter, D. F., Johnson, J. L., & Prochaska, J. M. (2007). Transtheoretical-based bullying prevention effectiveness trials in middle schools and high schools. *Educational Research, 49,* 397–414.

Lutgen-Sandvik, P., & Tracy, S. J. (2012). Answering five key questions about workplace bullying: How communication scholarship provides thought leadership for transforming abuse at work. *Management Communication Quarterly, 26,* 3–47.

Nansel, T. R., Overpeck, M., Pilla, R. S., Ruan, W. J., Simons-Morton, B., & Scheidt, P. (2001). Bullying behaviors among U.S. youth: Prevalence and association with psychosocial adjustment. *Journal of the American Medical Association, 285,* 2094–2100.

Olweus, D., Limber, S., Flerx, V. C., Mullin, N., Riese, J., & Snyder, M. (2007). *Olweus bullying prevention program schoolwide guide.* Center City, MN: Hazelden.

Roberto, A. J., & Eden, J. (2010). Cyberbullying: Aggressive communication in the digital age. In T. A. Avtgis & A. S. Rancer (Eds.), *Arguments, aggression, and conflict: New directions in theory and research* (pp. 198–216). New York, NY: Routledge.

U.S. Department of Education, Office of Planning, Evaluation and Policy Development, Policy and Program Studies Service. (2011). *Analysis of state bullying laws and policies.* Washington, DC: Author.

CATHARSIS THEORY

"I just needed to blow-off some steam" or "I just had to get that out of my system" are a few of the excuses that a person may give right after yelling at someone, punching the wall, or shooting down a platoon of enemy soldiers in a video game. Some go further to claim that they feel much better as a result. The notion that a person can rid himself or herself of negative emotions by acting aggressively, or witnessing violent acts in film or video games, has been a focus of popular psychologists for several decades. The relief that could come from "blowing off steam" is often called *cathartic relief*, and it is said to be good for you.

There has been little direct scientific evidence to support the idea that media viewing can lead to cathartic relief of negative emotions. Yet the possibility of catharsis continues to receive attention. The reason why catharsis continues to be examined might be because the idea seems to ring true for many of us. The conscious choice to relieve aggression by watching a movie or playing a video game rather than through physical assault sounds like a good idea. Can this ever be accomplished, or will media exposure only increase the desire to aggress? Does the media outlet matter (e.g., television versus video games)? Where did the notion of catharsis originate? This entry briefly summarizes the origins, theoretical mechanisms, and findings related to the principle of catharsis (sometimes called catharsis theory).

Cathartic Relief

The term *catharsis* is derived from the Greek word *katharsis*, a term that implies a process of purification through the act of purging. Written record of this concept can be traced back to the Greek philosopher Aristotle. He first used *katharsis* in a medical sense, referring to biological functioning, but he later implied that this process could also occur in an emotional context. Aristotle's writings in *Poetics* describe a process through which an audience that is viewing theatrical portrayals (either dramatic or comedic) may experience feelings of pity and fear. The experience of these feelings allows the viewer to purge these negative emotions and leave the theater in a balanced emotional state. Over the centuries some scholars have interpreted Aristotle's writings more broadly to mean that exposure to the actions of others may alleviate any negative emotional state, including anger, leaving the viewer in both an emotionally and physiologically relaxed state. Using this broad interpretation, cathartic relief can be conceptualized as the purging of negative emotions by viewing the actions of others (on stage, in television, in video games, etc.).

Catharsis in Psychoanalysis

Sigmund Freud believed that cathartic relief was essential in the treatment of hysteria (a catch-all condition characterized by seemingly irrational outbursts). Following the principles of psychoanalysis, Freud believed that recalling and verbally discussing a prior trauma could provide cathartic relief to hysterical patients. In this sense the patient is both the actor and the audience, experiencing the drama of the past event and ideally leaving the session freed of emotional distress.

Freud also believed that cathartic relief was necessary when dealing with the death wish (defined as an instinct that compels individuals to reduce negative stimulation, even though a complete elimination of negative stimulation is only achievable in death). Freud believed that the death wish could be managed by the expression of aggression. The death wish may compel us to hurt ourselves, but hurting ourselves cathartically relieves the need to continue hurting ourselves. Freud further surmised that individuals will often turn the death wish outward and aggress against others in an effort to cathartically relieve the death wish.

In the cases of both hysteria and the death wish, Freud changed Aristotle's original intent of catharsis, that viewing others purges negative emotions. Freud believed that relief could only come through self-expression. Yet Freud's death wish is often interpreted as a drive theory (i.e., individuals are innately driven to reduce negative stimulation), and a close examination of another drive theory (the frustration-aggression hypothesis) reveals how viewing media portrayals may reduce negative emotions.

Catharsis as a Drive

In 1939 John Dollard and his Yale colleagues published *Frustration and Aggression,* wherein they claimed that once an individual experiences a frustration (defined as the blockage of an intended goal), he or she will be driven to act aggressively (defined as inflicting injury against another individual) in an effort to relieve the negative emotions associated with the experience of the frustrations. The Yale group's frustration-aggression hypothesis stated that any goal, once thwarted, would create a need to aggress, and subsequent aggression would cathartically relieve the need to aggress further. "The expression of any act of aggression is a catharsis that reduces the instigation to all other acts of aggression" (Dollard, Miller, Doob, Mowrer, & Sears, 1939, p. 53).

Although the Yale group argued that aggression is the inevitable conclusion of a frustration, they also noted that this drive toward cathartic relief may be delayed if the frustrated individual fears punishment or fears failure in the production of an effectively aggressive act. Under these conditions of fear the individual may displace the aggression onto substitute targets or change the manner in which the aggression manifests. These suppositions proposed in the original 1939 book leave room for the possibility of catharsis as a result of media exposure.

Catharsis could occur through media exposure if following a frustration of goal attainment, and fearing punishment or failure, the individual chooses a substitute target for his or her aggression (i.e., displacement). This substitute target could take the form of a character in a film (e.g., "the bad guy") and the change in the form of aggression could move from immediate physical assault to delayed vicarious witness of assault (e.g., cathartic relief through witnessing the violent acts of others against the bad guy). A more tangible and direct substitute target could also be found in a video game. The displaced target in a video game would receive directed virtual aggression from the frustrated individual (e.g., the use of gunfire in an attempt to destroy the virtual target), potentially providing cathartic relief. The possibility of vicarious cathartic relief as a media effect has been examined several times, starting with work of Seymour Feshbach.

Catharsis as a Media Effect

Feshbach published a series of studies examining cathartic relief of aggression as a result of exposure to a vicarious aggressive activity. For example, using the language of drive theories, Feshbach (1961) hypothesized that cathartic relief could occur after viewing a violent film. "Participation in a vicarious aggressive act results in a reduction in subsequent aggressive behavior if aggressive drive has been aroused at the time of such participation" (p. 381). In other words, a provoked individual (aggressive drive aroused) who views a violent film (vicarious aggressive act) will gain cathartic relief from the film (reduction in aggressive behavior).

To test his hypothesis Feshbach employed a basic 2 × 2 (provocation × film) between-participants experimental design. First, in an effort to provoke the participants, the experimenters randomly assigned participants to either a verbal insult or no-insult condition. The insults "essentially disparaged the intellectual motivation and the emotional maturity of the students" (p. 382). Second, participants were randomly assigned to view either a violent or nonviolent film clip. The violent clip was taken from *Body and Soul* (1947) and featured a violent boxing prize fight, whereas the nonviolent film did not portray any violence. Third, participants then completed an aggressive word association task (a form of cognitive aggression) and an evaluation of the competency of the experimenter who had provoked them (a form of behavioral aggression).

Feshbach found that provoked individuals experienced cathartic relief after exposure to the violent film. These participants scored the lowest on both cognitive and behavioral aggression. Subsequent studies by Feshbach found similar results. For example, a field experiment by Feshbach and colleagues randomly assigned boys to watch a steady diet of either violent or nonviolent television programming over a period of several days. Results showed that the boys who watched the violent programs behaved less aggressively than did the boys who watched the nonviolent programs. The authors concluded that exposure to the violent programming had provided cathartic relief.

Although these studies suggest catharsis as a viable media effect, subsequent research on catharsis has been unable to replicate these findings. Furthermore, some have concluded that many of Feshbach's findings are invalid. Skeptical of catharsis theory, Dolf Zillmann and an Indiana University research team decided to test an alternative hypothesis using the same stimulus material used by Feshbach, the film *Body and Soul* (Zillmann, Johnson, & Hanrahan, 1973). They hypothesized that it was the film's happy ending that had reduced aggression, not cathartic relief from witnessing violent acts. To test this they provoked experimental participants with electric shock, randomly assigned them to view the film with or without a happy ending, and then allowed participants to deliver electric shock to their original tormentor. Findings showed that exposure to the happy ending reduced aggressive behavior. Participants who viewed the violence without a happy ending were more aggressive. These findings appear to directly contradict Feshbach's earlier work by demonstrating that the violence alone did not allow for cathartic relief.

The criticism of early findings in support of catharsis was not restricted to just one study. Critics have also offered an alternative explanation for the field experiment on children's exposure to violent television programming. The field experiment did not control for the entertainment quality of the programming across conditions. As a result, the boys in the nonviolent condition did not enjoy the programming as much as did the boys in the violent condition. Critics have argued that this lack of enjoyment may have led to the aggressive behavioral outbursts.

Catharsis Versus Cognitive Neoassociation

Although a series of studies showed support for catharsis, the findings of these studies were consistently invalidated. The principle of cognitive neoassociation offers a theoretical explanation for why this may be the case. This principle holds that memory can be conceptualized as a collection of networks consisting of nodes that represent thoughts and feelings. When individuals are primed with a certain concept (e.g., violence), they begin to access semantically related thoughts and feelings in their cognitive networks. This process of the spreading activation of semantically related thoughts and feelings offers an explanation as to why exposure to violence increases rather than decreases aggressive tendencies. As exposure to violence increases, semantically related thoughts increase, and this leads to an increased likelihood for aggressive behavior.

Cognitive network size may also increase over time. Repeated exposure to media violence may multiply the number of semantic nodes related to violence in one's semantic network. According to the availability heuristic, the greater the number of aggressive thoughts and feelings that are available in an individual's semantic network, the more likely it is that the individual will behave aggressively in a given situation.

The principle of cognitive neoassociation has been used as a guiding mechanism in several theoretical approaches (e.g., the general aggression model, script theory, social-cognitive theory), all of which conclude that exposure to media violence will increase aggression and not provide cathartic relief. Decades of research and hundreds of individual studies seem to demonstrate that exposure to passive media violence increases aggression. Yet there is reason to believe that catharsis could occur as a result of exposure to a more active media, such as a video game.

Catharsis and Video Games

A series of studies by Jack Hokanson and colleagues at Florida State University explain how a physical act (as opposed to a vicarious act) may offer cathartic relief. In one study (Hokanson, 1961) the experimenter provoked half of the participants with verbal insults, allowed the participants to retaliate by administering electric shocks to the provoker, and then measured if the retaliatory aggression provided cathartic relief in the form of reduced physiological arousal. Although no actual electric shocks were administered, participants were led to believe that if they pushed a button it would harm their provoker. The number, duration, and intensity (as measured by the amount of pressure applied) of the button pushes were recorded. Results revealed that those participants that applied the most pressure on the button experienced the greatest reduction of physiological arousal. In other words, cathartic relief was achieved by intensely pushing a button that was thought to harm another. This finding points to the possibility that pushing buttons on a video game controller may also provide cathartic relief provided those button pushes are believed to cause harm to others (e.g., shooting other players in a video game environment).

The possibility of catharsis as a result of violent video game play has been discussed by several researchers and was summarized in a meta-analysis by John Sherry (2007). After a careful examination of the video game effects literature, Sherry concluded that "there are some indications of support for the catharsis hypothesis." However, Sherry maintains that more research is needed before any definitive conclusions can be drawn. Studies that both (a) provoke participants and (b) expose participants to many types of violent video game play may demonstrate the potential for cathartic relief. When such a series of studies is completed we may then be able to draw a more complete conclusion concerning catharsis theory.

Chad Mahood

See also Aggression and Anger; Cognition: Schemas and Scripts; Uses and Gratifications Perspective of Media Effects

Further Readings

Dollard, J., Miller, N. E., Doob, L. W., Mowrer, O. H., & Sears, R. R. (1939). *Frustration and aggression.* New Haven, CT: Yale University Press.

Feshbach, S. (1961). The stimulating versus cathartic effects of a vicarious aggressive activity. *Journal of Abnormal and Social Psychology, 63,* 381–385.

Hokanson, J. E. (1961). The effects of frustration and anxiety on overt aggression. *Journal of Abnormal Social Psychology, 62,* 346–351.

Sherry, J. L. (2007). Violent video games and aggression: Why can't we find effects? In R. W. Preiss, B. M. Gayle, N. Burrell, M. Allen, & J. Bryant (Eds.), *Mass media effects research: Advances through meta-analysis* (pp. 245–262). Mahwah, NJ: Erlbaum.

Zillmann, D., Johnson, R. C., & Hanrahan, J. (1973). Pacifying effect of happy ending of communications involving aggression. *Psychological Reports, 32,* 967–970.

CENSORSHIP OF VIOLENT CONTENT

Research regarding media violence has surveyed a vast spectrum of media contexts and platforms, including television entertainment, news coverage, comic books, cinema, children's cartoons, music, advertising, and video games. It has been estimated that during roughly 70 years—the 1930s through the 1990s—hundreds of studies were conducted, with concluding evidence supporting the notion that exposure to media violence affected viewers' beliefs, emotions, and behaviors. More than a decade into the 21st century, media violence effects remains one of the most popular areas of research in mass communication and media effects. The start of a new millennium marked the emergence of a unified societal concern regarding media violence and its effects, especially the effects on children. With this increase in scrutinizing examination of the U.S. mass media, society at large began a heated debate over the role of government in the censorship of violent content and the ethical responsibility of the industries involved in the production and proliferation of violent content. With the introduction of technological innovations in communication and information distribution, and increased digital accessibility, societal concern about the influential power of media content on the attitudes, beliefs, and behaviors of audiences has increased.

To understand all sides of the censorship debate, it is important to understand what constitutes media violence, key research findings related to media violence exposure effects on viewers, and the major parties involved in the discussion of censorship. As with any long-term debate, it is essential to review the history and evolution of the opinions and major events related to the censorship of media violence in the United States. This particular review of the censorship of violence content in media focuses on the U.S. political and mass media environment. Around the world, societal approaches to media violence and the censorship or regulation of said violent content varies greatly from country to country and region to region.

Historical Perspective of Censorship of U.S. Media Content

"Censorship" holds an unpopular position within the vernacular of American society. Because the United States is a democracy with a free-market economy, its citizens have traditionally passionately upheld the right to freedom of speech afforded in the First Amendment to the U.S. Constitution. The political atmosphere in the United States has held a constant ebb and flow in regard to government involvement in censorship of the U.S. mass communication industry. Congress's involvement in the debate of content censorship, especially television, has been a reflection of society's growing concerns regarding the influence of media content on children, adults, and at-risk populations (the mentally ill and emotionally unstable). With every new form of communication that has been created in the 20th and 21st centuries, there has been nationwide debate to determine how best to protect the right to free speech while implementing parental controls for the protection of the nation's youth.

As radio blanketed the American culture in the 1920s, along with concurrent development of sound and color film in that decade, the Radio Act of 1927 was passed by Congress, giving a federal commission power to license stations, assign operating frequencies, and through a 1928 amendment, establish interstate and local stations. Because of inconsistency and dated radio, telegraph, and telephone communications regulations, Congress, at President Franklin D. Roosevelt's request, passed the Communications Act of 1934, putting all electronic communications businesses under purview of the Federal Communications Commission (FCC). This agency holds the responsibility of preserving healthy competition within the communication industry, managing the security of the United States' emergency communications system, protecting consumers' rights and interests, and fostering fair and safe technological innovation. In the ambiguous language of the 1934 act, the FCC could regulate in the "public interest, convenience and necessity." Because of this verbiage, the FCC has had a significant impact on questions of freedom through regulation of the media.

Throughout the 1930s, 1940s, and 1950s, the FCC rarely used the full extent of regulatory powers granted to it, but it was known to strongly suggest to networks that they "clean up" entertainment content in the event of viewer complaints. In the early 1900s, with the growth of filmmaking and cinema theaters throughout the United States, more than 45 local city and state censorship boards existed across the country, many controlled by religious organizations. These censorship boards controlled films' access to markets based on moral approvals (CARA, filmratings.com). Films would have to be granted approval in every market the film was to be

shown in. Eventually, the film industry's frustration with this disorganization led to the creation of the Motion Picture Association of America (MPAA) in 1922. This first step to self-regulation required all members—all major motion picture studios responsible for U.S. filmmaking—to submit movies to the Production Code Administration for approval prior to distribution. The first censorship code, the Hays Code—named in honor of the first MPAA president, Will Hays—was detailed and set extensive standards of what was deemed appropriate. For example, no criticisms of religion, no depictions of childbirth, no "lustful" kissing or "suggestive" dancing, and only the "correct standards of life" could be presented. Films were approved or disapproved by the Hays Code based on judgment of the content as moral or immoral. Individual communities would typically require a film to have been approved by the MPAA before making it available in cinemas.

The late 1950s was a scandalous time for the agency, during which its reputation was seriously tarnished when, for example, in 1958 the FCC commissioner resigned after it became known that he had accepted a bribe from an applicant for a television station license. Society's trust of mass media was jeopardized by the quiz show scandals, on which the FCC held hearings, revealing how producers had rigged the results of some shows. The hearings led to regulations to prevent future transgressions of a similar nature. As for the 1960s, television programming was known as the "vast wasteland" of media content plagued by the previous decade of mismanaged enforcement of regulations and conflict-of-interest scandals.

The 1960s and 1970s were a time of confrontation regarding the representation of minorities in media content as well as involvement and accessibility to management positions within mass communication companies. Innovations such as satellite communications and cable television required the FCC to develop regulatory standards for new markets. This time period also marked the first powerful content regulatory actions taken by the FCC. Alcohol and cigarette advertising on television were heavily regulated as to where, when, and how brands were allowed to market their products. Political campaign marketing saw the implementation of the "fairness doctrine" (also known as the Equal Time Rule) that caused controversy over issues such as equal air time for candidates from various parties and platforms. The fairness doctrine was challenged in 1969 in *Red*

Lion Broadcasting Co. v. Federal Communications Commission but was upheld on the grounds of frequency scarcity. And most relevant to media violence scholars, pressures from interested groups led to regulations limiting the hours during which various types of adult programming (violent content, sexual content, and profanity) could be aired.

Along with vast shifts in societal norms throughout the United States, the creative approach to filmmaking changed. The film and cinema industry was not collectively following the MPAA's Hays Code, and a new "open and frank" American movie style emerged. In April 1968 the U.S. Supreme Court upheld the decision granting states and cities the authority to prevent the exposure of children to books and films that could not be denied to adults. It became apparent that a new effective self-regulation system was needed or the government would step in to regulate U.S. filmmaking. With government discussion and societal pressures of increased regulation of film content, the MPAA's chair, Jack Valenti, approached the National Association of Theatre Owners (NATO) and what is today the Independent Film & Television Alliance (IFTA) to engage in five months of meetings with writers, directors, producers, actors, craft unions, critics, religious organizations, and the heads of MPAA member companies. The result was industry consensus that a new ratings system, run by an independent ratings body, would replace the Hays Code of approval or disapproval. This ratings system would give advance cautionary warnings to parents to help them make informed decisions about their children's movie viewing. In November 1968, the movie rating system was implemented. As a voluntary system, not regulated by the government, MPAA member company studios agreed to have all films rated, and members of NATO agreed to enforce the new ratings system by requiring identification of patrons at time of admission to shows. Rental stores and retailers also enforced the ratings system and identification requirements for movies released and sold on video. Although the rating categories and qualifications have been updated several times since its initial release, the MPAA's modern film-rating system is still, as of 2013, administered by the Classification & Ratings Administration (CARA), not by a government agency.

Scholars use various definitions of media violence when conducting media effects and mass communication research, but the content analytic work of George Gerbner garnered his definition of media violence wide attention. Gerbner (1972, p. 31) defined *violence* as "the overt expression of physical force against other or self, or the compelling of action against one's will on pain of being hurt or killed." His cultivation theory emphasized the cumulative effects of media violence exposure on the beliefs individuals hold about society. While his definition of violence is limited in that it only refers to physical violence, Gerbner's research catalyzed the debate of how media violence affects viewers.

During the deregulation era of the 1980s and 1990s, the FCC held that scarcity was no longer a consideration and formally abolished the fairness doctrine in 1987. The Telecommunications Act of 1996, signed by President Bill Clinton, aimed to replace laws that were seen as antibusiness and anticonsumer with laws that were intended to bolster market competition by deregulating the broadcasting market and promoting industry self-regulation regarding harmful content censorship. One of the more influential elements of this act was that it allowed for media cross-ownership, meaning the law was to "let anyone enter any communications business—to let any communications business compete in any market against any other." An additional element of the Telecommunications Act of 1996 was Title V's support for V-chip technology that enables parents to block television content based on ratings in an effort to protect children from exposure to indecent material or any content deemed inappropriate by parents and guardians. By January 2000, all television units 13 inches or larger were required to have V-chip technology. The FCC supported the development of this technology and worked to enforce its implementation to televisions in the United States. Congress, in § 551 of the Telecommunications Act of 1996, gave the television industry the first opportunity to establish a voluntary ratings system. By April 2000, the National Association of Broadcasters, the National Cable Television Association, and the MPAA established the TV rating system, also known as the TV Parental Guidelines requiring ratings, to be displayed on the television screen for the first 15 seconds of rated programming. Working in tandem with the V-chip, this rating system enables parents, as informed consumers on media content, to block programming with a certain rating from coming into their homes. Modeled after the MPAA movie ratings system, which many parents had been familiar with since the late 1960s, the TV Parental Guidelines rate programming that contains sexual, violent, or other material parents may deem inappropriate. The only television content not subject to the TV Parental Guidelines is news coverage and sports programming.

The millennium and early 21st century saw the most censorship-oriented research and government and activist group attention to media effects to date. On January 26, 2000, six professional health organizations issued a Joint Statement on the Impact of Entertainment Violence on Children. The statement included the signatures of all the presidents and executive officers of the six professional health organizations, including the American Academy of Pediatrics, American Academy of Child and Adolescent Psychiatry, American Psychological Association, American Medical Association, American Academy of Family Physicians, and American Psychiatric Association. A portion of the statement, paragraph 4, specified research findings that "point overwhelmingly to a causal connection between media violence and aggressive behavior in some children." Additionally, it referred to "the conclusion of the public health community, based on over 30 years of research, is that viewing entertainment violence can lead to increases in aggressive attitudes, values, and behavior, particularly in children" (Sparks, Sparks, & Sparks, 2009, p. 272).

The Children's Internet Protection Act (CIPA) was signed into law on December 21, 2000, requiring that primary and secondary schools and libraries in the United States use Internet filters and implement other measures to protect children from harmful content as a condition for receipt of federal funding (known as "E-Rate discounts" for telecommunications services and Internet access grants). Unlike the Communications Decency Act (Title V of the Telecommunications Act of 1996) and the Child Online Protection Act (1998), which were both deemed unconstitutional by the U.S. Supreme Court on First Amendment grounds, this law was found to be constitutional on June 23, 2003, by the U.S. Supreme Court. While the CIPA does not require the tracking of Internet use by minors or adults, it does require all Internet access to be filtered for minors and adults. Content that is obscene, pornographic, or harmful to minors must be filtered or blocked. The FCC subsequently instructed libraries to implement procedures for unblocking filters upon request by an adult without further enquiry into the reasoning, leaving the digression of what constitutes bona fide research up to the adult, as allowed by the CIPA.

A wide spectrum of media platforms and contexts has been used in the research of the effects of violent media content on audiences. Some of the most popular media recently included in this area of research include video games and mobile apps. As a response to growing concerns regarding video game content, the Entertainment Software Association (formally the Interactive Digital Software Association) established the Entertainment Software Rating Board (ESRB) in 1994 as a self-regulatory organization that assigns age and content ratings, enforces industry-adopted advertising guidelines, and ensures responsible online privacy principles for computer and video games in the United States and Canada. Since around 2005, several congressional bills aiming to regulate video game content and/or purchasing requirements (valid adult identification) have been proposed and ultimately stopped because of First Amendment violations. As of June 27, 2011, the U.S. Supreme Court ruled that video games are protected speech under the First Amendment in *Brown v. Entertainment Merchants Association.* The FCC and Federal Trade Commission have praised the ESRB as one of the most successful and effective self-regulatory campaigns, and the vast majority of retail stores prohibit unrated video games to be sold.

In 2003 Craig Anderson and colleagues summarized what could be said is the main consensus of modern media effects scholars in relation to violence research:

> Research on violent television and films, video games, and music reveals unequivocal behavior in both immediate and long-term contexts. The effects appear larger for milder than for more severe forms of aggression, but the effects on severe forms of violence are also substantial ($r = .13$ to $.32$) when compared with effects of other violence risk factors or medical effects deemed important by the medical community (e.g., effect of aspirin on heart attacks). The research base is large; diverse in methods, samples, and media genres; and consistent in overall findings. The evidence is clearest within the most extensively researched domain, television and film violence. The growing body of video game research yields essentially the same conclusions. (p. 81)

Growing Concerns Regarding Violent Media Content

Scholars often discuss the influence of the proliferation of media platforms and information sources on the increased availability and amount of media. While this technological advancement has many positive influences and utilities for society at large, it has also fostered a media consumption environment within which the audience is exposed to journalistic coverage of violence in every form of communication—written word, audio, video, and any combination of the three. Additionally, media platform proliferation has potentially increased the amount of promotional material and entertainment containing violent content seen by viewers overall. An increase in exposure to violent content may also be the result of the increasing integration of technologies such as computers, tablets, and smartphones into the everyday lives of Americans. This media platform integration has led to increased accessibility of information in terms of time and format of content availability. Not only are avid television show fans able to watch the most recent episode during its original air time, but digital video recorders as well as television content available on the Internet allow viewers full control of when, where, and how often they watch. Americans no longer have to wait for world news to air on evening television or to read about it in the next morning's newspaper; instead, they have access to 24-hour news coverage via communication networks on digital television, satellite radio, and vast wireless Internet accessibility on a wide range of mobile devices.

The 2010s have experienced gun violence in public places, including universities, movie theaters, shopping malls, and elementary schools. As of early 2013, in reaction to major recent events of public gun violence, such as mass shootings at an Aurora, Colorado, movie theater in July 2012 and at Sandy Hook Elementary School in Newtown, Connecticut, in December 2012, national discussions of updating gun regulations and increased censorship of media violence have become hot topics. Media effects research is expected to play a key role in the ongoing discussions regarding audience exposure to violent content and its influence on attitudes, emotions, and behaviors.

Mary Elizabeth Dunn

See also Effects from Violent Content, Short and Long-Term; Effects of Media Violence on Relational Aggression; Federal Communications Commission; First Amendment Protections and Freedom of Expression; Rating Systems, Film; Violence, Definition of

Further Readings

Anderson, C. A., Berkowitz, L., Donnerstein, E., Huesmann, L. R., Johnson, J. D., Linz, D., Malamuth,
N. M., & Wartella, E. (2003). The influence of media violence on youth. *Psychological Science in the Public Interest, 4*(3), 81–110.

Brown v. Entertainment Merchants Association, 131 S.Ct. 2729 (2011).

Caterino, B. (2009). Federal Communications Commission. In J. R. Vile, D. L. Hudson Jr., & D. Schultz (Eds.), *Encyclopedia of the First Amendment* (Vol. 1, pp. 441–443). Washington, DC: CQ Press.

Federal Communications Commission. (2012). *V-chip: Viewing television responsibly and the TV parental guidelines.* Retrieved from http://transition.fcc.gov/vchip

Gerbner, G. (1972). Violence in television drama: Trends and symbolic functions. In G. A. Comstock & E. A. Rubinstein (Eds.), *Television and social behavior*: Vol. 1. *Media content and control* (pp. 28–187). Washington, DC: Government Printing Office.

Harris, R. L. (2009). *A cognitive psychology of mass communication* (5th ed., pp. 4, 137, 257–290, 363). New York, NY: Routledge.

Red Lion Broadcasting Co. v. Federal Communications Commission, 395 U.S. 367 (1969).

Sparks, G., Sparks, C., & Sparks, E. (2009). Media violence. In J. Bryant & M. B. Oliver (Eds.), *Media effects advances in theory and research* (3rd ed., pp. 269–286). New York, NY: Routledge.

Websites

The Classification & Rating Administration (CARA); http://www.filmratings.com/filmRatings_Cara/#/about

Motion Picture Association of America (MPAA); http://www.mpaa.org/ratings/ratings-history

The TV Parental Guidelines; http://www.tvguidelines.org

CHARACTER DEVELOPMENT WITHIN VIOLENT CONTENT

Of the many media content dimensions that can influence the intensity of users' responses, a key factor is the extent to which portrayed characters are developed. Well-developed characters in media can elicit more powerful empathic and emotional responses, encourage media users to identify with characters, and enhance persuasion and imitation. However, underdeveloped characters can also have important effects, as they can encourage generalized, stereotypical judgments and responses in users. More specifically, character development is important to the potential effects of violent media content. The extent to which both perpetrators and victims of media violence are developed as characters may have strong influences on how media users respond to the violent messages they consume. This entry provides some definitions and terms associated with character development, describes the general role of character development in responses to media, and explains concepts and research findings dealing with audience responses to both well-developed and poorly developed media characters, both in media in general and more specifically in violent media content.

Definitions of Character Development

Character development can be understood most broadly as the way a character's background, traits, and behavior are revealed and portrayed over the course of a media narrative. For some researchers, particularly in literature and writing circles, a more specific distinction is made between the terms *character development* and *characterization*. In these cases, *character development* refers to the way a character's disposition and personality change over the course of a story because of events that occur during the plot, such as when Ebenezer Scrooge evolves from a selfish and greedy miser to a gleeful and generous philanthropist during the course of a night of tumultuous and supernatural life-changing experiences in Charles Dickens's novella *A Christmas Carol*. *Characterization* refers to the detail in which a character's existing traits are related in a story through detailed description of the character's background, appearance, dialogue, and behavior. For example, the characterization of Atticus Finch in Harper Lee's novel *To Kill a Mockingbird* takes place over the course of the entire novel; he is an honest, duty-minded, courageous, and humble hero throughout the story's narrative, but Mr. Finch's words and deeds establish the extent of these traits for the reader more and more over the course of the novel's plot even though his fundamental disposition is more or less the same at the end of the story as it is at the beginning.

When considering the overall extent to which a media character is richly portrayed, though, these distinctions may be unimportant because both the revelation of a character's traits in a story and the way that character's traits change over the course of a story are dimensions determining the richness of that character. Therefore, the term *development* is also used more generally to describe a character who encompasses both of these elements of character exposition and more. A well-developed character in a media narrative is a character whose traits

are revealed in sufficient detail that they are vivid, complex, and unique—often so much that some of a well-developed character's traits may be puzzling or surprising to a media user. A "flat" character is not particularly well-developed and may represent a simple archetype, while a "round" character is more deep and complex. For example, the Wicked Witch of the West in the novel and film versions of L. Frank Baum's *The Wizard of Oz* (along with most of the other characters in the story) might be considered a flat character representing a simple villain archetype, while the main protagonist, Michael Corleone, from the *Godfather* film trilogy based on Mario Puzo's novel of the same name might be considered a more complex round character: admirable and deplorable elements of his persona are revealed, his values change and evolve, and contradictory patterns in his behavior emerge. The extent to which a character in a media story can be described as "developed," then, is affected both by the characterization that is used to reveal the character in the story and by the developments that occur to change the character during the story's plot. Under this usage of the term, characters can be considered to be round and thoroughly developed or flat and underdeveloped whether they are dynamic characters whose traits change during a story or static characters whose traits are relatively constant throughout the story; the key to a character's development is how well those traits are described and how unique and complex they are.

The term *development* can therefore be used very specifically to describe either the changes in a character over the plot of a story (aka a character's "arc") or more generally to describe the extent to which a character is revealed as detailed, complex, and unique in a story. Given that in a general sense a character's detail and complexity are most relevant to an understanding of audience responses to media, the broader definition of *character development* as the extent to which a character is described and portrayed is the way the term is often applied in scholarship on media and media violence. The remainder of this entry also uses this more general definition of character development as the richness, detail, and complexity within which a media character is portrayed.

The Role of Character Development in Media Experience

Many dimensions of media content influence enjoyment of and emotional responses to media. One key element of a media narrative related to strong responses is the presence of conflict between characters toward whom an audience has developed strong feelings. Media effects researcher Dolf Zillmann and colleagues developed a conceptual approach to media enjoyment known as "affective disposition theory," which generally maintains that audience members' enjoyment of media is driven by the positive and negative feelings they develop toward media characters and their subsequent judgments about the results of conflicts between those characters. For example, media users will generally feel more positively when a character they like prevails in a conflict, and more negatively when a character they dislike is successful.

Furthermore, affective disposition theory predicts that the intensity of media users' responses to these plot outcomes will be stronger if the media users' feelings about a character are stronger. In other words, a media user will feel much more enjoyment when a character he or she enthusiastically likes succeeds than when a character the user feels positively toward, but with less passion, has similar success. Similarly, a villain's defeat will be relished by a media user more if the villain is adamantly despised than if the villain is disliked less intensely. Therefore, affective disposition theory (and a constellation of related perspectives referred to as "disposition-based theories") places both the direction and intensity of feelings toward characters at the center of media enjoyment. These general predictions of disposition theory have been supported not only in fictional dramas, but in a variety of media settings such as comedy, news, sports, and advertising. Whatever the setting and topic of a media narrative, a story that is effective at generating powerful positive and negative dispositions toward different characters is more likely also to make the media user experience feelings of suspense, excitement, and ultimately enjoyment of the narrative.

Crucial to a narrative's ability to create strong audience dispositions toward characters is the extent to which these characters are developed. More developed characters have their likeable and dislikeable traits more clearly and completely revealed in a media narrative, and affective disposition theory holds that these more fully developed characters will therefore elicit stronger judgments and more powerful positive and negative feelings from media users. Media users will feel more empathy toward protagonists who have been fully developed and more disdain for antagonists who are similarly well developed, and in turn they will fear more for well-developed protagonists when they are in danger, revel more in well-developed protagonists' victories over well-developed villains, and more intensely mourn the defeat of well-developed protagonists at the hands of well-developed villains.

A closely related idea is the concept of identification, which has been used to describe a few different but related responses to media characters. *Identification* is sometimes used to describe a process wherein a media user feels such a strong cognitive and emotional connection to a media character that the media user temporarily adopts the perspective of the media character, experiencing the media narrative as if through the perspective of the media character. This intensely vicarious experience, however, may be rare and brief among media users because of their awareness of the presence of the medium and their awareness of information and events that may not be available to the media character. Identification is also used to describe a less intense but more common and more enduring response to media characters wherein a media user simply perceives a media character's traits as either similar to the media user's existing traits or similar to the traits the media user would most like to have. This type of identification with media characters is often classified in one of two dimensions: "similarity identification" (also referred to by some as "homophily"), meaning the extent to which a media user perceives a media character as already having similar traits as the user, and "wishful identification," meaning the extent to which a media user desires to have the traits of a media character.

By either definition, identification plays a critical role in the social effects of media on audiences because it is the mechanism that may cause media users to imitate, emulate, and be persuaded by media characters. Identification, of course, tends to occur with protagonists and other characters who are viewed positively by users rather than with disliked villains. Identification can be enhanced by superficial characteristics of a media character, such as the character's attractiveness. More well-developed characters, though, may be more likely to elicit feelings of both similarity identification and wishful identification because their traits are revealed in more rich detail. Thus, a more well-developed character may induce greater feelings of identification in a media user, which in turn may lead to a higher likelihood that the media user may want to emulate the traits and behaviors of that character.

Audience Responses to Violence Involving Well-Developed Media Characters

Given that identification with media characters is tied to stronger effects of media content, it may come as no surprise that identification with violent media characters is important to the potential effects of media violence. Just as identification with media characters is related to increases in many other media effects, identification with violent media characters has been linked to increased effects of media violence on users' aggression. For example, children have been found to learn more aggressive behaviors from aggressive media characters when they identified with the aggressive characters. Wishful identification with violent media characters in both television and video games has also been associated with increased scores on aggression measures in youth. Media users with physically aggressive tendencies have also been found to identify more with aggressive characters in media, which may reinforce their aggressive tendencies.

Violence and aggression are prevalent in media content, particularly in electronic screen media such as television, film, and video games, so the potential for well-developed violent media protagonists to elicit stronger negative effects in users via identification may be of particular concern to the possible effects of media violence on users. That said, feelings of identification with violent characters may not always encourage aggression, because some media users may find the experience of identifying with a violent character to be unpleasant, frightening, or guilt inducing. Well-developed media characters who engage in media violence may also provoke more thoughtful responses about the harmful outcomes of that violence, which may lead to negative perceptions of violence and aggression.

Audience Responses to Violence Involving Poorly Developed Media Characters

Although media users generally tend to respond much more strongly to well-developed characters than to poorly developed characters, advanced development of characters is relatively rare in the media products that most concern researchers interested in the effects of media violence: violent programs in electronic media such as television, film, and video games. Compared with other media such as novels, the depth of character development in many television programs, movies, and video games is often limited, particularly in the case of the "action" genres that tend to contain the most violent content. In action-oriented electronic media, simple, narrowly defined characters are often the norm because action fare is less oriented around complex characters and plots than thrilling visual drama and fast-paced conflict. In fact, action genres often substitute violence for character development as a means to generate audience interest and excitement.

Although audience members' most powerful emotional responses are usually reserved for well-developed characters, the underdeveloped characters who populate the violent action narratives in screen media can also have powerful effects on users' perceptions and behavior through other psychological processes. Because the characters in violent action genres are not developed as unique and complex individual characters, they often represent common tropes, stereotypes, and character archetypes. Some of these stereotypes may mirror or caricature commonly held stereotypes about people in the real world. For example, an action film's stock villain might be a Muslim terrorist of Middle Eastern extraction included in reference to some high-profile acts of terror committed by Islamic extremists in recent history, or a video game protagonist in an inner-city setting may have to fight through a series of stereotypical Black street gang members evocative of widely held stereotypes about race and crime in the United States. The film's protagonist, meanwhile, may likely be a masculine young male who is eager to indulge in violence up to and including homicide to extract justice against his foes. Victims of violence, however, may more likely be female characters who passively await the arrival of a hero to rescue them.

All of these types of stereotypical character portrayals, though superficial enough to be almost hyperbole, may have subtle but important influences on their audiences. While an action film populated with one-dimensional and stereotypical characters may not inspire the deep emotional responses of a film containing more complex characters, the stereotypes represented by underdeveloped characters may create and reinforce media users' stereotypical views about violence, as well as its perpetrators and victims. Common stereotypical messages that violent media may portray through underdeveloped characters may include the inaccurate but unequivocally presented ideas that violence is an appropriate (or even necessary) behavior for a masculine person, that violence is justified when carried out as an act of vengeance, that women are attracted to violent men, that women are helpless against violence unless they are rescued from it by a man, that violence has limited serious consequences for its victims and perpetrators, and that some racial minorities have inherently violent tendencies.

Although no one violent media narrative may elicit powerful and thoughtful responses to these messages, the aggregate effects of thousands of stereotypical portrayals of violence involving underdeveloped characters may slowly make these stereotypes about violence more accessible when media users make judgments about the real word. Media researcher George Gerbner's cultivation theory posits that heavy use of media can slowly skew people's perceptions of reality, including judgments about violence, to more closely match the version of reality presented in media. Subsequent researchers have observed that these cultivation effects may be strongest when media information is not processed carefully. Therefore, the underdevelopment of stereotypical characters in much violent media content may be particularly conducive to long-term effects on real-world stereotyping; users of violent electronic media may frequently encounter stereotypical characters who do not inspire thoughtful reflection on the media narratives they populate, but instead the simple stereotypical messages they convey about violence may slowly and subtly accumulate in media users' memory and judgments about the real world. In this way, it is possible that the underdeveloped characters who are common to violent media may be as influential in the long term as more fully developed characters that engage audiences more powerfully—and perhaps even more so.

James D. Ivory

See also Films, Representation of Violence and its Effects in; First-Person Perspective, Violent Content From; Identity, Media Violence and Its Effects on; Narrative, Effects of Violent; Parasocial Relationships; Stereotyping in Violent Content

Further Readings

Bryant, J., & Miron, D. (2002). Entertainment as media effect. In J. Bryant & D. Zillmann (Eds.), *Media effects: Advances in theory and research* (2nd ed., pp. 549–582). Mahwah, NJ: Erlbaum.

Cohen, J. (2001). Defining identification: A theoretical look at the identification of audiences with media characters. *Mass Communication and Society, 4,* 245–264.

Eyal, K., & Rubin, A. M. (2003). Viewer aggression and homophily, identification, and parasocial relationships with television characters. *Journal of Broadcasting and Electronic Media, 47,* 77–98.

Gerbner, G. (1998). Cultivation analysis: An overview. *Mass Communication and Society, 1,* 175–194.

Hoffner, C., & Buchanan, M. (2005). Young adults' wishful identification with television characters: The role of perceived similarity and character attributes. *Media Psychology, 7,* 325–351.

Konijn, E. A., Nije Bijvank, M., & Bushman, B. J. (2007). "I wish I were a warrior": The role of wishful identification in the effects of violent video games on aggression in adolescent boys. *Developmental Psychology, 43,* 1038–1044.

Meyer, M. (2011). *The Bedford introduction to literature: Reading, thinking, writing* (6th ed.). Boston: Bedford/ St. Martin's.

Oliver, M. B., & Armstrong, G. B. (1995). Predictors of viewing and enjoyment of reality-based and fictional crime shows. *Journalism and Mass Communication Quarterly, 72,* 559–570.

Raney, A. A. (2006). The psychology of disposition-based theories of media enjoyment. In J. Bryant & P. Vorderer (Eds.), *The psychology of entertainment* (pp. 137–150). Mahwah, NJ: Erlbaum.

Signorielli, N. (2001). Television's gender role images and contribution to stereotyping: Past, present, future. In D. G. Singer & J. L. Singer (Eds.), *Handbook of children and the media* (pp. 341–358). Thousand Oaks, CA: Sage.

Slater, M. D., & Rouner, D. (2002). Entertainment-education and elaboration likelihood: Understanding the processing of narrative persuasion. *Communication Theory, 12,* 173–191.

Vorderer, P., Klimmt, C., & Ritterfeld, U. (2004). Enjoyment: At the heart of media entertainment. *Communication Theory, 14,* 388–408.

COGNITION: SCHEMAS AND SCRIPTS

Humans use cognitions to give meaning to their social world. Cognitions play a determinant role in interpreting situations, remembering the past, and guiding our behavior. Although in general, this process is adaptive, cognitions are sometimes dysfunctional, leading to behavioral problems such as aggressive behaviors. This entry describes the concept of schemas and some of the modalities of schemas that are relevant to understanding aggressive behavior, including person schemas, self-schemas, normative beliefs about aggression, relational schemas, and scripts.

The Concept of Schemas

Schemas are conceptualized as mental structures that contain expectations and general category knowledge—that is, knowledge about certain kinds of objects that we believe to be grouped together. This may include general expectations about oneself, others, social roles, and events. The theory of schemas suggests that we use such mental structures to select and process information from the social world.

As mental structures, schemas contain general and abstract knowledge about the features of a certain category, but they can also include more specific examples of the category, and information about how certain features are related to one another. Specifically, S. E. Taylor and J. Crocker (1981) proposed that schemas are hierarchically organized. At the highest level, they include general or abstract information about the features of the category, and at the lowest level of the hierarchy, they include specific examples of the schema (e.g., events or specific people). Moreover, schemas are connected to one another through networks. For example, an individual can have a schema referring to university psychology students that includes general features of psychology students, such as empathy and orientation toward other people. The schema will include a theory about how these features are related to one another. For example, it may include the idea that being interested in others can lead to developing an attitude of empathy toward other people's problems and feelings. In addition to the general features of the schema such as those mentioned, this schema will include specific examples of psychology students whom the individual has known. Last, the psychology student schema will be related to other schemas, such as university student, university, degree, exams, etc.

It would be difficult to function without schemas, because schemas provide us with a framework to lend meaning to the information we receive. Thus, they help us to achieve some sense of prediction and control over our social world. From this perspective, schemas are considered to be functional and essential for our adaptation. As existing mental structures, schemas help us to understand the complexity of social life. The concept of schema therefore emphasizes our active construction of social reality. Schemas guide our attention, perception, memories, and inferences.

Schemas help us to simplify reality. When we interpret events through the lens of schemas, we may not pay attention to apparently irrelevant perceptive details. This function of permitting fast and easy identification of examples and of guiding attention toward relevant information is very important because it simplifies cognitive processing, reducing the effort needed to lend meaning to our world, and frees other cognitive resources that may be necessary to deal with other tasks. Schemas also serve to lend meaning to behaviors that would otherwise be meaningless. This is known as *schema-consistent processing*.

However, this schema-consistent cognitive processing has a cost. Schemas can lead to errors and to ignoring aspects that, far from being irrelevant, are important. This problem is especially obvious when people are carried away by rigid and dysfunctional schemas, leading to biases in social information processing. Precisely, the origin and maintenance of violent behavior involves many dysfunctional cognitive schemas. The next section describes some types of particularly relevant schemas.

Types of Schemas

Person Schemas

Nancy Cantor and Walter Mischel (1979) described person schemas as abstract theoretical structures of personality traits or prototypes of people that enable us to categorize and make inferences about others. Person schemas imply an implicit personality theory, including expectations about what attributes of personality typically co-occur in other people.

Person schemas help us to answer the question, What kind of person is he or she? They help us to anticipate the nature of our interactions with specific individuals, lending a sense of control and predictability to social interactions. Numerous studies have shown that such schemas lead perceivers to attend certain information and ignore other information, to interpret ambiguous information consistently with the schema, and to recall the information that is consistent with or relevant to the schema. For example, if a teacher holds an aggressive child schema about a certain student, he or she will pay special attention to aspects that suggest aggressiveness in that child's behavior; he or she will tend to remember past events when the child behaved aggressively; and if he or she detects an intense emotion in the child, he or she will interpret this emotional state as anger.

Within the sphere of aggressive behavior, it has been found that people who frequently behave aggressively are usually characterized by schemas that imply the belief that people harm others deliberately. This type of schema leads to hostile attributions about others' intentions, which increases the probability that the individual will retrieve an aggressive script of how to behave.

Self-schemas

Self-schemas include abstract concepts about the self, which represent one's values, goals, and beliefs, and specific examples of one's past behaviors that are relevant to these attributes. Hazel Markus (1977) described self-schemas as cognitive generalizations about the self derived from past experiences, which organize and guide the processing of self-related information contained in the individual's social experience. Markus proposed that when a person has a solid idea about the self in some domain of behavior, this person is self-schematic, and domain-relevant information about the self is processed efficiently, confidently, and consistently. Furthermore, such information is recalled easily, and schema-inconsistent information is resisted. For example, if an adolescent has a self-schema as someone who is unattractive and clumsy in his or her interpersonal relations, this self-schema can lead him or her to recall situations in which he or she did not use social skills, attend signs of others' rejection in new situations, or interpret others' ambiguous gestures as signs of rejection. This interpretation could in turn activate a script that includes an aggressive action.

In recent years, self-schemas implying a grandiose view of oneself as a risk factor for aggressive behavior have awakened much interest. Authors such as Roy Baumeister and Brad Bushman have argued that children who have an extremely positive view of themselves and who believe they are better than others and should not have to follow the rules that govern the behavior of most people are especially vulnerable to acting aggressively in situations in which their self-esteem is threatened.

Normative Beliefs About Aggression

Normative beliefs play a central role in regulating aggressive behavior. These beliefs consist of cognitions about the appropriateness of aggressive behavior. They play a very important role guiding the search and selection of actions in social situations.

As with other cognitive schemas, normative beliefs can include various degrees of generalization. For example, they may consist of the belief that the use of aggression in general is appropriate to achieve one's goals, or they may consist only of the acceptance of certain forms of aggressive behavior (e.g., insulting) but not others (e.g., hitting). Likewise, normative beliefs can include information about specific situations in which the use of aggression is acceptable. For example, a youngster may believe

that aggression is adequate when the other person has also acted aggressively or that aggression is acceptable when it is exerted against a boy, but not against a girl.

Cognitive Scripts

Roger C. Schank and Robert P. Abelson (1977) proposed the concept of script for a representation of knowledge about events. A *script* is a cognitive schema that includes a predetermined, stereotyped sequence of actions that defines a well-known situation. Scripts for social situations are seen as having both procedural aspects to help guide social behaviors and semantic-declarative aspects to help the perceiver think about and understand the social situation.

Scripts provide the basis on which to anticipate the future and establish goals and plans for social situations. They enable an individual to organize strategies to achieve such goals by specifying the appropriate behavioral sequences to follow to attain the desired status. For example, the script of eating in a restaurant allows an individual to know the appropriate behavioral sequence when going to a restaurant: enter, wait until the waiter indicates where to sit, order drinks, look at the menu, order food, eat, pay, and leave. It also allows an individual to know how he or she should behave depending on the type of restaurant.

Scripts also imply sequences of expected behaviors and responses in a variety of situations, including conflicts with other people. This is why they have been used to understand aggressive behavior. Furthermore, exposure to media violence plays an important role in the learning and priming of aggressive scripts. Younger children may be more sensitive to this influence because their cognitions are less crystallized than those of older children. Thus, a child who is highly exposed to violent scenes in the media may learn aggressive scripts. Viewing violent scenes may also prime existing aggressive scripts, increasing physiological arousal and triggering an automatic tendency to imitate observed behaviors.

For instance, consider a young boy who has learned aggressive scripts through exposure to media violence. One day he observes that another child has taken away his ball at school. In this situation, the child may interpret the other child's behavior as a provocation and consequently retrieve a violent script of how to behave, consisting of pushing and hitting the other child in order to recover the ball. If his script repertory is heavily loaded with aggressive scripts stored in his memory, this will be more likely. Once the child retrieves an aggressive script to hit the other child, he evaluates the likely outcomes of the script and filters it through the normative beliefs about the use of aggression. If he anticipates that hitting the other child will solve the problem, if he does not anticipate negative outcomes for this action, and if he believes that it is okay to hit the other child, then he will enact the aggressive behavior.

Esther Calvete

See also Aggression and Brain Functioning; Aggressive Behavior; Aggressive Personality; Cognitive Psychology of Violence; Cognitive Script Theory and the Dynamics of Cognitive Scripting; General Aggression Model; Social Cognitive Theory; Social Learning From Media

Further Readings

Baldwin, M. W. (1992). Relational schemas and the processing of social information. *Psychological Bulletin, 112*(3), 461–484.

Cantor, N., & Mischel, W. (1979). Prototypes in person perception. In L. Berkowitz (Ed.), *Advances in experimental social psychology* (pp. 3–52). San Diego, CA: Academic Press.

Markus, H. (1977). Self-schemata and processing information about the self. *Journal of Personality and Social Psychology, 35*, 63–78.

Schank, R. C., & Abelson, R. P. (1995). Knowledge and memory: The real story. In R. S. Wyer, Jr. (Ed.), *Knowledge and memory: The real story* (pp. 1–85). Hillsdale, NJ: Erlbaum.

Taylor, S. E., & Crocker, J. (1981). Schematic bases of social information processing. In E. T. Higgins, C. P. Herman, & M. P. Zanna (Eds.), *Social cognition* (pp. 89–134). Hillsdale, NJ: Erlbaum.

COGNITIVE PSYCHOLOGY OF VIOLENCE

Although the subfield of psychology that has most often studied media violence has been social psychology, there are also numerous cognitive aspects of the experience of media violence. This entry looks at several of these. Although effects of media violence such as imitating violent behavior and desensitization toward violence are far better known, violent media also provide regular input to the construction of knowledge about real-world violence. Such cognitions have enormous implications for thought and behavior.

Cognition in Mass Communication Theories

Most of the major theories of mass communication effects have some cognitive aspects to them. Some of these theories and their respective cognitive aspects are discussed in this section.

Cultivation Theory

One theory with a central cognitive component is cultivation theory, which posits that repeated heavy media consumption inculcates the belief that the world is a very violent place, reflecting the hyperviolent nature of the world in entertainment and news media. In real life, 87% of crimes are nonviolent and 13% are violent, with only 0.2% of crimes being murders. On television, however, 87% of the crimes are violent and only 13% nonviolent, with a 50% of all crimes being murders—that is, a 250% increase over real life (Bushman & Anderson, 2001). Continued interaction with media and heavy exposure to violence cultivate this cognitive belief that the world is a very dangerous place. This belief can have numerous serious consequences, such as evoking nightmares or making one fearful of going outside or opening one's windows for needed ventilation so as not to become a victim of crime.

The induction of fear by violent media presupposes cognitive representation in several ways. A preschooler may be afraid of images and characters that look like distorted humans; for example, adults dressed as clowns, Santa Claus, or the Easter Bunny—all of which represent a major distortion of familiar humanity. However, a child in upper elementary or middle school may be more afraid of hypothetical dangers that a media character experiences; by this time the child's cognitive development is sufficiently advanced to allow him or her to think abstractly enough to imagine the danger that the hero is about to walk into. Thus, a child's level of cognitive development can determine what types of media images will evoke the most fear.

Social Cognitive Theory

Social cognitive theory posits the learning of behaviors through observational learning by watching others model them. Four cognitive subfunctions comprise observational learning from media. First, one must be exposed to the media example and attend to it. Second, one must be cognitively able to construct a memory representation for the event and use appropriate encoding strategies in order to remember that representation. Third, one must be able to translate this symbolic memory representation into action at a later time. Finally, motivation must develop to energize the performance of the behavior. Many factors can affect the degree of motivation developed. For example, a violent model who is attractive and is reinforced for behaving violently is more likely to be imitated than one who is unattractive or not rewarded for acting violently. Thus, several cognitive processes must occur in order for a behavior seen in media to be imitated.

Agenda-Setting Theory

Agenda-setting theory, although primarily developed to understand the processing of media news, is also relevant to violence. This perspective stresses that media tell us what to think about, or what is important. With the heavy coverage of violence in both entertainment and news media, the message is clear and strong that violent behavior is widespread and merits our attention. Moreover, this heavy coverage of violence subtly legitimizes its use to viewers' own conflict situations. For example, when a 30-second evening news report on a ball game spends most of that time covering a brawl, it is implicitly saying that fight is important.

Cognitive Schema/Script Theory

Perhaps the most centrally cognitive theory of media is cognitive schema/script theory. Applied to media, this framework says that people's initial perception, comprehension, and later reconstruction of memories of that content are guided by cognitive *schemas,* knowledge structures or frameworks that organize memory of people and events. A schema for an activity is called a *script.* People construct mental schemas/scripts based on life experiences and/or media exposure. For many people, life experience with violence is quite limited, so the relevant cognitive schemas may be informed largely, perhaps even entirely, from media. For example, for many viewers, schemas about surviving urban street battles, fighting against a home invader, or engaging in sword fighting develop primarily from media experiences such as playing video games or watching war movies.

Sometimes people learn social scripts about violence from media. For example, when viewers watch a movie about a man acting as a vigilante protecting

his neighborhood, they acquire a mental script for dealing with that situation. If viewers attempt to apply that script in real life, the consequences might be less successful than what is portrayed in the movie. The potential consequences of learning scripts from media become especially clear when considering a situation in which readers or viewers have little prior knowledge or scripts from their own life experience. For example, suppose a child's knowledge of dealing with muggers has resulted from watching cinematic adventure heroes trick and overpower a robber (e.g., *Home Alone*). If that child were to try that script on a real mugger by attempting the same moves as seen in the film, the consequences might be disastrous.

Sometimes scripts dealing with violence could actually be prosocial. Consider a movie dealing with a character's encounter with a playground bully. If well written and acted, the film could provide useful scripts for handling such intimidation productively. Because bullying was not taken seriously for a long time, many viewers or victims may have no mental script for productively dealing with it. Thus, a movie has the potential to suggest to victims some actions they might take to seek help and resist the bully. Beyond that, it could portray how one may expect to feel about being bullied, from whom to seek help, and to suggest what the effects of resisting a bully might be.

One consequence of holding such mental scripts is that they may later guide the drawing of inferences about people or events to be more congruent with these scripts. For example, someone with a negative schema about Mexican Americans might notice and remember mostly negative aspects about Latinos in a television show about gang conflict in East Los Angeles, whereas someone with a more positive schema might notice and remember different, more favorable information about Latinos from the same show. This *confirmation bias* directs people to notice examples and information consistent with their biases and fail to notice or remember information inconsistent with those biases.

In mass media, activation of a schema in the mind of an audience member may be triggered by some information in a television program, video game, print article, or website. It may also be triggered by certain formal features of a medium, such as flashbacks, montage, or sound effects in television or film. Young children generally do not understand these conventions and interpret the input literally, such as thinking that a flashback is a continuing new action. Part of the child's socialization to using a medium like television is to learn about these formal features and how to interpret them. For example, one way that children realized that video footage of the 2001 World Trade Center attacks or the 1986 *Challenger* space shuttle explosion were real, rather than a movie, was the lack of music in the background.

Often, much of the content in schemas or scripts is culture specific. The schema that members of one culture may hold may cause them to interpret the same story differently than members of a different culture. For example, a movie about an honor killing of an unfaithful wife by her husband's family may be seen as particularly grisly and horrific in cultures in which such practices are not prevalent or tolerated. Of course, cultural differences must be carefully considered by television producers in international programming sales.

Narrative Script

In addition to such specific content-based scripts, there are also more general cultural scripts—for example, a common narrative script for stories in Western culture. This narrative script is learned implicitly by young children from the time their parents start telling or reading stories to them. Such stories are composed of episodes, each of which contains an exposition, a complication, and a resolution. That is, the characters and setting are introduced (*exposition*), some problem or obstacle develops (*complication*), and that problem or obstacle is somehow overcome (*resolution*). People grow up expecting stories to follow this general script. Children's stories such as fairy tales do so explicitly ("Once upon a time there was a . . ."). Adult stories also follow the same script, but often in more complex fashion. For example, some of the complication may be introduced before the exposition is finished, or two subepisodes may be embedded in the resolution of a larger episode.

Entertainment media also use the narrative script to make their stories more readily understandable. Children's programs and cartoons follow the narrative script explicitly. Most television situation comedies and action-adventure shows also do so, although often in a somewhat more complicated fashion; for example, there may be two interwoven episodes (subplots), each with its own narrative structure. Children have well-developed story schema comprehension skills by around age 7, and such skills lead to better memory for the central story content, a reduction in processing effort, and

a greater flexibility of attention-allocation strategies. The principle of the cliffhanger, whereby the episode ends after the complication with no resolution, has been used in many primetime season finales to ensure the interest and return of viewers for the first show of the next season so that they can learn the resolution of the story.

A particularly common variation of the narrative script is the *myth of redemptive violence,* the idea that violence is sometimes necessary and desirable, even if regrettable, as part of the episode's resolution to defeat the bad guys and restore the good. This is a prevalent theme in action-adventure movies, video games, and even G-rated children's stories and movies. The idea of violence as necessary to preserve the social order and the greater good is such a strong cultural script that most people do not even notice it. Most police dramas, action-adventure movies, and even children's fairy tales and G-rated movies implicitly assume it. Stories that do not fit the myth of redemptive violence may not receive much attention. For example, instances of nonviolent social change receive much less coverage than wars in school history texts or as the basis for fictional stories. There are thousands of Western television shows, movies, and stories about violence between Whites and Native Americans; however, historical instances of European Americans and Native Americans treating one another well and coexisting successfully are almost unknown, although they did occur (e.g., in colonial Pennsylvania for most of the first century after English Quaker settlement began in 1682).

Decision Making

One major area where cognition is critical to the effects of media violence is that of judgment and decision making. For example, the decision to use violence after viewing a violent model is a cognitive choice. Many traditional risk and protective factors moderating behavioral violence may affect this decision. For example, media violence has been shown to disinhibit people's natural inhibitions against behaving violently. The decision to act violently may be an easier one to make after exposure to media violence has weakened the natural inhibitions against violent behavior. Such disinhibition is especially strong if the violent model is a respected character with whom the viewer identifies. Sometimes consuming the violent media may directly contribute to the loss of inhibitory control, as when someone playing many hours of first-person shooter video games specifically learns to "shoot first and ask questions later"—a useful strategy in such games but sometimes a recipe for tragedy in real life. This lowering of the threshold of deciding to act violently can have serious consequences.

Another area where decision making is important in understanding effects of violent media is in the decision to watch certain programming. Some people have stronger a priori preferences for violent media content than do others, and such people are more likely to choose to watch violent movies or play violent video games. For example, people who are male or who are by disposition more prone toward violence or sensation seeking enjoy violent entertainment relatively more than average, while those who are female or high in dispositional empathy show relatively less preference for violent entertainment.

Attention

Another cognitive dimension, *attention,* is clearly captured by media violence, and the more graphic the violence, the more successfully it captures attention. Once the viewer is paying attention, the content is much more likely to have other effects than if it had not been attended to. The desire to attract and hold viewers' attention can lead to ever-increasing graphic violence in a bid to capture the attention of a public desensitized to "typical" violence.

Memory

People remember many events from their lives, including media experiences. A few studies have used autobiographical memory techniques to study the impact of children's viewing of adult antisocial media, such as violence, without exposing young participants to the violence. This research asks participants to think of a specific movie, when they watched it, and the circumstances or people involved. For example, participants might be instructed to think of the overall experience of watching a frightening movie in their childhood (Harrison & Cantor, 1999). Following this, the frightening movie recalled is described in terms of the negative effects (e.g., insomnia, nightmares) or positive effects (e.g., enjoyment, mood elevation) experienced. Almost every young adult has memories of being scared by a violent movie seen in childhood (Hoekstra, Harris, & Helmick, 1999). Not only do they remember the experience, but they are able to recount their thoughts and feelings while watching it and many years afterward report the effects experienced.

Another common behavior involving memory for media is the use of movie quoting in social conversation. This is an almost universal behavior, at least among young adults, and appears to occur with little effort to remember. Although there are many purposes for quoting movies in conversation, the most common ones are to amuse oneself and amuse others.

Conclusion

When considering the impact of violence in media, part of this impact is cognitive in nature. People construct knowledge about violence in the world, and this knowledge influences attention, memory, and decision-making processes, which in turn influence behavior. Thus, an avenue of future research in the field of media studies is the cognition of violence.

Richard Jackson Harris

See also Cognition: Schemas and Scripts; Cognitive Script Theory and the Dynamics of Cognitive Scripting; Cultivation Theory; General Aggression Model; Media Effects Perspectives of Violence; Social Cognitive Theory; Social Learning From Media

Further Readings

Bryant, J., & Oliver, M. B. (Eds.). (2009). *Media effects: Advances in theory and research* (3rd ed.). New York, NY: Routledge.

Bushman, B. J., & Anderson, C. A. (2001). Media violence and the American public: Scientific facts versus media misinformation. *American Psychologist, 56,* 477–489.

Cantor, J. (1998). *"Mommy, I'm scared": How TV and movies frighten children and what we can do to protect them.* San Diego, CA: Harcourt Brace.

Harris, R. J., Cady, E. T., & Barlett, C. P. (2007). Media. In F. T. Durso (Ed.), *Handbook of applied cognition* (2nd ed., pp. 659–682). Chichester, UK: Wiley.

Harris, R. J., & Sanborn, F. W. (2013). *A cognitive psychology of mass communication* (6th ed.). New York, NY: Routledge.

Harrison, K., & Cantor, J. (1999). Tales from the screen: Enduring fright reactions to scary media. *Media Psychology, 1,* 97–116.

Hoekstra, S. J., Harris, R. J., & Helmick, A. L. (1999). Autobiographical memories about the experience of seeing frightening movies in childhood. *Media Psychology, 1,* 117–140.

Kirsch, S. J. (2006). *Children, adolescents, and media violence: A critical look at the research.* Thousand Oaks, CA: Sage.

COGNITIVE SCRIPT THEORY AND THE DYNAMICS OF COGNITIVE SCRIPTING

People's social behavior is controlled to a good extent by cognitive scripts learned through experience and observation of others' behavior. After being stored in memory, these cognitive scripts can be retrieved to guide behavior and solve problems.

A cognitive script indicates the sequence of behaviors that can be expected in a certain context, how the individual should behave in that context once the individual has assumed a role in the script, and what might be the expected consequences. By means of social learning, people acquire numerous scripts indicating how to act in such diverse situations as eating in a restaurant, attending a funeral, or going on a romantic date.

L. Rowell Huesmann (1988) applied the model of cognitive scripts to explain how children learn aggression-related knowledge structures from exposure to violence. In this context, the theory of cognitive scripts allows us to understand the development of habitual aggressive behavior. Its focus is the operation of the child's information-processing system in the presence of environmental and personal factors that facilitate aggressive behavior.

According to this theory, through observation, children learn not only simple behaviors but also complex and generalized social scripts. Once learned, these cognitive scripts can be retrieved from memory to guide information processing and future behavior. In this context, the aggressive cognitive scripts learned by children from observation of violent behavior in family, mass media, and other settings are especially relevant. Once learned, children can use these scripts to deal with and resolve their social interactions. Reviewing these cognitive scripts and obtaining positive consequences will cause the scripts to become chronically accessible and aggressive behavior to form part of the child's habitual behavioral repertoire. This entry describes the dynamics of this process and some of the most important factors that determine how it will take place.

Learning Cognitive Scripts

Cognitive script theory proposes that cognitive scripts are stored in memory through a two-component process: initial encoding of observed behaviors and their repeated rehearsal.

Initial script encoding takes place mainly from observation. Human beings have an innate tendency to imitate. At early ages, children are capable of imitating emotional expressions, and, subsequently, they begin to imitate motor behaviors, including aggressive behaviors such as shoving or hitting. As children grow, they begin to acquire scripts instead of simple behaviors through social learning. These cognitive scripts become increasingly complex and elaborate, including other schemas such as normative beliefs about the appropriateness of aggression and inferences about others' behavior.

For a sequence of behaviors to be encoded as a cognitive script, the child should attend the sequence of behaviors. Therefore, elements that favor attention will make encoding of a cognitive script more likely. Huesmann notes that if, at this phase, children perceive that the observed behavioral sequence is inappropriate and goes against the child's moral rules, then encoding the cognitive script may be impeded.

Aspects like the child's current mood in the observation phase can also influence initial encoding. If the child is angry at that time, he or she might judge the observed aggressive behaviors as acceptable, which favors encoding them. Likewise, new aggressive behaviors are more likely to be encoded if the child stores many instances of other aggressive behaviors in his or her memory than if he or she stores mainly examples of prosocial behaviors.

Moreover, from the social learning model, many factors influencing the acquisition of social scripts during the observation phase have been identified. Albert Bandura (1977) noted that children are more likely to learn a cognitive script if the model is similar to them, the model is attractive, the context is realistic, and the model's behavior is followed by reinforcing consequences. In addition, the process of learning social scripts by observation can be automatic and nonconscious, so that children are not aware of how these factors are influencing them.

Once a script is encoded, the child must perform a process of rehearsal in order for it to remain normally in memory. This rehearsal can take on numerous modalities, for example, simple recall of the original scene, fantasizing about it, acting out the scene, etc. According to Huesmann, the more elaborate the rehearsal, the stronger and more accessible the script will become. By means of elaborate review, the child can abstract and achieve a higher-order cognitive script, consisting of more general behavioral strategies than those initially observed and encoded.

Priming of Cognitive Scripts

G. H. Bower (1981) proposed a model of network association for memory. Memory is represented as a network of nodes wherein each node represents a concept or schema. The nodes are connected to one another by a network, so that when one node is primed, activation spreads through the network to the associated nodes. This network includes not only cognitive elements but also emotional states. Therefore, when one experiences an emotion (e.g., anger), this primes the schemas and scripts associated with this emotion.

When we learn new material, this is associated with the nodes that are active at the time of encoding. In this network of associations among nodes, schemas may be partially primed by associated stimuli in the environment. Applied to the field of aggressive scripts, exposure to violent cues can prime a complex system of networked associations linked to aggression-related emotions and schemas, increasing access to aggressive scripts. Access to these scripts in turn facilitates their acting as filters to interpret events and guide behavior.

Many elements can prime aggressive scripts. Diverse studies have shown that the cues habitually associated with violence, such as weapons, can prime aggressive scripts stored in memory. The same effect has been found for initially neutral stimuli that have been repeatedly associated with violence (i.e., the place where the child has repeatedly observed violent scenes) or for stimuli that were present in the original situation when the script was observed and encoded.

Multiple rehearsals of scripts can also strengthen connections between concepts, making scripts more accessible. According to Craig A. Anderson and Brad J. Bushman, multiple rehearsals create additional links between the new script and other schemas in memory. Thus, the number of paths through which the cognitive script can be primed increases. Moreover, multiple rehearsals contribute to increasing the strength of the links themselves.

In addition to aggressive cues and rehearsals, many factors can contribute to priming aggressive scripts. One of these factors is frustration or blockage of goal attainment. Similarly, provocations consisting of insults and physical aggressions can easily prime aggressive schemas and scripts. Concerning this, Anderson and Bushman (2002) have noted that many provocations can be seen as a type of frustration in which a person has been identified as the agent responsible for failing to obtain the goal. States of pain and discomfort can also contribute to priming scripts and schemas related to aggression.

The factor of arousal has received much attention because of its capacity to prime aggressive scripts. Arousal can sometimes be caused by exposure to violence. That is, observing violence can increase heart rate, electric skin conductance, muscular tension, and other psychophysiological parameters, and these in turn lead to aggressive actions. Many mechanisms have been suggested through which arousal can increase the risk of aggression. First, arousal provides energy and strength for action, and this is extensible to aggressive actions. Second, arousal is unpleasant for most people. Therefore, it can produce the same effect as exposure to pain or other unpleasant elements and, consequently, increase the tendency to act aggressively. The third mechanism is that, when arousal is very high, it can interfere with performance of complex tasks and self-regulatory processes, causing the child to have trouble inhibiting inappropriate behaviors or selecting more functional alternative behaviors. As a result, dominant scripts are more likely to be retrieved and executed.

A fourth mechanism takes place when a child who is aroused by observing a violent scene mistakenly attributes his or her arousal to another person's provocation. In these circumstances, it is more likely for the child to select and execute an aggressive script. A considerable number of studies have assessed the former effect under the label of "excitation transfer." This effect has been used to explain how observing violent scenes in the mass media can increase aggressive behavior by making individuals attribute their arousal to provocations that have nothing to do with the scenes that aroused them. Last, the child's arousal and emotional states play a particularly relevant role in the priming and execution of scripts. This aspect is addressed in the next section.

An important finding is that when a schema or script is repeatedly primed, it can become chronically accessible. When this happens, aggressive schemas and scripts become the individual's habitual internal state, and the individual automatically and frequently accesses these scripts to interpret new social encounters and to choose his or her course of action.

Evaluation of the Appropriateness of a Script

Throughout the diverse points of the process described previously, an evaluation of the appropriateness of the script can take place. This evaluation plays an important role in the determination of which scripts are stored in memory, which ones are retrieved and used, and which ones continue to be used in the future.

The first time that the script is evaluated occurs at the time of observation. If the child has normative beliefs about the inappropriateness of violence, he or she is less likely to encode the script in memory. The rehearsal of the script provides another opportunity to evaluate it. For example, a script that was initially accepted as adequate at the time of observation because the child was angry may subsequently be evaluated as inappropriate during the rehearsal.

Normative beliefs about the use of aggression, therefore, play an important role in determining which scripts are encoded in memory and subsequently executed. Concerning this, Huesmann and Lucyna Kirwil (2007) have emphasized the role of repeated exposure to violence. When children repeatedly observe violent scripts, they can experience an important change in their beliefs about violence. Children who initially may have thought that violence is rare and unaccustomed may come to believe that violence is unavoidable and forms part of the relations between people. This process has been called "cognitive desensitization" and leads to greater acceptance of violence, a more positive appraisal of aggressive behaviors, and more justification of aggressive acts that may be inconsistent with the individual's values. For example, a child may justify his or her aggression toward another child by thinking that the other child deserves it or even that it is "so he will learn to behave better."

The Role of Affects in Cognitive Scripts

Emotional states also play an important role in the theory of cognitive scripts. This role takes place at many steps of the process.

Mood can prime specific scripts because the nodes are associated in memory with autonomic activity and expressive patterns that usually accompany a particular emotional state. Thus, when a child enters a social situation in a prior state of anger, this emotion—including the component of physiological arousal—extends over the network and connects to aggressive schemas and scripts in associated memory, resulting in their priming.

Moreover, because emotional states can persist over time, a child may enter a social situation in an emotional state that has nothing to do with the situation, but his or her mood will influence his or her information processing, determining which elements the child will attend, how he or she will interpret them, and his or her course of action. For example, a child may leave the house angry because of an argument with his or her mother. When the child arrives at school, the child finds that another child is sitting at his or her desk. The child's angry mood can lead the child to interpret the other child's behavior as provocative and hostile. This in turn will prime a sequence of behaviors included in a script about how to act when other people provoke the child, taking away something that belongs to him or her.

Enacting Scripts

In previous sections, this entry mainly described the first phase of learning scripts—that is, the phase in which the child encodes and mentally reviews a script from observation of its performance by a model. But social learning also implies a second phase in which the child executes the script. In this second phase, the reinforcing consequences the child receives by imitating the behavior are highly responsible for whether or not the behavior will persist in the future. For example, a child may have observed violent scenes in his or her family setting in which a family member physically punishes another member when the latter disobeys or does something that annoys the former. The child may later imitate that behavior at school when other children do things that upset or oppose him or her. The child's behavior could serve to achieve his or her goals and prevent others from contradicting him or her. In this case, the child's behavior will be reinforced, increasing the likelihood of repetition in the future and of the script being consolidated as part of his or her habitual behavioral repertory. In contrast, imitating the observed behavior could have undesirable consequences for the child, such as the other children's rejection and his or her teacher's punishment. In this case, the child will be less likely to repeat the script in the future because it was punished.

The former example shows how the direct consequences of the execution of a script can play an important role in its persistence. In fact, once a script is retrieved from memory and before the child executes it, the child anticipates the consequences deriving from the behavior included in the script, and this evaluative process will, to a good extent, determine his or her decision to execute it or, contrariwise, to seek an alternative behavior. The following paragraphs examine in more detail how the process of script assessment takes place before its execution.

First, the child must be able to assess the consequences deriving from using the script. If the child decides that the consequences will be beneficial (e.g., obtaining some positive reinforcement or avoiding a negative one), then the probability of executing the script increases. It is important to take into account that, in this process of assessment of consequences, not only are the environmental consequences important but also the emotional state that the child anticipates experiencing when executing the script. If the child anticipates experiencing a high level of arousal when executing the script, and arousal is considered unpleasant or aversive, the child is less likely to execute the script. That is, if the child is aroused while thinking of the script and its consequences, then the use of the script will be inhibited. An implication of this is that people who feel less arousal when they think about aggression will be more likely to use aggressive scripts to solve problems in social situations.

Here, once again, repeated exposure to violence can have important effects. Research has proved that exposure to violence can lead to emotional desensitization through a process of habituation. That is, as children observe new violent scenes, they cease to experience emotional reactions to them. As a result, in the process of script assessment, children will experience less arousal when thinking of aggression and will anticipate a lower emotional reaction associated with executing the script. Therefore, repeated exposure to violence contributes to learning and executing aggressive scripts through the processes of cognitive and emotional desensitization. It should be taken into account that children differ in their capacity to anticipate the consequences of their behaviors. If the child focuses on the immediate consequences and less on the future, he or she is more likely to carry out the aggressive behavior.

Bandura's social learning model—and the anticipation of consequences—also includes another factor that he called *perceived self-efficacy*, which influences previously observed behavior. Bandura described perceived self-efficacy as the perception an individual makes of his or her own competence to complete a task and achieve his or her goals. This implies that it is not sufficient for the child to anticipate that the script will lead to positive consequences for aggressive behavior. It is also necessary for the child to assess whether or not he or she will be capable of executing the behavior competently and of achieving the established goals.

Huesmann notes that the most important component in script evaluation is the extent to which it is perceived as congruent with the child's internal self-regulation standards. This is where cognitive schemas consisting of normative beliefs about the appropriateness of aggression intervene, as described previously.

Last, the theory of scripts proposes various factors that contribute to the persistence of aggressive behavior. The first one is that the child may assess the consequences of the behavior in a biased manner. This can happen because the child focuses on a mistaken aspect or because the child is not capable of seeing all the consequences that follow the behavior. For example, a child who hits another child to get a ball from the other child may only perceive that he or she has gotten the ball, but not that this action involves other negative consequences, such as rejection by other children or a subsequent scolding by the teacher. Second, the child may lack a repertoire of alternative scripts that include prosocial forms of behavior to solve social problems. This may be because prosocial solutions are normally more complex and difficult to acquire than aggressive solutions. Third, the child develops schemas that justify violence, and therefore aggressive scripts are judged as appropriate. Last, the child can choose social settings in which aggression is acceptable, thus reducing the possibility of negative consequences for aggression.

Esther Calvete

See also Aggressive Behavior; Arousal and Aggressive Content, Theory and Psychology of; Cognition: Schemas and Scripts; Memory and Violence; Priming Theory; Social Cognitive Theory

Further Readings

Anderson, C. A., & Bushman, B. J. (2002). Human aggression. *Annual Review of Psychology, 53,* 27–51.

Bandura, A. (1977). *Social learning theory.* Englewood Cliffs, NJ: Prentice Hall.

Bower, G. H. (1981). Mood and memory. *American Psychologist, 36,* 129–148.

Huesmann, L. R. (1988). An information processing model for the development of aggression. *Aggressive Behavior, 14,* 13–24.

Huesmann, L. R., & Kirwil, L. (2007). Why observing violence increases the risk of violent behavior by the observer. In D. J. Flannery, A. T. Vazsonyi, & I. D. Waldman (Eds.), *The Cambridge handbook of violent behavior and aggression* (pp. 545–570). New York, NY: Cambridge University Press.

Comedic Violence, Effects of

Comedic violence refers to the depiction of violence in ways that are considered humorous. Attributions involve exaggerated, boisterous actions, farce, or other activities that may exceed the boundaries of common sense. Comedic violence is a type of broad, physical comedy that utilizes various representations of violence intended to provide comedic relief and entertainment for the audience. It originated from slapstick comedy—for example, a pie in the face or slipping on a banana peel—and evolved into more physical, violent actions such as being hit in the head with a hot iron or manually pulling out teeth. This entry briefly introduces comedic violence and discusses its evolution from slapstick comedy. More specifically, this entry focuses on the representations and effects of cartoon violence and comedic violence found in "gross-out" comedy films made popular in the 1990s and 2000s. The entry concludes with a discussion of the consequences of comedic violence in modern comedy.

Comedic Violence

Comedic violence evolved from slapstick humor, but it is now considered a subtype of aggressive humor. Aggressive humor is defined by E. Mavis Hetherington and Nancy P. Wray (1966) as the hostile intent to ridicule, deprecate, or injure. However, the explicit or implied presence of violence is not required in order for humor to be considered aggressive. Rather, comedic violence is a type of aggressive humor that depends primarily on actual or threatened physical harm for its humorous properties.

History of Comedic Violence

Slapstick humor can be found as early as Greco-Roman theater with *bômolochus,* or buffoons who would entertain audiences with their physical humor (e.g., hitting one another in the head, stomach, and buttocks areas) and practical jokes. This type of humor carried into 16th-century entertainment when Elizabethan playwright William Shakespeare incorporated slapstick humor into his work. For instance, his play *The Comedy of Errors* includes both chase scenes and beatings. Slapstick comedy continued to evolve into the 19th- and early 20th-century performances in U.S. vaudeville houses. However, it is most recognized for its prevalence during the silent movie era (ca. 1894–1929), when films did not have sound and the emphasis was on visual comedic effects. During this time, the pratfall, walking into walls, slipping on a banana peel, falling into mud, getting splashed with water or paint, and getting a pie in the face were all common stunts and gags. After the silent movie era, slapstick humor evolved and moved into cartoons, where comedic violence became a major component in shows such as *Tom and Jerry, Looney Tunes, Ren and Stimpy,* and *Ed, Edd n' Eddy.* Slapstick continues to be prevalent in modern comedy such as the gross-out films released in the 1990s and 2000s. *Dumb & Dumber, There's Something About Mary, The Hangover,* and *Jackass* were all popular among audiences, and all drew on comedic violence.

Physical Humor

Physical comedy is one of the oldest and most common forms of humor in entertainment. Watching another person fall down, receive a slap, trip over obstacles, run into walls, or perform a stunt has always been a popular source of entertainment for audiences of all ages. Physical comedy often depends on a sense of *schadenfreude,* the secret pleasure derived from witnessing the misfortune, real or imaginary, of the performer.

The "Jackass" Effect

There have been several incidents in which children and young adults have injured themselves or their friends while imitating stunts they saw on films and television. Many of these incidents were reported to have been inspired by the MTV show *Jackass,* a program in which Johnny Knoxville and his posse perform absurd stunts. Examples of the show's antics include hurling heavy medicine balls at one another in a pitch-dark room, allowing an alligator to bite Knoxville's nipple, and human bowling. In one episode, the cast used a machine to launch one another in grocery carts at 70 miles per hour. At one point, Bam Margera closes a loading dock gate, sending Ryan Dunn flying into the metal wall.

Among the *Jackass*-related mimicking incidents, a pair of boys in New England and another in Florida set themselves on fire. In Minnesota, a 19-year-old stopped traffic by running around in the rain carrying a chain saw and dressed only in a hospital gown. In another incident, a 16-year-old from Kentucky broke both his legs trying to jump over a car that was driving at him. It was reported that he was trying out a stunt he saw on a sneak preview of the show. After the accident, the stunt was pulled from the air.

Regarding a show like *Jackass* and others that depend heavily on comedic violence, it is possible that children and young adults may feel starved for attention or the recognition of their peers and see these stunts as a way to gain access into desired groups. As explicated within Albert Bandura's social learning theory (1977), children learn by imitating what they see around them, including what they see through media. They try out things that look interesting or have a perceived positive outcome and adapt them to fit their real-world situations. This includes violence and dangerous stunts. To this end, social learning theory suggests that people learn within a social context. This form of learning is facilitated through concepts such as modeling and observational learning—direct and vicarious. This was evidenced by one of Bandura's earliest research projects in this area that investigated circumstances under which children would imitate aggressive behavior. The children in the study were shown a film in which an adult starts hitting and kicking a Bobo Doll, a plastic punching bag with a red nose. The children who viewed the film in which the aggressor was rewarded demonstrated a considerable number of aggressive behaviors. Children who viewed the aggressor being punished showed limited imitation of the aggressor. This indicates that regardless of having acquired aggressive behaviors, these behaviors would only be acted out in favorable or rewarding circumstances. Therefore, if a child or young adult watches *Jackass,* he or she might think that imitating the stunts would result in the same popularity and fame Johnny Knoxville received. Or, at the very least, this could be viewed within the scope of the perceived social acceptance of peers. This is known as "observational learning." Observational learning enables a single model, in this case *Jackass,* to transmit new ways of thinking and behaving concurrently to countless people in widely dispersed locales. According to social learning theory, an individual can watch a show containing comedic violence and learn about human values, styles of thinking, and behavior patterns. Social behavior is learned by observing and imitating the actions of others. This suggests that the individual will then imitate the actions he or she viewed in the film or television show. This is evident in the number of incidents in which people admitted they were trying to replicate stunts seen on the show.

MTV runs a disclaimer on the program warning against attempting the stunts and saying it does not accept videotapes from people who want to get on the show. However, children do not respond to disclaimers the same as adults. This is due to the fact that a child's brain has not developed the capacity to weigh the potential long-term consequences of an action, even when those consequences are spelled out explicitly in a disclaimer. In fact, disclaimers could result in a "forbidden fruit" effect. Here, children would seek or act through the content because they are told not to by an authority figure.

Media Literacy as a Solution

Humorous elements in television and film are thought to signal to viewers that the seriousness of the events they are watching should be downplayed. As a result, material that should be seen as grave or dangerous is rendered whimsical or fun. Representations of violence that should be viewed as solemn and gruesome become comical. Therefore, the more comedic violence deviates from reality, the less likely the viewer will take the violent act or behavior seriously. In order for a viewer to perceive violence in television and film, he or she must witness a personal threat. For example, if the viewer watches a brutal beating or murder and it causes him or her to worry about his or her own safety, then the violence that caused the violent act will be perceived as such. Because comedic violence often deviates significantly from reality, it is difficult for the viewer to make a connection between the on-screen violence and a personal threat of violence. Thus, the level of violence associated with the television or film decreases.

Because children and young adults may be more susceptible to imitating acts viewed in the media, it is important for parents and educators to assist them with making the connection between on-screen violence and real-life personal threat. This can be achieved by increasing children's understanding of how media works and educating them about the real-life consequences that can result from partaking in the humorously violent acts they see on television or film. For example, a Taser shot to the head may seem funny when watching it on television, but it could be life threatening if reenacted off screen. Aside from stunts that could result in broken bones and head injuries, there are other nonphysical repercussions. Legal action could be taken if someone is injured or property is damaged while reenacting a stunt. Moreover, stunts and other violent acts are performed by professional actors and stuntmen who are trained to avoid incurring serious bodily injuries during the execution of a stunt. Thus, it is important that children and young adults understand the consequences and repercussions of imitating in the real world the comedic violence seen in the media.

Nicole Cunningham and Matthew S. Eastin

See also Bobo Doll Study; Effects From Violent Content, Short- and Long-Term; Fantasy Genre, Violence and Aggression in; Forbidden Fruit Hypothesis; Media Education and Media Literacy; Media Effects Perspectives of Violence; Social Cognitive Theory

Further Readings

Bandura, A. (1977). *Social learning theory.* Englewood Cliffs, NJ: Prentice Hall.

Bandura, A. (1994). Social cognitive theory of mass communication. In J. Bryant & D. Zillmann (Eds.), *Media effects: Advances in theory and research* (pp. 61–90). Hillsdale, NJ: Erlbaum.

Hetherington, E. M., & Wray, N. P. (1966). Effects of need aggression, stress, and aggressive behavior on humor preference. *Journal of Personality and Social Psychology, 4*(2), 229–233.

McIntosh, W. D., Murray, J. D., Murray, R. M., & Manian, S. (2003). What's so funny about a poke in the eye? The prevalence of violence in comedy films and its relation to social and economic threat in the United States, 1951–2000. *Mass Communication and Society, 6*(4), 345–360.

Potter, W. J., & Warren, R. (1998). Humor as a camouflage of televised violence. *Journal of Communication, 48,* 40–57.

COMPETITION, SPORTS, AND VIDEO GAMES

Competition is an important aspect of video games, and sports is a popular genre of video games involving competition. Unlike watching television or movies, playing video games is interactive in that a player's actions determine whether the protagonist wins or loses. This interactivity component of competition inherent in video games, especially sports-themed video games, has been a topic of study in media effects research. This entry focuses on competition in video games and its effects.

Historical Context

As a brief historical synopsis, video games first entered homes in 1972 with *Pong* and struggled to maintain sales—even during the late 1970s and early 1980s, when mainstream systems such as Coleco-Vision and Atari appeared on store shelves. Some claim this lull occurred because of a lack of imagination and poor game design (Apperley, 2006), mostly because of the limiting technology of the time. The video game industry did not flourish until Nintendo made its debut in 1985. In that year, Nintendo brought home gaming to new heights through its mass appeal and fresh game design of its Nintendo Entertainment System. Almost immediately, researchers questioned what learning effects video games like *Pac-Man* and *Super Mario Brothers* had on those who played them. With high-tech video game devices such as Microsoft Xbox, Nintendo Wii, and Sony PlayStation, or other gaming computers, gamers are playing in more realistic, detailed, and complex worlds than the first gaming experiences provided by Magnavox, Atari, and Coleco-Vision.

Video games are distinct from other media in a number of attributes. William Eveland utilized a continuum of relevant attributes for defining media; video games are defined based on where their attributes fall on each continuum. For instance, gaming is high on the *interactivity* continuum due to the necessity of constant controller manipulation to experience the game. Second, media is evaluated on *organization.* Video games typically involve low levels of linear information (albeit a game progresses in timed segments or moves to the next level after completing a level) and employ a more nonlinear structure through which the player may manipulate the action in infinite ways during play. Third, video games provide lots of *control* whereby the player can alter the pace, order, and amount of presentation (Barr, Noble, & Biddle, 2007). Fourth, video games typically are rich in *channel information,* such as video and stereo audio feedback and haptic experiences through gyroscopes in controllers. Fifth, *textuality* differs mostly by game genre (e.g., action, role playing, simulator, sports) or classification, but typically games employ textual symbols to indicate purpose of play, game status, and so on (e.g., time remaining, points cumulated, health status). The final attribute is *content*, which differs radically by gaming genre or classification, such as that of the *Entertainment Software Rating Board (ESRB)*. Distinctive features within the video game realm, however, include competition, either against the self or against a machine via a machine, and increased levels of interactivity and manipulation in comparison with earlier media.

With mounting evidence demonstrating prominent resource allocation toward video game play, it could be deduced that players spend more time with their gaming platforms than with guardians—and could be spending less time with cohorts than with games. Gaming has diffused into the culture and become such an integrated part of society that today's American adolescents more readily identify Nintendo's Super Mario than Disney's Mickey Mouse (Bensley & Eenwyk, 2001). Part of the attraction to games is the ability to escape. Games allow players to be different compared with their real-world selves. For example, nonathletic players can have professional football or basketball talent, which perhaps explains why sporting games have been dominant over the years.

The consumer market research group NPD Group offers evidence of sports games' popularity, stating that half of the top 10 selling games in the mid-2000s were sports games (e.g., *Madden NFL, NCAA Football, MVP Baseball,* and *NBA Live*)—and through the late 2000s, sales have remained congruent with past years. One of the most successful video game franchises belongs to EA Sports' *Madden* football series (and its offshoot, *NCAA Football*). This franchise annually holds the top spots in overall video game sales. Given their popularity, it is important to understand the outcomes from these gaming environments.

Competition

Many U.S. citizens strongly believe in competition and believe it to be a basic component of society—a necessary factor for achievement in economics, arts, science, and sports (Bonta, 1997). An element basic to competition is the inverse relationship of goal attainment between two people—as one advances toward achieving a given goal, the other moves further from it. All sporting events consist of competition, either interactive (e.g., football) or noninteractive (e.g., figure skating). Interestingly, Dolf Zillmann and colleagues (1989) argued that

competition promotes camaraderie and friendship, develops the mastery of general and unique motor skills that are attained through training, and is essential for character formation. Furthermore, competition affords people the ability to experience solidarity.

Much of the research has centered on the spectators of competitive situations; however, these competition concepts (e.g., camaraderie, friendship, motor skills) are deemed unattainable through spectatorship (i.e., passive viewing). Research has indicated a multitude of negative aspects from sports spectatorship—from riots, lootings, and killings to the halting of nation relations (see Zillmann, Bryant, & Sapolsky, 1989). Furthermore, no evidence exists that viewing sports concludes with a cathartic release, despite many hypotheses to the contrary. However, research has shown that spectatorship helps integrate and cement social circles, be it community, town, state, region, country, or world, by bolstering self-worth and societal belongingness. Sports is a common conversational subject, as evidenced by how much attention is given to sports in media (e.g., dedicated cable networks, newspaper sections, sports radio, electronic resources) and in Americans' lives, where many people discuss, watch, or read sports daily. More specifically, according to Bruce D. Bonta, American football represents the "competitive ethos" of the United States, thus binding people together. Within the United States, football is considered a central component of national pride, with both community and individual involvement.

Much research in the competition realm is based on spectatorship because studying the impact of participation as a favored identity has methodological constraints. However, gaming combines passive media (e.g., television) with interactive media (e.g., newspapers), representing a union of participation and spectatorship. With that said, engaging in a sports-themed video game is considered simulation, given that it is neither full participation nor complete spectatorship. A player is not literally engaged in the physical space of the game's physical boundaries; however, a player is not idly and passively viewing events as they unfold, either. In competition there are winners and losers, and a gamer must take credit for defeat as much as victory—in video game play, the gamer is attached to the game and team and is unable to separate the two. In this way, a football video game encompasses interactivity, involvement, manipulation of play, and competition outcomes as well as identification processes.

The relevancy of the teams playing is an important consideration in competition. In football, for example, two teams compete during a game; however, accessibility and salience of the player and opponent vary game by game. For this reason, certain groupings may come to a person's mind more readily than others, enhancing categorization and identification effects. For instance, Zillmann's research regarding competition indicates "Seeing a liked player struggle with a tough rival not only should be more suspenseful, but should also liberate more enjoyment than the safe play against a weak opponent" (Zillmann et al., 1989, p. 266)—meaning enjoyment increases in intensity as saliency of player and opponent increases.

Although few researchers have included sports as a genre in gaming effects, several studies have linked competition with aggression. Competition is inherently frustrating because of continual resistance toward one's reaching a desired goal. Leonard Berkowitz's research in the late 1980s and early 1990s has shown that aggression develops as a response to frustration. Moreover, frustration has been linked to priming aggressive thoughts and behavior.

Level of Competition

Research has indicated tightly contested games generally are more enjoyable than games won by a large margin. Suspense research typically involves passive viewing of narrative texts; therefore, what occurs during game play may be positioned differently because of active manipulation of gaming content. A gaming outcome may be situated as a magnitude of win or loss (i.e., closeness of the game). On a continuum of potential final score magnitude outcomes, the closer the outcome falls to the midpoint (i.e., a tie game), the greater competition increases due to the unpredictability of the game's resolution.

Moreover, research has indicated that enjoyment is dependent on emotional commitment; thus, close games are shown to intensify the competition outcome, whereby highly identified fans will experience greatest enjoyment winning a close game. Although it could be argued that close games may be more enjoyable because of their unpredictability, evidence exists that this may not matter as much as proposed. For instance, Nebraska fans thoroughly enjoy "seeing their highly rated football team not just defeat, but trample and humiliate an unheralded Indiana team" (Zillmann et al., 1989, p. 271).

To better understand the dynamic between winning and losing within the outcomes of enjoyment and hostility, Robert Griffiths delineated winning and losing further by examining the strength of win and lose. For instance, football incorporates many scoring options, such that a team may score in increments of 2, 3, 6, 7, or 8 points. Close scores are then defined by the possibility of a player having a chance to win or tie within one possession. Big wins were considered more than one possession ahead (with big losses more than one possession behind). Hence, the following score strength distinctions were made: *big win* (winning by 9 or more points), *close win* (winning by 1 to 8 points), *close loss* (losing by 1 to 8 points), and *big loss* (losing by 9 or more points). In the rules of college football, no ties can occur. Applying these parameters, Griffiths found score strength was a significant predictor of postgame play hostility. Hostility was reported greatest for big loss, followed by close loss, close win, and big win, respectively. Using a group comparisons test, only big loss and close loss, as well as big win and close win, were not significantly different from one another. Regarding enjoyment, score strength was a significant predictor. Winning big produced the greatest levels of enjoyment, followed by close win, close loss, and big loss, respectively. Using a group comparisons test, only close loss and big loss, and big win and close win, did not significantly differ from one another.

Additional Considerations

Because many research designs employ a "God" mode, whereby gaming action never ends, the gamer is exposed to aggression-inducing content for the duration of game play. However, this type of design lacks ecological validity of winning or losing. Competition outcome is a significant component of the affective response to the gaming experience. Winning produces enjoyment and losing produces hostility; however, being placed in a situation without the capability of resolution may inherently lessen the condition manipulation, producing small effects. Some players may feel frustrated by being placed in an unsolvable conflict; thus, these gamers may feel increased state hostility in all conditions because of the study design, not necessarily because of the gaming action or content. Or gamers may feel relaxed knowing they cannot lose, thereby attenuating hostility levels across all conditions. Research has not shown how gamers interpret never-ending gaming action in games that normally have natural resolutions. Thus, small effects from prior research may indicate greater effects when encompassing the competition outcome.

Researchers have indicated negative gaming effects are smaller than those of television or movies, but it was thought that they may simply be due to lack of funding or because gaming is a newer medium. Ultimately, though, as explicated previously, gaming is fundamentally different from watching television or movies because of interactivity and involvement in competition. Generally, a television viewer cannot win or lose, but simply passively observes action—whereas in gaming, whether the protagonist wins or loses is dependent on the player. This inherent function of competition is a necessary component to gaming effects research because of its influence on game play and game play effects. In this regard, competition outcome may best be posited as a situational input within Craig Anderson's general aggression model.

Matthew S. Eastin and Robert P. Griffiths

See also Aggression and Culture; Culture of Violence; Effects From Violent Media, Short- and Long-Term; General Aggression Model; Sports, Violence and Aggression in; Video Game Platforms, Effects of

Further Readings

Apperley, T. H. (2006). Genre and game studies: Toward a critical approach to video game genres. *Simulation & Gaming, 37*(1), 6–23.

Barr, P., Noble, J., & Biddle, R. (2007). Video game values: Human-computer interaction and games. *Interacting With Computers, 19*, 180–195.

Bensley, L., & Eenwyk, J. V. (2001). Video games and real-life aggression: Review of the literature. *Journal of Adolescent Health, 29*, 244–257.

Bonta, B. D. (1997). Cooperation and competition in peaceful societies. *Psychological Bulletin, 121*(2), 299–320.

Berkowitz, L. (1989). Frustration-aggression hypothesis: Examination and reformulation. *Psychological Bulletin, 106*, 59–73.

Berkowitz, L. (1990). On the formation of regulation of anger and aggression. *American Psychologist, 45*, 494–503.

Branscombe, N. R., & Wann, D. L. (1991). The positive social and self concept consequences of sports team identification. *Journal of Sport and Social Issues, 15*(2), 115–127.

Elverdam, C., & Aarseth, E. (2007). Game classification and game design. *Games and Culture, 2*(1), 3–22.

Jansz, J., & Martis, R. G. (2007). The Lara phenomenon: Powerful female characters in video games. *Sex Roles, 56*, 141–148.

Newman, J. (2002). In search of the videogame player: The lives of Mario. *New Media & Society, 4*(3), 405–422.

Riley, D. M. (2006). *The NPD group reports annual 2005 U.S. video game industry retail sales.* Retrieved from http://www.npd.com/dynamic/releases/press_060117.html

Vorderer, P., Hartmann, T., & Klimmt, C. (2003). *Explaining the enjoyment of playing video games: The role of competition.* Paper presented at the ACM International Conference Proceeding Series: Proceedings of the second international conference on entertainment computing, Pittsburgh, PA.

Zillmann, D., Bryant, J., & Sapolsky, B. S. (1989). Enjoyment from sports spectatorship. In J. H. Goldstein (Ed.), *Sports, games, and play: Social and psychological viewpoints* (pp. 241–278). Hillsdale, NJ: Erlbaum.

CROSS-CULTURAL PERSPECTIVES

Studying media through a cross-cultural lens—that is, from a perspective that allows for comparison among cultures—has advantages for understanding media effects. Cross-cultural research can identify the influence of different cultural norms on content effects such as violent media effects. It also can examine interactions between media violence and real-world violence in different cultures. In addition, it can observe different media effects between countries with well-developed media systems and those with limited media systems. Nonetheless, most media effect studies have been conducted mainly in the Western culture, specifically from an American or Anglo-Saxon perspective.

A few early studies in Brazil, Germany, and Scotland demonstrated that there have been similar incidents when media consumption and aggressive behaviors have been positively correlated. The initial cross-cultural study on global media violence was conducted in the 1980s. This study compared violent media and aggression across five countries (Australia, Finland, Israel, Poland, and the United States) and found that there is a similar violent media effect among these countries even though the content, access to media, and societal attitudes toward aggression differ. In the 1990s, another cross-cultural study was conducted within the European media environment. Here data indicated different usages of new technology among European countries; however, this research only focused on media-rich countries.

In response to growing concerns regarding the effects of violent media content, the United Nations Educational, Scientific, and Cultural Organization (UNESCO) conducted a multicultural analysis examining the influence of children's aggression in the real world (i.e., war and crime) and in media environments. Collecting data from 23 countries, this study was the first to include a large number of subjects and countries. To overcome the regional imbalance of previous studies, methods were employed to control for countries in a specific region, developmental status of countries, and culture.

To begin understanding cultural differences, the 23 countries were categorized into four regions (Africa, Asia/Pacific, Europe/Canada, and Latin America). There were different distributions of media outlets among them. In particular, European/Canadian regions had the highest television distribution, followed by Latin America and Asia. Africa has the lowest distribution of television. There were also cultural differences in perception of violence. For example, children in Europe and Canada considered a physical attack to be more severe aggression than verbal insults. However, children in Asia and Africa perceived verbal attacks as more severe than physical attack. In respect to the relationship between media violence and actual aggression, there was a cultural difference. While media violence is universal, children with high media exposure tended to connect media violence and real-world aggressive behavior. They also perceived aggression to be an effective way of solving conflicts and achieving preferred status. That is, when violence was repeatedly displayed in the media as "fun" and "thrilling," children tended to remember aggression within a rewarding context. Furthermore, children in high-technology or media-rich cultures showed a higher risk-seeking tendency than those in low-technology cultures. There was a tendency across all cultures for children to view aggressive media heroes as role models. Thus, even though the perception of violence varied, it is a general consensus among researchers that repetitive exposures to violent media created a more aggressive culture regardless of real-world experiences.

When Eastern and Western perspectives of media violence are compared, a difference in aggressive tendencies is found. For example, Eastern countries (e.g., China, Japan, and Korea) are collectivistic cultures; thus, they value moral disciplines and egalitarian commitment while devaluing competition and aggression. For example, statistics show lower rates of homicide and violent crimes in Japan compared

with the United States or other Western countries. Also, the contexts of violence in diverse media differ among Eastern and Western countries. Eastern television programs tend to depict the pain and suffering of victims of violent actions. In video games, people in Western cultures prefer action and sports games, whereas role-playing games are the most popular genre in Eastern cultures. Within this perspective, people in Eastern cultures tend to respond less aggressively to provocation than those who live in Western cultures. Children in Eastern cultures have relatively limited access to their own television sets and more parental monitoring than children in the United States and European countries.

Seungae Lee and Matthew S. Eastin

See also Aggression and Culture; Culture of Violence; General Aggression Model; International Perspective on Media Violence

Further Readings

Anderson, C. A., Shibuya, A., Ihori, N., Swing, E. L., Bushman, B. J., Sakamoto, A., Rothstein, H. R., & Saleem, M. (2010). Violent video game effects on aggression, empathy, and prosocial behavior in Eastern and Western countries: A meta-analytic review. *Psychological Bulletin, 136*(2), 151–173.

Groebel, J. (2002). Media violence in cross-cultural perspective: A global study on children's media behavior and some educational implications. In D. Singer & G. Singer (Eds.), *Handbook of children and the media* (pp. 255–268).Thousand Oaks, CA: Sage.

Huesmann, L. R., & Eron, L. D. (1986). *Television and the aggressive child: A cross-national comparison.* Hillsdale, NJ: Erlbaum.

Livingstone, S. (1998). Mediated childhoods: A comparative approach to young people's changing media environment in Europe. *European Journal of Communication, 13*(4), 435–456.

CULTIVATING CONTENT AND THE SOCIAL REPRESENTATION OF VIOLENCE

Media content can influence individuals' images, thoughts, and mental representations of the world in which they live. Cultivation theory proposes that individuals who spend more time watching television and other professionally produced media are more likely to have a perception of society that closely aligns with the most common media representations of social reality. Cultivation theory, as originally proposed, included only traditional media outlets; however, media consumption today not only includes this traditional mass media delivery of content but also is greatly affected by interactive media and its participatory sharing of information. Media consumers today are actively adding to the social communication of news and entertainment through creating, distributing, and consuming content delivered from media professionals and the general public, referred to as "user-generated content." To further delineate the role of socially produced and distributed media, this entry provides a brief overview of cultivation theory; defines user-generated content and socially created media; discusses realism, authenticity, and consumer "choices" with user-generated content; analyzes the impact of user-generated content on the news; and discusses associations of cultivated content and user-generated content in virtual and real worlds.

Cultivation Theory

Cultivation theory, originally developed by George Gerbner in the 1960s and 1970s, analyzes how television viewing affects individuals' construction of social reality and posits that a long duration of repeated exposure will alter one's perception of reality, including imagery and assumptions of public policies, to align more closely with the prolific mass media messages. After exposure to the display of an attitude or behavior in the mainstream media, a viewer will form thoughts or mental representations of the attitude or behavior. Repeated exposure to similar media content increases the likelihood a viewer will adopt these thoughts, create beliefs, and develop social perceptions that may not be congruent with what is witnessed in the world. Given this, viewing high levels of violent media content may cultivate a perception of higher rates of violence in society than actually exist. This is often termed *mean world syndrome* and is characterized by heightened mistrust of law enforcement and fear of crime.

Cultivation theory is one of the most widely published theories in mass communication research that focuses on the communication media itself. Research has investigated cultivation by studying the effects of a variety of television programming ranging from reality makeover shows that produce lower levels of self-esteem in viewers to local news programs that create an inflated fear of crime. These cultivated

perceptions of the real world, created through media content, can affect perceptions at both personal and societal levels. The power of cultivation has been shown to influence and uphold established ways of thinking. For example, as societal roles change (e.g., women's increased prominence in today's workforce), these new aspirations and beliefs are not reflected in societal perceptions and expectations because of the strength of cultivation.

Cultivation theory, which primarily investigates the impact of television exposure, has been criticized as having too narrow a focus. Additionally, critics of cultivation theory have questioned its measurability given the long-term nature of the effects. However, future work may become more robust as researchers analyze the fast-paced nature and impact of user-generated content in emerging digital environment communication methods.

User-Generated Content

The digital era and Web 2.0 technologies have dramatically changed mass media consumption by giving viewers more control and perceived ownership of the information they choose to access. Digital content no longer consists solely of information from traditional media that can be accessed at the convenience of the viewer; it also includes many virtual locations for creation and dissemination of the consumer's voice. Web 2.0 has created opportunities for consumers to actively engage in the media through user-generated content created by the general public. In addition to the creation of new content, sharing, commenting, rating, and editing content are many of the ways users have the opportunity to interact with the media. While the ability to publish personal content online has been available since the development of the Internet, Web 2.0 technologies have largely changed the ease of distribution. Through these many outlets, user-generated content differs from programming and messaging created by paid media professionals, and through the social creation of content has led the mass media landscape toward a user-centric model.

Online forums, games, personal blogs, content-sharing sites, and social media and networking sites create opportunities for participatory involvement in the development of news and entertainment stories, creating an environment that can be participant-led alongside the dominant media providers. Many of the popular sites for user-generated content include YouTube, Facebook, WordPress, Yelp, Wikipedia,

Reddit, and Flickr, along with many virtual world games and spaces, such as *SimCity* and *World of Warcraft*. The proliferation of user-generated content on sites like YouTube and various other content-sharing sites has fundamentally changed the way the majority of "connected" individuals are consuming mass media. These sites and spaces available for user-generated content allow consumers to connect with other consumers in a unique way, empowering the recipients of information. Individual control, both actual and perceived, is rising in comparison with industrial control of consumed media, creating opportunities for personalized media environments that can be accessed when and where desired. The presence of this content, and its more than 100 million streams viewed daily, create additional channels of media that may affect one's cultivated view of society.

As traditional media audiences decline, or at the very least segment, user-generated content sites create an opportunity for alternate perspectives and decentralized information seeking. The media environment today has an unprecedented number of available information sources. However, although societal trends are moving toward consuming a variety of information sources, the process is not as rapid as some may believe; many online users are still primarily visiting mainstream news sites. Future research focusing on user-generated content will allow scholars to investigate the critical intersection of mainstream news sources, popular entertainment, technology, and the community's response to widely publicized content.

Although user-generated content differs from television and other traditional media in its source, researchers have argued that some instances of these media may have the same effects as cultivation. User-generated content in game play is pervasive in today's society and is often accessed in ways that demand the attention and focus of the individuals exposed to the content through game navigation and play controls. Research that has focused on the cultivation effects after violent video game play has shown an increased prevalence of crime expectations. Future research may indicate that the impact of user-generated content outlets of many varieties is similar or greater in the cultivation of perceptions of society than traditional media alone.

Realism, Authenticity, and Consumer "Choices" in User-Generated Content

Much of our social reality, or the beliefs held about the world around us, is created by direct exposure

to objects and experiences, absolute realism, or the representations of these things and the meanings and associations that we assign to them—perceived realism. Although there is little agreement on the conceptualization of perceived realism, it has been widely used in research as the form of realism that moderates the media influence. Realism of media content can vary in the degree to which it is perceived as fiction or nonfiction, as well as how convincing the represented content presentation appears. Realism is often determined by the viewer and can lead to differing perceptions of the content. Knowledge of crimes and violence often comes from mass media instead of personal experience or contact, making the representation of crime in the mass media a prominent issue. When violent media is shown, the realism represented can have an impact on the degree to which it cultivates a perception of reality in the viewer. Given the higher prevalence of violence and crime in media when compared with the real world, and the subjective nature of viewing content, realism in both traditional media and user-generated content can be influential. Indeed, research has shown that realistic televised content has a greater impact on the cultivation of societal perception than the viewing of fictional content.

User-generated content differs from traditional media in that it is often published as a work in progress or in a format that invites other consumers to build or add to the content or discussion, making it seem more authentic. Information provided from the masses has enabled new crowd-sourcing approaches that are being implemented in the news, producing a remarkable breadth of knowledge as a result of the variety of perspectives. Some research has gone so far as to suggest that the collaborative nature of user-generated content can produce content of greater quality than that of the industry expert, even though this is still highly contested.

Many user-generated content sites provide opportunity and encourage individual customization of the media experience. Not only does this increase the potential for user identification with the media, it also allows the content to be further streamlined to fit the viewer's preferences. These highly customized media environments are often found to be highly congruent with the user's previous knowledge and current interests. The redundancy of information often screens out opposing viewpoints, which creates environments that further cultivate previously held beliefs and thus a call for an extension with a user-generated content focus to the cultivation literature.

Research has shown that this type of online experience will intensify attitudes and reduce ambivalence on a topic through a combination of the user's and the online platform's selectivity. The abundance of user-generated content available requires some type of introductory information, such as a thumbnail of a video or short description, to help viewers sort through and select from all the available content. *Bandwagon effects* occur when online videos are displayed with high viewing counts that often snowball other users into viewing the content. Additionally, these fragments of available content allow users and web technologies to further organize information through peer-selected ratings and other filtering algorithms. However, this type of filtering will often lead a viewer to the most popular media choice, not necessarily the most relevant or accurate.

Violence, News, and User-Generated Content

Violence is shown in the news through heavy representation and reporting of crimes on local, national, and international levels. Audiences believing that news sources report crime stories in a linear and comprehensive manner may be more susceptible to cultivate an inflated social perception of violence, since what is represented in the news, or is determined as newsworthy, is not a direct reflection of the world but rather a highly edited selection by journalism and media professionals. Historically, these gatekeepers have reported crimes in which the victims are more prominent and/or influential in a society, giving a higher perception of credibility and creating news media that are not necessarily representative of the common public. Furthermore, previous journalistic standards for eyewitness accounts were dependent on the status of the individual and required a certain degree of authority for trustworthiness.

Things are changing in the digital era, when news sources are no longer dominated by a select group of source creators who focus on the issues more pertinent to an elite population. Instead, today's news providers are evolving into organizations that more often highlight the behavior and topics of interest to the common citizen. As news coverage has transitioned to cover more stories related to the common public, the variety of source information has also slowly grown to include the public. Today's news sources change to accommodate the more participatory nature of news, and media consumption has affected the visibility and representation of the general concerns of the public. Web 2.0 dramatically increases the public's ability to participate in the spread of news, if not as dramatically in its content creation in the media industry. The proliferation of video uploads following tragedies or natural disasters attests to the changing dynamics of eyewitness accounts alone.

Through Web 2.0 technology, users are able to spread information to virtually unlimited audiences without involvement of intermediate parties. This ability to disseminate information may be one of the greatest technological advancements of user-generated content. YouTube and other user-generated content sites provide forums for society to further reinforce mainstream media as well as expand content in new directions. The opportunities for varying discourse in response to criminal activity and the fear of victimization can be perpetuated as a society grieves, copes, and processes information involved with these tragedies. This has been evidenced in the large reactions of video upload and comments created in response to nationally publicized crimes and events that create highly complex associations of connectivity.

As technology advances with public outlets and the flow of information (spread) quickens, reports have shown that up to a quarter of online news consumers have commented on a news story or blog, with small percentages also contributing with a picture or video. User-generated content posts, including YouTube videos, in response to real-world crime have the potential to include many discourses surrounding the crime, roles of potential fault or blame, broader policy issues, and varying responses to the news media and other posted content. This behavior was exhibited after the disappearance of Madeleine McCann, a British toddler, in 2008 when a plethora of widely consumed videos were posted to YouTube that contained a variety of content ranging from tributes to the victim to aggression and hostility toward the parents and/or authorities involved.

Interestingly, research has found that while hostile or violent content represents only a small portion of the user-generated content originally disseminated, it receives proportionally higher viewing and response rates. Hostile online postings are often a combination of remixed mass media segments presented with the users' content and opinion added in, as well as solely original content such as direct-to-camera addresses. Additionally, adverse comments are not only found in response to the hostile content, but often also in response to supportive postings, showing that antagonism is not limited to one categorically designed user-generated content. This flexible nature of user-generated content allows for dynamic interactions to go beyond the capabilities of traditional media in cultivating perceptions of society by expressing hostility through a dialogic exchange, with creators often having the most active voice.

Cultivated and User-Generated Content in Virtual and Real Worlds

Gaming is an arena of user-generated content that occupies a substantial amount of time in the lives of many youths and adolescents around the world. The amount of time spent playing games is comparable to the amount of time spent on schoolwork and other Internet activities in many areas of the world, with some studies showing that gaming is the most popular activity for many youths on home computers. Thus, this influx of virtual worlds and the amount of time spent immersed in these environments is creating a large research area for the role that games play in the construction of one's societal reality.

Simulation gaming, or games taking place in virtual worlds, consists of an interactive medium that allows players to inhibit and create alternate personae in an environment that is artificially rule-based, often simulating aspects of the real world without traditional space and time constraints. Simulation games often allow players to play the role of citizen or higher government official in dealing with crime and city planning, creating an opportunity for players to simplistically approach many of life's more complex phenomena. Generally speaking, gaming research is not decisively positive or negative on how it will affect the interactions and perceptions of the players and exposed content generators. Support for simulation gaming has shown evidence that educational content can lead to positive perception changes. Violent gaming, however, leads to greater controversy in benefits and detriments. Many studies have shown excessive gaming with violent content leads to negative consequences of cultivation, such as increased aggressive perceptions, thoughts, and behaviors; desensitization to violence in the real world; and increased stereotyping. Regardless of the violence, arguments are made for the benefits of these games regarding the skills acquired through cognitive development, such as pattern recognition and critical thinking, as well as decision-making and problem-solving abilities.

There is evidence that content from the real world has an impact on virtual user worlds and that, in turn, these worlds play a role in the cultivation of societal perceptions or expectations of real and idealized cities. Fear of crime has affected online environments as digital technology has enabled communities to utilize unique ways of collectively expressing their emotions, find identity, and make sense of the world. User-generated content has been found to create an overt sense of community and consensus of opinion. This outward personal expression can sometimes go as far as being seen as a public performance of grieving. User-generated content creates an alternate sense of community that depends on and utilizes communal knowledge.

Crimes related to children, especially murder or abduction, often provoke high levels of involvement in user-generated content environments for users to further understand the events or to provide outlets for expression. Not surprisingly, there is tremendous crossover of the real-world content into the virtual worlds. The impact of traditional media is visible when media content spills over into user-generated content arenas alongside other online outlets, as has been seen when posters for missing children in the real world are seen in the virtual streets of *Second Life* as a continuation of the public reaction to crime. Conversely, spending time in virtual world games has been shown to affect how players interpret their real worlds beyond the gaming experience.

Play of user-generated content and simulation games, such as *SimCity,* is correlated with altered expectations of city authorities and their role in crime and other city issues, including evaluated levels of distrust for city officials. The users gain experience in learning how things work, what things are, and how behaviors affect cities in these virtual worlds. The abstract concepts are then often applied to the user's life outside the gaming experience.

As shown through research and user trends, user-generated content is on the rise, and the effect of such content has both positive and negative consequences. Thus, although knowledge acquisition represents a positive effect, hostile and violent content can have negative consequences through cultivating effects.

Allison Lazard and Matthew S. Eastin

See also Cultivating Content and the Social Representation of Violence; Cultivation Theory; Realism of Violent Content, Real-World Violence on Television, and Their Effects; Social Cognitive Theory; Social Learning From Media; User Involvement in Violent Content, Effects of

Further Readings

De Keyser, J., & Raeymaeckers, K. (2012). The printed rise of the common man. *Journalism Studies, 13*(5–6), 825–835.

Gerbner, G., & Gross, L. (1976). Living with television: The violence profile. *Journal of Communication, 26,* 172–194.

Kennedy, J. (2010). Don't forget about me. *Journalism Studies, 11*(2), 225–242.

Morgan, M., & Shanahan, J. (2010). The state of cultivation. *Journal of Broadcasting & Electronic Media, 54*(2), 337–355.

Williams, D. (2006). Virtual cultivation: Online worlds, offline perceptions. *Journal of Communication, 56*(1), 69–87.

CULTIVATION THEORY

Perhaps no other perspective on media effects has generated such intense evaluation and controversy as cultivation theory. Television, as described by George Gerbner, the founder of cultivation theory, is the "dominant storyteller" in U.S. society—an object that is part of Americans' daily routine from birth until death. Based on this assumption, there is no pre-television experience; rather, Americans grow up in a televised world that helps shape perceptions of society. Essentially, cultivation theory posits that television helps provide viewers with lessons on U.S. cultural values and ideologies. Although Gerbner's ideas about cultivation originated nearly 50 years ago, television was, and still is, the most widely consumed channel of mass communication among U.S. citizens. Cultivation theory asserts that, unlike other forms of media, the public relies on television to help understand the social norms and values of U.S. society. This entry explores Gerbner's cultivation theory, including criticism and further refinements, and discusses the effects and moderating factors of cultivation.

Researching Media Content

Gerbner and his fellow researchers at the University of Pennsylvania began developing the cultivation perspective in the late 1960s by analyzing various television content. As part of the cultural indicators project, the seminal "message system analysis" studies assessed the dominant themes and messages present in media content. The late 1960s was a period of substantial violence and unrest in society. Thus,

initially, the content analyses were aimed at documenting the frequency and nature of portrayals of violence on television. However, these studies also addressed the portrayal of minorities, occupations, and gender roles. Results of those studies indicated that there were certain similar messages found across different television stations. Overall, rather than examining any one specific genre, message system analysis examined the sum total of all messages to detect broader themes consistent throughout television programming.

Cultivation Effects

The content analysis research laid the groundwork for assumptions regarding cultivation effects. Inherent in this original formulation is that television sends relatively consistent and homogeneous messages to a mostly diverse audience. More specifically then, because there are certain consistent patterns in television content, over time experience with these messages should lead to some viewer effect. Consequently, the theory suggests that indirect experience with television content will eventually displace one's personal experience when making a judgment about the real world. These effects will be most palpable for those individuals who spend more time in the television world, because these individuals should be expected to view the world differently than those individuals who watch less television. Although a topic for debate, heavy television viewers are traditionally viewed by cultivation researchers as those who are much less selective in what they watch compared with light television viewers. For those who view large quantities of television programming, the television experience has become ritualistic and habitual. Whereas light television viewers may rely on a personal experience when forming beliefs about the social world, heavy television viewers latch onto the information provided from television content as their source for information about the real world.

Methodologically, cultivation theory compares differences between light and heavy television viewers and perceptions of social reality. Following content analysis work to address whatever social issue is believed to be prevalent on television, survey methods are employed to examine what differences, if any, there are in beliefs about the social world between light and heavy television viewers.

When addressing how television affects audiences, cultivation researchers assume that this medium reinforces and sustains mainstream perspectives. Unlike other media effects theories that examine rapid changes in viewers' attitudes or behaviors, cultivation aims to provide an understanding of the gradual and subtle impact of the accumulation of television messages on viewers. Rather than attempting to link specific messages to violent behaviors, cultivation looks at how gradually, through continuous exposure, viewers develop certain worldviews. Initial findings showed that heavy viewing was linked to exaggerated perceptions regarding mistrust, danger, and victimization, as well as inaccurate estimations of the number of law enforcement professionals in the real world. Gerbner and colleagues came up with the "mean world syndrome" to describe an exaggerated perception by heavy viewers that most people cannot be trusted.

Although cultivation analysis grew out of interest in addressing violent content and has been applied frequently to this topic, the theory has subsequently been applied to a range of other social issues, including perceptions of dating, marriage, and gender roles; stereotypes regarding various ethnic groups; and politics. Furthermore, a large body of research has applied a cultivation perspective to address the link between television exposure and perceptions regarding the environment. Overall, heavy television viewers tend to be more skeptical of science yet optimistic about its promise. Depending on the research conducted, heavy viewers have been found either to be highly concerned about the environment or more apathetic toward environmental issues.

Cultivation theory has also frequently been used to help explain how media content influences health beliefs and behaviors. Specifically, cultivation theory has been used in research examining beliefs about cancer prevention, body image–related concerns and behaviors, doctor–patient concerns, smoking initiation, and psychosocial health issues such as low self-esteem. Additionally, an extensive body of research examines the role of television in creating distorted views of mental health. Overall, heavy television viewers are found to be less tolerant toward mental health and more fearful of those with mental health conditions.

Cultivation effects can further be broken down into *first-* and *second-*order effects. First-order effects relate to basic judgments regarding the frequency or estimate of something in the real world based on exposure to television content. For example, a perception formed through television that 5% of all people in the real world work in law enforcement would be an example of a first-order effect. Ultimately, these estimates are then compared to real-world data to assess accuracy. Second-order effects refer to values or attitudes that are formed or reinforced from viewing television content. First- and second-order judgments appear to be mostly separate effects that may only have a weak association with one another.

A meta-analysis found that differences in television viewing explain only roughly 1% of the variance in people's perspectives. While this overall effect size is small, cultivation researchers are quick to point out that these effects across studies have been fairly consistent and, furthermore, are influencing (albeit in small ways) the beliefs of very large groups of people. In addition, this small effect remains even after taking into account factors that may moderate effects, such as age, socioeconomic status, and gender.

Criticisms

General Television Content

The relatively straightforward hypothesis that heavy consumption of television content will ultimately shift one's beliefs about the real world has garnered significant attention from the social scientific community. Although many researchers have embraced the central arguments of cultivation theory, many of the core assumptions of this perspective have also faced intense criticism. In particular, critiques of the theory are linked to its methodological, conceptual, and analytical assumptions. First, while there is substantial research supporting the prediction that cultivation is linked to estimates of the real-world or first-order effects, many studies have failed to find similar, consistent results for more subjective attitudes or second-order judgments. In addition, because cultivation research involves a combination of content analysis methodology and surveys to test effects, there always exists the possibility that what coders perceive as evidence of a particular observation (i.e., violent acts) fails to be consistent with what viewers perceive that to be. This issue is particularly evident when addressing second-order judgments, because the coder is forced to make decisions regarding more subjective beliefs or attitudes of television content rather than more clear-cut manifestations. Other researchers have added that there are likely to be differences across viewers in the interpretation and meaning of television messages. Specifically, there is likely to be very little uniformity in interpretation of messages at any level. In addition, demographic factors such as gender, socioeconomic status, political beliefs, and religiosity have been found to qualify cultivation effects, challenging the broader assumption that all heavy viewers can be lumped into one category.

Another significant criticism involves how viewer involvement alters cultivation effects. Although the assumption that heavy television viewers, described as passive recipients of these messages, should theoretically be most influenced by messages, researchers have noted that attention, memory, and involvement were crucial in order for the learning subprocess of cultivation to proceed. Ultimately, viewer attention, rather than simple exposure, to media messages should determine whether content influences real-world beliefs. The argument linking involvement versus exposure is related, in part, to the competing perspective that exposure to one narrative or program leads to an immediate impact on viewers' beliefs and attitudes. In particular, rather than effects being traced to heavy long-term exposure to media messages, research has shown that one-shot exposure to certain programming may be sufficient to alter real-world beliefs and attitudes.

Other arguments suggest that the closer connection between specific groups and parental discipline may weaken cultivation effects. Finally, how real viewers perceive content to be, a factor related to narrative processing and involvement, has been found to alter the cultivation effects.

Genre-Specific Content

One of the major criticisms of cultivation stems from the original assumption that television is a coherent mass of messages that cuts across genres and storylines. Recent arguments by leading media effects researchers suggest that genre-specific messages are a more fitting area for uncovering cultivation effects. The television landscape has expanded to include thousands of channels that fit a variety of interests. Therefore, it may be naïve to assume that there are similar messages presented across such distinct genres. Ultimately, now, more than ever, people may selectively expose themselves to particular content to reinforce their beliefs. L. J. Shrum, a leading cultivation theory researcher, has provided strong evidence that genre-specific television viewing is a consistent predictor of cultivation effects, while general viewing is not correlated with either accessibility or social reality estimates. More recently,

genres including talk shows, television news, and makeover or cosmetic surgery programs have been tested to examine cultivation effects. Other studies have looked more in-depth at long-term exposure to specific programs to address cultivation effects. Arguably, these studies may technically not qualify as cultivation analyses; however, given the practical implications of studying specific genres, this concern appears to be of less relevance. However, many studies that examined both traditional cultivation effects (total television viewing) as well as effects related to genre-specific exposure found significant results for both relationships.

Moderating Factors

The numerous criticisms concerning cultivation effects have led to a variety of developments to isolate mechanisms that could help determine when cultivation effects would most likely occur.

Mainstreaming and Resonance

In an attempt to respond to various criticisms of cultivation theory as well as expand on its original foundation, Gerbner and colleagues introduced the concepts of mainstreaming and resonance as a revised explanation for effects. To account for individual differences, *mainstreaming* suggested that individuals holding more divergent attitudes from one another would be most influenced by heavy television viewing. In particular, eventually, individuals from more divergent groups (e.g., conservatives versus liberals) would converge on a more mainstream view of reality. Overall, differences in responses by viewers, which normally could be explained by differences in social, cultural, and political ideologies, would be weakened when examining responses of heavy viewers from those groups. Overall, given the (debatable) assumption that television over time continuously presents similar themes, mainstreaming predicts that heavy viewers with different personal experiences will develop a more similar view of reality than light viewers from their respective social groups. Researchers have also added to the initial mainstreaming assumptions by noting that those individuals whose personal experiences were most divergent from what was shown on television would be most influenced by increased viewing.

An opposing theoretical perspective, termed *resonance,* suggests that direct experience with certain issues, coupled with increased television viewing, would lead to a more reinforcing impact of exposure on real-world beliefs. For example, if television depictions of crime are similar to someone's personal experience (i.e., living in a dangerous neighborhood), this may resonate more with this viewer, amplifying cultivation effects.

Processes Underlying Cultivation Effects

While Gerbner did not offer any explanation for the specific processes occurring within viewers during exposure, this issue reflects arguably the most studied area within cultivation over the past 20 years. James Potter (1991) presented a revised model of cultivation subprocesses that included (a) general cultivation effects (heavy exposure to television content leads to changes in real-world beliefs) and (b) a learning, construction, and generalization process. The learning process strictly assessed the relationship between television exposure and perceptions about television. In particular, the model predicted that television exposure led to increased television-world estimates (first-order effects) and television-world beliefs (second-order effects). The construction process assessed the relationship between television-world estimates and beliefs and real-world estimates and beliefs, predicting that increases in television-world perceptions affected the real-world estimates (first order) and beliefs (second order). Finally, the model predicted that first-order effects in the television world would correlate with second-order effects in the television world, and that first-order effects in the real world would correlate with second-order effects in the real world. While the initial tests of this model were mixed, it does provide insight into the various subprocesses of cultivation.

Shrum delved more deeply into the cognitive process occurring within individuals that may influence cultivation effects. His research addressed how accessible certain information was from memory and whether information retrieval played an important role in explaining cultivation effects. In general, because heavy television viewers are exposed to certain themes more frequently than are light television viewers, it is much easier for the heavy viewer to retrieve this information from memory when primed or asked to reflect on it. Overall, because television provides the heavy viewer with frequent representations of certain social reality topics (i.e., crime victimization), heavy viewers should be more likely to form television-related cognitions. These television-related cognitions would therefore be more accessible for heavy television viewers than

for light viewers. Preliminary research in this area mostly supported these assumptions, with follow-up work extending these findings to second-order effects for topics such as marital discord.

Most recently, narrative processing has been studied as another potential intervening cognitive mechanism to explain cultivation effects. Helena Bilandzic and Rick Busselle (2008) described a model in which heavy involvement or engagement in a narrative is a central factor in the cultivation process. Such intense immersion into a narrative helps account for cultivation effects by altering viewers' real-world perceptions following each exposure. Similar to many recent studies of cultivation effects, the researchers addressed the link between narrative immersion and exposure to specific genres. Overall, they suggested that motivation is a crucial component of the cultivation process that leads viewers to select certain programming that will promote or facilitate greater engagement. Although findings from their initial work were mixed, results did show that genre-specific exposure was linked to increased narrative involvement into films of a similar genre.

Further Developments and Refinements

Given the unique attributes of the television medium, cultivation research has almost exclusively focused on the effects of exposure to mainstream programming. However, some recent literature points to the possibility of exploring cultivation effects in different channels and formats. In particular, a large body of work has examined cultivation effects linked to newspaper reading. While results of many of these studies vary, the significant relationships that have been found based on cultivation assumptions continue to stimulate additional research in this area. In addition, a few recent studies have examined the impact of video games on players' real-world estimates. One longitudinal study, in particular, conducted by Dmitri Williams (2006), examined the impact of online video game play on perceived real-world violence. The findings from this project showed that during the course of one month of game play, users shifted their beliefs about real-world danger (although isolated to only the violent situations depicted in the games).

Beyond the assessment of various media formats and channels, researchers continue to examine different types of effects that may be traced to cultivation assumptions. In particular, a burgeoning area of research assesses implicit or automatic reactions to media content as opposed to assessing more explicit judgments. This new area of research is consistent with other recent work that has examined differences across survey formats and the wording of questions when examining cultivation effects. Although only a small number of studies have implicit effects, the encouraging results suggest that researchers should continue to address more unique ways that cultivation may affect viewers.

Researchers have also linked cultivation theory to other dominant theoretical perspectives within the areas of media effects and persuasion to better explain differences in viewer perceptions. For example, cultivation effects have been explained through such popular psychological persuasion models as the theory of reasoned action and the elaboration likelihood model, and have been integrated with the media effects approaches of agenda setting and the third-person effect.

Christopher J. McKinley

See also Cultivating Content and the Social Representation of Violence; Effects From Media, Short- and Long-Term

Further Readings

Arendt, F. (2010). Cultivation effects of a newspaper on reality estimates and explicit and implicit attitudes. *Journal of Media Psychology, 22,* 147–159.

Bilandzic, H., & Busselle, R. W. (2008). Transportation and transportability in the cultivation of genre-consistent attitudes and estimates. *Journal of Communication, 58,* 508–529.

Morgan, M., & Shanahan, J. (2010). The state of cultivation. *Journal of Broadcasting & Electronic Media, 54,* 337–355.

Morgan, M., Shanahan, J., & Signorielli, N. (2009). Growing up with television: Cultivation processes. In J. Bryant & D. Zillmann (Eds.), *Media effects: Advances in theory and research* (3rd ed., pp. 17–42). New York, NY: Routledge.

Potter, W. J. (1991). Examining cultivation from a psychological perspective: Component subprocesses. *Communication Research, 18,* 77–102.

Shanahan, J., & Morgan, M. (1999). *Television and its viewers: Cultivation theory and research.* London: Cambridge University Press.

Shrum, L. J. (2007). Cultivation and social cognition. In D. R. Roskos-Ewoldsen & J. L. Monahan (Eds.), *Communication and social cognition: Theories and methods* (pp. 245–272). Mahwah, NJ: Erlbaum.

Shrum, L. J., & Bischak, V. D. (2001). Mainstreaming, resonance, and impersonal impact: Testing moderators of the cultivation effect for estimates of crime risk. *Human Communication Research, 27,* 187–215.

Williams, D. (2006). Virtual cultivation: Online worlds, offline perceptions. *Journal of Communication, 56,* 69–87.

CULTURAL VOYEURISM

New media technologies, ranging from hidden cameras and powerful telephoto lenses to the exponential growth of smartphones and the omnipresence of the Internet, pave the way today for an increasingly voyeuristic culture. It is a culture that thrives on watching revealing and authentic images of others' supposedly real and unguarded lives, often at the expense of the subjects' privacy. One form of voyeurism that challenges notions of individual and familial privacy, as well as social mores regarding the dead, involves the consumption of graphic, often sensational, images of real-life violence and death caught on camera. In some instances, more than just images are recorded, such as when the sounds of death (or possible death) are captured on 911 emergency calls and then released to the public. This entry explores such violence and death voyeurism (VADV). It initially examines different conceptions of voyeurism and then illustrates how lawmakers are enacting measures to thwart or slow the growth of VADV.

Conceptions of Voyeurism

At the heart of voyeurism is the activity of watching others. There are, however, several forms of voyeuristic watching in modern culture that must be distinguished from VADV.

For example, voyeurism can constitute a form of sexual deviance or disorder. This brand of voyeurism, according to the *Diagnostic and Statistical Manual of Mental Disorders* (American Psychiatric Association, 2000) often used by psychiatrists, centers on watching unsuspecting individuals who typically are naked or engaged in sexual conduct. The voyeur spies on them to achieve sexual excitement and gratification. This kind of voyeuristic behavior rises to the level of a sexual disorder when it is recurrent and leads to significant distress or impairment in the voyeur's social, occupational, or personal relationships.

Such sexual voyeurism also can constitute a crime under Peeping Tom laws. These laws, which exist in every state in the United States, frequently target peering through windows, doors, or other openings in a dwelling to observe an unsuspecting individual for purposes of sexual arousal. For example, Arizona Revised Statute § 13-1424 makes it a low-level felony to knowingly and without permission invade another person's privacy for the purpose of sexual stimulation.

While such laws traditionally were intended to stop individuals who physically trespassed onto property in order to spy with their own eyes, many states also have video voyeurism statutes that address high-tech peeping and surreptitious electronic recording. For instance, Louisiana's video voyeurism law, Louisiana Revised Statute 14:283, makes it a crime to use a recording device to observe, photograph, or film an unsuspecting person for a lewd or lascivious purpose. Even when prosecutions are successful, however, images obtained from video voyeurism can endure if they had been previously distributed via the Internet or uploaded to a website.

Beyond the realms of psychiatry and criminology, voyeurism generally suggests that some forms of looking at others are problematic or otherwise wrong. Indeed, the moniker "Peeping Tom," from which the statutes mentioned take their name, is derived from the legend of Lady Godiva. Tom was either blinded or killed—depending on the telling of the legend—for daring to peer out of a window at Lady Godiva as she rode nude on a horse through Coventry, England, to protest oppressive taxation. Tom's blinding or death suggests that some forms of looking are improper and merit punishment.

Voyeurism is problematic because it often represents an affront to societal values of privacy and autonomy. The voyeur intrudes, via his or her own eyes or electronic technologies, into physical areas of seclusion without the victim's knowledge, thus possessing power over the victim. Not only is the voyeur, by watching the unsuspecting victim, the taker of information in this relationship, but he or she also possesses power over the victim simply by knowing something the watched individual does not: that the individual, in fact, is being watched.

In contrast to such negative notions of voyeurism, the term sometimes is used in a more benign sense to describe the viewing of reality television programs. Unlike voyeurism as a form of sexual deviance, whereby an individual spies on another person, however, reality shows do not involve stealthful viewing. While most forms of voyeurism involve nonconsensual observation of unsuspecting people, the participants in reality television programs such as *Jersey Shore* and *Big Brother* are fully aware they are under observation. Another difference is that reality shows often are highly contrived and edited so that what viewers see may not be as real or authentic as it appears. Nonetheless, reality shows do allow audience members to peer voyeuristically into the lives of the shows' participants, at least providing viewers with the sensation of watching real people act out their lives.

The Voyeuristic Consumption of Images of Violence and Death

Gazing at images of death and violence in the media is nothing new. In January 1928, a photographer for the New York *Daily News* taped a miniature camera to his left ankle. He hid the camera from public view in order to capture an image of condemned murderer Ruth Brown Snyder's death in the electric chair at Sing Sing prison. The next day, the *Daily News* ran a full-page photograph of the deceased Snyder, still shackled and strapped to the chair, under the headline, "DEAD!"

Watching the grainy film taken by Abraham Zapruder of the assassination of President John F. Kennedy on November 22, 1963, might also be considered voyeuristic. Internet viewers on websites such as YouTube are able to see, again and again, a violent death caught on tape and spectate at the horrified reaction of the president's wife, Jacqueline Kennedy, as she scrambled out of the back seat.

The problem of the voyeuristic consumption of real-life images of death and violence is compounded in the Internet era. Once released, even old videos can go viral and remain forever available and easy to access. For example, television footage of Pennsylvania politician Budd Dwyer committing suicide by shooting himself in the mouth at a press conference in 1987 circulates now, more than a quarter-century later, on websites with names such as BestGore.com. While some television stations in 1987 chose, due to principles of journalism ethics, not to air the entire video and stopped short of showing the gunshot, today there is nothing stopping voyeurs on the Internet from repeatedly viewing it all.

Perhaps no example better illustrates this Internet-driven predicament over VADV than the case of Nikki Catsouras. She died in a gruesome car accident on Halloween in 2006 when the Porsche she was driving at more than 100 miles per hour slammed into a highway tollbooth. When members of the California Highway Patrol (CHP) arrived to investigate, at least one officer took photos of Catsouras's bloody, scalped, and nearly decapitated body in the crushed car. Two officers later admitted releasing the photographs to friends, and the images soon wound up on more than 2,500 websites, many of which contained jokes about the graphic photos. The parents of Catsouras successfully sued the CHP in *Catsouras v. California Highway Patrol* and ultimately reached a settlement of about $2.37 million in January 2012.

Sounds of death also make for voyeuristic listening fodder that seemingly satisfies some people's morbid and prurient interests. This is particularly true with 911 emergency calls involving celebrities that become part of the public record. For instance, in early 2012, an emergency phone call was made on behalf of actress Demi Moore. The caller is heard stating that Moore is shaking, convulsing, semi-conscious, and cannot speak. The incident prompted one California lawmaker to propose legislation that would shield such calls from public disclosure. Even when celebrities are not involved, 911 tapes can make for VADV fodder in the national media. That was the situation in 2010 when a 7-year-old boy from Norwalk, California, made a 911 call while hiding in a bathroom after three armed men broke into his home and held his parents at gunpoint. The tape, parts of which were played on news broadcasts and shows such as *Anderson Cooper 360°*, included the young boy pleading for operator Monique Patino to send police and soldiers to save him and his 6-year-old sister. The gunmen are heard breaking into the bathroom and yelling at the children, who ultimately were not physically harmed. The tape exists today on multiple websites. While it certainly made for voyeuristic listening, the tape also demonstrated the boy's courage and the operator's calm demeanor.

Legislative Pushback

In response to the VADV trend, some lawmakers are taking steps to protect familial privacy rights and to prevent the public release by government agencies of images of the dead. These laws only affect documents in the possession of government officials, such as coroners and the police. They are designed to balance the public's right to know with familial privacy concerns.

In 2011 Florida adopted a law, Florida Statute § 406.136, which generally prohibits government agencies and officials from disclosing photos, videos, and audio recordings that depict or record the killing of a person. Although surviving spouses may view such images and hear such recordings if they desire, the public and news media can only access them by proving to a judge that there is good cause for their disclosure. In making this determination, Florida judges must weigh three factors: whether the disclosure is necessary for public evaluation of governmental performance; the seriousness of the intrusion into the deceased's family's right to privacy; and whether similar information is already available in some other form. Those factors strike a balance between the public's right to know and the familial privacy interests of the deceased's relatives.

The Florida law was adopted partly in response to the death of Dawn Brancheau in early 2010. She drowned when a killer whale she was training at SeaWorld in Orlando, Florida, dragged her under water. Photographs and videos depicting Brancheau's death, including an underwater surveillance tape, ended up in the hands of local government officials, as well as the U.S. Occupational Safety and Health Administration. News organizations sought their release to determine whether better safety procedures might have saved Brancheau's life. Conversely, Brancheau's relatives tried to halt their release to protect their own privacy interests and to stop voyeuristic gawking.

In 2010 Georgia adopted the Meredith Emerson Memorial Privacy Act. The act exempts from Georgia's public records laws crime scene photos and videos, including ones produced by government agencies and by criminal perpetrators, that depict or describe a dismembered, decapitated, or mutilated person. Set forth in the Official Code of Georgia Archives § 45–16–27, the act allows disclosure of such images only if a judge determines the public interest in them outweighs privacy concerns asserted by the deceased person's next of kin. A trio of factors mirroring the Florida statute is used by judges in making this decision. The Georgia law was enacted after a journalist writing about Gary Michael Hilton, who was convicted of killing Meredith Emerson by cutting off her head along a Georgia hiking trail, asked the Georgia Bureau of Investigation for its file on Hilton pursuant to Georgia's open records law. The file contained photos of Emerson's nude, decapitated body. After Emerson's relatives went to court to prevent their release, Georgia lawmakers sprang into action to adopt the law ensuring the images would not be disseminated. This law and others like it censor real-life violent content in the name of protecting familial privacy interests.

Clay Calvert

See also Censorship of Violent Content; Legislating Media Violence: Law and Policy; National Television Violence Study; Realism of Violent Content, Real-World Violence on Television, and Their Effects; Television Violence

Further Readings

American Psychiatric Association. (2000). *Diagnostic and statistical manual of mental disorders* (4th ed., rev. text). Washington, DC: Author.

Baruh, L. (2009). Publicized intimacies on reality television: An analysis of voyeuristic content and its contribution to the appeal of reality programming. *Journal of Broadcasting and Electronic Media, 53*(2), 190–210.

Baruh, L. (2010). Mediated voyeurism and the guilty pleasure of consuming reality television. *Media Psychology, 13,* 201–221.

Calvert, C. (2000). *Voyeur nation: Media, privacy, and peering in modern culture.* Boulder, CO: Westview.

Catsouras v. California Highway Patrol, 181 Cal. App. 4th 856 (2010).

Doyle, T. (2009). Privacy and perfect voyeurism. *Ethics and Information Technology, 11,* 181–189.

Metzel, J. M. (2004). Voyeur nation? Changing definitions of voyeurism, 1950–2004. *Harvard Review of Psychiatry, 12*(2), 127–131.

CULTURE OF VIOLENCE

According to many theories, violence occurs when there is a breakdown in the social order and norms are no longer strong enough to rein in individuals' aggressive impulses. However, in a culture of violence, the opposite is true. Thus, in a culture of violence, aggression is often considered legitimate or even required by social norms.

The label "culture of violence" is usually a misnomer for what anthropologists call a "culture of honor." This distinction in terms is crucial in many cases, because "culture of violence" implies a culture in which any sort of violence is acceptable, whereas "culture of honor" implies a culture in which there are social norms that define some sorts of violence (and not simply any violence) as legitimate. People outside an honor culture often do not know the rules and cannot understand why people in honor cultures may hurt and kill one another over what seem like trivial matters (name calling, arguments over small amounts of money, an accident in which one person steps on another's shoes, and so on). Not understanding the cultural logic, those outside an honor culture may see a "culture of violence" defined by seemingly random or psychotic acts of aggression. This entry focuses on the culture of honor, specifically on its logic, development, and differences from other types of culture.

The logic of a culture of honor, however, defines one's honor in terms of the respect one can claim from others and the respect that others accord one. The latter element is crucial, because a person who does not have respect from others does not have honor, no matter how much self-respect he or she might have. For men, respect may be claimed based on one's virtue or virility (both are from the same Latin root word, *vir,* meaning man). Thus, a man of honor makes a claim based on a reputation for correct conduct (defined by the norms of his group) and a masculinity that asserts itself and makes it known that he will brook no disrespect. Thus, an honorable person needs to respond to threats, insults, and affronts, often with violence.

Honor norms such as these usually develop in places where there is inadequate enforcement of the law. In such places, there is no one to defend a person, no one to punish those who infringe on his or her rights, and no one to enforce agreements. Not being able to turn to the law, a person has to depend on him- or herself for protection. Insults or trivial incidents often take on extreme importance in these environments because these insults can be seen as probes or tests of one's mettle. A person who establishes that he or she will not tolerate even trivial infringements or slights establishes a reputation as one who cannot be messed with—on small matters and thus on big matters too.

Honor cultures can be distinguished from other sorts of cultures, such as a culture of *dignity* or a culture of *face.* In a culture of dignity, each person has inherent worth that is inalienable—it does not need to be socially conferred, and it can never be taken from the person. In a dignity culture, unlike an honor culture, one's worth is thus impervious to insults. The motto "Sticks and stones will break my bones but names will never hurt me" is an apt expression of this ideal. In a face culture, like a culture of honor, reputation is extremely important.

However, the context of face cultures is usually much different from that of honor cultures. Whereas honor springs up from milieus where the state is weak and self-protection is necessary, face cultures emerge in contexts where there is a well-established, settled hierarchy. In a face culture, one is entitled to respect for adequate performance of one's social role within the hierarchy; however, it is essential that one not overreach on status claims. Humility and harmony are key ingredients in a face culture because they allow the hierarchical system to function smoothly and with a minimum of turmoil. Insults and affronts are important in face cultures, but—unlike in honor cultures, where a person has to defend him- or herself and punish anyone who crosses him or her—punishments in face cultures are carried out by the group or administered by someone higher up in the hierarchy. Violent retribution for personal affronts in a face culture is to be eschewed for the sake of the overall harmony of the system.

Despite the emphasis on masculine honor, women in honor cultures also play extremely important roles. Their roles tend to be more variable across different sorts of honor cultures. Women may be repositories of family honor (needing to uphold norms of chastity and fidelity), they may act as enforcers of honor norms (goading men and boys into violence), or they may also participate in the violence themselves.

Of course, honor cultures, dignity cultures, and face cultures usually do not exist in pure form, because most societies are an amalgam. However, cultures that are often offered as prototypes include honor cultures such as those in the Mediterranean (especially the Middle East), Latin America, and the South of the United States; dignity cultures such as those of the northern United States and parts of northern Europe; and face cultures such as those found in East Asia.

Often, labels for particular regions gloss over a great deal of variation within a particular place. For example, street gangs of the inner cities, the Mafia, and prison subcultures—all of which operate outside the law—frequently run according to honor norms, usually without regard to whether the larger surrounding culture is defined by ideals of dignity, honor, or face.

Cultural institutions often do reflect—and perpetuate—the norms prevalent in the wider culture. For example, in the South of the United States, the laws with respect to gun control and self-defense are more lenient than those of the North. In one field experiment, employers in the South of the United States were likely to respond more warmly to job applicants who were convicted of honor-related crimes as compared with their northern counterparts. Furthermore, in one experiment examining media portrayals, college newspapers in the South of the United States (versus the North) wrote stories about (fictional) honor-related violence in a way that was more sympathetic to the perpetrator of honor-related violence, with southern news stories including more facts that mitigated his or her crime and made it seem more understandable. Thus, laws and policies, organizations and employers, and media portrayals often reinforce cultural norms about appropriate forms of violence.

Dov Cohen

See also Realism of Violent Content, Real-World Violence on Television, and Their Effects; Social Cognitive Theory; Social Learning From Media; Socialization of Violence in Media and Its Effects

Further Readings

Leung, A. K.-Y., & Cohen, D. (2011). Within- and between-culture variation: Individual differences and the cultural logics of honor, face, and dignity cultures. *Journal of Personality and Social Psychology, 100,* 507–526.

Nisbett, R., & Cohen, D. (1996). *Culture of honor.* Boulder, CO: Westview.

Peristiany, J. G. (Ed.). (1966). *Honour and shame: The values of Mediterranean society.* Chicago: University of Chicago Press.

Pitt-Rivers, J. (1968). Honor. In D. Sills (Ed.), *International encyclopedia of the social sciences* (pp. 509–510). New York, NY: Macmillan.

CYBERBULLYING, DEFINITION AND EFFECTS OF

When most people think of bullying, they conjure up images of two or more young people on the school playground verbally and/or physically harassing one another. Although this traditional form of bullying remains, recent years have witnessed another form of bullying known as *cyberbullying*. As discussed in this entry, although cyberbullying shares a number of features with traditional bullying, the two types of bullying differ from each other in critical ways. This entry defines cyberbullying, including an examination of factors that have impeded the development of a clear conceptualization of cyberbullying. Following this is an examination of the effects of cyberbullying for both victims and perpetrators.

Defining Cyberbullying

Although precise definitions of cyberbullying vary across studies, cyberbullying is generally defined as aggression that is intentionally and repeatedly carried out through an electronic venue (e.g., e-mail, blogs, instant messages, text messages, online games) against a target who cannot easily defend himself or herself. Importantly, though, researchers have had difficulty reaching a consensus on how to define cyberbullying. Varying definitions means that these same researchers are also then measuring cyberbullying in slightly different ways. Several variables that have impeded the ability of investigators to arrive at a common definition are discussed in the following paragraphs.

One key factor that has interfered with both the conceptualization and measurement of cyberbullying behavior is that cyberbullying can take many different forms. Nancy Willard (2006) has created a taxonomy of cyberbullying behaviors that illustrates the array of possible behaviors: flaming (i.e., an online fight), exclusion (i.e., removing or blocking individuals from listservs or buddy lists), harassment (i.e., repetitive, offensive messages sent to a particular target), impersonation (i.e., pretending to be the victim and electronically sending negative and inappropriate communications as if they were coming from the victim himself or herself), outing and trickery (i.e., soliciting personal information from someone and then electronically sharing that information with others without that person's consent), sexting, video recording of assaults or happy slapping and hopping (i.e., digitally recording physical assaults and then uploading the video to the Internet), and cyberstalking (i.e., stalking another person through the use of repeated threatening electronic communications). Given this list, identifying whether a particular electronic communication is or is not cyberbullying has, at times, proven to be elusive.

A second difficulty affecting the manner in which researchers conceptualize cyberbullying is that there are so many different venues through which the behavior can be perpetrated. Among these venues are electronic mail, text messages, instant messaging, online games, web pages, chat rooms, social network sites, and so on. Which venue emerges as the most common method for cyberbullying perpetration typically reflects the most common type of technology being used by a particular group of individuals. For example, among adolescents sampled over the years, instant messaging has been a common means of communicating online. Not surprisingly, then, it has also emerged as a common means of cyberbullying perpetration and victimization. As technology changes, however, so too will the means by which cyberbullying occurs. Toward that end, trends suggest that social network sites and text messaging are emergent venues of choice for cyberbullying.

Traditional Bullying Versus Cyberbullying

Given the extensive research attention that has been devoted to traditional bullying, particularly since the school shootings at Columbine High School near Littleton, Colorado, in 1999, one is inclined to think that our knowledge of cyberbullying should be well informed by our knowledge of traditional bullying. This is true to a degree in that traditional bullying and cyberbullying do share key features in common. Both traditional bullying and cyberbullying are acts of aggression that are typically repeated over time and that occur among individuals who have unequal amounts of power. This power may be reflected in physical differences, verbal acuity, social status, or technological expertise, to name a few. Even the perceived anonymity that often accompanies cyberbullying may give one individual more power over another.

Yet despite these elements that the two types of bullying have in common, they also differ in several critical ways. First, although people are never as anonymous as they perceive themselves to be, perpetrators of cyberbullying often hide behind screen names or send their communications from another person's account (i.e., impersonation, described earlier). In one study conducted in 2007 by Robin Kowalski and Susan Limber, just under 50% of the targets of cyberbullying reported that the perpetrator was a stranger or that they didn't know his or her identity. The anonymity that often accompanies cyberbullying opens up the pool of potential perpetrators. Research in social psychology on deindividuation has demonstrated that people will say and do things anonymously that they would not say and do in face-to-face interactions. Thus, individuals who might not consider engaging in face-to-face forms of bullying may, in fact, engage in electronic bullying, perhaps in retaliation for occurrences of traditional bullying.

There is another downside attached to the perceived anonymity of electronic communications. When people communicate face to face, perpetrators can read the emotional impact their behavior is having on the victim, and victims can more easily read the intent behind a perpetrator's behavior. With electronic communications, these markers of impact and intent are missing. Therefore, many perpetrators may be unaware of the full extent to which they are harming their victims, and some victims may misread the meaning behind the perpetrators' communications.

Cyberbullying and traditional bullying also differ in accessibility. Most traditional bullying occurs at school during the school day. Victims of cyberbullying, however, may be targeted at any time during the day or night. For example, people can leave posts on websites whenever they desire. Similarly, text messages can be sent at any time, even if the target doesn't check those messages. The nature of such electronic communications also opens up the potential audience relative to traditional bullying. Hundreds or thousands of people may see electronic posts on websites, and e-mails may be sent to hundreds of people at once.

Cyberbullying and traditional bullying also differ in the punitive fears attached to the behavior. With both traditional bullying and cyberbullying, victims show a strong reluctance to report their victimization. However, victims' reservations in reporting occur for different reasons. Victims of traditional bullying are reluctant to report their bullying because they fear that the individual who has been bullying them will find out and revictimize them. Targets of cyberbullying, however, fear that reporting their victimization will lead people in positions of authority (e.g., parents, teachers) to remove the means by which they are being victimized. Not wanting to have their technology taken away, they choose not to tell.

Cyberbullying and traditional bullying also are suspected to differ in the role that bystanders play. Most traditional bullying situations occur in the presence of others who typically adopt the role of bystanders or witnesses. Although these bystanders may not actively participate in the bullying, their failure to act on behalf of the victim can be taken as support for the bully. The role of the bystander in cyberbullying situations is a bit different and sometimes inadvertent. In a virtual chat room, the role of the bystander most closely resembles that in a traditional bullying situation, whereby the bystander simply "stands by" and witnesses online bullying occur between a victim and a perpetrator. However, in other cases, a bystander may engage in "cyberbullying by proxy," whereby another person uses the bystander's username to engage in cyberbullying. Alternatively, someone might forward an inappropriate e-mail or text message not having paid full attention to the content or without thinking about the impact of that behavior on the target.

In addition to the conceptual similarities and differences between cyberbullying and traditional bullying, researchers have empirically examined the overlap between the two types of bullying. Not surprisingly, the degree of overlap depends on the study being examined and the method by which the cyberbullying and traditional bullying are being perpetrated. However, involvement in the two types of bullying does appear to be related. Kowalski and her colleagues Chad Morgan and Susan Limber (2012) mapped out the direction of these relationships and found that involvement in traditional bullying, as either victim or perpetrator, bears the strongest relationships to involvement in cyberbullying as either victim or perpetrator. They also found that these relationships were stronger for females than for males.

Prevalence of Cyberbullying

The manner in which cyberbullying is conceptualized influences the prevalence rates that are reported. For example, researchers who ask a global question such as "Have you ever been cyberbullied?" tend to get very different prevalence rates than those who gather summary statistics from a series of questions asking whether participants have been cyberbullied through instant messaging, e-mail, text messaging, in a chat room, or on a website.

Prevalence rates are also tied to variations in the time parameters that are being used to assess cyberbullying. Researchers who ask whether cyberbullying has occurred within someone's lifetime will get much higher rates of occurrence than those who ask whether it has occurred within the past two months. Prevalence rates also vary with the criterion used to assess that cyberbullying has, in fact, occurred. Whereas some studies use a strict criterion that the behavior must have occurred two to three times a month or more, other studies use a more liberal criterion that the behavior need only have occurred once to be labeled as cyberbullying.

Finally, variability in prevalence rates also occurs with the age of the individuals sampled. Throughout most of cyberbullying's short history, its researchers have focused most of their attention on adolescents, believing that this is the population most likely to engage in this type of behavior. In the past couple of years, however, more attention has been given to prevalence estimates of cyberbullying among college students and older adults. In general, prevalence rates for cyberbullying victimization range from 10% to 40% among adolescent samples. Self-reported rates for perpetration tend to be somewhat lower, in the 7% to 12% range, depending on the study. In a 2012 study by Robin Kowalski, Gary Giumetti, Amber Schroeder, Heather Reese, more than 30% of college student respondents indicated that their first experience with cyberbullying occurred when they were in college. Among those who had also been cyberbullied in middle and high school, more than 40% said that the majority of the cyberbullying that they experienced occurred during college.

Effects of Cyberbullying

The consequences that follow from cyberbullying include the physical, psychological, social, and academic effects that the experience has for the victim and the perpetrator as well as the response that the victim offers to the perpetrator. Responses to cyberbullying vary widely, due in part to differences in the way individuals appraise the situation. These responses can range from doing nothing, a common response, to victims murdering the perpetrator or committing suicide. According to Richard Lazarus, people confronted with a potentially stressful situation engage in both primary and secondary appraisal. With primary appraisal, they evaluate whether the situation will have no effect on them, improve their well-being, or be stressful. If the situation is perceived as stressful, then individuals evaluate the harm, threat, and challenge posed by that situation and engage in a secondary appraisal process by which they determine whether they have the resources to deal with the stressful situation. This appraisal model highlights why victims and perpetrators frequently view cyberbullying situations very differently. Perpetrators appraise their behavior as having no impact on the well-being of the victim, whereas targets perceive the behavior as stressful. Additionally, the appraisal model illustrates why two victims might be affected differently by being targets of cyberbullying. One may appraise the situation as

less stressful than another and/or perceive that he or she has better resources to cope with the electronic bullying. Thus, the response of this individual to the cyberbullying will differ greatly from that of an individual who perceives the cyberbullying to be very threatening and who perceives himself or herself as having few resources to cope with it.

As a function of this appraisal process, additional physical, psychological, social, and academic outcomes of cyberbullying follow. These effects often mirror those that follow traditional bullying. Cyberbullying has been tied to tobacco, alcohol, and drug use, as well as eating disorders, anxiety and depression, reduced self-esteem, loneliness, and suicidal ideation. Targets of cyberbullying are also more likely to have poorer relationships with parents and peers than those not involved in cyberbullying. They also report being absent from school more, receiving lower grades, and having more difficulty concentrating compared with youth not involved with cyberbullying. Victims report experiencing a range of emotions including anger, sadness, embarrassment, fear, hurt, and confusion. These effects appear to be particularly strong for younger victims. As noted earlier, unlike victims of traditional bullying, victims of cyberbullying are unable to escape their victimization when they leave the schoolyard. Furthermore, the public nature of cyberbullying increases the potential humiliation that the victim may experience at the hands of the perpetrator.

The majority of the research on the consequences of cyberbullying has focused on targets of cyberbullying. Thus, we know less about the effects of this behavior on perpetrators. What we do know to date, however, is that, although perpetrators often report initially feeling positive emotions such as happiness after engaging in cyberbullying, they too experience negative effects of the behavior. Relative to those not involved with cyberbullying, perpetrators have been shown to have lower self-esteem, poorer academic performance, higher rates of substance abuse, increased loneliness, poorer social relationships, higher incidences of traditional bullying, and higher rates of delinquent behaviors. Some perpetrators also report feeling guilt and remorse following their cyberbullying behavior.

The group that seems to experience the most negative effects of cyberbullying is the bully/victim group. This group consists of the individuals who have been both victims of and perpetrators of cyberbullying. Even relative to victims only and bullies only, cyber bully/victims experience even higher levels of depression, anxiety, and suicidal ideation and lower levels of self-esteem and physical health.

The long-term effects of cyberbullying appear to be as bad if not worse than those attached to traditional bullying. In comparing the effects of cyberbullying and traditional bullying, however, it is important to keep in mind that many of the individuals involved in one type of bullying are also involved in the other type of bullying. This is important for prevention and intervention efforts directed at cyberbullying. Parents, administrators, and school counselors working with students who are involved with either type of bullying should immediately inquire whether the students are also involved in any other type of bullying.

Conclusion

In spite of conceptual and measurement issues that have plagued research on cyberbullying, as they do any relatively new research topic, the fact remains that cyberbullying is a problem among children and adults of all ages. The different venues by which cyberbullying can occur have presented problems in defining cyberbullying, but they present even more problems in the fact that they are ever-changing. This is confounded by the fact that the youth who are experiencing cyberbullying as either victims or perpetrators are digital natives who are trying to be helped by adults who are digital immigrants. This digital divide calls for the need for communication as everyone (e.g., students, teachers, administrators, parents, coworkers, supervisors, communities) works together to decrease the frequency with which cyberbullying occurs so that the negative effects stemming from it can be curbed.

Robin M. Kowalski

See also Aggressive Behavior; Bullying, Definition and Laws; Cyberbullying, Violent Content in; Cyberbullying Laws; Internet Violence, Influence on Society

Further Readings

Hinduja, S., & Patchin, J. W. (2008). Cyberbullying: An exploratory analysis of factors related to offending and victimization. *Deviant Behavior, 29,* 129–156.

Kowalski, R. M., Giumetti, G. W., Schroeder, A. W., & Reese, H. H. (2012). Cyber bullying among college students: Evidence domains of college life. In C. Wankel & L. Wankel (Eds.), *Misbehavior online in higher education* (pp. 293–321). Bingley, UK: Emerald.

Kowalski, R. M., & Limber, S. E. (2007). Electronic bullying among middle school students. *Journal of Adolescent Health, 41,* S22-S30.

Kowalski, R. M., Limber, S. E., & Agatston, P. W. (2012). *Cyberbullying: Bullying in the digital age.* Malden, MA: Wiley/Blackwell.

Kowalski, R. M., Morgan, C. A., & Limber, S. E. (2012). Traditional bullying as a potential warning sign of cyberbullying. *School Psychology International.*

Mason, K. L. (2008). Cyberbullying: A preliminary assessment for school personnel. *Psychology in the Schools, 45,* 323–348.

Patchin, J. W., & Hinduja, S. (Eds.). (2012). *Cyberbullying prevention and response.* New York, NY: Routledge.

Smith, P. K., Mahdavi, J., Carvalho, M., Fisher, S., Russell, S., & Tippett, N. (2008). Cyberbullying: Its nature and impact in secondary school pupils. *Journal of Child Psychology and Psychiatry, 49,* 376–385.

Tokunaga, R. S. (2010). Following you home from school: A critical review and synthesis of research on cyber bullying victimization. *Computers in Human Behavior, 26,* 277–287.

Willard, N. (2006). *Cyber bullying and cyberthreats: Responding to the challenge of online social cruelty, threats, and distress.* Eugene, OR: Center for Safe and Responsible Internet Use.

Ybarra, M. L., Boyd, D., Korchmaros, J. D., & Oppenheim, J. (2012). Defining and measuring cyberbullying within the larger context of bullying victimization. *Journal of Adolescent Health, 51*(1), 53–58.

CYBERBULLYING, VIOLENT CONTENT IN

Cyberbullying moves traditional bullying activities into the digital realm and adds new forms of aggression to the bully arsenal. It has become a significant issue for technology-savvy children and adolescents. This entry focuses on violent content in cyberbullying. It begins by defining cyberbullying and describing types of violent cyberbullying. It then gives specific examples of aggressive acts in high-profile cyberbullying cases before shifting to a review of research on the prevalence of different forms of cyberbullying.

Definition and Types of Violent Cyberbullying

According to noted experts Sameer Hinduja and Justin Patchin (2009), cyberbullying is defined as willful and repeated harm inflicted through electronic devices such as computers and cell phones. It may happen via e-mail or text messages, in chat rooms, on websites or social networking services, and in online video games or other virtual worlds. The channel through which cyberbullying takes place may affect the types of violent content possible, ranging from text-only to richer forms of aggression such as photos and video. Although bullying was around long before computers and other newer media technologies, Hinduja and Patchin identify distinguishing characteristics of cyberbullying: it can be anonymous; there is less inhibition about doing it; it is largely unsupervised; and it can potentially go viral, with content rapidly spreading among a large number of people.

Several common types of cyberbullying content have been identified, many of which may involve violence. Violent types of cyberbullying include the following:

Flaming, an Internet term for the communication of hostile or insulting messages online. This form of verbal aggression typically occurs without provocation in public forums such as chat rooms and discussion boards simply to personally attack an individual and/or incite his or her emotions.

Photoshopping (a reference to the Adobe Photoshop program), which, in the context of cyberbullying, involves modifying images or photos of a victim in a manner that embarrasses or otherwise harms him or her. This is often done by placing a photo of a person in some other environment or on another body. It could also extend to the doctoring of a photo to make it seem like a cyberbullying victim was the target or perpetrator of some violent act(s). For example, a victim's photo could be modified to make it look like he or she was beat up (such as through the addition of blood or bruises), or a gun or other weapon could be added to a victim's photo to make it appear as if he or she is violent.

Happy slapping (a term that originated in the United Kingdom) refers to an assault against an unsuspecting victim that is recorded (usually with a cell phone camera) and shared online. As noted by Hinduja and Patchin, happy slapping links traditional bullying with cyberbullying, since it entails physical, real-world abuse by a bully against a victim (as in traditional bullying) that is captured in digital form. The resultant photo or video can then be sent to others online, a phenomenon that has been enabled by sharing sites such as Facebook and YouTube.

Impersonation as a form of cyberbullying entails assuming the online identity of a victim (such as a Facebook or Twitter account with their name) and posting false, embarrassing, or incriminating information that appears to have come from them. This can be done by hacking into an account of a victim or creating a fake account under the victim's name.

Bombing involves using an automated computer program to send thousands of messages at the same time to a victim's e-mail account, causing it to fail or be disabled. As noted by researchers Esther Calvete, Izaskun Orue, Ana Estevez, Lourdes Villardon, and Patricia Padilla, this is a form of aggression with no parallel in traditional bullying. It could extend to other forms of malice by cyberbullies intended to disrupt the ability of a victim to use devices or applications.

Physical threats, finally, encompass any online activities by bullies that involve threatening a victim's safety or well-being. Physical threats are one of the most obvious forms of violent cyberbullying, and according to Hinduja and Patchin, it is the type of violent content online that warrants immediate attention from authorities, in the wake of high-profile incidents like the 1999 shootings at Columbine High School near Littleton, Colorado. Hinduja and Patchin reported that Columbine shooter Eric Harris threatened in a web diary to "kill and injure as many of you pricks as I can" (a blatant example of a physical threat) before the eventual attack on his classmates and teachers. Although reported by a parent months before the shootings, law enforcement officials failed to act on this evidence, something they would be much more likely to do today.

These represent specific types of cyberbullying, although there may be more. In a 2009 study reviewing the literature on cyberbullying, Heidi Vandebosch and Katrien Van Cleemput took a slightly different approach to characterizing content in cyberbullying. They first considered characteristics of traditional bullying and then extended them into similar and new bullying activities online. According to the authors, traditional bullying is direct and involves physical abuse such as punching. It can also be direct through property damage, verbal and nonverbal abuse, and social exclusion. Cyberbullying also has direct, physical forms, but in the digital world. Property damage can occur through bombing or sending viruses. Verbal abuse occurs through flaming. Nonverbal abuse may happen through the transmission of threatening images to a victim. And social exclusion may happen through exclusion from online groups. In addition, Vandebosch and Cleemput suggested that cyberbullying has indirect forms with no parallel in traditional bullying. These include (a) "outing" of entrusted information sent via e-mail or through some other private digital channel; (b) "masquerading," which is similar to what others have called impersonation; (c) spreading gossip through digital channels; and (d) taking part in an defamatory polling websites, such as those that ask to rate the attractiveness of victims. Within Vandebosch and Cleemput's typology, direct bullying forms (both real world and virtual) would be more likely to include violent content or be considered violent.

Case Examples of Violent Cyberbullying

To get a clearer picture of what particular types of violent content in cyberbullying look like, it is helpful to review case examples. These specific incidents also provide a depth of understanding concerning the phenomenon of cyberbullying in general. Since the advent of the Internet, several cases of cyberbullying have become high profile as a result of news media coverage. This section describes some of these incidents, with an emphasis on the violent content in them.

One of the most infamous examples of cyberbullying is the 2006 case of 13-year-old Missouri student Megan Meier. This incident included impersonation of a different type—the bully was a friend's mother (Lori Drew), who posed as a 16-year-old boy named Josh Evans on the social networking site MySpace. "Evans" befriended Meier before turning against her and becoming hostile. One of "his" last messages to her read, "You are a bad person and everybody hates you. Have a shitty rest of your life. The world would be a better place without you." Meier responded with "You're the kind of boy a girl would kill herself over." She committed suicide by hanging 20 minutes later. This incident received widespread attention and resulted in legislation against using the Internet for harassment.

Further examples of violent content are described on Drew Jackson's cyberbullying resource website. Lauren Newby, a Texas teen, was bullied by a former classmate on a web message board in 2001. An entire page on the site had the violent phrase "Die bitch queen!" repeated hundreds of times. Another post made fun of her multiple sclerosis by saying, "I guess I'll have to wait until you kill yourself which I hope is not long from now, or I'll have to wait until

your disease [M.S.] kills you." She was also called "a fat cow MOO BITCH" on the site, and this act of aggression escalated into offline violence. "MOO BITCH" was written in shaving cream outside of her house, and a bottle filled with acid was thrown at her front door.

In another incident from 2002, Canadian teen David Knight discovered that an entire website had been created to make fun of him. Visitors were asked to post comments against Knight and even his family, which resulted in pages of hateful comments. He was accused of being a pedophile and of using a date rape drug on young boys. E-mails were also directed at him, saying things like "You're gay, don't ever talk again, no one likes you, you're immature and dirty, go wash your face." A similar website was created in 2003 to insult and threaten a teen in England named Jodi Plumb. It made fun of her weight and even posted a date for her "death." A Michigan teen named Amanda Marcuson was bullied by classmates in 2004 after reporting them for stealing her makeup in class. She was called names via an instant messaging program when she got home, including "stuck up bitch." The bullying continued into the evening, and she was bombed by hostile messages on her cell phone while out, filling it to capacity.

Additional examples of violent content are spotlighted by Hinduja and Patchin in their book *Bullying Beyond the Schoolyard: Preventing and Responding to Cyberbullying* (2009). For example, a hate website was created by students in New Jersey in 2004 naming a school's "top five biggest homosexuals" and the "top 20 gayest guys and gayest girls." In another case from 2006, a seventh grader received e-mails threatening physical violence against her and family members because of their race. One line from a message read "all I got to say is that you better watch every move you make N***** and you can tell your older sister[s] the KKK will be after them [too] B****." In an example of happy slapping, six teenage girls were arrested in 2008 for kidnapping and assault after shooting a video of themselves beating up a female classmate. They intended to post the video online, in response to supposed negative comments made about them by the victim on MySpace.

Research on Cyberbullying Content

Although case examples give a depth of perspective on cyberbullying and help to humanize its victims, research on the phenomenon in general is also important to help gain a sense of the bigger picture. Almost all cyberbullying studies to date have involved surveys of young people designed to profile bullies and victims and document the prevalence and consequences of cyberbullying. Few (if any) content analyses have been done of cyberbullying, presumably because of difficulties with pooling a sample of such messages together. However, some surveys have asked young people about the types of cyberbullying they have experienced, and this is currently the best evidence available (beyond case examples) for general characteristics of violent content in cyberbullying.

In one of the largest and most relevant studies to date (published in 2010), Esther Calvete and colleagues surveyed 1,431 Spanish adolescents between the ages of 12 and 17 about cyberbullying behaviors. The researchers found that 44.1% of respondents engaged in at least one form of cyberbullying. Intentional exclusion from an online group was the most common type (20.2%), followed by posting negatives about a classmate on the Internet (20.1%), sending a link of such comments to others (16.8%), and hacking to send e-mails that could cause trouble for a classmate (18.1%). Note that these are not particularly violent forms of cyberbullying. Of the violent types described earlier, happy slapping was most common. The researchers uncovered two specific types of happy slapping: (1) videos of forcing others to do humiliating things (e.g., "cutting off the leg of a chair so they will fall when they sit and then recording them" or "making someone sing silly and then sending the video") (10.4%) and (2) videos of hitting or hurting another person (e.g., kicking a classmate or vagabond) (10.5%). Approximately 11% of respondents also reported sending happy slapping videos to others. Other violent or aggressive types of cyberbullying reported include sending threatening or insulting messages via e-mail (15.8%), sending threatening or insulting messages via cell phone (15.7%), and sending messages massively that include threats or are very intimidating (9.2%). Overall, boys displayed more cyberbullying behaviors than girls, with the differences most pronounced for happy slapping.

Vandebosch and Van Cleemput surveyed 2,052 primary and secondary school students (ages 10–18), with the goal of profiling bullies and victims of cyberbullying, in Belgium in 2005 for a study published in 2009. They also asked about the prevalence of what they called "potentially offensive Internet and mobile phone practices," or POP. The most frequent POP respondents reported being victimized by were threats or insults via e-mail or mobile phone

(33.7%). Vandebosch and Van Cleemput conducted their research before the ascension of social media, however, which somewhat limits the generalizability of their findings today.

Dorthy Wunmi Grigg studied cyberbullying through focus groups and individual interviews in a study published in 2010. Her British sample included a total of 32 primary school students, secondary school students, and adult participants (ages 8–54). All participants were asked open-ended questions related to cyberbullying. Results of thematic and interpretative phenomenological analyses revealed that the concept of cyberbullying may not capture the range of violent activities happening online, including those without repetition or imbalance of power as in many conceptualizations of cyberbullying. Grigg therefore suggests using a new concept, "cyber-aggression," to account for more types of violent online activity. Cyber-aggression would encompass all intentional harm inflicted through electronic means on a person or group (of any age) who perceive such activities as offensive, derogatory, harmful, or unwanted. This offers a broader approach to considering violent content online.

In *Bullying Beyond the Schoolyard: Preventing and Responding to Cyberbullying*, Hinduja and Patchin review the self-report studies conducted on cyberbullying before the publication of their book in 2009. In their most recent survey up to that point, of 1,963 middle school students in the United States, they found that 43% of respondents said they had experienced one or more of the following in the past 30 days: receiving an e-mail or instant message that made them upset, having something posted on their MySpace profile or a website that made them upset, being made fun of in a chat room, having something posted online that they didn't want others to see, or being afraid to go online. Their findings show that nearly half of respondents had an online experience that might be considered cyberbullying. The authors also charted several published studies of cyberbullying (by themselves and other authors) from 2002–2008 with percentages of adolescents in each who (a) reported being cyberbullied and (b) reported cyberbullying others. Both charts reveal a positive linear trend, suggesting that the problem of cyberbullying is getting worse over time.

Future Research

Much has been learned about cyberbullying through research, but more studies are needed, in particular content analyses. The research just reviewed gives some insight into cyberbullying content, but because it relies on self-report methods such as surveys and focus groups it may be missing some important aspects of cyberbullying messages, especially those related to violence. Content analyses can overcome the problems inherent in self-report techniques and provide a more accurate description of the form and content of violent cyberbullying messages, assuming a representative sample can be collected.

The international nature of cyberbullying research remains a strength and perhaps a weakness of this area of study. Because cyberbullying studies have been conducted in many different countries, it seems clear now that the problem exists all over the world. But this also raises questions about potential cultural differences in cyberbullying. Are patterns the same from nation to nation? To what extent do results in one country translate to others? Future research should compare cyberbullying across cultures and also document the prevalence and purveyors of cyberbullying in particular nations, such as the United States (where surprisingly little inquiry into cyberbullying has happened to date).

Cyberbullying research must also keep up with new technologies and applications, such as social media. As technologies and programs change, so may cyberbullying. Technological advancement even has the potential to alter some of the types of violent cyberbullying described earlier in this entry. For example, Photoshopping may become more video based as special effects software becomes more accessible and easy to use. Virtual (or computer-generated) representations of a victim might also be constructed and violently assaulted by bullies in purely digital form. This is already possible to an extent through avatar creation programs in video games, raising concerns about the potential for this kind of technology to be harnessed for the purpose of cyberbullying. As young people spend more of their lives online, bullies will likely find new ways to harass the digital selves of users, as they already have during the infancy of the Internet. Research in general can illuminate the problem of cyberbullying over time and help direct efforts at combating this pernicious new form of media violence. Automated computer content analysis programs could potentially be used to detect high-risk violent messages from cyberbullies and victims to prevent escalations of violence in the real world.

Paul Skalski and Julie Cajigas

See also Cyberbullying, Definition of; Cyberbullying, Effects of; Cyberbullying Laws

Further Readings

Calvete, E., Orue, I., Estevez, A., Villardon, L., & Padilla, P. (2010). Cyberbullying in adolescents: Modalities and aggressors' profile. *Computers in Human Behavior, 26*(5), 1128–1135.

Grigg, D. W. (2010). Cyber-aggression: Definition and concept of cyberbullying. *Australian Journal of Guidance and Counselling, 20,* 143–156.

Hinduja, S., & Patchin, J. W. (2009). *Bullying beyond the schoolyard: Preventing and responding to cyberbullying.* Thousand Oaks, CA: Sage.

Jackson, D. (n.d.). Examples of cyberbullying. Retrieved from http://www.slais.ubc.ca/courses/libr500/04–05-wt2/www/D_Jackson/examples.htm

Vandebosch, H., & Van Cleemput, K. (2009). Cyberbullying among youngsters: Profiles of bullies and victims. *New Media & Society, 11,* 1349–1371

CYBERBULLYING LAWS

With the advent of cybertechnologies, cyberbullying —bullying through electronic means—among children and youth has emerged as an issue of concern among youth, parents, educators, members of the media, and policy makers at the state and federal levels. Since 1999, legislators in nearly all states have passed laws addressing bullying, and many of these laws specifically address cyberbullying. These laws typically require that school districts develop policies to address bullying at school. In addition to these state anti-bullying laws, there are constitutional issues and other federal and state civil laws that affect how school personnel address bullying. There also are federal and state criminal laws that may criminalize some behaviors that are viewed as cyberbullying.

State Laws on Bullying and Cyberbullying

State laws on bullying did not exist prior to 1999. In the wake of the shootings at Columbine High School near Littleton, Colorado, there was a flurry of activity among state legislators, and within eight years, 30 states had passed laws on bullying. By 2012, 49 states had passed such laws. Laws addressing cyberbullying appeared somewhat later. In 2007 only five states had passed laws that explicitly addressed bullying through electronic communications, but within five years, the majority had done so.

Most state anti-bullying laws focus on the responsibilities of school personnel to address bullying. Typically, they require publicly funded school districts to develop policies about bullying. However, these laws vary dramatically in their definitions of bullying and cyberbullying and in the content and level of detail of their requirements. For example, some explicitly define bullying and note that it includes cyberbullying or bullying through electronic means; others fail to define bullying or leave it ambiguous as to whether cyberbullying is included within the scope of the law. Some laws apply to behavior that takes place only on school grounds or while using a school district's technology, such as when a student uses district-owned laptops or the district's computer networks when he or she is at home. Others cover behaviors that take place away from the school campus, even if a student is using his or her own technology, if the behavior creates a hostile environment at the school for a victim of bullying, if it infringes on the rights of a victim of bullying at school, or if it substantially disrupts the educational process. State anti-bullying laws also differ from one another in the extent to which they require or encourage the following: procedures for investigating incidents of bullying, disciplinary consequences for bullying, reporting of bullying incidents to district or state authorities, counseling or other support services for children involved in bullying, training for staff to address bullying, and prevention programs for students.

Other Relevant Federal and State Laws

Constitutional Provisions

Several amendments to the U.S. Constitution limit the ability of public school employees to restrict the speech of students, search student property, and discipline students for their speech. For example, under the First Amendment, student speech (including cyberspeech) is protected unless it is threatening; is lewd, vulgar, or profane; is (or appears to be) sponsored by the school; or disrupts the school or invades the rights of students. The Fourth Amendment's restrictions on unreasonable searches and seizures place some limits on the ability of school personnel to monitor and search Internet records for cyberbullying.

Federal and State Civil Rights Laws

Currently, there is no federal law against bullying or cyberbullying per se, but some victims of cyberbullying and their parents may sue public schools for damages under federal civil rights laws. Schools may violate an individual's civil rights if he or she is being harassed based on race, color, national origin, sex, or disability; if it is so serious that it creates a hostile environment; and if the harassment is not properly addressed by school personnel. Relevant civil rights laws are Title IX of the Education Amendments Act of 1972, which prohibits discrimination based on sex; Title VI of the Civil Rights Act of 1964, which prohibits discrimination on the basis of race, color, or national origin; and § 504 of the Rehabilitation Act of 1973 and Title II of the Americans with Disabilities Act, which prohibit discrimination on the basis of disability. State civil rights laws may have similar prohibitions.

State Negligence Laws

Under state negligence laws, students or their parents may sue school personnel for acting with negligence in responding (or failing to respond) to an incident of bullying. Negligence is a failure to exercise the level of care that a reasonable person would have exercised in a similar situation. It may involve doing something that a reasonable person would not have done, or failing to do what a reasonable person would have done in a similar context. Generally, an individual who sues school personnel for negligence in a case of cyberbullying must show (a) that the school personnel had a duty to foresee dangers for students in their care and had a duty to take steps to prevent these dangers, (b) that the personnel did not use reasonable care in light of these foreseeable dangers, (c) that the failure of the school personnel was a substantial factor that led to a student being harmed, and (d) that there were actual harms caused to a student.

Federal and State Criminal Laws

There are many federal and state laws that criminalize some behaviors that also may be classified as bullying, including laws related to cyberstalking, obscene electronic communications, harassment, preventing or interfering with school attendance. Federal and state child pornography laws and state sexting statutes may also apply in cases where incidents involve images of minors. Federal and state hate crimes also may apply in some situations of cyberbullying.

Conclusion

Since cyberbullying is a relatively recent phenomenon, the laws surrounding cyberbullying are new and continue to evolve. In recent years, many states have developed anti-bullying laws that require public schools to develop policies that address electronic forms of bullying (or cyberbullying). In addition to these state anti-bullying laws, there are constitutional considerations and civil and criminal laws that also must be considered. There remain uncertainties about how U.S. law may apply to forms of cyberspeech, particularly forms of cyberspeech that occur off school grounds.

Susan P. Limber

See also Bullying, Definition and Laws of; Cyberbullying, Definition and Effects of; Cyberbullying, Violent Content in; Internet Violence Laws; Legislating Media Violence: Law and Policy

Further Readings

Alley, R., & Limber, S. P. (2009). Legal issues for school personnel. In S. M. Swearer, D. L. Espelage, & S. A. Napolitano (Eds.), *Bullying prevention and intervention: Realistic strategies for schools* (pp. 53–73). New York, NY: Guilford.

Kowalski, R. M., Limber, S. P., & Agatston, P. (2012). *Cyber bullying: Bullying in the digital age* (2nd ed.). Malden, MA: Wiley/Blackwell.

Sacco, D. T., Silbaugh, K., Corredor, F. Casey, J., & Dohert, D. (2012). *An overview of state anti-bullying legislation and other related laws.* Retrieved from http://cyber.law.harvard.edu/sites/cyber.law.harvard .edu/files/State_Anti_bullying_Legislation_Overview_ 0.pdf

Srabstein, J., Berkman, B. E., & Pyntikova, E. (2008). Anti-bullying legislation: A public health perspective. *Journal of Adolescent Health, 42,* 11–20.

U.S. Department of Education, Office of Planning, Evaluation and Policy Development, Policy and Program Studies Service. (2011). *Analysis of state bullying laws and policies.* Washington, DC: EMT Associates.

Willard, N. (2007). *Cyber bullying and cyberthreats: Responding to the challenge of online social aggression, threats, and distress.* Champaign, IL: Research Press.

DEMOGRAPHIC EFFECTS

Although it is not without controversy, the general consensus in the scientific community has been that exposure to violence in the media is one of the contributing factors in the development of aggressive behavior. It has also been recognized that a number of demographic features (individual difference variables) meaningfully affect this relationship. Not only is an understanding of the influence of these factors essential to identifying the likely outcomes of viewing violent media, such awareness is also critical to determining appropriate methods for mitigating harmful effects. Thus, these individual differences in audience members affect both susceptibility and resilience to potentially harmful media messages and the mechanisms that may be involved in managing unintended and/or unfavorable responses. After describing the prevalence of violence in media, this entry discusses various individual differences and types of violent content that can influence the effects of media violence.

How Prevalent Is Media Violence?

Concern about the effects of exposure to media violence has stemmed from decades of empirical content analytic research that revealed that violence and aggression are staples in U.S. media. Beginning with early research by George Gerbner and colleagues, it has been well documented that our media environment is rife with displays of glamorized violence. For example, findings from the National Television Violence Study (NTVS; Smith et al., 1998) revealed that approximately 60% of programs on television contain violence—averaging to roughly six distinct acts of violence per hour. Moreover, NTVS data indicated that few acts are associated with pain, harm, or other consequences and that the perpetrators of these violent acts are often attractive characters.

Although it is probably not surprising that movies and video games are even more likely than television to contain such displays of violence and aggression, children's programming is more violent than primetime programming. Indeed, research by Barbara J. Wilson and colleagues (2002) revealed that nearly 70% of children's shows contain violence—averaging approximately 14 acts per hour.

Given the overall prevalence of violence in the media, it is helpful to understand the factors that may play a role in enhancing or reducing the effects resulting from exposure. Although these variables are numerous, there are several that have particular importance related to exposure to violent media content.

Why Do Demographic Effects Matter?

Simply put, individual difference variables speak to the issue of susceptibility. For example, it is easy to see how age (and by association cognitive ability) may be an important consideration in predicting fright responses to violent media content, with children and young viewers more vulnerable to such an outcome than adult audiences. Thus, different effects and different degrees of such effects are likely to vary based on known characteristics of the consumers.

Gender

Research exploring the role of gender in violent media effects has generally found that males tend to enjoy such content more than do females and experience less fear from exposure to such content. Notably, as meta-analytic evidence from Haejung Paik and George Comstock demonstrated, this content is also more likely to have a greater effect on males than females.

Children and Cognitive Development

Cognitive development has important implications for responses to violence in the media. Because younger children (e.g., preschoolers) are likely to pay greater attention to the physical and concrete features of stimuli (as opposed to internal motives of characters or conceptual features of media messages), there is greater potential for younger viewers to be influenced by attractive, likeable media models whose violent actions have gone unpunished. Moreover, younger children are less likely to distinguish fantasy from reality, increasing the potential for even cartoon depictions to serve as models of behavior. In addition, because temporal contiguity is important for the comprehension of media messages among young children, when the consequences of violent actions are separated by time from the behavior itself (e.g., separate scenes, complex plotlines, commercial breaks), they are less likely to be understood. To illustrate, early research by W. Andrew Collins (1973) demonstrated that younger viewers report greater aggressive responses when punishments for negative behaviors depicted in the media are temporally separated from the action.

Sensation Seeking

Sensation seeking is defined as a preference for and willingness to take risks to obtain intense and novel sensory experiences. Sensation seekers have been found to experience greater enjoyment from exposure to violent media content.

Empathy

Empathy can be defined as concern for the well-being of others and understanding of the emotions and feelings of others. Not surprisingly, then, the presence of empathy predicts that a viewer will experience less enjoyment of violent content in the media.

Aggression

Research has also demonstrated that those individuals who are higher in aggression reveal greater interest in and enjoyment of violent media content.

Machiavellianism

Similarly, those exhibiting Machiavellian personality (i.e., the tendency to use manipulation for personal gain) tend to experience greater enjoyment of violent media fare.

What Types of Violent Content Are Most Consequential?

Certainly, reactions to violent media are a function of the content features themselves, with individual difference variables more relevant (to a degree) to different features of the media. The research produced by the NTVS provides critical insights into these contextual cues.

Attributes of the Victim and Perpetrator

Attractive, likeable, and heroic perpetrators of violence are likely to encourage learning of aggression. Although this is the case for audience members of all ages, children view such features in a wider range of media models, including cartoon characters and fantasy figures. Although these attributes are also influential on the impact of exposure to the targets and victims of violence, in this case, these features are likely to encourage fear and anxiety in viewers.

Characteristics of Violence

Violence can be depicted in a number of ways. Notably, the type of presentation of violence has implications for the effects of exposure.

Graphicness, Realism, and Justification

Research on content features such as justification for violence, graphicness, realism, and use of weapons suggests that effects hold across all audiences. In other words, for males and females, young and old, and so on, justified violence (e.g., self-defense), as opposed to unjustified or malicious aggression, encourages imitation and learning. Similarly, the presence and/or use of weapons can encourage aggressive thoughts and behaviors in all audiences. Graphicness, particularly alongside prolonged exposure, can encourage desensitization and the learning of aggression. Finally, realism can encourage fright responses as well as aggressive attitudes or actions among both children and adults.

Pain and Suffering

When the targets of violence are seen to suffer or are associated with explicit injuries, both child and adult audiences are less likely to behave aggressively. Notably, however, such displays can prompt aggression in those prone to aggression.

Humor

The intersection of violence and humor is a complex issue and is represented in a variety of forms of entertainment. However, the work in this area provides limited and mixed conclusions with regard to (a) the influence of humor on aggression and (b) the influence of comedic displays of violence on subsequent aggression. In some cases, intense humor has been found to facilitate aggression, particularly among aggressive viewers. In other cases, the opposite was found. In other research, hostile humor (i.e., displays of violence or violent messages presented in a humorous manner) has been found to increase aggression among all audiences. Clearly, further research is needed to determine the nature of the relationship between humor and aggression.

Consequences of Violence: Rewards and Punishments

Ample research exists demonstrating that exposure to aggressive behavior that is positively reinforced encourages subsequent aggression. Notably, however, violence need not be rewarded in the media to encourage learning. Research by Albert Bandura (1965) demonstrated that among children, the failure to punish an otherwise antisocial behavior can serve as a reward, sanctioning the behavior. In other words, the absence of expected punishment or consequences prompts imitation and learning in the same manner as violence associated with an explicit reward.

Concluding Thoughts

Ultimately, the research on demographic effects suggests that not all audiences are equally susceptible or vulnerable to violent media. As such, these audience features are critical to understanding the nature and extent of the relationship between exposure and effects. Certainly, among the numerous factors known to affect this relationship (e.g., gender, aggression, empathy), the age/cognitive development

of the viewer appears to be among the most consequential. Furthermore, the features of media portrayals of violence appear to work in conjunction with the attributes of the consumer, influencing outcomes of exposure including learning, fear, and desensitization.

Dana Mastro

See also Aggression, Risk Factors of; Aggressive Behavior; General Aggression Model; Gender and Aggression; Comedic Violence, Effects of; National Television Violence Study; Social Cognitive Theory; Social Learning From Media

Further Readings

American Academy of Pediatrics. (2001). Media violence. *Pediatrics, 108,* 1222–1226.

Bandura, A. (1965). Influence of models' reinforcement contingencies on the acquisition of imitative response. *Journal of Personality and Social Psychology, 1,* 589–595.

Collins, W. A. (1973). Effect of temporal separation between motivation, aggression, and consequences: A developmental study. *Developmental Psychology, 8,* 215–221.

Gerbner, G., & Gross, L. (1976). Living with television: The violence profile. *Journal of Communication, 26,* 172–194.

Huesmann, L. R., Moise-Titus, J., Podolski, C., & Eron, L. (2003). Longitudinal relations between children's exposure to TV violence and their aggressive and violent behavior in young adulthood: 1977–1992. *Developmental Psychology, 39,* 201–221.

Oliver, M. B., & Krakowiak, M. (2009). Individual differences in media effects. In J. Bryant & M. B. Oliver (Eds.), *Media effects: Advances in theory and research* (pp. 517–531). Thousand Oaks, CA: Sage.

Smith, S., Wilson, B., Kunkel, D., Linz, D., Potter, J., Colvin, C., & Donnerstein, E. (1998). *National Television Violence Study* (Vol. 3). Thousand Oaks, CA: Sage.

Wilson, B., Smith, S., Potter, W. J., Kunkel, D., Linz, D., Colvin, C., & Donnerstein, E. (2002). Violence in children's television programming: Assessing the risks. *Journal of Communication, 52,* 5–35.

DESENSITIZATION EFFECTS ON SOCIETY

In the debate about potentially harmful effects of exposure to violent media, a central argument is that people who watch a lot of violent movies and television programs or play a lot of violent video games get used to the violence they see or enact in virtual reality and, as a consequence, find it less troublesome in the real world. This process is called "desensitization." According to the general aggression model (GAM), proposed by Craig A. Anderson and Brad J. Bushman (2001), desensitization to violence plays a key role in explaining how repeated exposure to violent media contributes to the development of an aggressive personality. This entry introduces desensitization as a theoretical concept for understanding how exposure to violent media may influence people's responses to real-world violence; presents research demonstrating desensitization in response to violent media stimuli; examines effects of desensitization on affect, cognition, and behavior; and discusses the implications of desensitization on users' media habits and learning opportunities for aggression.

Definition, Indicators, and Evidence of Desensitization

Desensitization is a general concept that refers to responses to emotionally charged stimuli. It describes the process by which a stimulus that initially elicits a strong physiological or emotional reaction becomes less and less capable of eliciting the response the more often it is presented. With each successive presentation, responses to the stimulus become weaker and eventually disappear altogether as the person habituates to the stimulus. In many domains of psychological functioning, desensitization is an adaptive process that over time enables individuals to reduce intense arousal and negative emotions associated with a particular stimulus. In the field of clinical psychology, the principle of desensitization has been applied successfully to the treatment of fear- and anxiety-related problems. In systematic desensitization therapy, patients are gradually exposed to the distressing stimulus while in a relaxed state of emotion and arousal that is incompatible with the negative emotional response evoked by the distressing stimulus.

With regard to violent stimuli, both in the media and the real world, desensitization can have a maladaptive effect. With repeated exposure, the initial fear response that people show when confronted with violence is weakened. This fear response, which is probably innate, is functional in alerting the organism to the threat of harm and activating protective behavior. It is associated with a negative

evaluation of violence and a strong desire to avoid it. Violence features prominently in the media, and it is presented as entertaining and rewarding. Thus, media violence meets the two critical conditions for desensitization: repeated exposure and a context incompatible with the negative emotional response to the distressing stimulus. Based on this reasoning, it is assumed that the more often people experience violence in the media, the less intense the fear response will be that is evoked by a violent media stimulus. This reduced fear response, in turn, is assumed to lead to a greater tolerance for violence; the disinhibition of aggressive behavior; reduced empathy with, and help for, victims of violence in the real world, and a weakening of moral evaluations of violence as wrong. The process of a decrease in negative emotions with repeated exposure to violent media stimuli is also called "habituation" to distinguish it from reduced responsiveness to real-life violence and greater propensity to show aggressive behavior, which is called "desensitization to real-life violence," in line with the differentiation suggested by Steven Kirsh (2012).

Desensitization to violence in the media can be apparent on three levels: (1) the level of arousal in the form of reduced physiological or neural reactivity, (2) the level of subjective emotional experience in the form of decreased fear and increased enjoyment of violent media presentations, and (3) the cognitive level in the form of a greater acceptance of violence as normal and acceptable. At the level of arousal, studies have used heart rate, blood pressure, skin conductance, or brain activity as indicators of desensitization. In a study with adolescents conducted by Maren Strenziok and colleagues (2011), short-term desensitization was demonstrated by a decrease in skin conductance, indicative of reduced arousal, in the course of watching violent videos. Using functional magnetic resonance imaging (fMRI) scans, this study also found a reduction in brain activity in the lateral orbitofrontal cortex involved in the regulation of emotional responses to situational stimuli. Furthermore, experimental studies have compared participants' responses to depictions of real-life violence on these physiological indicators following the presentation of either violent or nonviolent media stimuli. For example, in a study by Margaret H. Thomas, Robert W. Horton, Elaine C. Lippincott, and Ronald S. Drabman (1977), children who had previously seen an episode from a violent television program showed a lower galvanic skin response when presented with a videotape of a real-life altercation between other children than did those who had first seen a nonviolent television episode. Another study, conducted by Nicholas L. Carnagey, Anderson, and Bushman (2007), had college students play either a violent or a nonviolent video game before watching a videotape of real violence, showing that both heart rate and galvanic skin response while watching the scenes of real violence were lower among participants who had previously played the violent game.

Beyond demonstrating short-term desensitization in a single experimental session, there is evidence of long-term desensitization as a result of habitual use of violent media. Studies by Bruce D. Bartholow, Bushman, and Marc A. Sestir (2006), as well as by Strenziok and colleagues, have shown that habitual users of media violence displayed lower arousal to violent film clips and to depictions of real-life violence compared with people using violent media less frequently. This research has further shown that the reduced responsiveness by heavy users of media violence is specific to depictions of violent media stimuli and real-life violence and is not observed in response to nonviolent media contents and negative real-life stimuli unrelated to violence, such as images of disfigured babies.

At the level of subjective emotional states, there is further evidence of short-term as well as long-term desensitization to media violence. Patrícia Arriaga, Maria Benedicta Monteiro, and Francisco Esteves (2011) found that in the short run, playing a violent video game led to less discomfort when seeing images of real-life violence than playing a nonviolent video game. Barbara Krahé and colleagues also found that greater habitual use of violent media was linked to reduced anxious arousal by a violent film clip, but not anxious arousal by a sad clip. Desensitization as a result of frequent use of media violence not only is reflected in reduced negative affect, but it is also evidenced in greater enjoyment of violent media. Analyzing responses to a sequence of violent and funny film scenes, Kostas Fanti, Eric Vanman, Christopher Henrich, and Marios Avraamides (2009) found a curvilinear pattern of enjoyment for violent scenes across the sequence, with a decline after the first sequence followed by an increase after subsequent sequences. In contrast, enjoyment of the funny scenes showed a gradual decline. The study by Krahé and colleagues found that the higher people's habitual use of violent media, the more pleasant arousal they reported after watching a violent film clip, whereas habitual

media violence was unrelated to pleasant arousal to a funny clip.

Finally, evidence for cognitive desensitization comes from studies showing that both habitual use of violent media and short-term exposure to violent films or video games in experimental settings is linked to more positive attitudes about aggression and greater tolerance for violence.

Altogether, there is evidence of desensitization in reduced physiological arousal, reduced negative affect, and increased enjoyment of violence after short-term exposure to violent media stimuli and as a function of the habitual use of violent media over time. It was further shown that desensitization is specific to the violent content of the media stimuli and does not affect arousal and affective responses to other emotionally charged contents, such as sad or funny stimuli.

Effects of Desensitization

The weakening of the fear response through repeated exposure to violent media content is assumed to lead to several interlocking cognitive and affective outcomes that, in turn, affect both aggressive and prosocial behavior. The postulated paths from desensitization to increased aggression and reduced prosocial behavior are shown in Figure 1. In general terms, repeated exposure to violence in the context of entertainment is assumed to change the perception of real-life violence. It is less likely to be noticed, and seen as less serious, less condemnable, and more normal and acceptable. As a result of repeated exposure, media users develop a tolerance for violence as depicted in the media, and there is evidence that this tolerance translated into feelings, thoughts, and behaviors related to violence in the real world.

Decrease in Empathy and Disruption of Moral Evaluation

Desensitization to violence through exposure to violent media has been shown to decrease users' empathic concern for victims of real-life violence. Jeanne B. Funk and colleagues (2004) broadly define empathy as the capacity to perceive and experience the state of another person. It has a cognitive component in the form of perspective taking—that is, seeing the world from the point of view of another person—as well as an affective component in the form of sympathy or concern that involves sharing the feelings of the other person. There is evidence for both short-term effects of a single episode of

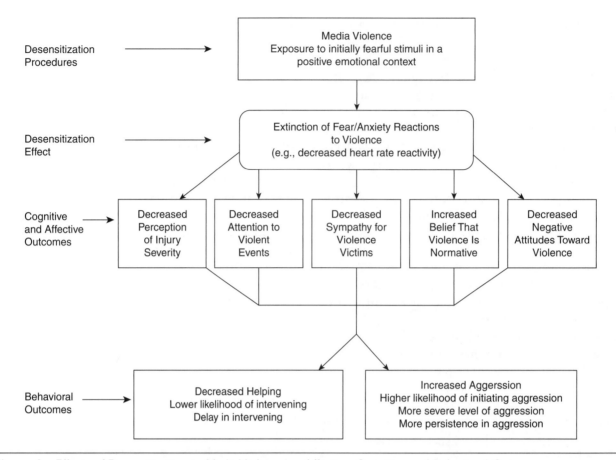

Figure 1   Effects of Desensitization to Media Violence on Affective, Cognitive, and Behavioral Outcomes

Source: Reprinted with permission from Bushman, B. J., & Anderson, C. A. (2009). Comfortably numb: Desensitizing effects of violent media on helping others. *Psychological Science,* 20, p. 274.

violent media use and long-term effects of habitual use of violent media, based on research with both children and adults. In studies with elementary school children, Funk and colleagues found negative associations between the intensity of media violence use and questionnaire measures of empathy as well as empathic responses to vignettes describing a child in distress. Among adults, Charles R. Mullin and Daniel Linz (1995) found that men who were shown sexually violent films subsequently expressed less sympathy for a victim of domestic violence and perceived her injuries to be less serious than did men in a control group.

By blunting empathic concern for others, desensitization as a result of exposure to media violence also impedes moral evaluation in situations in which behavior should be based on ethical principles and moral obligations. This is reflected in research by Ingrid Möller and Barbara Krahé (2009) that found a greater normative acceptance of aggression and

more positive attitudes toward violence in regular users of violent media.

Increase in Aggressive Behavior

By weakening the fear response to violence through exposure to violent media stimuli and the ensuing effects on reducing empathy and promoting a positive attitude toward violence, desensitization can disinhibit aggressive behavior. In Leonard Berkowitz's cognitive neoassociationist model of aggression (1993), fear and anger are seen as antagonistic emotional reactions that give rise to the competing responses of flight or fight. Reducing the flight impulse strengthens the fight response. In line with this proposition, decreased anxious arousal by a violent film clip predicted higher unprovoked aggression in a laboratory task. The less anxious arousal participants reported in response to a brief scene of violence, the louder the unprovoked aversive noise blast they administered to another person, as shown by Krahé and colleagues. Using the same aggression measure, another study by Christopher R. Engelhardt and colleagues (2011) found that participants behaved more aggressively after playing a violent compared with a nonviolent video game, and that the effect was mediated by reduced aversive motivation, indicated by event-related brain potential data, in response to depictions of real-life violence.

Decrease in Prosocial Behavior

The effect of desensitization to violence on reducing empathic concern for victims of violence seems that it would be less likely that help will be given to persons in need, yet few studies have examined the link between desensitization and helping behavior. In one study with elementary school children, it was found that children who had watched a violent film took longer to seek help from an adult when watching an altercation between two preschoolers than children who had watched a nonviolent film. Research by Bushman and Anderson showed that participants took longer to come to the help of the victim of a staged fight and rated the confrontation as less serious after playing a violent video game compared with a nonviolent game and that moviegoers who had just seen a violent film were less likely to help an injured person than those who had just watched a nonviolent film.

Implications of Desensitization to Media Violence

People are attracted to violent media for a variety of reasons and motivations. According to the uses and gratifications model, users choose media contents because of their capacity to satisfy particular needs. Among the needs satisfied by violent media contents is the search for new experiences, excitement, and arousal, as captured in the construct of sensation seeking. Sensation seeking varies as a function of developmental stage with a peak in adolescence, but it is also a relatively stable disposition that differs among individuals. A 2005 meta-analysis by Cynthia A. Hoffner and Kenneth J. Levine (2005) found a significant association between sensation seeking and enjoyment of media violence. The process of desensitization is counterproductive to the gratification of the need for excitement and stimulation that makes violent media appealing for users, particularly high sensation seekers. If, over time, violent media stimuli lose their capacity to elicit

emotional responses, ever more drastic and extreme violent stimuli are needed to keep up the desired level of arousal. This means that users' media diet will become increasingly more violent, thereby providing more opportunities for the social learning of aggression, the formation of aggressive scripts, and the positive evaluation of violence, all of which have been found to increase the risk of aggressive behavior. In addition, the experience of enjoyment when watching ever more violent movies or performing increasingly violent acts in a video game "sensitizes" users to associate violence with positive feelings, further contributing to the disinhibition of aggression.

Research on desensitization has focused on violent films and video games in demonstrating desensitization and its effects on responses to real-life violence. However, it is clear from content analyses, for example, by Stacy L. Smith and Aaron R. Boyson (2002), that violence also features prominently in songs and music videos that are highly popular among adolescents and young adults. Furthermore, verbal aggression and relational aggression, aimed at harming a person's social relationships, are widely present in the media over and above physical violence, as shown by Sarah M. Coyne and Emily Whitehead (2008). Although still awaiting empirical examination, the general principle of desensitization suggests that habitual exposure to media presenting verbal and relational aggression should increase users' tolerance of these forms of aggression in the same way as depictions of physical violence.

Barbara Krahé

See also Aggressive Behavior; Arousal and Aggressive Content, Theory and Psychology of; Effects From Violent Content, Short- and Long-Term; General Aggression Model; National Television Violence Study; Video Game Player and Opponent Effects

Further Readings

Anderson, C. A., & Bushman, B. J. (2001). Effects of violent video games on aggressive behavior, aggressive cognition, aggressive affect, physiological arousal, and prosocial behavior: A meta-analytic review of the scientific literature. *Psychological Science, 12,* 353–359.

Arriaga, P., Monteiro, M. B., & Esteves, F. (2011). Effects of playing violent computer games on emotional desensitization and aggressive behavior. *Journal of Applied Social Psychology, 41,* 1900–1925.

Bartholow, B. D., Bushman, B. J., & Sestir, M. A. (2006). Chronic violent video game exposure and desensitization to violence: Behavioral and event-related brain potential data. *Journal of Experimental Social Psychology, 42,* 532–539

Berkowitz, L. (1993). *Aggression: Its causes, consequences, and control.* Philadelphia: Temple University Press.

Bushman, B. J., & Anderson, C. A. (2009). Comfortably numb: Desensitizing effects of violent media on helping others. *Psychological Science, 20,* 273–277.

Carnagey, N. L., Anderson, C. A., & Bushman, B. J. (2007). The effect of video game violence on physiological desensitization to real-life violence. *Journal of Experimental Social Psychology, 43,* 489–496.

Coyne, S. M., & Whitehead, E. (2008). Indirect aggression in animated Disney films. *Journal of Communication, 58,* 382–395.

Engelhardt, C. R., Bartholow, B. D., Kerr, G. T., & Bushman, B. J. (2011). This is your brain on violent video games: Neural desensitization to violence predicts increased aggression following violent video game exposure. *Journal of Experimental Social Psychology, 47,* 1033–1036.

Fanti, K., Vanman, E., Henrich, C., & Avraamides, M. (2009). Desensitization to media violence over a short period of time. *Aggressive Behavior, 35,* 179–187.

Funk, J. B., Baldacci, H. B., Pasold, T., & Baumgardner, J. (2004). Violence exposure in real-life, video games, television, movies, and the Internet: Is there desensitization? *Journal of Adolescence, 27,* 23–39.

Hoffner, C. A., & Levine, K. J. (2005). Enjoyment of mediated fright and violence: A meta-analysis. *Media Psychology, 7,* 207–237.

Kirsh, S. J. (2012). *Children, adolescents, and media violence* (2nd ed.). Thousand Oaks, CA: Sage.

Krahé, B., Möller, I., Huesmann, L. R., Kirwil, L., Felber, J., & Berger, A. (2011). Desensitization to media violence: Links with habitual media violence exposure, aggressive cognitions and aggressive behavior. *Journal of Personality and Social Psychology, 100,* 630–646.

Möller, I., & Krahé, B. (2009). Exposure to violent video games and aggression in German adolescents: A longitudinal analysis. *Aggressive Behavior, 35,* 75–89.

Mullin, C. R., & Linz, D. (1995). Desensitization and resensitization to violence against women: Effects of exposure to sexually violent films on judgments of domestic violence victims. *Journal of Personality and Social Psychology, 69,* 449–459.

Smith, S. L., & Boyson, A. R. (2002). Violence in music videos: Examining the prevalence and context of physical aggression. *Journal of Communication, 52,* 61–83.

Strenziok, M., Krueger, F., Deshpande, G., Lenroot, K., van der Meer, E., & Grafman, J. (2011). Fronto-parietal regulation of media violence exposure in adolescents: A multi-method study. *Social Cognitive and Affective Neuroscience, 6,* 537–547.

Thomas, M. H., Horton, R. W., Lippincott, E. C., & Drabman, R. S. (1977). Desensitization to portrayals of real-life aggression as a function of exposure to television violence. *Journal of Personality and Social Psychology, 35,* 450–458.

DEVELOPMENTAL EFFECTS

Cognitive development can be especially important for those researchers interested in effects of media violence, because different developmental stages can lead to diverging perceptions and outcomes depending on the mental maturity of the audience. Theoretically, cognitive-developmental factors influence how depictions of violence are interpreted and perceived, and consequences of exposure depend on these perceptions. This entry discusses development's role in shaping children's perceptions of violent media and their ability to alter fear reactions, enjoyment of violent portrayals, acceptance of aggression, and perceptions of whether violence is justified. Theoretical mechanisms thought to explain these different effects on younger versus older audiences are also presented.

A number of studies have provided evidence that exposure to media violence can evoke fright reactions in both the short and long term. For example, research shows that exposure to media violence can lead to acute stress responses and anxiety. It is also thought that repeated exposure to media violence can cultivate a fear of victimization over time. However, only a handful of studies have specifically addressed development's role in shaping such reactions.

Research suggested that children's fear of violence depicted in news and other realistic content seems to increase with age. By contrast, children's fear of unrealistic violence in fantasy portrayals seems to decrease with age. Other research suggested that older children are more likely than younger children to react with fear to "implied violence" when it is not directly depicted. Younger children generally react only when stimuli seem to be directly threatening or violent. For example, younger children are more likely than older children to be fearful of nonviolent, benign, or beneficent characters that are portrayed in a grotesque or threatening manner, whereas older children can see past this type of portrayal. Children's cognitive development has been offered as an explanation for these different outcomes. Specifically, their abilities to distinguish reality from fiction, to engage in perspective taking, and to inhibit emotional responses to media violence are mechanisms that explain why these differences are observed. However, more research is needed to understand how these developmental factors change fear reactions to media violence, especially in the long term.

As with fear reactions, cognitive-developmental theory has also been central to understanding differences in story enjoyment between younger and older children. Early research in entertainment theory demonstrated that development plays an important role in enjoyment of violent punishment for a villain in a story. Audiences enjoy violence when the character being punished deserves it but find it abhorrent when the character is undeserving. Thus, as moral development leads to different perceptions of whether violence is justified versus unjustified, diverging outcomes in enjoyment of violence are observed. Specifically, whereas older children enjoy "equitable punishment," younger children often prefer seeing overly harsh, even violent retribution in story endings.

In addition to enhancing enjoyment, perceptions that media violence is justified may increase acceptance of aggression as a solution to social conflict. For example, an experiment showed that children over the age of 7 years were more likely to prefer a violent story ending after exposure to depictions of provoked (versus unprovoked) violence. However, it was predicted that children younger than 7 years of age would prefer harsh, violent punishment to a nonviolent outcome (regardless of provocation), because they generally see harsher retribution as more justified. Both of these observations have been explained in terms of moral development, which allows older children to see the provoked violence as more justified than unprovoked violence. In turn, this perception leads to enhanced enjoyment and acceptance of aggression. A number of studies have suggested this link. It is thought that justified portrayals minimize the pain and suffering of the victim and are perceived to morally condone violent behavior.

Cognitive-developmental frameworks (from Jean Piaget and Lawrence Kohlberg) have traditionally been used to explain these differences. Specifically, the cognitive-developmental frameworks of Piaget and Kohlberg suggested that if violent punishment is handed down from an authority figure, is unpunished or rewarded, or is perceived to satisfy to some egoistic concern, then younger children are more

likely to perceive the act as justified. By contrast, older children's perception of whether violence is justified depends on an inner sense of equity. Older children take into consideration other factors (such as the severity of a provocation) in their judgment. Also according to the cognitive stage framework, younger children will be more likely to perceive violence as justified if they see violence used to punish some misdeed—the more violent the punishment, the more justified it is perceived. By contrast, older children will be more likely to perceive violence as justified if it is proportional to the misdeed—not too mild and not too severe.

Newer research by cognitive scientists has begun to shed some light on the mechanisms responsible for these developmental differences. This research showed how the various mechanisms responsible for moral reasoning strategies (e.g., working memory capacity and response inhibition) are in the process of maturing throughout childhood and adolescence. When children must hold complex representations (such as stories) in mind, or inhibit emotional responses (such as a desire for retribution or a fear reaction), developmental differences are more likely to emerge. For example, it seems that younger children's diminished ability to hold a complex storyline in working memory leads them to use the severity of a villain's punishment as a "mental shortcut" to judge the punishment's appropriateness. In addition, younger children are less able to inhibit behavioral responses to threatening stimuli. More research is needed to tease apart the relationships between such developmental mechanisms and the manner in which they alter how violent portrayals are interpreted and perceived. Such an understanding would be valuable for media researchers as well as parents and childcare professionals who wish to understand the impact of violent media.

Robert Joel Lewis

See also Cognition: Schemas and Scripts; Cognitive Psychology of Violence; Cognitive Script Theory and the Dynamics of Cognitive Scripting; Ethical Development, Effects on; Exposure to Violent Content, Effect on Child Development; Longitudinal Research Findings on the Effects of Violent Content; Social Cognitive Theory

Further Readings

Krcmar, M., & Cooke, M. C. (2001). Children's moral reasoning and their perceptions of television violence.

Journal of Communication, 51, 300–316. doi: 10.1111/
j.1460–2466.2001.tb02882.x

Wilson, B. J. (2008). Media and children's aggression, fear,
and altruism. *The Future of Children, 18,* 87–118. doi:
10.1353/foc.0.0005

Zillmann, D. (1998). The psychology of the appeal of
portrayals of violence. In J. H. Goldstein (Ed.), *Why we
watch: The attractions of violent entertainment*
(pp. 179–211). New York, NY: Oxford University Press.

Drench Effects From Video Games

Conceptualizing the linkage between the drench hypothesis, proposed by Bradley S. Greenberg in 1988, and violent content in video games requires a modest examination of each phenomenon. The primary purpose of the original statement of the drench hypothesis was to offer an alternative to the cultivation hypothesis posited by George Gerbner and colleagues. The cultivation hypothesis proposed that the construction of social reality from television fiction occurs from repeated, persistent, and consistent portrayals of specific demographics (e.g., gender) or specific behaviors (e.g., violence). Such repetitious images account over time for the social beliefs attached to the content entities. This conception treats all occurrences as roughly equivalent and constitutes the cumulative drip-drip-drip effect. In contrast, the drench hypothesis poses that it would be more useful to concentrate on whether there is more impact from what can be termed "critical portrayals" than from the overall number of portrayals. This perspective argues that some television characterizations and some depicted social behaviors can be so forcefully presented as to account for a significant portion of the viewer's conceptions about that type of character and that type of behavior. In other words, the viewer bases impression formation and image construction more on the portrayal and behavior of one intensive, strongly presented character than on the portrayal and behavior of other, more passive characters.

Varying support for the drench hypothesis has been demonstrated in several content areas. The drench notion has been used to explain gender-related impressions from children's favorite television programs, the facial emotions of television characters, and the favorite shows of children as derived from their essays. In addition, the gender role attitudes of Latino adolescents and general gender stereotyping have been explored. Perceptions of race and prejudice have evolved in drench-based studies focused on women of color, affirmative action espousal, prejudice reduction, racial (and gender) counter-stereotypes, the recognition of racial stereotypes, and prejudice prevention. Sexual objectification and sexual behavior have had their share of examination in this rubric—for example, African American girls' focus on beauty, sexual attitudes, and sexual behaviors. Health-related conceptions of fatal diseases and medical professionals (i.e., doctors) have been studied. One-off image studies of the disabled and prostitutes also are available. But no known study has posed the possibility that aggressive responses to video games may be tempered or facilitated by the dynamic nature of differences among acts, scenes, or characters participating in the video game violence. The key content analyses of video game violence demonstrate relevant findings. These analyses of video game content have focused on the presence or absence of violence and/or hypersexuality of individual characters.

Nearly a third of all game playtime in E (Everyone)–rated games used intentional violence. In 60% of the games, injuring someone was rewarded or necessary for advancing to the next level, and 44% of games without a content descriptor for violence contained violent acts during more than a third of the games' duration. Furthermore, Kimberley Thompson and Kevin Haninger (2001) found a positive correlation between violent game play time and the frequency of deaths per minute. There was little sexuality found in E-rated games.

Concerning T (Teen)–rated games, Haninger and Thompson (2004) reported that 98% of their sampled games involved intentional violence for one-third of the game play time. This was in the context of 90% of the games requiring injury for advancement, and 7 in 10 requiring killing. In T-rated games, the kill rate was 61 human deaths per hour of game play. Furthermore, 1 in 5 games included sexual themes. "Games were significantly more likely to depict females partially nude or engaged in sexual behaviors than males" (p. 856). If the researchers expanded their definition of sexual themes to include "pronounced cleavage, large breasts, or provocative clothing" (p. 862), then nearly half the games qualified as containing sexual themes.

A theoretic rationale exists for the 2003 content analysis completed by Stacy L. Smith, Ken Lachlan, and Ron Tamborini. First, they sampled the most popular (based on sales figures) games across all age categories. This analysis corresponds closely to the choices made in tests of the drench hypothesis reviewed above. In addition to the frequency of violence, this content analysis examined the presence of justified and unjustified motives, the consequences of violent acts, rewards or punishments for violent acts, the explicitness of the violence, and the visual perspective of the player as perpetrator or victim. Video games for older children and adults, as compared with younger children and general audience games, had four times as much violence per minute and more deadly violence; more often featured human perpetrators and child perpetrators; more often targeted human victims; more often indicated that the violence was justified; and more often put the player in the first-person shooter perspective.

This last study connects well to the drench hypothesis. By examining the most popular games, the researchers acknowledged that some games gain far more attention and time from players. Teens and preteens spend hours and/or days playing the same game again and again, and it is those games that are more likely to yield formative impressions. Because the vast majority of games feature violence, what researchers expect to emerge from the "favorite" games are some related and strong impressions from the context of that violence. For example, if *Grand Auto Theft* features sanitize violence (i.e., little, if any, blood), justify much of the violent activity, and do not punish or reward the violent activity, then researchers would expect that players of such popular games would have a greater acceptance of violence as a means of problem solving.

It is primarily the content of the game that can create strong impressions. And content goes beyond mere incidents of violence to the means and outcomes of that violence and depictions of performing characters. For example, Lara Croft (*Tomb Raider*) is a beautiful, intelligent, and athletic archeologist who counters video game characterizations of females as merely sex objects. Playing that game in its several reincarnations may set a standard for players' impressions of females, particularly female players. Under the drench hypothesis, being exposed to such strong characterizations again and again for hours on end is expected to yield a greater impact than weekly viewing of a television show or multiple games with or without female adversaries.

It is difficult to identify a media-related activity that is more absorbing than video game play. One cannot also do homework, read a text, or prepare a meal while playing a video game, as one can when watching television or listening to music. The concentration required to perform and perform well makes one more apt to be a devotee of its explicit and implied messages. It is a primary and not a secondary activity.

Meta-analyses have demonstrated that exposure to violence in video games contributes to individual aggressiveness (Anderson et al., 2010) in much the same way that individual aggressiveness has been found with exposure to other mediated forms of violence. Anderson et al. noted in an interview, "We can now say with utmost confidence that regardless of research method—that is experimental, correlational, or longitudinal—and regardless of the cultures tested in this study [East and West], you get the same effects. And the effects are that exposure to violent video games increases the likelihood of aggressive behavior in both short-term and long-term contexts. Such exposure also increases aggressive thinking and aggressive affect, and decreases pro-social behavior." The question that remains for researchers is which video games and which game attributes are more likely to increase aggressive behavior.

Bradley S. Greenberg

See also Cultivation Theory; Drench Hypothesis; Effects From Violent Content, Short- and Long-Term

Further Readings

Anderson, C. A., Shibuya, A., Ihori, N., Swing, E. L., Bushman, B. J., Sakamoto, A., Rothstein, H. R., & Saleem, M. (2010). Violent video game effects on aggression, empathy, and prosocial behavior in Eastern and Western countries: A meta-analytic review. *Psychological Bulletin, 136*(2), 151–173. doi: 10.1037/a0018251

Gerbner, G., Gross, L., Morgan, M., & Signorielli, N. (1986). Living with television: The dynamics of the cultivation process. In J. Bryant & D. Zillmann (Eds.), *Perspectives on media effects* (pp. 17–40). Hillsdale, NJ: Erlbaum.

Greenberg, B. S. (1988). Some uncommon television images and the drench hypothesis. In S. Oskamp (Ed.), *Applied social psychology annual* (Vol. 8): *Television as a social issue* (pp. 88–102). Newbury Park, CA: Sage.

Haninger, K., & Thompson, K. M. (2004). Content and ratings of teen-rated video games. *Journal of the American Medical Association, 291*(7), 856–865. doi:10.1001/jama.291.7.856

Smith, S. L., Lachlan, K. A., & Tamborini, R. (2003). Popular video games: Quantifying the presentation of violence and its context. *Journal of Broadcasting and Electronic Media, 47*(1), 58–76.

Thompson, K. M., & Haninger, K. (2001). Violence in E-rated video games. *Journal of the American Medical Association, 286*(5), 591–598. doi:10.1001/jama.286.5.591

DRENCH HYPOTHESIS

Drench hypothesis focuses on differential effects of fictional or dramatic media messages on viewers. Media researchers often assume that media messages generate cumulative drip-drip-drip effects on the audience. Bradley S. Greenberg (1988), however, noted that some characters or presentations of fictional media, such as narrative film and television drama or situation comedy, can have drench (i.e., impressive) effects on some viewers. He suggested that not all portrayals have the same impact and that certain characters, rather than the collected mass of role characters, can have significant, lasting impacts. Diana Reep and Faye Dambrot (1989) empirically demonstrated that some fictional characters or presentations, rather than the accumulated images of numerous other characters and presentations, can have intense effects on viewers. Drench hypothesis assumes that effects of dramatized portrayals vary depending on how each viewer cognitively, and affectively, processes a particular presentation. Different viewers can perceive, interpret, and react to the content of a dramatic presentation in different ways. Drench analysis looks at the role of four major constructs in generating differential effects of fictional or dramatic media: message involvement, perceived realism, role affinity, and subject novelty. It is postulated that fictional or dramatic media can generate drench or impressive (i.e., intense) effects on viewers who exhibit high levels of message involvement, perceived realism, role affinity, and subject novelty.

A Boxing Analogy for Illustrating Drench Effects

Imagine a boxing event in which one boxer throws a punch to the other boxer, who is limited only to receiving or defending the punch. The impact of the punch can be determined by several factors. First, the thickness of the glove pad can make a difference in generating the impact of the punch. Suppose that the punch is thrown with a bare fist. The impact would be much greater than that through a glove. Second, the target boxer's defensive effort, or lack thereof, is an important factor. A punch thrown over the tightly covering arms of the target boxer cannot be very effective. What if the target boxer loosens his defense with his arms drooping? The less the defensive effort, the greater the impact of the punch. Third, the distance of the target boxer to the punching boxer would produce differential effects. To be fully affected, the target boxer needs to stand close enough to the puncher. If the target boxer stays too far from the puncher, the impact would become negligible. Last, the target boxer's body sturdiness (or lack thereof) would make a difference in the impact of the punch. That is, the less the body sturdiness, the greater the impact.

Likewise, imagine a person being exposed to a dramatic presentation. First, the thickness of the glove pad is likened to the viewer's perception of how realistic the dramatic presentation is (i.e., *perceived realism*). The viewer would be influenced more by messages that are perceived to be realistic than otherwise. Second, a lack of defensive effort by the target boxer is likened to how much the viewer likes the specific role character "throwing" certain messages to him or her. The construct of *role affinity* represents this aspect. It is plausible that when facing an attractive role character, the viewer would be more susceptible (i.e., exerting less defensive effort than otherwise) to the messages exhibited or advocated by the role character. Third, the distance between the punching boxer and the target boxer is paralleled to how deeply the viewer is involved in the presentation (i.e., *message involvement*). Just as a punch thrown to a target person standing too far does not produce much impact, messages sent to less involved viewers would generate less influence. Finally, just as the impact of a punch is greater for a target boxer whose body is fragile, dramatic messages would generate greater impacts on viewers who have not formed their attitudes and/or behavior related to the subject in concern (i.e., *subject novelty*) (see Table 1).

Message Involvement

Message involvement refers to the extent to which a media user engages in processing and construing the content of a media presentation. The level of involvement is determined by several factors. First,

Table 1   Boxing Analogy for Illustrating Drench Effects

Impact Factors in Boxing	Impact Factors in Fictional Media
Thickness (thinness) of glove pad	Perceived realism
(Lack of) defensive effort	Role affinity
Distance to the puncher	Message involvement
(Lack of) body sturdiness (target boxer)	Subject novelty

the viewer can become involved more deeply with exciting and suspenseful presentations than with tedious, boring ones. Second, the viewer who has a trait of greater fictional involvement is more likely to become absorbed in dramatic presentations. Finally, message involvement can also be influenced by situational elements such as the viewer's imminent needs and motives that either aid or deter his or her immersion in the presentation. While acknowledging that message involvement is determined by multiple factors, drench analysis examines the level of involvement manifested during a specific presentation. It is hypothesized that the greater the level of message involvement, the greater the impact of dramatized portrayals.

Perceived Realism

Perceived realism refers to the extent to which a viewer believes that the content of a dramatic presentation is likely to be seen or happen in the real world. It represents the real-world authenticity accorded to occurrences in a dramatized story. Dramatic media presentations are typically regarded as depicting reality, either actual or fantasized. It is possible that some presentations are perceived to be more realistic than others, depending on the viewer's implicit assessments on how closely people, settings, and occurrences portrayed resemble those in the real world and, therefore, how likely the story presented would take place in the real world. Viewers may perceive different levels of realism based on their own life experiences and psychological tendencies. It is hypothesized that the viewer perceiving more realism about a media presentation depicting violence as a means of solving life problems would be affected to a greater degree by the portrayals.

Role Affinity

Role affinity refers to the extent to which a viewer feels attracted to a specific role character in a dramatic presentation. According to Albert Bandura, adult models who are perceived to have attractive qualities have more influence on young people, while those who lack charming characteristics are generally ignored or rejected. Researchers have shown that when dramatic acts are performed by liked characters, the impacts on viewers are greater. Values, beliefs, attitudes, or behavioral styles advocated by a role character are likely to influence especially the viewers who feel high affinity with the character. Much concern has been raised about attractive characters showing undesirable behavioral practices and potentially affecting the viewers in adverse ways, as in film portrayals of violence (e.g., John Travolta and Samuel L. Jackson in *Pulp Fiction* and Woody Harrelson and Juliette Lewis in *Natural Born Killers*). It is plausible that if a liked character exhibits aggressive attitudes and behavior in fictional media, viewers feeling high affinity with the character are likely to be influenced as to the use of violence as a means of resolving conflict.

Subject Novelty

Subject novelty refers to the extent to which a viewer has prior exposure to the subject dealt with in dramatic portrayals. In a sense, drench effects are more plausible for younger viewers or those who have less experience and, therefore, less firm beliefs, attitudes, and behavioral inclinations in relation to the subject. A painting analogy would help the illustration of this aspect of drench effects. Suppose that someone is painting a picture on paper. It would be easy to recognize what is newly painted if the paper has not been much used yet (i.e., is white and clean). It would be harder to color new content if the paper already has other things painted. Likewise, the viewer who has less sturdy attitudes toward the subject (e.g., violent solutions to real-life problems) might be influenced to a greater extent by a dramatic presentation portraying violence.

C. Mo Bahk

See also Character Development Within Violent Content; Drench Effects From Video Games; Effects From Violent Media, Short- and Long-Term; Realism of Violent Content, Real-World Violence on Television, and Their Effects; Social Cognitive Theory;

Stereotyping in Violent Media Content; User Involvement in Violent Content, Effects of

Further Readings

Bahk, C. M. (2001). Drench effects of media portrayal of fatal virus disease on health locus of control beliefs. *Health Communication, 13*(2), 187–204.

Greenberg, B. S. (1988). Some uncommon television images and the drench hypothesis. In S. Oskamp (Ed.), *Applied social psychology annual, Vol. 8: Television as a social issue* (pp. 88–102). Newbury Park, CA: Sage.

Reep, D. C., & Dambrot, F. H. (1989). Effects of frequent television viewing on stereotypes: "Drip, drip" or "drench"? *Journalism Quarterly, 66,* 542–550, 556.

Effect Size in Media Violence, Research and Effects of

Effect size refers to the strength of a research finding. In the media violence research, effect size is most frequently used to determine the magnitude of the relationship between use of violent media and aggression. There are a number of different statistics that describe effect size, as well as a number of techniques for determining and pooling effect sizes across studies. Done well, an effect size estimate provides a reliable summary of the relationship between variables across a number of studies. For this reason, it is often invoked in discussions of the violent media literature.

What Is an Effect Size?

Effect sizes are the estimate of the magnitude of the relationship between variables. Many statistics reported in the research literature are estimates of effect size, including zero order correlations (e.g., Pearson's r), phi coefficient, regression coefficients, and so on. However, other statistics that many researchers rely on, those that determine statistical significance (e.g., chi-square, analysis of variance [ANOVA]), are not effect size estimates. Instead, these statistics represent the probability that an observed effect is not zero, given a particular population and variance. These statistics provide no information about the magnitude of the effect. Because the significance criteria are arbitrary, and significance is a function of sample size, tests of statistical significance are not particularly informative as to the strength of the relationship or difference between variables.

The most commonly used effect statistics in media violence research measure one of two things: (1) the degree of association between two variables or (2) the amount of difference between two dependent variables. Association effect is measured using correlation or regression statistics. These statistics constrain the relationship between the two focal variables to a linear (one-to-one correspondence) and then measure the degree to which the association between the two variables deviates from perfect association. These statistics are standardized such that possible scores vary between –1 and 1, with zero (0) indicating no relationship at all. The closer to 1 or –1, the more the association between variables is perfectly linear.

Difference statistics provide an estimate of the magnitude of difference between subjects in different experimental conditions. For example, a difference statistic reports how much higher subjects in the violent media condition scored on a measure of aggression than subjects in the nonviolent condition. Although difference statistics are rarely reported in journal articles, the most common difference statistic, Cohen's d, is easy to calculate if the authors report the means and standard deviations of the conditions. By pooling the standard deviations, Cohen's d provides a statistic that standardizes across studies that use measures of aggression that are on different scales.

Cohen's d has the added advantage of offering a recommended way to interpret the effect size. Cohen wrote that his statistic could be interpreted as follows: $d \approx .20$ can be considered a small effect size; $d \approx .50$ is a moderate effect size; and $d \geq .80$ is a large effect size. However, Cohen points out that these are general guidelines, and the interpretation varies according to subject area.

A common problem in social research has been that researchers often cannot conduct studies that are large enough to produce results that are definitive. However, if the results of several studies are pooled together, the preponderance of the evidence is much more trustworthy. Therefore, recent years have seen the rise of meta-analyses in the media violence literature in which researchers pool effect sizes across several similar studies to strengthen the trustworthiness of the conclusions.

An effect size estimate across a set of studies is determined by estimating the effect of each study or hypothesis, correcting the estimates for possible error, and then pooling the estimates in some diagnostic manner. The process of determining an overall effect size begins by collecting a census of all available research containing the focal variables. Collection ranges from simple access via journals to contacting an individual researcher for information. If a complete census is not collected, the effect size will be biased.

Effect Size Estimates of the Relationship Between Exposure to Violent Media and Aggression

Because of the political nature of the question and a number of contradictory results in the literature, there have been a number of meta-analyses conducted on media violence research. One of the earliest such studies, by F. Scott Andison, simply categorized results of 67 studies, with the majority of the studies categorized as weak positive and moderate positive. Wendy Wood, Frank Y. Wong, and J. Gregory Chachere, and Haejung Paik and George Comstock followed that study with meta-analyses that resulted in a weighted aggregate effect size of $d = .27$ and $d = .65$, respectively.

More recently, many meta-analyses have focused solely on the effects of violent video games on general aggression. John L. Sherry found an overall weighted effect size of $r = .15$ ($d = .30$), although the effect size was smaller for studies that used behavioral measures of aggression as compared to those that used pen-and-paper reports. Subsequently, Craig A. Anderson and colleagues published a series of meta-analyses with an effect size of around $r = .19$ ($d = .39$), dependent on the analysis they performed (e.g., different outcome measures, "best practices"

versus "not best practices" studies). Christopher J. Ferguson found that after correcting for publication bias the effect size for nonexperimental studies was reduced to $r = .06$ ($d = .12$) for aggressive behavior outcomes and $r = .11$ ($d = .22$) for aggressive thoughts, while the effect size for experimental studies was $r = .15$ ($d = .30$) for aggressive behavior outcomes and $r = .25$ ($d = .52$) for aggressive thoughts.

Some researchers have conducted meta-analyses that investigate more specific questions about the effects of violent media. Joanne Savage and Christina Yancey focused on studies in which the outcome measure could be related to actual criminal aggression. They found very small effects for actual criminality, $r = .04$ ($d = .08$), and among experimental studies, $r = .06$ ($d = .12$), with a little higher effect size of cross-sectional studies, $r = .16$ ($d = .32$), and longitudinal studies, $r = .12$ ($d = .24$). In a meta-analysis that looked at predictors of enjoying violent media content, Cynthia A. Hoffner and Kenneth J. Levine found that aggressive personality ($r = .28$, $K = 8$, $d = .58$) and sensation seeking ($r = .20$, $K = 6$, $d = .41$) were most strongly and positively correlated with liking violent media.

Problems and Caveats in Using Effect Size Estimates

Meta-analysis is a useful tool for detecting overall trends in the effect sizes of a research literature, but it comes with some important caveats. By reducing a large collection of research studies down to one statistic, a tremendous amount of information is lost. For example, variations in the manner in which variables are operationalized are lost. Meta-analysts attempt to compensate for this by conducting categorical analysis comparing behavioral, cognitive, affect, arousal, and so on. Craig Anderson and Brad J. Bushman (2002) have shown that lost information is not a problem in most cases.

Rules used for selecting studies for inclusion or exclusion can create two additional problems. Overly ambitious inclusion criteria can introduce excessive variance into the analysis, possibly even mixing "apples and oranges." However, Robert Rosenthal has suggested that studies can be weighted for "quality," such as the rating of the journal the work was published in or the use of best practices. However, any type of subjective judgment applied in meta-analysis brings suspicion of attempts to bias the findings.

A related problem is the "file-drawer problem," which is the possibility that unpublished studies, if included, could change the conclusions of the meta-analysis. This introduces the possibility of systematic publication bias. Timothy R. Levine demonstrated clear evidence of publication bias in the communication literature favoring studies with significant findings, so this is likely a problem in the media violence literature. A number of methods have been suggested for addressing the file-drawer problem, but they depend on untested assumptions as well.

Perhaps the most controversial issue with effect size estimates, whether for an individual study or pooled, is interpretation of the meaning. Some researchers contend that the results of the various media violence meta-analyses provide clear evidence that exposure to media violence leads to aggression. Others, looking at the same effect sizes, contend that the magnitude is so small that the real-world effects are trivial. While meta-analyses provide a reliable estimate of effect size that most researchers agree on, the ultimate meaning of that magnitude will always be subject to interpretation.

At best, effect size estimates and meta-analysis offer a qualified summary of a research literature that can be more rigorous than qualitative reviews. However, readers are advised to pay close attention to the caveats and assumptions in each meta-analysis.

John L. Sherry and Matthew Grizzard

See also Effects From Violent Media, Short- and Long-Term; Methodologies for Assessing Effects of Media; Violence in Media, Effects on Aggression and Violent Crime; Violence, Definition of

Further Readings

Browne, K. D., & Hamilton-Giachritsis, C. (2005). The influence of violent media on children and adolescents: a public-health approach. *Lancet, 365*, 702–710.

Cohen, J. (1994). The earth is round (*p* .05). *American Psychologist, 49*, 997–1003.

Hunter, J. E., Schmidt, F. L., & Jackson, G. B. (1982). *Meta-analysis: Cumulating research findings across studies.* Beverly Hills, CA: Sage.

EFFECTS FROM VIOLENT MEDIA, SHORT- AND LONG-TERM

Historically speaking, media scholarship has progressed from dated theories, such as the magic bullet theory, which argues the media is very powerful in its effects, to a more modern understanding through which researchers understand the individual differences among consumers and how they engage media. Within these advances, researchers have come to understand that media in general can have small to moderate effects upon individuals' cognitions, affect, and behaviors. Numerous theories abound that are used to account for violent media effects upon users. Some, such as media priming, work in the short term, while others, such as cultivation or social learning, predict long-term effects and consequences based on learned models of behavior. One area that has drawn criticism and concern is the consumption of violent media. Parental groups, nonprofit organizations, government organizations, and some academic researchers have often suggested that viewing such violence can lead to increases of aggression among viewers. To date, much research has supported significant correlations between violent media (television, movies, video games, music, etc.) and aggressive thoughts, affect, and behavioral intentions. For instance, a recent report commissioned by the International Society for Research on Aggression (ISRA) shows that violent media consumption can lead to increases of aggressive thoughts, emotions, and behaviors, and decreases in prosocial behaviors in the short and long term. While this link has been established, differences in how these effects are displayed can be seen in short-term effects and long-term consequences. To better address how violent media affects cognitions, emotions, and behaviors, it is important to explain the differences in how periodic and extended exposure can affect individuals.

Short-Term Effects Perspective

Imitation

One of the first concerns brought about by media violence was an individual's imitation or mimicry of depictions he or she viewed in the media. Early research showed that children often imitated movies and comic book characters when playing. If those depictions were violent, then so would be the imitative acts. Early experiments conducted by Albert Bandura showed that children often act in similar ways as the aggressive depictions they viewed when these depictions were rewarded rather than punished.

Cognitive Neoassociation and Media Priming

The cognitive neoassociative theory posits that a human's memory is made up of neural network nodes that correspond to an individual's behaviors, emotions, and thoughts that are connected via associative pathways. According to Leonard Berkowitz, when a thought or feeling is brought into focal awareness it may activate an associated node related to that thought or feeling. If this activation is strong enough, it will activate other similarly related nodes, thus creating a priming effect. Priming assumes that a stimulus can activate related nodes, increasing the likelihood that related concepts are also brought to mind. Simply put, media priming is based on the idea that a stimulus can activate associative nodes. Berkowitz's research (1984, 1990) proposed that aversive situations (foul odors, high temperatures, exposure to cold water) or depictions (disgusting or violent scenes) can produce aggression through negative affect. This negative effect may activate particular thoughts, memories, expressive motor actions, or physiological reactions. Media priming then suggests that because memories, thoughts, and feelings are connected via associative pathways, external activation of one or all of them may elicit automatic or controlled behaviors associated with those thoughts, memories, or feelings. Priming predicts that violent actions through media depictions of violence can prime semantically related thoughts, feelings, or behaviors about violence or aggression.

Excitation Transfer

Dolf Zillmann, a leading researcher of media effects, suggested that arousal or excitation associated with anger or aggression can influence cognitive processes. Thus, aggression may hinder an individual's ability to cognitively displace or reduce that excitation. However, in instances of moderate arousal, or in conjunction with mitigating information, individuals can likely displace their sense of anger or aggression. For instance, a snide remark or rude behavior elicited by an individual will not likely lead to anger or retaliation from the target if that behavior did not elicit anger (low arousal) or was attributed to the fact that the individual was under a lot of stress (mitigating circumstances). However, in instances of high arousal, an individual's ability to cognitively displace aggression or anger may be hindered and result in impulsive aggression. According to Craig Anderson's research on media violence, if two arousing events occur relatively close to each other, then a misattribution of one event to the other may occur, making an aroused individual more hostile. Thus, a person may experience an

anger-arousing event and then shortly afterward experience further arousal from another experience. In turn, a person may misattribute the second arousing event with the first and increase his or her level of anger or aggression. Thus, violent media, such as violent video games, violent musical lyrics, violent television, and violent movies, can produce aggressive arousal that causes misinterpretations of subsequent events and actions in aggressive assessments.

Long-Term Effects Perspective

Cultivation Theory

Cultivation theory was originally developed in order to explain the long-term consequences of television exposure. Cultivation deals more with responses and ways of thinking rather than on specific behaviors such as aggression. In some of his early research, George Gerbner reasoned that television was a source of maintaining and establishing conventional standards of beliefs and behaviors. Thus, television does not necessarily influence specific behaviors or attitudes; instead, it influences our beliefs about cultural values and perceptions of reality. Although television programs are often defined as somewhat different in terms of content and style, they may portray stable conceptions of social reality. In a 2002 study, Gerbner and colleagues suggested that "this is not to claim that any individual program, type of program, or channel (e.g., family programs, talk shows, sports networks, cooking channels, news channels, violent films, and so on) might not have some 'effects' of some kind or another; rather, it is to emphasize that we call 'cultivation analysis' focuses on the consequences of long-term exposure to the entire system of messages, in the aggregate" (p. 45).

Although cultivation theory has been widely applied to television research, a few researchers have extended its implications to violent video games. For instance, Dmitri Williams (2006) examined the effects of long-term online video game exposure to perceptions of real-world dangers. The researchers noted that the online gaming world was not very similar to the real world (i.e., it was similar to *Dungeons & Dragons*), but that it did contain large amounts of violence. Consequently, it was predicted that although the online world is not especially similar to the real world, cultivation effects may still occur. The results did show that through increased exposure to an online game participants increased their perceptions of violent crime occurring in real life. Thus, cultivation theory may also be applied to explain the effects or cultivation of perceptions regarding repeated exposure to violent video games, violent television, and in general repeated exposure to aggressive media.

Desensitization Theory

Desensitization has been suggested to occur in two ways: emotionally and cognitively. *Cognitive desensitization* is a process that occurs when a person, through repeated exposure to violence, comes to view subsequent violent occurrences as ordinary or low in consequence. *Emotional desensitization* occurs when a person, through repeated exposure to violence, does not have a strong affective reaction to previously disturbing stimuli. It could be argued that as a person repeatedly experiences media containing violent content these exposures could influence subsequent responses made by that individual. Acts of violence viewed by individuals could eventually come to be seen as acceptable ways to resolve conflicts or act toward another individual. Furthermore, "observing violence may arouse feelings associated with aggressive thoughts, but at the same time may reduce emotional reactions to the negative consequences of aggression for the victim" (Rule & Ferguson, 1986, p. 30). Thus, violent media may prime more aggressive thoughts and subsequently influence aggressive behaviors. However, viewing more violence (either through the media or direct experience) may lead to less emotional reactions in an individual. If violence comes to be seen as acceptable, subsequent reactions to violence may not be perceived to be harmful or deleterious. This may also influence an individual's attitudes about using aggression or violence in social interactions.

Jeanne B. Funk and colleagues (2004) examined whether or not preferences among schoolchildren for violent media would be associated with lower levels of empathy and stronger pro-violence attitudes. It was reasoned by Funk that cognitive desensitization would be reflected in stronger pro-violence attitudes and emotional desensitization through lowered empathy to real-life violence. Overall, research suggests that exposure to media violence from video games, television, movies, and the Internet can influence empathetic responses to real-life violence and pro-violence attitudes. To this end, desensitization influences individuals through lowered empathy and a stronger pro-violent attitude influenced by violent video games, violent movies, and television.

Script Theory

Scripts are guides for behavior based on past observations or direct experiences that come to be stored in memory for later use. L. Rowell Huesmann proposed a model to help account for the effects of media violence on children and adults. Similar to social cognitive theory, script theory includes reinforcement as a predictor of future use of stored scripts. Thus, if an aggressive behavior elicits a positive reward, then it will more likely be encoded for future use. Huesmann's research, conducted in 1986, mentions that "the more initially salient an observed aggressive scene is to the child, and the more the child ruminates upon, fantasizes about and rehearses the observed scene, the more likely it is that an aggressive script based on that scene is recalled and followed in a social problem-solving situation" (pp. 131–132). Also, the more realistic and the stronger the identification with the media character in the script, the more likely it is that a child will encode and store those aggressive behaviors.

That said, the processes of script theory may be psychologically different for children and older adolescents. For instance, younger individuals may encode new scripts because of their lack of observable scripts related to those behaviors. However, as suggested by Huesmann, older adolescents probably have more experience with such scripts, and it may be a simple cueing of already learned aggressive scripts that influence behaviors or thoughts. Consistent with Anderson's research, the aggressive scripts that are routinely rehearsed are more likely to be associated with other concepts in memory, thus making it more likely that it may be activated. Plus, routinely rehearsed or enacted scripts with each activation increase the strength and possibility that it will be enacted for future use. Individuals who routinely play violent video games or watch aggressive media may develop aggressive scripts for conflict situations. For example, the continual provocation through game play and required aggressive response will develop an aggressive script for conflict resolution. Furthermore, the violence of video games is likely to be rewarded; hence, the script is likely to be reinforced and accessible through repeated exposure.

Vincent Cicchirillo and Matthew S. Eastin

See also Arousal and Aggressive Content, Theory and Psychology of; Cognition: Schemas and Scripts; Cognitive Script Theory and the Dynamics of

Cognitive Scripting; Cultivation Theory; Effect Size in Media Violence, Research and Effects of; Excitation-Transfer Theory; General Aggression Model; Social Cognitive Theory

Further Readings

Anderson, C. A., & Bushman, B. J. (2002). Human aggression. *Annual Review of Psychology, 53,* 27–51.

Berkowitz, L. (1984). Some effects of thoughts on anti- and prosocial influences of media events: A cognitive-neoassociation analysis. *Psychological Bulletin, 95,* 410–427.

Berkowitz, L. (1990). On the formation and regulation of anger and aggression: A cognitive-neoassociationistic analysis. *American Psychology, 45,* 494–503.

Funk, J. B. (2005). Children's exposure to violent video games and desensitization to violence. *Child and Adolescent Clinics of North America, 14,* 387–404.

Funk, J. B., Baldacci, H. B., Pasold, T., & Baumgardner, J. (2004). Violent exposure in real-life, video games, television, movies, and the Internet: Is there desensitization? *Journal of Adolescence, 27,* 23–39.

Gerbner, G., & Gross, L. (1976). Living with television: The violence profile. *Journal of Communication, 26,* 173–199.

Gerbner, G., Gross, L., Morgan, M., Signorielli, N., & Shanahan, J. (2002). Growing up with television: Cultivation processes. In J. Bryant & D. Zillmann (Eds.), *Media effects: Advances in theory and research* (2nd ed., pp. 97–120). Mahwah, NJ: Erlbaum.

Huesmann, L. R. (1986). Psychological processes promoting the relation between exposure to media violence and aggressive behavior by the viewer. *Journal of Social Issues, 42,* 125–140.

Rule, B. G., & Ferguson, T. J. (1986). The effects of media violence of attitudes, emotions, and cognitions. *Journal of Social Issues, 42,* 29–50.

Williams, D. (2006). Virtual cultivation: Online worlds, offline perceptions. *Journal of Communication, 56,* 69–87.

Effects of Media Violence on Relational Aggression

Relational aggression is a nonphysical form of aggression that harms through manipulation of relationships and feelings of social acceptance and inclusion. There is increasing empirical evidence that media violence can lead to relational aggression among viewers. This phenomenon, by which media aggression can lead to types of aggression other than the form viewed, is often referred to as the "crossover effect."

This entry defines relational aggression, reviews empirical evidence for the effects of media violence on relational aggression, presents theoretical models that attempt to explain this crossover effect, and concludes with a discussion of the implications of this research for enhancing our understanding of media violence effects, particularly for females.

Relational aggression is distinct from both verbal and physical aggression. Although specific behaviors vary by developmental period, examples of relational aggression include social exclusion, use of the silent treatment, threats to withdraw love or friendship, and spreading rumors. Findings are somewhat inconclusive as to whether there are gender differences across the life span in the use of relational aggression; however, it is clear that girls and women typically use relational aggression more frequently than physical aggression. Relational aggression has negative consequences for adjustment and relationship quality; therefore, it is important to understand the role of various socializing agents, including the media, in the development and maintenance of these behaviors.

Correlational and experimental studies with children, adolescents, and adults have demonstrated that media violence leads to increases in relationally aggressive behaviors and cognitions among viewers. These effects have been demonstrated as a result of exposure to televised media violence, violent video games, and aggressive print media. Although there is some evidence that individual characteristics (e.g., preexisting aggression levels) and contextual variables (e.g., parental mediation) can alter these effects, there is currently limited research on moderators of the crossover effect.

There are at least two processes that may account for the link between media violence exposure and relational aggression among viewers. First, the general aggression model (GAM) suggests that viewing media violence activates aggression cognitions, increasing the likelihood that the viewer will engage in aggressive behavior. Although there is ample evidence that media violence activates cognitions related to physical aggression, it is only recently that studies have demonstrated similar effects of media violence on relationally aggressive cognitions. The specific processes underlying this activation need to be explored by future research. It may be that exposure to media violence increases the accessibility of general aggressive scripts in memory, including both physically and relationally aggressive thoughts. Alternatively, it may be that media violence primarily activates cognitions related to gender-normative forms of aggression. This latter process would explain the activation of relationally aggressive thoughts in response to exposure to media violence among women only.

A second process that may account for the link between media violence exposure and relational aggression among viewers is that long-term, cumulative exposure to media violence can lead to the development and maintenance of aggressive cognitions. Specifically, media violence exposure can result in hostile attribution bias, the tendency to attribute hostile intent to an individual's ambiguous negative action, as well as development of normative beliefs supportive of aggression. Additionally, both the GAM and George Gerbner's cultivation theory suggest that cumulative exposure to media shapes viewers' perceptions of reality and their beliefs and attitudes. These theories predict that long-term exposure to media violence will lead to beliefs that are consistent with media portrayals of aggression—namely that aggression is prevalent, acceptable, and effective. Research based on social information processing (SIP) models of aggression demonstrates that aggressive cognitions predict individual differences in aggressive behavior. Therefore, it is suggested that associations between media violence exposure and viewer aggression (both physical and relational) are mediated by aggressive cognitions, and existing research supports this premise.

The empirical link between media violence exposure and relational aggression has several implications that can help deepen our understanding of media violence effects. First, this research has demonstrated that media violence effects on aggressive behavior are broader than once believed. Media violence exposure can lead to increases in a variety of aggressive behaviors, not just physical aggression. Second, these findings dispelled the myth that concerns about media violence exposure should be focused on male viewers, who exhibit higher levels of physical aggression across the life span. Media violence may have similar harmful effects on the behavior of female viewers in the form of increased relational aggression. Further research should attempt to elucidate gender differences in this crossover effect and the specific cognitive mechanisms underlying this effect, as well as potential moderators.

Jennifer Ruh Linder

See also Attitude, Effects of Media Violence on; Cognition: Schemas and Scripts; Effects From Violent Content, Short- and Long-Term; Gender, Effects of Violent Content on; Gender and Aggression; General Aggression Model

Further Readings

Anderson, C. A., & Bushman, B. J. (2002). Human aggression. *Annual Review of Psychology, 53,* 27–51.

Card, N. A., Stucky, B. D., Sawalani, G. M., & Little, T. D. (2008). Direct and indirect aggression during childhood and adolescence: A meta-analytic review of gender differences, intercorrelations, and relations to maladjustment. *Child Development, 79,* 1185–1229.

Coyne, S. M., Nelson, D. A., Lawton, F., Haslam, S., Rooney, L., Titterington, L., Trainor, H., Remnant, J., & Ogunlaja, L. (2008). The effects of viewing physical and relational aggression in the media: Evidence for a crossover effect. *Journal of Experimental Social Psychology, 44,* 1551–1554.

Crick, N., & Dodge, K. (1994). A review and reformulation of social information-processing mechanisms in children's social adjustment. *Psychological Bulletin, 115,* 74–101.

EMERGENT PUBLIC HEALTH ISSUE: EFFECTS OF VIOLENCE

Violence is defined by the World Health Organization as "the intentional use of physical force or power, threatened or actual, against another person or against a group or community that results in or has a high likelihood of resulting in injury, death, psychological harm, maldevelopment, or deprivation." Violence takes many forms, including child maltreatment, youth violence, suicide, intimate partner violence, sexual violence, and elder abuse. Many of these behaviors occur in person, but violence can also be perpetrated through various forms of electronic media, such as cell phones, e-mail, and the Internet. There is no single cause of violence. Violence is the result of the complex interplay of individual, interpersonal, community, and societal factors. These factors include but are not limited to exposure to violence in the media, home, and community; poor problem-solving, communication, and social skills; drug and alcohol use; cultural norms that support violence as acceptable; and poverty. People in all stages of life can experience violence as victims, perpetrators, and/or witnesses, and these experiences can negatively affect physical, emotional, social, and economic health. The purpose of this entry is to outline the effects violence has on individuals and communities. Violence is a significant issue, but it is preventable. A public health approach to preventing violence and some evidence-based prevention strategies are also presented.

Violence-Related Mortality, Physical Injury, and Other Health Problems

Since 1965 homicide and suicide have been among the top 15 causes of death in the United States. In 2010, 55,035 individuals died as a result of violence (16,671 from homicide; 38,364 from suicide), an average of 151 each day. Adolescents and young adults have a disproportionately higher rate of violence-related mortality than other age groups. For instance, homicide is the third leading cause of death for young people ages 10 to 24 years, and homicide is the leading cause of death for African American youth. Suicide is the second leading cause of death among 10- to 34-year-olds.

Many more individuals experience physical injuries than premature death as a result of violence. In 2011 more than 2.4 million individuals required a visit to a hospital emergency room because of violence-related injuries. Of these injuries, nearly 487,800 were self-inflicted. The Administration on Children, Youth, and Families estimated that in 2010, 695,000 children were victims of child maltreatment. Of these youth, an estimated 78.3% experienced neglect, 17.6% physical abuse, 9.2% sexual abuse, 2.4% medical neglect, and 10.3% other forms of maltreatment described as threats of harm to the child and congenital drug addiction. Based on 2010 data reported by the Centers for Disease Control and Prevention, an estimated 3.2 million women and 2.3 million men reported experiencing severe physical violence from their intimate partners in the 12 months before they were surveyed. This intimate partner violence included behaviors likely to cause injuries, such as being hit with a fist or something hard, or beaten, kicked, and slammed against something. Furthermore, approximately 1 in 5 women and 1 in 71 men reported having been raped at some point in their lives. The true incidence of physical injury associated with elder abuse is uncertain because of limited monitoring at the national level and limited reporting of suspected cases to local and state protective services agencies. The best available estimates of the prevalence of elder abuse suggest that 1 to 2 million individuals age 65 or older have been abused, neglected, or exploited by persons on whom they depended for care, and many of these victims may have had associated physical injuries.

Experiences of violence can also increase the risk for other short- and long-term physical health problems. In addition to immediate physical problems, children who experience maltreatment have heighten risk for adverse health effects and chronic diseases as adults, including heart disease, cancer, lung disease, liver disease, obesity, high blood pressure, and high cholesterol. Violence by an intimate partner affects an individual's endocrine and immune systems through chronic stress or other mechanisms, which can increase the risk for irritable bowel syndrome, gynecological disorders, central nervous system disorders, and heart or circulatory conditions. Individuals who experience sexual violence have elevated rates of chronic pelvic pain, gastrointestinal disorders, gynecological and pregnancy complications, migraines and other frequent headaches, and back and facial pain. Exposure to youth violence can contribute to a range of other poor physical issues for youth, including smoking, obesity, high-risk sexual behavior, and asthma. Elder abuse can result in a range of physical injuries, such as broken bones and deficient nutrition and hydration, that can exacerbate any preexisting health conditions, increase susceptibility to new illnesses, and increase the possibility of death.

Emotional, Social, and Developmental Effects of Violence

Beyond the physical effects, many individuals who experience violence can have elevated rates of emotional, social, behavioral, academic, and occupational difficulties. The negative effects of violence can be experienced by those directly affected as well as by friends and family of victims, first responders, and people learning about the event from the media. These effects may be observable shortly after the violent incident or may not be obvious for many years. For instance, child maltreatment can impair brain development, resulting in long-term problems in cognition, language, and emotional and behavioral regulation. Relative to nonmaltreated peers, individuals who are maltreated as children can have increased rates of depression, anxiety, eating disorders, conduct disorder, and suicide attempts during their adulthood. Because of fear or experiences of violence as children, adolescents, or adults, individuals may avoid schools and employment settings, thereby limiting their academic and occupational potential and their opportunities to lead independent and productive lives. Youth exposed to violence or trauma in their homes, schools, or communities, or through the media, can have elevated rates of major depression, posttraumatic stress disorder, and substance use disorders as well as an increased likelihood of inflicting violence on others and themselves during adolescence and adulthood. Individuals who experience intimate partner violence may have various psychological consequences, including depression, antisocial behaviors, anxiety, sleep disturbances, and inability to trust others. Victims of sexual violence may experience immediate consequences, such as fear, withdrawal, and distrust of others, as well as chronic psychological conditions, such as depression, posttraumatic stress disorder, and social isolation. Individuals who experience elder abuse may have increased rates of depression and anxiety.

Compounding Effects of Multiple Victimizations

Being a victim of violence increases the risk for future victimizations and negative consequences. For instance, the experience of child maltreatment increases the likelihood of experiencing future assaults and bullying by peers, suicide, sexual violence, and intimate partner violence. Emerging research suggests that children and adolescents who experience multiple victimizations have a heightened vulnerability to severe emotional and behavioral problems. These youth with multiple trauma experiences have significantly higher rates of psychological distress, depression, posttraumatic stress disorder, substance use disorders, and delinquency than their nontraumatized peers or peers with less severe trauma histories. The developing research about cyberbullying or electronic aggression also showed that repeated victimization in person and through various forms of electronic media increases the risk for associated distress. For instance, young people are significantly more likely to report they were distressed when they were bullied by the same people online and in person compared with young people who were bullied by different people online and in person and young people who were only harassed online.

Effects of Violence on the Community

The damage resulting from violence extends beyond the perpetrators, victims, and witnesses. Violence can negatively affect the viability and productivity of communities by increasing health care costs, decreasing property values, and disrupting social

services. The total lifetime economic burden resulting from new cases of fatal and nonfatal child maltreatment in the United States is approximately $125 billion. The cost of deaths associated with violence in 2005 was $47.2 billion in combined medical and work loss costs. This figure underestimates the true economic burden of violence-related deaths because it does not account for costs associated with addressing nonfatal physical and emotional injuries of violence. Violence also results in other significant economic impacts, including the costs of arresting, prosecuting, incarcerating, rehabilitating, and reintegrating offenders, which are the fastest growing parts of many state budgets.

Public Health Approach to Preventing Violence

Although violence is often viewed as an inevitable part of life, like other significant public health problems violence is preventable. Public health, with its emphasis on a science-driven approach and collective action from diverse sectors, brings a focus on maximizing the benefits for the largest number of people. A public health approach to violence prevention is similar to a public health approach to addressing diseases and other harmful conditions—it applies scientific and programmatic expertise to preventing violence before it occurs. This approach involves (a) collecting data and coordinating multiple data systems to understand and monitor violence; (b) analyzing data to identify the populations and locations at greatest risk and to identify the factors that increase or reduce the likelihood of violence; (c) developing and testing violence prevention strategies; and (d) widely implementing violence prevention strategies that are based on the best available evidence.

Violence Prevention Strategies Supported by Research

No one factor causes violence, and there is no one definitive way to prevent violence. The likelihood of violence is influenced by the interaction of a variety of individual, interpersonal, community, and societal risk and protective factors. Prevention efforts work by reducing the multiple risk factors and increasing the many factors that buffer against the risk for violence. Prevention strategies that address risk and protective factors and that have demonstrated reductions in the likelihood of violence have been developed for many forms of violence.

The array of prevention strategies supported by research varies by the type of violence, and the risk factor addressed with most current evidence-based prevention strategies modify the individual's knowledge, skills, and interpersonal relationships. For example, some parenting and family relationship programs that have demonstrated reductions in child maltreatment and youth violence build positive caregiver–child relationships and teach effective communication strategies and use of nonviolent discipline strategies. Reductions in youth violence also have been shown by school-based programs that teach students anger management and interpersonal conflict skills and develop teachers' behavior management abilities. Evidence-based suicide prevention programs teach individuals about suicide and self-harm behaviors and ways to identify and cope effectively with emotions and stress and work to increase communication and problem-solving skills. Dating and sexual violence among adolescents have been shown to be reduced by a program that strives to change adolescent norms on dating violence and gender roles, improve conflict resolution skills, promote victims' and perpetrators' beliefs in the need for help and awareness of community resources for dating violence, encourage help-seeking by victims and perpetrators, and develop peer help-giving skills. Other identified risk factors for violence, such as media violence and cultural norms about the acceptability of violence, are only beginning to be understood, and prevention strategies that can reduce the impact of these risks and the likelihood of associated violence have not yet emerged.

Knowledge about practices, programs, and policies that seek to prevent violence continues to grow. Promising approaches that address broader community and societal influences on violence are beginning to emerge. For example, business improvement districts that create public–private partnerships and invest in local services and activities, such as street cleaning, security, and adding safe green spaces, are showing reduced rates of violent crime in select cities. Research also is showing which prevention strategies are ineffective. Examples of approaches that have been shown to be ineffective in reducing youth violence include Scared Straight, Drug Abuse Resistance Education (DARE), and the policy of transferring juvenile offenders to the adult criminal justice system. As the accessibility and use of social media and technology continue to grow, awareness about the significant public health issue of violence, its broad effects on individuals and communities,

and evidence-based prevention strategies has the potential to grow.

Corinne Ferdon

See also Aggression, Definition and Assessment of; Cyberbullying, Definition and Effects of; Effects From Violent Content, Short- and Long-Term; Sex in Media: Effects on Society; Violence, Definition of

Further Readings

Administration for Children and Families. (n.d.). *Child abuse and neglect.* Retrieved from http://www.acf.hhs.gov/acf_services.html#caan

Centers for Disease Control and Prevention. (n.d.). *Adverse childhood experiences (ACE) study.* Retrieved from http://www.cdc.gov/ace/about.htm

Centers for Disease Control and Prevention. (n.d.). *Violence prevention.* Retrieved from http://www.cdc.gov/ViolencePrevention/index.html

Dahlberg, L. L., & Mercy, J. A. (2009). History of violence as public health issue. *American Medical Association Virtual Mentor, 11,* 167–172. Retrieved from http://virtualmentor.ama-assn.org/2009/02/mhst1-0902.html

Ford, J. D., Elhai, J. D., Connor, D. F., & Frueh, B. C. (2010). Poly-victimization and risk of posttraumatic, depressive, and substance use disorders and involvement in delinquency in a national sample of adolescents. *Journal of Adolescent Health, 46,* 545–552.

Turner, H. A., Finkelhor, D., & Ormrod, R. (2010). Poly-victimization in a national sample of children and youth. *American Journal of Preventive Medicine, 38,* 323–330.

World Health Organization. (2013). *Health topics: Violence.* Retrieved from http://www.who.int/topics/violence/en

ETHICAL DEVELOPMENT, EFFECTS ON

Among the types of mediated depictions that have the ability to affect moral growth (e.g., sex, stereotypes, profanity, social relationships), the topic of violence has been the central focus of research. Despite this focus, there have been few studies looking specifically at developmental processes. Moreover, the theoretical frameworks used to study the effects of violence on moral development do not explain how the underlying emotional and intuitive components of moral judgment might change over time. Rather, theory tends to focus on social learning or cognitive-developmental moderators that do not identify moral judgment's basic motivational origins.

Traditional theory on ethical development conceives of morality as the product of rational processes, in which an individual consciously weighs evidence and infers culpability. By contrast, newer approaches in moral psychology stress the role of emotional and intuitive motivations that underlie moral judgment.

This entry discusses the theoretical frameworks used in past investigations of media violence's effect on children's ethical development, focusing on their main tenets and shortcomings. Last, newer approaches in moral psychology that have the potential to increase our understanding of media violence's effect on moral development are introduced.

Traditional Understandings

The early social-scientific theories on moral development come from Jean Piaget (1965) and later Lawrence Kohlberg (1984). Their cognitive-developmental approaches have continued to be influential in 21st-century literature on media violence. According to their cognitive-developmental models, morality is considered to be a set of rules to be learned and applied. As such, their theories proposed that moral judgment becomes more "advanced" as children's abstract reasoning abilities increase. Both Piaget and Kohlberg conceived of morality as justice and emphasized that moral advancement consists of an increasing reliance on justice in social judgments.

Piaget's framework consisted of two primary stages of moral growth. In the first stage, labeled the *heteronomous stage,* children's moral judgments are characterized by a dependence on authority, such as parents and teachers, as well as a focus on egoistic perceptions rather than perspective taking. In this stage, punishment handed down by an authority figure appears to be morally just. Observations have shown that when young children see harsh, violent punishment handed down or meted out by an authority figure, they interpret the severity of the punishment as an indicator of the misdeed's severity. Children in this stage use logic suggesting that the sterner a punishment is, the more justice has been served. Moreover, because young children do not consider others' intentions, the consequences of a misdeed (rather than motives) are more central in determining whether a behavior is perceived as morally just. Eventually, after children realize that their goals cannot be met by simple judgments based on authoritarian concerns or a focus on egoistic perceptions, they reach the *autonomous stage* of moral reasoning. In this stage,

children can better weigh the proportionality of a misdeed to its respective punishment. According to Piaget, moral judgments in this stage are based on an inner sense of equity. Cognitive reasoning is used to generate such equity-based moral judgments. Also, children advance from stage to stage through a type of mental conflict labeled *cognitive disequilibrium,* in which children actively construct meaning while engaged in cognitive reasoning.

Kohlberg later expanded Piaget's framework to include three major stages of moral growth (each with its own substages not discussed here). Like Piaget's, Kohlberg's concept of morality was based on justice. According to this framework, justice becomes more and more central to the judgment process, while other factors (such as a strong emotional desire for harsh revenge) become less salient as morality advances from stage to stage. The first major developmental period, which Kohlberg called the *preconventional stage,* is conceptualized much like Piaget's heteronomous stage. Children at this level of moral growth make judgments based on simple reward and punishment, authoritarian rules, and egoistic concerns stemming from an inability to engage in perspective taking. The second major stage in Kohlberg's scheme, the *conventional stage,* is characterized by the child taking into account the motives of others in a moral judgment. Children in this stage can recognize that violent behavior is less morally wrong if the perpetrator did not commit the violence intentionally. Judgments in this stage are also characterized by a greater ability to take into account proportionality and equity and to have a sense of empathy, consensus, and hierarchy with others that reinforces healthy interpersonal relationships and maintains social order. Kohlberg contended that not all individuals reach the final level of moral reasoning, labeled the *postconventional stage.* In this stage, individuals go beyond simple rules and are able to appeal to abstract moral certitudes about justice and individual rights while ignoring emotions that should be unrelated to justice.

Although there is an abundance of literature on cognitive development throughout the life span that goes beyond Piaget and Kohlberg, their cognitive-developmental models are still cited as foundational in studies of moral growth. Using these cognitive-developmental frameworks, research has shown that exposure to violent content is linked to authority-based moral reasoning strategies characteristic of the early stages of moral development. Also, measures designed specifically to assess developmental level through survey and interview techniques have been used to show that exposure to violent media is related to less advanced stages of moral reasoning in general. Moreover, experimental research applying cognitive-developmental models has demonstrated a causal link between exposure to violent content and moral growth. One line of research has examined "fantasy violence" (i.e., cartoon violence that young children are regularly exposed to) and has shown that it can lead children to utilize less advanced moral reasoning strategies compared with those not exposed to fantasy violence. To explain such findings, it has been proposed that when violence is portrayed as justified (versus unjustified), perspective-taking abilities may be hampered. This is because depictions of justified violence generally focus only on satisfying retributive concerns and minimize the salience of pain and suffering caused by retribution.

Despite their utility, the traditional cognitive-developmental approaches described have been criticized for a number of reasons. First, it has been noted that individuals generally do not fall "neatly" into one of the developmental stages outlined by Kohlberg. When responding to interview questions, study participants often use a mix of different reasoning strategies characteristic of multiple developmental levels. Second, it is often noted that development does not consist of the qualitative shifts suggested by the stage models of Piaget and Kohlberg. Rather, contemporary literature on cognitive development suggests that it advances continuously throughout childhood and adolescence, and that no definitive boundaries exist between different periods or phases of development. Third, the approach has been criticized for being culturally biased. Research has shown that postconventional moral reasoning is usually restricted to individuals who have a Western education. Despite the fact that individuals in non-Western cultures often use complex moral reasoning strategies to weigh multiple moral concerns, these individuals are generally not categorized as postconventional thinkers because they rely on criteria other than equity or justice in their moral decision making (e.g., traditionalism or moral purity). Finally, the approach assumes that moral judgment is a conscious, rational process, and that the motivations driving moral judgments are easily verbalized. The approach generally presents study participants with a moral dilemma and then asks them to articulate their thoughts about the dilemma. Individuals are then categorized into different developmental stages according to their verbalized responses. Newer approaches in moral psychology

claim that the majority of moral judgments occur intuitively and without conscious awareness, because most situations are not characterized by a dilemma or mental conflict that can evoke deliberative thought. Clear-cut situations in which an individual has committed a moral transgression do not typically stimulate conscious thought processes. Moreover, there is convincing evidence that individuals cannot always verbalize the motivations that determine their moral judgments, as discussed following. Before discussing such newer approaches, this entry first turns to another common framework in the study of media violence's effect on ethical development.

Albert Bandura's social cognitive theory is one of the most common frameworks for studying the effects of media violence. This literature has tended to link exposure to violent media to aggressive emotions, cognitions, or behaviors. The framework suggested that mediated depictions, such as superheroes triumphantly destroying evil through violent means, can validate, romanticize, or make trivial the use of violence. Bandura's framework emphasized the role of self-regulatory mechanisms, which are moral standards internalized through social experience. Mediated depictions may serve to selectively activate or disengage these internalized moral standards leading to inhibitory and disinhibitory effects. Disengagement of moral standards (through various mechanisms such as euphemistic labeling, dehumanization, or displacement of responsibility) can lead to moral transgressions such as violent behavior. Studies applying this framework have linked exposure to mediated violence (video games as well as traditional media) with aggressive outcomes such as disinhibition or moral disengagement. This is true for both correlational, survey-based research and experimental research conducted in the laboratory. Moreover, studies using this theoretical framework have shown that exposure to violent media as a young child is linked to an increased risk for aggressive behaviors later in life. Ultimately, certain depictions of violence may influence the self-regulatory mechanisms described by social cognitive theory, leading to disinhibition of violent motivations and moral disengagement. This process can be understood as having an impact on moral growth.

Newer Understandings

Whereas the cognitive-developmental models of Piaget and Kohlberg focused on an understanding of justice as the essence of morality, Bandura's social cognitive theory suggested that morality's essence consists of internalized social conventions. However, newer understandings in media and morality suggest that the essence of morality is innately dependent on universal, intrinsic motivations.

One such newer understanding comes from moral foundations theory (MFT). According to this framework, intuitive, rapid judgments about perceived behaviors create an immediate sense of "rightness" or "wrongness" that evokes a moral judgment. The framework has proposed that innate motivations govern a set of distinct *moral intuitions* that form the basis for all moral judgments. In its current form, MFT has identified six basic intuitive drives, labeled *care, fairness, liberty, ingroup loyalty, authority,* and *sanctity*. Each of these drives is thought to have emerged from human evolution as distinct fragments of mental circuitry that yield unconscious and automatic moral judgments to facilitate social behavior and group living. Literature has proposed that these moral intuitions may be functionally modular, in that each is used for a distinct type of social situation. Evidence for the framework's suggestion that moral judgment is unconscious and difficult to verbalize comes from an effect known as *moral dumbfounding*. This effect is illustrated when study participants are presented with a story about consensual incest (between a brother and a sister) without the possibility of reproduction. According to the story, the incestuous event is kept secret, brings the siblings closer together, and increases their overall happiness. Study participants generally have a strong emotional response and declare that the act was morally wrong, even when they acknowledge the absence of a victim in the story. The effect is labeled "moral dumbfounding" because even when participants acknowledge they have no reason for it, they often maintain their contention that the act was wrong on moral grounds.

Although MFT has posited that all humans are born with this "first draft" of six moral intuitions, cultural experience (including exposure to mediated violence) can influence the importance an individual or culture places on specific moral intuitions. Although no studies have thus far been framed in terms of developmental impact specifically, several studies have shown that exposure to morally relevant content can influence the importance placed on specific moral intuitions. This preliminary research has been conducted using both traditional paper-and-pencil surveys as well as newer research methods designed to tap unconscious attitudes in the laboratory.

Developmentally, emphasis on a specific moral intuition through repeated exposure to mediated or nonmediated messages should influence that intuition's impact on moral judgments. Continuous exposure to violence, for example, should lead to a decrease in the relative importance of the care intuition in moral judgments. This change in the relative importance of the care intuition should affect subsequent moral judgment. The significance of this change in relative importance can be seen especially when considering judgments that entail multiple salient moral concerns. In such a situation, it is often the case that one moral intuition must be sacrificed to adhere to another (e.g., in a moral dilemma). MFT has used dual-process logic to explain such a situation. This logic suggests that although most moral judgments are fast and automatic, conflict between incongruent moral concerns may lead to slower, deliberative judgments. If media violence has decreased the relative importance of the care intuition, then other concerns, such as allegiance to one's nation (ingroup loyalty), a desire for retribution (fairness), or deference to a superior (authority), may be judged as more important in the deliberative process and thus lead to a violent or aggressive outcome. For example, take the case of a gang member who is provoked or taunted by a member of a rival gang. If the relative salience of care for that gang member is less than the salience of ingroup loyalty and other salient concerns, such as retribution, then the likelihood for violent retaliation will increase.

Especially important to media violence's effect on ethical development, recent literature has discussed the reciprocal influence between media content and moral intuitions. To illustrate this process, consider an individual who places little emphasis on the care intuition. Such a person may have no trouble enjoying a gory, violent ending in which a protagonist gratifyingly slays an evildoer. This enjoyable experience can lead to a positive feedback cycle in which expectations learned from past media experiences drive future media choice behavior. Feedback occurs through repeated selections and exposures as the salience of care decreases and the ability to enjoy violence increases. If an individual's environment lacks messages upholding the care intuition, such a cyclical process could lead an individual to become polarized from mainstream views in terms of his or her endorsement of violent behavior. Such a process has been described by newer models in media theory, such as Ron Tamborini's (2011) model of intuitive morality and exemplars (MIME). Over time, such a reciprocal influence process may have a profound impact on moral growth. At this point, no study has examined the influence of media violence on moral intuitions over time. More studies, especially those using longitudinal methods, are needed to look at this reciprocal influence process to determine how the importance of moral intuitions changes developmentally and to understand the role of media violence in this process.

Overall, the various consequences of exposure to media violence for ethical development have been explored only in a preliminary way. Future studies need to apply newer understandings of moral psychology and media processes (such as MFT and MIME) as well as newer measurement techniques and longitudinal research methods. By mapping out the manner in which media violence affects developmental trajectories of underlying emotional and intuitive moral judgment components, researchers and practitioners will have better frameworks within which to understand media processes and to effect positive change.

Robert Joel Lewis

See also Cognitive Psychology of Violence; Developmental Effects; Exposure to Violent Content; Effects on Child Development; Longitudinal Research Findings on the Effects of Violent Content; Moral Development, Effects of Media Violence on; Social Cognitive Theory

Further Readings

Haidt, J., & Joseph, C. (2007). The moral mind: How five sets of innate moral intuitions guide the development of many culture-specific virtues, and perhaps even modules. In P. Carruthers, S. Laurence, and S. Stich (Eds.), *The innate mind* (Vol. 3, pp. 367–391). New York, NY: Oxford University Press. doi: 10.1111/j.1468–0017.2007.00302.x

Kohlberg, L. (1984). The psychology of moral development: The nature and validity of moral stages (Vol. 3). San Francisco: Harper & Row.

Krcmar, M. (2012). The effect of media on children's moral reasoning. In R. Tamborini (Ed.), *Media and the moral mind* (pp. 198–217). London: Routledge.

Krcmar, M., & Vieira, E. T. (2005). Imitating life, imitating television: The effects of family and television models on children's moral reasoning. *Communication Research, 32*, 267–294. doi: 10.1177/0093650205275381

Piaget, J. (1965). *The moral judgment of the child.* New York, NY: Free Press.

Tamborini, R. (2011). Moral intuition and media entertainment. *Journal of Media Psychology, 23*, 39–45. doi:10.1027/1864–1105/a000031

ETHICAL ISSUES IN RESEARCHING MEDIA VIOLENCE EFFECTS

Ethical issues that arise from researching potential effects of violent media on audiences parallel the ethical issues that arise from researching other social phenomena. The study of violent media effects necessarily involves human participants who answer survey questions, contribute to focus groups, respond to in-depth interviews, participate in laboratory or field experiments, and so on. The interests of participants presumably are balanced with the interests of the research. Scholars who conduct this research are asked by review mechanisms such as institutional review boards (IRBs) to set aside their ambitions and prejudices in favor of participants' safety and the priority of science.

Trust in the processes of scientific research and acceptance of research evidence is based, in part, on assurances that research is conducted and reported ethically. According to the European Commission on Research and Innovation, the public holds research and science in high regard. This trust is believed to be important to the process of disseminating knowledge and acting on that knowledge in discourse and public policy. In the United States, the Office of Research Integrity (ORI) oversees research funded by the National Institutes of Health (NIH). The ORI receives few allegations of misconduct each year. Of more than 25,000 grants, it initiates fewer than 50 investigations, and about one-third of these result in a misconduct finding.

In the field of media violence effects research, claims of ethics violations are infrequent. Subtle characteristics of research in a field with equivocal findings may lead some critics to make claims that researchers' intentions, accuracy, and bias result not from misconduct but rather from exuberance and impassioned debate. Nevertheless, it is worth reflecting on the traditions of ethical regulation of social research and reviewing the principles and regulations that determine ethics in social research, including media effects research.

Ethical Regulation of Social Research

The concise history of the principles, codes, and regulations that have led to current practices around ethics issues in social research is commonly linked to the end of World War II and the Nuremberg Doctors Trials in 1947. Of course, history is not so simple, and a longer and more complex origin timeline for ethics in social research reaches into antiquity. While the Nuremberg Doctors Trials found inhumane treatment of human subjects, the Prussian state had developed regulations for biomedical research at the turn of the century. Nevertheless, the trials permitted the research community to reflect on the Hippocratic Oath affirmed by doctors not to intentionally harm patients and extended the same principles to health and social science research involving human participants.

Significant events following the Nuremberg trials included the United Nations' Universal Declaration of Human Rights in 1948, the Declaration of Helsinki adopted by the World Medical Association (WMA) in 1964, the Australian National Health and Medical Research Council (NHMRC) 1966 Statement on Human Experimentation and Supplementary Notes to guide research and establish human research ethics committees (HRECs), and the United States' National Research Act and its creation of the United States' National Commission for the Protection of Human Subjects of Biomedical and Behavioral Research (NCPHSBBR) in 1974.

Publication of the *Belmont Report* by the NCPHSBBR (1979) established the ethical principles and guidelines followed by researchers in the United States today under the Code of Federal Regulations, Title 45, Part 46: Protection of Human Subjects. Although these major events punctuate the historical record on growing awareness and regulation of research ethics, many interstitial events of course lead to these milestones. Moreover, recent debate and consternation have followed these events, with concern that growing regulation of research ethics has occurred less to protect human participants in research and more to mitigate against legal risks as well as threats to the reputations of research institutions.

Regardless of conflicting views about the history and meaning of research ethics regulation, researchers and regulatory bodies around the world share the codes of ethical research. Hundreds of IRBs in the United States and thousands more internationally exist to review and enforce these codes of ethics. The overriding interest expressed in these is concern for the well-being of others and the priority of minimizing risk to participants for whom individual respect is paramount. Consequently, breaches of the code for ethical research practice are often found to occur not through deliberate violations but rather through technical problems and insensitive approaches to research that IRBs seek to prevent.

Guidelines applied by IRBs attempt to ensure research merit, integrity, justice, beneficence, and respect. Interest in research merit seeks to balance the quality of the proposed research as well as its potential contribution to knowledge and social welfare with the potential impact and harms that might be experienced by the research participant. Integrity considerations attempt to guide honest research conduct and communication of results. Just research accounts for fair participant recruitment and sampling procedures; appropriate burden on individuals or special groups of participants, such as students; and shared benefit from the research outcomes. In weighing beneficence, researchers and IRBs balance the level of benefit likely to result from the research against the potential risks that might be borne by participants. Finally, respect for participants as individuals recognizes different beliefs, customs, and cultural heritage, practices, and values.

These codes and guidelines are articulated to guide how research involving human participants is conducted, how it is reported, and how potential conflicts of interest that may arise from sources of funding and institutional relationships can be avoided.

Conducting Research

Engaging participants in ethical social research requires that participants are able to choose or consent freely to participate. In order to make this choice, participants must be fully informed about all the ways in which they would participate in the research and all the procedures they would be required to complete. For this reason, participants must have the intellectual capacity to comprehend the information researchers present to them. Minors, intellectually impaired individuals, and other groups not able to understand the details of the research procedures do not have the capacity to provide informed consent. In such circumstances, researchers are compelled to obtain consent through intermediaries such as adults, including parents, family, friends, or teachers, who serve as gatekeepers charged with protecting the dependents' interest.

Two additional concerns press on researchers who seek to engage participants and obtain informed consent. One is the potential to coerce participation either by offering unduly attractive incentives or incentives that may be of greater value to special populations (e.g., money paid to low-income earners such as students). The other concern is exploitation of power dependencies that may exist between researchers and participants. In a large proportion of the effects literature, school and university students are the population of interest. With school students, for whom the classroom teacher has the authority to direct participation, it is critical that researchers avoid enabling a power dependency to form. University students enrolled in a class of the researcher or the researcher's colleague or teaching assistant may fear consequences of nonparticipation; they may also anticipate grade-related benefits of agreement to participate and thus may feel compelled to participate. Departmental subject pools have been designed as a mechanism to overcome power dependencies, but these are subject to criticism for compelling students, nevertheless, to participate in research and for having the potential to invalidate the generalizability of a large body of psychological research.

A common dilemma that researchers must overcome is concealment. Media violence research is widely publicized in mainstream news media; consequently, participants' knowledge of the purpose of a study (particularly its hypotheses) may bias the way they respond to the study conditions. The balance that must be struck in this case is to limit concealment in a way that does not impinge on the capacity of the potential participant to make an appropriate decision about whether to proceed with involvement in the study. More difficult to manage are instances in which effects researchers determine it necessary to deceive participants in order to "throw them off the scent" of the purpose of the study to prevent participants responding or acting in a contrived or biased manner.

A necessity of experimental research on media effects is that participants are exposed to content that has the potential to harm them, for example, by causing physical or mental stress. Moreover, participants may be asked to perform tasks that have the potential to diminish their self-respect, such as performing a task that, ostensibly, harms another individual. Ethical conduct in media violence research is particularly problematic in this way because researchers who seek not to harm their participants should not produce the harmful effects that the research seeks to observe. These potential harms are minimized by contriving proxy conditions of violence and by ensuring that participants can opt out of the research at any time during the research trial, or by debriefing participants following the trial to ensure any potential harms are addressed and ameliorated.

Respect for and protection of privacy evolve from research ethics guidelines centered on respect and consent to participate. In public places, privacy is assumed to be less important than in private spaces. Similarly, participation in observational and question-asking research that does not identify individuals is assumed to diminish privacy violations. In such research, participants are entitled to expect that their individual answers, scores, and behaviors will not be divulged to others as part of the condition for their participation. Most social research ensures either anonymity for or confidentiality of the participant, depending on the nature of the research. Anonymous participation is common with large-sample surveys in which neither the researcher nor the reader of the research would in any way be able to identify the participant by his or her answers. Confidential participation is more common in experimental and other question-asking research such as focus groups and in-depth interviews in which the researcher knows the identity of the participant and can link the participant's responses to the manipulation or question but agrees not to divulge the identity of the participant associated with responses to the research.

Reporting and Publishing Research

Among the ethical issues that may arise from reporting and publishing research are plagiarism, multiple publication of the same research, data analysis errors, falsifying results, fabricating data, inadequate citing of resources, and making exaggerated claims about the implications of results in relation to public policy. In general, matters of ethics concerning publication focus on accuracy and honesty. Considerable guidance exists, particularly for media researchers, from the Association for Education in Journalism and Mass Communication (AEJMC) Code of Ethics approved by members in 2008. The AEJMC Code dedicates five of its eight principles to reporting and publishing ethics.

Avoiding plagiarism is the first principle in the AEJMC Code of Ethics. However, evidence for plagiarism and multiple publication misconduct is not part of published debates about media violence effects. Instead, it is generally recognized that pressures to publish research in order to advance the different careers of multiple authors and to meet production criteria set by some institutions lead to occasional claims of intellectual property theft and multiple publication from the same research. The code clarifies in the sixth principle that only original work not previously published should be submitted for publication.

Another of eight principles of the AEJMC Code calls on researchers to ensure the integrity of their research at every step of the process, from collecting data to analyzing it. In particular, the code makes explicit that fabricating data and concealing data that do not agree with the researcher's hypotheses, research agenda, or sponsor's goals are unethical. Similarly, the code tasks researchers with reporting results accurately and objectively. Methods and variations in procedures must be fully disclosed. Reports that differ from results simply to satisfy a research agenda are unethical. Moreover, whenever an error in the study is discovered, it is the responsibility of researchers to report this to the editor of the journal in which the research was published.

Avoiding Conflicts of Interest

Empirical research normally involves a number of financial costs, such as paying for access to participants; laboratory and field data collection costs; researcher time to design, field, and report research; and a number of administrative costs. It is reasonable to conclude that all research is funded to one degree or another. Funding sources include internal grants from researchers' institutions, external foundations and government grants, and private, industry, or client support related to applied research questions. It is a matter of ethics that funding sources are disclosed and that institutional relationships are declared to avoid concealment of conflicts of interest that may in fact or perception affect the impetus for and/or the conclusions from research.

The matter of conflicts of interest is complex in media violence research. Because media violence research may be driven by public concern, and because the fields of psychology and sociology tend to explore the causes and reduction of deviance, the inclination of researchers and the sources of their funding are to contribute to knowledge and policy with innovative research designs and definitive empirical outcomes. When entire professional bodies such as academic associations have professed definitive evidence from the body of research, they have also declared their positions in relation to the debate. For example, the American Psychological Association funds a large number and variety of research through scholarships, awards, and grants. Researchers supported with these resources are

encouraged to declare the funding source as part of the publication of their research.

Media Violence and the Ethics of Effects Research

Debates feature in every robust field of research, particularly those receiving media attention and those applied to the formation of public policy. Research on the effects of violent media on society receives considerable media and policy attention that produces lively debate. However, findings of media violence effects research have been contradictory across the literature on television and traditional mass media, and more recently on video games, particularly in government hearings such as those in the U.S. Supreme Court in 2011 and the Commonwealth of Australia in 2010. Contradictory findings and charged government debate have given rise to division and contestation between those who argue that evidence is consistent with the hypothesis that media violence produces aggression and those who argue that the evidence is not consistent with the effects hypothesis.

Although disagreements about the research may be impassioned, and claims of poor methods and interpretations of data feature regularly, claims of ethical misconduct are not forthcoming. Two substantive debates about violent media effects, one of historic merit and one of contemporary value, demonstrated the point. Neither explicitly questioned ethics, but both explored problems of methodology and interpretation, sometimes asking implicit questions of ethical propriety.

Cultivation and the Effects of Television Violence on Perceptions of Reality

In the early 1980s, Communication Research published a debate between George Gerbner and colleagues and Paul Hirsch on the effects of television on perceptions of violence in society, conceptualized in cultivation theory. Cultivation quickly grew in generative and heuristic value after Gerbner and colleagues published a series of papers on the Cultural Indicators Project and numbered "TV Violence Profiles" in which the authors first established "message system analyses" and then "cultivation analyses" from data provided by the National Opinion Research Center's (NORC) General Social Surveys and University of Michigan Institute for Social Research (ISR) survey data in order to identify a relationship between television drama content and, separately, perceptions of social reality ostensibly "cultivated" by heavy consumption of television content, which they reported to find.

Hirsch (1981a) reanalyzed the NORC and ISR data used by Gerbner and colleagues in support of their hypothesis. He did this both to provide reanalysis to test for replicability of results and to interrogate the statistical evidence that Gerbner and colleagues published in their reports. Hirsch reached conclusions that differed from those of the Gerbner group. Hirsh wrote that their cultivation hypothesis was not supported by the data. In his second examination of cultivation, Hirsch concluded that conceptual extensions to the hypothesis, namely "mainstreaming" and "resonance," were both illogical and unsupported by the data.

In their rejoinder to Hirsch's reanalysis and conclusion, Gerbner, Larry Gross, Michael Morgan, and Nancy Signorielli (1981) claimed that Hirsch's conclusions contained overstatement, exaggeration, and inaccuracy. Language used in their rejoinder featured passages that charged that Hirsch's position was "scientifically indefensible" and "false." In his rejoinder to Gerbner and colleagues, Hirsch (1981b) demonstrated the level of rancor and subtext over ethical considerations by taking umbrage at their claims that he had committed breaches of scholarly standards.

General Aggression Model and the Effects of Video Game Violence on Behavior

Three decades later, researchers of media violence effects have continued to question one another's conclusions. Attention on media violence effects has (generally) migrated from television drama and cultivation to computer games and the general aggression model (GAM). The GAM, advanced by Craig Anderson and colleagues in the early 2000s (Anderson & Bushman 2002), is a social cognitive theory of aggression that was developed over a period of years based on data collected primarily from student samples. The theory has been criticized by a number of scholars, particularly Christopher Ferguson and colleagues. These critics have claimed that supporters of the GAM are absolute in their view that their data support the theory and that GAM researchers use the theory to support moral, rather than scientific, positions.

The debate crystallized in 2010 when Ferguson and John Kilburn published a meta-analysis in the *Journal of Pediatrics* on research of violent media

(not just computer games) and aggression in relation to their public health risk. The authors claimed that publication bias and methodological problems plagued the field. In response, Fredrick Zimmerman and Victor Strasburger (2010) argued that the meta-analysis was flawed and that researchers with software can produce statistics that have little scientific value, claiming that their critics' research had little methodological rigor. The reply from Ferguson and Kilburn (2010) offered that Zimmerman and Strasburger made many errors, had omitted important information, and were polemical and dishonest to the point of misleading the public.

These debates highlight a number of ethical concerns. The first is that methodological limitations have troubled definitive findings intended otherwise for directed policy application. Consequently, researchers have been encouraged to support rather than falsify their research hypotheses. The second is that subjective, affective, and ego-involved attachment to theory has produced apparent bias in the presentation and contextualization of research. The third is that appropriate or accurate real-world applications of findings derived from empirical data have been problematic. Finally, haste to produce empirical outcomes has taxed some participants, particularly students who have served as convenient sources of observation. In turn, research findings may have been limited, and therefore their contributions may have been less meaningful through useful findings.

Conclusion

The study of ethics is itself a field of interpretation. Ethics, after all, is a branch of philosophy that deals with what is right or proper conduct and what is not. As with all fields, there are different approaches to determining right and proper research behavior, and these are commonly outlined in research methods textbooks popular in courses on media.

To protect the welfare and rights of research participants, questions of research integrity and ethical conduct by researchers are asked both before the research begins and once research is published. IRBs and HRECs will have reviewed much of the published research in the media effects literature before that research was undertaken. After publication, scholars will have considered the ethical conduct of research and the claims made by authors. Consequently, claims of research misconduct are uncommon.

In the field of media violence effects, the suite of methods available to researchers to explore their hypotheses is a limited one that struggles to establish a causal relationship, that cannot be challenged by rival explanations, between exposure to media violence on the one hand and aggressive behavior in audiences on the other hand. In short, scientists are left with attempting to use a variety of methods to get at the "truth" but fail to do so because the ideal experiment cannot be conducted: For if scientists had the capacity to manipulate and isolate critical variables, it would be unethical to do so because of the resulting harm that would be inflicted on those who participated in the research.

Jeffrey E. Brand

See also Cultivation Theory; Effect Size in Media Violence, Research and Effects of; General Aggression Model; Methodologies for Assessing Effects of Media; Priming Theory

Further Readings

American Psychological Association. (2012). *American Psychological Association: Conflicts of interest and commitments.* Retrieved from http://www.apa.org/research/responsible/conflicts/index.aspx

American Psychological Association. (2012). *American Psychological Association: Scholarships, grants, and awards.* Retrieved from http://www.apa.org/about/awards/index.aspx

Anderson, C.A., & Bushman, B. J. (2002). Human aggression. *Annual Review of Psychology, 53,* 27–51.

Association for Education in Journalism and Mass Communication. (2005). *AEJMC Code of Ethics Research: Recommended Ethical Research Guidelines for AEJMC Members.* Retrieved from http://www.aejmc.com/home/2011/03/ethics-research/

Brown v. Entertainment Merchants Association et al. 564 U.S. __ (2011).

Bushman, B. J., & Anderson, C. A. (2002). Violent video games and hostile expectations: A test of the general aggression model. *Personality and Social Psychology Bulletin, 28*(12), 1679–1686.

Chastain, G., & Landrum, R. E. (Eds.). (1999). *Protecting human subjects: Departmental subject pools and institutional review boards.* Washington, DC: American Psychological Association.

Commonwealth of Australia. (2010). *Literature review on the impact of playing violent video games on aggression.* Canberra: Australian Government Attorney-General's Department. Retrieved from http://bit.ly/W058P6

Dingwall, R. (2012). How did we ever get into this mess? The rise of ethical regulation in the social sciences. In K. Love & C. Pole (Eds.), *Ethics in social research* (pp. 3–26). Bingley, UK: Emerald Group.

European Commission. (2010). *Guidance note for researchers and evaluators of social sciences and humanities research* (draft). Brussels: Author. Retrieved from ftp://ftp.cordis.europa.eu/pub/fp7/docs/ethical-guidelines-in-ssh-research_en.pdf

European Commission. (2012). *Policy issues: Ethics in EU research.* Brussels: Author. Retrieved from http://ec.europa.eu/research/health/policy-issues-ethics_en.html

Ferguson, C. J., & Dyck, D. (2012). Paradigm change in aggression research: The time has come to retire the General Aggression Model. *Aggression and Violent Behavior, 17,* 220–228.

Ferguson, C. J., & Kilburn, J. (2009). The public health risks of media violence: A meta-analytic review. *Journal of Pediatrics, 154*(5), 759–763.

Ferguson, C. J., & Kilburn, J. (2010). Reply to Zimmerman and Strasburger. *Journal of Pediatrics, 156*(1), 169–170.

Ferguson, C. J., & Savage, J. (2011). Have recent studies addressed methodological issues raised by five decades of television violence research? A critical review. *Aggression and Violent Behavior, 17,* 129–139.

Freedman, J. L. (2003). Media violence and its effect on aggression: Assessing the scientific evidence. Toronto: University of Toronto Press.

Gerbner, G., Gross, L., Jackson-Beeck, M., Jeffries-Fox, S., & Signorielli, N. (1978). Cultural indicators: Violence profile, no. 9. *Journal of Communication, 28,* 176–207.

Gerbner, G., Gross, L., Morgan, M., & Signorielli, N. (1981). A curious journey into the scary world of Paul Hirsch. *Communication Research 8,* 39–72. doi: 10.1177/009365028100800102

Hirsch, P. M. (1980). The "scary world" of the nonviewer and other anomalies: A Reanalysis of Gerbner et al.'s findings on cultivation analysis part I. *Communication Research, 7,* 403–456. doi: 10.1177/009365028000700401

Hirsch, P. M. (1981a). On not learning from one's own mistakes: A reanalysis of Gerbner et al.'s findings on cultivation analysis part II. *Communication Research 8:* 3–37. doi: 10.1177/009365028100800101

Hirsch, P. M. (1981b). Distinguishing good speculation from bad theory. *Communication Research 8:* 73–95. doi: 10.1177/009365028100800103

Israel, M., & Hay, I. (Eds.). (2006). *Research ethics for social scientists.* London: Sage.

National Commission for the Protection of Human Subjects of Biomedical and Behavioral Research. (1979). *The Belmont Report: Ethical principles & guidelines for research involving human subjects.* Washington, DC: U.S. Government Printing Office. Retrieved from http://www.hhs.gov/ohrp/policy/belmont.html

National Health and Medical Research Council. (2007). *National statement on ethical conduct in human research*. Canberra: Australian government. Retrieved from http://www.nhmrc.gov.au/_files_nhmrc/publications/attachments/e72_national_statement_nhmrc_arc.pdf

National Health and Medical Research Council. (2011). *Research integrity*. Australian government: National health and Medical Research Council. Retrieved from http://www.nhmrc.gov.au/health-ethics/research-integrity

Office for Human Research Projections. (2009). Code of Federal Regulations, Title 45 Public Welfare, Department of Health and Human Services, Part 46, Protection of Human Subjects. Retrieved from http://www.hhs.gov/ohrp/policy/ohrpregulations.pdf

Olson, C. K. (2004). Media violence research and youth violence data: Why do they conflict? *Academic Psychiatry, 28*, 144–150.

Zimmerman, F. J. & Strasburger, V. C. (2010). Violence in media research. *Journal of Pediatrics, 156*(1), 168–169.

EXCITATION-TRANSFER THEORY

Initially proposed by Dolf Zillmann in the early 1970s, excitation-transfer theory (ETT) has been continuously tested and developed in a large range of communication contexts in the past few decades. The theory posits that cognitive awareness of the source of sympathetic excitation or arousal will decay before the excitation itself decays. Hence, residual excitation from the preceding stimulus tends to be misattributed to its subsequent stimulus and intensify emotional reactivity to the subsequent stimulus.

This theory is important to communication research because communication processes and behaviors are situated in contexts permeated with emotion and where successive emotion changes are an essential characteristic. For example, conversations—face to face or via social media—often unfold amid rapid topic and emotion changes. Similarly, media use typically involves switches between different content subjects with different emotions through changing channels, surfing websites, or multitasking with entertainment media and chores. For contextualized communication phenomena like these, ETT highlights the importance of recognizing and theorizing sequential dependencies in emotional responses to the changing environment and stimuli. In particular, the theory focuses on an enhancement effect on emotional reactivity to the present stimulus

and environment caused by residual excitation left over from preceding ones. Perhaps this excitation-transfer and emotion-intensification process is of special interest to media violence research because media violence is marked by its capability to elicit strong sympathetic excitation. This entry describes the conceptual framework and empirical support for ETT; examines ETT's application to media violence; and discusses critiques and theoretical developments.

The Conceptual Framework and Empirical Support

Excitation-transfer theory has its theoretical origins in psychology, physiology, and biology. Zillmann integrated and extended the excitatory potential concept from Clark Hull's drive theory from the 1940s, and Stanley Schachter and Jerome Singer's two-factor theory of emotion from the 1960s. Particularly, the influence of the two-factor theory on ETT is pronounced. The two-factor theory was part of the cognitive theories of emotion emerging in the 1960s. It proposed that the experience of an emotion is not only determined by physiological arousal, which is relatively generic across many emotions, but also a cognitive label on the physiological arousal, which is specific to the current situation. Extending the two-factor theory to sequential emotional experiences, ETT focuses on how asynchrony of the two emotional factors can occur, and what emotional and behavioral consequences can result from the asynchrony. More specifically, it theorizes "excitation" and the process of "transfer" of excitation as the following.

Excitation

Excitation-transfer theory conceptualizes excitation (or arousal) as the excitatory reactions of the sympathetic nervous system, or more precisely, dominance of the sympathetic system activation over the parasympathetic system activation. The sympathetic nervous system and parasympathetic nervous system are two branches and neural pathways of the autonomic nervous system. In general, the parasympathetic system helps maintain the body at rest, while the sympathetic system mobilizes energy resources to facilitate behavioral tendencies and actions, such as fight or flight. Intense emotional experience is associated with escalated sympathetic excitation. This is believed to have evolutionary adaptive functions: sympathetic excitation helps provide bursts of energy resources that enable an organism to execute appropriate actions in response to emotional stimuli in the environment, which are important to the organism's survival and prosperity. Furthermore, following the two-factor theory of emotion, ETT treats the sympathetic excitation as a nonspecific and unitary physiological activation and experience; it alone cannot determine an emotional experience. In experiments, the excitation is often operationalized by physiological measures such as electrodermal activities, blood pressure, heart rate, and perspiration.

Transfer

Excitation-transfer theory proposes that sympathetic excitation can be transferred from one stimulus to another because of misattribution of the source of the excitation. The misattribution results from asynchrony in cognitive and excitatory adaptation to environmental changes. Sympathetic excitation, partly mediated by hormonal changes (e.g., changes in norepinephrine and epinephrine), typically takes at least minutes to return to normal resting levels. Cognitive neural responses to environmental changes, however, can occur almost instantaneously. Thus, ETT posits that this difference in their speeds to adjust to environmental changes leads to asynchrony in physiological excitatory and cognitive changes. When an individual has cognitively switched to a later stimulus, the individual may still experience some of the sympathetic excitation evoked by earlier stimuli. However, according to the two-factor theory of emotion, individuals tend to causally attribute their emotional states to salient cues in their immediate environment. Therefore, the excitatory residue carries over into the present experience and is misattributed to the present stimulus.

A great amount of evidence has been accumulated over the past decades supporting the idea that excitation transfer is a common experience in our interpersonal, social, and mediated interactions.

The typical experimental paradigm for testing ETT is straightforward: first, individuals are exposed to a stimulus or a set of stimuli that can elicit sympathetic excitation at different levels of strength (e.g., high versus low); then, emotional reactivity to an immediately following stimulus is measured. The reactivity is expected to be stronger when the preceding emotional state has higher levels of excitation because a greater amount of residual excitation should be misattributed to the current state.

In experiments, excitation or residual excitation induced by the preceding stimulus is often ascertained by peripheral physiological measures, such as electrodermal activities, blood pressure, heart rate, and perspiration; subsequent emotional experience is often measured by self-report and behavioral measures. Using this experimental paradigm, excitation transfer has been demonstrated in various types of emotional reactions. For example, residues from sexual excitation can enhance emotional experiences such as anger and anxiousness, but they also can facilitate aggression as well as altruistic prosocial behavior; and excitation transferred from physical exercises can intensify subsequent anger and aggression. Various combinations of emotional sequences have been tested and show the robustness of the excitation-transfer phenomenon.

Media Violence, Aggression, and Excitation Transfer

Since its initial years, a primary application of ETT has been to understand how media violence affects subsequent emotional, cognitive, and behavioral responses, and in particular, aggressive behavior. According to ETT, the lingering arousal elicited by a preceding stimulus, such as a violent film, will intensify subsequent experience and behavior. One of the first ETT studies, published in 1971 in the *Journal of Experimental Social Psychology*, serves as a classic example of this research paradigm.

In the study, Zillmann tested residual excitation transfer from films to subsequent aggressive behavior. First, 12 male participants were recruited to pretest six film stimuli: two neutral films; two violent, aggressive sports films; and two highly arousing erotic films. Each film lasted 6–7 minutes, and the order of the films was counterbalanced. The participants watched the films individually. Their heart rate, skin temperature, and systolic and diastolic blood pressure were measured during watching each of the films, with sufficient time between the films to allow their physiological responses to return to resting levels. A single sympathetic activation score was computed using the physiological measures. Then, based on the sympathetic activation scores, a film clip for each experimental condition was selected: an educational film for the neutral condition, a prizefight film for the aggressive condition, and an erotic film for the arousing condition.

The main experiment involved 63 male undergraduate students. Each participant was told that the research was about the effect of punishment on learning, and he was randomly selected to play the role of a teacher while another "participant" (confederate) would play the role of a learner. In an initial interaction period, the participant received a total of nine 0.5-second 25-volt electric shocks from the confederate because of opinion disagreement between them, which in fact was scripted. This was intended to prod the participant to become aggressive toward the confederate. Then the participant started a "teaching" session. The participant watched one of the three stimulus films, which was said to be part of what the confederate was learning about. This was followed by a series of questions to the confederate regarding the film, and an apparatus informed the participant whether the confederate made an error or not. If an error occurred, the participant was instructed to punish the confederate by delivering an electric shock. The participant had control over the intensity of the shocks, which varied from 1 ("quite mild") to 10 ("rather painful"). As scripted, the confederate made 12 errors out of 20 questions. The intensity of aggressive behavior of the participant was operationalized by the intensity of the 12 electric shocks to the tormentor. As predicted by ETT, the intensity of the aggressive behavior was the highest in the erotic film condition, which was expected to produce the largest residual excitation, and the lowest in the neutral condition, which would produce the smallest residual excitation. The aggressive sports film was the second exciting among the three stimuli according to the physiological measures, and indeed led to the second intense aggression. The findings countered the simple content-based prediction that aggressive media content promotes aggressive behavior. Instead, they suggested that sympathetic excitation induced by media—whether from erotic films or televised sports—is a plausible mechanism for intensified aggressive behavior afterward.

A follow-up experiment by Zillmann, Aaron K. Katcher, and Barry Milavsky in 1972 extended the study by using emotionally neutral physical exercise to elicit physiological excitation. It also used a more complicated factorial experimental design to test whether aggressive instigation is necessary in the transfer of excitation to subsequent aggression. The experimental design was aggressive instigation (high versus low) × physical exercise (high versus low). The physical exercise of bike riding was used to elicit different levels of sympathetic excitation. As indicated by physiological measures of heart rate and systolic and diastolic blood pressure, sympathetic activation was higher in the more intense exercise condition. Subsequent aggressive behavior was operationalized by the intensity of electric shocks to the earlier instigator as in the 1971 study. The final data included 32 male students. Consistent with the 1971 findings, aggressive behavior increased with higher levels of sympathetic arousal elicited by more intense exercise and also increased with the increase of the initial instigation. Furthermore, the residual excitation interacted with the earlier instigation in that it intensified aggression when initial instigation was more prominent.

Later studies with similar designs have generated generally consistent findings in support of ETT. Experiments involving female participants have suggested that aggressive media sometimes fail to intensify later aggressive behavior among female participants, probably because the aggressive media fail to strongly excite them. Furthermore, in accordance with excitation-transfer predictions, there has been some evidence that arousing violent media not only can intensify retaliation and aggression but also pleasant experiences, such as music enjoyment.

Critiques and New Theoretical Development

As introduced, ETT was initially proposed in the 1970s and was directly influenced by Schachter and Singer's two-factor theory of emotion developed in the 1960s. At the time, most psychological theories, including the two-factor theory and ETT, were influenced by the general arousal theories of the 1950s and 1960s, which regarded emotional arousal as a generic and unitary physiological excitation. Increased arousal was thought to increase physiological activation in general. However, later research in psychophysiology suggested that physiological activation often is characterized by directional fractionation in the sense that during an arousing task, activation of some physiological systems may increase while activation of others may decrease. One important factor that determines different activation directions of physiological systems is another primary dimension of emotion along with arousal: hedonic valence, or how pleasant/positive or unpleasant/negative an emotion is.

Some researchers have suggested that ETT may need to consider not only the intensity of the emotional arousal but also its valence. Whether the preceding arousing stimulus is neutral, negative, or positive may affect emotional responses during the subsequent stimulus. Indeed, empirical studies testing the emotion congruence hypothesis have provided evidence showing that valence congruence of sequential stimuli or lack thereof may alter emotional and cognitive responses to the following stimulus. For example, a 1985 study by Nyla R. Branscombe examined how the emotional experience of viewing a negative or positive non-erotic film would be affected by preceding viewing of a negative or positive erotic film. The researcher did not observe the transfer of residual arousal, but she found the hedonic valence of prior messages lessened the emotional experience of subsequent messages when the valence of the prior message was incompatible with the subsequent message and when the messages were presented without any delay.

In a 2012 article, Zheng Wang and Annie Lang attempted to extend ETT to incorporate the emotional valence dimension from theoretical perspectives of J. T. Cacioppo's dual-motivational theory and Lang's limited capacity model of motivated mediated message processing. According to these motivational theories, emotion fundamentally stems from appetitive and aversive motivational activation. The two motivational systems have different activation functions. The appetitive system is featured by "positivity offset"—that is, it is more active than the aversive system in a neutral, non-arousing environment. The aversive system is featured by "negativity bias"—that is, it reacts more quickly and more intensely than the appetitive system when the aversive stimulus becomes more arousing. These features of motivational activation are evolutionarily and biologically plausible. Positivity offset encourages organisms to explore the environment in a relatively neutral and safe environment, while negativity bias helps protect organisms from sudden threats. These features have been shown to affect cognitive and emotional responses to media. In particular, emotional excitation is not generic or unitary, as assumed by ETT, but is fundamentally determined by which of the two motivational systems is activated—or sometimes both are activated. Thus, both arousing content and valence of stimuli are essential to the excitation-transfer process. Using physiological measures and a television context experiment, Wang and Lang provided evidence for conceptualizing excitation transfer as functions of dynamic activation of the appetitive and aversive motivational systems. The authors point out the importance of simultaneously considering both

the valence and arousal dimensions of emotion in understanding the excitation-transfer process.

Zheng Wang

See also Aggression and Affect; Aggression and Anger; Aggressive Behavior; Effects From Violent Media, Short- and Long-Term; Films, Representation of Violence and Its Effects in; General Aggression Model; Psychobiology of Violence; Sports, Violence and Aggression in; Television Violence

Further Readings

Branscombe, N. R. (1985). Effects of hedonic valence and physiological arousal on emotion: A comparison of two theoretical perspectives. *Motivation & Emotion, 9,* 153–328.

Zillmann, D. (1971). Excitation transfer in communication-mediated aggressive behavior. *Journal of Experimental Social Psychology, 7,* 419–434.

Zillmann, D. (1996). Sequential dependencies in emotional experience and behavior. In R. D. Kavanaugh, B. Zimmerberg, & S. Fein (Eds.), *Emotion: Interdisciplinary perspectives* (pp. 243–272). Mahwah, NJ: Erlbaum.

Zillmann, D., & Bryant, J. (1974). Effect of residual excitation on the emotional response to provocation and delayed aggressive behavior. *Journal of Personality and Social Psychology, 30,* 782–791.

Zillmann, D., Katcher, A. H., & Milavsky, B. (1972). Excitation transfer from physical exercise to subsequent aggressive behavior. *Journal of Experimental Social Psychology, 6,* 247–259.

Wang, Z., & Lang, A. (2012). Reconceptualizing excitation transfer as motivational activation changes and a test of the television program context effects. *Media Psychology, 15,* 68–92.

EXPOSURE TO VIOLENT CONTENT, EFFECTS ON CHILD DEVELOPMENT

The public's concern over media violence and its effects on children tends to focus heavily on the media's detrimental influence on children's aggressive behaviors. Many parents and educators as well as the popular press worry that exposure to violent content can lead to fighting with siblings at home, hitting peers in the playground, or even shootings on school campuses. Although these are serious issues, understanding a child's healthy development within the context of mediated violence is more complex than just framing it from a behavioral standpoint. The development of a child is multifaceted; hence, outcomes due to exposure to media violence vary in different aspects. Scholars in communication and developmental psychology have demonstrated the importance of studying this topic from perspectives that encompass a child's behavioral, physical, social, emotional, and cognitive development.

Each of these areas is distinctive. First, studies on behavioral development have addressed areas such as a child's ability to imitate and reproduce modeled behaviors like punching and kicking. This concern regarding imitation further leads to an examination of how the viewing of action-adventure programs can result in more imitative play rather than imaginative play. Second, studies on physical development examined weight gain and deteriorating eyesight from heavy exposure. Third, studies on social development have covered topics such as children's perception of gender roles and racial groups. Scholars warned against the danger of violent television that promotes tolerance of treating marginalized individuals with violence. Most recently, studies explored the impact of televised social aggression such as bullying, rumor spreading, and back-stabbing on children. Fourth, studies on emotional responses found that violent fantasy programs and news broadcasts provoke children's fear reactions. Research also suggested a link between media violence and emotional desensitization toward real-life violence.

Whether studying violent behaviors, perceived gender roles, or television-induced fears, scholars have often drawn upon cognitive-based theories for prediction and explanation. This entry introduces cognitive-based concepts that have been found to mediate media violence's impact on children's behavioral, social, and emotional development. Additionally, this entry focuses on findings based on television violence rather than video game violence, as there are more extensive and complete studies on television violence.

Cognitive-Developmental Theory

Studies that use the cognitive-based theories have posited that children are active but vulnerable viewers. Children's interaction with media violence should not be viewed as a one-way street. Children possess varying cognitive skills that can lead to different interpretations, comprehension, and evaluation of televised violence. As children mature, however, their cognitive skills improve. Consequently,

younger children with less developed cognitive skills are more vulnerable than older children. They are less capable of understanding media content the way it is intended to be understood. Nuances of televised violence like the appearance of a character, the perpetrator's motivation, and the type of action taken could easily be misinterpreted, ignored, or overgeneralized depending on a child's cognitive ability. Even older children are not as savvy as adults when processing violent content.

This view of children within the context of media violence has largely been influenced by Jean Piaget's cognitive developmental theory. Piaget argued that a child's capacity to learn through firsthand experience and mediated events is contingent on his or her progression through cognitive stages. Although distinct stage differences demarcated Piaget's cognitive-developmental theory from other cognitive theories, the theory has been controversial. The main criticism is that children do not necessarily progress through stages as uniformly as prescribed in Piaget's theory. Consequently, media scholars have placed less emphasis on the proposed stage differences and instead have acknowledged a qualitative difference between younger children (preschoolers) and older children (middle childhood).

Four specific cognitive skills introduced by Piaget's theory are particularly relevant to a child's ability to process media content. The four skills are (1) the ability to distinguish between fantasy and reality, (2) the ability to move from perceptual-based visuals to conceptual-based ideas, (3) the ability to draw inferences, and (4) the level of egocentrism, which determines a child's ability to take the perspectives of others. Past research has found these elements of children's cognitive development as predictors of aggressive attitudes and behaviors, moral evaluation of characters, and fear reactions.

Fantasy and Reality

One of the cognitive skills children develop as they mature from preschool to elementary school is the ability to distinguish between fantasy and reality. Preschool-aged children are not able to consistently differentiate between something that is imagined or created and something that exists in reality. They tend to believe that things that look real are real. For example, they believe that the television character the Hulk exists in real life. This lack of ability to make reality–fantasy distinction has been found to mediate children's willingness to imitate a character's violent behaviors as well as mediate children's fear responses toward violent television. Although findings suggest that children can differentiate fantasy from reality at around age 4 or 5 years, and that the older they get, the more they will dismiss fictional content as real, children's level of perceived television reality still varies. The more realistic the characters or behaviors seen on television, the more likely a child will be influenced by them. For instance, studies showed that children who thought televised violence to be real reported a higher tendency for physical and verbal aggression. Similarly, fear reaction studies found violent news content to evoke more fear from children than violent fictional content.

The importance of this cognitive skill led scholars to examine the complexity of children's perceived television reality and their developmental differences. To distinguish between fantasy and reality is more than just asking whether the program is fictional or realistic. The same fictional program can be perceived differently by different children, depending on what they focus their judgment on. Scholars have conceptualized perceived reality into various dimensions, including but not limited to magic window, identity, and plausibility. These dimensions are reviewed here because they not only demonstrate a child's developmental progression in comprehending television but also show the role of a child's perceived reality in facilitating the violent content's effects on aggressive behaviors and fear reactions.

Magic window refers to a child's view that television images are the representations of reality. They see television representation as a whole rather than a depiction consisting of many parts (e.g., script, actor, set). Children gradually move from this simplistic view of television as the "magic window" to a more complex phase in which they judge based on multiple cues. Two dimensions that demonstrate how older children gain the ability to use multiple criteria when judging television reality are identity and plausibility. *Identity* is the feeling of being the same as the character. The more similarity a child sees between him- or herself and a television character, the more real he or she perceives the character to be. And the more a character is perceived as a real-world individual, the more vulnerable a child is to the undesirable messages portrayed by the character. They are also more prone to imitate the behaviors of characters with whom they identify. Literature on identification found that boys tend to identify with aggressive characters more than do girls, and such

identification can result in negative consequences when violent behaviors are viewed.

The *plausibility* dimension of perceived reality points out that although older children understand television contents are scripted, they still judge some as more possible in real life than others. Consequently, an aggressive act on television that is deemed possible is more likely to influence a child than one that is deemed impossible. This cognitive skill is observed through studies on children's fear reaction to television. Joanne Cantor and colleagues found ample evidence over the course of 20 years that younger children are more frightened by events on television that would never happen, whereas older children are more frightened by events that could possibly happen. Many of the events studied were violence based, such as interpersonal violence, war, and natural disasters as shown in the news, which further illustrates how fantasy–reality distinction is crucial in the study of media violence and children.

It is clear that perceived television reality plays an important role in the effect of violent content on children. In fact, several studies incorporated it into their testing of effective school literacy curricula and parental mediation messages in hopes of mitigating the negative effects. They found that teaching children cognitive skills to dismiss perceived television programs as realistic portrayals of life can decrease the unwanted effects from televised violence. Fear reaction literature also found that older children benefit from cognitive strategies that explain the unrealistic aspect of fantasy depictions. With the technological advancement of 3D television and the proliferation of special effects and computer-generated imagery in video games, more and more scholars have underscored the relevance of perceived reality in the studies on media violence.

Perceptual and Conceptual Processing

Another cognitive skill relevant to children's interpretation of media violence is their ability to move from perceptual dependence to conceptual processing. *Perceptual dependence* refers to young children's cognitive limitation, which focuses more on salient features of media presentation such as vivid colors, sounds, and movements. Younger children pay close attention to things on television that are more concretely portrayed, such as the colorful costumes, animated appearance of characters, loud and flashy sound effects, and fast-paced and action-based behaviors. These images stay salient in younger children's minds more than do conceptual ideas, such as the personality of a character and motivation behind a behavior. Studies have shown evidence of a decrease in perceptual dependence as children get older. *Conceptual dependence* occurs as children reach middle childhood, when they slowly develop the ability to process more conceptual-based information presented on television. For example, Marina Krcmar conducted a series of studies on children's moral reasoning of televised violence and found that younger children focus their judgment of televised violence more on salient contextual cues, such as being punished because of a violent act; older children focus more on the motivation behind the violence, which is less easily portrayed visually.

Fear reaction literature also found evidence showing this perceptual to conceptual developmental trend. In an experimental study, young children were found to be more easily frightened by stimuli that appear frightening, whereas older children were more frightened by scary ideas. Extending this to violent news content, one study found children's fear from news on interpersonal violence, fires, accidents, and fantasy characters decreased with age, but fear toward war and suffering increased. The authors theorized that this was due to a more visually eye-catching and perceptual-based set of images in the former, which caused younger children to be more emotionally responsive.

Drawing Inferences

Similar to the ability to process conceptual ideas, children begin to develop the ability to draw inferences when they reach middle childhood. This ability is important to a child's comprehension of media violence because it can help them understand the context and plotline in which violence is portrayed. Studies found that younger children fail to understand abstract and thematic messages embedded in television shows. The older a child becomes, the better he or she is at recalling narratives, sequencing stories, and eventually making inferences about relationships and motivations. Although failing to make accurate inferences does not directly lead to aggressive behaviors, researchers did find that there is an influence on a child's choice of aggressive responses after viewing. Specifically, one study tested children's ability to connect motivation, aggression, and consequence for aggression with the interruption

of commercial breaks. Results show that even third graders had difficulty connecting punishment as the consequence for the aggression if there was a commercial break between the act of aggression and the consequence. This suggests that younger children run the risk of viewing violence in its vacuum without taking the storyline into consideration. In this case, children are interpreting violence independently from the consequences portrayed on screen. Scholars worry that because most consequences associated with violence appear toward the end of a violent show, young children will not be able to associate negative consequences with the violence. Without the negative outcome, children are more prone to judge violence as acceptable.

Taking Perspectives

The last cognitive skill informed by Piaget's cognitive developmental theory is a child's ability to take the perspectives of others. According to Piaget, young children are egocentric when processing the world around them. It is easier for them to acknowledge their needs and wants than to imagine the point of view of others. Like the other cognitive skills delineated, it is in middle childhood that children start developing the ability to think and feel from others' perspectives. Applying this concept to the realm of television violence, younger children are less capable of reasoning from the perspective of a television character. This then makes them less likely to use a character's motivation for aggression to interpret televised violence. Researchers further theorize that children's egocentrism along with perceptual dependency lead them to base judgments of televised violence on the punishment rather than the motivation because punishments or other consequences are more easily portrayed visually on television than is motivation.

Marina Krcmar and Patti Valkenburg examined children's exposure to fantasy violence and found that perspective taking mediates the impact of violent content on children's moral reasoning. They argued that violent shows often portray the storyline from the perspective of the perpetrator (the aggressor) rather than the victim. This one-sided presentation prevents children from learning from multiple perspectives. Consequently, violent television can discourage children from advancing the skills of perspective taking. Since most violent programs such as *Superman* and *Power Rangers* depict violence from the perspective of a heroic perpetrator who is trying to save the world, reinforcing such a perspective can also explain why studies are finding children to judge justified violence as acceptable.

To further illustrate the importance of perspective taking in children's interpretation of violent television, parental mediation literature suggested that parents encourage children to think about the negative outcomes of violence from the victim's perspective. This so-called fictional involvement as emphasized by adults while watching violent television with children has been found to be effective among boys in particular in preventing their post-viewing aggressive tendencies from increasing.

In summary, cognitive developmental theory helps media scholars to identify factors such as perceptual dependence, perceived reality, ability to make inferences, and perspective taking that mediate the effect of violent television on children's aggression, moral reasoning of interpersonal violence, and fear reaction.

Information Processing

The information-processing approach provides media scholars with another framework within which to study children's cognitive development. Instead of focusing on distinct developmental stages and various cognitive skills, the information-processing approach looks at children's minds as a whole and stresses the importance of experience on cognitive processing. As children gain more experiences, the cognitive structures become more elaborate. This approach compares the human mind to a computer and provides tools to analyze how information is attended to, encoded, stored, and retrieved in children's memory. Applying this to media violence, it is often helpful in explaining media effects on children as they mature, and after repeated exposure. For instance, children develop aggressive scripts from direct experiences with violence, but their experience viewing televised violence also plays a part. Consequently, the aggressive scripts become more complex and extensive as children watch more televised violence.

One specific area of research within this approach uses script and schema theory to hone in on how individuals obtain knowledge from experiences to build mental structures for all sorts of social interactions. Script, schema, and mental model are constructs often used interchangeably by effects studies to represent an individual's cognitive representation of people, things, events, and actions. However,

some argue that the mental model is broader than the script and schema because it also includes the series of events such as the related context that are used for problem solving and performing tasks. Children and media scholars borrow these constructs to study how children acquire them from within the television viewing context to guide their processing and retrieval of information. This includes characters' relationships with one another, motivation behind behaviors, character development, circumstances of events, and so on. Two outcomes most frequently studied using this approach are children's development of aggressive scripts, and mental models and gender role schema.

Rowell Huesmann and Leonard Eron used the script theory to explain how children retain aggressive scripts in their memory from past exposure to fantasy violence. The more violent the content a child is exposed to, the more likely he or she is to develop cognitive scripts that use violence as a solution for conflicts. In addition to exposure, the researchers further argued that the acquired scripts are reinforced if children rehearse them through imitative play. Violent video game literature often uses this same theory to stress the implication game playing might have on children's already acquired scripts because game playing provides multiple opportunities for the rehearsal of the learned aggressive scripts.

Krcmar and colleague argued that mental models are activated even by a single exposure to televised violence. They extended the aggressive script that focuses more on behavioral script to aggressive mental models that encompass cognitive structures that include context, events, and sequences as portrayed in televised violence. They also used the mental model approach to explain that more exposure to fantasy violence can evoke a child's use of certain moral reasoning. Furthermore, they use this approach to explain how the appearance of superhero characters (e.g., on lunchboxes and T-shirts) can activate aggressive mental models without the presence of the aggressive behavior as portrayed on television.

In addition to provoking aggressive scripts and mental models, television viewing has been found to develop children's gender role schema. Studies found that, from their exposure to television, children acquire specific expectations of how men and women should look and behave. More specifically, stereotypical portrayal of characters can lead children to have stereotypical attitudes. Television can even reinforce the already acquired schema to make them more accessible to children. The fear is that children will use the biased but easily accessible schema to guide them when interacting with people in real life. Although most studies examined television content in general rather than singling out violent programs, researchers who conduct content analysis of violent television as well as violent video games have argued that media violence can lead to stereotypical expectations toward different genders. That is, the prevalence of violent content with male aggressors and female victims could influence children's gender role expectations as they develop. For example, boys may expect to behave in a masculine way by exerting aggression as a solution to a problem, while girls may expect themselves to be protected by means of violence in a conflict situation.

In summary, the cognitive aspect of children's experience with mediated violence is often studied through the lens of the cognitive-developmental approach and the information-processing approach. Both provide perspectives through which to understand children's interaction with media violence, first at the cognitive level and also at the social, emotional, and behavioral levels.

Melissa M. Yang

See also Bobo Doll Studies; Cognition: Schemas and Scripts; Cognitive Script Theory and the Dynamics of Cognitive Scripting; Fear Reactions to Violent Content; Moral Development, Effects of Media Violence on; Priming Theory; Social Cognitive Theory

Further Readings

Bierwirth, K. P., & Blumberg, F. C. (2010). Preschoolers' judgments regarding realistic and cartoon-based moral transgression in the U.S. *Journal of Children & Media, 4*(1), 39–58.

Collins, W. A. (1975). The developing child as viewer. *Journal of Communication, 25*(4), 35–44.

Krcmar, M., & Hight, A. (2007). The development of aggressive mental models in young children. *Media Psychology, 10,* 250–269.

Levin, D. E., & Carlsson-Paige, N. (1994). Developmentally appropriate television: Putting children first. *Young Children, 49*(5), 38–44.

Nathanson, A. I., & Cantor, J. (2000). Reducing the aggression-promoting effect of violent cartoons by increasing children's fictional involvement with the victim: A study of active mediation. *Journal of Broadcasting & Electronic Media, 44*(1), 125–142.

Riddle, K., Cantor, J., Byrne, S., & Moyer-Guse, E. (2012). "People killing people on the news": Young children's descriptions of frightening television news content. *Communication Quarterly, 60*(2), 278–294.

Van Evra, J. (2004). *Television and child development.* Mahwah, NJ: Erlbaum.

FANTASY GENRE, VIOLENCE AND AGGRESSION IN

For as long as people have told stories, they have included make-believe characters, settings, and events in those stories. The fantasy genre has roots in the world's earliest surviving literature and traditions, and fantasy is represented today by many popular books, films, television programs, and video games. One common element across many fantasy works is the presence of violence. This entry explains definitions and characteristics of the fantasy genre, provides a brief history of the genre, and describes research and theory pertaining to the potential negative effects of violence in fantasy works.

Fantasy Defined

Generally, the fantasy genre includes fictional works of literature, films, television programs, video games, and other media featuring phenomena that do not exist in the natural world as a key characteristic of their settings, characters, plots, and themes. The settings, characters, and events of fantasy works are make-believe, and the worlds of fantasy works have different rules and parameters than the real world, although fantasy worlds contain their own internally consistent rules about what is possible within them.

Fantasy shares many similarities with the closely related genre of science fiction, as both include settings and events that do not exist in the present-day real world. The genres differ, though, because science fiction generally includes only elements that can be considered plausible within our understanding of hypothetically possible technological innovations and the laws of the real physical universe (such as discovery of intelligent life on another planet). Fantasy, meanwhile, includes elements that are impossible in our world at any time in the past, present, or future (such as the existence of fire-breathing dragons). Both fantasy and science fiction are therefore part of the broader genre of speculative fiction. The boundary between fantasy and science fiction is often blurry, though, and some works that contain elements of both science fiction and fantasy are also described as part of a hybrid genre known as science fantasy. The fantasy genre also shares many characteristics with the various mythologies of the ancient world, except that the fantasy genre is understood to be fiction produced as art and entertainment, while some mythologies were historically regarded as accurate descriptions of history and explanations of natural events.

Because the fantasy genre is, by definition, characterized by fantastic make-believe settings, its subject matter and themes vary widely. Consequently, the fantasy genre is divided into a range of more specific subgenres. Some of these subgenres include contemporary fantasy, which is fantasy cast in a present-day setting; dark fantasy, which is fantasy that contains elements consistent with the horror genre; and historical fantasy, which is fantasy cast in a setting that contains similarities with historical periods in the real world. (A particularly common and popular form of historical fantasy is medieval fantasy, which takes place in a setting similar to Europe's medieval period with the addition of make-believe elements.)

While works in the fantasy genre do not share a requisite set of plot characteristics, some plot elements are particularly common to fantasy works. Many fantasy stories center on combat and warfare between clearly identified good and evil factions or individuals. They often also feature a central heroic protagonist figure with one or more extraordinary abilities. Another common character in fantasy works is a consummate evil villain character whose abilities, powers, and resources dwarf those of any protagonists to the extent that the villain's victory may seem inevitable for much of the story's plot. Often, one or more hero characters must undertake a daunting quest involving travel and accomplishment of identified tasks in order to obtain requisite items, skills, or alliances necessary to defeat the story's evil antagonists. Many fantasy works also include magical objects and abilities, mythically inspired or originally devised animals and anthropomorphic humanoid "races," and settings generally reminiscent of medieval and ancient history. Some may also feature physical laws, geography, and cosmology that differ from those of our universe.

History of the Fantasy Genre

Although the fantasy genre is widely understood to have been first established in the mid-19th century, works with fantastic elements date back to the earliest known recorded stories. Famous epic poems throughout history, such as the *Epic of Gilgamesh* from ancient Mesopotamia, the *Mahabharata* and *Ramayana* from ancient India, Homer's *Iliad* and *Odyssey* from classical Greece, the Old Norse *Poetic Edda*, the medieval English *Beowulf*, and the medieval German *Nibelungenlied* all contain elements of fantasy, as do famous prose epics such as the Arabic collection *One Thousand and One Nights*. These and other fantastic historic works are not often classified as examples of the fantasy genre, though, because they all include elements from historical accounts, traditional legends and tales, or religious mythology; they are not works describing an original and deliberately fictional fantastic setting developed specifically for use in a unique literary work. Epic mythologies and traditional legends have nonetheless served as inspiration for many of the most well-known works of more modern fantasy. Similarly, other predecessors of the fantasy genre, including popular fairy tales of Renaissance Europe and the renowned plays of Elizabethan playwright William Shakespeare, included characters and plots common

to the fantasy genre but are not widely considered to be works of fantasy themselves.

The first true full-length fantasy novel, according to strict definitions of the genre, is widely believed to be *Phantastes*, which was penned by Scottish author George MacDonald and published in 1858. Another prominent 19th-century fantasy author was William Morris, who published *The Well at the World's End* in 1896. Some other popular works of early modern fantasy were written for children, such as Lewis Carroll's 1865 novel *Alice in Wonderland* and L. Frank Baum's 1900 novel *The Wonderful Wizard of Oz*. In addition to early novels and plays, the fantasy genre spread in the 1920s with the publication of inexpensive pulp magazines devoted to the genre, such as *Der Orchindeengarten* in Germany and *Weird Tales* in the United States. These publications launched the careers of noted fantasy authors such as Robert E. Howard, who is credited as the progenitor of the "sword and sorcery" fantasy subgenre, which is characterized by a focus on the action-packed escapades of a lone heroic warrior and is perhaps best exemplified by Howard's legendary fantasy hero Conan the Barbarian.

Although fantasy works had established a wide audience by the early 20th century, the publication of J. R. R. Tolkien's *The Hobbit* in 1937 and *The Lord of the Rings* between 1954 and 1955 brought the fantasy genre into mainstream popularity. Tolkien's books were not immediately worldwide bestsellers, but *The Lord of the Rings* eventually earned acknowledgment by several groups as the best book of the 20th century. Also achieving widespread attention was C. S. Lewis's seven-novel series *The Chronicles of Narnia*, published between 1950 and 1956. The popularity of the fantasy novel genre grew until Terry Brooks's 1977 novel *The Sword of Shannara* became the first fantasy novel to appear on the *New York Times'* best-seller list, where it reached the top ranking. Best-selling fantasy titles have been frequent since then, including J. K. Rowling's seven-novel *Harry Potter* series, which was published between 1977 and 2007 and is the best-selling book series of all time. The fantasy genre has also been well represented in other print literature, including comic books and graphic novels in particular.

The growth of the fantasy genre in literature during the 20th century was mirrored by increasing prominence of fantasy films during the same period, many of which emulated or directly adapted famous fantasy literature. A classic silent film is *The Thief of Baghdad*, a 1924 production with an Arabian setting reminiscent of *A Thousand and One Nights* that would be remade several times in the years to follow. Another early fantasy film was *The Wizard of Oz,* which was released in 1937 and remains perhaps the most beloved example of the genre. More fantasy films and films with fantasy elements borrowed from Greek, Roman, medieval, and Arabic mythology were released in subsequent decades. Notable examples include big-budget animated films such as Disney's *Alice in Wonderland* and *The Sword in the Stone.*

By the 1980s, a boom in fantasy films began with successes like *Conan the Barbarian,* Jim Henson's *The Dark Crystal* and *Labyrinth,* and *The NeverEnding Story.* More recent popular fantasy films have included the acclaimed three-film adaptation of *The Lord of the Rings* and the eight-film *Harry Potter* series, the latter of which is the highest-grossing film series in history. The fantasy genre has also been represented on television, particularly in recent decades. Successful small-screen fantasy series have included the daytime fantasy soap opera *Dark Shadows,* the contemporary fantasies *Beauty and the Beast* and *Highlander: The Series,* the medieval fantasy series *Xena: Warrior Princess,* the animated medieval fantasy series *Masters of the Universe,* and the critically acclaimed medieval fantasy series *Game of Thrones,* which is based on George R. R. Martin's *A Song of Ice and Fire* novel series.

Although the fantasy genre has been a considerable presence in literature, film, and television, its greatest impact has been on the video game medium. While early video games featured rudimentary simulations of sports and combat, the first video games to include narrative stories and themes were inspired by fantasy texts. They were also inspired by the paper-and-pencil role-playing game *Dungeons & Dragons,* which in turn borrowed heavily from J. R. R. Tolkien's famous books. In 1976 programmer Will Crowther completed the first version of the seminal text-based adventure game, *Colossal Cave Adventure,* which required the user to type commands to navigate an adventure setting featuring fantasy staples such as magic and fantastic species. *Colossal Cave Adventure* served as inspiration for the *Zork* text-based adventure game series, which was developed by researchers at the Massachusetts Institute of Technology beginning in 1977 and also included fantasy elements like magic items and otherworldly monsters.

University of Essex computer science students Roy Trubshaw and Richard Bartle were partially inspired by *Zork,* as well as *Dungeons & Dragons* and fantasy literature, when they developed a text-based role-playing game called *MUD (Multi-User Dungeon)* from 1978 to 1980 that could be played simultaneously by multiple players via the Internet. *MUD* spawned a genre of imitators. In the years since, fantasy themes have been a common feature of action and adventure games, and fantasy is a particularly dominant genre in computer role-playing games. Perhaps the best example of the fantasy genre's prominence in video games include *World of Warcraft,* a medieval fantasy game with Tolkienesque themes that was released in 2004 and has since become a dominant force in the online role-playing game market. *Dungeons & Dragons* and *The Lord of the Rings* have also been adapted as online role-playing games, illustrating the link between classic fantasy texts and the video game medium.

Prevalence of Violent Content in the Fantasy Genre

While some fantasy works depict little or no violence, many common plot characteristics of the fantasy genre are particularly conducive to violent content. The presence of an epic good-versus-evil conflict as a typical fantasy theme precipitates action and combat in many fantasy works, either via massive battles between armed forces or individual mortal combat between hero and villain characters. The quests and adventures that serve as a common plot device in fantasy works also frequently introduce violent foes to stand between fantasy protagonists and their goals. Additionally, the medieval setting of many fantasy works, particularly the sword and sorcery subgenre, tend to heavily feature combat with medieval-style weapons and armor. Finally, many fantasy works feature nonhuman species such as trolls, goblins, and orcs, and frequent and graphic portrayals of violence against these characters may sometimes be more palatable for fantasy authors, producers, readers, viewers, and players than depictions of human death on a comparable scale. Although it is difficult to determine what media genres are the most violent, works in the fantasy genre may be disproportionately likely to contain violence compared with many other genres.

Potential Effects of Violence in Fantasy

A large but increasingly disputed body of research has supported the presence of a relationship between consumption of media violence—particularly in television, film, and video games—and aggression in media users. Given that violence in fantasy works is common, the genre may be a source of concern for some researchers who have concluded that media violence represents a substantial causal risk factor for aggression in users. While research investigating the unique effects of violence in the fantasy genre is limited, there are some possible reasons why violence in the fantasy genre may pose a uniquely greater or lesser risk for negative effects compared with media content from other genres.

Research dealing with learning and imitation of media violence, much of it based on psychologist Albert Bandura's social cognitive theory, has identified several factors that may enhance the potential for media violence to be emulated and imitated. Findings have suggested that media violence may be particularly conducive to imitation when it is committed by an attractive role model, when it is justified, and when it is portrayed with minimal consequences for perpetrators and victims. Considering that a common motif in fantasy works is combat between a heroic protagonist and one or more villains as part of a noble quest, and considering that fantasy works may feature unrealistic powers that limit or reverse the serious effects of violence, it may be that the violence in fantasy works may encourage modeling of aggression and violence more than does violence in other genres. Furthermore, violence that is not portrayed in a realistic manner may not be taken seriously by media users, which may inhibit serious reflection about the harms of violence. Finally, the American Academy of Pediatrics maintains that children younger than 8 years of age may have difficulty distinguishing between fantasy and reality in media content. Consequently, they may not be aware that violence portrayed in fantasy works is not appropriate or safe in the real world.

That said, there are a number of reasons why violence in fantasy genres may have fewer negative effects than violence in other media genres. One factor that has been found to influence media violence is graphic realism; its more realistic visual depictions of violence may have more potential for negative effects on disinhibition and desensitization. Analyses of television content have observed that violence in live-action programs and programs featuring human characters is more likely to be extremely graphic than violence in animated programs and programs featuring fantastic nonhuman characters. With fantastic characters and animation both common in fantasy works, it is possible that violence in fantasy genres is portrayed with less graphic realism than is violence in other genres. Similarly, media violence that is perceived as unrealistic and implausible is less likely to have negative effects than media violence that is seen as realistic and possible. Fantasy works are, by definition, depictions of the impossible, so it is likely that users will see fantasy content as less plausible and consequently be less prone to negative effects—at least in the case of children older than 8 years of age who can clearly distinguish between fantasy and reality in media content.

Another area of media effects in which violence in fantasy works may differ from violence in media from other genres is in its potential for fear effects. Some research has indicated that frightening content that is seen as realistic may induce more fear in media users than content that is not seen as plausible, so frightening content in fantasy works may be less frightening than comparable content in works from other genres. However, young children have been found to be more frightened by distorted and unfamiliar-looking characters and settings than by more abstract frightening concepts, so the fanciful elements of some fantasy works may be more frightening to young children than other types of frightening media content.

In summary, the fantasy genre is a long-standing and prominent part of the media landscape, and often a violent one. Conceptual arguments and evidence regarding comparisons between the potential for negative effects of violence in fantasy works and that of works from other genres is somewhat conflicting depending on a number of dimensions. It is likely that broad conclusions about the effects of violence in the fantasy genre compared with other media genres are not possible, and individual forms and subgenres of the vast fantasy genre must be examined and interpreted uniquely in terms of potential negative effects.

James D. Ivory

See also Media Effects Perspectives of Violence; Realism of Violent Content, Real-World Violence on Television, and Their Effects; Social Cognitive Theory

Further Readings

Bartle, R. A. (2010). From MUDs to MMORPGs: The history of virtual worlds. In J. Hunsinger, L. Klastrup, & M. Allen (Eds.), *International handbook of Internet research* (pp. 23–39). Dordrecht: Springer.

Bushman, B. J., & Huesmann, L. R. (2001). Effects of televised violence on aggression. In D. G. Singer & J. L. Singer (Eds.), *Handbook of children and the media* (pp. 223–254). Thousand Oaks, CA: Sage.

Clute, J., & Grant, J. (Eds.). (1997). *The encyclopedia of fantasy*. New York, NY: St. Martin's.

Fowkes, K. A. (2010). *The fantasy film*. Malden, MA: Wiley-Blackwell.

Ivory, J. D. (2012). *Virtual lives: A reference handbook*. Santa Barbara, CA: ABC-CLIO.

Kirsh, S. J. (2006). Cartoon violence and aggression in youth. *Aggression and Violent Behavior*, 11, 547–557.

Potter, W. J., & Smith, S. (2000). The context of graphic portrayals of television violence. *Journal of Broadcasting and Electronic Media*, 44, 301–323.

Saricks, J. G. (2001). *The readers' advisory guide to genre fiction*. Chicago: American Library Association.

Tolkien, J. R. R. (1964). On fairy stories. In J. R. R. Tolkien, *Tree and leaf* (pp. 3–86). London: George Allen and Unwin.

Turco, L. (1999). *The book of literary terms: The genres of fiction, drama, nonfiction, literary criticism, and scholarship*. Hanover, NH: University Press of New England.

Wilson, B. J., Smith, S. L., Potter, W. J., Kunkel, D., Linz, D., Colvin, C. M., & Donnerstein, E. (2002). Violence in children's television programming: Assessing the risks. *Journal of Communication*, 52, 5–35.

FEAR REACTIONS TO VIOLENT CONTENT

The study of fear and fright reactions is important for media effects researchers because it fosters understanding of the natural and automatic reactions of viewers to specific contexts and situations. It is important to understand the effects of these events in order to grasp the power of media. According to Joanne Cantor (2009, p. 290), "fear is generally conceived of as an emotional response of negative hedonic tone related to avoidance or escape, due to the perception of real or imagined threat." Although people are capable of developing coping mechanisms, such as avoidance or denial, in response to fear-inducing media and experiences, the initial emotional and physiological responses to these situations are natural and unavoidable. Fear reactions to media are a well-developed area of research. A thorough review of the body of work is well beyond the scope of this entry, so this entry summarizes the physiological mechanisms responsible

for fear emotional responses in the human body and briefly introduces Cantor's three fear-inducing stimuli and events categories.

Physiological Reactions to Violent Content

The limbic system structures in the brain, such as the amygdala, hippocampus, and hypothalamus, are responsible for responses to emotions, memory formation, and behavioral motivations. More specifically, the amygdala is associated with fear- and fright-related emotions.[1] The automatic nervous system, composed of the sympathetic and parasympathetic branches, controls the human body's physiological reactions to emotions. The amygdala alerts the automatic nervous system via a complex neural network of signals. Generally, the sympathetic branch of the automatic nervous system responds to fear or fright emotions with what is classically known as the *fight-or-flight response*, which is associated with increased respiration, blood pressure, and heart rate as well as decreased digestion. Conversely, the parasympathetic branch of the automatic nervous system is responsible for physiological responses antagonistic to those of the sympathetic system, including decreased blood circulation and stimulated digestion. In her 2004 article "I'll Never Have a Clown in my House," Cantor analyzed the retrospective reports of adults and found that enduring, seemingly irrational effects on normal activities are common. Classic examples of this phenomenon include people who saw the movie *Jaws* as children feeling anxious when swimming in open water and people being frightened by fuzzy television screens after having seen the movie *Poltergeist*. In both of these examples, adults experience anxiety and a sense of fear when exposed to situations involving similarities to the movie narrative while consciously understanding and recognizing that their fears are irrational and unlikely to result in the outcome shown in the movie. Interestingly, this thought process and emotional response could possibly be explained by what Joseph LeDoux (1996) introduced as a two-system conceptualization of the neurophysiology of fear. In this dual-part mental mechanism, unconscious traumatic memories are stored in the amygdala and are highly resistant to change, while conscious memories involve appraisal processes and are stored in the hippocampus. This may account for the adult mind's inability to separate emotional responses to media exposures or situational triggers that induce memories associated with fear from rational thought and understanding of situational dangers. Psychophysiological methodologies, which use the automatic nervous system's physiological responses to monitor audience responses to content stimuli, can be paired with other traditional qualitative or quantitative measures to make inferences related to media effects research.

Fear-Inducing Stimuli and Events

As an expert in the area of fright reactions to media violence, Cantor has proposed, after reviewing literature on real-world fears and media fright reactions, three categories of stimuli and events that most often lead to audiences experiencing fear in reality and narratives. These situations include dangers and injuries, distortions of natural forms, and the experience of endangerment and fear by others. According to Cantor, these categories often occur in some combination and rarely are experienced alone.

The first category, dangers and injuries, encompasses a majority of all fear-inducing media. There are few situations, real or imaged, that produce fear without relating to an individual's perception of a threat of danger or injury. All fear-inducing events produced by Mother Nature, including natural disasters such as earthquakes, volcano eruptions, tornadoes, and hurricanes, are considered dangers and threats of potential injury whether in real life or mass media. Additionally, all interactions that relate to violent encounters, interpersonal, global, or universal, evoke fear in those involved as well as their audiences. All attacks on animals or by vicious animals are fear inducing as well. More modern concerns, the fear of large-scale industrial dangers and the fear of weapons of mass destruction, are prominent and popular in media as well.

The second category Cantor identified, distortions of natural forms, speaks to what are more commonly discussed as deformities and distortions of the natural form. This perception is not limited to the human body and includes all familiar organisms and, arguably, objects. These distortions are often portrayed in narratives as monsters, aliens, supernatural beings, and imagined creatures from other worlds or the worlds of specific narratives. In reality, these deformities and distortions include exposure to any deviation of the average or expected physical representation of a familiar form or object.

The third category of fear-inducing stimuli and events is the experience of endangerment and fear by others. This has to do with viewers responding to the situational depictions of emotional responses of characters, real or fictional. Vicarious emotional experiences, in which an audience member feels he or she somehow is the character or experiences empathetic emotions for the characters, is a common and powerful media exposure effect. Often, the purpose of media is to make the audience feel and relate to its characters in order to encourage empathy and increase a viewer's perception of having experienced a particular situation. In real life, these situations occur when exposed to the life events and actions of other relations, strangers, and animals.

Mary Elizabeth Dunn

See also Arousal and Aggressive Content, Theory and Psychology of; Censorship of Violent Content; Cognitive Psychology of Violence; Desensitization Effects on Society; Developmental Effects; Memory and Violence; News, the Presentation of Effects of Violent Content in; Psychobiology of Violence

Note

1. There has been major research, most notably that done by psychologist Helnrich Kluver and neurosurgeon Paul Bucy in 1939, that has identified the amygdala's key role in emotional responses to fear, but in no way should the reader take this statement to mean that the amygdala is solely responsible for emotional responses. In fact, aggressive and fearful behavior involves many areas of the brain and a variety of neural network levels (Myers, 2004).

Further Readings

Cantor, J. (2004). "I'll never have a clown in my house": Why movie horror lives on. *Poetics Today: International Journal for Theory and Analysis of Literature and Communication, 25,* 283–304.

Cantor, J. (2009). Fright reactions to mass media. In J. Bryant & M. B. Oliver (Eds.), *Media effects: Advances in theory and research* (3rd ed., pp. 287–303). New York, NY: Routledge.

Gilissen, R., Koolstra, C., Ijzendorrn, M., Bakermans-Kranenburg, M., & van der Veer, R. (2007). Physiological reactions of preschoolers of fear-inducing film clips: Effects of temperamental fearfulness and quality of the parent–child relationship. *Developmental Psychobiology, 49,* 187–195.

LeDoux, J. (1996). *The emotional brain: The mysterious underpinnings of emotional life.* New York, NY: Simon & Schuster.

Myers, D. G. (2004). Psychology. In *Modules* (7th ed., pp. 75–77). New York, NY: Worth Publishers.

FEDERAL COMMUNICATIONS COMMISSION

The Federal Communications Commission (FCC) was created by the U.S. Communications Act of 1934 to regulate interstate and international mass communications. Prior to the Communications Act of 1934, the communications industry in the United States was run by private enterprise, and there was little to no government regulation until the Radio Act of 1927. As radio stations grew in popularity, and with increasingly powerful transmitters, interference and overlapping of transmissions became a serious problem that led Congress to pass the Radio Act of 1927, giving a federal commission power to license stations, assign operating frequencies, and through a 1928 amendment, establish interstate and local stations. As radio, telegraph, and telephone communications laws became dated, Congress passed the Communications Act of 1934, which placed all electronic communications businesses under purview of the FCC. Under the act, the FCC was mandated with preserving healthy communication industry competition, managing the security of the United States' emergency communications systems, protecting consumers' rights and interests, and fostering fair and safe technological innovation.

According to the FCC website, "The FCC aims to support the nation's economy by ensuring an appropriate and competitive framework for communication; promote competition, innovation, and investment in broadband services and facilities; encourage the highest and best use of spectrum domestically and internationally; manage media regulations so that new technologies succeed; and to provide and securely defend the nation's communication infrastructure." Overseen by Congress, this independent U.S. government agency consists of five members (originally seven members and reduced to five in 1983), appointed by the president of the United States and confirmed by the U.S. Senate. The president selects one of the commissioners to serve as chair of the agency as well. Only three of the five commissioners may be members of the same political party at any given time, and none of the commissioners can have a financial interest in any commission-related business. The term

length for all commissioners is five years, with the exception of the filling of an unexpired term. The agency consists of bureaus and offices organized to fulfill objectives that include "the development and implementation of regulatory programs, the processing of applications for licenses and other filings, to encourage the development of innovative services, conducting investigations and analyzing complaints, as well as public safety and homeland security communication." While these bureaus and offices operate independently, they often collaborate to accomplish agency goals. In January 2002, the FCC restructured several of its bureaus, reducing the number of bureaus from seven to six. These six bureaus include Consumer and Government Affairs, Enforcement, Media, Public Safety and Homeland Security, Wireless Telecommunications, and Wireline Competition. The offices within the agency include Administrative Law Judges, Communications Business Opportunities, Engineering and Technology, General Counsel, Inspector General, Managing Director, and Media Relations.

The Media Bureau regulates services including amplitude modulation (AM), frequency modulation (FM), television, low-power television, translators, instructional television, and related broadcast auxiliary and direct-broadcast satellites. Additionally, the Media Bureau issues construction permits, operating licenses, and renewals or transfers of such broadcast licenses except for broadcast auxiliary services. All compliance by broadcasters with statutes and FCC policies is overseen by the media bureau as well.

The Consumer and Government Affairs Bureau is the public face of the commission. Responsible for all community outreach and education through the Consumer Center, this bureau handles and responds to inquiries and complaints. This bureau includes the Reference Information Center, the Office of Intergovernmental Affairs, the Disability Rights Office, the Office of Native Affairs and Policy, the Consumer Policy Division, the Consumer Inquiries and Complaints Division, the Consumer Affairs and Outreach Division, and the Web and Print Publishing Division.

The Enforcement Bureau houses 4 divisions, 3 regional offices, and 24 field offices to assist the commission and other government agencies in handling interference and unauthorized transmission cases throughout the country. The Investigations and Hearings Division is responsible for investigating alleged violations of telecom, media, and wireless transmission laws. The Market Disputes

Resolution Division consists of litigators responsible for adjudicating and mediating business-to-business disputes. By providing mediation, this bureau assists in enabling companies to resolve disputes without costly litigation. The Spectrum Enforcement Division has technical and engineering expertise, which it leverages to enforce the commission's rules relating to equipment marketing, hearing aid compatibility, unauthorized operations, and certain public safety issues. The Telecommunications Consumers Division is responsible for issues directly affecting consumers such as indecency and censorship regulations, telemarketing, closed captioning, and consumer privacy. Field teams, as the ground forces of the bureau, conduct routine on-site investigations; facility inspections; auditing of radio facilities, cable systems, and antenna structures; disaster recovery support; and assistance in carrying out special priorities of the commission.

The Public Safety and Homeland Security Bureau is responsible for fostering the enhancement of the security and reliability of the nation's communications infrastructure and public safety. The Public Safety and Homeland Security Bureau includes the Emergency Response Interoperability Center (ERIC) and three divisions: the Cybersecurity and Communications Reliability Division, the Operations and Emergency Management Division, and the Policy and Licensing Division. This bureau counsels other agencies and bureaus, makes recommendations to the commission, and acts for the commission under delegated authority in all situations related to public safety, homeland security, national security, emergency management and preparedness, disaster management, and ancillary operations.

The Wireless Telecommunications Bureau handles policies, procedures, and licensing of all wireless services. Additionally, this bureau produces an annual wireless industry assessment, the Mobile Wireless Competition Report, and manages interactive web tools to deliver key information to the public regarding wireless services. The Wireless Telecommunications Bureau consists of the Office the Bureau Chief and five divisions: the Actions and Spectrum Division, the Broadband Division, the Mobility Division, the Spectrum and Competition Policy Division, and the Technologies, Systems, and Innovation Division.

The Wireline Competition Bureau, known as the Common Carrier Bureau prior to January 2002's reorganization, regulates interstate telephone common carrier communications. A common carrier refers to a communication service business for public hire by individuals, companies, and organizations based on established rates.

Mary Elizabeth Dunn

See also Advertising Laws Regarding Violent and Aggressive Content; Censorship of Violent Content; Internet Violence Laws; Rating Systems, Film; Rating Systems, Television; Regulating Systems, Internet; Television Violence; Video Game Industry, Regulation Within the

Further Readings

Bennett, R. K. (2013). *The telecom wars: The history and future of telecommunications in the U.S.* CreateSpace.
Coase, R. H. (1959). The Federal Communications Commission. *Journal of Law and Economics, 2,* 1–40.
Hilmes, M. (2013). *Only connect: A cultural history of broadcasting in the United States.* Boston: Wadsworth/Cengage Learning.
Lacey, K. (2013). *Listening publics: The politics and experience of listening in the media age.* Cambridge, UK: Polity.
Zarkin, K. A., and Zarkin, M. J. (2006). *The Federal Communication Commission: Front line in the culture and regulation wars.* Westport, CT: Greenwood.

Website

Federal Communications Commission; http://www.fcc.org

Films, Representation of Violence and Its Effects in

The effect from the representation of violence in films, as in other media, has been an ongoing debate for decades. Violence in films has been a defining characteristic of Hollywood cinema since the silent film era (c. 1894–1929). Since then it has evolved and been reworked into various film genres ranging from action and horror and even to romantic comedies. The prevalence of cinematic violence continues to spark debate among those who believe the representation of film violence has a negative effect on the viewing audience and those who argue that its effect ends at being a form of entertainment. According to the American Psychiatric Association (APA), the one prevailing finding in media effects research has suggested that exposure to media portrayals of violence increases aggressive and violent behavior. However, although there is supporting literature for this assessment, some media researchers disagree. This entry discusses the increased prominence of violence in films; examines concepts and theory applied to explain the effects of film violence; and discusses why contradicting studies occur in research regarding effects of film violence.

Fewer Films, More Violence

Violence has become increasingly prominent in films over time. For example, researchers Helena McAnally, Lindsay Robertson, Victor Strasburger, and Robert Hancox (2012) analyzed the James Bond movie franchise, one of the world's longest-running and highest-grossing film franchises. Investigating 22 James Bond movies, starting with *Dr. No* (1962) and ending with *Quantum of Solace* (2008), the researchers found that the films have become more violent over time, with twice as many violent acts in *Quantum of Solace* as in *Dr. No*. Furthermore, in *Quantum of Solace*, Bond or his enemies were three times as likely to engage in serious acts of violence, such as punching, kicking, or using a weapon, as in the earlier films. In the study, slapping was considered a nonserious form of violence. It is estimated that approximately 33 characters die in *Quantum of Solace*, in which Bond prevents a faux environmentalist from hijacking Bolivia's water supply. In comparison, approximately 12 characters die in *Dr. No*, in which Bond foils Julius No's plan to use radio beams to sabotage a manned space mission.

Theoretical Concepts

A number of theories and concepts have been used to explain the effects of violent representations in film. An early theory used was cathartic symbolism, which suggested that the execution of an aggressive action under certain conditions reduces an individual's aggressive drive, thus diminishing the likelihood of further aggressive actions. The key point in the theory of cathartic symbolism was that the observed aggressive action did not necessarily need to be executed in reality, but rather could take place in the media. It was believed that decreased tolerance in the audience for the display and expression of anger had led to the formation of an environment in which individuals lacked sufficient options for the acceptable and safe release of frustrations and resentments. According to the theory of cathartic symbolism, rather than harboring anger and resentment until it

exploded and resulted in violence, aggravated individuals could release their anger by identifying with movie characters who beat and/or kill victims.

However, studies have revealed that when angry individuals were exposed to media violence, their aggressive propensities increased. This is in direct opposition to cathartic symbolism's key prediction that aggression should decrease after exposure to media violence. One concept that emerged in opposition to the theory of cathartic symbolism was disinhibition. Disinhibition suggests that watching violence on the screen reduces inhibitions toward violence. In such cases, violence is not only seen as a normal response to frustration and stress but also an acceptable solution in real life. As a result, this perception changes an individual's model code and attitude toward the use of violence.

Another concept frequently used to explain the effects of media violence is desensitization. Desensitization occurs when people become more accepting of real-life violence after repeated exposure to violent images via media. As a result, audiences begin to demand more extreme forms of violence on screen. The result is that desensitization becomes cyclical. The cycle starts with initial representations of violence in films, which, in turn, cause the audience to demand more explicit violence. As a result, filmmakers respond to these demands by making their films more graphic and violent. This cycle extends the audiences' desensitization to increasing levels of violence. To this end, the exposure to film violence increases the likelihood that people will behave aggressively and become less concerned about others. This is one possible explanation for the increase in serious acts of violence seen across the James Bond franchise. Additionally, researchers Ronald Drabman and Margaret Thomas (1974) found evidence of desensitization when they conducted a study to determine which children would be more likely to seek help after witnessing a fight. They found that children who viewed a violent film before watching a fight were less likely to report the incident to an adult than those children who had not seen the violent film. The results suggest that the children had become more tolerant of real-life violence because of exposure to the violent images seen in the film. However, other researchers argued against the desensitization effect, claiming that although desensitization may occur, it does not lead to a desensitization of new violent images.

The most common theory used to explain media effects is Albert Bandura's social cognitive theory, which suggests that people learn within a social context. This form of learning is facilitated through concepts such as modeling and observational learning. This was evidenced by a study investigating under what circumstances children would imitate aggressive behavior. The children in the study were shown a film in which an adult starts hitting and kicking a Bobo Doll, a plastic punching bag with a red nose. The children were divided into three categories: those who saw the aggressor being punished, those who saw the aggressor being rewarded, and a neutral group that saw no consequence for the behavior. The children who viewed the film where the aggressor was rewarded and those in the neutral group demonstrated a considerable number of aggressive behaviors. Children who viewed the aggressor being punished showed limited imitation of the aggressor. This indicates that regardless of having acquired aggressive behaviors, these behaviors would only be acted out in favorable or rewarding circumstances. Known as *observational learning,* it posits the enabling of a single model to transmit new ways of thinking and behaving concurrently to countless people in widely dispersed locales. For instance, using mass media, such as films, to form idea and behavior patterns is a form of observational learning. Therefore, according to social cognitive theory, an individual can watch a graphic, violent film and learn about human values, styles of thinking, and behavior patterns. Simply, social behavior is learned by observing and imitating the actions of others. This suggests the individual will then imitate the violence he or she viewed in the film. Thus, some researchers believe that viewing violent media results in real-life violence, specifically in cases in which individuals seem to be mimicking the violence seen on screen. However, a prosocial effect is also likely. If an individual views a film in which the villain is defeated and brought to justice, the individual may be dissuaded from mimicking the actions of the villain and instead imitate the actions of the hero or heroine.

Critiques of Media Violence Effects

There are two schools of thought in the debate on the effects of media violence. There are those who have argued that film violence increases imitation of violent and aggressive behavior and those who do not believe film violence leads to real-life violence. Those who believe in the mimetic effects of film violence have claimed that numerous studies indicate that media violence contributes to aggressive behavior in children, adolescents, and young adults. They also have argued that media violence influences audience perception and attitude toward violence. Support for these arguments dates to the Surgeon General's Scientific Advisory Committee report of 1972, *Television and Growing Up: The Impact of Television Violence.* The report emphasized that there is a causal relation between viewing violence and aggressive behavior. However, critics have argued that the report focused on a weak correlation between viewing violence and violent behavior, not an actual causal link. This purported weakness of the report has led other researchers to conclude that there is no substantial evidence that film violence affects crime or aggression. Researcher Jonathan Freedman (2002) came to this conclusion after reviewing more than 200 studies focusing on the impact of television and film violence on violent and aggressive behavior. Freedman argued that the majority of the studies were critically flawed in some way: Among other flaws, the studies exhibited difficulty relating laboratory testing to the real-life viewing experience. The studies also had problems with the researchers' expectations influencing the subject's behavior and the evaluation of that behavior. There were inconsistent findings and interpretations derived from field and real-life studies. More important, many studies on media violence show correlation, not causation. This is contrary to the claims made in the Surgeon General's Scientific Advisory Committee report. Moreover, it is counter to several meta-analytic reviews, including a study by Craig Anderson and Brad Bushman (2001) that suggested a positive relationship between exposure to violent content and postexposure aggression. To this end, media researchers who study the impact of violent content have attributed media as merely one factor that influences aggression behavior.

Future Debate

There are possible explanations for a link between film violence and real-life violence. For example, rather than film violence *causing* real-life violence, perhaps real-life violence only *resembles* film violence. As presented in much of the research looking at individual determinants of aggressive outcomes, it is possible that when exposed to violent content, aggressive people are more driven to, and more influenced by, media with violence. The idea that real-life violence may resemble film violence could be seen as a middle ground between both schools of thought. Although exposure to violent content may represent a single factor influencing aggression, arguing for no impact would imply the media have no influence. This would counter most disciplines that look at media effects, including advertising, political communication, and health.

Nicole Cunningham

See also Bobo Doll Studies; Catharsis Theory; Desensitization Effects on Society; Rating Systems, Film; Social Cognitive Theory; Social Learning From Media; Violence in Media, Effects on Aggression and Violent Crime; Violence, Definition of

Further Readings

Anderson, C. A., & Bushman, B. J. (2001). Effects of violent videogames on aggressive behavior, aggressive cognition, aggressive affect, physiological arousal, and prosocial behavior: A meta-analytic review of scientific literature. *Psychological Science, 12,* 353–359.

Bandura, A. (2004). Social cognitive theory for personal and social change by enabling media. In A. Singhal, M. J. Cody, E. M. Rogers, & M. Sabido (Eds.), *Entertainment education and social change.* Mahwah, NJ: Erlbaum.

Desilet, G. (2006). *Our faith in evil: Melodrama and the effects of entertainment violence.* Jefferson, NC: McFarland & Company.

Drabman, R. S., & Thomas, M. H. (1974). Does media violence increase children's toleration of real-life aggression? *Developmental Psychology, 10*(3), 418–421. doi: 10.1037/h0036439

Freedman, J. (2002). *Media violence and its effect on aggression: Assessing the scientific evidence.* Toronto: University of Toronto Press.

McAnally, H. M., Robertson, L. A., Strasburger, V. C., & Hancox, R. J. (2012). Bond, James Bond: A review of 46 years of violence in films. *Archives of Pediatrics & Adolescent Medicine,* 1–2. doi: 10.1001/jamapediatrics .2013.437

Pennell, A. E., & Browne, K. D. (1999). Film violence and young offenders. *Aggression and Behavior, 4*(1), 13.

Torr, J. D. (Ed.). (2001). *Violence in the media.* San Diego, CA: Greenhaven Press.

Torr, J. D. (Ed.). (2002). *Examining pop culture: Violence in film and television.* San Diego, CA: Greenhaven Press.

U.S. Office of the Surgeon General, Surgeon General's Scientific Advisory Committee on Television and Social Behavior, and National Institute of Mental Health. (1972). *Television and growing up: The impact of television violence: Report to the Surgeon General, United States Public Health Service, from the Surgeon General's Scientific Advisory Committee on Television and Social Behavior.* Rockville, MD: U.S. Department of Health, Education, and Welfare, Health Services and Mental Health Administration, National Institute of Mental Health.

FIRST AMENDMENT PROTECTIONS AND FREEDOM OF EXPRESSION

The First Amendment to the U.S. Constitution states, "Congress shall make no law . . . abridging the freedom of speech, or of the press." While the amendment speaks of Congress, it also protects expression against abridgment by state and local governments and by other branches of the federal government. Furthermore, although it speaks of speech and the press, the protections of the amendment reach other media, such as film and music. An interesting modern question concerns the First Amendment status of video games, which is the focus of this entry.

History

There were early cases, building on decisions that pinball machines were not included within the protection of the First Amendment, that exempted video games from First Amendment protection. These early games were simply seen as not containing the level of expression necessary for the First Amendment to come into play. Somewhat later, as the complexity of video games increased, some courts began to say that at some point the level of expression would be such that video games should be protected. As late as 2002, a federal district court concluded that video games did not enjoy protection (see *Interactive Digital Software Ass'n v. St. Louis Co.*). Although the trial court decision was reversed, with the appellate court seeing video games as presenting sufficiently good stories as to be protected, there may be something in the lower court's position that the government, and courts, should not distinguish among stories based on perceived value. Nonetheless, it is clear from the 2011 U.S. Supreme Court video games decision in *Brown v. Entertainment Merchants Association* that video games are protected by the First Amendment. Perhaps the more interesting issue at this point is whether less sophisticated games, and even pinball machines, can be left outside the scope of constitutional protection.

Limiting Children's Access to Video Games

The fact that a medium—speech, books, films, or video games—may be protected does not mean that all restrictions or abridgments are disallowed. For example, film is protected, but obscene films may be restricted or banned. Actual speech of a political nature is at the core of the First Amendment, but where it presents a "clear and present danger" of intentionally provoking imminent lawless action, it too may be prohibited. These examples point to two approaches to the recent issue of justifying limits on violent video game play by children. One approach has been to argue that, while video games may be protected, the violent content of certain games takes them outside the protection of the First Amendment. The other has been to argue that there is sufficient harm in children playing these games that play may be banned. Both approaches can apply to violence in any medium, and both played roles in the Supreme Court's *Brown* decision.

The state of California claimed that it could limit children's play in the same way that a number of states limit children's access to sexual material, even if that material would be acceptable for adults. The Supreme Court had upheld, in *Ginsberg v. New York* (1968), a statute that prohibited the distribution to children of sexually indecent material, even though the material was not obscene for an adult audience. In California's view, the state should have a similar opportunity to shield children from depictions of violence. A similar position had been accepted by the trial court in a case growing out of restrictions on violent video game play by children in arcades in Indianapolis (see *Amusement Mach. Ass'n v. Kendrick*), although the trial court's decision upholding the limitations was later reversed on appeal.

The majority opinion in *Brown* rejected the analogy to *Ginsberg*, stating that obscene material had historically lacked First Amendment protection, but violent material had not been excluded. That may well have been a misunderstanding of the state of law at the time of the framing of the Constitution and Bill of Rights. Obscenity, in that era, was not limited to sexual material. It is only with the 1896 case *Swearingen v. United States* that obscenity developed the sole focus on sex. The response of the states was to adopt additional statutes addressing violence. One of those statutes was struck down in *Winters v. New York* (1948). A three-justice dissent in that case noted that New York was one of 20 states having the same sort of legislation, with four additional states having similar statutes. The widespread existence of such statutes, together with an earlier lack of focus with regard to obscenity,

indicate a long history of limiting violent material, at least with regard to access by children.

The *Brown* majority pointed to language in *Winters* to the effect that the violent material at issue there contains "no indecency or obscenity in any sense heretofore known to the law." That language from *Winters* may itself express a lack of historical understanding. Furthermore, what the majority opinion did not mention was the caution expressed by the *Winters* court that, despite the vagueness concerns that motivated the court's decision, the decision should not be read as to prohibit the states or Congress "from carrying out their duty of eliminating evils to which in their judgment such publications give rise." Perhaps, then, the analogy to sexual obscenity should not have been so facilely dismissed. Nonetheless, it was dismissed and seems unlikely to serve in the future to justify any statutes similar to that struck down in *Brown*.

Justice Clarence Thomas, in his *Brown* dissent, took another approach to the idea of exceptions to the First Amendment. He argued that the framers of the Constitution would not have accepted the proposition that the First Amendment included a right on the part of children to obtain what material they might like without their parents' intercession, or a right on the part of strangers to the family to provide material to the family's children. That historical argument, along with other arguments, might have served to justify the states' limits. The majority rejected this argument, saying that, at most, it would justify a state prohibiting one who had been advised by a child's parents that the child was forbidden access. The Court would not allow the state the alternative of prohibiting access without the parents' positive intervention.

If the distribution of violent video games is not found to be within an exception to the First Amendment, then limitations on distribution to children must meet strict scrutiny. The limits must be necessary to, or narrowly tailored to, a compelling governmental interest. Courts have consistently held that the physical and psychological well-being of youth is a compelling governmental interest. The issue has been with the limits necessity to that well-being. This is where the role of science comes in. There must be a demonstration that harm is done to children who play these games.

Scientists, initially psychologists and more recently neuroscientists, have offered evidence of negative impact on children, but the *Brown* majority rejected the conclusions of the scientific community and did so with little to no analysis. The majority opinion seemed almost to ignore the scientific evidence. When it did comment on the scientific evidence, it asked for evidence that would be unethical and illegal to gather. The majority said that the only thing science has been able to show is a correlation between real-world aggressiveness and playing violent video games and that there is no demonstration of causation. But, as the dissent by Justice Stephen Breyer recognized, there are longitudinal studies and laboratory experiments that have established causation.

The majority also commented that an increase in feelings of aggression shown in laboratory studies is not the same as violence. Although the studies showed, for example, an increase in willingness to administer a loud noise after playing a violent video game and then being mildly provoked, the majority wanted more evidence. Yet it would be unacceptable for scientists to conduct a study in which children play violent video games, are strongly provoked, and are provided with deadly weapons. As the trial judge in the first of the video game cases, *Amusement Mach. Ass'n v. Kendrick,* said, "It is completely unremarkable that an academic study would use proxy variables to stand in for measures of actual harmful aggression. The prospect of controlled experiments with human subjects that could result in aggression inflicting actual harm raises a few ethical issues, to put it mildly. Surely the constitutionality of the law does not depend on whether such experiments have been conducted."

The majority seemed to base its view of the science mostly on the fact that, it said, the lower courts had rejected the scientific evidence. The lower courts themselves seem not to have been able to understand the science or were simply unwilling to let science, particularly statistical results of the sort established in psychology, serve to override First Amendment protections.

A telling example is the federal district court in *Entertainment Software Association v. Hatch* (D.Minn., 2006). The court, speaking of the work of the leading psychologist studying video games, said, "Dr. Anderson's meta-analysis seems to suggest that one can take a number of studies, each of which he admits to not prove the proposition in question and 'stack them up' until a collective proof emerges." But that is exactly what meta-analysis does, and although the statistical methods may have some complexity, the theory is intuitively easy to understand. As an intuitive example, player A getting

more hits than player B in any individual baseball game does not show him to be the better hitter. But stack up these insignificant results over the season, and it does show that player A is the better hitter.

Other judges seem to have concluded that the failure of an experiment to show correlation is evidence that there is no correlation (see, e.g., *Wilson v. Midway Games, Inc.*), but that conclusion may be unwarranted for two reasons. First, there may be an explanation for the lack of result. For example, the *Wilson* court cited an Australian study that found no correlation between aggression and playing a violent video game. But, the authors of the study themselves suggested that the result might be because they had used a game that was not very violent. In their study, using 8- to 12-year-olds, they "for ethical reasons" used a game rated as appropriate for those 8 years of age and older. Second, a failure to find correlation is not necessarily a demonstration that there is no correlation. There may even have been some correlation but a lack of statistical significance, and that might be the result of too small a sample to aensure a statistically significant result.

This rejection of the scientific evidence is not limited to statistically based studies but applies to neuroscience as well. There is neurological evidence showing a physical impact on the brain resulting from exposure to media violence. But, when the court in *Entertainment Software Association v. Blagojevich* (7th Cir, 2006) was confronted with evidence that the region of the brain responsible for judgment and inhibition was not fully functioning in children exposed to media violence, it said that that evidence did not mean that judgment and inhibition were not being exercised elsewhere in the brain, without providing any indication of where else in the brain these functions can occur.

Specifically, with regard to legislation aimed at video games, there has been a question of the tailoring of the statute to the harm addressed. The *Brown* majority questioned why the California statute was limited to video games, but psychologists have expressed particular concern about those games because of their interactive nature. Interactivity is said to provide a stronger learning environment. Here, too, the *Brown* majority seems to have dismissed the concerns of social scientists through a classic informal fallacy, equivocating on the word *interactive*. Accepting that video games are interactive, the Court said that so is all literature. Although literature may try to draw the reader into the story, the empathy it seeks differs from the participation found in video games. One would not want to fly with a pilot whose "interactivity" was limited to reading the biography of Charles Lindbergh or viewing a number of films in which pilots were the major characters. The interactivity that helps make one a good pilot is found in the flight simulator, and it is the flight simulator, rather than the book or film, that social scientists would assert is the equivalent of the participation found in video games.

Justice Breyer, in his *Brown* dissent, was the only justice on the Court to present an analysis of the studies. He provided two appendices, one with 115 studies supporting the legislature's concerns and the other with 34 that presented critiques or failed to find a correlation. He said, "I, like most judges, lack the social science expertise to say definitively who is right." The majority opinion used that admission to dismiss Justice Breyer's dissenting conclusions. The majority, however, seems to have ignored what Justice Breyer said immediately after his confession of a lack of expertise: "But associations of public health professionals who do possess expertise have reviewed many of these studies and found a significant risk that violent video games, when compared with more passive media, are particularly likely to cause children harm." He noted statements by the American Academy of Pediatrics, the American Academy of Child & Adolescent Psychiatry, the American Psychological Association, the American Medical Association, the American Academy of Family Physicians, and the American Psychiatric Association noting in excess of 1,000 studies pointing to a *causal* connection between media violence and aggressive behavior in children. This, despite Justice Breyer's own lack of scientific expertise, was sufficient for him to justify California's action.

Future Outlook

The *Brown* decision might be seen as a flat rejection of any possibility of science filling the role of demonstrating the necessity of restrictions on violent media to protect the physical and psychological well-being of youth. Yet the Court's conclusion on the science is necessarily contingent. All the Court could say is that the science, at this time, does not justify the limits. Scientific knowledge grows, and it may well be that that growth will eventually so firmly establish the harm done to children that any real scientific debate will be over. However, the nature of conclusions in psychological and social science studies, as in all statistical studies, also provides great opportunity for

those who are so inclined to reject their conclusions. All the studies state conclusions with a certain level of confidence. The free expression absolutist can always find that level of confidence inadequate. No matter how significant the result, there may still be some small doubt left, and a court can focus on that doubt. Courts are accustomed to conclusions being stated in an assertive manner with no doubt as to their validity and find it easy to reject the more measured conclusions of social scientists.

Perhaps the most likely scientific advance eventually to justify restriction will come from neuroscience, despite the early rejection of neuroscientific evidence. This new look at the issue, through functional magnetic resonance imaging, provides physical evidence that courts may find more difficult to dismiss. However, the decisions culminating in *Brown* may demonstrate a dogmatic unwillingness to accept the possibility that, outside of intentionally provoking violence, expression may ever cause harm sufficient to warrant limitation.

Kevin W. Saunders

See also Demographic Effects; Drench Effects From Video Games; Legislating Media Violence: Law and Policy; Video Game Industry, Regulation Within the; Video Game Player and Opponent Effects

Further Readings

Amusement Mach. Ass'n v. Kendrick, 115 F. Supp. 2d (S.D. Ind. 2000), *rev'd*, 244 F.3d 572 (7th Cir.).

Brown v. Entertainment Merchants Association, 131 S.Ct. 2729 (2011).

Entertainment Software Association v. Blagojevich, 404 F.Supp.2d 1051, 1066 (N.D. Ill. 2005), *aff'd*, 469 F3d 641 (7th Cir, 2006).

Entertainment Software Association v. Hatch, 443 F.Supp.2d 1065, 1069 n.1 (D.Minn. 2006).

Ginsberg v. New York, 390 U. S. 629 (1968).

Interactive Digital Software Ass'n v. St. Louis Co., 200 F. Supp. 2d 1126 (E.D. Mo. 2002), *rev'd*, 329 F3d 954 (8th Cir 2003).

Saunders, K. W. (1996). *Violence as obscenity: Limiting the media's First Amendment protection*. Durham, NC: Duke University Press.

Saunders, K. W. (2003). *Saving our children from the First Amendment*. New York, NY: New York University Press.

Swearingen v. United States, 161 U.S. 446 (1896).

Wilson v. Midway Games, Inc., 198 F.Supp.2d 167 (D. Conn. 2002).

Winters v. New York, 333 U.S. 507 (1948).

FIRST-PERSON PERSPECTIVE, VIOLENT CONTENT FROM

The first-person perspective is a formal technique of visual media wherein the camera assumes the point of view of a character. This technique allows the viewer to see and hear the world as if through the character's eyes and ears. While first-person perspective is sometimes used in film and television, violent content shown from this perspective is more frequently found in video games, most markedly in first-person shooter games. The first-person perspective is thought to exacerbate the effects of violent games through an increase in presence and an increase in identification with the violent character. There is growing evidence that first-person perspective taking stimulates particular neurological routes directly related to human self-consciousness. Increasingly, violent first-person shooter games have become associated with the military in both the entertainment and recruitment fields.

First-Person Violent Video Games

The first-person perspective is used extensively throughout the medium of video games, including racing games, flight simulators, and role-playing games. It is most notably employed in first-person shooter games. This genre emerged in the early 1990s with titles like *Wolfenstein 3D* and *Doom* and has maintained enormous popularity, with series like *Call of Duty* and *Halo* becoming some of the best-selling franchises in game history. In these games, players experience a three-dimensional world through the eyes of the protagonist, typically a White male situated in a warlike setting. The player sees the elements of the screen as if down the barrel of the virtual gun, sometimes with portions of the gun and the hand holding it detectable in the player's visual field. This formal combination of movement and targeting results in game play that is almost exclusively defined by combat. The connection between this genre and violent content is so pronounced that first-person shooters are frequently chosen as stimuli in studies linking violent games with aggressive outcomes.

Presence

Presence occurs when an individual is so swept up in the experience allowed through media—the sensory experience, the social experience of interacting with others, and the representation of the self—that it seems real. The first-person perspective in video games can help achieve this state, through the related concepts of *vividness* (the degree to which a mediated experience, as created through its formal features, is sensorially rich) and *interactivity* (the player's opportunity to shape the mediated experience, including but not limited to the *mapping* of the user's actions to actions that take place in the mediated environment).

Research has linked the experience of presence brought about by virtual reality gaming, which includes the first-person perspective, with aggressive outcomes, both when the aggression experienced in the game takes a form more likely to be relevant in day-to-day life, such as fistfighting, as well as when the aggression takes a more severe form, such as shooting. There is growing evidence to support the notion that the first-person perspective is a key feature of a vivid and interactive media experience that predicts presence, which, in turn, can increase the likelihood of an aggressive or hostile response.

Identification

Identification with media characters occurs when a viewer or game player experiences the emotions and thoughts of that character as if they were his or her own. Identification has been shown to increase the effect of violent media, and social cognitive theory suggests that individuals are more likely to emulate violent acts committed by characters with whom they identify. In video games, the ability to assume direct control of a character allows for high levels of identification. The vicarious experience provided by first-person-perspective games is believed to further increase identification. This perspective has been offered in several experiments that have manipulated point of view while assessing the influence of violent video games, though recent conflicting research may indicate a more complicated relationship among identification, perspective, and aggressive outcomes.

Relevant Neurological Processes

In cognitive neuroscience, individuals' conceptions of the self versus others derive from the representational capacities of the brain. The use of functional magnetic resonance imaging (fMRI) has demonstrated that the first-person perspective, manipulated in the laboratory through tasks carried out on a computer screen, is associated with activation of medial prefrontal regions of the brain, whereas the third-person perspective is associated with activation of other regions. The regions activated by first-person perspective taking are considered central to an individual's self-consciousness. The stimuli used in these experiments have evolved from static virtual images to those more dynamic in nature, and therefore more closely approximate video and computer games.

Links to the Military

First-person shooters have been linked closely to the military since their inception. In the early 1980s, Atari's *Battlezone,* a crude precursor to modern first-person video games, was adapted by the military to create the tank-training simulator, *Bradley Trainer.* In the mid-1990s, the U.S. Marines modified *Doom,* one of the earliest commercially successful first-person shooters, into training software for soldiers, and other branches of the military followed suit. Military themes have also dominated the commercial market. Many first-person shooters are set in a historical, contemporary, or futuristic military environment. These games range from the U.S. Army–produced *America's Army* to commercial franchises like *Call of Duty.* Scholarly critics such as Roger Stahl have critiqued these games as "militainment."

Erica Scharrer and Gregory Blackburn

See also Effects From Violent Media, Short- and Long-Term; Media Effects Perspectives of Violence; Media Violence, Definitions and Context of; User Involvement in Violent Content, Effects of; Virtual Reality, Violent Content in

Further Readings

Hitchens, M. (2011). A survey of first-person shooters and their avatars. *Game Studies, 11*(3). Retrieved from http://gamestudies.org/1103/articles/michael_hitchens

Krcmar, M., & Farrar, K. (2009): Retaliatory aggression and the effects of point of view and blood in violent video games. *Mass Communication & Society, 12*(1), 115–138.

Schneider, E. F., Lang, A., Shin, M., & Bradley, S. D. (2004). Death with a story: How story impacts emotional, motivational, and physiological responses to first-person shooter video games. *Human Communication Research, 30,* 361–375.

Vogeley, K., May, M., Ritzl, A., Falkai, P., Zilles, K., & Fink, G. R. (2004). Neural correlates of first-person perspective as one constituent of human self-consciousness. *Journal of Cognitive Neuroscience, 16*(5), 817–827.

FLOW THEORY

Flow theory, as suggested by Mihaly Csikszentmihalyi, posits that people feel happiest when they are in a state of flow. People experience flow in their everyday lives, professional performances, leisure activities, and entertainment media consumption. Flow has been one of the most prominent concepts of positive psychology. The concept has been examined over the past decade across various disciplines, including psychology, marketing, communication, education, organizational science, and cognitive neuroscience. This entry provides a definition of flow and the key characteristics of a flow state as well as a discussion about the theoretical and practical relevance of the flow construct to psychology of media violence. The entry concludes with a discussion about individual difference factors that moderate the effects of violent media enjoyment on flow.

Definition and Attributes

Flow is defined as an autotelic and intrinsically motivating experience. It is characterized by (a) focused attention to an activity with an accomplishable goal and interactive feedback; (b) loss of self-consciousness; (c) intrinsic reward, interest, and curiosity; (d) temporal distortion; and (e) optimal balance between the difficulty of the task and the skill of the performer or media user. *Focused attention* refers to intense concentration on or immersion in what an individual is doing at the present moment. *Loss of self-consciousness* means losing awareness of oneself when engaged in absorbing activities. This concept is relevant to feelings of self-presence, referring to a psychological state in which the boundary between the actual self and the virtual or mediated self is blurred. *Intrinsic reward* refers to inherently pleasurable and motivating activity for its own sake. *Temporal distortion* means losing track of time while engaging in a certain activity. For example, movie watchers and video game players often have a sense that time has passed more quickly than usual. *Optimal balance between challenge and skill,* referring to a match between the difficulty level of a certain task or activity and the cognitive ability or skill level of an individual, is an integral condition for experiencing a flow state. Too-easy tasks result in boredom, whereas too-challenging tasks result in frustration, thus hampering the realization of flow.

Flow and Media Enjoyment

Communication scholar John Sherry (2004) has argued that enjoyment of media results from a flow experience that is realized when there is a balance between media message contents and a user's ability to interpret that message. Driven by the neurophysiological perspective (NPP), communication scholars Rene Weber, Ron Tamborini, Amber Westcott-Baker, and Benjamin Kantor (2009) have theorized flow and media enjoyment as cognitive synchronization of attentional and reward networks. Media scholar Seung-A Annie Jin (2012) argued that physical presence, spatial presence (telepresence), and self-presence are important mediators that link the paths between antecedents to and consequences of flow in entertainment media. She also provided empirical evidence supporting the theoretical proposition that the fit between skill and challenge is a necessary condition for the emergence of flow across various video game genres.

Flow and Enjoyment of Violent Media

People enjoy violent media content in print media like books and in motion pictures like animations, television programs, and movies. Violent media depict characters being attacked or physically injured by others. Violence in media is enjoyable because it offers pleasurable gratifications. Research has suggested that people like violent films because they feature destruction or provide thrills, excitement, and unpredictability. Media psychologists Cynthia Hoffner and Kenneth Levine (2005) have claimed that it is possible that some violent content in media that produce negative emotions elicit interest or enjoyment.

Violent video games are the most popular violent interactive media. Video games provide unique opportunities for the balance between challenge and skill that can stimulate the neural correlates of flow. For example, when playing first-person-perspective shooter games like *Call of Duty* and third-person-perspective shooter games like *Max Payne,* experienced game players feel bored if they feel that it is too easy to kill the enemy. In contrast, inexperienced game players feel frustrated if they feel that it is too difficult to kill the enemy. Thus, the flow state in violent games is realized when users feel the challenge level provided by the game environments and content optimally matches their cognitive ability and skill levels. Also, successful performance is a positive prediction of flow in violent interactive media. Media psychologists Tilo Hartmann and Peter Vorderer have claimed that violent video games offer pleasurable aesthetics of destruction and stimulate excitement that results in pride or euphoria if the game player experiences success. These states of excitement and euphoria can increase psychophysiological arousal (i.e., a physiological and psychological state of being reactive to stimuli) and induce flow.

Individual Differences

Driven by Zuckerman's original conceptualization of sensation seeking, Hoffner and Levine propose that high sensation seekers enjoy stimuli that elicit negative emotions like fear because the intensity of these emotions helps them reach their optimal level of arousal. Sensation seeking and arousal needs are positively associated with a preference for and enjoyment of media violence. Jin found that video game users' playfulness, as one manifestation of autotelic personality, moderates the effects of the balance between skill and challenge on a flow state. The roles of individual difference factors, including sensation-seeking tendency, aggressiveness, and playfulness in inducing enjoyment and flow in violent media, merit future attention and further empirical tests.

Seung-A Annie Jin

See also Arousal and Aggressive Content, Theory and Psychology of; Presence Theory; Psychobiology of Violence; Video Games, User Motivations

Further Readings

Hoffner, C., & Levine, K. (2005). Enjoyment of Mediated Fright and Violence: A Meta-Analysis. *Media Psychology, 7,* 207–237.

Jin, S. A. (2012). Towards integrative models of flow: Effects of performance, skill, challenge, playfulness, and presence on flow in video games. *Journal of Broadcasting & Electronic Media, 56*(2), 169–186.

Sherry, J. (2004). Flow and media enjoyment. *Communication Theory, 14*(4), 328–347.

Weber, R., Tamborini, R., Westcott-Baker, A., & Kantor, B. (2009). Theorizing flow and media enjoyment as cognitive synchronization of attentional and reward networks. *Communication Theory, 19,* 397–422.

FORBIDDEN FRUIT HYPOTHESIS

Rating systems and warnings on violent and mature media content are intended to keep potentially harmful media out of the reach of children.

However, questions have been raised about whether these warnings and ratings could backfire by inadvertently making such content more desirable and attractive to children than it would be without affixed ratings. This notion is referred to as the *forbidden fruit hypothesis*. It has been the subject of much research—from explicit music, to television, movies, and most recently, video games. This entry illustrates the forbidden fruit hypothesis in the context of video game rating systems.

Video Game Ratings

Video game rating systems emerged because of rising concerns from parents and policy makers about negative effects of violent video games on youth. These concerns are supported by research concluding that exposure to such content can, in some situations, increase aggressive thoughts, emotions, and behaviors, and decrease empathy and prosocial behaviors in game players. Questions remain, however, about the best way to address concerns about negative effects of violent video games.

An intuitive reaction from the industry has been to implement a rating system (similar to other media rating systems) that categorizes games based on age-appropriate content. It is intended to assist parents in making informed decisions about their children's game selections. In the United States and Canada, the Entertainment Software Ratings Board (ESRB) assigns age and content ratings to video games. Ratings range from Early Childhood (EC 3+) to Mature (M 17+) and Adults Only (AO 18+). M- and AO-rated games are categorized as such because of violence, gore, sexual content, or mature language. In Europe, the Pan European Game Information system (PEGI) uses similar guidelines.

Unintended Negative Consequences of Media Rating Systems

Concerns have been raised that ratings may fail by inadvertently enhancing perceived likeability and desirability of "forbidden" media content. The forbidden fruit hypothesis was first raised in response to the parental advisory system introduced by the Recording Industry Association of America (RIAA), which flags mature content with a label reading "Parental Advisory Explicit Content." By clearly stating that some content should not be made accessible to children of certain ages, the restrictive warnings may increase desire to access the content among "forbidden" individuals.

Concerns have not been limited to RIAA ratings. Researchers have investigated television warnings appearing before violent programming, finding that they increase youth interest in violent programs, particularly when those youth are high in reactance (defined following). Further research has been conducted on the television V-chip parental monitoring device. Introduced as part of the Telecommunications Act of 1996, the V-chip was intended to work in conjunction with television ratings by allowing parents to block content of objectionable ratings. Research has found that programs receiving stronger parental advisories are viewed as more desirable by children, particularly boys. More recently, research on video game ratings has produced consistent findings. Age-restrictive labels increase attractiveness of video games in children, including both boys and girls, and in children as young as 7 years of age.

Reactance Theory

The forbidden fruit effect can be interpreted from the perspective of Jack Brehm's theory of psychological reactance (1966). The theory proposes that when a person's freedom to engage in a behavior is threatened or restricted, he or she will experience an unpleasant motivational state (referred to as *reactance*) that will encourage him or her to recapture that freedom. The more important the freedom is to the individual, the greater the motivational pressure to regain it. In the case of video game ratings, if a child perceives that a restrictive rating threatens his or her freedom to play that game, the child may become even more motivated to access it than he or she would have been if the child's freedom had not been threatened with an age-restricted rating.

Some researchers have proposed that such unintended negative effects may be avoided or reduced depending on how the rating system is presented. Specifically, if a rating is presented as descriptive (i.e., content based), rather than evaluative (i.e., age based, or cautionary), it may be less likely to elicit reactance, and, as such, it will be less likely to inadvertently increase desirability of the media content. For example, instead of labeling a video game "M" with an evaluative age-restrictive guideline ("should only be played by persons 18 years and older"), it could simply provide descriptive information ("contains intense violence"). This latter presentation also provides information about questionable content of the game, but it does not provide explicit advice about who should or should not play it. Although some research has found that evaluative ratings are more likely to elicit reactance (and subsequently enhance interest in the content), the general research consensus is that both descriptive and evaluative ratings have the potential to make media content more enticing to young people. Thus, regardless of how ratings are presented, they have the potential to increase interest in and desirability of media content among youth.

The finding that both descriptive and evaluative ratings can heighten children's interest in violent content is inconsistent with the reactance explanation of the forbidden fruit effect. From the reactance perspective, descriptive ratings (by not providing explicit age restrictions) should elicit *less* reactance than evaluative ratings and, as a result, prevent unintended negative reactions from youth. This illustrates that the forbidden fruit effect emerges not only due to reactance, but due to one or more additional factors. One suggestion offered is that regardless of how they are presented (evaluative or descriptive), ratings provide information about the likely presence of violence, sex, and mature content—topics that children and teens may find increasingly enticing and desirable.

Conclusions

Research consistently demonstrates a forbidden fruit effect of media rating systems. Content advisories intended to deter youth exposure to questionable content may actually increase desirability of and interest in such content. Rating systems that not only provide information to youth about the presence of mature and potentially enticing themes (e.g., violence), but also contain evaluative age-restricted guidelines (which may heighten psychological reactance) have been subject to particular scrutiny from researchers.

Catherine E. Goodall

See also Ratings Systems, Video Games; Video Game Industry, Regulation Within

Further Readings

Anderson, C. A., Shibuya, A., Ihori, N., Swing, E. L., Bushman, B. J., Sakamoto, A., Rothstein, H. R., & Saleem, M. (2010). Violent video game effects on aggression, empathy, and prosocial behavior in Eastern and Western countries: A meta-analytic review. *Psychological Bulletin, 136,* 151–173. doi:10.1037/a0018251

Bijvank, M. N, Konijn, E. A., Bushman, B. J., & Roelofsma, P. H. M. P. (2008). Age and violent-content labels make video games forbidden fruits for youth. *Pediatrics, 123,* 870–876. doi: 10.1542/peds.2008–0601

Brehm, J. W. (1966). *A theory of psychological reactance.* New York, NY: Academic Press.

Bushman, B. J., & Cantor, J. (2003). Media ratings for violence and sex: Implications for policymakers and parents. *American Psychologist, 58*(2), 130–141. doi:10.1037/0003-066X.58.2.130

GENDER, EFFECTS OF VIOLENT CONTENT ON

Gender is the sociocultural construction of biologic sex and therefore includes cultural, behavioral, biological, and psychological characteristics. In the United States, gender roles are based on heteronormative understandings of acceptable and unacceptable social behavior. *Heteronormativity* refers to sociocultural bias rooted in patriarchal institutions that privilege the male–female binary, contribute to stereotyped and sexualized understandings of certain bodies, and discipline those who transgress this dichotomy. Institutionalized hegemony and dominant heterosexual discourses contribute to and perpetuate social discrimination and gender violence within broader U.S. society. This heterosexist understanding of gender is reflected in U.S. film, print media, social media, and television. Individual and group acts of aggression toward women, LGBTQi (lesbian, gay, bisexual, transgender, queer/questioning, and intersexed) individuals, and other marginalized groups within the media in turn support and cultivate gender violence within the United States. This same media harnesses the potential to offer a counter-narrative on gender misrepresentation, stereotyping, inequality, and violence.

Gender Violence

Gender violence in any form reinforces gender inequity. Through intention and effect it sustains and perpetuates hegemonic male power. A pervasive worldwide phenomenon, historically gender violence was not recognized by political and legal institutions. Work by feminist, masculinities, and queer scholars have prompted domestic law within the United States and abroad to address causes, effects, and solutions to such violence. Legal change has been paralleled by new forms of violence emerging from globalization processes and modern technological innovations such as the Internet. Work aimed at eradication of gender violence has the dual task of progressing political and legal culture as well as developing innovative mechanisms that end silence associated with gender violence.

The primary sites of gender violence include the family, community, and state. While gender violence affects all genders, holistically, gender violence disproportionately affects females. Femicide, for example, is identified by international human rights law as an extreme form of misogynistic violence against women that is premised upon female subordination. Both in real life and as seen in the mass media, those living in poverty or under foreign occupation, women of color, and individuals who transgress heteronormative gender norms are at increased risk of gender violence. Occurring within public and private spheres, feminist research has indicated that gender violence is indiscriminate, negatively affecting all class, gender, ethnic, racial, national, religious, and age groups.

Gender violence is a historically and socially contextualized global phenomenon, yet it exhibits the universal themes of physical, psychological, and emotional trauma as well as tolerance by local communities and escalation during wartime. Due to its nonstatic nature and ability to reinvent itself when facing media coverage, policy change, and legal sanction, gender violence has been difficult to eliminate. Common forms of gender violence in the United States include age-related abuse; commercial sexual exploitation; domestic violence; eating disorders and bodily mutilation; glorified media and video game gender violence; incest; pornography; rape; restricted access to abortion, birth control, and health care; sexual assault; sexual harassment; workplace harassment; and media stereotyping.

Causes of Gender-Based Violence

The causes of gender violence are numerous. A predominant source of gender violence in the United States is the mass media, with pervasive violence found on television and in film. Television crime series such as *CSI: Las Vegas* and *Criminal Minds* commonly portray graphic depictions of female rape and assault. Shows like *The Sopranos* and *Sons of Anarchy* glamorize violence, often depicting female characters in traditional roles or as sex objects and male characters as impassive and justified in using violence. Films like *Fatal Attraction* (1987) and *The Hand That Rocks the Cradle* (1992) have reinforced traditional gender roles while concomitantly disciplining the "crazed" and rebellious woman. Finally, despite greater visibility for LGBTQi individuals, Hollywood films have continued to oversimplify issues of sexual orientation (e.g., *Brokeback Mountain*, 2005) and speak through a homophobic lens (e.g., *Seven Psychopaths,* 2012). Such renderings of gender and gender violence can reinforce stereotyping and related violence in the real world.

Multiple forms of gender violence also have been depicted in video games, music, and social media Internet websites. Video games such as *Grand Theft Auto* are filled with explicitly violent content and sexualized female bodies. Rap, hip-hop, hard rock, and heavy metal lyrics and music videos include misogynistic messages about female and queer bodies. Forms of gender violence on the Internet include sexist blogging, cyberbullying, child and Gonzo pornography, and commercial sexual exploitation or sex trafficking. Exposure to media violence can produce gender stereotypes, desensitize youth to violence, and teach adolescents that society tolerates male violence while simultaneously trivializing gender-based abuse. Such desensitization was witnessed in the 2013 Steubenville, Ohio, case involving the gang rape of a high school female, bystander

nonintervention, and subsequent cyberbullying through Tweets, Facebook pictures, and video.

Another source of gender violence is traditional sociocultural beliefs associated with gender power relations. Traditional, heterosexist thinking in the form of gender stereotypes exists in contemporary family relations, educational milieus, politics, and consumer settings. Gender stereotypes negatively influence behavior and perception of behavior at macro and micro levels. As students enter middle and high school, for example, they face gender norming through the kinds of courses and activities they are encouraged to pursue, fashion and sports magazine imagery, and clothing styles marketed at their age groups. Having been socialized by the mass media to assume passive gender roles, upon entering college many women, regardless of sexual orientation, are subject to sorority hazing, eating disorders, and/or falling victim to fraternity rape culture. Similarly, men face social pressures perpetuated by the mass media. This includes conforming to hegemonic, masculine characteristics or risk social isolation and discipline in the form of normalized heterosexual male talk about "sissies" and "faggots."

A final form of gender violence occurs because of state action and inaction. National and international state-operated institutions have coalesced to deprive women, individuals who transgress the gender hierarchy, and other marginalized groups of basic rights. Barriers to public service, equal pay for equal work, and autonomy over female health have been reduced, but they have not been fully eliminated because of state action and inaction. The state also maintains key forms of gender violence, including but not limited to failure to punish public officials who utilize harassment tactics in the media, military and U.S. border personnel involved in sexual assault, and those who foster rape cultures within U.S. prisons.

Effects of Gender Violence

Gender violence affects those targeted physically, psychologically, and emotionally. Regardless of form, gender violence can have short- and long-term negative family, health, and economic effects. Gender violence often results in the disruption of family and community life due to emotional withdrawal and depression. Physical gender violence such as rape can jeopardize female reproductive health through physical injury, sexually transmitted diseases, unwanted pregnancy, latent depression, and other health complications. Physical, psychological, and emotional trauma can be further complicated by the development of drug and alcohol use as well as by secondary victimization by social media and/or the state.

Gender violence also negatively affects female economic stability. Contributing to the labor force, for example, might prove difficult due to posttraumatic stress disorder that develops after the event. Given that male dominance is a perennial reminder of female vulnerability, gender violence creates an ostensible roadblock to achieving gender equality. Furthermore, everyday violence often is dismissed as illegitimate and reinforced by social and mass media conforming to heteronormative and heterosexist understandings of gender. The culture of fear created by media that perpetuate gender violence can restrict social mobility and participation in the political process. Such fear can limit progress toward true sociopolitical and economic equality within the United States and abroad.

Elimination of Gender Violence

As suggested by policy and media research, the mass media can help to reduce gender violence by encouraging parental guidance in selection of television, film, and music outlets for children. Media literacy research has suggested that more responsible depictions of violence, specifically the elimination of glorified male violence and the trivialization of female victims, will reduce violence within broader U.S. society. This suggests that rather than be desensitized to media violence, the teenagers in the Steubenville, Ohio, rape case who witnessed the crime would have intervened instead of occupying a bystander position. Based on critical media studies analyses, the Motion Picture Association of America (MPAA) could make its movie rating process more transparent and institute policies to more accurately rate movies containing glorified male violence directed at women. Toward these goals, increased public media literacy about gender violence might be achieved.

Feminist research has suggested that health care and counseling providers should utilize ethical methods when cases of gender violence are suspected. Specifically, they could operate within a medical paradigm that utilizes the mass media and works to reduce silence around gender violence. Research also suggests that health care and counseling agencies should publicly advocate for improved female access to health care and community education

about gender violence as well as ensure the availability of emergency contraception for victims of sexual violence.

Interdisciplinary and media literacy research has argued for a more sophisticated understanding of the linkages between and effects of violent content on gender. Educational curricula, programming, and policy also contribute to this understanding and arresting of broad-based gender violence. Education curricula and policy research have supported utilizing social media to prompt student discussion about gender violence through topics such as community building, gender stereotypes, teenage dating violence, and sex education.

Through Internet and video campaigns, feminist and queer activism has pushed U.S. and international human rights law to focus more acutely on the elimination of gender violence. Premised on the idea that all individuals should have equal institutional access, resources, and human rights, feminist and queer epistemology gives visibility to the multiple inequalities individuals face in private and public realms. In feminist theory specifically, the ability to make the invisible visible is accomplished through standpoint theory, or the idea that female knowledge is situated and therefore is best to explain all forms of female oppression.

Feminist efforts in the 1960s led to landmark U.S. legislation focused on gender discrimination and violence. This legislation includes but is not limited to Title VII of the Civil Rights Act (1964); Title IX of the Educational Amendments (1972); Hate Crime Statistics Act (1990); Violence Against Women Act (1994); and Hate Crime Prevention Act (1997). Work by feminists also pushed international human rights law to focus on global gender violence. Despite state resistance in the form of nonratification, UN conventions and protocols include but are not limited to the Convention on the Elimination of All Forms of Discrimination Against Women (CEDAW, 1979); Inter-American Convention on the Prevention, Punishment, and Eradication of Violence Against Women ("Convention of Belem do Para," 1994); Optional Protocol to the Convention on the Elimination of All Forms of Discrimination Against Women (2000); and the Yogyakarta Principles on the Application of International Human Rights Law in Relation to Sexual Orientation and Gender Identity (2006).

Many local, state, national, and international institutions work toward the elimination of gender violence. Through counseling services, education programs, social media campaigns, community outreach, academic scholarship, and policy implementation, gender violence has become a recognizable crime against humanity. At macro and micro levels, institutions offer numerous suggestions toward the permanent elimination of gender violence. Yet these same actors also may perpetuate gender violence. Operating from law and policy that favor male language, the state can shape how women and men view themselves and each other. Through political and legal mechanisms, state agencies determine the level of violence and coercion that is permissible against females and queer bodies. Policy makers therefore have an obligation to progressively integrate legal mechanisms that include gendered perspectives in the eradication of gender violence. As discussed in policy research literature, policy also can hold the system accountable for structural and individual abuses of power. These changes can be beneficial not only to the disproportionate numbers of women affected by gender violence but society as a whole.

Melinda A. Lemke

See also Attitude, Effects of Media Violence on; Cyberbullying, Definition and Effects of; Desensitization Effects on Society; Effects From Violent Media, Short- and Long-Term; Exposure to Violent Content, Effect on Child Development; Films, Representation of Violence and Its Effects in; Gender and Aggression; Identity, Media Violence and Its Effects on; Internet Violence, Influence on Society; Music Videos and Lyrics, Violent Content in; Pornography, Violent Content in: Effects of; Rape Perceptions; Sexualized Aggression; Socialization of Violence in Media and Its Effects; Violence, Definition of

Further Readings

Cornell, D. (Ed.). (2000). *Feminism and pornography.* Oxford: Oxford University Press.

Dumond, R. W. (2000). Inmate sexual assaults: The plague that persists. *Prison Journal, 80*(4), 407–414.

Falcón, S. M. (2007). Rape as a weapon of war: Militarized rape at the U.S.-Mexico border. In D. A. Segura & P. Zavella (Eds.), *Women and migration in the U.S.-Mexico borderlands.* Durham, NC: Duke University Press.

Faludi, S. (1991). *Backlash: The undeclared war against American women.* New York, NY: Anchor Books; Doubleday.

Holmes, R. M., & Holmes, S. T. (Eds.). (2002). *Current perspectives on sex crimes.* Thousand Oaks, CA: Sage.

Kelly, L. (1987). The continuum of sexual violence. In J. Hanmer & M. Maynard (Eds.), *Women, violence, and control* (pp. 46–59). Atlantic City, NJ: Humanities Press International.

Martin, P. Y. (2005). *Rape work: Victims, gender, and emotions in organization and community context.* New York, NY: Routledge.

O'Connell Davidson, J. (2005). *Children in the global sex trade.* Malden, MA: Polity Press.

Quinn, B. A. (2002). Sexual harassment and masculinity: The power and meaning of "girl watching." *Gender & Society, 16*(3), 386–402.

Sanday, P. R. (2007). *Fraternity gang rape: Sex, brotherhood, and privilege on campus.* New York, NY: New York University Press.

GENDER AND AGGRESSION

Consistent with popular wisdom, research has shown that men are more aggressive than are women; however, the size of this effect depends on several situational and perceptual factors. Men tend to engage in direct aggression, in which the target receives the harm, typically resulting in pain or physical injury for the target. For example, 95% of juvenile homicides are committed by young men. Men are more likely than are women to carry and use weapons, especially in conflicts with other men. Women are more likely to engage in indirect or relational aggression, in which the target receives psychological harm such as social exclusion and ostracism. The sex difference in physical aggression is larger in children than adults, perhaps because men learn to regulate aggressive responses and women may learn assertiveness, which is more consistent with the female gender role than aggression. This entry provides an overview of cognitive, social, and biological factors that have been identified in research to be related to sex differences in aggressive behavior. These variables may interact with the effects of viewing different types of media violence on aggression in men and women.

Cognitive and Social Factors That Affect Sex Differences in Aggression

Perceived Consequences of Aggression

Women are more likely to anticipate guilt and/or anxiety associated with aggression than are men and believe that their aggression would cause more harm to the target than do men. Women also tend to believe that their aggression is likely to cause danger to themselves more than do men. Men aggress more than do women when aggression is required rather than freely chosen, as is often the case in laboratory experiments. Studies on observational learning have shown that both girls and boys imitate aggression by a same-sex model more when they anticipate a positive consequence for aggressing.

Gender Role Socialization

Gender roles—societal expectations for how men and women should act—have been clearly linked to sex differences in aggressive behavior. When male and female participants feel deindividuated (anonymous, separate from their identity, and thus will not be held accountable for their actions), women have been shown to be as aggressive as men. Feelings of deindividuation can reduce women's feelings that they should not be aggressive because of gender role expectations, and thus they may express aggression. Furthermore, when aggression is viewed by others, women aggress less than men do in public settings, perhaps because of public violation of gender role expectations by women. Because the traditional male gender role is to be benevolent toward women, some studies have found that men are less aggressive toward women than toward men in public settings.

Men who endorse traditional masculine gender roles of hostility, defensiveness, and social dominance attitudes tend to be more aggressive than those who do not. Socialization of boys that involves restriction of emotional expression, which results in "male alexithymia," or the inability to articulate emotions, and transformation of emotions into aggression to achieve social dominance and to appear tough leads to development of aggressive response tendencies in boys.

Perceived Provocation and Anger

Laboratory experiments have revealed that when provoked by another person, men and women both respond aggressively. Consistent with this finding, anger does not predict sex differences in aggression; in laboratory experiments men have been no more aggressive when angered than have women. Thus, men and women may share the same degree of aggressive motivation when angered, but their means of expression in aggression may differ.

Sex of the Target

Laboratory experiments in which the sex of the target has been manipulated have revealed that when participants had the opportunity to aggress against a same-sex target (i.e., men–men; women–women), men were more aggressive than women. However, when opposite sex targets were provided, women were more aggressive against men than were men against women. This effect may be due to a suppression of aggression by men against the woman target because of the "gentleman" or "benevolent sexist" gender role for men. Men who endorse hostility toward women and hostile masculinity are more aggressive against a female target and less aggressive against a male target when provoked in the laboratory and also report having conducted more sexual aggression toward women than have men who do not endorse hostile attitudes toward women. This effect remains even after general aggressive attitudes are statistically controlled; thus, it does not seem to be the case that men who aggress against women are merely more aggressive people than those who are low in hostility toward women.

Tend and Befriend Tendencies in Women

Women have been shown to respond to stressful situations by nurturing the self and others, particularly children, and by affiliating with others, particularly other women, for social support and protection. This behavioral pattern has been found more in women than in men. Men tend to respond to stress and sympathetic nervous system arousal by "fight or flight." Recent evidence indicates this response in women may be related to increases in the hormone oxytocin in response to stress.

Biological Influences in Potentiating Aggressive Tendencies

The following section discusses potentiating biological factors that may undergird gender differences in aggressive response tendencies to provocative stimuli and influence emotional, cognitive, and behavioral responsiveness.

Hormonal Factors

Some evidence suggests that higher levels of prenatal androgens and later overall testosterone levels facilitate aggressive response tendencies. Specifically, higher levels of androgens have been predictive of higher self-reports of aggressive tendencies between men and women, increased boisterous play (i.e., rough-and-tumble wrestling), and, to a lesser degree, differences within men and women. Preliminary evidence implicates a moderating effect of cortisol, such that higher levels of cortisol decrease androgen influence in aggressive tendencies of men. In addition, preliminary evidence suggests estrogens have a modulating role in aggressive tendencies, with oxytocin, sex hormones, and endogenous opioids influencing the tend-and-befriend tendencies of women.

Biological Markers

The difference in the length of the second- and fourth-finger digit appears to be a marker of increased prenatal adrogenization and subsequent overall postnatal testosterone levels. While this digital marker can be found in females, it is far more typical in males. Men who are born with an additional Y chromosome, an XYY genotype, have been shown to display more aggressive behavior than average and are significantly overrepresented in penal institutions. These findings are from correlational studies; therefore, aggression in XYY samples may be due to related variables such as increased height, which may be associated with gaining power through intimidation or perceived provocation from peers.

Mirror Neurons

Mirror neurons have been proposed to play an important neurological role in social cognition and interpersonal ability along with emotional recognition. Recently, research examining gender differences while observing others' behaviors suggested differences in anatomical structures and neuronal response activation in the human mirror neuron system. For example, preliminary evidence suggested that females show a greater amount of activation and gray matter in areas associated with mirror neurons as well higher activity when processing stimuli related to self and other empathic interactions. Although any conclusions from this research would be premature, it may be a promising field of inquiry for ferreting out gender differences as a result of neuroanatomical structure and basis of reactivity and understanding aggressive interpretation and response.

Implications for Media Violence Exposure Effects

Because distinct factors are associated with aggressive responses in men and women, the two sexes may differ in reactions to depictions of these factors in television shows, movies, music, and video games. In fact, observational learning may be most likely to occur for each sex when factors to which they are sensitive are present. Boys and men may be particularly likely to imitate direct aggression performed by male protagonists who are provoked by a male, particularly with a weapon. Depictions of men gaining social dominance and other rewards through use of physical aggression may also increase the likelihood of imitation by male viewers. This tendency is particularly a concern if the man perceives that this aggression is normative, expected of him, and associated with positive consequences. Depictions of masculinity as being devoid of emotional expression other than anger may further develop aggressive tendencies in men.

When women are exposed to media depictions of aggression, they are more likely to view the perspective of the target of the aggression and feel empathy for him or her. Women may be more likely to feel fear associated with perceived danger for the target when viewing stressful situations and aggression, which may increase tendencies to affiliate with other women. Girls and women may be more likely than men to imitate depictions of relational aggression if they perceive that it is normative, associated with social approval, and expected of women. When the target is depicted as provoking the aggressor and therefore is perceived as "deserving" of the aggressive acts, women may be likely to think the aggression is justified and an appropriate response. Finally, forms of media in which women feel anonymous and/or adopt a different character's persona, such as in a video game or a social media site, may increase aggressive behavior in women.

Kathryn B. Anderson and Debra L. Corey

See also Aggression and Brain Functioning; Developmental Effects; Effects of Media Violence on Relational Aggression; Gender and Aggression; Gender, Effects of Violent Content on; Gender Stereotypes, Societal Influence on; General Aggression Model; Stereotyping in Violent Content

Further Readings

Anderson, C. A., & Anderson, K. B. (2008). Men who target women: Specificity of target, generality of aggressive behavior. *Aggressive Behavior, 34*, 605–622.

Archer, J. (2004). Sex differences in aggression in real-world settings: A meta-analytic review. *Review of General Psychology, 8*(4), 291–322.

Carre, J. M., & Mehta, P. H. (2011). Importance of considering testosterone-cortisol interactions in predicting human aggression and dominance, *Aggressive Behavior, 37,* 489–491.

Eagly, A. H., & Steffen, V. J. (1986). Gender and aggressive behavior: A meta-analytic review of the social psychological literature. *Psychological Bulletin, 100*(3), 309–330.

Feder, J., Levant, R. F., & Dean, J. (2010). Boys and violence: A gender-informed analysis. *Psychology of Violence, 1*(5), 3–12.

Hyde, J. S. (1984). How large are gender differences in aggression? A developmental meta-analysis. *Developmental Psychology, 20,* 722–736.

Knight, G. P., Guthrie, I. K., Page, M. C., & Fabes, A. (2002). Emotional arousal and differences in aggression: A meta-analysis. *Aggressive Behavior, 28,* 366–393.

Taylor, S. E., Klein, L. C., Lewis, B. P., Gruenewald, T. L., Gurung, R. A. R., & Updegraff, J. A. (2000). Biobehavioral responses to stress in females: Tend-and-befriend, not fight-or-flight. *Psychological Review, 107,* 411–429.

GENDER STEREOTYPES, SOCIETAL INFLUENCES ON

Gender is the sociocultural construction of biologic sex. It comprises cultural, behavioral, biological, and psychological characteristics. Gender identity, therefore, is a socially constructed and fluid construct. This understanding of gender is integral to recognizing gender stereotypes and other forms of social misrepresentation within the United States. Gender stereotypes continue to be manifest within all forms of popular media, including film, print media, television, and social media like Facebook and Twitter. Stereotypes that construct heteronormative gendered representations of class, race/ethnicity, and social location influence individual and group (mis)understanding of gender. This knowledge construction process reinforces dominant discourses, thereby affecting social access, participation, equity, and respective policy change.

Gender Roles and Identity

In the United States gender roles are rooted in heteronormative understandings of acceptable and unacceptable feminine and masculine behavior. *Heteronormativity* refers to sociocultural bias rooted in patriarchal social, political, economic, and legal institutions that privilege the male–female binary over same-sex relationships. Given that the male–female binary is considered normative, lifestyles or relationships that transgress this dichotomy are socially disciplined, subject to prejudice, and/or denied access to many societal institutions.

Expectations about femininity and masculinity are socialized through various venues, including but not limited to the mass media, education, family, religion, law, government, and workplace. Such exposure influences the ability or inability of individuals to transcend socialized constructions of gender identity. Beginning in the 1950s, feminist theory, and later male and queer studies, sought to challenge heteronormative modes of gender role construction. Certain feminist, as well as lesbian, gay, bisexual, transgender, queer/questioning, and intersex (LGBTQi), activists advocate a more fluid understanding of gender performance so to stymie misunderstandings about sexual identity and eradicate gender stereotyping. From this perspective, privileging heteronormative relationships operates only to buttress the supposed normalcy of heteronormative behavior. Such privilege also shores up gender hierarchies that subject women, LGTBQi individuals, and those who transgress the gender regime to stereotyping, misrepresentation, underrepresentation, and prejudice.

Gender Stereotypes

Stereotypes are generalized and/or exaggerated ideas about groups, subgroups, and/or individuals within society. Stereotypes are inaccurate understandings of identity that operate to discount the multidimensionality that exists within an individual. Stereotypes disregard, for example, the ways gender intersects with class, race/ethnicity, sex, and historical context. Stereotypes limit individual ability to process new information or positively affect new relationships, and therefore they prompt the development of prejudice.

Stereotypes proliferate within group situations, during encounters with those who differ from one's own peer group, and/or when one is forced to defend one's self-image and esteem. Stereotypes also manifest in situations when individuals are outsiders or minorities within a majority situation. Research, for example, has documented stereotypes used against lone females studying and working in science, technology, engineering, and mathematics (STEM) fields and corresponding gender gaps in academic performance across all female demographic groups.

Gender stereotypes occur when heteronormative characteristics are applied to individuals without considering sociopolitical, economic, or historic contexts. Learned in social settings such as education and work, as well as through visual media like television and film, gender stereotypes maintain heteronormative understandings of gender and pigeonhole gender identity. Gender stereotypes about groups, subgroups, individuals, and corresponding behavior obscure reality as well as subject individuals to increased levels of social scrutiny and discipline for performing tasks outside their supposed gender roles.

Since the 1960s, feminists within media studies and feminist activists have critiqued the ways women are stereotyped in media texts as "unnatural," "abnormal," "witches," "sluts," "whores," "bitches," "she-men," "butches," "dykes," and "anti-family." Although many of these terms are representative of specific historical contexts, stereotypical rhetoric can subsist and evolve. The term *feminazi*, for example, was coined in the early 1990s by Rush Limbaugh, but it remains a key term in a rhetorical arsenal directed at assertive women. Black and Chicana feminists, as well as queer theorists, also document the additional burdens, stereotypes, and ways that women of color and LGBTQi individuals must negotiate public institutions differently than their White and/or heterosexual female counterparts. Their work points to ways gender stereotypes operate not only to the detriment of women and LGBTQi individuals, but to all living within the United States.

Societal Influences on Gender Stereotypes in the United States

In the United States gender stereotypes intricately are tied to predetermined heteronormative expectations about femininity and masculinity. Derived from long-standing Western patriarchal tradition, gender stereotypes assume there only are female and male genders and that both are heterosexual. In this vein, gender identity and gender stereotypes are not mutually exclusive but rather reinforcing. In the United States discussions of gender and sexuality in educational textbooks, television, Internet blogs, music, and workplace break rooms reinforce heteronormativity, which in turn buttresses gender stereotyping. As such, gender stereotyping includes widespread consensually held descriptive and prescriptive norms about oppositional female and male behavior.

In the United States, although inequality exists within and between subgroups of women and men, historically all women and nonheterosexual individuals have had less status and societal access than have White heterosexual men. Such inequality can be traced to English laws of coverture used in the American colonies. Middle-class White norms that emerged in the 1800s known as the "cult of domesticity" or "true womanhood" laws operated to deny married women rights associated with property, earnings, jury duty, divorce, children, and sexuality. Supporting stereotypes about female inferiority and "separate spheres" ideology, the U.S. Supreme Court, for example, denied women access to law school in *Bradwell v. State of Illinois* (1873) and the right to vote in *Minor v. Happersett* (1875). Furthermore, laws protecting White male rights to physically discipline their wives and concerning female property ownership existed through the 19th century, with laws designed to protect women from domestic violence not passed until the late 20th century. Women of color faced the double burden of a history based in slavery, denial of citizenship, and discrimination, and of having White norms of femininity imposed upon their communities.

Despite inequalities in law and social economy, women made inroads to education through the establishment of Vassar College (1865), Wellesley College (1872), Smith College (1875), Bryn Mawr College (1885), Barnard College (1889), and Radcliffe College (1894). Well into the 20th century, gender stereotypes maintained older false ideas that female presence in higher education would weaken curriculum standards, that institute prestige would decline, and that women would be unsexed. By 1901, females gained access to public elementary and secondary education; however, educators such as G. Stanley Hall relied on gender stereotypes to argue that coeducation would rob girls of their femininity and boys would be made effeminate. Pedagogical progressives like John Dewey also reinforced gender stereotypes by advocating for public education on the grounds that certain natural characteristics could be learned from and therefore beneficial to the opposite sex.

These and other historic forms of discrimination are tied to normative female gender characteristics of motherhood, care, irrationality, emotions, submissiveness, sexual objectification, and natural or physical weakness. As a result of the history of slavery and race relations in the United States, women of color face the double bind of stereotypes based on their gender, race/ethnicity, and/or class, including but not limited to being characterized as "sexually aggressive," "animalistic," "unintelligent," "mammies," and "welfare queens." Given that White men historically have dominated the public sphere, supposed male gender role characteristics came to include "breadwinner," "rationality," "scientific inclination," "competitiveness," "assertiveness," "sexually aggressive," and "independent thinking." Those men who do not exhibit these characteristics risked being stereotyped as "girls," "losers," "sissies," "homos," and "faggots." Although women, men, and LGBTQi individuals have entered social institutions that have traditionally been off limits (e.g., women lawyers and engineers; male nurses and stay-at-home dads; open service in the military), many occupations in the United States remain strongly gendered. As a result, gender stereotyping and harassment persist in public and private spaces.

Exaggerated ideas of women and men are perpetuated in private and public milieus. In families, through observation, imitation, reward, and punishment, children implicitly and explicitly learn gender-appropriate and inappropriate behaviors. Children also are socialized toward traditional gender roles through the toys, clothes, behavior, interests, and levels of assertiveness they are encouraged to pursue. Barbie dolls, toy kitchen sets, and youth beauty pageants, for example, are marketed to girls, while play guns, action figures, and violent video games are marketed to boys.

Gender norming and concomitant gender stereotypes continue throughout middle years and adolescence as a result of parental behavior as well as through interactions with peers and teachers. Youth are particularly susceptible to stereotype threat in peer situations. *Stereotype threat* involves the experience of fear or anxiety in a social situation in which an individual has the potential to experience a negative stereotype about her or his identity or group. Messages received from fashion magazines, film, the Internet, music, and television also sustain gender stereotyping in adolescence. For example, television series such as *The Bachelor* and *The Bachelorette* reinforce stereotypes about single women and men and the exaggerated heteronormative characteristics teenagers should replicate, and reality shows like *Survivor* and MTV's *Road Rules Challenge* reinforce traditional gender norms. Gender stereotyping continues into adulthood, operating to underpin heteronormativity. Regardless of interests or gender identity, that a woman upon graduation from college will marry and have children remains a stereotypical assumption that women and men must confront.

Resistance to Gender Stereotypes

Stereotypes have endless expression within everyday life and broad ideology. Stereotypes can be subtle and nuanced or resound in the most perverse rhetoric. Traditionally held understandings of gender roles and identity eventuate in the creation and perpetuation of gender stereotypes while also failing to take account of those genders existing on a continuum. Gender stereotypes within social institutions restrict the possibilities of culture in the United States. Regardless of accuracy, gender stereotypes negatively influence behaviors, interactions, and perceptions at macro and micro levels. In summary, gender stereotypes operate as overly simplistic understandings of gender that obscure and/or pigeonhole gender identity, limit individual and/or group access to social institutions, and eventuate in gender-based discrimination.

Given that gender roles and corresponding stereotypes are culturally derived, they are inscribed and resisted differently throughout the United States. In the United States, feminist researchers and activists of all backgrounds have sought to end stereotyping, racial invisibility, and media imagery that sexually objectifies women, thereby also eliminating sexual harassment, racial discrimination, and violence in public spaces. Queer theorists have examined and proposed ways to ameliorate the detrimental impacts gender stereotypes have on those within the LGBTQi community. A landmark achievement, the Matthew Shepard and James Byrd, Jr. Hate Crimes Prevention Act (2009), for example, allows the Department of Justice to prosecute crimes motivated by a victim's actual or perceived gender, gender identity, and sexual orientation. LGBTQi activists also have pushed for greater visibility in popular culture, specifically the increased presence of queer bodies on cable television.

Backed by social science research, rights groups have pushed for legislation that addresses negative social factors influencing and resulting from gender stereotyping. Such research and activism have been moderately successful at state, national, and international levels. A major victory at the international level has been the United Nations Convention on All Forms of Discrimination Against Women (CEDAW, 1981). As the United Nations' principal gender rights treaty, among other stipulations CEDAW requires that states modify sociocultural practices to eliminate prejudices based on the supposed superiority, inferiority, or stereotyped roles of women and men. Although the United States signed CEDAW on July 17, 1980, it has not ratified or acceded to the convention and therefore is not legally bound to its provisions.

Melinda A. Lemke

See also Advertising, Influence on Society; African Americans in Media, Character Depictions and Social Representation of; Asians in Media, Character Depictions and Social Representation of; Latinos in Media, Character Depictions and Social Representation of; Media as a Reflection of Society; Sex in Media, Effects on Society; Social Learning From Media; Stereotyping in Violent Content

Further Readings

Bastow, S. (1992). *Gender: Stereotypes and roles.* Pacific Grove, CA: Brooks/Cole.

Beauvoir, S. (1949). *The second sex (Le deuxième sexe).* C. Borde & S. Maloyany-Chevallier (Trans.). New York, NY: Knopf.

Bradwell v. State of Illinois, 83 U.S. 130 (1873).

Butler, J. (1999). *Gender trouble: Feminism and the subversion of identity.* New York, NY: Routledge.

Cook, R. J., & Cusack, S. (2010). *Gender stereotyping: Transnational legal perspectives.* Philadelphia: University of Pennsylvania Press.

Dines, G., & Humez, J. M. (Eds.). (1995). *Gender, race, and class in media: A text-reader.* Thousand Oaks, CA: Sage.

Faludi, S. (1991). *Backlash: The undeclared war against American women.* New York, NY: Anchor Books; Doubleday.

Matthew Shepard and James Byrd, Jr. Hate Crimes Prevention Act, 18 U.S.C. § 249 (2009).

Minor v. Happersett, 88 U.S. 162 (1875).

Ortner, S. B., & Whitehead, W. L. (Eds.). (1981). *Sexual meanings: The cultural construction of sexuality.* New York, NY: Cambridge University Press.

Riley, D. (1988). *Am I that name: Feminism and the category of "women" in history.* New York, NY: Macmillan.

Sloop, J. M. (2004). *Disciplining gender: Rhetorics of sex identity in contemporary U.S. culture.* Boston: University of Massachusetts Press.

United Nations Convention on the Elimination of Discrimination Against Women (1979). UNGA A/RES/34/180.

Wittig, M. (1992). *The straight mind and other essays.* Boston: Beacon Press.

GENERAL AGGRESSION MODEL

General aggression model (GAM; Anderson & Bushman 2002) is a comprehensive and integrative theoretical framework within which multiple social, cognitive, and developmental theories are incorporated to aid comprehension of and research on human aggressive behavior. Some of the more prominent (but not the only) theories that GAM incorporates include cognitive neoassociation theory, social learning theory, and behavioral script theory. Each theory offers crucial insight into understanding the reasons why people behave aggressively. This entry outlines the processes of GAM, especially with regard to media effects, and discusses the extensions of GAM to other research topics.

Processes

General aggression model can be broadly broken down into two sets of related processes. *Proximate processes* are those that are immediately related to aggressive behavior. *Distal processes* are those that influence short-term processes through long-term aggressive behavioral tendencies.

Proximal Processes

Proximal processes can best be understood by examining a single-cycle episode of GAM (see lower portion of Figure 1). A single episode begins with two forms of input. The first of these forms is the situation, factors within the present event that can influence social behavior. The second of these forms of input involves intrapersonal factors. These are individual differences—person factors—that may directly influence behavior, such as mood or trait aggressiveness, or may moderate the effects of situational factors.

In the next stage of GAM's single-cycle episode, proximate processes influence internal states. The primary internal states of interest concern affect, cognitions, and physiological arousal, each of which interacts with the others (e.g., heart rate increases following frustration). General aggression model does not state which of these internal states are affected by which input variables; that is the task of more specific research. Instead, GAM specifies

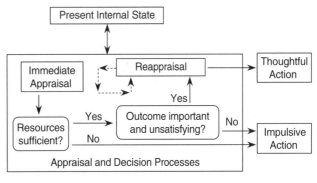

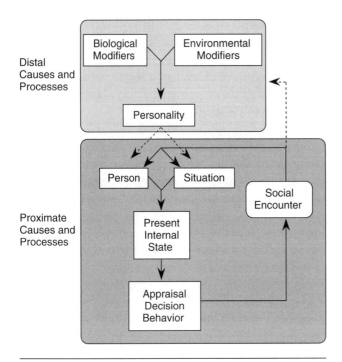

Figure 1   The General Aggression Model: Single-Cycle
and Distal Processes

Source: Anderson, C. A. & Carnagey, N. L. (2004) Violent
evil and the general aggression model. Chapter in A. Miller
(Ed.) *The Social Psychology of Good and Evil* (p. 183).
New York, NY: Guilford Publications. Copyright Guilford
Press. Reprinted with permission of The Guilford Press.

that factors that ultimately influence the likelihood
of aggressive behavior do so through at least one
of these three types of internal states. For example,
research has demonstrated that the short-term effects
of media violence on aggressive behavior are mediated primarily by aggressive cognitions. However,
aggressive affect and physiological arousal also play
a part in some cases.

The single-cycle episode of GAM continues with
decision and appraisal processes (Figure 2). It posits
that the contents of an individual's internal state both
influence and are influenced by these decision and
appraisal processes. Research regarding individuals'
attributions (e.g., Anderson, Krull, & Weiner, 1996)
has shown that after a significant event occurs, an
individual will immediately attempt to determine why
it occurred. This initial appraisal can occur without
conscious awareness. Furthermore, the appraisal may
include behavioral response options. For example,
if someone believes he or she has been provoked, a
retaliatory response may occur as an immediate reaction. If an individual does not have the time, motivation, or cognitive resources to further evaluate his or
her initial attribution, then an impulsive, reactionary

Figure 2   Appraisal and Decision Processes Within the
General Aggression Model: Expanded View

Source: Anderson, C. A., & Bushman, B. J. (2002). Human
aggression. *Annual Review of Psychology, 53*, 27–51.

decision will occur. However, if time, motivation, and
cognitive resources are available, the individual must
decide whether his or her initial attribution is both
important and unsatisfying. If this is not the case, and
the initial attribution is either unimportant or satisfying, then an impulsive behavior will likely occur. If
this is the case, then one or several reappraisals of
the event will occur. Reappraisals will continue to be
made until the individual is satisfied with the attribution or until a response is required, in which case
a thoughtful action will likely occur. Thoughtful or
impulsive actions can be either aggressive or nonaggressive, and reappraisal of events does not necessarily guarantee that an initially hostile attribution will
be altered by reappraisal.

After an impulsive or thoughtful appraisal is
made, the ensuing behavior then feeds into the ongoing social encounter. The social encounter then influences the situational input for the next behavioral
cycle. This process is one basis for GAM's proposed
violence escalation cycle (Figure 3). When a hostile
attribution is made, it can be considered a triggering event for the violence escalation processes. These
hostile attributions may occur as a result of any
range of events, from mild provocation (e.g., being
bumped in the hallway) to severe provocation (e.g.,
being insulted). After being provoked, an individual
is likely to retaliate in a more severe manner than
warranted by the initial provocation. The individual
who made the initial perceived or actual provocation
is then likely to respond with an even more severe
retaliation, which leads to continued repetitions of
the cycle. General aggression model posits that media
violence (as well as other risk factors) influences the
knowledge structures that individuals retrieve when
making attributions to a significant event. They

therefore increase the likelihood that a triggering event is perceived as hostile and guide the perceived appropriate behavioral response. Research has demonstrated that a minor triggering event is more likely to initiate a violence escalation cycle for individuals high in trait aggressiveness than for nonaggressive individuals.

Distal Processes

General aggression model also incorporates several developmental processes in its understanding of aggressive behavior (see upper portion of Figure 1). These distal processes focus on how continued exposure to aggression-related stimuli (such as media violence) develops long-term aggressive personalities. There are two primary types of factors that influence the development of an aggressive personality. The first type involves biological modifiers such as arousal, serotonin levels, hormonal imbalances, and the possession of disorders such as attention deficit hyperactivity disorder (ADHD). The second type involves environmental influences on what people learn and believe. These may include harsh

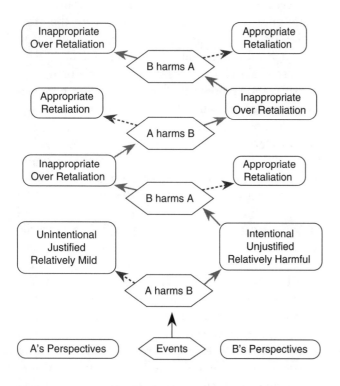

Figure 3   The Violence Escalation Cycle

Source: Anderson, C. A. & Carnagey, N. L. (2004) Violent evil and the general aggression model. Chapter in A. Miller (Ed.). *The Social Psychology of Good and Evil* (p. 181). New York, NY: Guilford Publications. Copyright Guilford Press. Reprinted with permission of The Guilford Press.

or inconsistent parenting, cultural and community influences, peer influences, exposure to violence, and poverty. General aggression model proposes that these two types of modifiers interact with each other to influence the development of aggressive (or nonaggressive) personalities.

At its most fundamental level, GAM is considered a social cognitive model of aggression. As individuals continually interact with aggression-related stimuli, they learn, rehearse, and reinforce aggression-related knowledge structures, and each interaction serves as a learning trial. Furthermore, observational learning plays a key role in the development of aggressive tendencies. Individuals do not simply imitate aggressive behavior but also use the behavior of others as a model through which to draw inferences to help determine when aggressive responses are appropriate. As individuals find themselves in situations that repeatedly evoke aggressive thoughts, feelings, and behaviors, they continually develop aggression-related knowledge structures. These knowledge structures are then "tapped into" when individuals interpret events and make decisions, ultimately leading to an increased likelihood of aggressive behavior. If the emitted aggressive behavior tends to be successful—in other words, if it is reinforced by the environment—then such thought, feeling, and action patterns (scripts) become more likely avenues of response in future situations. Of course, if the environment (e.g., parents, peers) does not reinforce aggressive behaviors, and especially if it instead rewards nonaggressive solutions to conflict, then a nonaggressive behavior style becomes more likely.

One of these proposed underlying processes involves *desensitization,* defined as a reduction in negative emotion–related physiological reactions to viewing, thinking about, and planning real-life violence (Carnagey, Anderson, & Bushman, 2007). *Physiological reactivity* is defined as the change in various forms of negative emotional arousal such as heart rate, perspiration, and skin conductance. Multiple studies have established a relationship between exposure to violent media and subsequent desensitization. As individuals become desensitized to violence, they experience a lessened negative emotional and physiological reaction to thoughts about violence, essentially reducing normal emotional inhibitions to behaving aggressively. In short, violence is experienced as less aversive and seen as more acceptable.

Nicholas L. Carnagey and colleagues examined the effects of violent media on desensitization by randomly assigning participants to play a violent or nonviolent game and measuring physiological arousal both before and after game play. Subsequently, participants viewed clips of real-life violence and had their physiological arousal measured a third time. Participants who had played the violent game showed significantly reduced physiological reactions to viewing the clips of real-life violence compared with those who had just played a nonviolent game. Similarly, Brad J. Bushman and Craig A. Anderson (2009) examined the effects of media violence on helping behavior. Specifically, their studies involved participants who played either a violent or a nonviolent game (Study 1), or who watched either a violent or nonviolent movie (Study 2), and were then given an opportunity to help a person in need. In both studies, media violence exposure decreased helping behavior.

A second process through which exposure to media violence leads to long-term developments of aggressive behavioral tendencies comes from the development of aggressive attitudes and beliefs. General aggression model points out that positive beliefs and attitudes toward violence should lead to increased aggressive behavior. For example, when aggressive responses are considered more socially appropriate, individuals may be more likely to engage in aggressive behavior. General aggression model argues that as aggressive behavior is positively reinforced, attitudes and beliefs toward aggressive responses to provoking situations are increasingly perceived as appropriate. This notion is supported by a variety of studies in which playing violent games was associated with more positive attitudes toward violence. When positive attitudes toward violence were taken into account, the relationship between violent video game play and aggression was nearly extinguished. Longitudinal research has demonstrated that playing violent video games was associated with increased likelihood of believing aggressive responses to be appropriate 30 months following initial exposure. Furthermore, these beliefs were associated with increased aggressive behavior. This suggests that one of the routes through which violent media exposure leads to aggressive behavior is by supporting and reinforcing positive attitudes and beliefs toward violence.

Another way in which individuals develop long-term aggressive behavioral tendencies is through the development of aggressive behavioral scripts. A behavioral script is a mental representation of what events should occur given any social situation, such

as what to do in a fast-food restaurant. Such scripts guide our interpretation of events that we witness, but they also guide our behavior. Although many behavioral scripts are universal within a given culture, others are more regional or even idiosyncratic.

With regard to aggressive behavior, behavioral scripts inform individuals how and when aggressive responses are appropriate in a given social scenario. Road rage, intimate partner abuse, and child abuse all appear to have scripted aggressive behaviors at their core. Our experiences and individual characteristics dictate, to some extent, what behavioral scripts are encoded. As individuals are repeatedly exposed to violence, whether in the form of violent media or real-life violence, they develop and reinforce aggressive behavioral scripts. As these scripts become increasingly available, individuals are more likely to retrieve and use them when deciding when aggressive responses are most appropriate. Contrastingly, for those who are not frequently exposed to violence, fewer scripts are developed, and for scripts that do exist, automatic retrieval is less likely. This tendency is reflected in research demonstrating that long-term exposure to violent video games is positively associated with an increased likelihood of perceiving ambiguous behavior as aggressive. Furthermore, short-term violent video game exposure has been shown to increase the accessibility of aggressive behavioral scripts.

The formation of individuals' long-term aggressive tendencies as a result of violent media exposure is also related to the development of aggressive perceptual schema. Perceptual schemas are knowledge structures that individuals draw upon to identify objects and scenarios. For example, individuals are able to identify a vehicle by drawing upon what is known about the qualities of vehicles (e.g., the object moves, has wheels or some type of engine). However, individuals also use perceptual schema to identify complex social scenarios such as provocation by collecting and interpreting the variety of "cues" associated with provocation (e.g., an angry facial expression). These knowledge structures contain nodes that are linked together in semantic memory. Aggressive concepts such as "murder" are repeatedly paired with similar concepts such as "gun" or "stab." Therefore, when one of these concepts, or nodes, is activated, other associated nodes are also activated. As events continually prime one or more nodes within an associative network (such as aggression-related concepts), they reinforce the network, making other nodes within that network more likely to become activated. For instance, some research has demonstrated that viewing aggression-related pictures (e.g., guns) led to faster responses to aggression-related words (e.g., *injure*) than to nonaggressive words. Similarly, research has been conducted testing this hypothesis using word-fragment completion tasks. In these tasks, participants are asked to fill in the blanks of words that can be completed to form either aggressive or non-aggressive words. For example, the word fragment *explo_e* can be completed with the word *explode* or *explore*. Other research has shown that participants were more likely to complete word fragments with aggressive words after playing a violent game than after playing a nonviolent game.

Longitudinal research has further elucidated the relationship between violent media exposure and aggressive perceptual schema by studying a group of elementary school children at two points during the school year over a six-month period. They found that for children who were repeatedly exposed to violent video game play, increases in hostile attribution biases were more likely. General aggression model posits that as these children continually reinforced aggression-related nodes within their semantic network, these aggression-related concepts became more heavily used, relied upon, and available. When encountering an ambiguous situation, they were therefore more likely to draw upon aggression-related concepts, ultimately leading to a tendency to interpret the ambiguous behavior as aggressive.

Other research has also examined the relationship between violent media exposure and aggressive perceptual schema using a different but related method. This research demonstrated that college students who are exposed to high amounts of violent media are more likely to display highly accessible aggressive self-images. Taken as a whole, these studies appear to demonstrate that exposure to violent media influences the development of long-term aggression-related knowledge structures, and as individuals are exposed to violent media, these knowledge structures are activated and reinforced in the moment. It is important to note, however, that this collection of discussed knowledge structures is not an exhaustive list but includes some of the most important and well-researched to date.

Theoretical Extensions

General aggression model has been applied heavily to research regarding the effects of media on aggression and is one of the most cited contemporary theoretical models in media effects research on aggression. However, its applications are not merely limited to media effects research, nor was it ever intended as merely a model for media effects. Instead, as a general model of aggression, GAM can be and is applied to numerous other aggression research topics. These include (but are certainly not limited to) provocation, intimate partner violence, intergroup violence, global climate change effects on violence, and suicide. Another prominent example involves the "weapons effect." It has been long understood that the presence of a weapon leads to an increase in aggressive behavior. As was mentioned previously, GAM predicts that this occurs as a result of the knowledge structures associated with weapons. Because weapons are often closely linked in memory to aggression-related concepts (e.g., murder, kill), activation of a single concept (e.g., the presence of a weapon) leads to a spreading activation of similar concepts. However, GAM points out that this spreading activation is dependent on any given individual's personal history and the nature of the knowledge structures that are activated.

Research by Bruce D. Bartholow and colleagues (2005) directly tested this by recruiting participants who reported their leisure activities either to include hunting or to not include hunting. In their first experiment, they determined that hunters reported more positive and less aggressive associations with guns used for hunting than did nonhunters. In their second and third experiments, exposure to images of hunting guns was associated with higher levels of aggressive thoughts and behavior for nonhunters as compared to hunters. This effect, according to GAM, occurs as a result of the associations that hunters have regarding guns used for hunting. Because these individuals view guns used for hunting as a tool for leisure and sport rather than aggression and harm toward other people, fewer aggression-related concepts are simultaneously activated—leading to lessened aggressive responses compared with those whose knowledge structures strongly connect guns used for hunting with aggression and harm toward others.

General aggression model has also been modified to apply to nonaggressive learning tendencies in what is called the general learning model (GLM). Of course, not all media depict violent content. For example, some media, including video games, portray prosocial content. Theoretically, many of the same processes through which individuals develop aggressive tendencies will also apply to (in this case) prosocial tendencies. Much like GAM, exposure to prosocial content in media leads to both long-term and immediate prosocial tendencies. Other research has demonstrated that individuals who played more prosocial games were more likely to behave prosocially in the future. Furthermore, playing a prosocial game increased the likelihood of a student participant helping another student in need.

Craig A. Anderson and Christopher Groves

See also Cognition: Schemas and Scripts; Cognitive Psychology of Violence; Cognitive Script Theory and the Dynamics of Cognitive Scripting; Effects From Violent Media, Short- and Long-Term; Interactive Media, Aggressive Outcomes of; Longitudinal Research Findings on the Effects of Violent Content; Social Cognitive Theory; Social Learning From Media; Video Game Player and Opponent Effects

Further Readings

Abelson, R. P. (1981). Psychological status of the script concept. *American Psychologist, 36,* 15–29.

Anderson, C. A., Benjamin, A. J., & Bartholow, B. D. (1998). Does the gun pull the trigger? Automatic priming effects of weapon pictures and weapon names. *Psychological Science, 9,* 308–314.

Anderson, C. A., Buckley, K. E., & Carnagey, N. L. (2008). Creating your own hostile environment: A laboratory examination of trait aggression and the violence escalation cycle. *Personality and Social Psychology Bulletin, 34,* 462–473.

Anderson, C. A., & Bushman, B. J. (2002). Human aggression. *Annual Review of Psychology, 53,* 27–51.

Anderson, C. A., & Carnagey, N. L. (2004). Violent evil and the general aggression model. In A. Miller (Ed.), *The social psychology of good and evil* (pp. 168–192). New York, NY: Guilford.

Anderson, C. A., Carnagey, N. L., Flanagan, M., Benjamin, A. J., Eubanks, J., & Valentine, J. C. (2004). Violent video games: Specific effects of violent content on aggressive thoughts and behavior. *Advances in Experimental Social Psychology, 36,* 199–249.

Anderson, C. A., & Dill, K. E. (2000). Video games and aggressive thoughts, feelings, and behavior in the laboratory and in life. *Journal of Personality and Social Psychology, 78,* 772–790.

Anderson, C. A., Gentile, D. A., & Buckley, K. E. (2007). *Violent video game effects on children and adolescents: theory, research, and public policy.* New York, NY: Oxford University Press.

Anderson, C. A., Krull, D. S., & Weiner, B. (1996). Explanations: Processes and consequences. In E. T. Higgins & A. W. Kruglanski (Eds.), *Social psychology: Handbook of basic principles.* New York, NY: Guilford.

Bandura, A. (1986). *Social foundations of thought and action: A social-cognitive theory.* Englewood Cliffs, NJ: Prentice-Hall.

Bartholow, B. D., Anderson, C. A., Carnagey, N. L., & Benjamin, A. J. (2005). Interactive effects of life experience and situational cues on aggression: The weapons priming effect in hunters and nonhunters. *Journal of Experimental Social Psychology, 41,* 48–60.

Berkowitz, L. (1984). Some effects on thoughts on anti- and prosocial influences of media events: A cognitive neo-association analysis. *Psychological Bulletin, 95,* 410–427.

Bushman, B. J., & Anderson, C. A. (2009). Comfortably numb: Desensitizing effects of violent media on helping others. *Psychological Science, 20,* 273–277.

Carnagey, N. L., Anderson, C. A., & Bushman, B. J. (2007). The effect of video game violence on physiological desensitization to real-life violence. *Journal of Experimental Social Psychology, 43,* 489–496.

DeWall, C. N., Anderson, C. A., & Bushman, B. J. (2011). The general aggression model: Theoretical extensions to violence. *Psychology of Violence, 1,* 245–258.

Gentile, D. A., Anderson, C. A., Yukawa. S., Ihori, N., Saleem, M., Ming, L. K., Shibuya, A., Liau, A. K., Khoo, A., & Sakamoto, A. (2009). The effects of prosocial video games on prosocial behaviors: International evidence from correlational, experimental, and longitudinal studies. *Personality and Social Psychology Bulletin, 35,* 752–763.

Moller, I., & Krahe, B. (2009). Exposure to violent video games and aggression in German adolescents: A longitudinal analysis. *Aggressive Behavior, 35,* 75–89.

Uhlmann, E., & Swanson, J. (2004). Exposure to violent video games increases implicit aggressiveness. *Journal of Adolescence, 27,* 41–52.

GENETICS OF AGGRESSIVE BEHAVIOR

In many respects, aggression serves as the raw material that drives conduct problems across the life course. Whether assessing difficult temperament in infancy and toddlerhood, self-regulation deficits in childhood, delinquency in adolescence, or criminal violence in adulthood, aggression—defined as a behavior directed toward another person with the intention of doing harm (Anderson & Bushman, 2002)—is the fundamental, elemental construct that is involved. *Aggression* is an umbrella term that captures diverse forms of harm-causing conduct, such as proactive aggression (instrumental planning to harm), reactive aggression (impulsive, affective reaction to real or perceived threat), direct aggression (overt physical infliction of harm), and indirect aggression (relational aggression involving gossip and social exclusion). This entry focuses on genetics as a factor in aggressive behavior, including heritability and genetic variants.

The first step toward understanding the genetics of aggressive behavior is to assess the heritability of aggression using twin studies. Behavioral genetics research has used twin data to statistically estimate and disaggregate variance in antisocial conditions into three components: genes, shared environmental factors, and nonshared environmental factors. The extent that antisocial conditions are caused by genetic factors is known as *heritability* and indicated as h^2. The extent that antisocial conditions are caused by environmental factors that are common to twins, such as family conditions, is known as *shared environment* and indicated as c^2. The extent that antisocial conditions are caused by environmental factors that are unique to twins such as their peer associations is known as *nonshared environment* and indicated as e^2.

Based on data from diverse samples selected across nations, psychologists have shown that aggression is substantially heritable. In a U.S. sample, Laura A. Baker and colleagues (2007) studied multiple symptom measures of antisocial behavior, including diagnostic counts for conduct disorder and ratings of aggression, delinquency, and psychopathic traits obtained through self-reports, teacher ratings, and caregiver ratings. The broadest composite measure of antisocial behavior spanning all raters was profoundly heritable (h^2 = .96). A related study with the same data found that proactive or cold-blooded aggression is also moderately heritable (h^2 = .50) compared with reactive or hot-blooded aggression (h^2 = .38) (Baker, Raine, Liu, & Jacobson, 2008).

Based on data from the Netherlands Twin Register, Edwin J. C. G. van den Oord, Frank C. Verhulst, and Dooret I. Boomsma (1996) examined the underpinnings of problem behaviors and found heritability estimates were moderate to high across twin pairs. These included total problems (h^2 = .38), externalizing problems (h^2 = .60), oppositional behavior (h^2 = .66), aggressiveness (h^2 = .69), and over/hyperactivity (h^2 = .65). Based on twin data from the Quebec (Canada) Newborn Twin Study,

van Lier and colleagues (2007) reported a similar heritability estimate for aggression (h^2 = .66). A 2011 summary review of research and meta-analyses indicated that aggression is 50% heritable (Tuvblad & Baker, 2011).

The moderate-to-high heritability of aggression leads to the next step: finding genetic variants that are associated with it and related antisocial conditions. One of the most studied susceptibility genes for aggressive antisocial behavior generally and temper specifically is the monoamine oxidase A (MAOA) gene. MAOA is a catabolic enzyme that is involved with regulating serotonin, norepinephrine, and dopamine in the synapses. Localized to chromosome Xp11.23, the variable number of tandem repeats polymorphism (MAOA-uVNTR) produces alleles with low activity and high activity. The low-activity allele is the risk allele and reflects MAOA deficiency.

Several researchers have utilized MAOA as a promising candidate gene for understanding the neurogenetic bases of aggression. Joshua W. Buckholtz and Andreas Meyer-Lindenberg (2008) developed an explanatory model for how MAOA alters the neurogenetic architecture of aggression. They suggested that MAOA in particular alters serotonin and norepinephrine levels during development of the corticolimbic circuit, which results in impairments in social decision making and affect regulation. This compromises the ability to interpret ambiguous social interactions and perceptions of potential threat. This explanatory model squares with links of MAOA to impulsive, reactive aggression, such as a bar fight. The landmark study of Brunner Syndrome identified five males in a single family with a complete and selective deficiency of MAOA activity caused by a glutamine to thymine mutation that changed a glutamine (CAG) codon to a termination (TAG) codon. The result in affected males is borderline mental retardation and severe forms of aggressive behavior toward persons, such as attempted rape, and property, such as arson (Brunner, Nelen, Breakefield, Ropers, & van Oost, 1993).

Because of its relationship to anger and aggression, MAOA has been referred to as the "warrior gene." Rose McDermott and colleagues (2009) conducted a novel experimental study to evaluate the warrior reputation of the MAOA polymorphism. In their study, subjects were able to punish those they believed had taken money from them by administering hot, spicy sauce to their opponents in the course of a simple economic power-to-take game in which subjects were informed that 20% or 80% of their money had been taken. Those with the low-activity MAOA allele reacted in a particularly aggressive manner to provocation and displayed more intense and frequent aggressive responses. The study is noteworthy because it confirmed a role of MAOA genotype to provocation and aggressive response in an experimental design.

Another newsworthy study on the warrior gene examined the relationship between MAOA and gang activity. Based on data from the National Longitudinal Study of Adolescent Health, Kevin M. Beaver and colleagues (2010) found that low-MAOA activity alleles conferred an increased risk of joining a gang among males but not among females. Moreover, this genotype also predicted among gang members those who used weapons during a fight. Theirs was the first study to link MAOA and a serious form of aggression among gang members. Leanne M. Williams and colleagues (2009) studied electrical brain activity and antisocial personality traits among 210 participants with low or high MAOA alleles. They found that those with the low-activity MAOA genotype showed alterations in brain electrical activity that were most apparent for negative emotions, such as overt anger. In addition, these individuals had higher scores on an index of antisocial traits.

Genetics research on aggression is in its infancy, and only a handful of the approximately 25,000 human genes have been investigated. As criminology becomes more interdisciplinary and genetic data sets become more widespread, scholars will increasingly identify candidate genes and environmental moderators, such as media violence exposure, that increase the likelihood of assorted aggressive acts.

Matt DeLisi

See also Aggression, Definition and Assessment of; Aggression, Risk Factors of

Further Readings

Anderson, C. A., & Bushman, B. J. (2002). Human aggression. *Annual Review of Psychology, 53,* 27–51.

Baker, L. A., Jacobson, K. C., Raine, A., Lozano, D. I., & Bezdjian, S. (2007). Genetic and environmental bases of childhood antisocial behavior: A multi-informant twin study. *Journal of Abnormal Psychology, 116,* 219–235.

Baker, L. A., Raine, A., Liu, J., & Jacobson, K. C. (2008). Differential genetic and environmental influences on reactive and proactive aggression in children. *Journal of Abnormal Child Psychology, 36,* 1265–1278.

Beaver, K. M., DeLisi, M., Vaughn, M. G., & Barnes, J. C. (2010). Monoamine oxidase A genotype is associated with gang membership and weapon use. *Comprehensive Psychiatry, 51,* 130–134.

Brunner, H. G., Nelen, M., Breakefield, X. O., Ropers, H. H., & van Oost, B. A. (1993). Abnormal behavior associated with a point mutation in the structural gene for monoamine oxidase A. *Science, 262,* 578–580.

Buckholtz, J. W., & Meyer-Lindenberg, A. (2008). MAOA and the neurogenetic architecture of human aggression. *Trends in Neurosciences, 31,* 120–129.

McDermott, R., Tingley, D., Cowden, J., Frazzetto, G., & Johnson, D. D. P. (2009). Monoamine oxidase A gene (MAOA) predicts behavioral aggression following provocation. *Proceedings of the National Academy of Sciences of the USA, 106,* 2118–2123.

Tuvblad, C., & Baker, L. A. (2011). Human aggression across the lifespan: Genetic propensities and environmental moderators. *Advances in Genetics, 75,* 171–214.

van den Oord, E. J. C. G., Verhulst, F. C., & Boomsma, D. I. (1996). A genetic study of maternal and paternal ratings of problem behaviors in 3-year-old twins. *Journal of Abnormal Psychology, 105,* 349–357.

van Lier, P., Boivin, M., Dionne, G., Vitaro, F., Brendgen, M., Koot, H., et al. (2007). Kindergarten children's genetic vulnerabilities interact with friends' aggression to promote children's own aggression. *Journal of the American Academy of Child and Adolescent Psychiatry, 46,* 1080–1087.

Williams, L. M., Gatt, J. M., Kuan, S. A., Dobson-Stone, C., Palmer, D. M., Paul, R. H., et al. (2009). A polymorphism of the MAOA gene is associated with emotional brain markers and personality traits on an antisocial index. *Neuropsychopharmacology, 35,* 1–13.

Grand Theft Auto

Released by Rockstar Games (then DMA Design) in October 1997, *Grand Theft Auto* is a series of cross-platform, multigeneration video games known for their focus on antisocial, crime-based narratives as well as their introduction of nonlinear "sandbox" game play to action-adventure video games. A typical *Grand Theft Auto* game involves the player taking the role of an upstart criminal working his way into the confidences of an organized crime system by working as an errand boy and taking on jobs of increasing difficulty, risk, and reward. Earlier versions of

Grand Theft Auto were nonspecific regarding player motivations (usually suggesting an implicit motivation for material wealth), while later games focused more heavily on character development—often providing a narrative that attempted to justify the player's violent criminal acts as acts of revenge or for the protection of family and friends. The *Grand Theft Auto* franchise is considered a commercial success, selling more than 124 million copies worldwide across dozens of game systems as one of the 10 top-selling game franchises of all time. Most games in the *Grand Theft Auto* series are rated M for "Mature" by the U.S.-based Entertainment Software Review Board for violence and suggestive themes; they rely heavily on narratives that mix satire and social commentary (such as *Grand Theft Auto: San Andreas*'s focus on drugs and gang warfare in early 1990s Los Angeles). *Grand Theft Auto* is considered to be one of the most influential games in the history of the medium in part because of its successful implementation of sandbox gaming and in part for its intense focus on antisocial behavior as the core of game play. This entry focuses on *Grand Theft Auto*'s unique place in the discourse on media violence.

Freedom of Motion, Freedom of Action

"If you're armed with weapons and a strong disrespect for authority, you might just want to take that Body Count song to heart and become a cop killer." This was the introduction to a GameSpot.com review of a European-localized iteration of the original *Grand Theft Auto* in May 1998, and it speaks to the game's dual focus on sandbox gaming and violent actions. In this review, the commentator talks about the nearly 6,000 miles of drivable road and the expansive urban environments reminiscent of New York City, Miami, and San Francisco that serve as a digital playground on which to play out fantasies of crime and violence akin to popular movies such as *The Godfather* and *Scarface*. Game play unfolds in a series of missions, and although mission destinations were usually fixed, *Grand Theft Auto* allows players to take any number of different routes and strategies to achieve mission objectives. However, all of these routes are steeped in violent criminal activity, from the theft of vehicles to get from one mission to the next, to the murder of rival crime bosses, police officers, and innocent bystanders who might interfere with the player's objectives. Because of this, how much

freedom *Grand Theft Auto* truly provides the gamer can be challenged: gamers are free to move where they please, but they are required to engage in violent criminal activity to advance the game narrative. From this, a central question for scholars concerns how these violent criminal actions might affect gamers.

Murder and Make-Believe

Theories of media violence have provided informative yet conflicting rationales as to how players might be influenced by the game play in *Grand Theft Auto*. Social cognitive learning theory explains that an individual's behavior is influenced by his or her empirical environment—that is, individuals learn through observation. Paying attention to and remembering the violent criminal actions of *Grand Theft Auto*—particularly relevant because video game players actively engage in action rather than passively observing it (such is the case when watching television)—is thought to encourage their replication. For the motivation to commit the acts in the real world, script theory argues that repeated exposure to these behaviors results in the development of violent and antisocial cognitive schema in players, and the general aggression model similarly argues that repeated exposure to media violence teaches individuals to respond in kind to provocation in the real world. Beyond the formation of violent criminal scripts, others, including researchers and policy makers, to name a few, are concerned about desensitization to crime and violence in the real world as well as about the moral disengagement required for individuals to enjoy the game resulting in moral disengagement from similar real-world action. These theories, combined with *Grand Theft Auto*'s popularity, suggest that the social criticism the game has received from scholars and public officials for being what now-disbarred U.S. attorney and activist Jack Thompson labels "murder simulators" that make violence "pleasurable and attractive" may be warranted.

Critics contend, however, that *Grand Theft Auto*'s satirical portrayal of violent crime is more clever than sinister and represents a semantic "magic circle" in which players can engage in a fantasy world of crime and punishment in which the rules of the real world are not meant to apply. Newer perspectives of morality and entertainment have suggested that moral disengagement processes function such that media users suspend real-world notions of morality so that they are free to enjoy the on-screen actions in products such as *Grand Theft Auto* without fundamentally accepting them as appropriate. Moreover, some researchers have argued that engaging in antisocial violent acts in a virtual world such as *Grand Theft Auto* helps dissipate similar feelings before they are able to gestate in the real world, although empirical support for this catharsis approach to media violence has been sparse. Related to this, video game researcher Ian Bogost argued that the intense moral panic reactions to games such as *Grand Theft Auto* are precisely the goal of such games: to expose users to absurd and unacceptable situations (such as the problems associated with inner-city crime and rampant drug addiction) so that they can be critiqued; a similar view has been raised by the Australian Institute for Public Affairs, which argues that the game play of *Grand Theft Auto* is in itself a test of individual morality but not a cause of it. Yet some scholars and public officials have argued that issues of fantasy violence and gunplay in *Grand Theft Auto* are of lesser importance than the manner in which the franchise portrays minorities and ethnic groups—often deriving humor and entertainment from their derision.

Nicholas David Bowman

See also Catharsis Theory; *Grand Theft Auto*, Social Representations in; Media as a Reflection of Society; Social Learning From Media; Video Games, User Motivations; Weapons, in Violent Media Content, Use, Policy, and Effects of

Further Readings

Bandura, A. (1977). *Social learning theory*. New York, NY: General Learning Press.

Kutner, L., & Olson, C. K. (2008). *Grand theft childhood: The surprising truth about violent video games and what parents can do*. New York, NY: Simon & Schuster.

MacDonald, R. (1998, May 6). *Grand Theft Auto* review. *Gamespot.com*. Retrieved from http://www.gamespot .com/grand-theft-auto/reviews/grand-theft-auto-review-2547751

Raney, A. A. (2011). The role of morality in emotional reactions to and enjoyment of media entertainment. *Journal of Media Psychology, 23*(1), 18–23.

Weber, R., Ritterfeld, U., & Kostygina, A. (2006). Aggression and violence as effects of playing violent video games? In P. Vorderer and J. Bryant (Eds.), *Playing video games: Motives, responses, and consequences*. Mahwah, NJ: Erlbaum.

GRAND THEFT AUTO, SOCIAL REPRESENTATIONS IN

Although the popular video game franchise *Grand Theft Auto* is often maligned for using violent criminal activity as the focal point of game play, a deeper look into the game shows a narrative in which humor and entertainment are derived from the derision of minorities and women, and a general satirical look at crime as a central part of urban spaces. Although the goal in creating this content is likely social commentary rather than bigotry, the presence of such bigotry has been a cause for concern for scholars and public figures sensitive to the franchise's immense popularity—selling 124 million copies since its release in October 2007. This entry focuses on minority portrayals, misogynistic themes, and the gritty portrayal of urban life in *Grand Theft Auto* by reviewing research and commentary on these topics; it also discusses counterarguments that the humorous portrayals in *Grand Theft Auto* should alleviate concerns over their potential effects on gamers by providing context.

Minority and Ethnic Portrayals

Cultural studies professors Anna Everett and S. Craig Watkins (2008) have argued that video games such as *Grand Theft Auto* can be understood as racialized pedagogical zones (RPZs) that serve as a semantic classroom in which the player can learn to create and perpetuate racial bias. These RPZs are thought to be particularly effective because they provide intrinsically attractive environments in which players can rehearse and retain scripts related to discrimination and stereotype that transfer to real-world thoughts, actions, and beliefs. Focusing on *Grand Theft Auto 3*—the first game in the series to feature the realistic, immersive 3D environments, high-resolution graphics, and narrative-driven game play for which the series has come to be known—media researchers Mikolaj Dymek and Thomas Lennerfors (2005) noted the more prominent minority and ethnic portrayals in the game, including a violent and flamboyant gang of Colombian drug lords, an Italian mafia family reminiscent of *The Godfather* and *Casino*, a group of African American hip-hop gangsters engaged in an ongoing and brutal turf battle set in the projects of the fictitious Liberty City (*Grand Theft Auto*'s version of New York City), and a centuries-old Japanese

Yakuza marked by its strict hierarchal structure and commitment to loyalty and honor. These stereotypes, while hardly the invention of *Grand Theft Auto*'s producers, Rockstar North, are viewed as further perpetuation of minority and ethnic stereotypes already prevalent in other media, and the fact that they are interactive is thought only to reinforce their effect on users' thoughts toward those groups portrayed. Critical race theory further argues that such portrayals foster a perspective that racism is normal rather than abnormal in modern society, and the interactive nature of such portrayals in *Grand Theft Auto* works to strengthen this normative perspective. In 2008 Rockstar North acknowledged that racial portrayals in *Grand Theft Auto: Vice City* were perhaps inappropriate and removed dialogue between Cuban and Haitian gangsters in response to a defamation lawsuit by the Haitian-American Grassroots Coalition.

Misogyny

In January 2004, former U.S. Senator Joseph Lieberman expressed concern at the "horrendous" game play featured in *Grand Theft Auto: San Andreas,* making specific mention of how the video game allowed players to liaison with prostitutes to increase the player's health and, if desired, mug and murder the prostitute afterward. Although many public officials have gone on record to criticize the general violent themes in *Grand Theft Auto,* Lieberman took specific issue with the franchise's portrayal of women, calling on the makers of *Grand Theft Auto* and the entertainment industry as a whole to "treat women with respect." Lieberman's concerns were not assuaged when video game hackers found a previously hidden mini-game in *Grand Theft Auto: San Andreas* called "Hot Coffee" that allowed the player to simulate domineering oral and vaginal sex with his in-game girlfriend as part of game play. Lawmakers, including U.S. Senator Hillary Clinton, accused the game's producers, Rockstar North, of intentionally hiding the mini-game to avoid an Entertainment Software Rating Board (ESRB) rating of AO, for "Adults Only," which may have hindered sales. In general, women in the *Grand Theft Auto* universe, most often portrayed as prostitutes or subordinate romantic interests, rarely occupy positions of respect; later women in the series are depicted as increasingly central characters to the game's narrative but tend to use their

sexuality as a tool in their criminal successes. To date, a female character has not been a playable character in a *Grand Theft Auto* game.

Urban Life and Criminality

A popular application of cultivation theory is the explanation of the mean world effect—the notion that mediated portrayals of society (particularly urban society) as dangerous and crime-infested spaces foster within audiences an assumption that all urban spaces are dangerous and crime-infested. The cultivation effect has received substantial empirical support; this is particularly troubling, given the steady decline in criminal behavior (particularly in the United States) since the late 1960s. Yet the prevailing theme in all *Grand Theft Auto* games has been one of crime as a normative and necessary part of survival in urban life. Beyond the petty and violent crimes highlighted by *Grand Theft Auto,* the portrayal of widespread drug use and easy access to guns and prostitutes is believed to suggest and perpetuate an unrealistic and controversial view of life in urban spaces, particularly within audiences who have no regular contact with urban environments other than their experiences playing *Grand Theft Auto.*

Humor and Context as Coping

Critics of the social representations in *Grand Theft Auto* have ample content to criticize. However, some scholars have questioned whether the presence of content alone is a sufficient precondition for an assumed media effect. Some critics of *Grand Theft Auto* overlook the game's clear satirical approach, claiming that the game is intended to be a commentary on racism, misogyny, and urban portrayals rather than a celebration of them. Humor theorists, including psychologist Sigmund Freud, have acknowledged that satirical humor is often tendentious and intended to dehumanize the target individual or group while also recognizing that satire serves to reveal the absurdity of humorous situations. For *Grand Theft Auto,* using satire to highlight negative stereotypes is a tool to allow audiences to unmask and think more critically about the logic of such portrayals—a similar approach was taken by Norman Lear and his critically acclaimed television show *All in the Family,* a show heralded for its sardonic commentary on race relations in the United States during and following the civil rights movement. A media literacy perspective would similarly encourage audiences to learn the implicit messages intended by the game's producers rather than focusing solely on the surface-level content. If video games such as *Grand Theft Auto* indeed serve as RPZs, it can be argued that the lessons learned can be pro- as well as antisocial.

Nicholas David Bowman

See also African Americans in Media, Character Depictions and Social Representation of; Attitude, Effects of Media Violence on; Cultivation Theory; Gender Stereotypes, Societal Influence on; *Grand Theft Auto;* Media as a Reflection of Society; Social Learning From Media; Violence in Media, Effects on Aggression and Violent Crime

Further Readings

Delgado, R., & Stefanic, J. (2000). *Critical race theory: An introduction.* New York, NY: New York University Press.

Dymek, M., & Lennerfors. (2005). Among pasta-loving Mafiosos, drug-selling Colombians, and noodle-eating Triads: Race, humour, and interactive ethics in *Grand Theft Auto III. Proceedings of the Digital Games Research Association 2005: Changing Views—Worlds in Play.* Vancouver, British Columbia.

Everett, A., & Watkins, S. C. (2008). The power of play: The portrayal and performance of race in video games. In K. Salen (Ed.), *The ecology of games: Connecting youth, games, and learning.* Cambridge, MA: MIT Press.

Freud, S. (1960). *Jokes and their relations to the unconscious* (J. Strachey, Trans.). New York, NY: Continuum.

GROUP AGGRESSION

Although research has suggested that there is no single way to define today's game player, it has indicated that gaming environments such as those containing multiple players are growing in popularity. Massive multiplayer online gaming (MMOG) environments have provided researchers with innovative opportunities to integrate research areas such as interpersonal, group, and mass communication. Thus, grounded in the media effects and psychology literature as well as group dynamics research, this entry examines the influence of group size on video game play. Specifically, it connects the influence that group size can have on aggression.

Since the 1990s research regarding video game content and its effect on antisocial outcomes, such as aggression, has increased. Meta-analyses conducted by Craig Anderson and colleagues substantiate the positive relationship between violent video game play and aggressive outcomes. Within the field of communication, investigators have utilized several theories to explain human aggression, including arousal theory, excitation transfer, and social cognitive theory. From these theoretical frameworks, a model on human aggression known as the general aggression model (GAM) was developed by Anderson and colleagues.

The GAM merges the situational context of violent exposure with the individual's person-attributes as a framework for understanding violent media effects. Craig Anderson and Brad Bushman described the process as the "activation and application of aggression-related knowledge structures stored in memory (e.g., scripts, schemas)" (2002, p. 1680). The GAM is generally known through its single-episode model that demonstrates how the individual inputs of environment and person influence internal states of cognition (i.e., state hostility), affect, and arousal. Situational inputs in gaming research oftentimes include exposure to violent or nonviolent content. Person variables can include gender, attitudes, long-term goals, traits, and so on. In terms of violent game play, the game's content and the player's person-attributes combine to prime aggressive cognition, arousal, and aggressive affect. Because each gaming session is considered a learning opportunity for real-world behavior, over time and repeated exposures, knowledge structures made more accessible through confrontational situations become increasingly difficult to change. To this end, each time an aggressive response is performed through play, a knowledge structure is made or strengthened and may be called upon in contexts within and outside the gaming environment. In this way, the GAM indicates the activation and application of aggression scripts are nothing more than rehearsed knowledge structures and these structures are not medium dependent and thus learned behavior within game play can be activated during a real-world encounter.

The GAM is not without alternative voices. For example, when researching both hostility and prosocial effects from playing *Asheron's Call 2,* a game where violent action during play was not forced or directed at other players and is generally considered a more community oriented game, Dmitri Williams and Marko Skoric observed increased prosocial feelings from play. Also supporting the potential for prosocial effects, Nick Yee asserts that given the socioemotional nature and amount of positive conversations taking place between players during play, MMOGs should be considered collaborative environments.

Group Game Play

Although numerous research projects have examined gaming components, few have accounted for situations such as group motivation, game type, and in-game behavior. Different gaming experiences could influence aggressive cognition and subsequent aggression tendencies and behaviors another way. The current entry addresses the dynamics of three factors that influence the effects from violent game play: group motivation, group size, and in-game verbal aggression.

When looking at younger and older populations, group size influences competitiveness. Smaller groups, generally defined as two players, are considered less competitive than larger groups. Here, early research suggests that as groups increase from two to seven people, disagreements and antagonism increased (Bales & Borgatta, 1955). Later research suggested that larger groups are more directly competitive because direct competition and dominance occurs across the entire group and thus no single person is offended. Furthermore, larger groups are thought to provide greater anonymity, allowing people to compete openly toward individual player goals. Supporting these earlier studies, recent examinations of group size, such as that by Joyce Benenson and colleagues (2001), found that children in larger groups displayed greater competitive behavior than those in two-person groups.

Motivation and Group Game Play

A common situation manipulation that helps researchers to understand game play effects is motivation—competitive play versus cooperative play. Because of the inherent difference in the desired outcome of each task situation, these situations are often considered types of goal structures. For instance, in a competitive setting, the advancement toward one person's goal inversely relates to another's ability of goal attainment. Conversely, in cooperative situations, advancement toward a goal is shared by everyone in the group.

Competition historically has been linked with aggression. It is believed that aggression develops as a response to frustration. Competition is inherently frustrating because a person is blocked from a desired goal. In terms of video game play, one player attempting to reach a goal negatively affects the chances of the second player achieving the same goal. Alternatively, cooperative game play allows all players to work together toward the same goal of winning. Using this logic, research has consistently indicated that competitive situations produce frustration, conflict, anger, aggression, and arguments, whereas agreement and affiliation are associated with cooperative situations.

Group Size and Gender

In addition to group size effects, much of the group dynamics research has examined the interaction between gender and group size within the context of group competition. Some researchers have found that males typically compete more in larger groups, while females typically compete more in smaller group settings. However, recent research has indicated that although children believe larger groups as more competitive than smaller ones, gender differences were not apparent. Furthermore, research by Anderson and colleagues at Iowa State University as well as Eastin and Griffiths failed to find gender difference for hostility when looking at competitive gaming. Thus, while the literature genearlly acknowledged that men are more competitive than women, research on how gender and competitiveness are influenced by group size within the context of video game play is less conclusive.

Group Size and Communication

Verbal aggression, within interpersonal literature, is generally viewed as an attack on another's concept of self. Verbal aggression includes such behaviors as verbal character attacks; comments regarding competence, physical appearance, and personality; and general teasing, profanity, and hostile threats. From these behaviors, researchers have connected aggressive communication to aggressive behavior in adults and youth. Therefore, research has suggested that those who verbalize aggression would subsequently think and behave more aggressively. This remains consistent with the notion of scripting in the GAM.

Game play factors such as group size and competitive interactions are thought to increase state hostility after game play; however, these gaming situations have also been found to influence forms of verbal aggression. For instance, in an early study conducted by Robert F. Bales and Edgar F. Borgatta, comparison of dyads to groups containing three, four, five, six, and seven participants found that larger groups displayed greater conflictual language. Similar to the literature investigating group size and aggressive behavior, Bales and Borgatta suggested that greater anonymity afforded in larger competitive groups increased tension, disagreements, and aggression. In the early 2000s, Benenson and colleagues supported earlier work when they reported that larger groups were more competitive and subsequently produced a less positive atmosphere. Furthermore, research has shown that a person who naturally has trait hostility has hostile cognitions and exhibits aggression-related behavior, one of which is verbal aggression. Due to existing hostile response scripts, antisocial verbalizations should be readily accessible and in line with factors such as game content. To this end, research indicates that group size, competition, and trait hostility have a direct and indirect effect on state hostility through verbal aggression.

Integrating gender into this somewhat complex scenario, research has indicated that males use verbal aggression more than females for social status gains. More specifically, Benenson's research confirmed Bales and Borgatta's findings that indicate when faced with a competitive situation, males tend to be more verbally aggressive.

Although communication has been incorporated into gaming for some time, the relatively recent development of live chat provides new opportunities for players.

Within game play, Pena and Hancock used the cues-filtered-out approach to examine the frequency of positive and negative text messages between game players. The cues-filtered-out perspective predicts the lack of social cues and level of anonymity provided online will increase depersonalization and subsequent negative forms of communication. In their research, Pena and Hancock found both negative and positive communication. However, note as predicted, players displayed significantly more positive text-based communicative acts (37) than negative (14). While this research increased current understanding of the amount and tone of text messages during multi-user game play, it was text-based and did not look at the effects of such communication.

Integrating verbal aggression and competitive group game play, Matthew Eastin at The University of Texas at Austin recently conducted a study and concluded that the situational input of group size significantly included short-term post–game play hostility. Furthermore, this study suggested that when state hostility is heightened, hostile expectation bias increases—meaning that as the number of game players increase in competitive play, verbal aggression and state hostility increase. In this way, player behaviors act as a mediating factor to aggressive cognitions experienced from play.

While research is still needed within the area of group game play, recent innovative research has proven effective at increasing the knowledge-base of video game play research. That is, as researcher continues to look beyond simple definitions of play to include more game-based situations, we will gain a better understanding of when violent game play can have a negative effect on youth.

Matthew S. Eastin

See also Cognition: Schemas and Scripts; Cyberbullying, Violent Content in; Demographic Effects; Gender, Effects of Violent Content on; General Aggression Model; Social Cognitive Theory; Trait Aggression

Further Readings

Anderson, C. A. (2004). An update on the effects of violent video games. *Journal of Adolescence, 27,* 113–122.

Anderson, C. A., & Morrow, M. (1995). Competitive aggression without interaction: Effects of competitive versus cooperative instructions on behavior in video games. *Personality and Social Psychology Bulletin, 21,* 1020–1030.

Bales, R. F., & Borgatta, E. F. (1955). Size of group as a factor in the interaction profile. In A. P. Hare, E. F. Borgatta, & R. F. Bales (Eds.), *Small groups: Studies in social interaction* (pp. 495–512). Toronto, Ontario: Random House.

Benenson, J. F., Nicholson, C., Waite, A., Roy, R., & Simpson, A. (2001). The influence of group size on children's competitive behavior. *Child Development, 72,* 921–928.

Bonta, B. (1997). Cooperation and competition in peaceful societies. *Psychological Bulletin, 121,* 299–320.

Bushman, B. J., & Anderson, C. A. (2002). Violent video games and hostile expectations: A test of the General Aggression Model. *Personality and Social Psychology Bulletin 28*(12), 1679–1686.

Deutsch, M. (1993). *The resolution of conflict.* New Haven, CT: Yale University Press.

Eastin, M. S. (2007). The influence of competitive and cooperative group game play on state hostility. *Human Communication Research, 33,* 450–466.

Eastin, M. S., & Griffiths, R. P. (2009). Unreal: Hostile expectations and social game play. *New Media & Society,* 509–531.

Kiesler, S., Siegel, J., & McGuire, T. W. (1984). Social psychological aspects of computer-mediated communication. *American Psychologist, 39,* 1123–1134.

Maccoby, E. E. (1990). Gender and relationships. *American Psychologist, 45,* 513–520.

Pena, J., & Hancock, J. (2006). An analysis of socioemotional and task communication in online multiplayer video games. *Communication Research, 33,* 92–109.

Rice, R. E., & Love, G. (1987). Electronic emotion: Socioemotional content in a computer-mediated communication network. *Communication Research, 14,* 85–108.

Roberto, A. J., Meyer, G., Boster, F. J., & Roberto, H. L. (2003). Adolescents' decisions about verbal and physical aggression: An application of the theory of reasoned action. *Human Communication Research, 29,* 135–147.

Williams, D., & Skoric, M. (2005). Internet fantasy violence: A test of aggression in an online game. *Communication Monographs, 72,* 217–33.

IDENTITY, MEDIA VIOLENCE AND ITS EFFECTS ON

Although the role of identity in media processing and effects has been widely discussed, only a small number of empirical studies have examined this issue in the context of exposure to violent media. Broadly speaking, the influence of identity as well as identification can be seen in everything from media selection and avoidance to processing media messages, to interpreting media messages, to learning from media, to more straightforward media effects (such as aggression). It is hardly an overstatement to say that issues of identity and identification have the potential to influence nearly every aspect of media uses and outcomes in the context of violent media.

Conceptualizing Identification and Identity

The concepts of identification and identity are not synonymous. Nevertheless, aspects of identification and identity are often related and may become intertwined when viewing media. Although identification with media characters is typically thought to include some degree of perceived association with a media character, it has been conceptualized in a number of ways.

As research by Jonathan Cohen (2001) described, *identification* with media figures can be thought of as a state in which audience members take on the identity and viewpoint of the characters. This may occur because viewers like or are attracted to the characters, or because they perceive themselves to

be similar to the characters in some way. Thus, the viewer becomes psychologically distant from his or her role as an audience member and processes the messages from the perspective of the characters. Although this may be only a fleeting experience of identification, it can be intense and is likely to include not just thoughts but also emotions. However, Cohen also noted that identification is more than just adopting the attitudes and feelings of the character; it should be understood as absorption into the character such that the viewer has internalized the character's perspective and feels *with* the character (rather than *for* the character).

Identity, more specifically, often refers to a sense of belonging with a particular group and the influence of that group membership on one's conceptualization of self. This definition, derived from thinking rooted in Henri Tajfel's (1978) social identity theory, is meaningful because the implication is that such memberships not only define our self-concepts but are used to make group comparisons to support positive self-distinctiveness. Accordingly, they govern how we interpret the social world when salient. Such identities (known as *social identities*) are consequential to media exposure because they meaningfully contribute to selection and interpretation processes as well as effects of exposure. As research by Dana Mastro (2012) has suggested, group identification can influence how we interpret media messages and judge figures in mass media content. For sample, for viewers highly identified with their groups, exposure to aggression or crime in the news can lead them to have more unfavorable and punitive evaluations when the suspect is an outgroup member.

Indeed, research has demonstrated that both identity and identification play important roles not only in what we select and avoid in the array of media offerings available to us but how we make sense of and respond to the content.

Media Choices

Jake Harwood's (1999a, b) research on social identity gratifications has shown that consumers actively select media messages that support meaningful group identities and avoid or reinterpret messages that threaten group identity. More specifically, his work has demonstrated that identification with salient groups (in his work, age groups) is predictive of media consumption patterns, even above personal factors. This notion was further explored in research by Jessica Abrams and Howard Giles (2007, 2009) that showed that audiences will avoid content that threatens their (group) identity and seek out content that will support identity needs. In testing this claim, Abrams and Giles surveyed African Americans and Latinos regarding their television use and their racial/ethnic group identification. Their results revealed that consumers, particularly those who were highly identified with their groups, made strategic media usage decisions based on identity concerns. And these selection or avoidance decisions had an impact on evaluations of self and others.

Identification can also arise from personality-based attributes such as aggression. In fact, research by L. Rowell Huesmann (1984a, b) has indicated that aggressive children appear to identify more with aggressive characters in the media.

Altogether, this research has suggested that identity features of consumers are critical to consider when conceptualizing violent media effects. If the groups, traits, and states individuals identify with can predict what they select from the media, and these choices produce a pattern of exposure to violence and aggression, then certain groups may be at even higher risk for aggression and violence, fear, and/or desensitization.

Media Effects

Although it may fluctuate, identification is meaningfully related to learning and (potentially) modeling depicted behaviors. In line with Albert Bandura's social cognitive theory, identification with media characters can enhance the perception of rewards and/or consequences associated with the character's behaviors. Such associations can therefore increase the likelihood of engaging in rewarded behaviors,

even antisocial behaviors such as violence and aggression. More specifically, identification (in this case, a connection with or similarity to the media figure) has been argued to increase a viewer's belief that he or she can successfully reproduce the behavior being enacted, particularly if the viewer is high in self-efficacy. Correspondence along any variety of features, including age, gender, ethnicity, and the like, can increase the potential for viewers to identify with media characters. To illustrate, results from research by Cynthia Hoffner and colleagues (2005) has suggested that audiences identify more strongly with characters of the same gender. They attribute this association to perceived similarity.

In Bandura's experimental research, participants (both children and adults) were shown media models engaging in aggressive behavior and were either rewarded or punished for their actions. Those who viewed the rewarded aggression were more likely to engage in similar physically and verbally aggressive behavior. This was argued to occur, at least in part, as a result of identification with the model. It should be noted, however, that nearly all viewers appear to be more likely to reproduce rewarded behaviors.

More generally, but in a similar vein, longitudinal research by Huesmann and colleagues demonstrated that exposure to violent media, particularly among boys, is associated with both later aggression and criminality. Here, identity is seen as additionally important in that aggressive children are more likely to identify with violent characters, and such identification predicts subsequent aggressive fantasizing and aggressive behavior. In one work of note, Huesmann and Leonard Eron (1986) tracked the television viewing of 758 U.S. children and 220 Finnish children over a three-year period and assessed the influence of identification and exposure (among other things) on concurrent and subsequent aggression. This research found that for girls in the United States and boys in both countries, exposure was predictive of aggression (both current and future). Importantly, identification with television characters enhanced this association among boys.

Identification also affects media socialization processes. As work by W. James Potter (1988) revealed, the more television individuals watch, the more crime and violence they perceive there to be in the real world; this relationship is even more pronounced among those who identify with television characters. In fact, his work has indicated that this relationship dissolves when viewers have low levels of identification with media characters.

Finally, identity may also contribute to stress responses to media content, as well as other health-related outcomes. Eric Dubow and colleagues' research (2009) has suggested that identification with violence (i.e., because of personal experience with violence) is associated with greater stress and poorer health as a result of exposure to violent news in particular.

Dana Mastro

See also Social Cognitive Theory; Social Learning From Media; Uses and Gratifications Perspective of Media Effects

Further Readings

Abrams, J., & Giles, H. (2007). Ethnic identity gratifications selection and avoidance by African Americans: A group vitality and social identity perspective. *Media Psychology, 9,* 115–134.

Abrams, J., & Giles, H. (2009). Hispanic television activity: Is it related to vitality perceptions? *Communication Research Reports, 26,* 247–252.

Bandura, A. (1986). *Social foundations of moral thought and action.* Englewood Cliffs, NJ: Prentice Hall.

Cohen, J. (2001). Defining identification: A theoretical look at the identification of audiences with media characters. *Mass Communication & Society, 4,* 245–264.

Dubow, E. F., Huesmann, L. R., & Boxer, P. (2009). A social-cognitive-ecological framework for understanding the impact of exposure to persistent ethnic-political violence on children's psychosocial adjustment. *Clinical Child and Family Psychology Review,* 113–126.

Harwood, J. (1999a). Age identification, social identity gratifications, and television viewing. *Journal of Broadcasting and Electronic Media, 43,* 123–136.

Harwood, J. (1999b). Age identity and television viewing preferences. *Communication Reports, 12,* 85–90.

Hoffner, C., & Buchanan, M. (2005). Young adults' wishful identification with television characters: The role of perceived similarity and character attributes. *Media Psychology, 7,* 325–351.

Huesmann, L. R., & Eron, L. D. (1986). *Television and the aggressive child: A cross-national comparison.* Hillsdale, NJ: Erlbaum.

Huesmann, L. R., Eron, L. D., Lefkowitz, M. M., & Walder, L. O. (1984a). The stability of aggression over time and generations. *Developmental Psychology, 20,* 1120–1134.

Huesmann, L. R., Lagerspetz, K., & Eron, L. D. (1984b). Intervening variables in the TV violence–aggression relation: Evidence from two countries. *Developmental Psychology, 20,* 746–775.

Mastro, D., & Atwell Seate, A. (2012). Group membership in race-related media processes and effects. In H. Giles (Ed.), *The handbook of intergroup communication* (pp. 357–369). New York, NY: Routledge.

Potter, W. J. (1988). Three strategies for elaborating the cultivation hypothesis. *Journalism Quarterly, 65,* 930–939.

Sparks, G., & Sparks, S. (2002). Effects of media violence. In D. Zillmann & J. Bryant (Eds.), *Media effects: Advances in theory and research* (pp. 269–285). Hillsdale, NJ: Erlbaum.

Tajfel, H. (1978). *Differentiation between social groups: Studies in the social psychology of intergroup relations.* London: Academic Press.

INTERACTIVE MEDIA, AGGRESSIVE OUTCOMES OF

Although concern about effects of media on aggression dates back centuries, and concern about effects of modern electronic media has been widespread since the late 20th century, the advent of new interactive media such as video games has led to increased concern about the unique effects of violence in these interactive media on aggression in their users. As is the case with television and films, most popular commercial video games contain violence as a central element of their narratives. Although television and films can expose viewers to graphic violence frequently and in contexts that glorify violent behavior and trivialize its consequences, interactive media such as video games can immerse their users even further in violent content by allowing users to take part in simulations of violent behavior that is often rewarded in the games.

The active involvement of video game users in simulating violent acts has prompted researchers to speculate that the interactive nature of violent video games may lead them to have more pronounced effects on aggression than other violent media. Although this speculation has a strong basis in established theoretical mechanisms related to learning and imitation, there has been limited evidence to indicate that violence in interactive media has uniquely strong effects on aggression compared with other media. At the same time, others have argued that speculation about particularly strong effects of violence in interactive media on aggression is based in fears of the new medium and unfamiliarity with it. Finally, some have suggested that although violence in interactive media may not influence aggression more than other media at this time, advances in interactive media technology may lead to stronger effects in the future. This entry briefly summarizes scholarship dealing with the potential unique effects of violence in interactive media, focusing primarily on conceptual explanations and empirical evidence related to the effects of violent video games.

Theoretical Explanations

A prominent though disputed body of research has indicated that for some people, exposure to violent media can make aggressive thoughts more accessible, increase aggressive feelings, and increase the likelihood of aggressive behavior. This relationship between media violence and aggressive thoughts, feelings, and behaviors in media users has been observed with interactive video games as well as with other media like television and films. Furthermore, a number of conceptual arguments have been used to support speculation that interactive portrayals of violence may affect aggression more than do other media.

Perhaps most common is the explanation that people learn behaviors—good or bad—best when they are actively involved in the learning process. Multiple theoretical frameworks related to learning of behavior, most notably Albert Bandura's social cognitive theory (formerly social learning theory), have stipulated that greater attention to instructions and examples leads to enhanced memory of the observed material and consequently more learning of new behaviors. Social cognitive theory and other perspectives also note that learning is enhanced when an observed behavior is practiced and rehearsed, reinforcing the behavior in the memory of the person practicing it. Although violence in media such as television and film may be consumed passively, violent interactive media such as video games encourage the user to actively attend to their content and participate in a simulation of violent behavior that may lead to more negative effects.

Another frequent explanation for why violence in interactive media may have uniquely strong effects is that the most common violent interactive media, namely popular video games, typically reward the user for rehearsing violent behaviors. Social cognitive theory predicts not only that learning is enhanced by focused attention and active rehearsal, but also that a person is most likely to learn from examples when a positive motivation for the learned behavior is provided. Violent interactive video games often provide built-in motivation for modeling violent behavior by encouraging or requiring users to engage in simulated violence to advance in the game, accrue in-game rewards, and advance the game's interactive narrative to encounter new content.

Finally, violent interactive media often encourage users to personally identify with the perpetrators of violent acts in the content. Social cognitive theory and related approaches claim that media users may model aggression in violent media more when they personally identify with a perpetrator of violence in media. This identification may occur because the media user either already perceives himself or herself as similar to the violent media character or because the media user sees the violent media character as a role model to be emulated. Like other media, violent interactive media such as video games often portray heroic violent characters who are physically attractive and likeable, but violent interactive media also encourage identification because they often place the media user in the perspective of these characters. Users of violent video games are often placed in the roles of violent characters under their control, and many interactive games such as popular first-person shooter games also display their content from a violent character's point of view, further encouraging the user to identify with the featured character.

There are also some reasons why violence in interactive media may have weaker effects on aggression than violence in other media. Violent video games' imagery does not usually present truly photorealistic representations of actors, as do television and film, and realistic visual depictions of violence in media are known to influence aggressive responses more than less realistic depictions. Therefore, violence in video games may increase aggression less than more photorealistic violence in television and film, although any such discrepancy may diminish as video game technology grows more advanced over time. Additionally, although other frameworks predict that users' active involvement with violent content in interactive media may increase effects of that content on aggression, an alternate prediction is that users' active involvement with violent video games may distract from their attention to the violent content and limit its effects.

Empirical Evidence

Although some theoretical mechanisms have stated that violence in interactive media such as video games may predict stronger effects on aggression than non-interactive media such as television and films, research evidence supporting this prediction is mixed. Comparing the effects of interactive media to other electronic media is challenging because the different media are used in different settings, by different audiences, for different purposes, and for different amounts of time. Therefore, it is challenging to compare the effects of violence in interactive and non-interactive media by comparing the magnitude of effects observed in different studies that have focused on those different media. Furthermore, it is also difficult to design a controlled experiment comparing effects of violence in interactive and non-interactive media because it would be nearly impossible to accurately create stimulus conditions comparing the experience of viewing different media, such as a violent movie and a violent video game, while keeping all other content consistent to isolate comparison of the interactive and non-interactive formats. The different media have different content structures, so replicating the same content for both an interactive medium and a non-interactive medium would likely result in content that is notably inappropriate for one or both of the media formats. For example, video games and films may both be guided by a narrative story, but the two media may differ along dimensions such as repetitiveness of their content, the amount of dialogue they include, the photorealism of their imagery, and the length of time it takes to complete them. Therefore, it is difficult to design studies that allow direct comparisons between the effects of violent content in interactive and non-interactive media.

Given these challenges, studies attempting to compare the effects of violence in interactive and non-interactive media have produced mixed and inconclusive results. Simple comparisons among studies on effects of violence in video games, television, and film have sometimes found the effects of the different media to be comparable, have at other times found effects of video game violence to be stronger than those of non-interactive media, and have also found effects of video game violence to be weaker. These inconsistencies exist in part because there is some dispute about the appropriateness and validity of measures of aggression used in the different studies. Other studies have asked survey participants to report their long-term previous exposure to violent video games and violent non-interactive media and then examined correlations between

these forms of media exposure and participants' aggression levels using a number of measures. Some of these studies have suggested that prior exposure to violent video games is a stronger predictor of aggression than prior exposure to violent non-interactive media, but others have not. Additionally, the findings of these correlational surveys have provided little definitive evidence for effects of one medium or another, as the correlations they observe could be due to some other existing difference in the tendencies of people who use different media. Last, some studies have attempted more direct comparisons by comparing effects of violence in two conditions, such as a children's cartoon and a violent game, or by comparing the effects of either playing or watching the same violent game, but these studies have also produced mixed results. It is also difficult to interpret the implications of these studies for comparing effects of violence in interactive and non-interactive media; there are many differences between playing a violent game and watching a violent cartoon aside from the degree of interactivity involved, and watching a video game does not accurately replicate the experience of using genuine non-interactive media. Thus far, then, the conceptual argument that violence in interactive media may be more harmful than violence in non-interactive media is popular and widely considered to be plausible, but it has limited support in the existing research evidence.

Policy

Based in part on the inconclusive nature of research comparing effects of violence in interactive and non-interactive media, attempts to regulate violence in interactive media more strictly than non-interactive media in the United States have thus far been unsuccessful. Most notably, the Supreme Court of the United States ruled in 2011 that a California law regulating minors' access to violent video games was unconstitutional because it regulated video games more than other media when there was not adequate evidence to support discriminating between the risks presented by interactive and non-interactive forms of media. Some Supreme Court justices concurring with the opinion noted, though, that future research and technological developments in video games might lead to measurably different effects of interactive and non-interactive media. As video games and the research examining their effects both become increasingly advanced, it is likely that we will see more research attempting to definitively compare the effects of interactive and non-interactive media.

James D. Ivory

See also Drench Effects From Video Games; General Aggression Model; Presence Theory; Social Cognitive Theory; User Involvement in Violent Content, Effects of; User Trends Toward Aggressive Games; Virtual Reality, Effects of Violent Content in

Further Readings

Anderson, C. A., Gentile, D. A., & Buckley, K. E. (2007). *Violent video game effects of children and adolescents: Theory, research, and public policy.* New York, NY: Oxford University Press.

Brown v. Entertainment Merchants Association, 131 S.Ct. 2729 (2011).

Gentile, D. A., & Anderson, C. A. (2003). Violent video games: The newest media violence hazard. In D. Gentile (Ed.), *Media violence and children* (pp. 131–152), Westport, CT: Praeger.

Gentile, D. A., & Gentile, J. R. (2008). Violent video games as exemplary teachers: A conceptual analysis. *Journal of Youth and Adolescence, 37,* 127–141.

Ivory, J. D., & Kalyanaraman, S. (2009). The effects of technological advancement and violent content in video games on players' feelings of presence, involvement, physiological arousal, and aggression. *Journal of Communication, 57,* 532–555.

Tamborini, R., Eastin, M. S., Skalski, P., Lachlan, K., Fediuk, T. A., & Brady, R. (2004). Violent virtual video games and hostile thoughts. *Journal of Broadcasting and Electronic Media, 48,* 335–357.

Weber, R., Ritterfeld, U., & Kostygina, A. (2006). Aggression and violence as effects of playing violent video games? In P. Vorderer & J. Bryant (Eds.), *Playing video games: Motives, responses, and consequences* (pp. 347–361). Mahwah, NJ: Erlbaum.

INTERNATIONAL PERSPECTIVE ON MEDIA VIOLENCE

The July 20, 2012, Aurora, Colorado, cinema shootings of more than 70 people (58 injured and 12 killed) by a 24-year-old man, James Egan Holmes, at a late-night screening of the new Batman film *The Dark Knight Rises* shocked people around the world. As with similar mass shootings, it raised questions about the link between violence in the media and violent behavior, and whether an international public health response involving parents, professionals, the media, and policy makers is needed to reduce the effects of media violence on children's and young adults' thoughts and behavior.

Link Between Media Violence and Violent Behavior

Although there is strong evidence for negative effects on schoolchildren who view violent images in the media, making them more aggressive in the short and long term, the research evidence for older children, teenagers, and young adults has been inconclusive. The small amount of quality research has suggested that boys are more likely to show aggression after viewing violent media than are girls, and that violent acts by heroes (e.g., Batman) are more influential than violence from villains (e.g., the Joker).

What is clear is that Batman and other superhero films, with their associated merchandise and toys, are often directly marketed at children, whom many health professionals and parents consider to be too young to see the violent imagery portrayed in the film. However, there seems to be little concern about children and young people viewing adult scenes of violence in comparison with worry about adult sex and nudity for all forms of media. Only when violence is seen within a sexual context is it considered to have serious consequences for mental health, according to Craig A. Anderson and colleagues (2003). Parents who allow their children to view adult DVDs or computer games unsupervised may be unaware of the neurological changes that can occur for children, which, according to René Weber, Ute Ritterfield, and Klaus Mathiak (2006), can damage children's mental health in relation to feelings of aggression and fear. Although many parents do not wish their children to see violent imagery as a form of entertainment in the context of a story or game play before the children are ready for it, that may not always be possible. For instance, a film may be given an age-restricted rating (e.g., R or NC-17 by the Motion Picture Association of America, or 12 certificate by the British Board of Film Classification), but toy shops may be filled with merchandise linked to the film that is aimed at younger children. Not surprisingly, these children may then have a strong desire to see a film that is age inappropriate. Indeed, John L. Sherry (2001)

Table 1   Public Health Recommendations to Reduce the Effects of Media Violence on Children and Adolescents

Parents:

1. Parents should be made aware of the risks associated with children viewing violent imagery as it promotes aggressive attitudes, antisocial behavior, fear, and desensitization.
2. Parents should review the nature, extent, and context of violence in media available to their children prior to viewing.
3. Parents should assist children's understanding of violent imagery appropriate to their developmental level.

Professionals:

4. Offer support and advice to parents who allow their children unsupervised access to inappropriate extreme violent imagery as this could be seen as a form of emotional abuse and neglect.
5. Educate all young people in critical film appraisal, in terms of realism, justification, and consequences.
6. Exercise greater control over access to inappropriate violent media entertainment for those young people in secure institutions.
7. Use violent film material in anger management programs under guidance.

Media producers:

8. Media producers should reduce violent content and promote antiviolence themes and publicity campaigns.
9. When violence is presented, it should be in context and associated with remorse, criticism, and penalty.
10. Violent action should not be justified or its consequences minimized.

Policy makers:

11. Policy makers should monitor the nature, extent, and context of violence in all forms of media and implement appropriate guidelines, standards, and penalties.
12. Education in media awareness should be a priority and a part of the school curricula.

Source: Browne, K. D., and Hamilton-Giachritsis, C. E. (2005). The influence of violent media on children and adolescents: A public health approach. *The Lancet, 365,* 702–710.

found that effect size for media violence on young people increased over time as the violent imagery became more sophisticated and explicit, and this trend continues.

Kevin D. Browne and Catherine E. Hamilton-Giachritsis (2005) have suggested that the effects of violent imagery on the screen in television, films, DVDs, and interactive computer games are not the same for every person. The importance each television or film scene or computer game image has to an individual, and the meaning he or she ascribes to it, is determined by the individual's background and the context in which the content is viewed. For example, experiencing "real" violence in the home may have a considerable effect on how violence on the screen is perceived and adopted as an example of acceptable behavior, with volatile reactions seen as a way of having power and control over others. These volatile reactions may then be triggered by media violence and incorporated into a preexisting antisocial behavioral repertoire.

The general aggression model and some empirical research support the suggestion that individuals from violent backgrounds and those predisposed to aggressive behavior may be more susceptible than others to the impact of watching and interacting with violent images. Thus, it is important to develop this line of inquiry to consider the impact of violent imagery on mental health difficulties, especially when linked to alcohol or drugs as state-dependent learning.

Violent computer games, film, and television may reinforce the distorted thoughts and antisocial behaviors of those already predisposed to violent behavior; however, for those individuals not predisposed to violence, research has shown that such nonviolent individuals may become desensitized to violent imagery by frequently watching violent television and film. Young people who offend against others have been shown to be characterized by low self-esteem (feeling easily threatened), by distorted ideas about physical confrontation, by low empathy for others, by self-centered moral values, and by a preference for violent DVDs or computer games.

Long-term outcomes for children and young people viewing media violence are difficult to establish, partly because of the methodological difficulties in linking behavior with past viewing. In addition, there is only weak evidence from correlation studies linking media violence directly to crime.

Research has shown that teenagers and young adults from violent homes are already predisposed to antisocial behavior and delinquency, and this predisposition influences their increased preference and memory for violent images from media entertainment and computer games. Compared with other teenagers and young adults, they are more likely to act out violent scenes and incorporate what they see into their violent acts.

Therefore, violent media entertainment and computer games have the potential to actively increase the frequency of violent behavior in those teenagers and young adults who are already predisposed to aggression as a result of adverse past experiences. By contrast, other teenagers and young adults have a passive response to violent images and are more likely to develop a fear of crime and be desensitized to violence by others.

International Approach

The World Health Organization has highlighted the necessity of adopting a public health approach to the prevention of violence and the reduction of mortality and morbidity in societies. Its *World Report on Violence and Health* specifically mentions the need to address violence in the media as a part of an overall prevention strategy—and for community, health, and social services in each country to be involved in the prevention of media violence and the control—especially availability—of firearms and other weapons that can help turn fantasy into reality.

From an international public health perspective, there is a need for parents and policy makers to take an educational rather than censorial approach to media violence. Table 1 provides a number of public health recommendations in relation to reducing the effects of media violence on children and adolescents. In addition, media effects researchers, such as Amy I. Nathanson and Joanne Cantor (2000), and Marcel W. Vooijs and Tom H. A. Vandervoort (1993), have proposed that parents and teachers share in the viewing of violent material with children and help them critically appraise what they

see, in terms of its realism, justification, and consequences. In this way, parents and teachers can reduce the impact of violence imagery. Furthermore, it has been suggested that media producers need to recognize the potential impact of their violent images on vulnerable audiences who may not have the capacity to see the violence in the context of the story.

Kevin Browne

See also Audience Interpretation of Media Violence, Effects of; Desensitization Effects on Society; Effects From Violent Media, Short- and Long-Term

Further Readings

Anderson, C. A., Berkowitz, L., Donnerstein, E., Huesmann, L. R., Johnson, J. D., Linz, D., Malamuth, N. M., & Wartella, E. (2003). The influence of media violence on youth. *Psychological Science in the Public Interest, 4,* 381–410.

Anderson, C. A., & Bushman B. J. (2001). Effects of violent video games on aggressive behavior, aggressive cognition, aggressive affect, physiological arousal, and prosocial behavior: A meta-analytic review of the scientific literature. *Psychological Science, 12*(5), 353–359.

Browne, K., & Hamilton-Giachritsis, C. (2005). The influence of violent media on children and adolescents: a public-health approach. *The Lancet, 365*(9460), 702–710.

Cooley-Quille, M., Boyd, R. C., Frantz, E., & Walsh, J. (2001). Emotional and behavioral impact of exposure to community violence in inner-city adolescents. *Journal of Clinical Child Psychology, 30*(2), 199–206.

DeWall, C. N., Anderson, C. A., & Bushman, B. J. (2011). The general aggression model: Theoretical extensions to violence. *Psychology of Violence, 1*(3), 245–258.

Ferguson, C. J., San Miguel, C., & Hartley, R. D. (2009). A multivariate analysis of youth violence and aggression: The influence of family, peers, depression and media violence. *Journal of Pediatrics, 155*(6), 904–908.

Huesmann, L. R. (1999). Symposium: The effects of childhood aggression and exposure to media violence on adult behaviors, attitudes, and mood: Evidence from a 15-year cross-national longitudinal study. *Aggressive Behavior, 25*(1), 18–19.

Huesmann, L. R. (2007). The impact of electronic media violence: Scientific theory and research. *Journal of Adolescent Health, 41*(6): S6–S13 (Supplement).

Jolliffe, D., & Farrington, D. P. (2004). Empathy and offending: A systematic review and meta-analysis. *Aggression and Violent Behavior, 9*(5), 441–476.

Krug, E. G., Dahlberg, L. L., Mercy, J. A., Zwi, A. B., & Lozano, R. (Eds.). (2002). *World report on violence and health.* Geneva: World Health Organization.

Nathanson, A. I., & Cantor, J. (2000). Reducing the aggression-promoting effect of violent cartoons by increasing children's fictional involvement with the victim: A study of active mediation. *Journal of Broadcasting & Electronic Media, 44*(1), 125–142.

Pennell, A. E., & Browne, K. D. (1998). Young offenders' susceptibility to violent media entertainment: Implications for secure institutions. *Prison Service Journal, 120,* 23–27.

Pennell A. E., & Browne, K. D. (1999). Film violence and young offenders. *Aggression and Violent Behavior, 4*(1), 13–28.

Savage, J. (2004). Does viewing violent media really cause criminal violence? A methodological review. *Aggression and Violent Behavior, 10*(1), 99–128.

Sherry, J. L. (2001). The effects of violent video games on aggression: A meta-analysis. *Human Communication Research, 27,* 309–331.

Vooijs, M. W., & Vandervoort, T. H. A. (1993). Teaching children to evaluate television violence critically: The impact of a Dutch schools television project. *Journal of Educational Television, 19*(3), 139–152.

Weber, R., Ritterfield, U., & Mathiak, K. (2006). Does playing violent video games induce aggression? Empirical evidence of a functional magnetic resonance imaging study. *Media Psychology, 8*(1), 39–60.

INTERNET BLOCKING

Internet blocking, also known as *Internet filtering* or *content control,* is the use of hardware or software to restrict access to undesirable online content. Blocking is distinct from *monitoring,* which tracks online behavior without preventing access, although both functions are often found together in software applications. Filtering of pornographic and political material receives the most attention, but violent online videos and video games, cyberbullying threats, images of violent behavior, and hate group websites can also be blocked. This entry describes Internet blocking technology and examines its efficiency, prevalence, and social impacts.

Blocking Technology

Content can be blocked by individual users through their web browsers, computer operating systems, or client-side computer programs such as NetNanny or by Internet service providers (ISPs), network managers, or search engines. The crudest forms restrict Internet access by configuring operating systems to require passwords when logging on or opening web browsers, or with tamper-proof physical locks that disable hardwired Internet connections or power cords. Address filtering employs black lists that block forbidden web addresses or white lists that allow access only to acceptable websites. Keyword filters block URLs of websites or images that contain forbidden words, such as derogatory terms used by hate groups. Content ratings of "old media" products, such as TV-MA or R-rated videos, are also used by filtering software. Collaborative filtering enlists users and content providers to participate in the filtering process by labeling content. Pattern recognition software detects nudity and might conceivably be designed to detect fistfights or hostile spoken words as well.

Efficiency

Content filtering has technical and social limitations. Both overblocking of desirable content and underblocking of unwanted material are frequent errors. Address filtering requires continual updating of black lists (or white lists). Blocking of specific content within websites, such as music and videos, relies on the content rating systems of entertainment industries that either do not incorporate violence (e.g., Recording Industry Association of America's Parental Advisory labels) or that focus more on sex than violence (e.g., Motion Picture Association of America film ratings). Pattern recognition of video remains a significant technical challenge. Internet blocking techniques are susceptible to circumvention both by those whom they are intended to protect and by content providers. Computer-savvy children have a variety of anti-blocking techniques at their disposal: passwords can be guessed, fraudulent accounts established, computers carried to outlets without parental lockouts. And tips for evading filtering software are readily available online and through youth subcultures. Content providers can disseminate new addresses that redirect users to blocked ones or copy material to new websites.

Prevalence

National surveys from the mid-2000s found that filtering software was used in a third of UK and more than half of U.S. homes. Workplace filtering through corporate firewalls is widespread, although it is primarily targeted to pornography and illegal activities rather than violent or aggressive content. The Children's Internet Protection Act (CIPA) of 1999 requires filtering in U.S. schools and libraries that receive public (E-Rate) funds for computers, and filtering is universal in U.S. schools and participating public libraries. CIPA is aimed primarily at sexual content, but individual organizations determine what is appropriate content for children, so filtering of violent content also likely occurs, but the extent is unknown. Among nations, China suppresses postings about violent protests by its citizens. Egypt shut down the Internet during the Arab Spring uprising of 2011, as Iran had done in 2009, in part to prevent the spread of images of violent antigovernment protests. France and Germany block words and images related to Nazism and Holocaust denial, and the European Union is implementing automated filtering of child pornography and possible terror-related websites.

Social Impacts

In a national U.S. survey, it was found that filtering software was associated with reduced exposure to unwanted sexual content in homes that used it compared with those who did not; however, a third of children in the filtered homes still reported unwanted exposure, and filtering made no difference among 16- to 17-year-olds. A UK study found no significant relationship between filter use and reduction in risk of exposure to violent content. Significant censorship and privacy issues are raised by Internet blocking. Children, employees, and citizens may perceive filtering software as a violation of trust or be frustrated when conducting harmless Internet searches that lead to determined circumvention efforts. Blocking of terror and hate group websites with violent content and filtering of images from political demonstrations raise civil liberties issues in countries that value freedom of speech.

Robert LaRose

See also Internet Content, Effects of Violent; Internet Violence, Influence on Society; Internet Violence Laws

Further Readings

Akdeniz, Y. (2010). To block or not to block: European approaches to content regulation, and implications for freedom of expression. *Computer Law & Security Review, 26*(3), 260–272.

Burt, D. (2002). The facts on filters. Seattle, WA, N2H2. Retrieved from http://www.ntia.doc.gov/legacy/ntiahome/ntiageneral/cipacomments/pre/aclj/ExhibitA.pdf

Deibert, R. J., Palfrey, J. G., Rohozinskiand, R., & Zittrain, J. (Eds.) (2008). *Access denied: The practice and policy of global internet filtering.* Cambridge, MA: MIT Press.

Gomez Hidalgo, J. M., Sanz, E. P., Garcia, F. C., & Rodriguez, M. D. B. (2009). Web content filtering. *Advances in Computers, 76,* 257–306.

Leberknight, C. S., Chiang, M., & Wong, F. M. F. (2012). A taxonomy of censors and anti-censors: Part I–Impacts of Internet censorship. *International Journal of E-Politics, 3*(2), 52–64.

Lenhart, A. (2005). *Protecting teens online.* Pew Internet and American Life. Retrieved from http://www.pewinternet.org/~/media//Files/Reports/2005/PIP_Filters_Report.pdf.pdf

Livingstone, S., & Helsper, E. J. (2008). Parental mediation of children's Internet use. *Journal of Broadcasting & Electronic Media, 52*(4), 581–599.

Yan, Z. (2009). One law with two outcomes: Comparing the implementation of CIPA in public libraries and schools. *Information Technology and Libraries, 28*(1), 6–14.

Ybarra, M. L., Finkelhor, D., Mitchell, K. J., & Wolak, J. (2009). Associations between blocking, monitoring, and filtering software on the home computer and youth-reported unwanted exposure to sexual material online. *Child Abuse & Neglect, 33*(12), 857–869.

INTERNET CONTENT, EFFECTS OF VIOLENT

Many academicians and laypeople alike are worried that there are negative ramifications to the violence that is often encased in digital entertainment. This issue received national attention after the 1999 school shootings at Columbine High School near Littleton, Colorado. The investigation of the shootings revealed that the shooters had been heavy users of violent video games and websites. Many worried that exposure to such violence leads to desensitization in children. These worries are not unjustified; research has suggested that exposure to violent content impairs emotional regulation that would normally allow a child to trigger an empathetic response. The lack of an empathetic response increases the likelihood of aggressive behavior.

Children become desensitized when they begin to perceive violence as mundane and inevitable rather than uncommon and unlikely (Slater, 2003). Once this belief is held, it is likely that children will find no need to censor their violent behavior. Desensitization is thought to occur as the result of the lack of consequences in violent media. An increase in tolerance for violent behavior was shown in Ronald S. Drabman and Margaret Hanratty Thomas's 1974 study and was later confirmed in 1994 by Fred Molitor and Kenneth William Hirsch.

Violent entertainment content does not affect everyone equally. In the work of Michael Slater, some adolescents were found to be more inclined to seek out violent content and were subsequently affected by it more so than others. Adolescents who lacked ties with socialization agents such as school, family, and peers tended to gravitate toward peer groups with deviant norms. The adolescent may respond to the perceived alienation by these groups with anger, which has also been found to predict deviant behavior. Traits, along with sensation seeking (i.e., the need for novel experiences), can be representative of social dysfunction. It is speculated that these traits, along with alienation, may lead adolescents to seek out violent content. Interactive computer-mediated violence may even serve as a way for an adolescent to act out violent fantasies on the alienating parties.

This entry discusses various types of violent Internet content, including gaming, pornography, cyber-aggression, and pro-suicide content, and their effects.

Violence in Online Gaming

In a review of 16 studies conducted between 2005 and 2009, Victoria Anne Sublette and Barbara Mullan (2012) found no evidence suggesting that multiplayer online games affected the physical or psychosocial health of the players; they did, however, find evidence of addiction. One common stereotype of online gamers is that they are lacking in social skills and do not seek opportunities to interact with others. Contrary to this misconception, online gaming does not necessarily deteriorate socialization. Some players have active social lives while also cultivating relationships with other players within their online worlds.

Today, the concern about exposure to violent content seems to be largely focused on video games. This may be because its active nature sets it apart from other screen-based entertainment. Players do not consume content in a passive manner but actively interact with a virtual environment and choose and execute violent strategies for which they

are then rewarded. Not only do video games offer positive enforcement, but they present violence as justified and without negative consequences (Funk, 1995). The presentation of violence as justified, the reward that follows it, and the perception of violence as the norm may lead to the development of pro-violence attitudes.

Pornography and Violence

In addition to video gaming, pornography is a prominent source of violence online. Although not all pornography is considered violent, all types of pornography, including violent pornography, are becoming more common online. A primary concern of researchers has been that portrayals of women in violent sexual encounters will lead to violence against women offline. Exposure to violent or degrading pornography has been shown to increase aggression against women by men in laboratory and experimental settings, including acceptance of interpersonal violence against women, acceptance of rape myths, the belief that some women enjoy being raped, and fantasizing about rape. However, studies have also found no such effects in men who do not have preexisting inclinations. The availability of sexually explicit media on the Internet increased dramatically between 1995 and 1999, yet reports of sexual assault in the United States decreased during this time period (Fisher & Barak, 2001).

There also appears to be no significant effect on aggression toward women in a laboratory setting after men's repeated exposure to violent pornography. Neil M. Malamuth and Joseph Ceniti's 1986 study observed men in a laboratory setting and measured their level of aggression toward women by instructing them to assign a level of punishment via aversive noise. The men in this study had been exposed to four weeks of violent, nonviolent, or no pornography prior to participating in the lab experiment. Although the men in this study viewed full-length films and read texts in analog form, the results of the study deserve mentioning because both forms of content are available online.

Many researchers have suggested that individuals with a predisposition toward sexually explicit media will seek out sexually explicit media with antisocial content and are more likely to be affected by it. For this reason, Internet pornography may be more dangerous than traditional means of access. Individuals with this predisposition now have the ability to seek violent, sexually explicit media easily, anonymously, and repeatedly, and may then be affected by it. This, combined with sensation-seeking behaviors, previously discussed, may be particularly dangerous.

Cyber-Aggression

As children use the Internet to fulfill their social and entertainment needs, an issue that has plagued children in the physical playground has followed them online. Many studies have reported that cyber-aggression occurs in equal frequency to traditional aggression. Only 79% of adolescents who reported themselves as being cyber-aggressors knew their victims personally. However, this behavior may not be random acts of meanness. Cyber-aggression often occurs as a reaction to an event that happened on school grounds. Although the relationship between traditional and cyber-aggression has not been clearly established, evidence has suggested some overlap between the two worlds.

There is a perception that cyber-aggression is not met with any consequence to the aggressor because of the anonymity allowed by the Internet. Research has shown, however, that there are consequences for these individuals. Data collected from group assessments involving 192 children in the 3–6 grade levels showed that cyber-aggression can lead to social problems at the individual, relationship, and group levels (Schoffstall & Cohen, 2011). Cyber-aggression was correlated with loneliness and lower self-worth, lower peer optimism, fewer mutual friendships, and lower ratings of social acceptance and popularity. Anonymity, though, is thought to allow females to be equally aggressive as males (Schoffstall & Cohen, 2011).

It is important to note that cyberbullying and cyber-aggression are not synonymous. Corrie L. Schoffstal and Robert Cohen (2011) define *bullying* as "any behavior that is intended to harm, repeatedly and over time, characterized by an imbalance of strength or power, and such that the victim does not feel he or she can stop the interaction." Cyber-aggression does not have to be repeated or involve a relationship characterized by an imbalance of power. Cyberbullying is rare and occurs in only 21% to 25% of online harassment cases. It cannot be said whether traditional or cyberbullying is more damaging. Some forms of cyberbullying are reported by students to have less impact than traditional bullying. Studies have generally shown that cyber- and traditional bullying have similar negative effects on victims, including effects on school performance,

depression, social anxiety, low self-esteem, and sadness and hopelessness. In a survey of 5,862 students from three countries (Italy = 1,964; Spain = 1,671; England = 2,227) in grades 8, 10, and 12, researchers found that anger was the most common emotional impact of both traditional and cyberbullying. The feeling of being "defenseless" was the least reported emotional response to cyberbullying. Rosario Ortega and colleagues (2012) also found a greater impact on girls, younger students, and those facing frequent rather than occasional occurrences. It is important that researchers continue to study cyberbullying prevention because its effects have been shown to be emotionally damaging and in some cases has even led to suicide.

Personal Violence Online: Pro-Suicide Content

Pro-suicide web content is becoming commonplace. Websites that provide pro-suicide information are now gaining visibility and are topping search engine results, making them accessible to those at risk. Researchers, politicians, teachers, and parents, to name a few, are concerned that portrayals of and advice pertaining to suicide, along with cyberbullying, will encourage those at risk to follow through with plans of suicide. A review of the literature showed that the presence of pro-suicide content online has increased in recent years; however, the verdict is still out on how this content affects suicide rates globally.

A 2008 study by Lucy Biddle and colleagues analyzed search results for suicide-related keywords and found that 30% of the pages found conveyed mostly information about suicide methods and were largely encouraging of suicide. Many of the sites included suicide success stories, pictures of those who had committed suicide already, and suicide notes. Another function of these sites is to help those contemplating suicide find suicide pacts, other individuals who will commit suicide with them. Access to pro-suicide content may lead individuals who are at risk to carry out suicide plans after being informed and encouraged. If information on this self-inflected violence does lower thresholds, as Michael Westerlund (2011) speculates, this would be an effect similar to the desensitization of violence. Some research suggests that any correlation between suicide and suicide-related search volume may also be due to an increased interest in suicide during periods of high suicide death rates (i.e., individuals searching for suicide terms to find more information about recent deaths), leading to an increase in suicide-related searches. However, a content analysis of search volume data collected by Google Insights for suicide-related searches in Japan between 2004 and 2009 found no significant correlation between suicide rates and the search terms *suicide* or *suicide method*.

Laura F. Bright

See also Cyberbullying, Definition and Effects of; Cyberbullying, Violent Content in; Desensitization Effects on Society; Pornography, Violent Content in; Pornography, Violent Content in: Effects of

Further Readings

Biddle, L., Donovan, J., Hawton, K., Kapur, N., & Gunnell, D. (2008). Suicide and the Internet. *British Medical Journal, 336,* 800–802.

Drabman, R. S., & Thomas, M. H. (1974). Does media violence increase children's toleration of real-life aggression? *Developmental Psychology, 10*(3), 418–421.

Espelage, D., & Swearer, S. (2003). Research on school bullying and victimization: What we have learned and where do we go from here? *School Psychology Review, 32*(3), 365–383.

Fisher, W. A., & Barak, A. (2001). Internet pornography: A social psychological perspective on Internet sexuality. *Journal of Sex Research, 38*(4), 312–323.

Funk, J. B. (1995). Video violence. *American Academy of Pediatrics News, 16,* 21.

Malamuth, N. M., & Ceniti, J. (1986). Repeated exposure to violent and nonviolent pornography: Likelihood of raping ratings and laboratory aggression against women. *Aggressive Behavior, 12*(2), 129–137.

McCarthy, M. J. (2010). Internet monitoring of suicide risk in the population. *Journal of Affective Disorders, 122*(3), 277–279.

Molitor, F., & Hirsch, K. W. (1994). Children's toleration of real-life aggression after exposure to media violence: A replication of the Drabman and Thomas studies. *Child Study Journal, 24*(3), 191–207.

Ortega, R., Elipe, P., Mora-Merchan, J. A., Genta, M. L., Brighi, A., Guarini, A., Smith, P. K., Thompson, F., & Tippett, N. (2012). The emotional impact of bullying and cyberbullying on victims: A European cross-national study. *Aggressive Behavior, 38*(5), 342–356. doi: 10.1002/ab.21440

Schoffstall, C. L., & Cohen, R. (2011). Cyber aggression: The relation between online offenders and offline social competence. *Social Development, 20*(3), 587–604. doi: 10.1111/j.1467-9507.2011.00609.x

Slater, M. D. (2003). Alienation, aggression, and sensation seeking as predictors of adolescent use of violent film, computer, and website content. *Journal of Communication, 53*(1), 105–121.

Sublette, V. A., & Mullan, B. (2012). Consequences of play: A systematic review of the effects of online gaming. *International Journal of Mental Health Addiction, 10*(1), 3–23. doi: 10.1007/s11469-010-9304-3

Westerlund, M. (2011). The production of pro-suicide content on the Internet: A counter-discourse activity. *New Media Society, 14*(5), 764–780. doi: 10.1177/1461444811425221

INTERNET VIOLENCE, INFLUENCE ON SOCIETY

The Internet offers immediate access to just about any type of media violence imaginable. The web offers uncensored violent writings, photos, videos, and games all within a single medium, giving it an unprecedented amount of violent content. Among adolescent users, immediate access to such content is also harder to supervise. With Internet connections on laptops and personal computers that are often housed in the privacy of an adolescent's bedroom, along with the addition of Internet access on cell phones, parental policing of the Internet activity of today's youths can be far more difficult than policing their television viewing, the books they read, the console video games they play, and any further adolescent usage of other traditional media. Moreover, the interactive nature of the Internet encourages users to share and even participate in violent behaviors. The distinct nature of violence on the Internet raises many questions about potential effects. This entry considers the influence of Internet violence on society. It begins by defining Internet violence and societal-level effects. It then reviews research on the societal influence of media violence. It concludes with future considerations for research and policy.

Preliminary Definitions: Internet Violence and Societal Effects

Internet violence includes both violent content and violent behavior online. In one of the few book chapters focusing broadly on Internet violence, Ed Donnerstein (2011) offered a typology of what Internet violence entails. At an initial level, he proposed, the medium makes all previous forms of violent media available to users, including print, film, television, and video game violence. It also adds "extreme" violence to the mix, such as footage of real-life executions, terrorist and hate sites, and other violent content that would be restricted from traditional media. Moreover, the Internet allows users to actively participate in media violence. They can send, create, and upload violent content. They can play violent games. And through social media, they can be perpetrators of real-life violence (when they communicate aggressive messages) or victims of violence (through cyberbullying). The vastness and sometimes starkly realistic nature of violence on the Internet, along with its participatory dimension, suggest a host of possible effects.

Although much of media theory and research has focused on individual-level effects, the enormous global popularity of the Internet has undoubtedly had a larger-scale impact. Here, the effects of Internet violence on life in general and criminal behaviors are discussed, beginning with two major examples.

Prominent Examples of Internet Violence and Societal Effects

One example of the societal influence of Internet violence can be seen in the popularity of websites containing videos of real-life violence. The Internet not only makes extreme violence available, but evidence has suggested that a large segment of society is seeking out this previously taboo content. In a critical study titled "Internet Spectatorship on Body Horror," Sue Tait (2008) wrote about Ogrish.com (now Liveleak), a popular website providing uncensored access to real-life violence. The original Ogrish.com included footage of accidents, suicides, and crime scenes. The site also became a repository for war-related footage during the second Iraq war and gained notoriety during the mid-2000s for hosting the beheading videos of Daniel Pearl (executed in 2002) and Nick Berg (executed in 2004). Tait notes that prior to the site's sale in 2006, the Berg video had been downloaded 15 million times, and each of the site's 19 other beheading videos had been downloaded several million times. Note that these numbers are just from one site—there were likely many others sources on the Internet providing access to the footage. The high viewership of these and other gruesome videos can be taken as an indicator of large-scale effects. People are now seeing real acts of violence they would otherwise not be able to view, increasing societal-level access to previously forbidden images.

A second prominent example of the Internet's influence on society can be seen in what journalist Jill Smolowe (and others) call "mean girl" copycat incidents, such as the beating of Florida teen Victoria Lindsay by a group of teens. The assault of Lindsay was captured on video and posted on YouTube, where it became a viral video sensation with millions of views. According to Smolowe (2008), the county sheriff involved in the case called the attack "absolutely animalistic" and said the perpetrators lured the victim to the home for the purpose of filming the beating and putting it online. It was not an isolated incident, however. One girl interviewed by Smolowe said she watches girl fights on the Internet "all the time," leading some to speculate about the extent to which girls and others are lured into perpetrating violence for the fame that it can bring. Just about anyone can shoot video today, and the participatory nature of the Internet allows them to share those videos with others. Because violence sells, it makes sense that some would use aggressive behavior to garner attention. This raises questions about the extent to which society is becoming more violent as a result. However, very few studies to date have specifically addressed Internet violence, and even fewer have examined its influence at a societal level.

Research on Societal Effects of Internet Violence

Of the research that has been done on the influence of Internet violence on society, studies by Michele Ybarra and colleagues (2008) that focused on aggressive outcomes have presented some of the most compelling findings. One investigation involved a survey of 1,588 youths ranging in age from 10 to 15 years. In the survey, respondents were asked if they had visited each of the following types of websites in the past 12 months: a hate site; a "snuff" site; a Satanic rituals site; a site showing pictures of war, death, or terrorism; or a site showing cartoons of stick people or animals being aggressed against. These items were intended to represent exposure to Internet violence, along with questions about the proportion of visited sites that contained violence involving real people and violence involving cartoons. The survey also included measures of (a) exposure to other violent media (including television, video games, and music), (b) the extent to which respondents engaged in seriously violent behavior (including acts likely to result in murder, aggravated assault, robbery, and sexual assault), and (c) control variables (including individual, family, school, peers, and community factors). Results of the survey revealed that 38% of youths had visited one or more of the violent website types, and approximately 5% of the total respondents had engaged in one or more forms of seriously violent behavior in the previous year.

When Ybarra and colleagues looked at the statistical relationships between variables, they found that heavy exposure to Internet violence involving real people, compared with no such exposure, was associated with a five times greater likelihood of engaging in real-life violent behavior. This relationship emerged even after controlling for other risk factors such as anger proclivity, substance abuse, poor parenting, delinquent peers, and community violence. Heavy exposure to Internet violence was also found to be the form of media exposure most likely to relate to seriously violent behavior, surpassing television, video games, and music. The researchers concluded that, among violent media forms, Internet violence seems particularly concerning and may offer insights into young people's seriously violent behavior. They cautioned against interpreting their findings as causal, however, given the correlational nature of their study.

In a follow-up longitudinal study of 10- to 15-year-olds over a three-year period, Ybarra and colleagues (2011) found exposure to X-rated, sexually violent material to be associated with a six times greater likelihood of self-reported sexually aggressive behavior, including in-person sexual assaults and sexual harassment or solicitation through communication technologies. Studies of cyberbullying have also looked at online aggression of this nature, which appears to be on the rise. In Ybarra's research, the effect of sexually violent media on aggressive outcomes did not hold for exposure to nonviolent X-rated material. The Internet features copious amounts of both violent and nonviolent sexually explicit material, and consistent with research on pornography effects, violent pornography appears to be the most harmful. The easily accessible combination of sex and violence online represents another area of concern about the influence of Internet violence on society.

Future Considerations for Internet Violence and Society

The unique aspects of Internet violence, along with the compelling findings from studies on its effects, call for more research specifically addressing this topic. As Donnerstein notes, unlike traditional media for exposure to violence (which has been the subject of thousands of scientific studies), there is general consensus that considerably more research is needed on the influence of the Internet on children and adolescents. This includes research on Internet violence effects, which have only been examined in a handful of studies. Future research on Internet violence can help fill a major void in the literature by employing different methodologies (particularly ones better establishing causality), examining additional variables (including macro-level outcomes), and studying more populations (such as adults and racial and ethnic groups).

With a firm body of research on Internet violence in place, parents, policy makers, and others can make informed decisions. The scant amount of evidence on Internet violence effects to date suggests that it may be more problematic than other forms of media violence. At the very least, it adds another log to the fire of risk factors for violence in society.

Paul Skalski and James Denny

See also Internet Blocking; Internet Content, Effects of Violent; Internet Violence, Influence on Society; Internet Violence Laws

Further Readings

Donnerstein, E. (2011). The media and aggression: From TV to the Internet. In J. Forgas, A. Kruglanski, & K. Williams (Eds.), *The psychology of social conflict and aggression.* New York, NY: Psychology Press.

Smolowe, J. (2008, April 28). Mean girls. *People.* Retrieved from http://www.people.com/people/archive/article/0,,20196197,00.html

Tait, S. (2008). Pornographies of violence? Internet spectatorship on body horror. *Critical Studies in Media Communication, 25*(1), 91–111.

Ybarra, M. L., Diener-West, M., Markow, D., Leaf, P. J., Hamburger, M., & Boxer, P. (2008). Linkages between Internet and other media violence with seriously violent behavior by youth. *Pediatrics, 122*(5), 929–937.

Ybarra, M. L., Mitchell, K. J., Hamburger, M., Diener-West, M., & Leaf, P. (2011). X-rated material and perpetration of sexually aggressive behavior among children and adolescents: Is there a link? *Aggressive Behavior, 37*(1), 863–874.

INTERNET VIOLENCE LAWS

Concerns regarding Internet violence have increased as access to and use of the Internet have become ubiquitous in U.S. society. High-profile acts of violence, particularly regarding children and bullying that extends beyond the schoolyard, have increased awareness of the capability of individuals to use the Internet to cause harm. In response to this awareness, governmental units have responded by attempting to implement various laws or policies to halt Internet violence. This entry examines the types of Internet violence that lawmakers have targeted, the legal framework surrounding legislation targeting forms of Internet violence, and the effectiveness and limitations of these laws.

General Types of Internet Violence

U.S. lawmakers have generally focused on cyberbullying, cyberstalking, cyberharassment, hate speech, and recording and/or distributing video of acts of violence. Although each of these types of violence has corresponding offline laws and legal precedent, the emergence of the Internet has pushed these laws beyond their expected application. The Internet has provided new venues for violence, intensified contact with violence, and altered the manner in which people experience violence. This section addresses these types of violence and differentiates them from their offline counterparts.

Cyberbullying

Bullying, particularly of children by their peers, has received significant media coverage during the first decade of the 21st century. The behaviors of concern for bullying and cyberbullying are acts of physical violence or threats of physical violence, intimidation, and/or identification as being outside of the social norms and being treated as an outsider. Schools have made attempts to curb these types of behaviors, but the Internet has created opportunities for these types of behaviors to extend beyond the school grounds themselves, making it increasingly difficult to curtail.

Cyberstalking and Cyberharassment

Stalking and harassment behaviors are similar to bullying behaviors but include adult populations as well. Harassment behaviors include unwanted communication or interaction that persists following a request to cease. Stalking behaviors, by contrast, include threats or intimidation. These threats may be made to an individual, family unit, or specific group. One can be harassed, however, without being stalked. The Internet has created more opportunities for harassment because digital communication tools are varied and ubiquitous. Stalking behaviors may also be enabled via the Internet because of the increased resources available to identify and monitor targets.

Cyberhate Speech

Hate speech in general has been a concern in the United States for many years. The U.S. Supreme Court has addressed hate speech as early as 1949 in the case *Terminiello v. Chicago* and as recently as 2011 in *Snyder v. Phelps*. Hate speech covers any form of racist, bigoted, or extremist messages. The use of electronic communication technologies (such as cell phones, websites, e-mail, etc.) to propagate hate speech is considered cyberhate speech.

Recording and Distributing Violent Content

The creation of violent content has also been a historical concern of the United States. Of particular interest for this entry is the emergence of "crush" and "snuff" videos or films. Crush films depict the abuse of animals, often ending with the death of the animal. Crush films also include violence against human beings, but without the death of the person. This is of particular concern to advocates of homeless citizens because they are often targeted or enticed to be in these films with nominal money or resources. Snuff films are a growing concern, but their existence is debated. These films depict the murder of a human being for entertainment purposes. Video depictions of murder (such as beheadings, etc.) that are not considered snuff films appear online. The differentiation between these is in the purpose; entertainment is the key component of a snuff film.

Online Differences

As mentioned previously, each of these behaviors has comparable offline legal frameworks. However, what makes these behaviors unique and of concern to lawmakers is the scope and intensity that the Internet provides. Although the ability to physically commit violence via electronic communication is limited, the threat of violence is damaging to targets of violence. The Internet increases the ability of perpetrators to engage and expose their targets to threatening messages. Whereas violence was once primarily committed in a geographic space, the Internet creates affordances for nongeographically bound interactions.

In addition to the potentially increased access to targets, the Internet also creates a larger viewing audience for acts of violence. Victims of violence can now be publicly targeted to audiences of several hundred to several hundred thousand, increasing the effect felt by the target. In addition to the violence itself, the target may also feel the pressure of a larger audience to their victimization, potentially increasing the psychological impact of the violence itself. Theories regarding mass audience behavior online (such as the social identity model of deindividuated effects) suggest that this audience may also feel more at ease in perpetuating acts of violence as well.

Finally, victims of acts of violence online experience the possibility of being targeted by anonymous sources. This has ramifications for the effectiveness of antiviolence legislation but can also make the act of violence more intimidating and threatening to the target. When the source of violence is unknown, the target is put in a position of great ambiguity, which can intensify the impact of violence. This may be particularly true of bullying behavior because it is likely that peers are involved, but which peers are unknown. The anonymous nature of some Internet violence can erode social trust beyond what might be experienced in offline acts of violence.

Because of these potential impacts of violence in online environments, legislators have responded to concerns of their constituents by attempting to create legal frameworks that include electronic communication. The following section discusses these attempts in general.

Laws and Internet Violence

Laws regarding Internet violence have primarily arisen as a state as opposed to federal issue. Although the U.S. federal government has had discussions and proposed bills (2009 was the most recent), at the time of publication, federal law does not address directly any of the Internet violence issues discussed in this entry.

Cyberbullying

Of the 50 U.S. states, 49 of them have laws that specifically address bullying behaviors. The only exception is the state of Montana, where some of the behaviors included in bullying are covered under preexisting laws, such as laws regarding assault, and so on. Forty-nine states require policies regarding bullying, which minimally make an allusion to electronic devices and media as a venue in which bullying can occur. A majority of states (43 in total)

also empower schools to sanction students who are in violation of bullying policies.

This support for cyberbullying victims is limited. Whereas 49 states have bullying laws, only 16 states specifically address cyberbullying behaviors. The number of states with laws including off-campus behavior—the likely scenario for most cyberbullying—is even smaller. Only 10 states recognize bullying, cyberbullying, or offline bullying that occur outside of school grounds. This creates potential enforcement issues that are discussed later in this entry.

Finally, states vary significantly regarding the punishment for bullying and cyberbullying behavior. A total of 12 states treat bullying and cyberbullying as criminal offenses ranging from misdemeanors to felonies. This suggests that the states are willing to recognize bullying but require very little in terms of consequence. Schools are overwhelmingly given authority to address incidents on their property, but they are limited in prosecutorial power and sanctions.

The states that include all of the elements discussed are limited to three. Arkansas, Louisiana, and Tennessee each have laws that specifically recognize cyberbullying, treat various forms of bullying as criminal offenses, and recognize that bullying that occurs digitally away from school grounds constitutes bullying. Missouri, Nevada, and North Carolina are similar to these states except that they do not currently recognize cyberbullying that occurs outside of school property. Finally, New York has recently proposed amendments that would classify bullying and cyberbullying as criminal offenses and already recognize off-campus behavior as bullying or cyberbullying. The remaining states vary in their treatment of cyberbullying, but as indicated previously, the majority of states are addressing this issue with laws of some sort.

Cyberstalking and Cyberharassment

The U.S. federal government, in addition to several states, has passed laws that pertain to cyberstalking and cyberharassment. Federal law prohibits the use of Internet services or connected devices to harass an individual or family, or to transmit threats. This is a purposefully broad law that allows for new technologies to emerge and still fall within the definition of Internet services or connected devices. More specific laws also exist at the federal level. For example, the

Violence Against Women Act specifically mentions electronic communication as a venue for stalking and harassing that would fall under the jurisdiction of the law.

States have also created their own laws to address cyberstalking and cyberharassing. These laws tend to be more general in nature and may account for the paucity of cyberbullying laws in these states. All 50 states have laws that deal with either cyberharassment or cyberstalking in some form. New Mexico and Nebraska, however, do not specifically identify the Internet or electronic communication in their statues. Instead, each state provides broad language that includes contacting an individual in any manner, regardless of medium, therefore effectively including digital communication. These laws range in severity of criminal offense from misdemeanors to felonies.

Cyberstalking laws address the use of electronic devices to instill fear in an individual or an individual's family. This includes threats of violence and threats of death. These laws also tend to identify behaviors through which a person can threaten violence. Examples of these behaviors include using electronic communication or devices to make false statements about individuals or gain access to individuals, gathering information in order to make threats, and the false representation of a person (which would include identity theft). Because of the potential threat of violence or death posed by these behaviors, these laws tend to classify cyberstalking behavior as a felony charge that includes significant fines and possible jail time.

By contrast, cyberharassment is typically classified as a misdemeanor because of the lack of credible threat. Once a threat is made, a case would be covered under cyberstalking law. Cyberharassment includes repeated contact that is deemed by the target to be unwanted. Unlike cyberstalking, cyberharassment law recognizes the behavior as being an annoyance that does not pose a credible threat of violence.

Cyberhate Speech

Cyberhate speech does not necessitate a specific target. Instead, cyberhate is the use of extreme speech, terrorist speech, bigoted speech, and/or racist speech that can be intimidating to those who experience it. Specific individuals may also be targeted with cyberhate speech, but that is not a requirement of cyberhate speech as defined.

Anti–hate speech and anti–cyberhate speech legislation has been proposed at the U.S. federal level as parts of laws pertaining to decency. For example, the Communications Decency Act included provisions limiting the type of speech permitted by extremist groups both offline and digitally. The U.S. Supreme Court, however, has repeatedly ruled that such broad limitations are in violation of the U.S. Constitutions First Amendment's protection of free speech. The Court has argued that concerns for free speech, including hate speech, is protected speech in that it contributes—even minimally—to the marketplace of ideas that contribute to the health of a democracy. States have similarly attempted to curb cyberhate speech, but those attempts too have been ruled unconstitutional because of First Amendment protections.

Although general cyberhate speech is not protected, there are limitations. When hate speech is directed toward an individual, electronically or not, the laws regarding cyberharassment and cyberstalking provide targets with legal protection. Additionally, speech that is specific in a threat or attempt at intimidation is not protected under the First Amendment. As a consequence, hate speech on the Internet as a general rule is not illegal, but targeted threats of violence toward an individual or small group would not be protected and would permit legal recourse.

Depictions of Violence Online

The last laws discussed in this entry relate to the recording and distribution of violent content on the Internet. Similar to cyberhate speech law, much of the content included under these laws (crush or snuff videos) is protected under the First Amendment. Although U.S. federal and state proposals have been made to address these issues, the U.S. Supreme Court has generally sided with free speech over limiting depictions of violence. As recently as 2010, the Supreme Court, in *United States v. Stevens,* invalidated a law that generally prohibited crush videos on the grounds that the statute was overly broad.

Although general bans at the federal level have failed, more specific state proposals may have more success. For example, the state of New York has proposed legislation that would make the recording and distribution of violent crimes a felony offense. This law, and proposals similar to it, may be able to pass First Amendment protection defenses on the grounds that the violent acts being filmed are (a) illegal acts in the state in which they occur at the time they occurred and (b) that there is potential financial gain for those distributing the content. In order for these proposed laws to pass concerns of constitutionality, both of these considerations must be met.

Effectiveness and Limitations

As discussed previously, both the U.S. federal government and individual state governments are increasingly addressing concerns regarding Internet violence by enacting legislation aimed at curtailing emergent methods of intimidation, threats, and depictions of violence. Although these laws have moved to include online interactions, they face some limitations on their effectiveness because of the nature of the Internet itself.

One of the greatest limitations of Internet violence laws in general is the ability of perpetrators to remain anonymous. Victims of cyberbullying, cyberstalking, and cyberharassment are not always aware of the identity of those targeting them. Without this ability to identify perpetrators, law enforcement faces several challenges to enforcing the law. First, without knowing who the perpetrator is, victims of Internet violence may be reluctant to report incidences. Victims of cyberstalking and cyberharassment in particular tend to report instances to their Internet service providers (ISPs) as opposed to law enforcement. Although the ISP may be able to assist victims in effectively blocking future contact, this strategy can be limited if perpetrators use new accounts or different devices to continue stalking and harassing. Law enforcement is also limited in the type of information officers are able to use from ISPs when addressing Internet violence cases. U.S. civil liberty law protects the privacy of users, including those who may be engaging in violent or threatening behavior.

Another concern is the technological abilities of perpetrators to hide their identities. Although ISPs can track Internet protocol (IP) addresses, there are programs that enable users to hide their IP addresses and other identifying digital information and maintain anonymity. The use of open networks (such as public wi-fi, public Internet hotspots, or open wireless networks) can also enable perpetrators to hide their identities and make it difficult for victims and law enforcement to make use of the laws designed to protect individuals from Internet violence.

The various state laws can also lead to prosecutorial problems. Although perpetrators of Internet violence often know their targets, the Internet allows violence to occur across state lines, creating problems of jurisdiction. If identifiable, there may be disagreement between states regarding which law is applicable: those of the state in which the target lives or those in which the perpetrator lives. These issues have been preceded by cases involving indecency laws and pornography, because it is not always clear which state's laws are in effect. Although these issues are resolved within the judicial system, this process can be both time and resource depleting for targets. This is often a discouragement to bringing suits in civil court and can tie up resources in criminal court.

The final concern regarding the limitations of the effectiveness of these laws is that they are applicable within the United States only. International law regarding Internet violence is significantly more variable than the differences between states previously discussed. Some countries have considerably less protection than the United States, making it difficult to prosecute Internet violence. Internet traffic can also be routed through various countries, making the jurisdiction of these laws significantly more difficult to determine. There are other countries, by contrast, with fewer protections of speech rights; these laws could therefore create problems for U.S. citizens in that their speech would not be protected if consumed outside of the United States. These jurisdiction problems pose the greatest limitation to Internet violence laws, and there has yet to be a global consensus regarding what constitutes Internet violence and the appropriate regulation of Internet violence.

Paul Zube

See also Advertising Laws Regarding Violent and Aggressive Content; Bullying, Definition and Laws of; Cyberbullying Laws; Regulating Systems, Internet; Violence, Definition of

Further Readings

Broderick, M. (2010). Supreme Court avoids crushing the First Amendment: Why the decision in *United States v. Stevens* was important for the preservation of First Amendment rights. *Denver University Law Review, 88*, 557.

Franks, M. A. (2010). The banality of cyber discrimination, or, the eternal recurrence of September. *Denver Law Review Online, 87*, 5. Retrieved from http://papers.ssrn.com/sol3/papers.cfm?abstract_id=1569202

Hinduja, S., & Patchin, J. W. (2009). Bullying beyond the schoolyard: Preventing and responding to cyberbullying. Thousand Oaks, CA: Sage.

Snyder v. Phelps, 562 U.S. ___, 131 S.Ct. 1207, 1214 n.1 (2011).

Terminiello v. Chicago, 337 U.S. 1 (1949).

Tsesis, A. (2009). Dignity and speech: The regulation of hate speech in a democracy. *Wake Forest Law Review*, 44.

United States v. Stevens, 559 U.S. ___, 130 S.Ct. 1577 (2010).

LATINOS IN MEDIA, CHARACTER DEPICTIONS AND SOCIAL REPRESENTATION OF

Portrayals of Latinos (and diverse groups in general) in the media play a meaningful role in the development of social perceptions regarding Latinos, particularly among audience members with little or no real-world contact with them. These perceptions ultimately can influence a range of societal outcomes, including prejudice and discrimination, as well as policy decisions. Accordingly, it is important to systematically document these media depictions and examine the effects of exposure on audiences. Notably, both the quantity and the quality of these portrayals have been implicated in the outcomes associated with exposure. Specifically, these characterizations (a) speak to perceptions of group standing and status, (b) define norms of treatment and expectations about interethnic contact, (c) prompt cognitive and emotional responses that govern interethnic interactions, and (d) influence policy decisions.

Quantity of Character Depictions

Although U.S. Census data reveal that Latinos are the largest racial/ethnic minority group in the United States (at approximately 16% of the population), they constitute only about 4% of the characters on television. In fact, content analyses of television over the past 50 years have repeatedly demonstrated that Latinos are represented at a rate well below their real-world proportion of the population. Research by Dana Mastro and colleagues indicates that, unlike other racial/ethnic groups who have seen their rate of representation rise over the decades (such as African Americans), the proportional representation of Latinos has been on the decline.

Children's programming offers a more favorable picture. According to research by Naeemah Clark and Stephynie Perkins (2007), approximately a quarter of contemporary children's programs (with identifiable race-related figures) have featured Latino characters. Comparatively, however, this is less promising than it may appear, because African Americans and Asian Americans are each depicted in more than half of children's shows. In children's commercial advertising, Latinos appear in less than 10% of advertisements, but according to research by Hae-Kyong Bang and Bonnie Reece (2003), Latinos are the primary figure in nearly three-fourths of these ads. No ads feature Latinos exclusively.

Quality of Social Representations

As summarized in Clint Wilson, Félix Gutierrez, and Lena Chao's work (2003), the portrayals of Latinos in early television programming relied heavily on long-standing stereotypical characterizations seen in film, such as criminals, Latin lovers, hot-tempered males, and female spitfires, as well as inept objects of derision—with broken English a staple among these figures. By the 1970s, the infrequent roles associated with Latinos focused primarily on two types of characterizations: the streetwise *barrio* family and the Latin lover. Many of these figures were noteworthy because they were lead roles in popular programs (as opposed to minor or background characters). In the 1980s, the tremendous popularity of shows like *Miami Vice* and *L.A. Law* led to changes in representations of Latinos. During this time, roles for Latinos centered nearly exclusively on the legal system, with Latinos seen as both law defenders and law breakers. This casting trend was even more prominent in the 1990s. As research by Mastro and Bradley Greenberg (2000) demonstrated, 77% of Latinos on primetime television during this decade appeared in crime dramas. Notably, the majority of these Latino characters were law enforcers as opposed to criminals (at least with major and minor characters). Nonetheless, they were still less likely than their White or African American television counterparts to appear in recurring or main roles. Moreover, one-quarter of Latino appearances were on a single program (*NYPD Blue*).

According to Children Now, approximately three-fourths of Latinos in more contemporary television programming appear on situation comedies and crime dramas. Across the board, they are less likely than other racial or ethnic groups to appear in high-status occupations and are four times more likely to be characterized as domestic workers. Analyses by Mastro and Elizabeth Behm-Morawitz (2005) provided additional insights into these characterizations. Their research indicated that the typical Latino character on primetime television is a family member involved in discussions about crime. They are portrayed as less articulate, less intelligent, lower in job authority, more seductively dressed, younger, and lazier than their peers on television. In addition, alongside African Americans, Latinos are the most hotheaded characters on primetime television.

The research on television news coverage of crime conducted by Travis Dixon, Daniel Linz, and colleagues has indicated that Latinos (as well as African Americans) are portrayed as crime perpetrators more often than are Whites. However, this rate is below real-world arrest reports for Latinos. Their work reveals that the same pattern emerges in depictions of Latino youth in crime news. However, in representations as victims in crime news on television, Latinos also are seen at rates lower than Whites and real-world crime data. In addition, coverage of crime on television news is more likely to present prejudicial information (e.g., existing arrest records) when the defendant is Latino (versus White), particularly when the case involves a White victim.

Concluding Thoughts

Exposure to the types of images known to be associated with Latinos (as described previously) is not without consequence. Research has consistently revealed that short-term and long-term exposure to even a small number of unfavorable Latino characterizations on television can influence (a) the development and structure of social perceptions of Latinos among non-Latino viewers, (b) diversity-related policy preferences, and (c) interethnic judgments and behaviors. In addition, exposure to negative representations of Latinos among Latino audience members can have a range of harmful psychological consequences.

Dana Mastro

See also African Americans in Media, Character Depictions and Social Representation of; Asians in Media, Character Depictions and Social Representation of; Character Development Within Violent Content

Further Readings

Bang, H.-K., & Reece, B. (2003). Minorities in children's television commercials: New, improved, and stereotyped. *Journal of Consumer Affairs, 37*, 42–67.

Children Now. (2004). *Fall colors, 2003–2004: Prime time diversity report.* Oakland, CA: Children Now.

Clark, N., & Perkins, S. (2007, May). *Parts of the scenery, leaders of the pack, one of the gang: Diversity on children's programs.* Paper presented at the annual meeting of the International Communication Association, San Francisco.

Dixon, T., Azocar, C., & Casas, M. (2003). The portrayal of race and crime on television network news. *Journal of Broadcasting & Electronic Media, 47*, 498–523.

Dixon, T., & Linz, D. (2000a). Overrepresentation and underrepresentation of African Americans and Latinos as lawbreakers on television news. *Journal of Communication, 50*, 131–154.

Dixon, T., & Linz, D. (2000b). Race and the misrepresentation of victimization on local television news. *Communication Research, 27*, 547–573.

Dixon, T., & Linz, D. (2002). Television news, prejudicial pretrial publicity, and the depiction of race. *Journal of Broadcasting & Electronic Media, 46*, 112–136.

Mastro, D. (2009). Effects of racial and ethnic stereotyping. In J. Bryant & M. B. Oliver (Eds.), *Media effects: Advances in theory and research* (3rd ed., pp. 325–341). Hillsdale: NJ: Erlbaum.

Mastro, D. (2009). Racial/ethnic stereotyping and the media. In R. Nabi & M. B. Oliver (Eds.), *The Sage handbook of mass media effects* (pp. 377–391). Thousand Oaks, CA: Sage.

Mastro, D., & Behm-Morawitz, E. (2005). Latino representation on primetime television. *Journalism & Mass Communication Quarterly, 82,* 110–130.

Mastro, D., & Greenberg, B. (2000). The portrayal of racial minorities on prime time television. *Journal of Broadcasting & Electronic Media, 44,* 690–703.

Mastro, D., & Tukachinsky, R. (2012). Cultivation and perceptions of marginalized communities. In J. Shanahan, M. Morgan, & N. Signorielli (Eds.), *The cultivation differential: State of the art research in cultivation theory* (pp. 38–60). New York & Berlin: Peter Lang.

Wilson, C., Gutierrez, F., & Chao, L. (2003). *Racism, sexism, and the media: The rise of class communication in multicultural America.* Thousand Oaks, CA: Sage.

Legislating Media Violence: Law and Policy

Media violence has long been an issue for lawmakers, generally because of concern over the negative effects it is believed to have on those—primarily children—who are exposed to it. However, for all the attention and concern given to violence in various forms of media, policy makers have had little success in taking legislative action to address the issue. A major reason for this is that media violence is generally protected by the First Amendment to the U.S. Constitution, seriously limiting the options available to legislators to restrict or prohibit media violence. For example, a number of states have passed laws attempting to restrict minors' access to violent video games, but those laws have uniformly been declared unconstitutional for violating First Amendment free speech rights. The primary law in effect to deal with violence in the media is the V-chip law, which requires technology to be included in television sets that parents can use to block content to which they do not want their children exposed. This entry first examines legislative efforts to deal with media violence in general and then focuses on attempts to deal with violence in various forms of media: television, video games, movies, music, and the Internet.

Legislative Strategies on Media Violence

The main strategy of the U.S. Congress to deal with media violence has been to hold hearings, typically calling on witnesses from the industry, scholars who study television violence and its effects, and representatives of parent and child advocacy groups. These hearings are often used by Congress to express concern about media violence and its effects and call on the industry to take action on the issue. This approach, sometimes referred to as "regulation by the raised eyebrow," avoids raising First Amendment free speech issues because that does not constitute formal legal action. However, the approach is typically not effective, because the media industries often fail to address the issue in a manner that satisfies Congress.

Historically, congressional attention on media violence has been more focused on reducing the levels of violence in media consumed by children or in getting the industry to present violence in a more responsible manner. However, the focus in the early 2000s has shifted in two other directions. One area of more recent congressional activity has focused on restricting the marketing of violent entertainment products to children. This effort largely began after a wave of school shootings in the late 1990s, particularly those at Columbine High School near Littleton, Colorado, in 1999. There was some evidence in the Columbine shootings that the two high school students who shot and killed a number of classmates and teachers were avid consumers of violent video games and movies, and violent media was blamed by some as playing a role in this and other school shootings. Following Columbine, President Bill Clinton asked the Federal Trade Commission (FTC) to study the marketing of violent entertainment to children. This study, released in 2000, found that the movie, music, and electronic game industries typically marketed violent entertainment products to children that their own ratings systems classified as being inappropriate for children.

Many entertainment industry segments, including those just mentioned, operate their own industry rating systems, generally rating their products according to the age groups for which these products are appropriate or inappropriate. Oftentimes, these age-based ratings are accompanied by content ratings that indicate the particular type of content—violence, for example—that prompted the age-based rating. These rating systems are voluntary industry systems that are advisory in nature: they are meant to provide parents with information about the content of media products to assist them in deciding which products to allow their children to consume. They do not carry the force of law, though: No laws are broken when a minor gains access to a product that is rated as being inappropriate for minors. However, the industries studied were criticized for targeting minors in the marketing plans for products that were rated as inappropriate for them.

Furthermore, in its report the FTC noted that minors were frequently able to purchase or gain access to media products rated as inappropriate for them. With the release of this report, Congress held hearings and introduced bills on the topic. Although none of those bills became law, Congress still shows interest in the issue. For its part, the FTC has conducted a series of follow-up studies. Generally, those studies have found improvement by the movie and electronic game industries in not marketing violent entertainment products to children, but there is much progress still to be made by the music industry.

The other area of focus for Congress in recent years has involved ratings systems. The legislative proposals in this area have largely focused on promoting or requiring accuracy in media product-rating systems. One related proposal that seems to generate a fair amount of interest among policy makers is encouraging or requiring a universal rating system that would apply across media types, as opposed to the different systems applied to different types of media at the time this entry was written. The belief behind these proposals is that such a system would be easier for parents to use and understand. No such efforts, however, have had much success.

Television

Congress has shown the most concern and activity over television violence in comparison with violence in other forms of media. There are a few reasons for this. First, television is in nearly every home in the United States and is used by the U.S. population more than any other form of media. Second, television stations are licensed by the government through the Federal Communications Commission (FCC). This gives the federal government authority over television that it does not have over other forms of media. Third, broadcast television receives the least amount of First Amendment protection of all forms of media, giving the government more leeway to regulate television programming than it does to regulate the content of other forms of media. The reason for this lower level of protection is that there are a limited number of television station licenses that can be granted, so not everyone who wants a license can be granted one—a concept referred to as "scarcity."

Congress has passed more laws to address violence on television than in any other form of media. The most significant of these laws instituted the V-chip requirement. The V-chip is a technology that is required to be included in most television sets sold in the United States since 2000. This technology works in conjunction with an industry-developed rating system that rates programs based on the age groups for which they are appropriate and identifies particular types of potentially objectionable content—such as violence—that those programs contain. Parents can use this technology to block programs with content they do not wish their children to see. Because parents, rather than the government, are blocking programming, use of the V-chip does not violate the First Amendment.

Two other laws passed by Congress to deal with television violence did not have much impact. The first, which went into effect in 1990 and was the first law passed by Congress to deal with television violence, gave the industry a three-year antitrust exemption, the purpose of which was to allow the industry to work to develop standards to lessen the negative effects of television violence. The law, however, required no action by the industry; whether the industry took advantage of the opportunity provided by the law was entirely voluntary. The only result of this law was that the industry agreed to air audience advisories before violent programs. Many observers, however, believed the industry largely failed to follow through on this promise. The other law dealing with television violence, passed in 2007, directed the FCC to investigate and report to Congress on the existence, availability, and promotion of content-blocking technologies and other parental empowerment tools. The FCC provided Congress with the report required by this law in 2009.

The other main regulatory proposal frequently advanced in Congress to deal with television violence is a "safe harbor" proposal, although as of 2012 this has not come close to being passed into law. Under such a law, violent programs could not be shown during hours when a large number of children are in the viewing audience, effectively limiting violent programming to the late-night and overnight hours. Such a proposal is similar to the "safe harbor" currently in effect for indecent broadcast programming: programming containing offensive sexual content on broadcast television stations. However, indecency is given less First Amendment protection than is violent content. Although the indecency safe harbor has been ruled constitutional under the First

Amendment, it is not at all clear that a violence safe harbor would be constitutional. Nevertheless, this has not prevented the proposal from being introduced several times in Congress since the 1990s. Since the implementation of the V-chip requirement, the violence safe harbor proposal has been narrowed to apply only to violent programming not blockable by use of the V-chip. Thus, if such a proposal were to become law, it would apply only to violent programming not rated for violence under the V-chip rating system.

Other common legislative proposals dealing with television violence involve the requirement of studies on the issue of television violence to be conducted by various entities and the gathering of complaints from the public about television violence. In addition, proposals have been introduced that call for the institution of a family viewing hour or the creation and offering of family-friendly tiers of programming by cable and other multichannel program providers. Programming during this time or on these tiers would be appropriate for viewing by a family audience.

Video Games

In the 1990s and first decade of the 21st century there was a great deal of activity in state legislatures to restrict or prohibit minors' access to violent video games. A number of laws were passed that aimed to do this; however, those laws were unable to survive court challenges. Many of the laws modeled their definitions of the violent content subject to the law on the legal definition of obscenity, a category of offensive sexual content without redeeming value that is not protected by the First Amendment. However, sexual content and violent content are treated differently under the First Amendment, with violent content receiving greater First Amendment protection than sexual content. Thus, modeling definitions of violence on the definition of obscenity in laws aimed at violent video games was unsuccessful.

Another problem with laws seeking to restrict minors' access to violent video games involved the definition of video game violence subject to the law. When restricting or prohibiting speech protected by the First Amendment, the speech subject to that law typically must be defined both specifically and narrowly. To date, courts have not been satisfied with legislators' attempts to define the video game violence they were targeting in a manner that makes it clear exactly what types of violence are subject to

the law and that targets only that violence necessary to achieve the objectives of the law.

A final major problem with many of the violent video game laws involved the evidence presented by the government to support the need for the laws. Courts have been reluctant to accept the social-scientific evidence presented to them as establishing that exposure to violent video games causes minors to act violently or aggressively or has other negative effects on them. In this regard, courts tend to note that the research establishes correlation—but not causation—of exposure to violent media and negative effects in violent media consumers.

In addition to state legislature interest in the issue, the U.S. Congress also showed much interest in regulating violent video games in the first decade of the 21st century. There were generally two types of proposals that seemed popular with legislators. The first would make it illegal to rent or sell games rated Mature or Adults Only to minors. The other focused on ensuring that video game ratings were accurate. Although a number of bills were introduced along these lines, none was enacted into law.

Movies

Congress has passed only one law dealing with violence in the movies in the modern era. That law, passed in 2005, made it clear that the use of filtering technologies to edit or skip content deemed to be offensive or inappropriate, including violent content, was not a violation of copyright law. It should be noted that such editing is confined to home viewing of films only, and that the law prohibits making fixed copies of movies so edited.

Legislative action to deal with violence in movies was more common in the early days of the film industry than in more recent decades. This is due in part to a 1915 Supreme Court decision that held that movies were not entitled to protection under the First Amendment. This made it much easier for the government to attempt to regulate film content. There was much more action during this time period, however, at the state and local levels than at the federal level. Many jurisdictions created censorship boards that would screen films and often require cuts to be made to them before granting approval to screen such films in a particular area. Violence was one of the types of content of concern to censorship boards.

In 1952 the Supreme Court reversed its earlier decision and found that movies were entitled to

First Amendment protection. This made it much more difficult for censorship boards to operate without violating the First Amendment, and during the 1960s and 1970s many censorship boards ceased operation. Since that time, legislators have continued to express concern about film violence. In the early 2000s, much of that concern was directed at the marketing of violent movies to children, particularly for films rated by the industry as inappropriate for children. Legislative proposals have been advanced to prohibit such marketing practices, but none has become law.

Music

In the mid-1980s, the Parents Music Resource Center successfully brought the attention of Congress to the messages provided by the lyrics in some popular music. Although the group's efforts were originally inspired by sexually explicit lyrics, the organization's concerns grew to include lyrics describing or promoting violence as well. It was partly a response to pressure from this group that led to a series of congressional hearings on albums with explicit lyrics. Congress has on occasion held hearings on the issue of explicit song lyrics, with particular concern focused on violent messages contained in heavy metal and rap music. To date, however, no legislation has been enacted to deal with the issue.

With this pressure and the threat of potential legislation on the topic, the recording industry responded by agreeing to place parental advisories on recordings with explicit lyrics. In regard to violence in music, Congress has expressed concern over the shortcomings of the recording industry's advisory system and its implementation. Since 2000, Congress has also been concerned about the recording industry's marketing practices, which have been found to target children for recordings with parental advisories, as well as the ease with which children are often able to purchase or access music with explicit lyrics. These practices, documented in a series of FTC reports, have been targeted in proposed legislation, but none of those proposals has become law.

Internet

There has been more focus in Congress on attempting to restrict or prohibit sexual content on the Internet than on violent content. Thus, Congress attempted to restrict minors' access to Internet content that was indecent or harmful to minors, but those laws were struck down by the courts as unconstitutional.

A major reason why these laws were invalidated involved the existence of blocking and filtering technologies, which can be used by parents to help limit the content their children are exposed to online. The Supreme Court noted that the use of these technologies by parents was preferable from a First Amendment perspective to government restrictions or prohibitions on Internet content. The Court also noted the use of such technologies was more effective in blocking objectionable content than were the laws enacted by the government. Such reasoning would likely apply to any legislative efforts to restrict minors' access to violent content online. Other than attempts to restrict minors' access to violent online games, covered by much of the legislation discussed in the video game section of this entry, there do not appear to have been many serious legislative attempts to regulate violence on the Internet.

Joel Timmer

See also Censorship of Violent Content; Federal Communications Commission; First Amendment Protections and Freedom of Expression; Rating Systems, Film; Rating Systems, Television; Rating Systems, Video Games

Further Readings

Black, G. D. (1994). *Hollywood censored: Morality codes, Catholics and the movies.* Cambridge, UK: Cambridge University Press.

Clements, C. (2012). Note: Protecting protected speech: Violent video game legislation post–*Brown v. Entertainment Merchants Ass'n. Boston College Law Review, 53,* 661–692.

Cooper, C. A. (1996). *Violence on television: Congressional inquiry, public criticism, and industry response: A policy analysis.* Lanham, MD: University Press of America.

Federal Trade Commission. (2000). *Marketing violent entertainment to children: A review of self-regulation and industry practices in the motion picture, music recording and electronic game industries.* Washington, DC: U.S. Government Printing Office.

Hamilton, J. (2000). *Channeling violence: The economic market for violent television programming.* Princeton, NJ: Princeton University Press.

Paulson, K. A. (2004). Regulation through intimidation: Congressional hearings and political pressure on America's entertainment media. *Vanderbilt Journal of Entertainment Law and Practice, 7,* 61–89.

Rowland, W. D., Jr. (1983). *The politics of TV violence: Policy uses of communication research.* Beverly Hills, CA: Sage.

Ruschmann, P. B. (2010). *Regulating violence in entertainment*. New York, NY: Chelsea House.

Signorielli, N. (2005). *Violence in the media: A reference handbook*. Santa Barbara, CA: ABC-CLIO.

Timmer, J. (2004). Incrementalism and policymaking on television violence. *Communication Law and Policy, 9*, 351–385.

LINEATION THEORY

Lineation theory is a broad theory that provides a big-picture explanation of the mass media phenomenon. It grew out of a major critique of the practices and findings in the large literature of published research about the media. This entry presents a description of lineation theory first. Next, the entry shifts the focus to violence and shows how the theory presents explanations as answers to four major questions that have concerned media violence researchers and policy makers over the years.

Overview of Lineation Theory

Lineation theory integrates constructs and propositions across the entire range of the mass media phenomenon. With its 140 constructs and 56 propositions, it is much broader than other media theories, which typically focus on one type of effect, one type of message, or one type of audience process.

The foundation for lineation theory's system of explanation is a conceptualization of "mass" media that was developed to serve two purposes. First, it was constructed to overcome the limitations inherent in past conceptualizations that relied on definitional elements such as audience size, audience type, and kind of channel of transmission. Second, it was developed to capture the essential characteristics of the new media environment, with its technological convergence across channels of transmission, the digitization of messages, the interactive nature of audiences, and the condition of information saturation that requires most exposures to take place in an automatic state of attention. From this foundation, the theory builds its explanation in four areas (media organizations, audiences, messages, and effects) and then ties those explanations together across these four major facets of the mass media phenomenon.

Within the media organization facet, lineation theory's key construct is the "line of thinking," which explains how mass media organizations make decisions about how to attract their audiences, then condition them for repeated, habitual exposures. Additional explanatory propositions illuminate the mass media organizational goals, strategies, and practices.

Within the audience facet, the key explanatory constructs are exposure states and information-processing tasks. *Exposure states* refer to the qualitatively different states (automatic, attentional, transported, and self-reflexive) in which audience members can experience any given media message. The *information-processing tasks* are filtering, meaning matching, and meaning construction. By placing the focus on exposure states and information-processing tasks, lineation pushes the role of motives and gratifications into the background. It foregrounds the importance of examining how the mass media organizations condition audience exposure patterns so that audience members' filtering and meaning-matching decisions are automatic, and their meaning construction decisions are highly constrained. These two constructs are also essential to explaining how the media exert their influence and shape effects.

Within the facet of media messages, lineation theory's key construct is the narrative line, which is reflected in a variety of formulas that producers use to craft their messages. In order to be successful storytellers, producers of mass media messages need to learn these basic formulas, then exhibit the talent to work variations off those standard formulas. Audiences also use these formulas to set their expectations for each media message and to guide them through the messages efficiently.

Within the media effects facet, lineation theory's key construct is the "line of influence," which is the path through the constellation of factors that interact with one another in various ways to bring about effects in both individuals as well as more macro units of institutions and the public. The media's role in this process is to exert one of four types of influences: triggering of something that already exists within a person (such as a memory, an emotion, behavior, etc.), altering something that already exists (such as an attitude, belief, or behavioral pattern), reinforcing something, or acquiring something new.

In the synthesis used to construct lineation theory, W. James Potter sorted through the media literature in an effort to identify patterns of practices that have been most useful in increasing understanding about the phenomenon of the mass media. He characterized past media research as having a Generating-Findings perspective through which media scholars have been concerned with exploring the breadth of the media phenomenon by trying out a wide variety of methods, concepts, and definitions for those concepts. He argued that while this perspective has been valuable in generating a large literature filled with useful insights, the literature has now become highly fragmented, making it increasingly difficult to calibrate the relative importance of different findings and integrate them into a big picture of knowledge structure about the mass media. Potter argues that there needs to be a major shift in mass media scholarship into what he calls a Mapping-Phenomenon perspective, which is characterized by building depth over breadth through a higher degree of programmatic empirical research along with much more focus on construct explication, critical analyses of literatures, and synthesis of findings. Potter offers lineation theory as a first step in guiding the evolution from the Generating-Findings perspective to the Mapping-Findings perspective.

The theory was named *lineation* because the metaphor of "line" is featured so prominently. The key explanatory constructs include the "narrative line" to explain message formulas, the "line of thinking" to explain how people in media organizations make decisions, and the "line of influence" to explain how elements within media messages along with factors in the audience and environment work together to bring about effects. Also within the media audience facet, the line is a threshold that separates the qualitatively different exposure states.

Lineation and Media Violence

Lineation theory grew out of Potter's work on media violence in the 1980s and 1990s, and many of the ideas in lineation theory were introduced in *On Media Violence* (1999). This section illustrates how lineation theory provides explanations as answers to four questions about media violence: (1) Why do the media continue to rely on violence in their messages? (2) Why do audiences with their continued exposures support this high prevalence of violence in media messages? (3) How is violence portrayed in media messages? (4) What is the effect of exposure to media violence?

Why Do the Media Continue to Rely on Violence in Their Messages?

Scholars who analyze media content have frequently reported high levels of violence in both informational and entertainment messages. The National Television Violence Study found that more than 60%

of all fictional television shows across all genres and day parts (specific portions of the day for broadcast scheduling) presented at least one act of violence. This widespread use of violence in television messages has been consistently high ever since the early days of television. This raises the question about why violence has been used so much and so consistently over the decades. Lineation theory provides two explanations as an answer to this question: the orienting reflex in humans and the conditioning by the media.

The orienting reflex, which is hardwired into the brains of all humans, directs the sense organs to monitor a person's environment for potential threats. When a sound or an image signals a threat, a person's attention is directed toward that threat, and often the body is aroused as it goes into fight-or-flight mode. This orienting reflex and the arousal it often triggers provide a degree of pleasure, so humans continue to engage in these. Because these processes are thousands of years old, they have not yet adapted to the challenges posed by mediated messages, so the triggering of a person's orienting reflex or fight-or-flight reaction is the same with real-world stimuli as with stimuli from mediated messages. Producers of mediated messages can stimulate the orienting reflex in a variety of ways, but the easiest way to elicit this reflex is to present cues that signal life-death implications, such as violence.

Over time, people are exposed to many media messages that use violence to stimulate arousal followed by a satisfying outcome to the characters involved in the violent stories. This tends to condition audiences to regard violence in stories as leading to feelings of pleasure in the form of safe arousal, because audiences get to experience the arousal without having to suffer the negative consequences they would experience if the violence occurred in the real world.

Producers of media messages know that the cost of attracting and maintaining audiences is high, as is the risk for failure. Therefore, producers rely on proven techniques to reduce their risk of failure. Featuring violence in storytelling is a proven technique to draw audience members' attention, involve them in a story as they experience the pleasure of arousal, and deliver the additional pleasure of an easy-to-understand resolution to the action.

Why Do Audiences Support This High Prevalence of Violence in Media Messages?

Although there are many examples of people complaining about the high degree and wide prevalence of violence in media messages, the messages that feature violence continue to attract audiences in large numbers. Lineation theory explains that this continued support can be traced to two factors: easy-to-follow story formulas and long-term conditioning.

The formulas used to present violence in media messages are very simple. Young children easily learn these formulas and then use that knowledge to make sense of violent messages in an efficient manner the rest of their lives. The generic formula for violence in storytelling specifies that a good character with whom the audience identifies is egregiously wronged by evil characters using violence early in the story. The good character continues to be wronged unjustly (along with his or her friends and family) by the evil characters, building up to a climax in which the good character eventually uses violence to subdue the evil characters and thereby stop their mayhem. The story ends with the good characters being successful in restoring peace and harmony. This formula is easy for everyone to follow; it draws them into the action through life-death suspense; and it provides a satisfying resolution.

Because the media violence formula is so prevalent, audiences have been exposed to it many times and have become conditioned by it. Audiences know that such stories will be easy to follow and understand. They can recognize the good and evil characters with almost no effort. They trust they will be swept away by the action and experience a range of strong emotions. And they know that at the end of the story, they will feel emotionally spent and satisfied with the narrative journey.

How Is Violence Portrayed in Media Messages?

Content analyses of the way violence is portrayed in the media continually find a high prevalence of certain elements. Very few instances of violence on television are graphic—that is, there is little blood and gore. The consequences of the violence are rarely depicted; victims of violent acts are rarely shown suffering physically, emotionally, or financially. More frequently the use of violence is rewarded, or at least not punished. And the good characters (heroes) are as likely to engage in violence as are the bad characters (villains), with the difference being that the villain violence is not justified while the hero violence is justified.

This pattern of elements depicts violence as sanitized, trivialized, and glamorized. Producers sanitize the portrayals of violence by avoiding graphicness, thus reducing the chance of offending audiences.

Producers trivialize the violence with humor and fantasy (as in cartoons). Producers glamorize the violence by showing larger-than-life villains and heroes in order to attract audiences and lead them to identify with certain characters.

Lineation theory regards these patterns as narrative formulas that producers use to construct new stories. Successful producers follow these formulas closely enough so that audience members can easily follow their stories, but producers also need to employ minor variations from the formula so as to surprise and entertain audiences.

What Is the Effect of Exposure to Media Violence?

After nine decades and an estimated 6,000 published studies on media effects, there is still a controversy over whether the media are responsible for effects on individuals and society, what those effects are, and what is the prevalence of those effects. Social scientists who believe the media exert effects point to the consistency of findings on certain effects in the large literature. However, among policy makers and the public at large there is a lack of understanding about the range of effects and the role violence plays in bringing about those effects. Lineation theory explains that there are three factors that serve as barriers for greater awareness about effects from exposure to violence in media messages. First, the studies in the literature are largely focused on what lineation theory characterizes as Groups-Differences strategy rather than a Target-Degree strategy. This means that researchers have depended more on explaining small differences in means across treatment groups in experiments rather than in documenting changes (knowledge, attitudes, beliefs, or behaviors) in a person over time as a result of media exposures.

Second, the value of the Groups-Differences strategy has been its discovery of potentialities rather than actualities. This means that the use of laboratory experiments with controls is a strong method to isolate one effect and a small set of causal factors to determine whether or not an effect will occur in a group of people or not. The weakness inherent in this method is that this control creates an artificial situation that largely ignores the real-world situation of overwhelming message choice, distractions, simultaneous exposures, and audience members' naturalistic meaning matching and meaning construction processes. It also stimulates an exposure state of attention rather than relying on other exposure states, especially automaticity that is far more common in everyday life. Although the results of such studies are often valuable in identifying particular effects and particular factors of influence, these results do not provide much insight into the size of effects or how widespread the effects are in the real world.

Third, the theories and models that have been developed to explain media influence are relatively weak because they consider few factors that occur in a person's everyday life. They favor attribute variables (such as gender, age, and socioeconomic status) over more active influences (such as degree of gender role socialization, cognitive maturity, and lifestyle beliefs). They default to simple relationships among variables (symmetrical and linear) rather than testing for more complex relationships that are more common in the everyday lives of humans.

Although lineation theory provides a critique of the limitations in the research, it does not ignore the value of that research—that is, the shortcomings in the literature are viewed as limitations in the value of the research, not as factors that invalidate those results. Lineation theory recognizes that the literature to date has clearly identified the potential for several dozen different effects that people can experience from exposures to media violence. Furthermore, the theory highlights scores of factors that have been found useful in the process of influence.

W. James Potter

See also National Television Violence Study

Further Readings

National Television Violence Study. (1998). Thousand Oaks, CA: Sage.

Potter, W. J. (1999). *On media violence*. Thousand Oaks, CA: Sage.

Potter, W. J. (2009). *Arguing for a general framework for mass media scholarship*. Thousand Oaks, CA: Sage.

Potter, W. J. (2012). *Media effects*. Thousand Oaks, CA: Sage.

Longitudinal Research Findings on the Effects of Violent Content

Longitudinal studies of media violence effects are conceived as a way to overcome the limited causality of correlational studies without resorting to the artificial design of laboratory experiments that are lower in external validity. These studies search for various types of effects in the target audience—from the most passive (rising fear levels and changes in victimization likelihood assessment) to the most active (physical aggression). Common to all longitudinal studies is the assumption that the effect of media violence is not something that can be witnessed immediately in response to a single exposure to specific media content. A cumulative pattern of behaviors and opinions that supposedly gradually develop throughout months or even years and can be predicted by and attributed to routine contact with violent media is replacing the simplistic S-R model of laboratory experiments, according to which exposure to media violence directly and immediately brings about an associated violent reaction. Because of the routine nature of media consumption, longitudinal effects studies use exposure to popular repetitive content as their major independent variable and rarely refer to extremely violent material that is not part of the mainstream media.

Longitudinal studies can be classified by their design: epidemiological or panel. Panel studies can be further classified according to the medium on which they focus (television and films, video games and Internet gaming sites, cross-media). This classification distinguishes effects by their type (individual behavior in panel studies, crime rates in epidemiological studies) and helps media researchers in associating specific media with particular effects. This entry discusses these classifications as well as the general limitations of longitudinal studies.

Epidemiological Studies

Epidemiological studies conceive of the mass media (and particularly violent television programming) as an epidemic that contaminates society and leads to violence and crime. The speed with which this epidemic progresses is closely related to the speed with which the media become readily available to different sectors in society.

Epidemiological studies are macro-scale observations that look at total numbers. They do not follow behaviors or opinions of specific persons, but compare crime rates across a period of time and associate them with media penetration. A widely cited 1989 study by Brandon S. Centerwall compared homicide trends in the United States, Canada, and South Africa just before the introduction of television and a decade after it had been introduced. This research found a 90% increase in the annual incidence of homicides in some societal sects, but it ignored important factors that might have played a part in the rising levels of violence: changes in age distribution (with larger numbers of younger people, because of the baby boom, who are prone to violent behavior), urbanization (cities are more abundant with violent crime than rural districts), and the violent political struggle against apartheid (in South Africa). Even though the typical television programming (at least in the United States) has maintained a rather steady level of violence for decades, the rate of violent crime per capita has been declining steadily since the early 1990s. In this regard, a time series analysis of crime statistics conducted by Karen M. Hennigan and colleagues (1982) concluded that the introduction of television broadcasting to different parts of the United States between the late 1940s and mid-1950s was consistently associated with increases in larceny but not with changes in the level of violent crime, burglary, or auto theft, even though the latter were the most often seen crimes on the home screen in those years, as Dallas W. Smythe showed in 1954 in the first-ever published content analysis of TV violence.

Epidemiological studies were able to demonstrate a somewhat more robust (although not perfect) connection between media penetration and violence in small communities to which television broadcasting arrived late. This allowed comparing unwired townships with townships that were already wired. An observational study in 1986 by Tannis MacBeth Williams examined the level of aggression among children who lived in a remote Canadian village that had not received a television signal until the mid-1970s and compared it with the level of aggression of children who lived in wired villages. This study also measured the level of violence in the unwired village after it had been wired and detected significant differences, which suggests that the introduction of television broadcasting does lead to increase in violence. Still, a lengthy critique composed by Jonathan L. Freedman in 2002 contended that because before the advent of broadcasting violence level in the wired and nonwired villages was similar, the comparability of the villages and the validity of the findings remained in doubt.

More recent research in this category compared the violence level of schoolchildren in St. Helena—a small British colony located in the south Atlantic Ocean—before and after television broadcasting (and electronic media in general) became available to its denizens in the mid-1990s.

The researchers—Barrie Gunter, Tony Charlton, David Coles, and Charlie Panting (2000)—detected an increase in the level of violence of boys, but no considerable changes were found among the girls. Interestingly, the time devoted to television viewing (with the exception of cartoons) was not directly related to aggressive behavior.

The St. Helena study was probably the last of its kind, because in the first decade of the 21st century it is practically impossible to find communities with no access to violent media content of some kind. Like the other epidemiological studies, the St. Helena research offered evidence that television violence has some impact on macro-level measures, but the significant findings did not connote a perfect scheme of effects that can be logically attributed to the content.

Panel Studies

Panel studies follow people who are in a critical period of cognitive formation (mainly kindergarten, primary school, and junior high students) and examine their media exposure habits as well as their violent behavior (or proneness to violent conduct) over a significant period of time. The lags between measurements fluctuate considerably, from a couple of months to 22 years. Until the 21st century, researchers were mostly interested in measuring the long-term effects of television viewing, but with the coming of the Internet and the thriving of a gaming culture, a plethora of studies positing playing video games and browsing Internet gaming sites as the predicting variable have been published.

Regardless of medium, the main challenge in panel studies remains to establish a positive correlation between the level of exposure to violent media at T1 (first measurement) and the frequency of violent conduct (or lack of prosocial behavior) at T2 (second measurement). The existence of such a correlation is considered indirect proof of causality because the time order of model components is clear. As Freedman's critique from 2002 postulated, no significant correlation should exist between violence level at T1 and media exposure at T2, because the existence of such a relationship may suggest that violent people choose to consume violent media rather than become violent because of the media they have consumed.

Panel Studies Focused on Television

The longest panel study ever made surveyed young people from New York when they were 9 years old, when they were 19 years old, and when they were

31 years old. After the second measurement, in 1977, the researchers—Monroe Lefkowitz, Leonard Eron, Leopold Walder, and Rowell Huesmann—reported a positive correlation between the boys' preference for violent programming when the first measurement took place and their consequent violent behavior (indicated mainly by peer nomination). No similar effect was noted among the girls. A similar pattern was observed in the second-longest study (17 years), conducted in 2002 by Jeffrey G. Johnson and colleagues, and was explained by the fact that the programming watched by boys is more violent than the shows girls tend to watch.

The third phase of the New York study was expanded into a cross-cultural comparison that included children and adolescents from the United States, Australia, Finland, Israel, the Netherlands, and Poland in an attempt to establish the universality of long-term media violence effects. The researchers, Rowell Huesmann and Leonard Eron (1986), reported significant longitudinal effects in Poland and Israel (only among city children—not in a rural community). No effects were observed in the Netherlands, Finland, and Australia. In the United States, the effect this time was significant for girls but not for boys. In 1982 J. Ronald Milavsky and colleagues published another mass-scale U.S. study from the 1970s that found that among primary school children only a minority of the violent indicators were significantly related to television viewing habits 3 years earlier. The small number of significant findings in this study brought attacks on the authors, who had received funding from a major television network, and—according to Rowell Heusmann and Laramie Taylor (2003)—chose violence measures that rarely yield effects because of their brutality. In contrast, in 1975 Elizabeth D. McCarthy and colleagues found that longer viewing hours are significantly associated with higher scores on fighting and delinquency indices among junior high pupils five years later. McCarthy and colleagues also found a small (but significant) correlation between television viewing levels at T1 and lower grades at T2. This finding was replicated by Daniel R. Anderson and colleagues in 2001, but only for girls, and mainly when viewing action-adventure programming (the most violent genre in television drama) was entered into the equation instead of total viewing time. Similarly, in 1984 Jerome L. Singer, Dorothy G. Singer, and Wanda S. Rapaczynski reported a significant correlation

between watching action-adventure programming at T1 and acting violently at T2 (a year later), but no such relationship was noted for total viewing.

The pattern of effects in European studies is no less complex. A 1992 Dutch study by O. Wiegman and M. Kuttschreuter found that all the correlations between viewing violent programs in primary school and violent behavior and lack of prosocial behavior in high school vanish when the level of aggression at T1 is controlled for. In Finland, the time devoted to television viewing in childhood was found by Vappu Viermo (1996) to be negatively related to aggression among adolescent males but positively correlated with violence among adolescent females. In Germany, however, Barbara Krahé and Ingrid Möller (2010) found that habitual exposure to media violence in high school was negatively related to empathy and positively related to aggression one year later.

Panel Studies Focused on Video Games and Internet Gaming Sites

The increasing realism of violence in video games brought researchers in the first decade of the 21st century to investigate the long-term impact of gaming. In 2008 Anderson and colleagues reported an approximately 1% covariance between playing violent video games and manifesting aggression toward peers half a year later among Japanese teens. Another Japanese study from the same year by Akiko Shibuya and colleagues investigated younger students and yielded different scores for boys, who became more aggressive one year after playing video games in which violence was justified, and girls, who strengthened their antiviolence positions. Further inconsistency came from a 2009 German study by Möller and Krahé that found significant positive correlations between playing violent games using the console or the Internet and scoring higher on some violence measures, but it also pointed at small negative correlations or no relationship at all with other indicators of aggression. In contrast, in Canada, T. Willoughby, P. J. Adachi, and M. Good (2012) found that playing violent video games in early adolescence does predict higher levels of aggression four years later, whereas playing nonviolent video games does not predict any change at the level of aggression. This finding supports the hypothesis that video games socialize gamers to internalize violent solutions to problems.

Cross-Media Longitudinal Studies

Cross-media longitudinal studies (all of them conducted in the United States) included a plethora of media conduits among the independent variables, often combining exposure to new media (video games, Internet gaming sites) and to traditional mass media (television shows, theatrical films, rental DVDs) into an overall media consumption measure.

In 2006 Jamie M. Ostrov, Douglas A. Gentile, and Nicki R. Crick correlated parental reports concerning preschoolers' media contact with data regarding the toddlers' aggression provided by their school. Measurements were taken every eight months for two years. The results pointed at a moderate ($r = .3$) correlation between exposure to violent content of any medium and relational and verbal aggression (among girls) and physical aggression (among boys). Christopher J. Ferguson (2011) criticized this research for not paying enough attention to control variables and for using measures that are not rigid enough. When he repeated the study, employing a large set of potentially moderating variables (family-related factors, peers violence, neighborhood delinquency) and using official legal definitions of violent delinquent behavior as a dependent variable, no significant correlations between playing video games or watching violent programs on television at T1 and violence at T2 were noted. A 2011 cross-media longitudinal study by Douglas A. Gentile, Sarah Coyne, and David Walsh examined 10-year-olds for their media preference habits, self-reports of aggression, teachers' reports of the students' aggression, and peer nomination of aggressive and prosocial students. After controlling for parental involvement in media consumption, preference for violent media at T1 remained modestly ($r = .3$) and positively related to physical aggression at T2 (five months later), weakly ($r = .1$ to $r = .2$) and positively associated with relational aggression and verbal aggression, and modestly ($r = .25$) but negatively related to prosocial behavior.

Appreciation of Panel Studies

The capability of panel studies to retain respondents for many years is commendable, although an attrition of nearly half of the subjects in the longer studies, such as Heusmann and Eron's aforementioned 22-year lag panel research, is raising problems. Also problematic is the inconsistency of the scores across gender or differences between countries. It is true that positive correlations between media consumption at T1 and aggressive tendencies at T2 outnumber positive correlations between aggressive tendencies at T1 and media consumption at T2, but it is also true that—compared with media consumption—aggressive tendencies at T1 are a much stronger predictor of aggressive tendencies at T2, as Lefkowitz and colleagues have demonstrated. This means that even if television viewing in childhood is responsible for some of the violent behavior of adults, initial proneness to violence (along with external factors such as genetics, parenting style, educational background, and economic condition) probably has a larger role in nurturing violence, as Ferguson (2010) suggests in his critique.

Limitations

Longitudinal studies constitute an edifice of knowledge that attributes some influence on the violent behavior and fears of some people (mainly children) who are exposed to popular violent content in the media for a long period of time. Although the effects are quite frequently robust enough to pass the significance threshold, most of them remain in the small effects territory ($r = .1$ to $r = .2$). Such correlations are not in line with Centerwall's provocative statement that television violence is the reason for no fewer than 10,000 homicide cases that occurred in the United States between the early 1950s and the late 1980s.

The most consistent findings come from early studies and from research that was conducted in small communities soon after their residents had been exposed to modern media. Perhaps the expectation to find larger longitudinal effects in Western societies that have been for years accustomed to the media is naïve, especially when longitudinal research lacks an undisputed cognitive mechanism that could explicate the effects. According to Ferguson (2010), genetics, family history, peer pressure, and other sociopersonal and educational factors are more influential on aggressive behavior than is watching mainstream television programming or playing typical video games. However, some longitudinal effects can be observed despite numerous moderating and intervening factors, which should not be taken lightly.

Amir Hetsroni

See also Effect Size in Media Violence, Research and Effects of; Effects From Violent Media, Short- and Long-Term; Gender, Effects of Violent Content on; Violence in Media, Effects on Aggression and Violent Crime

Further Readings

Anderson, D. R., Huston, A. C., Schmitt, K. L., Linebarger, D. L., Wright, J. C., & Larson, R. (2001). Early childhood television viewing and adolescent behavior: The recontact study. *Monographs of the Society for Research in Child Development, 66*(1), (2001), 1–154.

Anderson, C., Sakamoto, A., Gentile, D. A., Ihori, N., Shibuya, A., Yukawa, S., Naito, M., et al. (2008). Longitudinal effects of violent video games on aggression in Japan and the United States. *Pediatrics, 122*(5), 1067–1072.

Centerwall, B. S. (1989). Exposure to television as a risk factor for violence. *American Journal of Epidemiology, 129,* 643–652.

Ferguson, C. J. (2010). Media violence effects and violent crime: Good science or moral panic? In C. J. Ferguson (Ed.), *Violent crime: Clinical and social implications* (pp. 37–56). Thousand Oaks, CA: Sage.

Ferguson, C. J. (2011). Video games and youth violence: A prospective analysis in adolescents. *Journal of Youth and Adolescence, 40*(4), 377–391.

Freedman, J. (2002). *Media violence and its effect on aggression: Assessing the scientific evidence.* Toronto: University of Toronto Press.

Gentile, D. A., Coyne, S., & Walsh, D. A. (2011). Media violence, physical aggression, and relational aggression in school-age children: A short-term longitudinal study. *Aggressive Behavior, 37*(2), 193–206.

Gunter, B., Charlton, T., Coles, D., & Panting, C. (2000). The impact of television on children's antisocial behavior in a novice television community. *Child Study Journal, 30*(2), 65–90.

Hennigan, K. M., Del-Rosario, M. L., Heath, L., Cook, T. D., Wharton, J. D., & Calder, B. J. (1982). Impact of the introduction of television on crime in the United States: Empirical findings and theoretical implications. *Journal of Personality and Social Psychology, 42,* 461–477.

Heusmann, L., & Eron, L. (1986). *Television and the aggressive child: A cross-national comparison.* Hillsdale, NJ: Erlbaum.

Heusmann, L., & Taylor, L. (2003). The case against the case against media violence. In D. A. Gentile (Ed.), *Media violence and children: A complete guide for parents and professionals* (pp. 107–130). New York, NY: Praeger.

Johnson, J. G., Cohen, P., Smailes, E. M., Kasen, S., & Brook, J. S. (2002). Television viewing and aggressive behavior during adolescence and adulthood. *Science, 295,* 2468–2471.

Krahé, B., & Möller, I. (2010). Longitudinal effects of media violence on aggression and empathy among German adolescents. *Journal of Applied Developmental Psychology, 31*(5), 401–409.

Lefkowitz, M., Eron, L., Walder, L., & Huesmann, L. (1977). *Growing up to be violent: A longitudinal study of the development of aggression.* Oxford, UK: Pergamon.

McCarthy, E. D., Langner, T. S., Gersten, J. C., Eisenberg, J. G., & Orzeck, L. (1975). Violence and behavior disorders. *Journal of Communication, 25,* 71–85.

Milavsky, J. R., Stipp, H. H., Kessler, R., & Rubens, W. S. (1982). *Television and aggression: A panel study.* New York, NY: Academic Press.

Möller, I., & Krahé, B. (2009). Exposure to violent video games and aggression in German adolescents: A longitudinal analysis. *Aggressive Behavior, 35*(1), 75–89.

Ostrov, J. M., Gentile, D. A., & Crick, N. R. (2006). Media exposure, aggression and pro-social behavior during early childhood: A longitudinal study. *Social Development, 15*(4), 612–627.

Shibuya, A., Sakamoto, A., Ihori, N., & Yukawa, S. (2008). The effects of the presence and contexts of video game violence on children: A longitudinal study in Japan. *Simulation & Gaming, 39*(4), 528–539.

Singer, J. L., Singer, D. G., & Rapaczynski, W. S. (1984). Family patterns and television viewing as predictors of children's beliefs and aggression. *Journal of Communication, 34,* 73–89.

Smythe, D. W. (1954). Reality as presented by television. *Public Opinion Quarterly, 18,* 143–156.

Viermo, V. (1996). Factors in childhood that predict later criminal behavior. *Aggressive Behavior, 22,* 87–97.

Wiegman, O., & Kuttschreuter, M. (1992). A longitudinal study of the effects of television viewing on aggressive and prosocial behaviors. *British Journal of Social Psychology, 31,* 147–164.

Williams, T. M. (1986). *The impact of television: A natural experiment in three communities.* New York, NY: Academic Press.

Willoughby, T., Adachi, P. J., & Good, M. (2012). A longitudinal study of the association between violent video game play and aggression among adolescents. *Developmental Psychology, 48*(4), 1044–1057.

MARKETING OF VIOLENCE

Early research defined *media violence* as the act or threat of injuring or killing another person portrayed in the popular media. More recently, researchers have broadened the definition to include the depiction, act, or credible threat of physical force intended to harm. A large body of literature has pointed out the potential dangers of violent media and its influence on viewers, especially youth. Simply put, much of the research has indicated that there is a connection between viewing violent programs and displaying aggression in real life.

Violence is popular and frequently portrayed in media. Moreover, entertainment industries have commercialized violence to attract more customers. Movies, television, music, and video games contain stories including violence and killings. This is the paradox faced by society: people object to televised violence but at the same time are saturated with and often seek violent media content. This entry examines both the attraction to violent content and the marketing of violent content.

Attraction to Violent Media Content

Theories in psychology have long explored media violence and its effects on viewers. Theories of aggression suggest that watching violence can be enjoyable. According to this theory, people can experience power and cathartic discharge of instinctive aggression via vicarious violence. Other theoretical perspectives have suggested that people learn inhibitations through socialization. Thus, when people see violence, they feel empathy toward victims and avoid watching the pain.

Looking specifically at effects, media violence research has suggested that there are individual differences in preference for violent programs that are dependent on an individual's personality. Also, there are group differences at the demographic, societal, and cultural levels. For example, studies have found that low-income youth enjoy watching violent programs more than do middle-class youth. However, it is hard to measure how violence influences the popularity or the success of media content, in part because much media contain some degree of violence. Furthermore, program popularity is not determined solely by a program's violent content. Actors and actresses, genre, and marketing efforts, to name a few, also contribute to popularity.

After reviewing more than 1,000 studies, the American Medical Association concluded that watching media violence can increase children's aggressive attitudes, values, and behaviors. Specifically, children who are exposed to violent programs tend to see violence as a way of resolving conflicts. Consuming media violence also can desensitize youths and children to violence in real life and alter the perception of danger, of mistrust, and of fear in the world. Furthermore, when children experience media violence during their younger developmental years, they are more likely to engage in violent and aggressive behaviors at later periods of life.

Marketing Violence

Marketing violence to children can be traced to the early 1980s. In 1984 the Federal Communications

Commission rescinded commercial guidelines for children's television programs. After this deregulation, the selling of products linked to specific television programs was deemed permissible, opening a Pandora's box of marketing to children. In addition, the quantity of media violence has drastically increased. At the end of the 1990s, it was estimated that the average child sees 8,000 murders and 100,000 violent actions from television before junior high school. Furthermore, other media such as video games and the Internet have increased the amount of violence to which youths and children are exposed. In particular, approximately 80% of video games contain violence, and more than two-thirds of children have access to the Internet, which enables them to watch all types of violence.

The video game market expanded considerably over the past decade, and much of the commercial growth was among older youths and children. Producers of video games have used television, gaming magazines, and the Internet to advertise and promote new games. Moreover, the cross-platform content distribution has allowed video game producers to reach consumers multiple times. Because playing violent video games involves perpetrating violent acts, some researchers have suggested that video games are harmful to children. Researchers such as Matthew Eastin at The University of Texas at Austin believe that this active component increases the negative impact on young players compared with merely watching the violent acts. In the early 1990s, the video game industry responded to criticism about the potential harm of violent video games by creating the Entertainment Software Rating Board (ESRB). The ESRB was designed to guide parents in selecting appropriate video games for their children, thus protecting children from video game violence. The ESRB developed four unrestricted ratings and two restricted ratings: Early Childhood (eC), Everyone (E), Everyone 10+ (E10+), Teen (T), Mature 17+ (M), and Adults Only (Ao). Even though the rating system is voluntary, many video games carry ESRB ratings, and some retail stores do not sell unrated video games. Research has indicated that some violent M-rated games are often marketed to boys younger than 17 years. And T-rated games have expressly targeted children under age 13.

A report by the Federal Trade Commission showed that 90% of R-rated movies are advertised through online websites and more than one-third of the website users are under age 17, even though the R (Restricted) rating requires children under 17 years of age to be accompanied by a parent or adult guardian. Furthermore, underage admission to R-rated films is not uncommon, and youths between 13 and 16 years old have purchased R-rated DVDs. Higher-rated violent content tends to glamorize the violence, and youths may interpret the content as acceptable and exciting. Children and youths are particularly vulnerable to media violence because they do not have the capability of connecting the punishment shown later with the earlier violence shown. They also tend to focus on overt and vivid aspects of violent content such as weapons and blood rather than motivations and intentions beneath the surface of violence. This seeking of higher-rated content, regardless of medium, can be explained through the forbidden fruit hypothesis—the desire to have what you are told you cannot have. As such, parents may find marketing efforts difficult to balance with their regulation of media content.

Seungae Lee and Matthew S. Eastin

See also Advertising, Influence on Society; Advertising, Violent Content in; Advertising Laws Regarding Violent and Aggressive Content; Desensitization Effects on Society; Forbidden Fruit Hypothesis; General Aggression Model

Further Readings

Diener, E., & DeFour, D. (1978). Does television violence enhance program popularity? *Journal of Personality and Social Psychology, 36*(3), 333–341.

Huesmann, L. R., Dubow, E. F., & Yang, G. (2012). Why it is hard to believe that media violence causes aggression. In Karen E. Dill (Ed.), *The Oxford handbook of media psychology*. New York, NY: Oxford University Press.

Levin, D. E., & Carlsson-Paige, N. (2003). Marketing violence: The special toll on young children of color. *Journal of Negro Education, 72*(4), 427–437.

Pitofsky, R., Anthony, S. F., Thompson, M. W., Swindle, O., & Leary, T. B. (2000). *Marketing violent entertainment to children: A review of self-regulation and industry practices in the motion picture, music recording and electronic game industries*. Report of the Federal Trade Commission. Retrieved from http://www.ftc.gov/reports/violence/vioreport.pdf

MEDIA AS A REFLECTION OF SOCIETY

In his landmark mass communication theory reader, noted media theorist Denis McQuail (2010) wrote that the mass media can often be thought of as a metaphorical mirror, reflecting myriad events in social and physical worlds. Such a metaphor seems at odds with notions of agenda setting and media effects by suggesting that media hold up a faithful reflection of the current societal mores, norms, and social structures rather than causing them to be as they are portrayed. Indeed, McQuail's mirror as metaphor is not new; it was invoked during the 19th and 20th centuries to describe the way news and data about society were conveyed in newspapers—some of the earliest newspapers often used this metaphor in their publication mastheads—with references to newspapers such as the *Recorder, Chronicle, Observer, Sentinel,* and more bluntly *The* (Altoona, Pennsylvania) *Evening Mirror* (1876).

Yet such a metaphor assumes a normative approach to media production—that is, it tends to specify what newspapers (or rather, media in general) ought to do for society rather than what they do in practice. After all, a mirror's reflection becomes a bit strained and distorted depending on which way one tilts it and where one is standing. Such a metaphor might explain, for example, recent research that has suggested that perceptions of media bias are largely the result of one's ideological stance rather than objective content analyses. To this end, this entry discusses specifically the notion of the media as a mirror of the most violent urges of society, and how these are reflected (or not) in the mass media.

How Audiences (Historically) Affect Media

The media as mirror metaphor was particularly popular during the limited effects paradigm of mass communication research that spanned from the early 1940s (with Carl Hovland's research into the ineffectiveness of the U.S. Army's *Why We Fight* films in increasing soldiers' motivations to fight in war) to the early 1960s (with Joseph Klapper's 1960 treatise *Effects of Mass Communication* suggesting, among other things, that media portrayals tend to reinforce rather than shift widely held societal norms). To put it simply, the research approach assumed that mass media did not have an appreciable effect on viewers,

but rather media content was a reflection of mores and norms in society.

In this line of reasoning, the media can be examined as a reflective tool for portrayals of idealized societal values. Anecdotal examples of such reflections can be found in the analysis of both the Vietnam War coverage (which tended to focus increasingly on the human tragedy and toll of the war as public opinion became less supportive of the war effort) and civil rights coverage of the 1960s (which similarly shifted to coverage corruption and coercion of government as national sentiment became increasingly supportive of racial desegregation and equality). In both cases, we saw largely held public sentiments toward events (antiwar sentiment in the former, pro-equality sentiment in the latter) causing a shift in media coverage to appease those sentiments rather than coverage setting the agenda for public discussion. A more modern approach to this line of reasoning can be found in Ron Tamborini's (2011) model of moral intuitions in media entertainment (MIME) that discusses how media audiences' shared social mores can be used by content producers to craft similarly valenced messages in support of the same—following an assumption that audiences are more likely to select and enjoy content that speaks to their worldviews than against them (claims similar to those made by Klapper).

If one assumes that media present a distorted reflection of society, one comes to the notion that media cultivate certain ideas and beliefs about society. Yet it is not the media per se that are the inventors of frames of reference or images of social groups, nor of the collective history of a nation. Rather, mass media are charged with the task of putting these together into consistent and repetitive narratives that become sources of information for people about society and their places in it. This makes the society presented in mass media both a vehicle for social and cultural change and a vessel for cultural stagnation and homogenization.

Violent Content as Representative of Violent Culture

Stemming from a concern about the potential effects violent media were having on society at large, researchers began to record and quantify the frequency and types of violence in mass media.

One of the most relevant research programs on media violence and crime was launched in 1968 by

George Gerbner and colleagues at the Annenberg School of Communication at the University of Pennsylvania. Specifically concerned with societal effects of crime and violence, Gerbner's Cultural Indicators Project recorded the number of violent acts in programming as well as the demographics of perpetrators and victims. This research suggested that although there was (and perhaps still is) a lot of violence on television, it is not representative of real life in frequency or type. In general, their project demonstrated that violent crimes were far more common on television than in everyday life. As well, racial minorities were overrepresented as criminal offenders, and law enforcement and crime overall were also overrepresented than real-life instances. Finally, Gerbner demonstrated that, over time, heavy television viewers were far more likely to align their perceptions of reality with those representations on television—in this case, representations of a violent and criminal social world—than with statistics of violence and criminal behavior. This *cultivation effect* suggests that rather than the media reflecting society, heavy viewers of television may instead be reflecting images and attitudes presented in the mass media.

The 1990s saw one of the largest content analysis projects of this type when the National Television Violence Survey (NTVS) updated Gerbner's findings by content analyzing all U.S. television content from the time period 1994 to 1997. Researchers involved with the NTVS considered the frequency of violence as well as contextual factors of televised violence, namely, the justification for violence, the consequences of violence, how violence was depicted (considerations such as showing sanitized and bloodless acts compared with gory and blood-soaked ones), the repetition of violence, and the weapons involved. Notable findings included that most of the violent acts portrayed on television tended to be justified (the perpetrator was aggressing in a morally or legally sanctioned manner), realistic (the violent act was neither sanitized nor glorified), unpunished (the perpetrator was not arrested or sanctioned for the act), with minimal consequences for victims (victims were rarely shown experiencing pain or suffering), and committed by attractive protagonists (perpetrators were often socially and sexually desirable). Focusing again on frequency, an unexpected finding of the NTVS studies was that the raw number of violent acts on television increased substantially during the three years the study was conducted. Such data might suggest that for U.S. television audiences, violent entertainment in media is something produced

with regularity, perhaps because of a cultural attractiveness to violence as well as a desire for more crime (and associated justice) programming. Put together, as has been suggested by studies on moral foundations, this could suggest a culture placing high importance on justice restoration using extreme measures if necessary.

Other cultures have conducted similar research on crime and violence, such as research that examined the content of Israeli television programming and found an overrepresentation of violent property crime as well as the reporting of extraordinarily violent deaths as common to newspaper obituary sections. Such content, especially the content of obituaries, might be interpreted as reflective of a society that is facing a relatively high threat level because of the political instability of the Middle East—in particular, deaths due to terrorist activities such as bombings and rocket strikes in major population centers. Although the obituary content is perhaps a realistic representation of singular violent acts, its overrepresentation, combined with a heavy focus on entertainment fare with justified violence again suggests a culture placing a high importance on retribution.

New Media, New Representations

Thus far this entry has focused primarily on mass media messages such as those on television—or what Gerbner labeled "the great storyteller of our generation." Yet this notion of a great storyteller has been challenged in the face of a newer media landscape that provides many more options to the modern media consumer. As researchers move away from the one-to-many approach of message production to a more individualized one-to-one approach, the notion of media as a passive reflection of society becomes open to question.

New media advocate and scholar Clay Shirkey (2008) has argued that new message production systems such as those in social media platforms—Facebook, Twitter, and YouTube among the more popular—have ushered in a participatory media culture in which the users may shape the mediated information that they consume. A prominent example of such a participatory culture would be the Arab Spring uprisings of 2010, in which social media users (largely younger, well-educated technology users) were able to spread individualized and localized messages of dissent into more shared and nationalized movements. An abundance of anecdotal and scientific data has suggested that although many of the target regimes were successful in molding and shaping traditional media messages to support and advance a hegemonic message (often labeling the protests and protestors as radical movements by small and frivolous aspects of society), they were unable to control the messages produced and distributed through social media channels. Put another way, although state-controlled media systems had been notoriously successful in cultivating a cultural view supporting their base of power, newer media systems—controlled by the users themselves—allowed for countercultural messages to be crafted and disseminated by political dissidents to an audience far larger than the traditional coffee shop or subbasement.

On a smaller scale, studies of news sourcing from U.S. journalists have suggested that social media sites provide as much as 20% to 40% of the news leads for the daily working reporter. Major news sources such as CNN.com have introduced programs that allow viewers to write their own news stories (CNN's iReporter) in a way that borrows structurally from YouTube's user-generated entertainment content-sharing system. Regarding violent media content, there does not seem to be an abundance of crime and violent media on social media pages— at least from the user-generated content. Indeed, although content analysis of social media channels is scarce, anecdotal evidence suggests that users who share traditional media content seem largely to mirror the popular (and often violent) headlines and programs of the day; users who generate and share their own created content tend to focus far more on non sequitur comedic videos, Internet memes and jokes (such as the popular "I can haz cheeseburger" images), music videos; and other content largely categorized as personal expressive narrative bits— or what scholar Ananda Mitra (2010) has named *narbs*. In general, it might be argued that new media have provided the tools for a generation to shape its own media content rather than being shaped by a generation of media content—that is, crafting a mirror rather than looking into one.

Nicholas David Bowman and Allison Eden

See also Aggression and Culture; Censorship of Violent Content; Cultivating Content and the Social Representation of Violence; Cultivation Theory; Culture of Violence; Desensitization Effects on Society; Gender Stereotypes, Societal Influence on; Media Violence, Definitions and Context of; National Television Violence Study

Further Readings

Gerbner, G., & Gross, L. (1976). Living with television: The violence profile. *Journal of Communication, 26*(2), 172–194.

Hallin, D. (n.d.). *Vietnam on television*. Chicago: Museum of Broadcast Communications.

Howard, P. N., & Hussain, M. M. (2011). The role of digital media. *Journal of Democracy, 22*(3), 35–48.

Klapper, J. T. (1960). *Effects of mass communication*. New York, NY: Free Press.

McQuail, D. (2010). *Mass communication theory* (6th ed.). London: Sage.

Mitra, A. (2010). Creating a presence on social networks via narbs. *Global Media Journal, 9*(16), 1–18.

Shirkey, C. (2008). *Here comes everybody*. New York, NY: Penguin.

Tamborini, R. (2011). Moral intuition and media entertainment. *Journal of Media Psychology, 23*(1), 39–45.

MEDIA EDUCATION AND MEDIA LITERACY

Concern about the impact of media violence on youth has led to the identification of strategies to mitigate potential adverse effects. One of the most viable approaches has been media literacy. Media literacy results from an inquiry-based pedagogy for developing critical thinking skills to understand, analyze, and reflect on media messages, media audiences, media effects, and media industry practices. The goal of media literacy education is to empower individuals with the knowledge, skills, and competencies they need to think critically, communicate effectively, and participate fully in society. With advances in digital technologies enabling media consumers also to become content creators, media literacy is viewed as a prerequisite for the inquiry and self-expression necessary to navigate the ever-changing media and social environments safely and responsibly. This entry discusses the conceptual framework for media literacy, describes the nature of media literacy education and scholarship, and summarizes the effectiveness of media literacy interventions for media violence in the evolving participatory digital culture.

Conceptualizing Media Literacy

Media literacy is an expanded conceptualization of literacy brought about by the emergence of new technology. Just as people needed to be able to read and write to participate fully in society after the printing press was invented, people need to be able to comprehend and think critically about what they watch, hear, read, and create using different media forms that are essential for full involvement in a participatory digital society. Media literacy encompasses the integration of all forms of literacy: *print literacy*, the ability to read and write; *audiovisual literacy*, the ability to understand and use sounds and images; and *digital or information literacy*, the ability to search, find, evaluate, organize, and use information from a wide range of sources and media formats. *Media literacy* is most commonly defined as the ability to access, analyze, and evaluate the different aspects of media technology, messages, and audiences and create content using a variety of media forms. These abilities drive the conceptualization of media literacy and media literacy education.

Although scholars approach media literacy from different perspectives, most have emphasized a similar set of conceptual understandings that focus on the following core concepts. A media literate individual understands that media messages are constructed for particular purposes; each form of media uses a unique combination of techniques, or creative language with a specific set of rules, to construct messages that convey meaning using language, text, visual images, motion graphics, sound, music, and multimedia formats; media messages contain embedded values, points of view, and ideologies that selectively represent reality; people interpret messages and create their own meaning based on their individual skills, beliefs, and experiences; media messages are produced within economic, social, political, historical, and aesthetic contexts; and media messages can influence values, beliefs, attitudes, behaviors, and the democratic process.

Reconceptualizing Media Literacy in the Digital Age

As media screens and platforms merge and converge, spawning ever-increasing ways to communicate with one another, new technologies are yet again expanding the conceptual framework of literacy. New definitions interconnect media literacy with digital citizenship and information literacy and encompass multidimensional capabilities critical to communicating effectively with new media and contributing responsibly to a participatory culture. In the digital age, individuals need to understand the strengths

and limitations of the various media technologies, reflect on their choices and consequences as media consumers and creators, and act responsibly and ethically in the changing social, economic, political, and cultural environments. The reconceptualization repositions media literacy in a civic context in which citizens of all ages are well-informed, engaged, and responsible media consumers and creators who have the repertoire of social skills, cultural competencies, and communication tools essential for full involvement in the evolving participatory digital society.

Expanded definitions of media literacy emphasize the abilities to *access* or find, understand, and share appropriate and relevant information and ideas effectively using media technologies; *analyze* message content in terms of source, purpose, point of view, target audience, and potential effects and *evaluate* its quality, reliability, credibility, and accuracy; *create* content using multiple media formats and techniques appropriate for communicating with the intended audiences; *reflect* on the impact personal experiences and values have in consuming, creating, and sharing media messages responsibly and ethically and assess the potential effects of individual communication choices on oneself and others; and *act* or participate individually and collaboratively to share knowledge and solve problems using interactive media technologies with family and peers, at school and work, and in diverse communities from local to global levels.

Another aspect of digital and media literacy abilities is the notion of new media literacies. New media literacies are social skills and cultural competencies needed for full involvement in the participatory culture that build on abilities individuals bring to their interactions with new media and expand their cognitive capacities in meaningful ways. For example, new media literacies emphasize the capabilities to multitask digital media forms, engage in play to problem-solve, assume alternative identities for self-discovery, create stories across media platforms, appropriate cultural artifacts to produce new meanings, construct simulations to learn about real-world processes, collaborate with others toward common goals, and negotiate across diverse communities recognizing and respecting multiple perspectives.

The Nature of Media Literacy Education

Toward the end of the 20th century, the media literacy education movement began to establish itself worldwide. Although some countries have mandated curriculum-driven media literacy education, many continue to encounter obstacles in institutionalizing media literacy standards in schools. Media literacy instruction has been most commonly incorporated across K–12 curricula; however, it is not confined to traditional formal school settings. Media literacy and youth media production programs have been implemented in informal settings such as after-school programs, summer camps, youth clubs, community organizations, and faith-based groups. With the proliferation of new media technologies, digital and media literacy is gaining recognition as a 21st-century skill and gaining support in mainstream education. In addition, digital and media literacy instruction is finding its way into college and university courses, adult lifelong learning programs, parent education, and professional development trainings for teachers, health practitioners, and youth advocates.

Given media's ubiquitous presence in everyday life, media educators recommend that school-based instruction partner with parent education and community programs to provide comprehensive media literacy training. Active parental mediation has been found to influence children's learning from media and even reduce the impact of media violence on them. Because the home is where most children first use media and acquire their initial media skills, parents can help children make meaningful media choices, nurture critical thinking, and take advantage of teachable moments that provide opportunities for learning, reinforcing, and practicing media literacy skills, regardless of settings.

Teachable moments are unplanned circumstances that lend themselves to offering children insight into a certain issue or situation beyond their cognitive, emotional, and moral reasoning abilities. For example, parents watching television with their children may question a character's decision to use aggression to solve a problem, leading to a family discussion in which they share their own values and explore alternative ways to resolve conflict. Or a news report about a teen bullying incident captured on video that went viral may prompt parents to talk to their children about what might have provoked it, how the victim might feel, what they would do if they witnessed bullying, and the judgment involved in videotaping and disseminating it online. In media literacy education, teachable moments often can be more effective than a direct question and can bridge formal and informal learning.

Not only do the teaching and learning of media literacy reach beyond school settings, the study and practice of media literacy encompass diverse disciplines. Media literacy scholars and practitioners include those in media and cultural studies, communication, journalism, television, film, education, psychology, women's studies, public health, and library and information sciences. As the field of media literacy gains multidisciplinary momentum, there has been increasing interest in media literacy as a practical strategy for youth violence prevention, conflict resolution, health promotion, and other areas that affect young people's well-being. Media literacy strategies also have been applied to detect false advertising claims; analyze news bias; assess the trustworthiness of websites; counterbalance sexual objectification of women in media representations; discourage stereotyping by race, gender, and sexual identity; enhance positive body image to preempt eating disorders; decode food marketing techniques to promote healthy eating; deter alcohol, drug, and tobacco use among youth; facilitate participation in civic life; and promote digital citizenship.

The Effectiveness of Media Literacy Interventions for Media Violence

Although the efficacy of media literacy programs has not always been explicitly measured, there is an emerging body of evidence demonstrating media literacy to be an effective intervention for reducing media's influence on aggression and antisocial behaviors among children and adolescents. The term *intervention* refers to the media literacy lesson and the experimental treatment used to test which specific features of the lesson produce the most significant results. Generally, one group receives the treatment, and the results are compared with another group that received a variation of the treatment or to a control group that did not receive the treatment.

The majority of these studies have analyzed classroom-based curriculum interventions specially designed to provide media literacy skills to reduce the effects of viewing violent television among children and adolescents. Media literacy instruction has generally included a series of lessons and interactive activities about the nature of media storytelling and production techniques, media audiences and effects, and the role media play in young people's lives. The studies vary in rigor, pedagogical approach, and experimental design, including media literacy treatment, frequency and duration of intervention, session facilitator, and participant age and skill level. Thus, identifying which specific media literacy strategies are most effective, for which children and under which circumstances, is difficult. Nonetheless, some factors have emerged as ones that can be effective in lessening the impact of media violence.

The specific outcomes depend on the objectives of the media literacy intervention. The most common goals have focused on reducing the amount of exposure to violence and lessening susceptibility to the effects of violent content. Media literacy interventions typically have targeted high-risk factors identified by media effects studies that affect aggressive and antisocial thoughts, attitudes, and behaviors. These factors include violence that is committed by attractive characters—particularly "good guys" or superheroes—for justified reasons and that goes unpunished, shows minimal pain or harm to the victims, and seems realistic to the viewer. For younger audiences, these portrayals of violence pose a more serious risk of harm because children under age 7 years have difficulty distinguishing reality from fantasy, and the portrayals may motivate them to mimic the aggressive behavior.

Although some scholars contend that reducing exposure to media violence is not a media literacy strategy in and of itself, others have maintained that learning to self-regulate media behavior and make informed choices is a media literacy skill that can lessen media's influence on aggressive tendencies. There has been evidence that decreasing children's media exposure, even without targeting violent content, can significantly decrease their antisocial behavior. Several methods have been used to help children manage their media time and be more selective in their media habits. Children have been encouraged to monitor and limit the overall time they spend watching violent programming or playing violent video games, restrict access to certain violent content, or participate in a media turnoff activity in which they disconnect from technology for a set period of time.

Given the prevalence of violence in media content and conclusive evidence about its effects, reducing exposure to violence can be an important factor. However, changing children's media habits in order to filter violent content, either by reducing overall media time or restricting exposure to media violence, is virtually impossible because of the pervasiveness of violence in entertainment, news, and advertising across media screens. Moreover, spending as much time as children do in the media world, their vicarious media experiences can supersede their firsthand personal experiences. This is especially true for

children who watch similar types of violence repeatedly and imitate it in their play behavior. Consuming one candy bar is not likely to have harmful health effects, but eating junk food over several years poses a significant risk of obesity and other health problems. In the same way, watching one act of media violence is usually negligible, but watching thousands of violent actions over years of viewing poses a significant risk of harmful effects.

Factual Knowledge Versus Critical Analysis

Media literacy interventions to reduce children's susceptibility to viewing violence have yielded promising results. The most common approaches involve imparting factual information about media and media production, critically evaluating media storytelling, and providing hands-on experience with the production process. Although certain strategies have been found to be more effective than others, most have indicated the need to integrate media literacy throughout K–16 education. One of the challenges for researchers and educators is identifying which approaches and specific intervention features are most beneficial to developing media literacy skills at different ages and stages of development.

Taken together, media literacy lessons that emphasize critical analysis of media content, encourage emotional involvement with the characters, and require students to actively process what they learned have been more effective than providing only facts about media and media production techniques in lessening the effects of media violence. For example, students tended to be more critical of violence, perceive it as unrealistic and unjustified, and express less involvement with aggressive characters when they were encouraged to challenge inaccurate beliefs about the realism and use of violence, or evaluate perpetrators as being uncool and unpopular, or consider the victim's feelings before viewing a violent program, or think about children like themselves who might experience harmful effects from viewing violence. However, learning that characters are actors, the fighting is faked, and camera angles and special effects make the action look real tend to increase children's knowledge about media's technical aspects but not reduce their susceptibility to violent content. Of particular note is a media literacy intervention that moderated the influence of media violence on at-risk youth in the juvenile justice system and helped them develop responsible decision-making skills to resist impulses that can result in violence, substance abuse, or prejudice, particularly when they discussed what they learned with their peers.

Under certain conditions, the intended media literacy lesson can backfire and actually increase susceptibility to aggressive tendencies. Known as a *boomerang effect,* this unintended outcome has been attributed to the specific mediation strategy. Lessons that focus on facts without critically analyzing or actively processing what is learned can result in children being more willing to use aggression. Researchers underscore the importance of testing a media literacy violence curriculum before instituting it as a lesson plan to avoid potential boomerang effects.

Media Violence and the Role of Media Literacy in the Digital Age

When the media literacy movement emerged, media audiences were largely media consumers, television was the dominant medium in children's lives, and media violence was one of the main concerns. Media audiences are no longer only media consumers because technological innovations enable them to create as well as consume content. Television still has a major presence and media violence continues to be a primary concern, but now television competes with new media that have inadvertently morphed mediated violence into new social and ethical concerns specific to the participatory culture. The result is a growing list of problematic behaviors, such as cyberbullying and other forms of online harassment, that make youths vulnerable to electronic aggression perpetuated through digital technologies as well as an ongoing debate about the role of media literacy education. At the heart of the debate is whether media literacy education should emphasize protection versus empowerment.

Some scholars have stressed media literacy skill building to protect individuals from potentially harmful effects of engaging in a media activity for enjoyment, while others have focused on media literacy strategies to empower individuals to evaluate media content critically for themselves. Still others have strived to achieve a balance between protecting and empowering individuals. They have acknowledged that the research evidence and public concern about the impact of media violence and electronic aggression on youth make the issue inherently about protection and counteracting harmful effects. At the same time, these researchers want to help youths become critical thinkers who can communicate effectively, responsibly, and respectfully in the participatory digital culture.

As researchers have documented the ways in which youths inhabit the new media world, policy makers, public health experts, and Internet safety proponents have called for media literacy education that simultaneously empowers and protects individuals as they actively participate in digital communities. The goal is to provide the essential knowledge, skills, competencies, and lifelong learning opportunities to maximize the benefits and minimize the risks of living in a digital society.

Bobbie Eisenstock

See also Cyberbullying, Definition and Effects of; Interactive Media, Aggression Outcomes of; Media Effects Perspectives of Violence; Pediatricians and Media Violence; Social Learning From Media

Further Readings

American Academy of Pediatrics. (2010). Media education. *Pediatrics, 126*(5), 1012–1017.

Aspen Institute Communication and Society Program. (2010). *Digital and media literacy: A plan of action.* Washington, DC: Author.

Byrne, S. (2009). Medial literacy interventions: What makes them boom or boomerang? *Communication Education, 58*(1), 1–14.

Cantor, J., & Wilson, B. (2003). Media and violence: Intervention strategies for reducing aggression. *Media Psychology, 5,* 363–403.

Collier, A., & Nigam, H. (2010). *Youth safety on a living Internet: Report of the Online Safety and Technology Working Group.* Retrieved from http://www.ntia.doc.gov/legacy/reports/2010/OSTWG_Final_Report_060410.pdf

Jenkins, H. (2006). *Confronting the challenges of participatory culture: Media education for the 21st century.* Chicago: MacArthur Foundation.

Jeong, S., Cho, H., & Hwang, Y. (2012). Media literacy interventions: A meta-analytic review. *Journal of Communication, 62*(3), 454–472.

Moore, J., Dechillo, N., Nicholson, B., Genovese, A., & Sladen, S. (2000). Flashpoint: An innovative media literacy intervention for high-risk adolescents. *Juvenile and Family Court Journal, 51*(2), 23–34.

National Association for Media Literacy Education. (2007). *Core principles of media literacy education in the United States.* Retrieved from http://www.namle.net/wp-content/uploads/2009/09/NAMLE-CPMLE-w-questions2.pdf

Wilson, C., Grizzle, A., Tuazon, R., Akyempong, A., & Cheung, C. (2011). *Media and information literacy: Curriculum for teachers*. Paris: UNESCO.

Worthen, M. (2007). Education policy implications from the expert panel on electronic media and youth violence. *Journal of Adolescent Health, 41*(6), S61–S63.

MEDIA EFFECTS PERSPECTIVES OF VIOLENCE

There can be no doubt that violence, in the form of realistic (as opposed to theatrical, comic, or cartoonish) portrayals of intentional physical harm to another, is readily available in the mass media. By the age of 18 years, a typical child will have been exposed to 40,000 acts of murder and more than 100,000 other acts of violence on television or in the movies. The existence of this media violence has generated a great deal of research, much of which has focused on questions of media effects—primarily whether watching violence in the media somehow leads to increased violence in society, perhaps by influencing the minds of viewers through modeling or habituation. The results of more than 100 laboratory experiments have effectively demonstrated that violent media can, indeed, have a causal influence on the likelihood of aggressive behavior (Anderson & Bushman, 2002).

But the ready availability of media violence raises other important questions beyond its effects. Viewers are not generally forced to watch violence; they view it as a *choice*. Despite the presence of violence in the media, there are other nonviolent options available that are in fact more popular. Even though a large part of the viewing audience has no interest in or may even be repelled by media violence, the focus of this entry is on the many persons who have consistently enjoyed graphic and gruesome violent images and stories and have been doing so for much of human history. Little research has addressed the question of why some viewers make that choice, why horrific violent images are such a popular element in human art and literature. In order to fully understand the effects of media violence, it is necessary to put that violence into a context that takes account of the forces and factors that motivate viewers to watch it. What is the attraction? Why do large sections of the public seek out and find pleasure in watching violence in the mass media of television, film, video, and computer games? Although there is much that is not yet understood, this entry offers a brief overview of psychological theory and research that attempts to provide some insight into the appeal of media violence.

The Emotional Appeal of Violent Images

At the most basic level, bloody and brutal fictional depictions of violence may be inherently appealing. Whether we're talking about rubbernecking at the scene of an accident or being captured by the iconic images of Hannibal Lecter or Freddy Krueger, some people seem to find simple (although perverse) pleasure, even thrill, in the depiction of cruelty and horror, especially when presented in the safe, imaginary playground of art. To some extent, this can be understood in terms of the depth and power of the *emotional experience* these scenes produce. There is a vast array of feelings, both negative and positive, that are elicited by these images: excitement, disgust, fascination, horror, tension and release, joy, dread, and many more. Perhaps the very variety of individual responses is itself a source of appeal. But beyond that, there are a number of questions that need to be addressed. Violence often involves images of humans in great pain. Usually, those images elicit concern, empathy, pity, sorrow in viewers. What then explains how those same images produce positive emotions in some of us? And how is it that when people experience negative and discomforting emotions, such as anxiety and fear, in the presence of violent images, they continue to be drawn to them? Several psychological approaches may help make sense of these conundrums.

It must first be acknowledged that fiction and reality are different, and most viewers know it. What is unacceptable in reality, when others are truly hurting, may be a source of fascination or delight in fiction, when there is a suspension of disbelief and the perceived hurt is not subject to the same moral restrictions and human empathy that operate in the real world. Echoing Friedrich Nietzsche, Dolf Zillmann (1998) has suggested that the simple opportunity to overcome the social taboos that accompany the open expression of otherwise unsanctioned or inappropriate emotions may, in some ways, be liberating. Being unable or unwilling to violate social norms in real life, there may be enjoyment in seeing those norms violated by others. For example, *schadenfreude*—experiencing pleasure from another's pain—is not an especially noble human tendency, but when it occurs in response to an imaginary or fictional character on screen, there is an emotional distance that prevents that feeling from becoming too disturbing.

Part of the intrinsic appeal of violent images may also be related to our evolutionary heritage. Violence and aggression may have evolved as an adaptation to basic survival challenges, such as competing for resources, defending against attacks, gaining status, and attaining access to sexual resources. Given greater intrasexual competition among males than among females for access to sexual resources, there is also evolutionary logic for the common finding that males are more physically aggressive than females and that males are more excited than females by the prospect of physical combat. That males are also more interested in viewing violent media (e.g., Goldstein, 1998) has suggested that the appeal of such images may bear some connection to evolutionary processes. To the extent that depictions of aggressive or violent acts offer valued and adaptive information, the stimulus features of media aggression may be inherently attractive.

The Sensory Appeal of Violent Images

The sensory appeal of some destructive media images may be enjoyed for its own sake, completely apart from the story that is being told (Sparks & Sparks, 2002). Some people may genuinely delight in the sensory experience of watching even horrendous, albeit fictional or imaginary, human disaster. As suggested by a number of psychological theories, violent imagery, because of its intense sensory nature, its complexity, and its real-world novelty, may increase levels of sensory stimulation or arousal, which can be a very rewarding experience, especially in a safe, familiar environment. The sensory appeal of some violent mayhem may also be a function of its aftereffects. That is, some viewers may eventually come to seek out the anxiety and even terror associated with terrifying images because, with repeated exposure, the initial fear of the viewing experience tends to give rise to great pleasure.

Violent Images in Narrative Context

In addition to elements of violent scenes that are intrinsically appealing, it is important also to recognize contextual elements that lead people to enjoy violence. Perhaps the most critical contextual factor contributing to its appeal is not what violence *is*, but rather what violence *does*. Most media violence occurs in the context of a compelling narrative involving transgression and retribution, the victory of good over evil, and the triumph of protagonists over antagonists. Just as in real-life experiences of treachery and revenge or betrayal and reversal of fortune, similar media narratives allow the viewer to effectively identify with the characters and make moral judgments, cognitively and emotionally, about the "perfect bastards" and the "suffering heroes." When those judgments are consistent with the viewer's inherent sense of justice, when "sweet" revenge is achieved, the viewer's worldview is confirmed in a very powerful and rewarding way. So it may not necessarily be the violence itself that is the principal attraction for most people, but rather the instrumental value of violence in achieving a fair and satisfying moral goal.

This narrative structure is so well established that even before the final resolution is achieved, there is usually strong anticipation of the characters' fate. Although the "bad guy" may momentarily have the upper hand, the viewer can anticipate that he'll get what he deserves, producing a kind of "forepleasure" in the innocent victim's suffering. The popularity of films like *Dirty Harry* and *Die Hard* clearly suggest that many people find violence to be an acceptable way to tell stories, particularly when that violence is used in the pursuit of justice.

Viewer Characteristics

Another approach to the appeal of violence has focused not on the nature or context of the violent images but on certain preexisting aspects of the viewer. That is, the way one thinks or behaves may influence what one chooses to watch. More specifically, prior aggressive behavior may predispose persons to seek out media violence. Allan Fenigstein (1979) put that causal relationship to the experimental test. Research participants were either primed to have aggressive thoughts (Study 1) or were induced to behave in an aggressive way toward another participant (Study 2). Compared with the appropriate control groups, those in the manipulated aggression conditions showed a greater interest in viewing violent media. That is, those who engaged in aggressive behavior were more likely to want to see media images of others behaving aggressively. Related to this finding, other studies have found that those who are high in personality measures of aggressiveness also choose to view more aggressive programming and enjoy it more. Research has also shown that even those who are simply preoccupied with violence, because it is such a significant part of their world, were more likely than those from a safer environment to expose themselves to violence in the media.

The increased interest in watching violence as a function of the existence of aggression in one's past or present life may be attributed, in part, to a desire to view images that are, in some way, related to oneself. As suggested by the aphorism "Imitation is the sincerest form of flattery," witnessing behavior like one's own may offer important psychological rewards. Not only does it affirm and justify one's behavior (and identity) through social comparison and perceived consensus, it may also offer insight and understanding into one's own aggressive actions that may sometimes be accompanied by confusion or uncertainty.

These findings suggest that the well-established correlational relationship between media violence and aggression is a function of reciprocal causal links: media violence increases aggression, but at the same time, aggression increases media violence, in the sense that it increases the interest in viewing it. This bidirectional model of influence suggests the possibility of a vicious cycle in which aggressive thoughts or actions lead to the viewing of violence, which then leads to further acts of aggression, and so on, an idea that has been supported by research. In summary, the relationship between fiction, in the form of media violence, and the consciousness (and unconsciousness) of those exposed to it is so complex that it is impossible to isolate one from the other in terms of cause and effect. Media violence appeals to and reflects the behaviors, values, and beliefs that exist in some parts of society; and it also offers a powerful mechanism for the transmission of ideas and actions, both old and new.

Allan Fenigstein

See also Aggression, Risk Factors of; Arousal and Aggressive Content, Theory and Psychology of; Effects From Violent Media, Short- and Long-Term; Excitation-Transfer Theory; General Aggression Model; Media Rating Systems; Media Violence, Definitions and Context of; Methodologies for Assessing Effects of Media; National Television Violence Study; Television Violence

Further Readings

Anderson, C. A., & Bushman, B. J. (2002). Media violence and societal violence. *Science, 295*, 2377–2378.

Fenigstein, A. (1979). Does aggression cause a preference for viewing media violence? *Journal of Personality and Social Psychology, 37*, 2307–2317.

Goldstein, J. (1998). Why we watch? In J. Goldstein (Ed.), *Why we watch: The attraction of violent entertainment* (pp. 212–226). New York, NY: Oxford University Press.

Sparks, G. C., and Sparks, C. W. (2002). Exploring the attractions of violent entertainment. In J. D. Torr (Ed.), *Violence in film and television* (pp. 114–126). San Diego, CA: Greenhaven Press.

Zillmann, D. (1998). The psychology of the appeal of portrayals of violence. In J. Goldstein (Ed.), *Why we watch: The attraction of violent entertainment* (pp. 212–226). New York, NY: Oxford University Press.

MEDIA RATING SYSTEMS

Media rating systems serve several goals. First, they inform children and caregivers about the potential harmfulness of audiovisual products for children below certain ages. Second, they help the entertainment industry comply with legal requirements protecting children from harmful media exposure. Third, they put into practice the notion of harmful media content, thus enabling authorities to determine whether the entertainment industry complies with such requirements. In addition to offering an overview of the organization and implementation of media rating systems worldwide and the factors that ensure a valid rating system, this entry discusses three factors that are relevant regarding the effectiveness of media ratings: (1) the acceptance of media ratings by the public, (2) the compliance and support by the (entertainment) industry, and (3) the potential that the ratings will make risky commodities more appealing to young viewers, a phenomenon known as the *forbidden fruit effect*.

Media ratings are a vital element of any system aimed at restricting children's access to harmful media content. However, several factors may diminish their effectiveness in practice. Whereas governments and health care organizations are concerned about the risks associated with exposure to harmful media content, the entertainment industry is for-profit, and the public may prefer easy access to media content. Whether media ratings are an effective means to restrict underage access depends on both the relevant legislation and the extent to which all relevant parties comply with and support the ratings.

Organization and Implementation of Media Ratings

To protect children and adolescents and to inform caregivers about violent or otherwise harmful media content, media ratings have been introduced in many countries. Media ratings serve as a tool for restricting access and exposure to harmful media. Consisting of age pictograms or cautionary advice (also known as *evaluative ratings*) and/or content-warning pictograms (*descriptive ratings*), media ratings can be placed on covers, posters, packaging materials, and other advertising materials and can also be shown at the start of a television program or movie. Like traditional advertising and packaging material, the ratings provide cues and information to help parents and caregivers make informed decisions regarding the media consumption of their children.

Media ratings are used worldwide, and many countries have introduced their own rating systems with their own ratings and regulations. In most countries, media rating systems are based on complex regulatory systems that include combinations of public and private regulation at various regulatory levels (including international, regional, and national legislation, self- or co-regulation, funding, and distribution of information) (Dorbeck-Jung, Oude Vrielink, Gosselt, Van Hoof, & De Jong, 2010). In the case of governmental legislation, a law is promulgated or enacted by a legislative or governing body and the government is responsible for maintaining the law and punishing violators. Self-regulation involves the regulations established within an industry. Here, the industry's own interest is prominent, but the goals of the regulation extend beyond making a profit. When the government is explicitly involved in self-regulation activities, this is called *co-regulation,* and it means that the industry and the government cooperate to formulate the conditions of regulation.

The existence of so many complex regulatory systems and the fact that most countries have their own rating system leads to differences regarding the functions of the ratings (see Table 1), accompanied by differences on an operational level (e.g., the compulsoriness of the classifications and the

position and size of the ratings on audiovisual products, resulting in different degrees of emphasis). In television, there are differences regarding the restrictions on broadcasting time, the number and types of television networks involved (government-owned television networks versus their commercial counterparts), the moment the rating is shown (during the entire program or a limited number of times), and the appearance of the ratings (mostly ratings are shown as a number in a small box in a particular color, lettering [e.g., PG, meaning Parental Guidance Suggested in the United States], or by means of a verbal announcement beforehand).

Most countries have their own systems of coding media products (with differences regarding codes, coders, and coding process), which may result in very different ratings per country. A transparent and uniform coding procedure is essential to ensure a valid rating system. Other relevant principles for a valid system include a high level of penetration and coverage and a clear complaint procedure. *Penetration* refers to the number of producers, distributors, and television broadcasting stations that join the (often voluntary) systems, and *coverage* refers to the total number of ratings placed on audiovisual products. Finally, a complaint procedure should be accessible such that only a relatively small effort to issue a complaint is necessary when rules are not followed. Furthermore, the procedure should be made public in a clear way, and the handling of a complaint should not take too long. If a complaint is valid, sanctions should be imposed.

Acceptance by the Public

Caregivers are the gatekeepers of the media products that children are able to consume. To facilitate this process, media ratings are essential tools, providing clear information about the media products. Therefore, in many countries, caregivers are the main target group of media ratings. Studies on the acceptance and preferences of caregivers have generally

Table I Function of Media Ratings per Regulatory Level

	Legislation	*Co-regulation*	*Self-regulation*
Informing caregivers and children	x	x	x
Helping industry comply with the law	(x)	x	x
Helping authorities enforce the law	x	x	(x)

x = main function, (x) = additional function

shown that they want ratings describing the content of a television program, motion picture, or game rather than general information about the appropriateness or harmfulness of the content. This preference may stem from caregivers having different ideas about the degree of harm produced, accompanied by their strong belief that they know their children better than anyone. Additionally, caregivers expect different effects regarding boys and girls and different effects based on the age of the child. Caregivers want to decide for themselves what is best for their child but need information to make informed decisions. Descriptive ratings are therefore favored more than evaluative ratings. In general, media ratings are valued by caregivers, who use them as guidelines that inform and assist them in identifying the applicability of media products for their children. Moreover, most caregivers indicate that they believe that media ratings are useful and necessary even though differences exist in usage regarding the various media (with higher usage for motion pictures followed by television programs, video and computer games, and music products). Last, because the ratings systems differ greatly by country, how the ratings are interpreted may differ.

Compliance and Support by the Industry

Whether minors are actually protected from harmful media content depends not only on the organization and implementation of the ratings and the acceptance by the caregivers but also on the extent to which the industry complies with these age restrictions. In the case of media ratings, the industry includes stores selling media products such as DVDs and games; movie theaters; and broadcasting stations airing television programs. To enhance acceptance within the entertainment industry, relevant factors include sufficient overlap of private interests with public interests (e.g., reputational considerations and forestalling legislation), the existence of specific pressures to comply with rules (e.g., internal and external surveillance activities), a small number of actors in a highly organized and homogeneous sector, and a high degree of social responsibility within the industry with a general concern for taking the rules seriously (Dorbeck-Jung et al., 2010).

In a recent large-scale compliance study, the level of compliance by the (Dutch) entertainment industry with the age restrictions imposed by media ratings was examined (Gosselt, Van Hoof, & De Jong, 2012). In that study, adolescents attempted to buy media products for which they were too young according to the classification in department stores, toy stores, CD/DVD stores, game shops, DVD rental companies, libraries, and movie theaters. In spite of self-reported compliance and an overall positive attitude from the vendors toward the classification systems, the rates of compliance were poor. Second, to examine the compliance with the age classifications by television broadcasting companies—relating to coverage (the extent to which ratings are assigned to programs), broadcasting time (programs that are classified for older age groups mostly are not allowed to be broadcast before a certain time slot), and size of the pictogram and screening time—a content analysis showed that compliance was also rather poor. This finding showed that introducing media ratings alone is not enough. Despite their implementation, it is easy for minors to access harmful media content.

Recent survey data gathered among vendors have indicated that three factors are important for vendors in their decision whether to comply with the media rating systems: their personal acceptance of the systems (Do they intrinsically feel minors should be protected and do they think the current rating system is the most appropriate one to use?), their perceptions of the legal basis for the ratings (Is there a legal basis for the ratings?), and the perceived degree of surveillance (What happens when one does not comply?) (Gosselt et al., 2012). Without sufficient knowledge of the rules, parties cannot act according to the rules. Additionally, vendors must be capable of following the rules, which means that practical barriers that could decrease compliance (e.g., aggressive behavior on the part of consumers) should be reduced. Last, the willingness to comply depends on two factors: the attitudes toward the regulations (intrinsic motivation) and their estimations of the consequences of violations (extrinsic motivation). These three factors show that it is important not only to inform vendors about the existence of the media rating systems and the meaning of the ratings but also to provide information about the importance and validity of the systems and their legal backgrounds (e.g., the legal basis of the age classifications and warning labels) and to facilitate them in complying with the media ratings.

The Occurrence of a Forbidden Fruit Effect

As many studies have indicated, in general, legal age restrictions lead to a decrease in consumption.

However, in addition to this so-called threshold effect, there has been speculation regarding the possible occurrence of a negative side effect. There are two competing theories about the likely effects of media ratings: the *tainted fruit theory* and the *forbidden fruit theory*. The tainted fruit theory predicts that the ratings will make restricted commodities less attractive, whereas the forbidden fruit theory predicts that the ratings will make such commodities more attractive. The term has its roots in the biblical story surrounding Adam and Eve, who are warned by God not to eat from the tree of knowledge of good and evil in the garden of Eden. However, Eve picks a fruit from the tree and persuades Adam to eat it. The forbidden fruit effect is connected to psychological theories such as *reactance theory* and *commodity theory*. Reactance theory assumes that people like the freedom to behave according to their own wishes. When this freedom is threatened, they experience psychological reactance—an unpleasant emotional state that motivates them to restore the threatened or lost freedom. Commodity theory predicts that any commodity that is perceived as unavailable, that cannot be obtained, or that can be obtained only with much effort will be valued more than commodities that can be obtained freely. Therefore, in addition to the expected positive effects of the ratings (the threshold effect), it is reasonable to assume that media ratings may have adverse effects as well.

Most studies have suggested that age ratings and warning pictograms may indeed have a forbidden fruit effect on children and adolescents An overview by Brad J. Bushman and Joanne Cantor (2003) showed that high age ratings and content warnings have a forbidden fruit effect on children and adolescents (from 8 to 17 years old), who find such products more attractive. However, when children are younger than 8 years old, a so-called tainted fruit effect may occur: high age ratings and content warnings decrease the attractiveness of media for them. In sum, the attractiveness decreased until the age of 8, increased until about age 22, and then decreased. Differences were found for male and female participants, with higher effect sizes among boys than girls. In their meta-analysis, Bushman and Cantor included studies on television programs, movies, games, and music. They did not report significant differences across the types of media products. The meta-analysis that Bushman and Cantor reported on employed various methods that have been used to establish the occurrence of forbidden fruit effects.

In addition to consumer surveys that have been conducted, the strongest form of evidence has been based on experimental research.

However, a possible flaw in these earlier studies concerns the artificial nature of the stimulus materials used (with much emphasis on the ratings and relatively little verbal and/or visual information about the media product). Using a more realistic approach (by means of actual covers of media products in combination with actual media ratings placed on the actual position in normal size), a recent experimental study did not detect a forbidden fruit effect. The results showed that age ratings and content warning pictograms did not appear to make potentially harmful media products more attractive to children and adolescents (Gosselt et al., 2012). The underlying psychological mechanisms of the forbidden fruit hypothesis may still be valid, but the placement of the pictograms on DVDs and games may be too insignificant to trigger such reactions in real life. In all, more studies are needed to explore whether media ratings indeed can have a forbidden fruit effect in practice and under which circumstances.

Conclusion

After rules for media ratings are developed by government and/or industry, the general public becomes involved. When media products are made to appear to be a type of forbidden fruit, minors may judge media products that are subject to age limits as more attractive. Whether this process occurs within the current context requires further exploration.

It is important to monitor whether all parties involved know, accept, and comply with the rules. Media ratings target several groups: children and adolescents, caregivers (the public), the industry and/or retail, and policy makers. Multiple studies on the acceptance of media ratings have indicated that self-reported support for the media ratings is reasonable. This concerns both the public and the industry. However, when analyzing compliance figures, it becomes clear that self-reported support and actual support are not the same. Regarding individual vendors, we know that three factors are important: knowledge, ability, and motivation.

For media ratings to protect children effectively from harmful media, the ratings require facilitation of the vendors and enforcement strategies to increase the knowledge, ability, and motivation of the selling personnel to comply with the rules. Facilitation may be prompted through interventions focusing on the need for and usefulness of media ratings and skills that are needed to prevent noncompliance with the ratings. Such interventions may have a positive effect on compliance because both ability and motivation aspects are addressed. In addition to facilitating vendors, enforcement checks are required to associate violations of the rules with negative consequences. Enforcement checks will be effective only when vendors are aware of them and are periodically informed about their results and consequences. Therefore, a valid and visible system of external surveillance must be developed to affect the vendors' perceived risk of being caught for noncompliance and to emphasize the legal basis of complying with the ratings.

Jordy F. Gosselt, Joris J. van Hoof, and Menno D. T. De Jong

See also Rating Systems, Film; Rating Systems, Television; Rating Systems, Video Games

Further Readings

Bushman, B. J., & Cantor, J. (2003). Media ratings for violence and sex: Implications for policymakers and parents. *American Psychologist, 58*, 130–141.

Dorbeck-Jung, B. R., Oude Vrielink, M. J., Gosselt, J. F., van Hoof, J. J., & De Jong, M. D. T. (2010). Contested hybridization of regulation: Failure of the Dutch regulatory system to protect minors from harmful media. *Regulation & Governance, 4*, 154–174.

Gentile, D. A., Humphrey, J., & Walsh, D. A. (2005). Media ratings and movies, music, video games, and television: A review of the research and recommendations for improvements. *Adolescent Medicine Clinics, 16*, 427–446.

Gosselt, J. F., De Jong, M. D. T., & van Hoof, J. J. (2012). Effects of media ratings on children and adolescents: A litmus test of the forbidden fruit effect. *Journal of Communication, 61*, 1161–1178.

Gosselt, J. F., van Hoof, J. J., & De Jong, M. D. T. (2012). Media rating systems: Do they work? Shop floor compliance with age restrictions in the Netherlands. *Mass Communication and Society, 15*, 335–359.

MEDIA VIOLENCE, DEFINITIONS AND CONTEXT OF

The term *media violence* refers to any acts of physical force directed toward animate beings in mass communication outlets such as movies, television programs, computer and console video games, newspapers, magazines, comic books, and so on. Violence has been ubiquitous in the media especially since the beginning of the television era. Indeed, the National Television Violence Study (NTVS), the largest study conducted in the 1990s to assess media violence, concluded that about 60% of the 10,000 sampled programs contained violence that most of the time had lethal consequences. The popularity of violence portrayed in media has created concern among the public and policy makers and has led scientists to embark on a mission to determine whether and how media violence exerts a negative influence on the personality and behavior of people and especially young children. A plethora of studies on the topic have shown that both brief and chronic exposure to media violence leads to an increase of aggression. This entry provides an overview of the major scientific findings that shed light on how media violence affects people.

Overview

The media revolution of the 20th century has brought about new means of entertainment. The beginning of the century marked the advent of the cinema, the 1960s–1970s the popularization of television broadcasting, the 1970s–1980s the introduction of video and computer games, and the Internet infiltrated people's homes in the mid- to late 1990s. Along with these new forms of entertainment came greater exposure to violent events. Indeed, even one of the first movies ever made, *The Great Train Robbery* (1903), contained several violent scenes (e.g., knocking unconscious a train operator, killing a messenger and a passenger, shooting and killing all the bandits) within its 12-minute duration.

The rise in popularity of television watching since the 1960s has correlated strongly with the rate of violent crimes in the United States and has led scientists around the world to ponder whether a causal link exists between the exposure to media violence and real-life aggressive behavior. This question is discussed in the next section.

Media Violence and Real-Life Aggressive Behavior

Television executives have often claimed that television programming represents merely a mirror into a violent society and is not the source of societal violence. But is this really the case? In an article published in the *American Psychologist* in 2001, prominent media violence scientists Brad Bushman and Craig Anderson discussed evidence suggesting that violence in television programs is overrepresented compared to violence in society. They cited research showing that although 87% of the crimes occurring in the real world are nonviolent, only 13% of the crimes shown on television are so. Notably, whereas half of the violent crimes shown on television are murders, only 0.2% of crimes are murders in real life. The prominence of violence in television programs has sparked a scientific debate around the effects that media violence exposure might exert on the personality and behavior of people, and especially young children. On the one hand, media violence exposure may function in a number of ways that make people more aggressive and thus more likely to commit violent acts in their everyday lives. On the other hand, it is possible that violence in media such as television and films may serve a cathartic function. That is, by viewing violent acts in media people may release their aggressive impulses and refrain from carrying out these acts. This hypothesis has been around since the time of Aristotle, who claimed that viewers experience emotional release when viewing the protagonists of plays experience negative events. Although plausible, this catharsis hypothesis has not been supported by scientific research. Instead, studies carried out on the topic since the 1960s, using a variety of methodologies ranging from correlational approaches to laboratory experimental designs, have provided evidence that exposure to media violence leads to increased real-world aggression. Although some argue that the relation between media violence and aggression found in correlational studies is spurious, with constructs such as trait aggression held responsible for both aggressive behavior and preference for violent media, studies using experimental methodologies with highly controlled designs have refuted such accounts and verified the presence of causal links. Research aimed at uncovering the underlying mechanisms that subserve the effects of media violence on behavior is presented next.

Mechanisms and Mediator Variables

In a meta-analytic review of studies carried out to investigate the effects of violent video games, Anderson provided evidence documenting that exposure to violent video games is causally linked to increases in aggressive behavior, aggressive cognition, aggressive affect, and cardiovascular arousal as well as decreases in helping behavior. In fact,

the evidence for a causal link between media violence and aggression is so overwhelming that Anderson claimed that the "scientific debate over whether media violence has an effect is over" (2004, p. 114). Indeed, the focus of recent research has shifted from the question of "Does media violence increase aggression?" to the question of "How does violence increase aggression?" Thus, more recent research focuses on identifying the mechanisms and variables that underlie the causal relation between media violence and aggression. In general, studies show that repeated exposure to violence in entertainment media is a major contributor to aggressive and violent behavior in real life by instigating imitation, making real-world violence more acceptable, distorting viewers' perceptions of real-world crime and violence, desensitizing viewers to the suffering of victims of violence, and increasing the accessibility of violent constructs in memory.

Albert Bandura and colleagues' 1961 and 1963 studies on social learning provide an example of how passive exposure to violence can affect behavior in children by means of imitation. In these experiments, young children between 3 and (about) 6 years of age who observed an adult physically and verbally abusing a Bobo Doll were subsequently more likely to adopt the same type of behavior toward the doll than were children in a control group. These differences in aggressive behavior were further exaggerated when the adult model was of the same sex as the child, suggesting that gender is a moderator variable. According to the experimenters, observing the adult exerting aggression toward the doll lowered the children's aggressive inhibitions by giving them the impression that violent actions are acceptable. Importantly, the 1963 study provided evidence that the imitation effects are present regardless of whether children observed aggression toward the doll as a real-life event or in a film or even in cartoons. Although these studies have been criticized on various grounds (e.g., the videos could have functioned as instructions to children), they have typically been regarded as clear evidence that people's behavior can be influenced through observational learning and mimicry.

Bandura's studies showed that imitation of violent actions, and possibly the adoption of the belief that aggressive actions are acceptable, may result from observing violent content. More recent studies have suggested that media violence may influence behavior by causing desensitization to violence. *Desensitization* refers to the diminished emotional responsiveness to a negative or aversive stimulus after repeated exposure to it. After prolonged and/or repeated exposure to media violence, an observer may become emotionally and cognitively desensitized to media violence. Desensitization to media violence was observed in many studies conducted in the 1980s. These studies found that individuals who experienced high levels of television violence in the past were more likely to be desensitized to violent film clips compared with those who had watched only small amounts of television violence. A 2007 study conducted by psychologist Nicholas Carnagey and colleagues showed that children who were highly exposed to video game violence in the past showed lower responsiveness to real-world violence and were more likely to judge violence as pleasurable compared with children who were not extensively exposed to video game violence. Furthermore, other studies provided evidence that children's exposure to movie or video game violence results in pro-violence attitudes (cognitive desensitization) and lower empathy or sympathy for the victims of violence (emotional desensitization). Thus, it seems that chronic media violence exposure has lasting effects on viewers' attitudes toward violence and viewers' empathy toward the victims of violence through the process of desensitization.

Although studies generally have documented desensitization to media violence by showing that people's reactive responses to violent media are diminished after chronic experience, desensitization has also been observed with short-term exposure to media violence. In a study conducted by Kostas Fanti and colleagues in 2009, participants viewed nine 2-minute video segments that included either violent actions or comedic episodes; their reactivity was measured using a questionnaire that was administered after each video segment. Results revealed the presence of a curvilinear relationship between time (i.e., number of scenes already watched) and both levels of enjoyment and sympathy for the victims of the violent acts. The violent segments initially produced aversive responses that tended to increase in intensity after the participants watched the first few segments. However, with later scenes participants' levels of enjoyment increased and their sympathy levels decreased dramatically. That is, even after watching four to five violent scenes, participants showed evidence of desensitization to the violent content of the films. Notably, although differences were found in the overall scores of people reporting involvement in real-life aggression acts and those

who did not, desensitization was identified in both groups of participants.

Cognitive and emotional desensitization—the reduced emotion-related physiological reactivity to negative events such as violent acts—have often been linked to physiological arousal. Initial exposure to media violence typically produces aversive responses such as fear, increased heart rate, perspiration, discomfort, and disgust. Studies have provided evidence that exposure to violence in video games leads to physiological desensitization. In one study, participants played either a violent or a nonviolent video game for 20 minutes and then watched videos of real-life violence for 10 minutes. Measures of heart rate and galvanic skin response were taken before and after video game playing as well as during video viewing. Results showed that although heart rate increased from before the game to after the game, the increase was equal in violent and nonviolent game conditions. However, whereas heart rate remained at the same level for the violent game condition during violent video viewing, it increased in the nonviolent condition. Also, although galvanic skin response levels were equal for the two game conditions in pre- and postgame measurements, they decreased substantially during video viewing, but only in the violent game condition. No such decrease was found in the nonviolent condition in which a small, nonsignificant increase was observed. Importantly, none of the effects reported were mediated by trait aggressiveness. Thus, the results cannot be explained by individual differences in the susceptibility to media violence. Overall, these findings indicated that playing a violent game, even for a short time, can physiologically desensitize people to real-life violence.

Evidence for short-term desensitization to media violence also comes from studies that used event-related potentials, which is a noninvasive method that measures the brain's response resulting from a cognitive event. One such study investigated the links among violent game experience, desensitization, and aggression. Participants with varying levels of prior violent game experience were exposed to a task in which violent or negative nonviolent pictures were occasionally presented within a series of neutral images. Electrophysiological signals were recorded during the picture-viewing task. Subsequently, participants carried out a version of the competitive reaction time task. In this task participants were given the impression that they were competing with another participant in a task that entailed fast reactions to auditory tones. In reality, however, whether or not a participant wins in a given trial was predetermined. Following winning trials, participants were given the opportunity to punish their opponents by delivering a loud noise to their ears. The intensity and the duration of the noise were used as measures of aggression. Results revealed the presence of a lower-amplitude P300 event-related potential component for participants with greater violent game exposure when viewing violent pictures, but no differences in P300 amplitude were observed for negative nonviolent and neutral pictures. Because previous studies had shown that larger P300 amplitudes are elicited by stimuli that are judged to be inconsistent with the context, the decrease of the P300 amplitude when viewing violent pictures was regarded as evidence for desensitization to violence. Furthermore, smaller P300 amplitudes for violent pictures were associated with higher aggression scores in the competitive reaction time task. Importantly, these findings remained significant even after controlling for individual differences in trait aggression. Thus, these findings have suggested that chronic exposure to violent games results in desensitization to violence, causing people to behave more aggressively.

In addition to mimicry and desensitization, media violence may function to alter people's perceptions about violent acts. Attractive heroes in action movies are often engaged in violence toward others, resulting in the glamorization of violent acts. Their actions almost always remain unpunished, with the protagonists showing no remorse or guilt for their actions. Glamorization of violence is even more prevalent in recent ultra-violent console and computer games, where the player adopts the perspective of the game protagonist to carry out violent acts and crime toward others. Thus, not only is the player of video games actively engaged in simulated violence—which has been shown by research to have even more dramatic consequences on personality and behavior than passive exposure—but he or she may also come to believe that violence is justifiable and attractive. Furthermore, media violence is not only glamorized, but it is also sanitized. That is, the consequences of media violence in movies are most often not portrayed realistically. Protagonists in action movies are shown to exhibit little pain after being violently hit or shot and recover easily from blows that in real life would have been fatal. As a result, viewers may develop misperceptions about how severe the consequences of various violent actions are and become more likely to resort to violence in real life.

Future Directions

Research on the effects of media violence on personality and behavior has shown negative consequences on humans and young children in particular. Although a number of different mechanisms and mediating variables have been proposed to explain the causal link between exposure to media violence and aggressive behavior, further research is still needed to pinpoint all involved variables and their possibly complex interrelations. Furthermore, the increasing intensity and the novel type of violence that appears on media today leave scientists with the task of determining whether even higher effect sizes can be obtained in studies of modern media. Finally, policy makers may want to pay close attention to scientific findings to inform their decisions with regard to media violence.

Kostas A. Fanti and Marios N. Avraamides

See also Bobo Doll Studies; Desensitization Effects on Society

Further Readings

Anderson, C. A. (2004). An update on the effects of violent video games. *Journal of Adolescence, 27,* 113–122.

Bandura, A., Ross, D., & Ross, S. A. (1963). Imitation of film-mediated aggressive models. *Journal of Abnormal and Social Psychology, 66,* 3–11.

Bartholow, B. D., Sestir, M. A., & Davis, E. B. (2005). Correlates and consequences of exposure to video game violence: Hostile personality, empathy, and aggressive behavior. *Personality and Social Psychology Bulletin, 31,* 1573–1586.

Bushman, B. J., & Anderson, G. A. (2001). Media violence and the American public: Scientific facts versus media misinformation. *American Psychologist, 56,* 477–489.

Carnagey, N. L., Anderson, C. A., & Bushman, B. J. (2007). The effect of video game violence on physiological desensitization to real-life violence. *Journal of Experimental Social Psychology, 43,* 489–496.

Fanti, K. A., & Avraamides, M. N. (2011). Desensitization to media violence. In M. Paludi (Ed.), *The psychology of teen violence and victimization* (pp. 121–133). Santa Barbara, CA: Praeger.

Fanti, K. A., Vanman, E., Henrich, C. C., & Avraamides, M. N. (2009). Desensitization to media violence over a short period of time. *Aggressive Behavior, 35,* 179–187.

Kunkel, D. (2007). *The effects of television violence on children*. Hearing before the U.S. Senate Committee on Commerce, Science, and Transportation. Retrieved from http://www.apa.org/about/gr/pi/advocacy/2008/kunkel-tv.aspx

Oliver, M. B. (1994). Portrayals of crime, race, and aggression in "reality based" police shows: A content analysis. *Journal of Broadcasting and Electronic Media, 38*, 179–192.

MEMORY AND VIOLENCE

Memory processes play an important but often overlooked role in the media violence literature. Scholars who study media violence effects have tended to approach the issue of memory in one of two ways. First, several theoretical perspectives have relied on memory as a mechanism that can explain the effects of exposure to media violence. Second, some researchers have focused specifically on audiences' memories for media violence as outcomes of exposure. Both perspectives are described in this entry, after a brief review of different types of memory processes and systems.

Types of Memory

There are numerous ways of conceptualizing human memory. Some scholars have categorized human memory based on time (i.e., short term versus long term) whereas others have viewed memory as consisting of multiple, independent systems. For example, some scholars have argued that human memory can be categorized into two overall systems: the declarative memory system and the nondeclarative memory system. *Nondeclarative,* or *implicit memory,* refers to memory without awareness. For example, memory for skills and habits—such as driving a car or using a remote control—fall under the category of nondeclarative memory. *Declarative memory* refers to memories that can be described and involve awareness.

Declarative memory can further be categorized into subsystems that include semantic memory and episodic memory. The *semantic memory system* is memory for factual information: the Beatles' first #1 song, or the name of the director of the film *Pulp Fiction. Episodic memory* refers to memory of events in which a person was personally involved. Memories of a first date or a person's whereabouts on September 11, 2001, would constitute episodic memory.

As the following sections illustrate, some media violence researchers have focused on nondeclarative memory processes, whereas others have studied declarative memory.

Memory as a Mechanism Leading to Effects

Leonard Berkowitz's (1984) priming theory is an example of a framework that employs nondeclarative memory processes to explain media effects. Priming theory adopts what researchers refer to as a *cognitive neoassociationistic framework,* which views human memory as a collection of networks. Each network in our brain consists of nodes that are connected by pathways. Nodes are modules that represent memories for events (e.g., seeing a scary movie on a date), people (e.g., a boyfriend), locations (e.g., the cabin by the lake), and even emotions (e.g., fear). Priming research also adopts a concept called *spreading activation* to explain the activation of nodes in an associative network. As explained by researchers Allan Collins and Elizabeth Loftus (1975), spreading activation occurs when a node is triggered or primed. The node then radiates along the pathways in memory and activates other related nodes in its network. This process of spreading activation renders nodes temporarily accessible in memory.

Within the field of media effects, the priming framework has been used to study short-term effects of exposure to violent media. When audiences are exposed to violent content in the media, the violent content triggers related nodes stored in memory, and these nodes in turn can activate other related memories. For example, researcher Brad Bushman (1998) exposed individuals to either violent or nonviolent videotapes. After exposure, they were asked to rate homonyms that had both violent and nonviolent meanings (*mug, sock*) in terms of their level of aggressiveness. The study found that participants who had viewed the violent content perceived the homonyms as being more violent than those who had viewed the nonviolent clip, and thus the authors concluded that violent media had primed aggressive memory networks.

Although priming is a short-term phenomenon, this framework has also been used to explain long-term effects of violent media exposure. Whereas one-time exposure to a stimulus increases the temporary accessibility of nodes in memory, repeat exposure to a stimulus can lead to *chronic accessibility*. Chronic accessibility occurs when a node is highly accessible in memory even in the absence of a recent prime. Therefore, frequent exposure to media violence can render related nodes in memory accessible on an ongoing, chronic basis.

The fact that media violence can increase the accessibility of violent thoughts in memory on both short and chronic bases is used by many media scholars to explain media violence effects. Scholars Vincent Price and David Tewksbury (1997), for example, proposed that chronic accessibility might be responsible for the effects found in cultivation research. L. J. Shrum (1996) went one step further and formulated a "heuristic processing model" to explain cultivation effects. According to Shrum's model, individuals will use the information that is most accessible to them when making judgments about how frequently events occur. Thus, heavy viewers of violent television believe the real world is a violent place because they are relying on easily accessible constructs in memory—constructs that became accessible because of recent or frequent exposure to media violence. Finally, Craig Anderson's general aggression model (GAM) also relies on memory accessibility to explain violent media effects. According to the GAM, violent media content is one example of an input variable that affects audiences' cognitions, emotions, and physiological arousal states. More specifically, the model predicts that media violence can increase the accessibility of violent thoughts, which could in turn lead to aggressive behaviors depending on how individuals appraise a particular situation.

Finally, L. Rowell Huesmann's (1998) information processing approach to media effects also relies on nondeclarative memory processes to explain media effects. According to Huesmann, the human brain is analogous to a computer, with a memory system that stores data and an executive program that helps us to process inputs and generate outputs. Similar to the cognitive neoassociation approach to memory, Huesmann also views memory as a series of nodes and links. Huesmann expanded upon the connectionist approach, however, by incorporating the concepts of schema and scripts. The term *schema* refers to a structure encoded in memory that represents knowledge about a subject. A *script*, on the other hand, is a schema that links together events in a sequence. For example, many people have scripts for what they can expect to occur when dining in a fancy restaurant. In general, we acquire schema and scripts through repeat experience with stimuli and events or by observing others.

According to Huesmann, when individuals are exposed to media violence, they will search for a script in memory to guide behavior. Aggressive individuals will have more elaborate networks of social scripts that emphasize the role that aggression should play in problem solving. At the same time, a person's mood or arousal level at the time of exposure could also affect the script that will be selected from memory to guide behavior. Once media audiences have selected a script from memory, they will evaluate the script and behave according to the script. Thus, the information processing perspective relies on information stored in memory—in the form of scripts and schema—to predict how media violence might lead to aggressive behaviors on the part of audience members.

Memory as an Outcome

A handful of media violence researchers have explored people's memories for violent media content as outcomes in and of themselves. Most common are the studies that explore audience members' autobiographical memories for media violence. According to William Brewer (1986), autobiographical memories are memories of the self and tend to be personal, long lasting, and significant. For some scholars, the term *autobiographical memory* is synonymous with episodic memory, although others do not equate the two directly. Communication researchers have explored audience members' autobiographical memories for memorable, one-time experiences with media content, such as watching a romantic movie on a date or viewing sexually explicit television programs or movies.

Much of what we know about autobiographical memories for violent content comes from studies of frightening media conducted by researchers such as Richard Jackson Harris, Steven Hoekstra, and Joanne Cantor. Although not all frightening films include violence, the results of their studies have suggested that violent media content has a significant impact on audiences, resulting in vivid, detailed memories for the content as well as the viewing circumstances. For example, these studies all confirmed that holding a memory for violent, frightening media content is a somewhat universal experience. Harris and colleagues (2000, 2004) found that nearly 100% of young adult participants could remember watching a scary movie in the context of a romantic date. Furthermore, most of the remembered movies were R-rated, violent slasher films. Hoekstra and colleagues (1999) found that nearly all young adults in their study could remember a specific time during childhood when they were frightened by a slasher film. In a study by Kris Harrison and Joanne Cantor (1999), 90% of young adults could remember a specific movie or television that had scared them in the past. Furthermore, the young adults in their study wrote vivid, detailed descriptions of the content they could remember. A vast majority of the content they remembered and wrote about included descriptions of violence, such as mentions of blood and bodily injuries.

Participants in these research projects also held detailed memories of the viewing circumstances. For example, they reported remembering their reactions to the violent content, such as fear, anxiety, and sleep problems. They could also remember details about the context of viewing, such as where they were when they viewed the film, with whom they viewed the film, and who had decided to watch the movie. The results of these studies, therefore, have demonstrated that people do in fact have very detailed long-term memories of memorable experiences with media violence.

More recent research by Karyn Riddle and colleagues has focused more specifically on memories for violent media content, demonstrating some of the consequences of having detailed memories for media violence. In this study of young adult college students, participants were asked whether or not they could remember a specific movie or television program viewed in the past that was violent. Of all participants, 75% could remember a specific instance, and they wrote essays describing the violence they could remember. Those essays were then coded for vividness, which entailed counting up the number of references to blood, guts, and gore. Guided by Shrum's heuristic processing model of cultivation effects, Riddle and colleagues (2011) proposed that people who hold vivid memories for media violence should have those memories easily accessible in memory, which should in turn affect social reality beliefs about real-world violence. Indeed, the findings of that study revealed that young adults who included vivid details in their essays about blood and gore gave higher estimates of real-world violence than those who wrote less vivid essays.

Thus, the limited research on memories for violent media has suggested that audiences often have detailed memories for violent content seen in the past. They also have vivid memories for the viewing circumstances in which they saw violent media.

These findings are very important, given the high accessibility of vivid memories. After all, holding vivid memories for violent media content can in turn affect people's ongoing beliefs and attitudes. One important issue that must be addressed, however, is the veracity of audience members' memories. Indeed, it would be extremely difficult to determine the accuracy of media audiences' memories for media violence seen in the past. Nonetheless, even memories plagued with errors are important to study, because they still have the potential to guide our thoughts, attitudes, and behaviors.

Karyn Riddle

See also Cultivation Theory; Fear Reactions to Violent Content; General Aggression Model; Priming Theory

Further Readings

Anderson, C. A., & Dill, K. E. (2000). Video games and aggressive thoughts, feelings, and behavior in the laboratory and in life. *Journal of Personality and Social Psychology, 78,* 772–790.

Anderson, J., & Bower, G. (1973). *Human associative memory.* Washington, DC: V. H. Winston.

Berkowitz, L. (1984). Some effects of thoughts on anti- and prosocial influences of media events: A cognitive-neoassociation analysis. *Psychological Bulletin, 95,* 410–427.

Brewer, W. F. (1986). What is autobiographical memory? In D. Rubin (Ed.), *Autobiographical memory* (pp. 25–49). Cambridge: Cambridge University Press.

Broadbent, D. E. (1958). *Perception and communication.* New York, NY: Pergamon.

Bushman, B. J. (1998). Priming effects of violent media on the accessibility of aggressive constructs in memory. *Personality and Social Psychology Bulletin, 24,* 537–545.

Cantor, J., Mares, M.-L., & Hyde, J. S. (2003). Autobiographical memories of exposure to sexual media content. *Media Psychology, 5,* 1–23.

Collins, A. M., & Loftus, E. F. (1975). A spreading-activation theory of semantic processing. *Psychological Review, 82,* 407–428.

Harris, R. J., Hoekstra, S. J., Scott, C. L., Sanborn F. W., Dodds, L. A., & Brandenburg, J. D. (2004). Autobiographical memories for seeing romantic movies on a date: Romance is not just for women. *Media Psychology, 6,* 257–284.

Harris, R. J., Hoekstra, S. J., Scott, C. L., Sanborn, F. W., Karafa, J. A., & Brandenburg, J. D. (2000). Young men's and women's different autobiographic memories of the experience of seeing frightening movies on a date. *Media Psychology, 2,* 245–268.

Harrison, K., & Cantor, J. (1999). Tales from the screen: Enduring fright reactions to scary media. *Media Psychology, 1,* 97–116.

Hoekstra, S. J., Harris, R. J., & Helmick, A. L. (1999). Autobiographical memories about the experience of seeing frightening movies in childhood. *Media Psychology, 1,* 117–140.

Huesmann, L. R. (1998). The role of social information processing and cognitive schema in the acquisition and maintenance of habitual aggressive behavior (pp. 73–109). In R. G. Geen & E. Donnerstein (Eds.), *Human aggression: Theories, research, and implications for policy.* New York, NY: Academic Press.

Neath, I., & Suprenant, A. M. (2003). *Human memory* (2nd ed.). Belmont, CA: Wadsworth.

Nelson, K. (1993). The psychological and social origins of autobiographical memory. *Psychological Science, 4,* 7–14.

Nisbett, R. E., & Ross, L. (1980). *Human inference: Strategies and shortcomings of social judgment.* Englewood Cliffs, NJ: Prentice-Hall.

Pillemer, D. B. (1992). Remembering personal circumstances: A functional analysis. In E. Winograd & U. Neisser (Eds.), *Affect and accuracy in recall: Studies of "flashbulb" memories* (pp. 236–264). New York, NY: Cambridge University Press.

Price, V., & Tewksbury, D. (1997). News values and public opinion: A theoretical account of media priming and framing. In G. A. Bennett & F. J. Boster (Eds.), *Progress in communication sciences: Advances in persuasion* (Vol. 13, pp. 173–212). Greenwich, CT: Ablex.

Riddle, K., Potter, W. J., Metzger, M. J., Nabi, R. L., & Linz, D. (2011). Beyond cultivation: Exploring the effects of frequency, recency, and vivid autobiographical memories for violent media. *Media Psychology, 14,* 168–191.

Roskos-Ewoldsen, D. R., Roskos-Ewoldsen, B. & Carpentier, F. R. D. (2002). Media priming: A synthesis. In J. Bryant & D. Zillmann (Eds.), *Media effects: Advances in theory and research* (2nd ed., pp. 97–120). Mahwah, NJ: Erlbaum.

Rumelhart, D. E. (1980). Schemata: The building blocks of cognition. In R. J. Spiro, B. C. Bruce, & W. F. Brewer (Eds.), Theoretical issues in reading comprehension: Perspectives from cognitive psychology, linguistics, artificial intelligence, and education (pp. 33–58). Hillsdale, NJ: Erlbaum.

Schacter, D. L., & Tulving, E. (1994). What are the memory systems of 1994? In D. L. Schacter & E. Tulving (Eds.), *Memory systems 1994.* Cambridge, MA: MIT Press.

Schank, R. C. (1982). Dynamic memory: A theory of learning in computers and people. New York, NY: Cambridge University Press.

Shrum, L. J. (1996). Psychological processes underlying cultivation effects: Further tests of construct accessibility. *Human Communication Research, 22,* 482–509.

METHODOLOGIES FOR ASSESSING EFFECTS OF MEDIA

There are myriad methods for assessing media effects in both traditional and digital environments, from basic surveys to netnography to neuromarketing. This entry reviews a selection of quantitative and qualitative research methods that are currently used to examine consumer behavior, and thus media effects. The entry focuses on tried-and-true methods of assessing media effects as well as new exploratory research that is being done in the physiological and neuromarketing space.

Surveys and Consumer Panels

Surveys using consumer panels are an effective and efficient method for collecting consumer responses to media from a representative sample of consumers. Online surveys and traditional mail panels differ from each other only in the medium through which they are given: Internet versus print. Thus, online surveys have essentially the same strengths and weaknesses as traditional mail surveys. However, the use of the Internet to assess media effects exaggerates some of the weaknesses associated with surveys. During any survey data collection, participants will eventually reach the point of "satisficing" if they lose interest or become impatient for whatever reason. Satisficing occurs when participants begin to focus on simply completing the survey rather than providing accurate answers to the questions. This can happen for a number of reasons, but the most common cause is poorly designed or long surveys. The self-administered nature of online surveys exacerbates this behavior because there is no researcher present to engage the participant. To prevent satisficing, T. Downes Le Guin and colleagues (2012) have recommended that both off- and online surveys should be kept as short as possible, employ simple language, and have a well-organized design.

Many researchers have argued that the design of an online survey creates an experience for participants that will be similar to their experiences during other web-based activities. Therefore, surveys should include visual and interactive features that can be supported by the Internet. Surveys must be enjoyable and engaging (or at least not a burden) for participants, otherwise participants will quickly move on to one of the many other activities that the Internet has to offer. Some of these new design techniques include drag-and-drop features rather than radio buttons for selecting answers, and the use of color and images to define answer categories. Other research has shown that participants prefer more traditional HTML-based survey designs over interactive designs that focus on rich media. Rich media designs may lead to unintended results and are more likely to suffer survey abandonment, which can be counterproductive to the research project.

Media Effects Experiments

To overcome the control issues associated with online surveys, many researchers have looked to both on- and offline experiments to assess media effects in a more controlled environment. Some researchers have used laboratory facilities to conduct experiments in which the participants can be observed as they participate in the experiment; this observation can be both visual and physiological (e.g., eye tracking, galvanic skin response). In such an environment, researchers can limit the impact of confounding variables while also monitoring the capture of participants' choices and behaviors. Despite advances in technology and the use of computers in experiments, researchers are still aggregating their participants in a physical location during their data collection. If experiments were to be conducted online, researchers would be able to reduce the costs of their projects; however, the validity and reliability of the results would suffer. Similar to online surveys, online experiments would suffer not only from satisficing but from other control complications as well. Some researchers speculate that despite this cost advantage, experiments do not commonly take place online because many researchers are apprehensive about their ability to recruit and pay participants via the Internet as well as achieve internal validity.

Physiological Data Tracking

Physiological measures are appealing because they can in some ways add validity to research. The qualitative and quantitative measures that are used to gauge participants' responses to media have often relied on the participants' ability to assess their own attitudes and emotional responses and their willingness to disclose honest information to the

researcher. Physiological research methods work around this limitation by providing researchers with data, which for the most part cannot be directly controlled by the participant. Researchers have found that traditional methods lack the ability to measure "the subconscious, intuitive, and purely emotional aspects of communication with consumers" (Ohme, Reykowska, Wiener, & Choromanska, 2009, p. 22; also see Braidot, 2005; Kenning, Plassmann, & Ahlert, 2007). One example of this occurred when recall and behavioral testing showed discrepancies in the outcomes of two similar advertisements. The difference between the two advertisements was so minor that postexperimental interviews revealed that participants were unable to detect a change between the ads yet reacted differently to each. In cases like this one, participants were unable to analyze their own responses and disclose them to the researcher, and physiological data have helped to better inform the researcher of the occurring effect. There are a variety of physiological responses to consider when conducting media effects research, including but not limited to (a) electromyography (EMG), (b) galvanic skin response, and (c) functional magnetic resonance imaging (fMRI).

A common way to measure participants' physiological response to stimuli has been the probe startle reflex. This method requires researchers to measure participants' involuntary physical responses to sudden stimuli such as loud noises, flashes of bright light, or bursts of air. One common physical response is an involuntary eyeblink that can be measured by using electromyography. EMG testing records the physiological properties of facial muscles, including participants' eyeblinks through the sensors placed over the orbicularis occuli muscle group located just below the eye. Although orbicularis occuli is the most common muscle tested, researchers can also monitor the response of other facial muscles such as zygomaticus major (located in the cheeks) and the corrugator supercilii (located between the eyebrow and the bridge of the nose). By probing participants' startle reflexes, researchers can obtain measurable results of participants' genuine reaction to stimuli. This gives validity to researchers' results because participants will not have the opportunity to intentionally or unintentionally disclose inaccurate information regarding their responses. Other measurable physical responses include heart rate, blood pressure, respiratory rate, and sweat conductance. Researchers can even use galvanic skin response measures to detect palpitations in the skin.

Researchers also need to monitor subconscious brain activity that may lead to behavioral outcomes. One way of doing this is to use electroencephalograms (EEGs) to analyze brain waves produced by the participants' cortexes. EEG machines have high temporal resolution, which allows them to detect changes in brain activity in real time, making them well-suited tools to measure responses to rapidly changing stimuli. Although this feature makes EEGs superior to fMRIs (which have a lag time of a few seconds) for detecting change, the EEG is limited to readings of the cortex. The EEG also has a longer standing in media research than the fMRI, going back to the early 1970s. EEGs have been used to measure viewers' attention to various types of media, including advertising, the intensity of the emotional reactions elicited by specific aspects of media, and comprehension and retention of the media content.

Neuromarketing

Neuroscience approaches can benefit media research because they allow researchers to better understand how media affect viewers at a cognitive level. For instance, using brain-imaging techniques, researchers can detect changes in brain patterns during exposure to media. This could be particularly useful when studying the effects of media violence, for example. During exposure to varying degrees of media violence, researchers may see an increase in emotional reactivity or the lack of activity, signifying habituation or desensitization to violence. Brain imaging has also proved that consuming television may not be as passive an activity as researchers in the 1970s thought. Research has shown a collaboration of 17 separate areas of the brain while subjects viewed edited visual action sequences. These areas include face and object recognition, control of attention, cognitive interpretation of the layout of space, interpretation of intention, interpretation of biological movement, memory, sequential comprehension, and holistic perception.

Without the bridge between communication research and neuroresearch, we may have continued to regard television as a passive experience. These examples have shown that media researchers cannot understand the full effects that media have on viewers without collaboration with researchers in other fields. There have been many important discoveries in neuroscience regarding emotion that can be transferred to media research. It has been found that a majority of "emotional processing occurs below conscious awareness; despite the importance of emotions, humans have limited ability to describe their emotional world; emotional and memory systems are dynamic and change moment-to-moment in response to the environmental context; and the emotional centers are intimately interconnected with the cognitive centers of the brain and receive information prior to and influence cognitive processing and behaviors" (Marci, 2006, p. 381). The transfer of information among researchers in various fields has been slow, however, because of the lack of consistency in defining the term *emotion*. Despite the growing prominence of neuroimaging techniques such as fMRIs, there are still many areas of the brain that cannot be credited with specific functions. There is also a lack of evidence for correlations between specific neurological responses and discrete emotions like happiness, sadness, fear, or anger.

By learning the basics of neuroscience, communication and media effects researchers can collaborate with neuropsychologists to advance knowledge of communication psychology. Without some understanding of neurological processes, communication and media researchers and their neurophysiology colleagues will lack a common language. Another obstacle that may be faced when conducting media effects research is the cost of fMRI equipment used to collect data on neurological activity. Also, many fMRI machines are reserved for clinical purposes and medical research. Although most hospitals and major clinics have machines capable of providing information useful for nonmedical research purposes, there is a shortage of personnel with the knowledge needed to conduct data collection using fMRI machines compared with clinical observation (Anderson et al., 2006; Bradley, 2007).

Focus Groups

The Internet holds several advantages for researchers who have chosen a qualitative research method. Access to participants through the Internet can reduce project lead times and field times, lower the cost, allow the researcher to cross international boundaries, and gain access to busy professionals who may not have had time to participate otherwise. However, there are also severe limitations to qualitative research conducted online versus face to face. Unlike traditional qualitative research methods, researchers will not be able to observe participants' nonverbal communication or their reaction to the researcher or others around them. The Internet also offers anonymity to participants; therefore, researchers can never be certain whom they are allowing into their subject pool.

Among the online qualitative methods that are emerging are online focus groups. Much like traditional focus groups, these are group discussions led by the researcher. This discussion takes place in a virtual space, such as a chat room, where participants are able to see the responses and comments of their peers and the moderator. All participants are online at the same time to allow for direct interactions to happen in real time. Clients and other observers have access to the discussion, and all content can be saved for further analysis. Several services exist for this type of research, including Skype, Face Time, and WebEx.

Netnography

Netnography is a fairly new term that refers to a type of ethnographic research that is conducted using online communities. The word itself is a hybrid form of *Internet* and *ethnography*. When conducting netnographies, researchers may employ ethnographic techniques such as observation to develop a qualitative analysis of communities that arise from computer-mediated communication. Researchers can either be participatory or nonparticipatory agents within the community. They may also ask community members to write autobiographies. Researchers who choose to conduct netnographic research may benefit from the growing use of the Internet, its ease of access, and its abundance of rich information.

Just as in other cultural studies, researchers conducting netnographies must gain admittance into the community they are trying to explore. First, they must identify an online community that will best serve their research question. To ensure that a particular community meets the needs of the researcher, the researcher must learn the focus of the community by reviewing commonly discussed topics and group member profiles. Researchers must be willing to review multiple communities before selecting one to study. Once the community has been selected, data collection can begin. Netnographies provide two sources of data: content that can be pulled directly from communications taking place among community members, and the researcher's own observations regarding community members and their interactions. The data will be analyzed and interpreted in a way similar to other qualitative research models: coding, content analysis, and data linking. In their analysis of the data, researchers must bear in mind that netnographies, unlike ethnographies,

provide them only with participants' communicated statements, responses, and intentions. Researchers will not be able to observe the acts that community members carry out outside the virtual world. Participants involved in netnographies should be informed of the researcher's presence and intentions and have access to some or all of the research text at the end of the project.

Content and Rhetorical Analysis

Content analyses are the study of text, verbal, or visual communications and can be used as either quantitative or qualitative research methods. When used in a qualitative research design, content analyses are used to evaluate the underlying meaning of content rather than provide numeric values. This method is less linear and standardized than most quantitative methods. Although content analyses have come under criticism in the past for being time consuming, they can be as easy or as difficult as the researcher chooses. Each research design will be different based on the topic the researcher is interested in, and there are no set guidelines for data analysis. As a qualitative method, content analysis lends itself well to the analysis of user-generated content created on the Internet as well as exploratory research related to media effects in the traditional space. Researchers can use it to understand the meaning of the communication taking place between users, make connections, and draw inferences. The primary difference between traditional content analyses and content analyses conducted online is the use of text and visual communication materials that have been created by users within the virtual space of the Internet.

Like content analyses, rhetorical analyses examine text and visual communication between users, but rather than analyzing what is being said, its focus is on how those messages are delivered. In one study looking at fantasy themes within the websites of online hate groups, for example, the researcher analyzed the text for symbolic cues, characters, plotlines, settings, and sanctioning agents in order to determine the overall theme. In this example, the elements surrounding the material, rather than the message itself, were the subject of interest.

Laura F. Bright

See also Cross-Cultural Perspectives; Effect Size in Media Violence, Research and Effects of; Effects From Violent Media, Short- and Long-Term; Media Effects Perspectives of Violence; National Television Violence Study; Psychobiology of Violence

Further Readings

Anderson, D. R., Bryant, J., Murray, J. P., Rich, M., Rivkin, M. J., & Zillmann, D. (2006). Brain imaging: An introduction to a new approach to studying media processes and effects. *Media Psychology, 8*(1), 1–6. doi: 10.1207/S1532785XMEP0801_1

Belz, F. M., & Baumbach, W. (2010) Netnography as a method of lead user identification. *Creativity and Innovation Management, 19*(3), 304–313. doi:10.1111/j.1467–8691.2010.00571.x

Bradley, S. D., Angelini, J. R., & Sungkyoung, L. (2007). Psychophysiological and memory effects of negative political ads. *Journal of Advertising, 36*(4), 115–127.

Braidot, N. P. (2005). *Neuromarketing: Neuroeconomia y negocios.* Buenos Aires, Argentina: Norte-Sur SL.

Cacioppo, J. T., Bernsten, G. G., Larsen, J. T., Poehlmann, K. M., & Ito, T A. (2000). The psychophysiology of emotion. In M. Lewis & J. M. Haviland-Jones (Eds.), *Handbook of emotions* (173–191). New York, NY: Guilford.

Cacioppo, J. T., & Petty, R. E. (1985). Physiological responses and advertising effects: Is the cup half full or half empty? *Psychology & Marketing, 2*(2), 115–126.

Couper, M. P., Singer, E., Tourangeau, R., & Conrad, E. G. (2006). Evaluating the effectiveness of visual analog scales: A web experiment. *Social Science Computer Review, 24*(2), 227–245.

Downes-Le Guin, T., Baker, R., Mechling, J., & Ruyle, E. (2012). Myths and realities of respondent engagement in online surveys. *International Journal of Market Research, 54*(5), 613–633. doi: 10.2501 /IJMR-54-5-613-633

Duffy, M. E. (2003). Web of hate: A fantasy theme analysis of the rhetorical vision of hate groups online. *Journal of Communication Inquiry, 27*(3), 291–312. doi: 10.1177/0196859903252850

Elo, S., & Kynga, S. H. (2008). The qualitative content analysis process. *Journal of Advanced Nursing, 62*(1), 107–115. doi: 10.1111/j.1365–2648.2007.04569.x

GMI Interactive Whitepaper. (2011). *Redesigning Mintel's online brand research survey to re-engage respondents and improve data quality.* Bellevue, WA: Global Market Insight.

Horton, J. J., Rand, D. G., & Zechhauser, R. J. (2011). The online laboratory: Conducting experiments in a real labor market. *Experimental Economics, 14*(3), 399–425. doi: 10.1007/s10683–011–9273–9

Kenning, P., Plassmann, H., & Ahlert, D. (2007). Applications of functional magnetic resonance imaging for market research. *Qualitative Market Research, 2*(10), 135–152.

Malinoff, B. (2010, June 3–4). *Sexy questions, dangerous answers.* CASRO Technology Conference, New York.

Marci, C. D. (2006). A biologically based measure of emotional engagement: Context matters. *Journal of Advertising Research, 46*(4), 381–387. doi: 10.2501/S0021849906060466

Miller, C. (2009, May 28–29). *Respondent technology preferences.* CASRO Technology Conference, New York.

Murphy, F. C., Nimmo-Smith, I., & Lawrence, A. D. (2003). Functional neuroanatomy of emotion: A meta-analysis. *Cognitive, Affective, & Behavioral Neuroscience, 3*(3), 207–233.

Neuendorf, K. A. (2002). *The content analysis guidebook.* Thousand Oaks, CA: Sage.

Ohme, R., Reykowska, D., Wiener, D., & Choromanska, A. (2009). Analysis of neurophysiological reactions to advertising stimuli by means of EEG and galvanic skin response measures. *Journal of Neuroscience, Psychology, and Economics, 2*(1), 21–31.

Reid, D. J., & Reid, F. J. M. (2005). Online focus groups: An in-depth comparison of computer-mediated and conventional focus group discussions. *International Journal of Market Research, 47*(2), 131–162.

Sleep, D., & Puleston, J. (2011). *Measuring the value of respondent engagement: Summary of research findings.* Bellevue, WA: Global Market Insight.

Strube, S. N., & Zdanowicz, Y. (2008, February 5–6). *Maximizing respondent engagement through survey design.* CASRO Panel Conference, Miami.

Thomas, R., Bremer, J., Terhanian, G., & Couper, M. P. (2007, September). *Truth in measurement: Comparing web-based interviewing techniques.* ESOMAR Congress, Berlin.

MORAL DEVELOPMENT, EFFECTS OF MEDIA VIOLENCE ON

The corruption of children's moral values due to media violence has long been a significant concern among media scholars, parents, educators, and policy makers. However, studies examining the effects of media violence on children's moral development have been scarce in comparison with other areas of media violence research. Despite this, a handful of studies have produced empirical evidence showing televised violence's relation to children's moral development. Researchers have turned to well-established psychology theories on moral development as their theoretical frameworks. These theories include the cognitive developmental approach developed by Jean Piaget and Lawrence Kohlberg, the affective approach developed by Martin Hoffman and Nancy Eisenberg, and the socialization approach developed by Albert Bandura. Given that the narratives of most violent media content deal with justice-based moral issues such as good versus evil and right versus wrong, most studies have chosen to examine effects on moral development through the lens of the cognitive developmental approach. Specifically, this approach provides a method to understand children's moral development by assessing both their moral judgment and moral reasoning.

Of all media scholars, Marina Krcmar and colleagues have studied this topic most extensively. Borrowing from the cognitive developmental perspective, they conceptualized moral development as the ways children make ethical judgments. The same line of research has identified *moral judgment* as a child's ability to tell right from wrong when asked to make an ethical choice, whereas *moral reasoning* is a child's ability to verbally explain the decision he or she makes. To further aid understanding of how studies have used cognitive developmental approaches as their theoretical backbone, this entry (a) reviews Piaget and Kolhberg's theory on moral development, (b) identifies moral characteristics that shape children's ability to make judgments and articulate moral reasoning, and (c) examines empirical research findings on television violence and moral development.

Moral Developmental Theories

Piaget and Kohlberg's theories play a huge role in the cognitive approach of moral development. Both theories are deeply rooted in the constructivist viewpoint that focuses on how internal constructions are established and developed through the course of childhood. Their theories ask the question of how children provide explanations (i.e., moral reasoning) for their moral judgments throughout their developmental stages. Children are viewed as active agents who can construct logical ideals through exchanges of perspectives with others. Furthermore, they achieve moral maturity by actively taking perspectives of others rather than passively internalizing moral standards and judgments handed down by socializing agents (e.g., parents, teachers, or television).

In his classic study, Piaget used stories depicting children's transgressions, such as breaking glass, as ways to assess children's developing moral judgment. He found that children process differently according to their cognitive developmental differences. Younger children, under approximately age 9, exhibit heteronomous morality by using rules handed down by authority figures such as socialization agents when making judgments, whereas older children slowly develop more autonomous reasoning by first constructing a sense of fairness and justice through "You scratch my back, I scratch yours" or "tit-for-tat" morality before reaching the true autonomous morality of reciprocity (i.e., "Do as you would be done by" morality).

Kohlberg used moral dilemma scenarios, such as one that pitted the moral judgment of stealing against saving a dying person, to understand children's moral reasoning. His theory posited that as each individual matures, they go through stages of development that move them toward moral maturity. Although their methods of assessment were different, Kohlberg's stage theory was strongly influence by Piaget's views.

Characteristics of Moral Developmental

Whether it is from Piaget's heteronomous morality to autonomous morality or Kolhberg's immature to mature stages of moral reasoning, the quintessential characteristics that mark children's moral development are egocentrism, perspective taking, and reciprocity. Younger children are egocentric in the sense that they are limited to unidimensional thinking. They have difficulty keeping track of multiple situations. In sociomoral development, preschoolers' moral judgments are often limited by salient punishment and authority figures. They have the tendency to make decisions by focusing on one feature of a situation at a time. Before the age of approximately 7 years children lack the ability to take the perspective of others because egocentrism limits them to considering events from their own perspective. They do not yet possess the ability to differentiate between self and others, nor can they consider the interests of others. Consequently, judgment strategies are either based on immediate self-need or superficial cues such as visible consequences rather than the abstract psychological interests or motivation of others. To summarize, due to egocentrism and lack of a perspective-taking ability, younger children's moral judgments are based on obedience to rigid rules and authority, avoidance of punishment, and individualistic concerns.

As children develop, they move from superficial physicalistic features to an understanding of reciprocity. However, the first traces of reciprocity are usually demands for equal exchanges of favors, which both Piaget and Kohlberg do not consider as ideal mature moral reasoning. This tit-for-tat morality lacks full awareness of another's intentions and thoughts. For example, in an interpersonal aggression context, explanation for reciprocity morality sounds like this: "If somebody hits you two times, you should hit them back two times—fair and square."

By approximately age 9, children's moral judgment shifts from the understanding of pragmatic equal exchange reciprocity to mutual trust in relationships. Therefore, reciprocity goes beyond self-interest to the awareness of other people's expectations and feelings. This, then, is the beginning of a more mature and sophisticated reasoning. Generally speaking, older children, after approximately age 9, make greater use of intentional information in their moral judgments than would younger children. They pass from the superficial level to the abstract level. They begin to develop the ability to take the perspectives of others, consider others' feelings and thoughts, and exercise reasoning strategies that reflect more of a "do as you would be done by" morality. At this point, behavior is judged based on intention for the first time. One caveat for children's ability to role-take is their limited social experience. Kohlberg stressed that children tend to practice reciprocity moral reasoning only in close interpersonal contexts, such as among family members or close friends. In other words, children are more likely to take the perspectives of those with whom they come in contact or with whom they are most familiar.

Televised Violence and Children's Moral Development

Research indicates that exposure to both fantasy and realistic violence correlates with the use of less sophisticated moral reasoning strategies. For example, one study found that frequent violence viewers have the tendency to choose authority-based or punishment-based reasoning strategies over perspective-taking strategies. As delineated earlier, immature moral reasoning due to egocentrism often entails interpretations that focus either on rules handed down by authority figures or on consequences such as punishment for a violent behavior. Not showing preference for reasoning that prescribes ideal reciprocity and perspective taking suggests that televised violence can encourage children to use less advanced moral reasoning.

One reason why heavy viewing of fantasy violence encourages children to choose more immature moral reasoning over mature ones is the nature of televised violent narratives. These narratives often put emphasis on a hero's perspective that legitimizes and glorifies violence without clear negative consequences and punishments. Without a clear, tangible outcome to aggression, children have no salient features upon which to base their judgments. Additionally, heroes and villains portray the most stereotypical images of right versus wrong and good versus evil. As pointed out previously, Kohlberg's theory posited that children, given their limited social experience, practice ideal reciprocity only under close interpersonal context. As a result, they base many of their moral judgments on less familiar people (i.e., TV characters) and on a stock of stereotypes (i.e., who is nice and who is mean). This serves as another possible reason why even older children with heavy violent media consumption are still likely to view heroes who engage in violent behaviors to be natural and acceptable.

It is important to note that effects of televised violence on children's moral reasoning should not be treated uniformly. Research has shown that the choice between different reasoning strategies is dependent on both contextual features of the violence as well as children's developmental differences. Violence shown as provoked or justified is perceived differently from violence shown as unprovoked or unjustified. For instance, children tend to judge unjustified violence as wrong, but wider variance exists in judgment toward justified violence. Additionally, children offered up more sophisticated explanations for their moral judgment toward justified violence than unjustified violence. Although justified violence yielded more variance in children's moral reasoning, justified violence on television is often portrayed as restitution for harm or revenge. It generally reflects the concept of the tit-for-tat morality that both Piaget and Kohlberg categorized as immature morality. Again, media's portrayal of violence seems to be providing models of, or simply reinforcing, immature moral reasoning.

As for developmental differences, though some mixed results were reported across studies, one study did find younger children to judge unpunished violence as more acceptable than punished violence, and older children to judge provoked violence as more acceptable than unprovoked violence. This again underscores how exposure to media violence can reinforce younger children's use of superficial criteria such as physical punishment for their moral judgment.

Besides mapping out the connection between different types of televised violence and children's use of different moral judgment or reasoning, studies have also devised instruments to better measure children's moral reasoning as it reflects their judgment of violence depicted on television. One instrument includes interpersonal violence dilemmas used to assess children's moral developmental stages through interview methodology, while another instrument is a close-ended self-administrative scale that also measures children's moral reasoning on interpersonal violence.

Scholars have just started exploring media violence's impact on children's moral development. To date, the majority of the studies have been on televised violence; only one has focused on video gaming. More attention should be paid to other effects of media violence, and studies examining televised violence should explicate in further detail the intricate relationship between different contextual features of television violence and children's moral developmental characteristics. Last, putting a greater emphasis on the cognitive approach doesn't mean minimizing the relevance of the other approaches. In fact, future research should explore how affective and socialization approaches provide further insight into media violence's effect on moral development.

Melissa M. Yang

See also Exposure to Violent Content, Effects on Child Development; Media Effects Perspectives of Violence; Media Violence, Definitions and Context of; National Television Violence Study; Television Violence

Further Readings

Bierwirth, K. P., & Blumberg, F. C. (2010). Preschoolers' judgment regarding realistic and cartoon-based moral transgressions in the U.S. *Journal of Children and Media, 4*(1), 39–58.

Krcmar, M., & Cooke, M. C. (2001). Children's moral reasoning and their perceptions of television violence. *Journal of Communication, 51,* 300–316.

Krcmar, M., & Curtis, S. (2003). Mental models: Understanding the impact of fantasy violence on children's moral reasoning. *Journal of Communication, 3,* 460–478.

Krcmar, M., & Valkenberg, P. M. (1999). A scale to assess children's moral interpretations of justified and unjustified violence and its relationship to television viewing. *Communication Research, 26*(5), 608–634.

Krcmar, M., & Vieira, E. T. (2005). Imitating life, imitating television: The effects of family and television models on children's moral reasoning. *Communication Research, 32*(3), 267–294.

Lemal, M., & Van Dan Bulck, J. (2009). Television and children's moral reasoning: Toward a closed-ended measure of moral reasoning on interpersonal violence. *Communication, 34*(3), 305–321.

Vieira, E. T., & Krcmar, M. (2011). The influence of video gaming on U.S. children's moral reasoning about violence. *Journal of Children and Media, 5*(2), 113–131.

MUSIC VIDEOS AND LYRICS, VIOLENT CONTENT IN

One of the fundamental concerns driving the interest in violent content in music lyrics and videos is whether such content influences consumers' thoughts and behaviors in a deleterious way. Available evidence has demonstrated that there is indeed a link between violent content in music lyrics and videos and subsequent attitudes and perceived social norms toward violence, as well as aggressive thoughts and behaviors. However, the relationship between violent content and violent behaviors is multifaceted and influenced by a wide range of additional factors. There is ample evidence that violent content has been present in music throughout recorded history—with varying degrees of overt references to and graphic descriptions of violence that have become of increasing concern in recent decades. This concern has been accelerated by the advent of music videos, which emerged as a new form of entertainment in the early 1980s and became extremely popular in a very short period of time.

Background and Context

Concerns about the harmful effects of explicit content in music have been directed at a wide range of so-called problem music styles, including jazz, bebop, early rock and roll, heavy metal, and rap, among others. This phenomenon has been fairly well chronicled, and because much attention has been trained on particular forms of music, violent content that may be included in other styles of music has often been overlooked.

Themes of violence in music have long been a part of the lyric content and the attendant visual productions, spanning across many genres of music and over a very long period of time. For example, the Camille Saint-Saëns opera *Samson and Delilah* depicts a climactic conclusion of Samson bringing down stone columns and crushing his adversaries. As some observers have pointed out, popular music began attracting the most widespread controversy and calls for censorship when White artists began incorporating elements of the music of Black America—jazz, blues, and rhythm and blues (R&B). In the 1980s, the focus of concern was on heavy metal and hard rock bands such as Guns 'n' Roses, Cinderella, and Def Leppard. The Parents Music Resource Center (PMRC) and other critics pointed to cases in which life seemed to imitate art, as when in 1986 a 16-year-old boy in California shot himself while listening to Ozzy Osbourne's song "Suicide Solution." Perhaps the most influential development in popular music in the past three decades has been the rise of hip-hop and rap, bringing aspects of inner-city culture into the mainstream. These genres have their own high-profile critics, Bill Cosby and Spike Lee among them, who have argued that some of this music glorifies criminality, ignorance, and misogyny. Arguably, one of the key differences that has emerged in more recent history is the inclusion of increasingly graphic content in both lyrics and music videos—with some subgenres within the broader styles of metal and rap becoming strongly associated with graphic violent imagery.

The role of violent content in music lyrics and videos and its ability to influence real-world behaviors was scrutinized in the aftermath of particularly salient instances of violence—such as homicides (including the influence the music of the band AC/DC was posited to have on convicted serial killer Richard Ramirez) and school shootings (most notably Columbine High School near Littleton, Colorado, but also shootings in Jonesboro, Arkansas; Paducah, Kentucky; and Pearl, Mississippi). In the public dialogue around these events, some of the questions that emerged have pertained to the styles of music and particular musical artists that the perpetrators listened to and enjoyed. In these cases, the reactionary nature of the broader public interest in the links among musical preferences, lyric content, and criminality was evident. Inferences and assumptions of causality were also evident.

Scholars have been somewhat cautious in ascribing music and other media with causal significance. Music can alter attitudes, as experiments have shown. In survey research of adolescents, scholars found that metal and rap music were correlated with poor grades, sexual activity, drug use, arrests, and behavior problems in school. Still, the correlation between music preferences and certain types of

behavior does not necessarily signify causation. In fact, studies have shown that dispositional traits such as self-esteem, distrust, and aggression lead individuals to certain preferences in music and in behavior. In other words, music preference and behavior may indeed be effects of the same cause (or set of causes), and the claim that certain types of music can *cause* antisocial behavior is difficult to support with strong empirical evidence. It has been hypothesized that people with certain dispositional traits (anger, distrust) may be more inclined to choose aggressive music. This music then reinforces and amplifies the trait, increasing the likelihood, people will act in aggressive ways.

How (and How Much) Violence Is Depicted in Music Videos

A significant percentage of music videos have been found to show acts of violence, with some estimates indicating that 15% of all music videos portray violence in at least one form. Analyses have revealed that there are differences in the amount of violence depicted in music videos across various networks, including MTV, VH1, and BET. Specifically, MTV and BET were found to have a greater percentage of videos depicting violence than VH1. Furthermore, there are differences between each of these networks in terms of the nature of the violence portrayed—most notably in terms of the identities of perpetrators and victims of violence. For example, the violence in videos that were shown on MTV featured a greater number of White perpetrators and White victims, while those shown on BET featured more Black perpetrators and victims of violence.

In addition to violence across race, many music videos also portray negative behaviors toward women. In one study, rock videos were found to elicit antagonistic attitudes toward women in much the same way that pornography elicits such attitudes. Indeed, the sexual objectification of women is a common theme of both rock and rap videos. Many rap videos feature the male rapper in a position of dominance over a group of women. Moreover, these women are often dressed in revealing clothing and repeatedly appear to be lusting after the musician or group.

Violence has been used in the context of music videos to produce strong emotional responses in viewers, and in several examples there has been a concerted effort to use exceptionally graphic violence. Consider the singer M.I.A.'s 2010 YouTube video for the song "Born Free," which depicts the capture and slaughter of individuals with red hair at the hands of men dressed in military attire. In this instance, there was a significant level of online discussion and debate about the portrayal of graphic violence as part of a broader social commentary. The nature and intensity of this violence pushed far beyond what would be broadcast on television. With broadcast television losing some reach to sites such as YouTube that have fewer content filters, there are new challenges for those concerned about the messages in video and music. This is especially important considering that YouTube is the most popular website among children, according to a 2009 FTC report.

The Effects of Exposure to Violent Content

One of the most pronounced areas of impact for violent content in music videos (and perhaps to a lesser extent, lyrics) is its influence on perceptions of social norms around violence. That is, those who view violent content are increasingly likely to see violence as an appropriate response to people, situations, and events. Also of interest are the findings that exposure to violence in the context of music videos does not increase the favorability of viewer response, but rather has been associated with negative reactions including anxiety and fear. In other words, a viewer need not enjoy the content of a video to react in a negative manner. Studies also show that such negative reactions, particularly fear, are much stronger when elicited by visual stimuli (such as a music video) than when elicited by lyric descriptions alone.

Aggressive music can also have an impact on how someone perceives his or her environment. Experiments have shown that after hearing a song replete with violent lyrics, subjects interpreted ambiguous words such as *stick* in an aggressive way. Findings do not support the idea that violent music acts as a catharsis, giving people a "release" of aggressive feelings. On the contrary, it seems that violent lyrics can put the listener into an aggressive state of mind that negatively alters his or her perception of the world. Such perceptions can be self-fulfilling. Because of music's effect on perception, a metal listener may tend to view others as aggressive even when they are not. This misperception may lead the metal listener to respond to relatively benign behavior by others with suspicion and aggression, and one can expect the listener's social environment to react negatively too. When conflict results, it serves to reinforce the metal listener's image of the world as dangerous and dog-eat-dog. As such, the listener's expectations may be fulfilled.

One of the empirically established effects of violent content in music videos and song lyrics more generally has been that the presentation of violence has been consistently associated with increased levels of aggressive thoughts. In this way, when violence is depicted, it may position aggressive responses to confrontations as a viable, if not socially approved, method of addressing conflict. Thus, the portrayal of violence in music videos has the potential to increase the viability of violence in the consideration set of responses to conflict. This has important implications for how conflict is perceived and also how it is addressed and resolved.

Also important in the discussion of violence in music videos is the portrayal of victims and aggressors, which can build and reinforce racial and gender stereotypes. The intersection of sex and violence in music videos also has the potential to influence a decrease in the perception of severity of violence against women among male viewers. Because the audience for music videos includes adolescents, the extent to which violence is portrayed in the context of sexual relationships has implications for the development of perceived expectancies and social norms regarding what is viewed as more or less permissible.

There are still open questions regarding how long the negative effects remain influential on a viewer's attitudes and behaviors. Many of the studies elicit responses from participants immediately following the viewing of a violent video. And although much evidence shows that there is a negative reaction immediately after watching a video with violent content, more data regarding the long-term impact are needed before drawing more general conclusions about violent content's effect on behavior. However, there are reasons to think the effects could be long-lasting. The so-called activation frequency hypothesis argues that those categories—such as violence, misogyny, or materiality—that are activated frequently have a larger influence upon behaviors. Thus, if viewers are repeatedly exposed to violent content, this content may be more behaviorally influential. Furthermore, because many people, including children and adolescents, spend several hours every week listening to music or watching music videos, it remains plausible that the violent content therein may affect behavior in a negative way.

Of course, most people do not react violently to music videos and lyrics. Those people who do react violently represent a relatively small percentage of the total population of music consumers. However, when dealing with violence, a small percentage can make a big impact. If even a low percentage of music listeners are driven to acts of violence, the consequences could be severe. Recent studies have shown that those who do commit violent acts are more likely to be fans of music with violent lyrics (such as heavy metal) than are those who do not commit such acts. This has led some researchers to look beyond the causal question of whether or not violent music itself engenders antisocial behavior. Instead, they argue, attention should be paid to the amplifying effects of violent music on youths who are already at risk. The question is thus not whether music may or may not induce certain negative attitudes and behaviors, but rather how violent content can amplify such moods if they are already present in the listener.

Congress and Parental Warnings

With the advent of music videos, musical performers were able to augment the music and lyric content with imagery that could be used to complement the material that was portrayed in their music. Corresponding with the development and increased popularity of music videos, the issue of violent content in music and videos has been considered, discussed, and debated in political as well as scientific contexts. Specifically, there have been congressional hearings to address sexual and violent content in music—most notably those convened in the mid-1980s by the Parents Music Resource Center. Susan Baker and Tipper Gore, wives of politicians James A. Baker and Al Gore, founded the PMRC, and the group enjoyed considerable influence in getting the issue into the public eye. In these hearings, a wide and disparate range of musicians came before Congress to address the issue of violent, sexual, and occult content in music that was assumed to be causing significant harm to children and adolescents who were prime consumers of the music. One of the key outcomes was the development of parental warning labels that were designed to advise parents of "explicit" content and that would be prominently featured on the cover art of a given recording. However, these hearings also demonstrated a very clear tension between the concern about potential harmful effects of violent content in music lyrics and freedom of speech and artistic expression. Subsequent congressional hearings about the prevalence and impact of explicit and violent content in music and lyrics have similarly run into this same tension, most recently focusing on hip-hop music in 2007.

The music industry has proven adversarial to the position of the PMRC and the Federal Trade Commission (FTC), the industry's regulator, both of whom have maintained for nearly two decades that the music industry markets adult-themed music to children and adolescents. The FTC has somewhat limited power to enforce its recommendations, including its push for clear warning labels on all explicit content. However, although industry compliance is inconsistent, the FTC has helped shape the music industry profoundly.

According to the FTC industry report to Congress in 2009, nearly all of the top albums with warning labels were also released as edited versions. These "clean" versions accounted for nearly one-quarter of the album sales for those releases. In general, the FTC noted an improvement in industry standards on its marketing of explicit content. The regulator found no ads for explicit content music in teen magazines, and it reported fewer ads for such content on websites frequented by teens and children than in previous studies. When buying music online, the FTC reported that warning labels were prominent and readable. However, from a comparative perspective, the industry's television advertising has lagged far behind these standards, with only half of the ads for explicit content displaying a warning. Also, television ads for explicit music appeared on television shows with large teen audiences.

Further Research

One area requiring further study is the impact of the Internet on the consumption of violent music videos and lyrics. Since most websites do not maintain standards as strict as those of television, the Internet makes increasingly violent and explicit content available. Additionally, the fact that videos are available on demand and without charge on many websites such as YouTube makes this content easily accessible. Finally, the advent of new technologies on which to view these videos—such as smartphones, computer tablets, and laptops—allows content to be viewed outside of one's living room or away from one's desk. Additional research is needed to properly assess the impact that this new wave of technologies will have on the behavior of music consumers going forward.

Anthony F. Lemieux, Jason Levitt,
and Jay Wood

See also Exposure to Violent Content, Effects on Child Development; First-Person Perspective, Violent Content From; Media Ratings Systems; Rap Lyrics, Effects of Violent Content in; Sexualized Aggression; Stereotyping in Violent Media Content

Further Readings

Alcorn, L. M., & Lemieux, A. F. (2010). The effect of sexually explicit rap music on sexual attitudes, norms, and behaviors. In Tamara E. Ivanova (Ed.), *Music: Composition, interpretation, and effects.* Hauppauge, NY: Nova Science Publishers.

Anderson, C. A., Berkowitz, L., Donnerstein, E., Huesmann, L. R., Johnson, J. D., Linz, D., et al. (2003). The influence of media violence on youth. *Psychological Science in the Public Interest, 4,* 81–110.

Anderson, C. A., Carnagey, N. L., & Eubanks, J. (2003). Exposure to violent media: The effects of songs with violent lyrics on aggressive thoughts and feelings. *Journal of Personality and Social Psychology, 84,* 960–971.

Baxter, R. L., De Riemer, C., Landini, A., Leslie, L., & Singletary, M. W. (1985). A content analysis of music videos. *Journal of Broadcasting and Electronic Media, 29,* 333–340.

Caplan, R. E. (1985). Violent program content in music video. *Journalism Quarterly, 62,* 144–147.

Council on Communications and Media. (2009). Impact of music, music lyrics, and music videos on children and youth. *Pediatrics, 124,* 1488–1494.

Federal Trade Commission. (2009, December). *Marketing violent entertainment to children: A sixth follow-up review of industry practices in the motion picture, music recording and electronic game industries.* Report to Congress. Retrieved from http://www.ftc.gov/os/2009/12/P994511violententertainment.pdf

Johnson, B., & Cloonan, M. (2009). *Dark side of the tune: Popular music and violence.* Burlington, VT: Ashgate.

Johnson, J. D., Adams, M. S., Ashburn, L., & Reed, W. (1995). Differential gender effects of exposure to rap music on African American adolescents' acceptance of teen dating violence. *Sex Roles, 33,* 597–605.

North, A., & Hargreaves, D. (2008). *The social and applied psychology of music.* New York, NY: Oxford University Press.

Rich, M., Woods, E. R., Goodman, E., Emans, S. J., & DuRant, R. H. (1998). Aggressors or victims: Gender and race in music video violence. *Pediatrics, 101*(4), 669–674.

Smith, S. L., & Boyson, A. R. (2002). Violence in music videos: Examining the prevalence and context of physical aggression. *Journal of Communication, 51*(1), 61–83.

Took, K. J., & Weiss, D. S. (1994). The relationship between heavy metal and rap music and adolescent turmoil: Real or artifact? *Adolescence, 29,* 613–621.

NARRATIVE, EFFECTS OF VIOLENT

Violent narratives are a common theme in media. A *violent narrative* is defined as a plot, with characters involved in ongoing relationships, featuring the use of intentional verbal or physical aggression intended to harm others. Violent narratives in media have been documented for well over 50 years in television and film and now extend to other media such as smartphones, iPods, and video games. Although the relative frequency with which violence appears in media has remained flat over the years, depictions of violent acts are more explicit and audiences are more engaged with violence than ever before. Implications for interacting with violent narratives are discussed.

The purpose of this entry is to (a) introduce the reader to the history of violent narratives commonly encountered in media; (b) provide an overview of the frequency and nature of violent narratives in popular media, such as television, motion pictures, and video games; (c) describe the amount and frequency with which audiences spend time with media on a daily basis; (d) explain theoretical mechanisms for how and why audiences become immersed in narratives; (e) explain the consequences of exposure to violent narratives; and (f) offer ways to ameliorate the potential negative effects of violent narratives.

History of Violent Narratives in Media

Violent narratives are regularly encountered in media. Television, a staple of American life since the 1950s, is one medium that demonstrates the frequency of violent narratives. As early as the 1960s,

the first systematic study of television content and its effects, the Cultural Indicators Project (CIP), found that two out of three television programs featured some form of violence. That trend in violent narratives in television continues in the early 21st century.

George Gerbner created the CIP, a large empirical undertaking, to investigate his belief about television as "America's storyteller." The multifaceted study largely consisted of two parts: a content analysis that tabulated the frequency of various portrayals in television, and an investigation of the effects of viewing such content. Portrayals of violence were one category of the phenomena measured, and Gerbner sought to determine how they shaped audience's perceptions about police activity and fear of victimization.

The CIP revealed that violent depictions permeated two-thirds of television programming regardless of genre (excluding news and sporting events, which were omitted from coding). Regarding effects of viewing violent content, heavy viewers (those who watched an average of 4 or more hours of television per day) were more likely to endorse a fear of victimization than light viewers (those who watched an average of fewer than 2 hours per day). Thus, most television programs include some form of violent or aggressive theme, and effects occur for audiences who watch a lot of television. More recent studies of television content have revealed that violent themes and narratives continue apace.

Frequency and Nature of Violent Narratives in Media

The prevalence of violence extends to other media as well. Violent narratives are widespread in motion pictures. Almost all contemporary popular films include violent storylines or subthemes. Of the top-grossing films each year for the past 55 years, 89% have included portrayals of violence. Sex differences in violent portrayals are notable; males are consistently portrayed more than are females in violent and aggressive acts. Female characters have been depicted in violent and aggressive acts at an increasing rate over time. Moreover, although females are less likely than males to be in lead roles in films, they are more likely over time to engage in graphic and explicit representations of violent acts. This suggests that audiences are developing increased tolerance for violent storylines.

Violent narratives in music lyrics are prevalent in two genres in music: heavy metal and rap. Lyrics frequently include the use of physical and verbal aggression, and at times rely on themes of violence against women.

Video games routinely use explicit brutality and increasing gore and realism to gain traction with audiences. This invites players into a more immersed virtual reality of the violent narrative. Video games create worlds of fantasy (e.g., imagined realms) or realistic experiences (e.g., military training). Games are becoming increasingly realistic by incorporating 3D, Surround Sound headsets, and virtual reality goggles. To this end, video games can be considered a modern-day venue in which to engage in violent narratives.

Audience Exposure to Media on a Daily Basis

Data from a nationally representative survey published in 2010 showed that among 8- to 18-year-olds, media usage has risen sharply over the past five years. On average, youth interact with entertainment media more than 7 1/2 hours each day. Since 2004, that is a 1 1/4-hour increase. The increase, in large part, is due to the proliferation of smartphones and MP3 players such as the iPod. Youth between the ages of 8 and 18 spend an average of 49 minutes each day multitasking on smartphones. Time spent on smartphones is split among watching television, listening to music, and playing video games.

Viewing television programs remains the largest media use segment. Television viewing has increased to an average of 4 1/2 hours per day, but the platform has changed. Youth rely less on regularly scheduled television programs and instead opt for recorded programs, or they view programs online and on smartphones. Following television program

viewing, music listening (2 1/2 hours per day) and video gaming (1 1/4 hours per day) are the most popular media. Time spent viewing films decreased over the 5-year period (2004–2009) and averages 25 minutes per day. Thus, apart from sleep and school, youth spend the majority of their leisure time interacting with media.

Theoretical Mechanisms to Explain Effects of Violent Narratives

At its very core, cultivation theory explains why audiences come to believe that television storylines are real. Indeed, cultivation theory, posited by Gerbner, asserts that television is America's storyteller. By repeating violent and crime-oriented themes throughout television, audiences adopt the norms and portrayals on television as real.

The cultivation process happens through two primary processes: mainstreaming and resonance. *Mainstreaming* is the process of television blurring, blending, and bending reality to a single reality for all. In essence, television becomes the one common story among all groups in society, sending a consistent message (for a critique see Potter, 1993). *Resonance* is a pronounced effect of viewing violent narratives on television for those who previously experienced violence in real life. Viewing violent content is like getting a double dose of reality and reliving the violence all over again. Other theories relating to a narrative quality also explain why viewers come to have changed beliefs after viewing violent storylines.

Walter Fisher's narrative paradigm (1985) claimed that people are natural storytellers. He believed that people are rational and make decisions based on the logic of stories. Stories provide a basis for "good reasons" by which humans make decisions about how to behave. Audiences evaluate whether stories provide good reasons by what Fisher calls *coherence* and *fidelity*. Coherence is how well a story "hangs together," and, alternatively, fidelity is how well a story "rings true" for audience members. To the extent that a story fits together and resonates with audiences, it provides a logical argument on which to base decisions in life.

Transportation theory also explains why violent narratives may affect audiences. Building upon the work of Victor Nell and using a term coined by Richard Gerrig, Melanie Green and Timothy Brock (2000) developed *transportation theory*, meaning that audiences are figuratively taken to the world created by the narrative. The theorists have claimed that while a viewer is in a transported state in which the narrative world becomes his or her reality, three processes are simultaneously occurring.

The first process is a *cognitive* process wherein one's thoughts are intensely focused on the twists and turns of the unfolding plot. A viewer surmises what might happen next in the story, and he or she might play out "what if's" in certain scenarios to determine the possible outcomes. Time slips away, and the viewer might even become unaware of what is happening in the room around him or her. Consequently, the person is less likely to counterargue (question) the plot.

The second process is an *affective* process through which the person becomes emotionally involved in a story. The audience member comes to know the characters in the plot and responds emotionally to the events. As such, the person may feel great satisfaction, relief, and elation when likable characters triumph over evil or avoid tragedy. However, he or she might feel suspense, terror, or hatred when the disliked character is about to succeed or gets away with immoral crimes. These all contribute to one's emotional involvement with a narrative.

The third process is one of *visual imagery*. Figuratively, these are images in the mind's eye. Visual imagery occurs when one is able to conjure up an image of the narrative scene in one's mind. These images persist and become the world of the narrative. Thus, when all three processes are occurring (cognitive, affective, and visual imagery), one becomes transported into the narrative world.

Effects of becoming transported are that audience members' beliefs may shift to those of the narrative. Without realizing it, audience members who are transported may have adopted the narrative world, if only temporarily, as their own. Attitudes and beliefs change to be more consistent with those of the narrative than before.

Effects of Violent Narratives

Television

Violent narratives are an ingrained part of our daily lives. Narrative entertainment television programs are the most common source of enjoyment. A narrative's ability to convey experiences, whether fact or fiction, depends on audience members' ability to become immersed in the story. Although people may seek out entertainment programs for enjoyment, at times they may emerge from the experience with changed beliefs.

Studies over the past several decades have found that viewing violent television programming is associated with more aggressive attitudes and behaviors and that these behaviors persist over time (for critiques see Ferguson & Kilburn, 2009; Wilson, Stover, & Berkowitz, 2009). These study designs included experiments, meta-analyses, cross-sectional surveys, and longitudinal studies. Oftentimes, studies have examined the effects with adults, but much of the literature has focused on children and their receptivity to programming.

Children are exposed to violent narratives at an early age. There is a small but statistically significant association between consumption of violent television programming and increased physical aggression in children younger than 10 years of age. This association is more pronounced for boys than girls. Higher consumption of violent fare is associated with greater intentions to harm others and often is associated with less empathy for others' suffering. Thus, greater consumption of violent narratives in young children is associated with greater inclination for physical aggression, more aggressive thoughts, and less empathy for others.

Subtle effects of engaging with violent narratives are also likely to occur. Indirect aggression is the intention to harm in ways not directed at the target but ultimately designed to harm him or her. Examples of indirect aggression are spreading rumors, damaging a person's belongings, and intentionally excluding a person from a group for the purposes of hurting his or her feelings. Studies show children as young as preschoolers watching cartoons with violence exhibit this effect.

Frequently, young children are introduced to violent narratives through slapstick cartoons. *Tom & Jerry* and *Wile E. Coyote and the Roadrunner* are examples of slapstick cartoons. A common misconception is that children like violence in cartoons. This is not the case. Instead, studies have shown that *action* is a motivating force for children viewing slapstick cartoons, and intentional infliction of harm is not the main attraction.

One reason for concern about young children viewing violent narratives is that violent narratives may prime children to act in ways they see modeled in cartoons. Thus, in ambiguous situations, children are apt to interpret actions or to respond aggressively. Second, violent narratives form the basis for scripts in which children learn to act later on. Fisher's narrative paradigm claims that stories give people "good reasons" to act. If a story hangs together well, children are likely to learn from that story that aggression is the appropriate way to behave.

Music Lyrics and Music Videos

MP3 players, such as iPods, are the second most popular form of media used by youth. Violent narratives are present regularly in several popular genres of music, such as heavy metal and rap music. There have been a limited number of studies on the effects of listening to violent lyrics. A clear pattern has emerged, however, with cross-sectional surveys. Listeners of violent lyrics have, statistically, significantly more hostile and aggressive thoughts than do listeners of nonviolent lyrics. The cause of this association, however, has not been discerned.

Additional studies have been conducted to study aggression associated with viewing violent music videos, yet these studies have been beset by methodological problems. From the studies using music videos and examining their association with aggression, a few patterns have emerged. First, even young children who viewed violent music videos endorse more aggressive attitudes than their peers who did not view violent videos. Additionally, children who view violent music videos have been rated by teachers as more physically aggressive, indirectly aggressive, and less helpful than children who did not view violent videos. College students who cite heavy metal and rap music preferences rate higher on aggression and maladaptive behaviors, such as behavior problems in school and arrests. Women who view violent music videos rate date rape as more acceptable than do women who do not watch violent videos. Taken as a whole, listening to or viewing violent music videos clearly goes hand in hand with aggression. More rigorous studies are needed to tease out the links with violent narratives.

Video Games

One of the more popular pastimes in recent history, violent video games are a hit with audiences of all ages. A number of studies have been conducted on video gaming over the past decade, and from these studies meta-analyses have been conducted. A pattern has emerged about video game players: people who play games featuring violent storylines display significantly more aggressive thoughts, aggressive emotions, physiological arousal, and less helping behavior than people who do not play violent video games. This finding was consistent even after parsing out studies whose methods were

deemed problematic. Therefore, engaging with a medium that requires not only viewing and listening to violent narratives, but active participation in aggressive behavior, has been associated with aggressive thoughts, emotions, and behaviors.

Film

Violent narratives are replete in motion pictures as well. Numerous experiments have demonstrated that viewing violent narratives causes audience members to act more aggressively than audience members who watch films with nonviolent narratives. Motion pictures pose a special venue for media effects because of their narrative format and the setting in which movies are often viewed: in a darkened theater where attention is focused and distractions are minimized. Transportation theory claims that the more cognitive, emotional, and visual imagery devoted to processing the storyline, the more likely it is that one will become transported into the story. The greater the transportation, the more likely beliefs are to be consistent with story. Therefore, if most movies focus on themes of violence, and characters solve problems with aggressive actions, viewers are likely to walk away from the stories with similar thoughts.

Strategies to Mediate Effects of Violent Narratives

Parents can use several strategies to reduce the negative effects of violent narratives on children. The first step is to limit the amount of time a child spends with media. Less exposure to violent narratives is associated with less aggressive attitudes and behaviors. A number of professional organizations (e.g., American Medical Association) follow the recommendations of communication scholars and formally endorse "No television before age 2" and to limit screen time to no more than 2 hours of quality programming each day after age 2. Other steps include talking with children about what parents find acceptable in media, discussing why or why not, and providing media literacy training. Taken together, these approaches may minimize effects of violent narratives in media.

Summary

Across a number of media, violent narratives are commonly associated with increased aggressive attitudes, beliefs, emotions, and arousal, and less helping behavior. Several concerns arise from this:

(a) television is a medium that introduces violent narratives to children at a very young age and continual exposure to violence persists into adulthood; (b) violent themes are repeated across numerous platforms; and (c) violent video games are increasingly realistic and immersive.

Violent narratives across media present a homogeneous theme, indicating that violence is a part of our culture and an acceptable way to deal with problems. Moreover, with the increasing popularity of violent video games, their immersive qualities and explicit depictions of gore are of concern as gamers devote time to enacting violent behaviors. Thus, across a number of media, there is audience engagement with violent narratives from an early age and well into adulthood, with a propensity for more aggressive attitudes and behaviors than those who do not view or interact with violent media.

Carmen Stitt

See also Aggression, Risk Factors of; Aggression and Culture; Aggression and Youth; Attitudes, Effects of Media Violence on

Further Readings

Anderson, C. A., & Carnagey, C. L. (2009). Causal effects of violent sports video games on aggression: Is it competitiveness or violent content? *Journal of Experimental Social Psychology, 45,* 731–739.

Boxer, P., Huesmann, L. R., Bushman, B. J., O'Brien, M., & Moceri, D. (2009). The role of violent media preference in cumulative developmental risk for violence and general aggression. *Journal of Adolescence, 38,* 417–428.

Ferguson, C. J., & Kilburn, J. (2009). The public health risks of media violence: A meta-analytic review. *Journal of Pediatrics, 154,* 759–763.

Fisher, W. (1985). The narrative paradigm: An elaboration. *Communication Monographs, 52,* 347–367.

Gentile, D. A., Coyne, S., & Walsh, D. A. (2010). Media violence, physical aggression, and relational aggression in school-age children: A short-term longitudinal study. *Aggressive Behavior, 37,* 193–206.

Gerbner, G. (2002). Telling stories, how do we know what we know? The story of cultural indicators and the cultural environment movement. In M. Morgan (Ed.), *Against the mainstream: The selected works of George Gerbner* (pp. 485–491). New York, NY: Peter Lang.

Green, M. C., & Brock, T. C. (2000). The role of transportation in the persuasiveness of public narratives. *Journal of Personality and Social Psychology, 79,* 701–721.

Morgan, M., & Shanahan, J. (2010). The state of cultivation. *Journal of Broadcasting & Electronic Media, 54,* 337–355.

Potter, W. J. (1993). Cultivation theory and research: A conceptual critique. *Human Communication Research, 19,* 564–601.

Weaver, A. J., Jensen, J. D., Martins, N., Hurley, R. J., & Wilson, B. J. (2011). Liking violence and action: An examination of gender differences in children's processing of animated content. *Media Psychology, 49,* 49–70.

Wilson, H. W., Stover, C. S., & Berkowitz, S. J. (2009). Research review: The relationship between childhood violence exposure and juvenile anti-social behavior: A meta-analytic review. *Journal of Child Psychology and Psychiatry, 50,* 759–779.

NATIONAL TELEVISION VIOLENCE STUDY

The National Television Violence Study (NTVS) was a major investigation into violent content on U.S. television, the use of ratings and advisories, and the influence of public service messages about violence. Funded by the National Cable Television Association (NCTA) for $3.3 million, it began in the summer of 1994 and ran through 1998 with the publication of its third and final annual report. During that period, the project took place primarily on four university campuses and involved a dozen principal investigators, a score of advanced graduate students, more than 200 undergraduates as trained coders of television content, and more than 1,700 other people as participants in experiments and surveys.

Overview

In the early 1990s, public criticism of violence in the media spiked in response to several high-profile shootings by students in public schools (such as those at Columbine High School near Littleton, Colorado, in 1999 and Westside Middle School near Jonesboro, Arkansas, in 1998). The U.S. Congress responded with hearings that increased pressure on the media, especially television, to cut back the amount of violence or at least label programs with violence to warn viewers. In response to this pressure, the Cable Television Association agreed to fund research that would increase knowledge about the amount of violence in their programming and the usefulness of labeling violence programming. After issuing a call for proposals that attracted submissions from a variety of experts on media violence, the NCTA awarded a $3.3 million contract to a group of communication scholars who proposed a series of studies to document the amount and type of violence across the television landscape, the use of viewer advisories and ratings about violence, and the effects of antiviolence messages on adolescents. Calling itself the National Television Violence Study (NTVS), the project was designed and executed by media scholars from the University of California at Santa Barbara, University of Texas at Austin, University of Wisconsin at Madison, and University of North Carolina at Chapel Hill.

The project also created an advisory council so as to benefit from the best thinking from a wide range of stakeholders in the issue of media violence. This council included representatives from the following professional organizations: American Bar Association, American Medical Association, American Psychiatric Association, American Academy of Pediatrics, Society for Adolescent Medicine, National Education Association, National Parent Teachers Association, American Society of Criminology, American Psychological Association, American Sociological Association, and International Communication Association. It also included representatives from the following media industry organizations: American Federation of Television and Radio Artists; Directors Guild of America; Producers Guild of America; Writers Guild of America; Caucus for Producers, Writers, and Directors; and the National Cable Television Association. The advisory group met in person annually with the principal investigators. Although the principal investigators relied on advice from members of the advisory council, the project was designed as a scientific study that was not constrained by the political agenda of any media organization,

The NTVS research was conducted as follows. The examination of the use of content ratings and advisories was conducted at the University of Wisconsin at Madison under the direction of principal investigator Joanne Cantor. The study of the effects of antiviolence messages on adolescents took place at the University of North Carolina at Chapel Hill under the direction of principal investigators Frank Biocca and Jane Brown. The examination of how violence was portrayed in reality television programming was conducted at the University of

Texas at Austin under the direction of principal investigators Ellen Wartella, Chuck Whitney, Wayne Danielson, and Dominic Lasorsa. Finally, the largest part of the project, the examination of the prevalence and context of violent portrays in fictional programming across the entire television landscape, was conducted at the University of California at Santa Barbara with principal investigators Edward Donnerstein, Dale Kunkel, Daniel Linz, W. James Potter, and Barbara Wilson.

Content Analysis of Fictional Programming on Television

The NTVS conducted an analysis of the content of nearly 10,000 hours of television programming across 23 broadcast, cable, and independent channels of U.S. television. Individual programs were randomly selected so that the resulting sample would represent the total television landscape of fictional programming over a three-year period beginning in the fall of 1995.

Violence was defined as any overt depiction of a credible threat of physical force or the actual use of such force intended to physically harm an animate being or group of beings. Violence also included certain depictions of physically harmful consequences against an animate being or beings that result from unseen violent means. Each program was examined at three levels (individual act of violence, scene in which the violence occurred, and program) so that the context (or meaning) of the violence could be assessed in addition to the prevalence of the violence. Contextual variables focused on the way the violence was portrayed, such as its degree of graphicness, humor, the use of weapons, type of perpetrators (demographics, attractiveness, motives, degree of punishment or reward), and type of victim (demographics, attractiveness, degree of harm).

Across the three years, more than 54,000 acts of violence in fictional television programs were identified and analyzed. Within this representative sample, 62% of all programs were found to present at least one act of violence, and the average rate of violent acts presented across the entire range of fictional programs was found to be 6.8 acts per hour. Of even more importance than prevalence and rate to the investigators was context. The study included an examination of 28 contextual characteristics across the three levels of narrative analysis (the violent act, the scene, the television program).

The findings about the context of violence indicated that the violence was largely sanitized, trivialized, and glamorized. As to sanitizing, the violence was rarely presented as graphic; blood and gore were totally absent in 6 out of 7 violent scenes. Also, in more than 40% of all violent portrayals, there was no depiction of harm or pain to the victims. As to trivializing violence, 42% of the violence was presented in a humorous context. As to glamorizing, the good characters (or heroes) were as likely to commit acts of violence as were the bad characters (or villains); also, fewer than 30% of all acts of violence were portrayed as being punished. In addition, about one-quarter of all violent acts displayed guns, and another one-third of acts depicted the use of another kind of weapon. These figures about the prevalence, rate, and context of violent portrayals were found to be stable; that is, they did not fluctuate significantly across the three years of programming that were analyzed. Furthermore, these figures were close to the rates of prevalence and contextual patterns found in previous analyses of violence in television programming.

Content Analysis of Nonfictional Television

The violence in nonfictional programming was analyzed at the University of Texas at Austin. *Nonfictional programming* was defined as reality programming that presented actual current or historical events or circumstances. This included news, public affairs, interviews, talk shows, and documentaries. These researchers used the same definition of violence as given previously, with one exception: they also coded for talk about violence.

In their analyses of more than 1,400 randomly selected nonfictional programs, they found that about 39% of nonfictional shows presented visual depictions of violence, and another 10% of those programs presented only talk about violence. Thus, the prevalence of violence across the landscape of nonfictional programming was found to be less than the prevalence of violence across the landscape of fictional programming. The researchers found that violence in nonfictional programming was more likely to appear in the daytime than at night. Also, they found large variations across genres, with police shows being the most violent and talk shows being the least violent. As with the findings of the analyses of fictional programming, the context formula is the same; that is, graphic portrayals are rare, guns are used in about one-third of all violent acts, and the

majority of perpetrators were not depicted as being punished for their acts.

Ratings and Advisories

The main question motivating the research conducted at the University of Wisconsin at Madison was, Do program ratings and advisories about television violence work? Data were generated through interviews with elementary and middle school children. They found that advisories about violence increased the attractiveness of violent programs for boys but did not have an effect on girls. However, when the advisories were worded as "viewer discretion advised," they did have an effect on girls by reducing their interest in viewing the program.

In another study, researchers watched how children interacted with their parents when advisories preceded programs. They found that there was talk about the advisories and that children were very likely to avoid the violent programs when parents were present. In a third study, researchers found that among college students, the ratings and advisories had no effect on their desire to watch various programs.

In a fourth study, the researchers examined how frequently advisories appeared to television programs. They found that only 4% of programs were preceded with an advisory in 1995, but two years later, advisories were found to precede two-thirds of programs with violence.

Antiviolence Messages

The main question motivating the research conducted at the University of North Carolina at Chapel Hill was, Are antiviolence messages effective? Researchers conducted a series of 7 experiments on 200 adolescents to determine whether 15 public service announcements (PSAs) designed by the cable industry itself were effective. The findings indicated that PSAs with a narrative format (dramatic plot with fictional characters) were more interesting and arousing to adolescents than PSAs that featured a "talking head." However, the narrative PSAs were not found to reduce adolescents' attitudes about violence and aggression. In a subsequent study, the researchers analyzed the content of 100 antiviolence PSAs and found that more than three-quarters presented an act of violence that was followed by no negative consequences to the perpetrators. The researchers then designed an experiment that showed participants a PSA that ignored negative consequences, showed the perpetrator being paralyzed by handgun violence, or showed the perpetrator being killed. The findings indicated that presenting death to the perpetrator was the most effective PSA in changing attitudes, followed by depicting paralysis; PSAs that ignored negative consequences were found to be the least effective.

Conclusion

The NTVS is generally regarded as the most extensive and rigorous study of portrayals of violence across the entire landscape of U.S. television, along with the use and effectiveness of program advisories and ratings and antiviolence PSAs. Not only did it generate a long list of authoritative findings, but it contributed methodological innovations in the areas of sampling, training of coders, measuring reliability, and analysis of programming characteristics at multiple levels of narrative.

W. James Potter

See also Content Analysis; Cultivating Content and the Social Representation of Violence; Effects From Violent Media, Short- and Long-Term; Exposure to Violent Content, Effects on Child Development; Media Effects Perspectives of Violence; Media Rating Systems; Media Violence, Definitions and Context of; Social Cognitive Theory; Social Learning From Media

Further Readings

National Television Violence Study. (1996). *National Television Violence Study* (Vol. 1). Thousand Oaks, CA: Sage.

National Television Violence Study. (1997). *National Television Violence Study* (Vol. 2). Thousand Oaks, CA: Sage.

National Television Violence Study. (1998). *National Television Violence Study* (Vol. 3). Thousand Oaks, CA: Sage.

Potter, W. J. (1999). *On media violence*. Thousand Oaks, CA: Sage.

NEWS, THE PRESENTATION AND EFFECTS OF VIOLENT CONTENT IN

Violent content in the media is not limited to the movies and television shows for entertainment. Each day, millions of Americans are presented with violence in the news through some medium, whether television, radio, or the Internet, and a considerable amount of coverage is devoted to stories of crime and violence. Additionally, the availability of news through 24-hour channels means that news consumers can receive their news any time of the day.

The news media serve an important function in that they are many people's link to the rest of the world. In fact, research has shown that up to 96% of Americans rely on the media for news on crime. However, the news that they receive may be skewed in favor of stories of violent crime because some news outlets may follow the long-standing mantra, "If it bleeds, it leads" when deciding which stories to present. For example, a television newscast may air four crime stories back to back at the beginning of the broadcast. As such, research suggests that up to 65% of television news coverage and 25% of newspaper space are allocated to stories of crime and violence.

Because violent crime stories may be out of the ordinary and are often sensational in nature, they can easily capture an audience and entice viewers to come back for more. As a result, some people may develop a distorted perception of how prevalent crime in general, and specific types of crime in particular, actually are. Additionally, some people may develop distorted perceptions of exactly who is committing the crimes and who are the victims, which can lead to stereotyping of certain groups, such as minorities, women, and juveniles.

A number of effects result from violent content in the news. News media companies may experience an increase in ratings and/or sales. In addition, violent content in the news may shape public and political agendas through news consumers' and politicians' responses to crime and violence. Violent content in the news may also increase fear among residents, both on local and national levels, and may have adverse effects on children, such as promoting aggression and violence. Violence in the media may also contribute to fostering racism and a cultural divide among U.S. citizens. This entry focuses on how news is constructed and presented and the effects of violent content on audiences.

Constructing News

The amount of violence that is present in the world in the early 21st century creates a challenge for news media organizations. They must determine how much information, if any, to share with audiences. Not all events that occur will become news events, and as such, not every crime incident will receive coverage. Those that do receive coverage are assigned a level of newsworthiness by television producers, newspaper editors, and other media executives that determines where and how the events are presented. Some of the considerations involved in such a decision include the journalistic style of the media organization, its intended target audience, and whether coverage of the event will increase ratings or sales.

The news is essentially a product that media outlets want to sell to consumers. Following the economic principle of supply and demand, this creates a need to produce news both quickly and efficiently. The media rely on a number of official sources, which may include law enforcement and criminal justice personnel. These sources serve a number of functions. First, they are able to provide the media with consistent and credible information. Second, they are able to provide the information at a limited cost or time expenditure by the news media organizations. These factors also contribute to the decisions regarding which stories become the most newsworthy and which stories receive less or even no coverage.

Constructing news is a dynamic, fluid, and ongoing process. When a story breaks, media organizations collect information, construct the story, and disseminate it to the public. From there, members of the public consume the story and then relay their approval or disapproval back to the media organizations. If the audience favors a particular story, the media organizations will likely continue to produce stories on the same or a similar topic in an effort to keep the audience interested. However, if there is disapproval from a large contingent of the news consumers, the media organizations may turn to other stories.

Television and Internet news organizations, as opposed to other media organizations, are able to broadcast news 24 hours a day, 365 days per year, allowing for a continuous stream of news content, including "breaking" news. Although many newspapers have added online editions to their coverage span, stories that break after the paper has gone to press must wait until the following day for coverage in print. News stories that are published in magazines experience an even greater lag in time between the story breaking and coverage being printed, even in instances of a weekly magazine (such as *Time*). In many instances, such magazines are unable to cover a story as it breaks, but they are able to provide their readers with in-depth coverage, providing a more detailed and complete picture of the news event.

Distorting the Picture

As mentioned, crime news may be distorted in the media, both in terms of how much crime is occurring as well as who are the victims and offenders. Statistics show that crime in the United States has been and continues to be on the decline; yet it is frequently the focus of news coverage. Research has shown that crime stories can account for up to 65% of news coverage (depending on the format). Homicides, in particular, are often distorted in the media because of their sensational nature. While other crimes, such as property crimes (theft, burglary, etc.), are more common, homicides, which account for less than 1% of violent crimes, typically receive the most coverage and better placement (front-page coverage in newspapers or lead stories in television broadcasts) above other stories.

Researchers have focused on understanding why homicide stories garner such attention in the media. Some researchers have noted that newsworthiness is often ascribed to victims whom the media deems to be more "worthy," such as women, children, the elderly, multiple victims, or those who are wealthy. Increased newsworthiness affords these victims better placement, more follow-ups, and lengthier amounts of coverage (in respect to word counts or time allocated on air). Other researchers have found that in localities where homicide is more common, cases with atypical circumstances, or those that deviate most from what is considered to be normal, may receive elevated coverage.

When a particular phenomenon is rare, such as in the case of school shootings or mass shootings, the disproportionate amount of attention it garners helps to fuel the misconception of its actual prevalence. When word breaks of stories such as the shootings at Columbine High School near Littleton, Colorado (1999), Virginia Tech University (2007), a movie theater in Aurora, Colorado (2012), or Sandy Hook Elementary School in Newtown, Connecticut (2012), the news media immediately reports such incidents. The sensational nature of these events may immediately capture the audience, and media organizations may continue to cover the story, adding new details as they become available. Yet, regardless of other events that may be going on locally or nationally, the media tend to focus on the same event over and over until another highly sensationalized case of crime or violence takes its place (see Downs, 1972). However, the amount of coverage devoted to these stories may give people an inaccurate sense of how frequently (or infrequently) they occur. In reality, school shootings occur fewer than 10 times per year (on average), and mass shootings occur at similar rates. A person has a greater likelihood of being struck by lightning than being the victim of either of these incidents. Similarly, the reporting of the terrorist events of September 11, 2001, and coverage of the events in the 10 years following the attacks have made some viewers more fearful of terrorism, even though its prevalence has not increased. The amount of news coverage devoted to such events can make it seem as though these events are occurring more frequently, which can in turn have varying effects on the audience.

Affecting the Audience

Although the majority of news consumers will never directly be the victims of crime, violent content in news can have effects on them. For instance, stories that are local tend to have a greater impact on audiences than national stories because of the close proximity, which increases the chances that the news consumer knows someone who was directly involved in the violence. Stories presented at a national level may give news consumers an increased sense of safety in that the violence is occurring elsewhere.

Fear of crime is one of the most studied responses to violent news content. Fear of crime is driven by the disproportionate coverage of violent news events as compared with their actual frequency. Thus, some people may believe a specific type of crime occurs more frequently than it does, or that they may be more likely to be a victim of violence when, in fact, their likelihood of victimization is low. For example, portrayals of violence in the news often indicate that street crimes are commonplace, implying that these are the serious crimes of which people should be most afraid. Presenting violence in the news may give some people a distorted understanding of the differences between criminals and noncriminals— differences that may not be as severe as the public is led to believe. It can also make people more fearful of strangers, when, in fact, most violence is committed by persons the victims know.

Adults are traditionally considered the target audience for news coverage; however, research has suggested that news can also have effects on children. Although children may not actively seek to watch televised news, they may be present when their parents watch the news, and children's reactions to violent news content may be shaped by their parents' reactions. Particularly sensationalized news stories can have an impact on young children, who are unable to differentiate between reality and sensationalism, which can increase their levels of fear of crime and violence. In addition, research has suggested that children may become more aggressive the more they are exposed to violence in the media.

Audience members may alter their behavior as a response to the violence presented in the news and any subsequent fear of crime. Such behavioral changes may include altering how or when they leave their homes, withdrawing or isolating themselves from their community, or perceiving their community to be a threat to themselves and their families. Audience members' attitudes toward punitive responses to crime may also be altered, whereby a person demands harsher punishment for less severe actions. As with children, adult audience members may also become more aggressive and violent in response to news coverage of violence.

Affecting Public Opinion and Policy

The effects of violent news coverage extend beyond the individual viewer. Violent content and the reactions it elicits can shape the greater public opinion as well as drive policy. When there is an outcry from citizens regarding the threat of violence they perceive to be real because of what they consume from news coverage, policy makers may seek to address their constituents' concerns by introducing legislation aimed at controlling violence, such as a "three strikes law" mandating harsh sentences for repeat offenders or by reallocating funds for crime control.

Politicians may use the news media as a means of advocating a particular issue, such as gun control, increased screening at airports, more funding for law enforcement agencies, or other crime-related policies. For example, a politician may appear on newscasts in support of a crime control policy or legislation.

Violence in the news does more than shape public opinion about policy issues. It can also serve to shape racial attitudes and can even promote racism. The media tend to report minority-on-White crime more often than more commonplace minority-on-minority crime. Such news coverage focuses on minority offenders, particular those who are African American, which constructs a concern over Black dangerousness. Minority offenders are usually cast opposite a White victim. However, when the victim part of a minority, the media tend to construct the story in a way that makes the victimization a result of the victim's own actions, which can result in perpetuating fear among Whites and inflating their perceived risks of victimization and fear of crime.

Additional Considerations

While the news media may have an attentive audience, there are a number of issues that may help to perpetuate the disparity between news coverage and reality that one may want to consider when examining news media effects. First, in an effort to inform the public as soon as possible, news organizations may report incomplete information because all pertinent facts may not yet be available or uncovered. In other instances, reported information may later be found to be inaccurate, and some media outlets may not clarify this for audiences when the inaccuracy becomes known.

Second, because reporters may continue to report on a news event after the initial event, the audience may believe there is a need for continued concern. For example, television news reporters continued to report from outside the accused Aurora movie theater shooting suspect James Holmes's apartment building even though police had removed the incendiary devices from inside Holmes's apartment and declared the area safe. Such ongoing reports may inadvertently lead viewers to conclude that a threat still exists, furthering fear and apprehension of an issue that has already been addressed.

As researchers have pointed out, the news media are often a window to the world for news consumers. What is seen through that window may be more likely to be considered real than what actually occurs in the world. Therefore, understanding how news is presented and what effects it has on its audience

is critical to understanding the actuality of violence beyond the news.

Jaclyn Schildkraut

See also African Americans in Media, Character Depictions and Social Representation of; Attitude, Effects of Media Violence on; Audience Interpretation of Media Violence; Effects of; Effects from Media, Short- and Long-Term; Gender, Effects of Violent Content on; Marketing of Violence; Media Violence, Definitions and Context of; Television Violence; Violence in Media, Effects of the Representation of

Further Readings

Cantor, J., & Nathanson, A. I. (1996). Children's fright reactions to television news. *Journal of Communication, 46*(4), 139–152.

Cerulo, K. (1998). *Deciphering violence: The cognitive structure of right and wrong.* New York, NY: Routledge.

Chiricos, T., Eschholz, S., & Gertz, M. (1997). Crime, news, and fear of crime: Toward an identification of audience effects. *Social Problems, 44*(3), 342–357.

Downs, A. (1972). Up and down with ecology: The issue-attention cycle. *Public Interest, 28*, 38–50.

Gans, H. J. (1979). *Deciding what's news.* New York, NY: Pantheon.

Gilliam, F. D., Iyengar, S., Simon, A., & Wright, O. (1996). Crime in black and white: The violent, scary world of local news. *Harvard International Journal of Press/ Politics, 1*(3), 6–23.

Jewkes, Y. (2004). *Media and crime.* Thousand Oaks, CA: Sage.

Robinson, M. B. (2011). *Media coverage of crime and criminal justice.* Durham, NC: Carolina Academic Press.

Romer, D., Jamieson, K. H., & Aday, S. (2003). Television news and the cultivation of fear. *Journal of Communication, 53*(1), 88–104.

Surette, R. (1992). *Media, crime, and criminal justice: Images and realities.* Pacific Grove, CA: Brooks/Cole.

Parasocial Relationships

Parasocial interactions and parasocial relationships constitute a form of involvement with media personae that entails the experience of intimacy and companionship with media figures. This entry discusses such parasocial bonds and summarizes research into whether they lead to selective exposure to and learning from media violence.

The term *parasocial interactions* was first introduced in 1956 by Donald Horton and R. Richard Wohl. They noted that some television viewers engage in one-direction, quasi-social interactions with media performers. Parasocial interactions refer to viewers' experiences during media exposure, but over time, parasocial interactions can grow into parasocial relationships that endure across multiple media encounters and can persist outside the context of media exposure. As such, parasocial relationships constitute the mediated equivalent of social relationships. Empirical research has drawn many similarities among formation, maintenance, and dissolution of interpersonal relationships and parasocial relationships. For instance, like social relationships, parasocial relationships rise from interpersonal attraction. Furthermore, parasocial relationships are facilitated by psychological characteristics that make individuals more inclined to engage in relationships in general. Finally, termination of either type of relationship is emotionally distressing.

Parasocial interactions and parasocial relationships have been conceptualized as a distinct form of media engagement that differs from other modes of media involvement, such as identification with characters. In a parasocial relationship, a viewer bonds with a media persona without merging his or her self-concept with the character. That is to say, a viewer interacts with the media figure as with another person, whereas in the case of identification, a viewer temporarily suspends his or her self-concept and steps into the character's shoes by adopting the character's emotional and cognitive perspective.

Parasocial relationships have the potential to contribute to media effects in general and to media violence effects in particular in two ways. First, parasocial relationships can serve as a motivational factor, guiding selective exposure to violent media. Second, parasocial relationships might constitute a mediating variable that carries out the effects of media exposure.

Parasocial Relationships and Exposure to Media Violence

Uses and gratifications theory maintains that media consumption is, at least at times, instrumental and purposeful. Audience members actively select media outlets that can satisfy particular psychological and sociological needs. For example, media consumers may select certain media content to alleviate boredom or to satisfy their need for surveillance and acquiring accurate knowledge about the world. Because parasocial interactions and parasocial relationships are associated with enjoyment, individuals seeking entertainment are likely to selectively consume media content that maximizes parasocial interactions and parasocial relationship opportunities.

With repeated exposure to a particular media figure, viewers come to know him or her better and develop a more elaborate relational schema that, in turn, sets positive expectations of future media exposure. In other words, past parasocial interactions experiences enhance subsequent preferences for media content featuring the liked character. It is, therefore, logical to conclude that previously established parasocial relationships with any given violent media persona will be associated with further exposure to the violent media character.

Research has found that parasocial interactions motivation is positively associated with relaxation, information, and entertainment television-viewing motivations. Intensity of parasocial interactions with media figures, such as soap opera protagonists and news anchors, is related to preference for these programs. However, parasocial interactions and parasocial relationships appear to be less important motivating factors in exposure to violent media content. Alan M. Rubin, Paul Haridakis, and Keren Eyal found that parasocial interactions with a television talk-show host is an important predictor of exposure to a nonviolent talk show (*The Oprah Winfrey Show*), but parasocial interactions play a relatively minor role in viewers' exposure to an aggressive television talk show (*The Jerry Springer Show*). Their findings suggest that selective exposure to aggressive talk shows is driven by a uniquely different set of motivations, such as taking enjoyment from voyeuristic and humiliating aspects of the program. Relational gratifications and affinity with the host, however, play little role in viewers' seeking of aggressive talk shows.

The seemingly low importance of parasocial relationships in viewers' preference for aggressive media is consistent with the findings of Eyal and Rubin's (2003) study on the relationship between children's trait aggression and intensity of their parasocial relationships with violent media characters. Given that parasocial relationships resemble interpersonal relationships, it was hypothesized that the same precursors of social attraction will also be meaningful in the formation of parasocial relationships. One such factor is homophily (i.e., similarity), such that individuals tend to be attracted to other people similar to themselves. In the context of violent media, this line of reasoning suggests that aggressive individuals are more likely to form parasocial bonds with aggressive characters.

Despite this sound theoretical rationale, the results of the study conducted by Eyal and Rubin did not support this hypothesis. Controlling for gender, viewers' trait aggression does *not* predict parasocial relationships with aggressive characters. The researchers did, however, find that aggressive viewers experience greater identification with aggressive characters, namely, they are more likely to vicariously share the characters' experiences. Identification and parasocial interactions are moderately correlated, such that viewers who identify with a given character are more likely to engage in parasocial interactions with this character, but the two psychological processes do not necessarily co-occur. In fact, Eyal and Rubin found that parasocial interactions moderate the association between viewers' aggression and identification with violent characters, such that this effect becomes even stronger when viewers also engage in parasocial interactions.

Empirical research has suggested that, contrary to the uses and gratifications hypothesis, parasocial relationships are not an important predictor of selective exposure to violent media. However, existing parasocial relationships with violent media personae can enhance other forms of involvement with violent media (e.g., identification with the violent characters). Such involvement, in turn, can intensify media effects.

Parasocial Relationships and Effects of Violent Media

Several theories have explicated the mechanisms linking parasocial interactions and parasocial relationships with media effects of violence.

Socialization

Media personae can serve as powerful role models that promote learning of specific behaviors and adoption of abstract values. Parasocial relationships and parasocial interactions provide conditions in which, according to social cognitive theory, learning and production of internalized behaviors are particularly likely to occur.

First, preexisting parasocial relationships with media figures increase attention to messages featuring the parasocial friends. Second, parasocial relationships and parasocial interactions intensify viewers' emotional and cognitive responses to the program viewed. Third, parasocial relationships promote media consumers' discussion of the show with others, thereby reinforcing the lessons extracted from the media. Thus, if a viewer experiences parasocial relationships with a television character, he or she will pay more attention to the character's violent or prosocial actions, will engage in mental rehearsal of these behaviors, and therefore will be more likely to learn the modeled aggressive or prosocial message.

Media role models can also shape media consumers' self-identity. Affinity with media personae, whether celebrities or fictional characters, allows viewers to envision alternative selves. A number of studies have shown that parasocial relationships empower viewers, boost their self-esteem, and raise their sense of self-worth. Parasocial relationships can also enhance viewers' self-efficacy and increase certainty in their ability to realize their aspirations. On a societal level, parasocial relationships can lead to increased social efficacy, such that individuals come to believe in their power as a community to change their social reality. According to social cognitive theory, self-efficacy and collective efficacy are important precursors of reenacting a learned behavior. Furthermore, affinity with media personae can shift media consumers' ideals and set new personal goals. Admirers strive to imitate their idols' behaviors, appearances, and beliefs and change their self-perception. Thus, parasocial relationships catalyze the socialization function of media.

From a social learning theory standpoint, parasocial relationships and parasocial interactions have the potential either to reduce or enhance viewers' violence, depending on the specific behaviors modeled by the observed media personae. Parasocial relationships with aggressive role models promote viewers' aggression or approval of violence, whereas parasocial relationships with media figures who model prosocial behaviors have the opposite effect.

Persuasion

In addition to social learning, parasocial relationships and parasocial interactions can facilitate media effects through heuristic persuasion. Specifically, in an interpersonal communication context, liking is an important factor that increases social influence and reduces reactance to persuasion. Because parasocial interactions and parasocial relationships are, in many respects, similar to social relationships, mediated relationships can also reduce audiences' ability to resist the persuasive power of the media.

Parasocial Contact

The intergroup contact hypothesis maintains that intergroup tensions and violence, to a large extent, result from uncertainty and anxiety involved in encountering a member of an unfamiliar, foreign group. Thus, positive interactions with likable and prototypical outgroup members can produce positive attitudes toward these individuals and the outgroup as a whole. Although the intergroup contact hypothesis originally accounted only for interpersonal relationships between members of different groups, the theory was subsequently extended to a mediated context. It was suggested that parasocial contact with positive outgroup media characters would be sufficient to hamper intergroup hostility.

Empirical Support

Few published studies have specifically examined the possible effects of parasocial relationships and parasocial interactions on subsequent aggression. In a survey of children in southern Sweden conducted in 1976, Elias Hedinsson found that parasocial relationships are positively associated with perceptions of violence in society among 13-year-olds but not 11-year-olds. More recently, Adam Earnheardt found that parasocial relationships with athletes are related to admiration, which in turn, results in greater tolerance of violence.

In examining prosocial effects of media, studies have provided support for the mediated contact hypothesis using measures of identification, liking, and affinity (although not parasocial interactions per se). These studies have demonstrated that involvement with minority characters or with majority-group characters modeling positive relationships with minority groups can diminish prejudicial feelings. However, despite the compelling theoretical grounds for hypothesizing a relationship between parasocial relationships and media effects, a recent meta-analysis revealed that, overall, parasocial relationships have relatively small impact on media consumption outcomes. Compared with other forms of involvement, such as transportation and identification, parasocial relationships yield a very weak effect on the viewers. Thus, future research needs to carefully examine the differences among the impact of parasocial relationships, parasocial interactions, and other forms of involvement on violence and intergroup feelings.

Practical Implications

The possible negative consequences of parasocial relationships with aggressive characters lead to increased concern about the quality of role models offered by media to young viewers, particularly boys. It has been argued that glorification of violence and the association between masculinity and aggression have negative impacts on children who are developing their own identities.

At the same time, efforts have been made to exploit parasocial relationships as a mechanism of media effects to promote socially desirable outcomes. Education-entertainment programs, such as the soap opera *Soul City* in South Africa, are specifically designed to generate audience relationships with the characters, and through this involvement, reduce public tolerance for domestic violence. Finally, given the potential of parasocial contact with media characters to improve viewers' perceptions of other social groups, it is particularly important for media to present a more integrated and egalitarian cast of characters.

Riva Tukachinsky

See also Social Learning From Media; Stereotyping in Violent Media Content; User Involvement in Violent Content, Effects of; Uses and Gratifications Perspective of Media Effects

Further Readings

Cohen, J. (2001). Defining identification: A theoretical look at the identification of audiences with media characters. *Mass Communication and Society, 4*, 245–264.

Eyal, K., & Rubin, A. M. (2003). Viewer aggression and homophily, identification, and parasocial relationships with television characters. *Journal of Broadcasting & Electronic Media, 47*, 77–98.

Hoffner, C. (2009). Parasocial and online social relationships. In S. L. Calvert & B. J. Wilson (Eds.), *The handbook of children, media, and development*. Oxford, UK: Blackwell.

Klimmt, C., Hartmann, T., & Schramm, H. (2006). Parasocial interactions and relationships. In J. Bryant & P. Vorderer (Eds.), *Psychology of entertainment* (pp. 291–313). Mahwah, NJ: Erlbaum.

Papa, M. J., Singhal, A., Law, S., Pant, S., Sood, S., Rogers, E. M., & Shefner-Rogers, C. L. (2000). Entertainment-education and social change: An analysis of parasocial interaction, social learning, collective efficacy, and paradoxical communication. *Journal of Communication, 50*(4), 31–55.

PEDIATRICIANS AND MEDIA VIOLENCE

In 1983 the American Academy of Pediatrics (AAP), an organization of pediatricians dedicated to the health and well-being of children and adolescents,

established a five-person Task Force on Children and Television to begin informing the academy about media influences on children and adolescents. Since then, pediatricians have come to recognize the important role that media play in the lives of their young patients (see Figure 1). Dozens of studies published since the early 1990s in *Pediatrics* and in *Archives of Pediatrics & Adolescent Medicine* attest to the fact that media can potentially affect virtually *every* concern that pediatricians and parents have about children and adolescents—aggressive behavior, school performance, sleep, sex, drugs, eating disorders, language acquisition, even depression, suicide, and attention-deficit disorder (Strasburger, Jordan, & Donnerstein, 2012). Because pediatricians treat the majority of America's children and have access to their parents, they represent one of the best sources of educating the public about healthy media habits and potential problems with the viewing of media violence.

Timeline

The medical community as a whole began focusing attention on media violence in the 1950s, when the first U.S. Senate hearings were held questioning whether media violence leads to real-life aggression. Many significant events and publications have ensued.

In 1972 the U.S. surgeon general issued a special report on the public health effects of media violence, entitled *Television and Growing Up: The Impact of Televised Violence: Report to the Surgeon General*, that was based on a growing and nearly unanimous body of evidence. A few years later, a child

Figure 1   A Satirical View of the Pediatric Research on Television

Source: Patrick O'Connor/*The Kent-Ravenna, Ohio Record Courier.* Reprinted with permission.

psychiatrist in Seattle who later became Benjamin Spock's coauthor, Michael Rothenberg, issued a clarion call for action on media violence in a leading medical journal, the *Journal of the American Medical Association*. At the time, he cited 146 articles in behavioral science journals, representing 50 studies involving 10,000 children and adolescents, and concluded, "The time is long past due for a major, organized cry of protest from the medical profession in relation to what, in political terms, I consider a national scandal" (Rothenberg, 1975, p. 1046).

In 1982 the National Institute of Mental Health (NIMH) issued *Television and Behavior: Ten Years of Scientific Progress and Implications for the Eighties*, a comprehensive review of the research on children and media, including media violence and its effects. This served as the basis for further research, funding, and public health efforts for at least the next decade.

In 2000 the AAP was joined by the American Medical Association, the American Academy of Child and Adolescent Psychiatry, and the American Psychological Association in testimony before Congress addressing concerns about media violence. In 2001 the U.S. surgeon general published *Youth Violence*, a comprehensive report on media violence in which he asserted that media violence is a significant causal factor in real-life aggression.

The Federal Communications Commission released its own report on TV violence, *In the Matter of Violent Television Programming and Its Impact on Children*, in 2007, and agreed with the surgeon general that there is "strong evidence" linking media violence to real-life aggression in children. Finally, in 2012 the AAP made the issue of children, adolescents, and the media part of its strategic plan—one of its top three priorities for the coming years (see Figure 2).

In addition, the AAP has issued four major policy statements on children, adolescents, and the media, beginning in 1990 and as recently as 2009 (Committee on Communications, 1990, 1995; Committee on Public Education, 2001; Council on

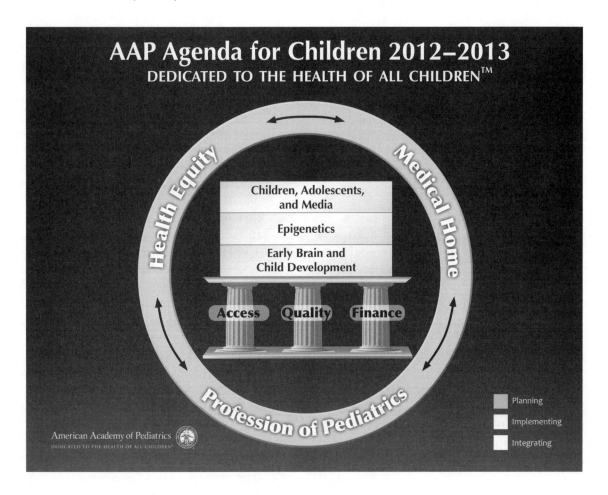

Figure 2   As of 2012, the Issue of the Media Is One of the Top Three Priorities for the American Academy of Pediatrics
Source: American Academy for Pediatrics.

Communications and Media, 2009). These statements tend to attract significant media attention and help to educate the general public about media effects. Other major organizations have issued similar statements, including the American Psychological Association (Schmidt, Bickham, Branner, & Rich, 2008) and the International Society for Research on Aggression (2012).

Recommendations

Beginning in the 1990s, the AAP began distributing specific recommendations to its pediatrician membership regarding how to counsel parents about their children's media use. These recommendations, as outlined by the Council on Communications and Media, include the following:

1. Limit the total amount of children's entertainment screen time to less than 2 hours per day.

2. Avoid screen time for infants younger than 2 years of age.

3. Make children's bedrooms media-free: in particular, a child's bedroom should be free of television sets or any electronic device with Internet connectivity.

4. Monitor closely what media children watch.

5. Co-view media with children and discuss any objectionable content with them.

Research

Initially and for several decades, studies on the impact of media violence on children's aggressive behavior appeared solely in the psychology and communications literature—in journals that pediatricians and other doctors may not routinely read. The impact of the AAP's Task Force on Children and Television began to be felt in the 1990s, when both *Pediatrics* and *Archives of Pediatrics & Adolescent Medicine* began publishing original research articles and commentaries. These have contributed significantly to the efforts of the outstanding researchers in this area (e.g., Bushman & Huesmann, 2012). As the official journal of the AAP, *Pediatrics* has published numerous studies and commentaries on the issue of media violence, particularly since 2004:

- In 2004 a study of 365 pediatricians in Minnesota by Douglas A. Gentile and colleagues found that the pediatricians agreed with the

academy's recommendations about children, adolescents, and media but were skeptical about how effective they could be in counseling parents. In the same year, Tina L. Cheng and colleagues' study of 922 parents found that half reported "always" limiting their children's violent television viewing but 73% believed their children viewed television violence at least once a week anyway.

- A study of the top 100 films from 1994 found that the rating did not adequately predict the frequency of violence in the films (Jenkins, Webb, Browne, & Kraus, 2005).

- In a study of 180 parents of children 6 to 13 years old, A. B. Jordan and colleagues (2006) found that most of the children spent at least 3 hours per day watching television and that few parents had rules restricting total television time.

- Victor C. Strasburger authored two commentaries in 2006 and 2007 that questioned why pediatricians underestimate the media's influence and discussed how they could take action against media violence.

- In a study of the top-grossing PG-13 films from 1999–2000, Theresa Webb and colleagues (2007) found that 90% contained violence, with nearly half of the violence of lethal magnitude.

- Keilah A. Worth and colleagues conducted a survey of more than 6,500 preteens and teens in 2008 and found that 40 of the most popular violent movies were seen by an estimated 12.5% of 22 million U.S. adolescents ages 10 to 14 years old. All were rated R. Also in 2008, one of the first reports on new media, conducted by Michele L. Ybarra and colleagues, found that 5% of the 1,588 10- to 15-year-olds surveyed had engaged in seriously violent behavior in the past year and that 38% reported exposure online to violence.

- Shari L. Barkin and colleagues' 2008 study of 137 pediatric practices showed that just a minute or two of office-based counseling by pediatricians could prevent approximately 900,000 children and teens from being exposed to media violence each year.

- A unique longitudinal study by Craig Anderson and colleagues (2008), consisting of three different samples (181 Japanese high school students ages 12 to 15 years, 1,050 Japanese students ages 13 to 18 years, and 364 U.S. third through fifth graders ages 9 to 12 years), found that playing violent video games is a significant risk factor for later aggressive behavior.

- Parents of 94 young children reported an average of 12 hours of screen media per week, and only 35% of the parents could correctly identify the expert recommendations for children older than 2 years of age in a 2009 study by Jeanne B. Funk and colleagues.
- Dayna M. Maniccia and colleagues' 2011 meta-analysis of interventions to reduce children's screen time identified 29 studies. Interventions achieved small but statistically significant reductions in screen time.
- In 2011 Michele L. Ybarra, Kimberley J. Mitchell, and Josephine D. Korchmaros surveyed 1,588 preteens and teens 10 to 15 years of age, studying the youths for three consecutive years, and found that violent text messaging and Internet bullying increased over time.

Advocacy

The AAP has advocated for a variety of potential solutions to the problem of children being exposed to media violence. In addition to suggesting how pediatricians (and other health professionals who see children) can counsel parents about media, the academy has worked closely in Washington, D.C., with other public health–oriented groups to support legislation such as the Children's Television Act of 1990, designed to increase the amount of educational television, and the still unpassed CAMRA Act (Children and Media Research Advancement Act), which intends to direct federal funding toward research on the effects of electronic media on children. The AAP has also suggested that Congress fund an updated NIMH Report on children, adolescents, and the media. For many years in the 1990s, the academy also maintained a presence in Hollywood with its Media Resource Team, which interacted with the creative community in an effort to accurately publicize child health issues.

Victor C. Strasburger

See also Developmental Effects; Ethical Development, Effects of; Exposure to Violent Content, Effects on Child Development; Longitudinal Research Findings on the Effects of Violent Content; Moral Development, Effects of Media Violence on

Further Readings

American Academy of Pediatrics, American Academy of Child and Adolescent Psychiatry, American Psychological Association, American Medical Association, American Academy of Family Physicians, & American Psychiatric Association. (2000, July 20). *Joint Statement on the Impact of Entertainment Violence on Children. Congressional Public Health Summit.* Retrieved from http://www.aap.org/advocacy/releases/jstmtevc.htm

American Academy of Pediatrics, Task Force on Children and Television. (1984). *Children, adolescents, and television.* Elk Grove Village, IL: Author.

Anderson, C. A., Sakamoto, A., Gentile, D. A., et. al. (2008). Longitudinal effects of violent video games on aggression in Japan and the United States. *Pediatrics, 122,* e1067–e1072.

Barkin, S. L., Finch, S. A., Ip, E. H., et al. (2008). Is office-based counseling about media use, timeouts, and firearm storage effective? Results from a cluster-randomized, controlled trial. *Pediatrics, 122,* e15–e25.

Bushman, B. J., & Huesmann, L. R. (2012). Effects of violent media on aggression. In D. G. Singer & J. L. Singer (Eds.), *Handbook of children and the media* (pp. 231–248). Thousand Oaks, CA: Sage.

Cheng, T. L., Brenner, R. A., Wright, J. L., Sachs, H. C., Moyer, P., & Rao, M. R. (2004). Children's violent television viewing: Are parents monitoring? *Pediatrics, 114,* 94–99.

Committee on Communications. (1990). Children, adolescents, and television. *Pediatrics, 85,* 1119–1120.

Committee on Communications. (1995). Media violence. *Pediatrics, 95,* 949–951.

Committee on Public Education. (2001). Media violence. *Pediatrics, 108,* 1222–1226.

Council on Communications and Media. (2009). Media violence. *Pediatrics, 124,* 1495–1503.

Federal Communications Commission. (2007, April 25). *In the matter of violent television programming and its impact on children.* Statement of Commissioner Deborah Taylor Tate. MB docket No. 04–261.

Funk, J. B., Brouwer, J., Curtiss, K., & McBroom, E. (2009). Parents of preschoolers: Expert media recommendations and ratings knowledge, media-effects beliefs, and monitoring practices. *Pediatrics, 123,* 981–988.

Gentile, D. A., Obert, C., Sherwood, N. E., Story, M., Walsh, D. A., & Hogan, M. (2004). Well-child exams in the video age: Pediatricians and the American Academy of Pediatrics guidelines for children's media use. *Pediatrics, 114,* 1235–1241.

Jenkins, L., Webb, T., Browne, N., Afifi, A. A., & Kraus, J. (2005). An evaluation of the Motion Picture Association of America's treatment of violence in PG-, PG-13-, and R-rated films. *Pediatrics, 115,* e512–e517.

Jordan, A. B., Hersey, J. C., McDivitt, J. A., & Heitzler, C. D. (2006). Reducing children's television-viewing time: A qualitative study of parents and their children. *Pediatrics, 118,* e1303–e1310.

Maniccia, D. M., Davison, K. K., Marshall, S. J., Manganello, J. A., & Dennison, B. A. (2011). A meta-analysis of interventions that target children's screen time for reduction. *Pediatrics, 128,* e193–e210.

Media Violence Commission, International Society for Research on Aggression (ISRA). (2012). *Aggressive Behavior, 38,* 335–341.

Office of the Surgeon General. (2001). *Youth violence.* Rockville, MD: Author.

Pearl, D., Bouthilet, L., & Lazar, J. (1982). *Television and behavior: Ten years of scientific progress and implications for the eighties.* Rockville, MD: National Institute of Mental Health.

Rothenberg, M. B. (1975). Effect of television violence on children and youth. *Journal of the American Medical Association, 234,* 1043–1046.

Schmidt, M. E., Bickham, D. S., Branner, A., & Rich, M. (2008). Media-related policies of professional health organizations. In S. L. Calvert & B. J. Wilson (Eds.), *The handbook of children, media, and development* (pp. 502–526). Malden, MA: Blackwell.

Smith, A. (1952). Influence of TV crime programs on children's health. *Journal of the American Medical Association, 150,* 37.

Strasburger, V. C. (2006). "Clueless": Why do pediatricians underestimate the media's influence on children and adolescents? *Pediatrics, 117,* 1427–1431.

Strasburger, V. C. (2007). Go ahead punk, make my day: It's for pediatricians to take action against media violence. *Pediatrics, 119,* e1398–e1399.

Strasburger, V. C. (2012). Schools and media. *Pediatrics, 129,* 1161–1163.

Strasburger, V. C., Jordan, A. B., & Donnerstein, E. (2012). Health effects of media on children and adolescents. *Pediatric Clinics of North America, 59,* 533–587.

U.S. Surgeon General's Scientific Advisory Committee on Television and Social Behavior. (1972). *Television and growing up: The impact of televised violence: Report to the Surgeon General.* Publication No. HSM 72–9090. Rockville, MD: National Institute of Mental Health, U.S. Public Health Service.

Webb, T., Jenkins, L., Browne, N., Afifi, A. A., & Kraus, J. (2007). Violent entertainment pitched to adolescents: An analysis of PG-13 films. *Pediatrics, 119,* e1219–e1229.

Worth, K. A., Chambers, J. G., Naussau, D. H., Rakhra, B. K., & Sargent, J. D. (2008). Exposure of U.S. adolescents to extremely violent movies. *Pediatrics, 122,* 306–312.

Ybarra, M. L., Dierner-West, M., Markow, D., Leaf, P. J., Hamburger, M., & Boxer, P. (2008). Linkages between Internet and other media violence with seriously violent behavior by youth. *Pediatrics, 122,* 929–937.

Ybarra, M. L., Mitchell, K. J., & Korchmaros, J. D. (2011). National trends in exposure to and experiences of violence on the Internet among children. *Pediatrics, 128,* e1376–1386.

PEER INFLUENCE ON VIOLENT CONTENT EFFECTS

The concept of peers is very important in the literature of adolescent psychology. This is because teens are at an age when they spend a significant amount of time with their friends and greatly value the opinions of their peers. Developmental psychologists such as Jean Piaget and Harry Stack Sullivan underscore the importance of friendships in the socioemotional development of adolescents. This entry examines the impact of peer influence on the effects of violent content among adolescents (ages 12 to 20). A brief review of the role of peers in adolescence is presented before exploring research on peer influence on media use and peer mediation of violent content.

The Role of Peers in Adolescence

Scholars often refer to adolescence as a transitional stage from childhood to adulthood, with developmental challenges such as identity formation, need for independence, and sensation seeking. As teens work their way through this transitional time, sources of socialization such as peers, media, family, and school provide them with different contexts in which to work out these challenges. According to Jeffrey Jensen Arnett (1995, 2007), of all the socialization agents on teens, media and peers share the most in common. Both provide teens with the freedom to make choices concerning their own socialization. Teens have control over with whom they associate and what media they consume. Arnett has argued that although parents (or other adult socializers) might have rules for their teenagers' choices of peers and media, these restrictions are difficult to implement. Because teens spend more time alone or with friends than with their parents, parents can be faced with challenges when attempting to exert their influence on teens. Furthermore, according to James Youniss, peers provide the opportunity for teens to exchange values and ideas on an equal footing. Social reality is constructed together with teens' peers rather than taught or handed down by adults. As a result, peers are crucial in shaping teens' lives.

Peer relationships can lead to positive or negative influences, although most studies have focused on the undesirable effects. Examples of this include peers initiating behaviors that involve substance use, cheating, risky driving, and youth violence. Studies also found that peer norms are very influential on teens' sexuality. Some studies have even measured peer delinquency as a predictor of risky behaviors.

The word *influence* tends to suggest an adolescent's vulnerability to his or her peers' manipulation, but the most recent view among researchers in peer relationships has shifted the passive perspective to an active one. That is, in the context of a healthy adolescent's development, they argue that the adolescent is actively selecting friends according to his or her interests and preferences rather than passively accepting them. An adolescent associates with peers who will provide validation and approval of his or her values and lifestyle in an effort to test and form an identity. It is when problematic peer socialization arises that passivity happens. This can include a lack of peer interactions because of exclusion, or undesirable peer interaction because of teasing or bullying. This form of peer influence through isolation and victimization can lead to emotional stress and behavioral problems.

Peer Influence on Media Use

As suggested by the active audience perspective from the uses and gratification theory, teens actively choose media based on their needs and wants. Moreover, they adapt their media choices to their developmental needs. Although very little communication research has empirically investigated peer influence on media use, some studies have theorized the relationship. For instance, scholars have argued that peer influence plays a role in teens' music preferences, especially heavy metal music. Music provides a venue in which teens can feel a sense of belonging. Youth subcultures characterized by heavy metal music or punk-style music provide ways for teens to fulfill their developmental need of identity formation. Although studies have identified peers' roles in teens' preference for heavy metal music, there is a distinct lack of research on the intricate interplay between peer influence and the effects of objectionable lyrics. This is particularly relevant considering the frequency of sexist and violent anti-female attitudes promoted in the lyrics of heavy metal music.

Scholars have also posited that peers provide teens with an arena in which to experiment the different roles learned from television. They receive feedback from their peers as a means to develop independence as well as self-identity. Peer feedback in the form of peer pressure was found to be a determinant of teens' exposure to indecent television content. Similar to peer pressure, a need for social acceptance can influence a teen's choice of films as well. More specifically, the data from one study have suggested that when in the presence of male friends, female teens tend to comply with the male peers' preference for violent or action films when renting videos. Another study examining peer victimization found that teens who are not socially accepted by their peer group and are teased or bullied reported watching more violent movies, playing more violent video games, and visiting more websites that describe or recommend violence.

Peer Mediation of Violent Content

Although research in psychology has explored peers' role in adolescence, and research in communication has produced some work linking peer influence with media use, there exists only one published study in the field of communication that has examined peer influence and violent content. Amy Nathanson (2001) looked at teens' orientation to antisocial television (e.g., containing violent or sexual content) in relation to both parental and peer mediation. She conceptualized peer mediation as a two-dimensional construct that includes peer discussion and peer co-viewing of television. Using college students' retrospective data, Nathanson compared self-reported data on parental mediation with that of peer mediation and found that peer mediation of antisocial television occurred more often than parental mediation. Furthermore, she found that discussion of antisocial television is related to adolescents' aggression by fostering positive orientation toward the television content. Nathanson postulates that peer discussions and co-viewing can encourage the undesirable outcomes of antisocial television.

An unpublished conference paper borrowed Nathanson's conceptualization of peer mediation and examined peer discussion and peer co-play within the context of violent video games. The study also found peer mediation to predict adolescents' aggression more than did parental mediation.

Researchers looking to further the knowledge of peer influence on violent content should consider looking into violent content such as music lyrics, video games, and websites that encourage violence. Relevant theoretical concepts that can be used to inform this line of research include adolescents' developmental challenges, uses and gratification theory, and peer mediation.

Melissa M. Yang

See also Aggression in Youth; Music Videos and Lyrics, Effects of Violent Content in; Rap Lyrics, Effects of Violent Content in

Further Readings

Arnett, J. J. (1995). Adolescents' uses of media for self-socialization. *Journal of Youth and Adolescence, 24*(5), 519–533.

Arnett, J. J. (Ed.). (2007). *Encyclopedia of children, adolescents, and the media.* Thousand Oaks, CA: Sage.

Brandtzaeg, P. B., & Heim, J. (2009). Children's electronic gaming content preferences and psychological factors: Is there a connection? *Nordicom Review, 30,* 69–86.

Dalessandro, A. M., & Chory-Assad, R. M. (2006, June). *Comparative significance of parental vs. peer mediation of adolescents' antisocial video game play.* Dresden, Germany: Instructional and Developmental Communication Division, International Communication Association,

Nathanson, A. I. (2001). Parents versus peers: Exploring the significance of peer mediation of antisocial television. *Communication Research, 28*(3), 251–274.

Roe, K. (1995). Adolescents' use of socially disvalued media: Toward a theory of media delinquency. *Journal of Youth and Adolescence, 24*(5), 617–631.

Strasburger, V. C., Wilson, B. J., & Jordan, A. B. (2009). *Children, adolescents, and the media.* Thousand Oaks, CA: Sage.

PORNOGRAPHY, VIOLENT CONTENT IN

The word *pornography* is most often used as a general referent for content depicting nudity and explicit sexual acts that is used by consumers to achieve sexual arousal. Some cultural critics have speculated that pornography is a powerful agent of sexual socialization. In particular, anti-pornography feminists have asserted that pornography eroticizes sexual aggression against females, increases the probability that males will sexually aggress against females, and increases callousness and indifference to female victims of sexual aggression. Such assertions have led social scientists to quantitatively explore the extent and nature of sexual violence in

pornography. This entry synopsizes the findings of this research.

Definitional Considerations

The results of assessments of sexual violence in pornography have depended on analysts' definition of *violence*. Analysts' definitions to date have varied along five dimensions: (1) only some analysts count verbal aggression as violence (e.g., "You're nothing but a stupid whore!"); (2) only some analysts count unintentional harm as violence (e.g., unintentional gagging during penile oral sex); (3) only some analysts count acts that do not ultimately lead to harm as violence (e.g., spanking that does not physically harm the target); (4) only some analysts count consensual aggression as violence (e.g., consensual hair-pulling); and (5) only some analysts count coercion as violence (e.g., threats, or taking advantage of power differences, such as a supervisor coercing a subordinate). Naturally, analysts employing more inclusive definitions find higher rates of violence; analysts employing more exclusive definitions find lower rates of violence. To explore the uppermost boundaries of pornographic violence, this entry reports results from studies that employed inclusive definitions of violence when definitional differences have yielded conflicting findings.

Violence Categories and Themes

The following violence categories and themes have been assessed in studies of violence in pornography: overall prevalence of violence, overall prevalence of physical violence, most common types of physical violence, rape myth–supporting portrayals (i.e., behavior in which a target is forced into sex but ultimately enjoys the encounter), rape or use of force, verbal violence, consequences of violence, and gender of aggressor and target. Summary findings for each category or theme are reported next (when available) for the media most commonly studied by pornography analysts.

Books

Analyses of pornographic books have found that up to 20% contain physical violence. The most common types of physical violence are bondage and use of weapons. Rape myth–supporting portrayals were found in nearly all instances of forced sex in one study; the use of force to obtain sex occurred in approximately one-third of sexual encounters. Sexual violence is nearly always perpetrated by males against females.

Magazines

One study of pornographic magazines found that up to 25% of scenes depicted violence. The most common types of violent images are of bondage, pushing, and shoving. Rape depictions have been documented in up to 5% of images. Verbal violence has been found in up to 8% of scenes. Males are usually the perpetrators of violence; females are almost always the targets.

Movies

A study of the best-selling and most rented pornographic movies found that 88% of scenes contained physical violence (spanking and gagging being the most frequent violent acts). Forty-nine percent of scenes contained verbal violence. Females were targets of violence 94% of the time; males were perpetrators 70% of the time. A similar study of the most rented pornographic movies found that aggressors never experienced any negative consequences for their behavior. Rape myth–supporting portrayals were found in 14% of scenes in another study. A study of "triple-X" movies found that rape occurred in 31% of violent scenes.

Internet

Due to its breadth, assessing the Internet for pornographic violence is a daunting—if not impossible—charge. Few have taken up the task. Existing attempts have sacrificed breadth for depth, selecting a highly specific portion of the Net for analysis (most often sexual bulletin boards). One study of pornographic stories on a popular sexual Usenet discussion board found that 41% described rape (in such disturbing detail the author of the study eventually sought psychological counseling to help her come to terms with what she had read). The two other most common forms of violence were bondage and discipline. Pedophilic sex was described in 19.4% of stories. A separate study of the same bulletin board found that 85% of violence victims were female. A study of images posted in 17 different sexual bulletin boards found that 10% depicted bondage and discipline. Another study attempted to locate sites specifically devoted to rape. Thirty-one sites were located using keyword searches (e.g., "rape," "bitch," "forced sex") in search engines such as Yahoo! and Altavista. Examples of titles found were "Real Brutal Rape Videos," "Raped and Abused Teens," and "The Rapist Archives."

Conclusion

Studies of pornographic books, magazines, movies, and Internet content have found that violence is both infrequently and frequently depicted in pornography. Conclusions reached about the prevalence of violence in pornography depend largely on the medium studied, the specific act of violence analyzed, and the definition of violence employed. Nevertheless, existing research supports several contentions made by pornography critics: both physical and verbal violence are depicted in pornography; the violence depicted can be extreme; aggressors generally go unpunished; males are typically the perpetrators of aggression; and females are almost always the targets.

Paul J. Wright

See also Arousal and Aggressive Content; Catharsis Theory; Desensitization Effects; General Aggression Model; Pornography, Violent Content in: Effects of

Further Readings

Bridges, A. J., Wosnitzer, R., Scharrer, E., Sun, C., & Liberman, R. (2010). Aggression and sexual behavior in best-selling pornography videos: A content analysis update. *Violence Against Women, 16,* 1065–1085.

Linz, D., & Malamuth, N. (1993). *Pornography.* Newbury Park, CA: Sage.

Wright, P. J., Donnerstein, E., & Malamuth, N. M. (2012). Research on sex in the media: What do we know about effects on children and adolescents? In D. G. Singer & J. L. Singer (Eds.), *Handbook of children and the media* (pp. 273–302). Thousand Oaks, CA: Sage.

PORNOGRAPHY, VIOLENT CONTENT IN: EFFECTS OF

The term *pornography* has been loosely applied to many forms of explicit (and even nonexplicit) depictions of sexual behavior. What depictions are considered pornographic depends to a large extent on the political and religious orientation of those who use these descriptions. Within the aggression research community, however, there has generally been a consensus as to the definition of violent pornography. This material depicts sexual coercion in a sexually explicit context. For many years researchers have been studying the effects of sexually violent pornographic material on male viewers in particular. In one line of research, the effects of depictions of rape have been examined. In another line the effects of exposure to films that depict graphic violence against women, often juxtaposed with mildly sexual scenes (slasher films), have been studied. This entry discusses research on the effects of violent content in pornography and other films of a sexual nature.

Research Findings

The results of these studies have consistently revealed that several types of negative effects occur after exposure to sexual violence. For example, certain men are sexually aroused (e.g., penile tumescence) from viewing these violent images. Sexual arousal from aggression against women is also associated with a set of beliefs in which male dominance and female submissiveness are perceived as natural and justified and the view that male–female relationships are fundamentally adversarial. Additional research has indicated that men are likely to become desensitized to violence against women after viewing this material and later report calloused attitudes about rape. Men also show increased aggression against women in the laboratory.

As with other mass media depictions of rape, a common theme in violent pornography is that women derive pleasure from sexual aggression. In violent pornography, however, the effects might be accentuated by the explicit portrayals of sex and violence. It has been hypothesized that viewing an act of aggression in which the victim responds in a positive manner by showing pleasure might reduce aggressive inhibitions and justify aggressive behavior. The research supports this assumption.

Additional research has suggested a link between self-reports of sexually violent behavior outside the laboratory and rape depictions in the media—but this link is indirect. In speculation about these more complicated mediated effects, researchers have suggested that sexually violent media may affect men's attitudes, which, if combined with several other factors, may in turn affect aggressive behavior in naturalistic settings. This implies that exposure to sex and violence in the mass media is not the most or even one of the most powerful influences on sexually violent behavior. Rather, it may be only one of the many factors that interact to affect responses. The nature of the effect and the degree of influence of sexually violent media will often depend on, among other things, the

psychological background of the person exposed to the media stimuli and the sociocultural context in which exposure takes place.

Special Case of Nonexplicit Sexually Violent Media

Another line of research has examined the effects of films that juxtapose nonexplicit sexual scenes with graphic violence against women. The films in this category, often labeled "slasher" films, are usually R-rated because they are not sexually explicit. Recent inquiries into media violence have begun to consider the implications of exposure to these types of sexually violent materials because of the opportunities for exposure to such materials to young adolescents within the confines of R-rated cable and the Internet. Sexual violence in the media includes explicit sexualized violence against women, including rape, and images of torture, murder, and mutilation. Empirical research on the impact of sexual violence found in slasher films has revealed antisocial effects on both male and female college-age viewers. In one study males were exposed to five full-length slasher films over a period of two weeks. After each film, emotional reactions, perceptions of violence in the films, and attitudes toward women in the films were measured. Following exposure, the men evaluated a videotaped trial involving a female victim of sexual assault as part of an ostensibly unrelated study.

The results indicated that subjects experienced decreases in anxiety and depression between the first and last day of viewing. Subjects also perceived less violence in the films and evaluated the films as less degrading to women over time. Most important, subjects exposed to the filmed violence against women expressed less sympathy for the victim portrayed in the rape trial than did control groups who had not been exposed to such films. In an earlier study, subjects who viewed sexually violent films also judged the victim in a rape trial as less injured than did control subjects.

In summary, research consistently has indicated that exposure to depictions of violence against women either juxtaposed with mildly erotic scenes (slasher films) or in the form of sexually explicit or nonexplicit rape scenes results in callousness toward female victims of violence, especially rape victims, and other antisocial attitudinal, perception, and behavioral effects. Two important caveats need to be reiterated. First, these effects can occur without explicit sexual content. Many of the rape-related depictions used in the research described would not be considered pornographic. In the lines of research noted, it appears to be the message about violence against women that is important in producing antisocial effects. The mere presentation of consenting sex, no matter how explicit, did not facilitate antisocial outcomes. Second, the effects in these studies are strongest for men who *already* possess certain attitudes or who are predisposed to sexual violence in some way. Specifically, the behavioral effects occur most consistently for those who possess calloused attitudes about rape. These distinctions are crucial for the legal and educational solutions we might consider.

Finally, stronger effects might be expected for younger viewers because they lack the critical viewing skills and the experience necessary to discount the myths about women and sexual violence. To a young adolescent who is searching for information about sexual relationships, sexual violence in popular films (and on the Internet) may be a potent formative influence on attitudes toward sexuality. A young teenager's first exposure to sex may come in the form of a mildly erotic but violent movie such as a slasher film. This film would not be restricted because it did not carry an X rating. It could easily be seen today with the advent of new technology.

Edward Donnerstein

See also Cultivating Content and the Social Representation of Violence; Cultivation Theory; Pornography, Violent Content in; Priming Theory; Rape Perceptions; Sexualized Aggression; Social Learning From Media

Further Readings

Donnerstein, E. (2011). The media and aggression: From TV to the Internet. In J. Forgas, A. Kruglanski, & K. Williams (Eds.), *The psychology of social conflict and aggression* (pp. 267–284). New York, NY: Psychology Press.

Hald, G. M., Malamuth, N. M., Yuen, C. (2010). Pornography and attitudes supporting violence against women: Revisiting the relationship in nonexperimental studies. *Aggressive Behavior, 36,* 14–20.

Linz, D., & Malamuth, N. (1993). *Pornography.* Newbury Park, CA: Sage.

Vega, V., & Malamuth, N. (2007). The role of pornography in the context of general and specific risk factors. *Aggressive Behavior, 33,* 104–117.

PRESENCE THEORY

The theory of presence examines how people use communication technologies to expand their psychological and physical reach. Originally limited to teleoperation, or operating a machine at a distance, and virtual reality, the theory has been growing in popularity and application. The theory is multidimensional and has been studied in a variety of disciplines. Presence has been applied to the study of media violence in an attempt to understand the influence of media violence on some media users. The theory of presence is sometimes referred to as the theory of telepresence. This entry explains the theory of presence and discusses research into whether it influences the effects of media violence.

Conceptual Framework

Presence is a psychological state in which media users suspend their conscious experience of mediated experiences (i.e., video games, virtual reality, television). The result is a sensation of immersion or feeling a connection with the mediated content or characters. This connection has been characterized as a sense of being there, feeling a part of the action, or an emotional connection. A sense of presence is achieved through an interaction of media form (i.e., screen size), media content (i.e., violent video games or verbally aggressive sitcoms), and characteristics of the individual media user. This interaction is a process that leads to varying levels of presence during a media exposure. The theory has been studied to examine the impact of media content on aggression after exposure to violent media content.

History of Presence

The theory is highly interdisciplinary and has been studied in the fields of communication, cognitive science, psychology, computer science, art, and philosophy. The term was originally coined by Marvin Minsky in the early 1980s as a description of how technology might allow for the extension of the human body during teleoperation. Over the past 30 years, the theory has been adopted by research in a wide variety of media experiences, including highly immersive communication technologies such as virtual reality, clinical psychological treatment via desktop virtual environments, and popular media (i.e., video games, television, movies).

Subdimensions of Presence

Presence is a multidimensional concept with three subdimensions. The subdimensions are spatial or physical presence (i.e., feeling of being in the environment or perception of mediated environment), immersion (i.e., engagement and/or attention), and social realism (i.e., degree of naturalness or similarity to the real world). All of these subdimensions have been examined both individually, to assess the influence of different communication media, and in combination, to examine the impact of presence on media effects. Research results have demonstrated that the subdimensions are separate and that each has a unique impact on media effects. For example, social realism is a stronger predictor of presence for men than for women.

Cognitive Explanations for Presence

Cognitive psychology has offered a possible explanation for why people experience presence. Presence is viewed as the outcome of an intuitive experience-based metacognitive judgment that controls our action in either the real or virtual worlds. One model suggests there are three poles: mental imaginary space, physical space, and virtual space. The interaction of these three poles provides a continuum of presence sensations.

Presence and Media Violence

Within communication, a number of researchers have studied presence and its influence on the enjoyment of and effects of violent content. Because of the interactive nature of video games, most of these studies examined violent video games using experimental methodology.

The studies of presence and violent content have not reported consistent results. In fact, several studies have reported contradictory findings. There have been results reporting that participants who play highly violent video games report lower levels of presence, while other studies report participants felt more presence. Likewise, the influence of sensations of presence also has led to conflicting reports. Some studies have reported presence leads to more aggressive thoughts, while others did not find a relationship between the variables.

There is some consistency among the studies of the contribution of individual characteristics of the media user. The type of content employed in the study, gaming experience, and genre preference all contribute to the level of presence sensations reported by participants.

Additionally, media user characteristics, including gender, have been found to affect reported levels of aggression, aggressive thoughts, and presence. Within media violence studies, we also see the three subdimensions of presence functioning uniquely.

Cheryl Campanella Bracken

See also Narrative, Effects of Violent; Realism of Violent Content, Real-World Violence on Television, and Their Effects; Screen Size and Violent Content, Effects of

Further Readings

Biocca, F. (2003, May). *Can we resolve the book, the physical reality, and the dream state problems? From the two-pole to a three-pole model of shifts in presence.* Presented at the EU Future and Emerging Technologies, Presence Initiative Meeting. Venice, Italy.

Bracken, C. C., & Skalski, P. (2010). *Immersed in media: Telepresence in everyday life.* New York, NY: Routledge.

International Society for Presence Research. (2000). *The concept of presence: Explication statement.* Retrieved from http://www.ispr.info

Lombard, M., & Ditto, T. B. (1997). The heart of it all: The concept of presence. *Journal of Computer-Mediated Communication, 3*(2). Retrieved from http://jcmc.indiana.edu/vol3/issue2/lombard.html

Waterworth, J. A., Waterworth, E. L., Mantovani, F., & Riva, G. (2010). On feeling (the) present: An evolutionary account of the sense of presence in physical and electronically-mediated environments. *Journal of Consciousness Studies, 17*(1–2), 167–178.

PRIMING THEORY

Research on the depictions of violence and aggression in the media has garnered a significant amount of attention from social scientists. A number of theoretical models have been developed to help understand whether or not seeing violent content in the media is associated with increased levels of aggression in the lives of viewers. A component that many of these theories have in common is the concept of "priming." This entry outlines the concept of priming, describes some of the key findings of priming research focused on aggression in the media, explains how priming has been used in two social psychology theories focused on media and aggression, and describes how priming can be used in future research examining the effects of violent content in the media on society.

Overview of Priming

The concept of priming originated in cognitive psychology and has been described as "the effect of some preceding stimulus or event on how we react . . . to some subsequent stimulus" (Roskos-Ewoldsen, Klinger, & Roskos-Ewoldsen, 2007, p. 53). Studies have often described the use of priming tasks to manipulate the accessibility of information in people's memories. Therefore, priming is inherently connected to the concept of accessibility. That is, priming focuses on understanding how the media make certain pieces of information more accessible in viewers' memory.

Priming uses the network model of memory as the theoretical grounding explaining how media make certain pieces of information more accessible in the human brain (Roskos-Ewoldsen et al., 2007). The network model describes memory as an assortment of nodes that represents different pieces of information (Anderson, 1983). For instance, people likely have nodes in their memory for general concepts like "sports" and specific nodes for subsets of these larger concepts (e.g., baseball, basketball, football, soccer). Moreover, in our memories, each of these nodes is attached to other pieces of information. For instance, most sports would be connected to the node "ball." However, different sports may be connected to different concepts. The concept of "baseball" is likely associated with nodes such as "bat," "summer," and "home run." By contrast, football would likely be connected to nodes such as "goal posts," "fall," and "touchdowns." Therefore, seeing the word *baseball* or *football* will activate different sets of nodes. Because these two sports make different sets of nodes accessible in memory, watching these two sporting events may have different effects on a variety of outcome variables. For example, compared with watching a baseball game, taking in a football game may result in more aggressive thoughts becoming accessible in memory, which could translate into aggressive behaviors.

Scholars have highlighted the importance of recency (i.e., how recently the information was primed) and intensity (i.e., how intense was the priming event) to understand priming effects (Roskos-Ewoldsen et al., 2007). Priming has generally been

described as a short-term effect, in that information becomes temporarily more accessible in memory. Indeed, research has shown that a delay of 30 minutes decreases the effects of primed information when judging political candidates.

Similarly, Wendy L. Josephson's (1987) study that examined the effects of media violence on aggression in viewers found a decrease in aggressive behaviors in the second and third periods of a floor hockey game compared with the first period, which indicates that the effect of the priming event must have diminished with time. A second variable is the intensity of the priming event. Intensity could be thought of as the number of occurrences of a priming event or the duration of the event. In essence, seeing a slasher horror film in its entirety will have a greater priming effect on viewers than seeing only one scene from the same movie.

Scholars have also explained that recency and intensity may interact when examining the priming effects. That is, greater intensity will result in greater accessibility of the primed information. Moreover, the priming effects of intense events have been shown to dissipate more slowly than the primed information for a less intense event.

Priming Effects of Violence and Aggression

Studies have demonstrated priming effects across different manipulations and media content using a wide range of dependent variables. Specifically regarding violent or aggressive outcomes, these studies have shown strong evidence that a variety of manipulations, such as showing people a picture of a gun, getting people to think about competition, or suggesting that participants are about to watch a violent film, prime violent and aggressive cognitions.

Findings have indicated that consuming violent media content via movies, television, music, and video games makes aggressive feelings and thoughts more accessible in viewers' memory. This set of studies also indicates that priming effects can occur across a wide variety of dependent variables. For instance, watching violent media has been shown to increase trait hostility, levels of aggressive tendencies, reaction times identifying aggressive words, preference for aggressive programming, and engaging in aggressive behaviors while playing a competitive sport. David R. Roskos-Ewoldsen and colleagues (2007) have provided evidence that violent media does indeed prime aggressive cognitions. Their meta-analysis showed a statistically significant priming effect across a series of studies they identified as focusing on priming and aggression.

There is also evidence that priming effects vary across individual difference variables. For instance, trait aggression and hypermasculinity have both been shown to moderate the main effects of aggressive primes. In essence, these studies have shown increases in aggression to be greater among those with high levels of trait aggression and hypermasculinity. Roskos-Ewoldsen and colleagues' (2007) meta-analysis also showed a statistically significant priming event by trait aggression interaction on aggressive outcomes.

Application of Priming to Violence Theories

Priming has served as the linchpin for two theoretical models focused on predicting aggressive actions: the neoassociation model (Berkowitz, 1990) and the general aggression model (GAM; Anderson, 1997). Leonard Berkowitz (1990) uses the network model of memory to explain that primed negative affect (i.e., negative emotions) activates similar and related concepts in memory. Specifically, he explained that negative affect activates "anger-related feelings, action tendencies, and thoughts and memories" (p. 497). In essence, events that elicit negative reactions make aggressive nodes accessible in individuals' memories that make the individuals more likely to engage in aggressive behaviors.

Similarly, Craig Anderson's GAM model explains that priming is an important factor in understanding aggressive behaviors. The GAM model expands on Berkowitz's theory by adding individual-level factors and an appraisal and decision process about how to act. Specifically, the GAM notes that situational and individual-level factors interact to prime cognitions, affect, and arousal. In essence, the situation primes nodes associated with aggression in people's memory, an effect that varies based on individual difference variables such as trait aggression. Depending on their appraisal process, people will act impulsively or thoughtfully. In this theory, the priming of aggressive cognitions, affect, and arousal play a key role in understanding whether people will engage in impulsive or thoughtful aggressive actions.

Future of Priming Research

Priming will continue to play an important role in the scholarship focused on aggression. Although much of the research has focused on the short-term effects of priming on aggressive behaviors, scholars have started to explain that continuous priming of information in memory could make aggressive cognitions chronically accessible in one's memory. Alexander Todorov and John A. Bargh have explained that continuous priming of aggression could increase the likelihood of people acting aggressively in social situations.

The potential for aggressive cognitions to be chronically accessible in memory is more likely in the early 21st century than previously because the fragmentation of media has given people greater control over the media content they consume. This increase in control could lead people with aggressive tendencies to consume aggressive media content more frequently. For instance, Michael D. Slater and colleagues (2003) found a reinforcing spiral in which aggressive people would seek out aggressive media content, which then increased their levels of aggression. In this process, people watch violent media content that primes any aggressive tendencies they may have. With aggression primed in their memory, these people then seek out additional aggressive media content, which keeps the aggressive pieces of information accessible in their memory. This is particularly important because continuous priming means that environmental cues become less important in triggering aggressive behaviors. In essence, people who have aggressive thoughts chronically accessible in their memory do not need to consume aggressive content to have aggressive cognitions available in their memory (Chen & Bargh, 1997). The inevitable consequence of priming is that having these cognitions accessible will most likely cause an accidental bump to be interpreted as an act of aggression, which could lead an individual to respond in turn with a violent action.

Priming remains an important factor in the theoretical models that attempt to explain the relationship between media use and aggressive behaviors. Extensive research has shown that violent content in the media indeed primes the aggressive parts of people's memory. Moreover, priming has played an integral part in theoretical models that outline the sociological and psychological processes in which media use leads to aggressive behaviors. Because the accessibility of information is so important for understanding the effects of media, scholars will continue to study and apply priming to future studies examining the effects of violent media content on society.

Jay Hmielowski

See also Aggression, Definition and Assessment of; Aggression, Risk Factors of; Aggression and Affect; Aggression and Anger; Aggressive Behavior; Effects From Violent Media, Short- and Long-Term; Excitation-Transfer Theory; General Aggression Model; Memory and Violence; Media Effects Perspective of Violence; Media Violence, Definitions and Context of

Further Readings

Anderson, C. A. (1997). Effects of violent movies and trait hostility on hostile feelings and aggressive thoughts. *Aggressive Behavior, 23,* 161–178.

Anderson, C. A., Anderson, K. B., & Deuser, W. E. (1996). Examining an affective aggression framework: Weapon and temperature effects on aggressive thoughts, affect, and attitudes. *Personality and Social Psychology Bulletin, 22,* 366–376.

Anderson, C. A., & Bushman, B. J. (2002). Human aggression. *Annual Review of Psychology, 53,* 27–51.

Anderson, C. A., Carnagey, N. L., & Eubanks, J. (2003). Exposure to violent media: The effects of songs with violent lyrics on aggressive thoughts and feelings. *Journal of Personality and Social Psychology, 84,* 960–971.

Anderson, C. A., & Morrow, M. (1995). Competitive aggression without interaction: Effects of competitive versus cooperative instructions on aggressive behavior in video games. *Personality and Social Psychology Bulletin, 21,* 1020–1030.

Anderson, J. (1983). *The architecture of cognition.* Cambridge, MA: Harvard University Press.

Bargh, J. A., Chen, M., & Burrows, L. (1996). Automaticity of social behavior: Direct effects of trait construct and stereotype priming on action. *Journal of Personality and Social Psychology, 71,* 230–244.

Berkowitz, L. (1984). Some effects of thoughts on anti- and prosocial influence of media events: A cognitive-neoassociationistic analysis. *Psychology Bulletin, 95,* 410–427.

Berkowitz, L. (1990). On the formation and regulation of anger and aggression: A neoassociationistic analysis. *American Psychologist, 45,* 494–503.

Berkowitz, L., & Rogers, K. H. (1986). A priming effect analysis on media influences. In J. Bryant & D. Zillmann (Eds.), *Perspectives on media effects* (pp. 57–81). Hillsdale, NJ: Erlbaum.

Bushman, B. J. (1998). Priming effects of media violence on the accessibility of aggressive constructs in memory. *Personality and Social Psychology Bulletin, 24*(5), 537–545.

Chen, M., & Bargh, J. A. (1997). Nonconscious behavioral confirmation processes: The self-fulfilling consequences of automatic stereotype activation. *Journal of Experimental Social Psychology, 33,* 541–560.

Eastin, M. S. (2006). Video game violence and the female game player: Self-and opponent gender effects on presence and aggressive thoughts. *Human Communication Research, 32*(3), 351–372.

Higgins, E. T., Bargh, J. A., & Lombardi, W. (1985). Nature of priming effects on categorization. *Journal of Experimental Psychology: Learning, Memory, & Cognition, 11,* 59–69.

Josephson, W. L. (1987). Television violence and children's aggression: Testing the priming, social script, and disinhibition predictions. *Journal of Personality and Social Psychology, 53*(5), 882–890.

Langley, T., O'Neal, E. C., Craig, K. M., & Yost, E. A. (2006). Aggression-consistent, -inconsistent, and -irrelevant priming effects on selective exposure to media violence. *Aggressive Behavior, 18*(5), 349–356.

Leyens, J. P., & Dunand, M. (1991). Priming aggressive thoughts: The effect of the anticipation of a violent movie upon the aggressive behaviors of the spectators. *European Journal of Social Psychology, 21,* 507–516.

Roskos-Ewoldsen, D. R., Klinger, M. R., & Roskos-Ewoldsen, B. (2007). Media priming: A meta-analysis. In R. W. Preiss, B. M. Gayle, N. Burrell, M. Allen, & J. Bryant (Eds.), *Mass media effects research: Advances through media analysis* (pp. 53–80). Mahwah, NJ: Erlbaum.

Roskos-Ewoldsen, D. R., Roskos-Ewoldsen, B., & Carpentier, F. D. (2009). Media priming: An updated synthesis. In J. Bryant & M. B. Oliver (Eds.), *Media effects: Advances in theory* (pp. 53–80). Mahwah, NJ: Erlbaum.

Sherry, J. L. (2001). The effects of violent video games on aggression: A meta-analysis. *Human Communication Research, 27*(3), 409–431.

Slater, M. D., Henry, K. L., Swaim, R., & Anderson, L. (2003.) Violent media content and aggression in adolescents: A downward-spiral model. *Communication Research, 30,* 713–736.

Todorv, A., & Bargh, J. A. (2002). Automatic sources of aggression. *Aggression and Violent Behavior, 7,* 53–68.

PSYCHOBIOLOGY OF VIOLENCE

There clearly are linkages between violence and psychobiology—the mental functioning and behavior in relation to other biological processes—but how they are linked depends on the individual, the context, and the researcher's interpretation. Studies employing modern biological techniques and media expressions of violence (rather than assessments based on questionnaires, staged situations or direct observation of participation in real life, or sporting events) have simply not, as yet, been carried out. However, some research on violent video games has found effects on aggression. A longitudinal study with German adolescents, conducted by Ingrid Moller and Barbara Krahe (2009), revealed that playing violent electronic games had a long-term effect on later physical (but not indirect/relational) aggression. A later study by Matthias Bluemke, Monika Friedrich, and Joerg Zumbach (2010) suggested that even short participation in such games increased implicit aggressive self-concepts in German students without markedly altering either heart rate or skin conductance measured to assess arousal. This entry looks at research that has studied the relationship between psychobiology and violence.

The first complicating factor is that *any* behavioral expression involves a complex interplay among biological factors (genes, neural circuits, neurotransmitters, hormones, etc.), situational determinants (the context), and accumulated positive and negative experiences of individuals participating in the encounters. Violence (unlike feeding or sexual behavior, where there is a relatively easily identified basic utility) has the added complications of being subject to external value judgments (so-called negative apperception) and being deemed, in some way, to be excessive. Different people (depending on age, gender, and background) can judge the same events very differently. An event that is viewed or heard may be perceived as realistic or not (as in some cartoons and games). In looking at what is considered aggression, researchers have found that actions that look remarkably similar (such as hitting or kicking) may serve offensive (competitive), defensive, or even predatory functions. The presumed function could easily color the viewer's perception of the action.

An array of biological factors can be linked to activities that can be classified as violence. This is, however, far from being a one-way street. Biological factors may alter the propensity for expressing certain actions, but participation in the activities (or even exposure to them) often changes the individual's physiology, which might well lead to the individual having changes in mood that alter his or her probability of showing responses that could be subsequently labeled as violent by observers.

There appear to be few direct studies on media violence and psychobiology, but the linkages between biological factors and the propensity for producing actions that can be perceived as violent have been substantially reviewed (e.g., Brain, 2000), and these offer potentially fruitful areas for investigation. Varied individual responses to images, songs, or game events might well be influenced by genetics, although it would be an oversimplification of the science to attribute violent behavior to a "gene for violence." Factors such as gender, developmental or adult exposure to psychoactive drugs, and even diet also can influence individuals' response to violence. An illustration of how difficult it is to separate out the possible actions of individual biological factors on responses to and participation in violence is clearly evident when one notes that the effect of gender (which is itself partly due to genes on the so-called sex chromosomes, partly a consequence of early hormonal exposure in the so-called androgenization process, partly due to self-image, partly to social factors, and partly a consequence of the adult hormonal profile), which is very likely to change how individuals respond to the sensory input to which they are exposed. Propensities for showing particular individual responses might also vary in subjects with nervous systems subtly changed as consequences of developmental or adult exposure to legal, illegal, or prescribed psychoactive drugs. Modern imaging approaches to central nervous system activity could clearly be used to study the effects of putatively violent media exposure on neurobiological activity. Paul F. Brain (2000) noted that "substances such as glucose, caffeine, alcohol, tryptophan (an amino acid), environmental lead, food additives, vitamins and minerals have all, at various times, been investigated as potential influences on antisocial behavior." Some of these could influence how individuals respond to media input and whether those same individuals perceive responses they choose to make as appropriate or not. Brain (1997) pointed out that one of the likely reasons why alcohol is said to fuel aggressive responses in barroom contexts is that arguments appear to escalate because the drink-impaired participants lose the ability to respond to each other in socially acceptable ways. In this context it has been shown that individuals with different ratings of the trait for dispositional anger vary in their physically aggressive responses to violent and nonviolent video games (Engelhardt, Bartholow, & Saults, 2011).

The most likely candidates for linking psychobiological responses to media images are the neurotransmitters of the central nervous system and the hormonal changes within the circulatory system (some of which clearly alter mood and feelings or traits and states). Neurotransmitters act relatively acutely and have been linked to reward or hedonistic systems (a reason why some psychoactive drugs—and possibly games—are addictive). Psychoactive compounds have been associated with violence in a number of ways. For example, many psychoactive drugs (e.g., alcohol, cocaine, and benzodiazepines) can influence neural development in the offspring of addicted mothers. Their ingestion by older individuals clearly alters how the users perceive and should respond to the variety of sensory inputs to which they are exposed. Albert J. Reiss and Jeffrey A. Roth (1993) note, however, that individual differences apart from biological processes affect the relationships between violent behavior and the use of alcohol or other psychoactive drugs.

Hormones are generally more chronically acting and would seem to be prime candidates for linking exposure to violent media input to subsequent behavioral change. Modern technologies (e.g., enzyme immunoassay) enable some steroid hormones of the adrenal glands and gonads to be accurately measured in salivary samples that, unlike blood samples, can be taken without stressing the subject and thus changing the very thing one is trying to measure. Although psychobiological investigations of aggression have tended to concentrate on adrenal steroids (both glucocorticoids, such as cortisol, and adrenal androgens, such as dehydroepiandrosterone), gonadal steroids (androgens and estrogens), and the classic "emergency" catecholamine adrenalin, hormones appear to "talk to each other" so that many other often unrecorded factors (e.g., insulin and growth hormones) are also likely to be changed. Focusing on single hormones, however, gives one a partial view of the pattern of physiological change.

Some hormones appear to have direct effects on central nervous system activity (they are bound within particular neural locations and alter the firing rates of neurons), but they may also have indirect signaling effects on participants in social interactions by altering their anatomical appearance or even odor production. It is well established that sex steroids can change aggressive feelings. Indeed, a meta-analysis of studies that use both the Buss-Durkee Hostility Inventory score and measure plasma testosterone titer produced a low but positive relationship between these two measures. One should emphasize, however, that elevated testosterone levels are linked to angry mood rather than to expressed behavior. Certain categories of sexually aggressive male offenders have altered levels of particular hormones (notably dehydroepiandrosterone). Saliva (free rather than protein-bound) concentrations of testosterone have been positively correlated with self-rated spontaneous aggression, and such hormonal measures have been correlated with the degree of violence involved in crimes for which young U.S. male prisoners were convicted (Dabbs, Frady, Carr, & Besch, 1987).

Studies involving conflict in staged sporting encounters have also proved revealing. Some studies have confirmed that male winners in both physical (e.g., tennis) and intellectual (e.g., chess) contests have elevated levels of testosterone, whereas losers show declines in this hormone (Booth, Shelly, Mazur, Tharp, & Kittok, 1989; Mazur, Booth, & Dabbs, 1992). The chess finding is particularly important because physical activity (profound in many sports) produces quite marked changes in these hormonal levels. Interestingly, it has been suggested that winners show these changes only when they feel they "deserve it"; the "lucky" winners of raffles do not show this physiological change. More recently, Stefano Parmigiani and colleagues (2009) showed that in karate fighters where testosterone and cortisol were measured before and after ritualized and actual paired conflict revealed that losers had both higher pre- and post-fight levels of cortisol than winners but also showed higher levels of harm avoidance and anxiety and lower levels of novelty seeking in questionnaire assessments. The observed correlations between biological and psychological measures suggest that either psychometric tests predict hormonal responses in specified contexts (here in an actual competitive encounter) and/or that hormonal responses might be used to infer the personality traits of an individual and his or her likely responses in the specific situation.

Although the focus on individuals exposed to violent input from media sources is generally concerned with desensitization and imitation of the violent actions, there is also a literature (reviewed in Brain, 1997) showing that human and animal victims of threat and attack can be subtly damaged by the induction of endocrine, psychological, and immunological changes that impair mental health and disease resistance. It is not impossible that some individuals might find some kinds of media input threatening. Although one would not expect them to show elevated competitiveness or desensitization, they might well become hyperdefensive and respond in ways deemed inappropriate.

Recent developments in the ability to accurately assess physiological changes (especially hormones), and the increased sophistication of measures of psychological change, may spur new research into psychobiological responses to violence, including responses to violent media such as news items, televised sports, video games, and cartoons.

Paul F. Brain

See also

Further Readings

Bluemke, M., Friedrich, M., & Zumbach, J. (2010). The influence of violent and nonviolent computer games on implicit measures of aggressiveness. *Aggressive Behavior, 36*, 1–13.

Booth, A., Shelly, G., Mazur, A., Tharp, G., & Kittok, R. (1989). Testosterone and winning and losing in human competition. *Hormones and Behavior, 23*, 556–571.

Brain, P. F. (1987). The physiology of the unicorn. *Politics and the Life Sciences, 6*, 43–47.

Brain, P. F. (1997). Alcohol's effects on physiology and "aggression": What is the nature of the link? In S. Feshbach & J. Zagrodzka (Eds.), *Aggression: Biological, developmental and social perspectives* (pp. 51–65). New York, NY: Plenum Press.

Brain, P. F. (2000). The biology of aggression. In E. E. & N. Bittar (Eds.), *Principles of medical biology* (pp. 103–113). Greenwich, CT: JAI Press.

Dabbs, M. J., Frady, R. L., Carr, T. S., & Besch, N. F. (1987). Saliva testosterone and criminal violence in young adult male prisoners. *Psychosomatic Medicine, 49*, 174–182.

Engelhardt, C. R., Bartholow, B. D., & Saults, J. S. (2011). Violent and nonviolent video games differentially affect physical aggression for individuals high vs. low in dispositional anger. *Aggressive Behavior, 37*, 538–545.

Mazur, A., Booth, A., & Dabbs, J. (1992). Testosterone and chess competition. *Social Psychology Quarterly, 55*, 70–77.

Moller, I., & Krahe, B. (2009). Exposure to violent video games and aggression in German adolescents: A longitudinal analysis. *Aggressive Behavior, 35*, 75–89.

Parmigiani, S., Dadomo, H., Bartolomucci, A., Brain, P. F., Carbucicchio, A., Costantino, C., et al. (2009). Personality traits and endocrine response as possible asymmetry factors of agonistic outcome in karate athletes. *Aggressive Behavior, 35*, 324–333.

Reiss, A. J., & Roth, J. A. (Eds.). (1993). *Understanding and preventing violence*. Washington, DC: National Academy Press.

Psychopathology and Susceptibility to Violence

Over the course of their lives, many people succumb to their aggressive urges. Jealous husbands may abuse their wives, rejected youth may lash out toward their rejecters, and healthy experimental participants may blast annoying strangers with aversive and prolonged noise. But how much of aggression is due to abnormal mental processes? How do such pathological thoughts, feelings, and behaviors influence an individual's susceptibility to commit violent acts? Each form of mental illness is unique, and as such, the avenues through which any form of psychopathology can influence aggressive behavior are idiosyncratic. This entry addresses the relation of psychopathology to aggressive behavior, focusing on several specific mental illnesses, and discusses the effect of media violence on the susceptibility to violence in those with mental illness.

Depression

According to the American Psychiatric Association, depression is a major mental illness characterized by chronic sadness, a lack of interest in most activities, weight change, problems sleeping, loss of energy and ability to concentrate, and thoughts of death. Ronald C. Kessler and colleagues (2005) found that roughly 6.7% of U.S. adults meet criteria for major depressive disorder, classifying 30.4% of these cases as "severe." Although depression is characterized by lethargy, it is also associated with an approach-related behavior, namely aggression. In a study by Maurizio Fava and colleagues (1991), depressed people, compared with nondepressed controls, reported greater frequency of aggressive outbursts. In another study, Hyeonsook Shin (2010) found that children who report elevated levels of depression show increased levels of aggression six months later. In an authoritative review of the literature, Charles S. Carver, Sheri L. Johnson, and Jutta Joorman (2008) showed that risk factors for depression are also closely associated with impulsive aggression. Emil F. Coccaro and colleagues (1997) found that low serotonergic functioning, which is a core feature of depression, is robustly closely associated with impulsive aggression and violence. These findings are also consistent with Leonard Berkowitz's (1993) cognitive neoassociation theory, which predicts that negative affect increases the risk aggression.

Social Anxiety

Social anxiety, as defined by the American Psychiatric Association, is a pervasive psychiatric disorder characterized by persistent fear and distress regarding potential negative evaluations from others. Research has shown that social anxiety places people at risk for suicidal ideation, suicide attempts, and substance use disorders. Although social anxiety is frequently associated with behavioral inhibition—a motivational direction in sharp contrast to the approach-related nature of aggression—a certain subtype of social anxiety disorder can be associated with higher levels of aggression. Recent research by Todd B. Kashdan and colleagues (2009) identified two classes of social anxiety disorder that bore distinct associations to aggression. The "classic" subtype was characterized by heightened behavioral inhibition and lower aggression. In contrast, a second "atypical" subtype was associated with impulsivity and heightened aggression. Thus, social anxiety can serve as a resiliency or risk factor for aggression.

Intermittent Explosive Disorder

According to Kessler and colleagues (2006), people with intermittent explosive disorder (IED) engage in recurrent episodes of aggressive acts that are out of proportion to the severity of the provocation. Moreover, IED patients' aggressive outbursts cannot be explained as a result of another mental disorder or a response to a psychotropic substance. In any 12-month period, approximately 3.9% of U.S. adults meet criteria for IED (Kessler et al., 2006). Research has shown that people with IED, compared with those without IED, have higher levels of anger, make more hostile attributions when confronted with socially ambiguous cues, and exhibit stronger amygdala activation in response to provocation. Compared with people without IED, people with IED are prone to engage in relational aggression, impulsive verbal aggression, aggressive driving, and physical violence.

Attention Deficit/Hyperactivity Disorder

Attention deficit/hyperactivity disorder (ADHD) is a disorder marked by inattention and hyperactivity. It frequently begins in childhood and persists through adulthood. According to the Centers for Disease Control and Prevention, parent-reported ADHD is on the rise in the United States, from 7.8% in 2003 to 9.5% in 2007. ADHD is associated with heightened aggression during childhood, adolescence, and young adulthood. These findings suggest that ADHD is reliably associated with higher aggression across various stages of human development.

Borderline Personality Disorder

Borderline personality disorder (BPD) is characterized by emotional instability, chaotic relationships, and angry outbursts, as noted by the American Psychiatric Association. Borderline personality disorder is somewhat rare; the National Institute of Mental Health notes that it occurs in approximately 2% of the U.S. population, especially in young women. Donald M. Dougherty and colleagues (1999) found that people with BPD show heightened levels of aggression. Indeed, a review of the BPD literature concluded that "impulsive aggression is an important trait underlying disorders such as borderline personality disorder" (Skodol et al., 2002, p. 952).

Psychopathy/Conduct Disorder

Psychopathy, as defined by Robert D. Hare and colleagues (1990), is a disorder marked by callous, unemotional, and impulsive or antisocial behavior. Sylvain Nouvion and colleagues (2007) concluded that psychopaths tend to engage in cold, calculated, unemotional, and premeditated proactive aggression. Despite the stereotype of the psychopathic murderer, most people who commit murder are not psychopathic, according to Sherrie Williamson, Robert Hare, and Stephen Wong (1987). Because most murders occur as a result of fits of rage, they tend not to fit the profile of the psychopath. Nonetheless, psychopathic traits can be considered a risk factor for aggression.

Schizophrenia

The American Psychiatric Association defines schizophrenia as a disorder characterized by delusions, hallucinations, and other disturbances in affect, cognition, and behavior. Research has shown that schizophrenic individuals display an increased susceptibility with committing aggressive acts, such as violent crimes, including homicide. Peter Cheung and colleagues (1997) found that violent individuals with schizophrenia, compared to nonviolent individuals with schizophrenia, had auditory hallucinations (in the form of internal voices) that had more negative affect, vocabulary, and tone. Furthermore, violent individuals with schizophrenia had a more difficult time coping with these voices, as evidenced by the increased ability of the voices to make them angry.

Psychopathology and Violent Media

Do forms of mental illness make people more susceptible to the ability of violent media to increase aggression? Preliminary evidence for just such a phenomenon exists in Jeanne B. Funk and colleagues' (2002) finding that the preference for violent video game play is associated with troubled thoughts, maladaptive internalizing, anxiety, depression, and behavioral problems among adolescents. Furthermore, Tom Grimes, Eric Vernberg, and Teresa Cathers (1997) found that children with psychiatric behavioral disorders responded to violent videos by reporting less empathy toward the victims of the violent act and that the violence was more justified than did the controls. Together, these results demonstrate that violent media may interact with psychopathology by (a) being viewed as more appealing by individuals with mental illness, and (b) reinforcing mental processes consistent with psychopathy, namely diminished empathy and increased approval of violent acts. Future research into the effects that violent media has on individuals with psychopathology and the ultimate influence this has on aggressive and violent tendencies is necessary.

David S. Chester and C. Nathan DeWall

See also Aggression, Definition and Assessment of; Aggression, Risk Factors of; Trait Aggression; Violence in Media, Effects on Aggression and Violent Crime

Further Readings

American Psychiatric Association. (2000). *Diagnostic and statistical manual of mental disorders* (4th ed.). Washington, DC: Author.

Berkowitz, L. (1993). *Aggression: Its causes, consequences, and control.* McGraw-Hill Series in Social Psychology. New York, NY: McGraw-Hill.

Buckner, J. D., Eggleston, A. M., & Schmidt, N. B. (2006). Social anxiety and problematic alcohol consumption: The mediating role of drinking motives and situations. *Behavior Therapy, 37,* 381–391.

Carver, C. S., Johnson, S. L., & Joormann, J. (2008). Serotonergic function, two-mode models of self-regulation, and vulnerability to depression: What depression has in common with impulsive aggression. *Psychological Bulletin, 134,* 912–943.

Centers for Disease Control. (2010). Increasing prevalence of parent-reported attention-deficit/hyperactivity disorder among children—United States, 2003 and 2007. *Morbidity and Mortality Weekly Report, 59*(44), 1439–1443.

Cheung, P., Schweitzer, I., Crowley, K., & Tuckwell, V. (1997). Violence in schizophrenia: Role of hallucinations and delusions. *Schizophrenia Research, 26*(2–3), 181–190.

Coccaro, E., Kavoussi, R., Berman, M., & Lish, J. (1998). Intermittent explosive disorder—revised: Development, reliability, and validity of research criteria. *Comprehensive Psychiatry, 39,* 368–376.

Coccaro, E. F., Kavoussi, R. J., Cooper, T. B., & Hauger, R. L. (1997). Central serotonin and aggression: Inverse relationship with prolactin response to d-fenfluramine, but not with CSF 5-HIAA concentration in human subjects. *American Journal of Psychiatry, 154,* 1430–1435.

Coccaro, E. F., Noblett, K. L., & McCloskey, M. S. (2009). Attributional and emotional responses to socially ambiguous cues: Validation of a new assessment of social/emotional information processing in healthy adults and impulsive aggressive patients. *Journal of Psychiatric Research, 43,* 915–925.

Crystal, D. S., Ostrander, R., Chen, R. S., & August, G. J. (2001). Multimethod assessment of psychopathology among DSM-IV subtypes of children with attention-deficit/hyperactivity disorder: Self-, parent, and teacher reports. *Journal of Abnormal Child Psychology, 29,* 189–206.

Dougherty, D. M., Bjork, J. M., Huckabee, H. C., Moeller, F. G., & Swann, A. C. (1999). Laboratory measures of aggression and impulsivity in women with borderline personality disorder. *Psychiatry Research, 85,* 315–326.

Eronen, M., Tiihonen, J., & Hakola, P. (1996). Schizophrenia and homicidal behavior. *Schizophrenia Bulletin, 22*(1), 83–89.

Fava, M., Rosenbaum, J. F., McCarthy, M. K., Pava, J. A., Steingard, R. J., & Bless, E. (1991). Anger attacks in depressed outpatients and their response to fluoxetine. *Psychopharmacology Bulletin, 27,* 275–279.

Funk, J. B., Hagan, J., Schimming, J., Bullock, W. A., Buchman, D. D., & Myers, M. (2002). Aggression and psychopathology in adolescents with a preference for violent electronic games. *Aggressive Behavior, 28*(2), 134–144.

Galovski, T., Blanchard, E. B., & Veazey, C. (2002). Intermittent explosive disorder and other psychiatric co-morbidity among court-referred and self-referred aggressive drivers. *Behaviour Research and Therapy, 40,* 641–651.

Glazer, W. M., & Dickson, R. A. (1998). Clozapine reduces violence and persistent aggression in schizophrenia. *Journal of Clinical Psychiatry, 59*(Suppl. 3), 8–14.

Grimes, T., Vernberg, E., & Cathers, T. (1997). Emotionally disturbed children's reactions to violent media segments. *Journal of Health Communication, 2*(3), 157–168.

Hare, R. D., Harpur, T. J., Hakstian, A. R., Forth, A. E., Hart, S. D., & Newman, J. P. (1990). The Revised Psychopathy Checklist: Descriptive statistics, reliability, and factor structure. *Psychological Assessment: A Journal of Consulting and Clinical Psychology, 2,* 338–341.

Kashdan, T. B., McKnight, P. E., Richey, J. A., & Hofmann, S. G. (2009). When social anxiety disorder co-exists with risk-prone, approach behavior: Investigating a neglected, meaningful subset of people in the National Comorbidity Survey Replication. *Behaviour Research and Therapy, 47,* 559–568.

Kessler, R. C., Chiu, W. T., Demler O., & Walters, E. E. (2005). Prevalence, severity, and comorbidity of twelve-month DSM-IV disorders in the National Comorbidity Survey Replication (NCS-R). *Archives of General Psychiatry, 62,* 617–627.

Kessler, R. C., Coceara, E. F., Fava, M., Jaeger, S., Jin, R., & Walters, E. (2006). The prevalence and correlates of DSM-IV intermittent explosive disorder in the National Comorbidity Survey Replication. *Archives of General Psychiatry, 63,* 669–678.

Kessler, R. C., Crum, R. M., Warner, L. A., Nelson, C. B., Schulenberg, J., & Anthony, J. C. (1997). Lifetime co-occurrence of DSM-III-R alcohol abuse and dependence with other psychiatric disorders in the National Comorbidity Survey. *Archives of General Psychiatry, 54,* 313–321.

Lindqvist, P., & Allebeck, P. (1990). Schizophrenia and crime: A longitudinal follow-up of 644 schizophrenics in Stockholm. *British Journal of Psychiatry, 157*(3), 345–350.

McCloskey, M. S., Berman, M. E., Noblett, K. L., & Coccaro, E. F. (2006): Intermittent explosive disorder–integrated research diagnostic criteria: Convergent and discriminant validity. *Journal of Psychiatric Research, 40,* 231–242.

McCloskey, M. S., Lee, R., Berman, M. E., Noblett, K. L., & Coccaro, E. F. (2008). The relationship between impulsive verbal aggression and intermittent explosive disorder. *Aggressive Behavior, 34,* 51–60.

McCloskey, M. S., Phan, K., Angstadt, M., & Coccaro, E. (in press). Amygdala dysregulation to angry faces among patients with intermittent explosive disorder. *Neuropsychopharmacology.*

Murray-Close, D., Ostrov, J. M., Nelson, D. A., Crick, N. R., & Coccaro, E. F. (2010). Proactive, reactive, and romantic relational aggression in adulthood: Measurement, predictive validity, gender differences, and association with intermittent explosive disorder. *Journal of Psychiatric Research, 44,* 393–404.

National Institute of Mental Health. (2011). *Borderline personality disorder.* Retrieved from http://www.nimh.nih.gov/health/publications/borderline-personality-disorder-fact-sheet/index.shtml

Nouvion, S. O., Cherek, D. R., Lane, S. D., Tcheremissine, O. V., & Lieving, L. M. (2007). Human proactive aggression: Association with personality disorders and psychopathy. *Aggressive Behavior, 33,* 552–562.

Shin, H. (2010). Does depression moderate or mediate the relations between deficits in competence and aggression? A short-term longitudinal study of Korean children. *School Psychology International, 31,* 331–352.

Skodol, A. E., Siever, L. J., Livesley, W. J., Gunderson, J. G., Pfohl, B., & Widiger, T. A. (2002). The borderline diagnosis: II. Biology, genetics, and clinical course. *Biological Psychiatry, 51,* 951–963.

Williamson, S., Hare, R. D., & Wong, S. (1987). Violence: Criminal psychopaths and their victims. *Canadian Journal of Behavioural Science, 19,* 454–462.

RACE-BASED ATTRIBUTES IN VIDEO GAMES, INFLUENCE ON HOSTILITY

Researchers have established a positive relationship between video game play and hostility. Matthew S. Eastin and colleagues furthered this research area by uncovering the complex nature of game play in the contexts of self, character, and opponent. Findings have suggested that trait and cultural-based norms influence how players are affected by game play and their aggression-related outcomes. This entry reviews the gaming literature by examining the influence of race-based attributes of self, character, and opponent on aggression outcomes.

Research has been conducted to identify the relationship between violent video game play and aggression. Craig Anderson and Brad Bushman (2002) have empirically developed a general aggression model (GAM) to better understand why exposure to violent media increases human aggression. As a conceptual platform, the GAM provides a framework for understanding violent media effects through the activation of aggression-related knowledge structures. For example, the model indicates that during violent video game play, personal and situational inputs pool to prime aggressive cognition, aggressive affect, and arousal. During each game play session, scripts learned through play are more readily accessible and available for automatic activation. Similar to Leonard Berkowitz's cognitive neoassociation model, aggressive ideas activated during game play involuntarily prime other semantically related ideas—prompting game players to experience aggressive thoughts outside the game environment.

Recently, using the GAM as a general framework, Eastin's research examined certain features of video games that may interact to predict aggressive outcomes. For instance, research has indicated that avatar gender and opponent gender influence aggressive thoughts among female participants. Moreover, Eastin demonstrated how the type of environment, type of game play, and competitor type influence hostile expectations during conflict situations. Finally, Eastin also reported that gaming in larger groups and expressing hostile thoughts during game play increases hostile outcomes.

Stereotyping by Race Among White Audiences

Over the past two decades White Americans' stereotypes of Blacks have shifted because of a broader liberalization of racial attitudes in the United States, a decrease in overt expressions of anti-Black sentiment, and a reduction in stereotypical depictions of Blacks in the media. Compared with early media portrayals in which Blacks were often characterized as lazy, violent, and living primarily in poverty-stricken areas, recent entertainment media have represented Blacks as educated and belonging to the middle class. Still, Travis Dixon and Dana Mastro (2005), two researchers in the area of race and media, have suggested that negative Black stereotypes continue to persist in the media. In Dixon and Mastro's research, Blacks are thought to be largely relegated to appearances in racially segregated situation comedies in which the least diversified repertoire of characters is offered. Moreover, news media make associations between Blacks and negative issues such as violent crime, drugs, poverty, and welfare by situating these stories alongside images of Blacks.

Stereotypical images found in the media are easily accepted because they are simple and generally have little ambiguity. Stereotypes lead to self-perpetuating expectations about specific groups and their members that direct attention to information that is consistent with the stereotypes. Adjective list studies in social psychology reveal that Whites list *violent* and *criminal* as traits most typical of Blacks. Racial stereotyping is not limited to those with racial prejudices. When researchers have controlled for levels of prejudice, both high- and low-prejudice Whites are equally knowledgeable of Black cultural stereotypes (Devine, 1989).

Theories of accessibility and automatic activation can be used to explain the potential priming effect of racial stereotypes about Blacks. Here, *accessibility* refers to the ease with which information stored in memory reemerges and dictates the ease with which specific stereotypes are automatically activated. Automatic activation pertains to the spontaneous triggering of certain well-learned sets of associations that have been cultivated through repeated activation. According to Kai Sassenberg and Gordon B. Moskowitz (2005), the activation of racial stereotypes can occur without one's awareness. Stereotypes about Blacks have a long history of repeated activation in the culture and are therefore likely to be easily accessible to Whites.

Race-based stereotypes can be activated by mere exposure to a person from the stereotyped group or symbolic cue associated with the stereotype. Research by Osei Appiah (2013) has indicated that the simple presence of Black characters in media, even when depicted in nonstereotypical roles, invoke stereotypes. Furthermore, research has suggested that Whites respond faster to negative Black stereotype traits when these traits are followed by a Black prime. This has been substantiated through social psychology research, which has shown that the same behaviors performed by Black and White individuals are interpreted very differently by Whites and Blacks. Whites have viewed Blacks as more guilty and aggressive than White ingroup members performing the same behavior. For example, Whites identified guns faster when primed with Black faces

vis-à-vis White faces but also misidentified tools as guns more often when primed with Black faces (Payne, 2001). Similarly, White children were more likely to attribute negative behavior or aggression to Black perpetrators than to White perpetrators engaged in the same behavior (McGlothlin & Killen, 2006). Many Whites lack direct interaction with a wide variety of Blacks, and studies have indicated that when Whites are exposed to racial stereotypes in the media their negative attitudes about racial groups are reinforced. This is especially true among Whites who lack substantial interaction with a diverse population. Lacking much opportunity for repeated close contact with a wide variety of Blacks, Whites rely heavily on racial material presented in the media for cataloging Blacks.

Turning to media, the impact of stereotypes may be examined through interactive mediated experiences such as video games, which often encourage the player to take on perceived attributes of the game's central character. As outlined by Eastin and colleagues, a White person who plays as a Black character in a video game—particularly a violent game—may conjure up and act out readily available stereotypical images that characterize Blacks as aggressive and violent. As a result, a White gamer playing as a Black character may activate stereotypes of Blacks' aggression and not only have more aggressive thoughts but also unconsciously act out the aggressive or violent stereotype by playing more aggressively.

Subscribing to Negative Stereotypes

Research has demonstrated that Blacks are generally aware of negative stereotypes associated with their group. Past research has suggested that many Black respondents perceived Whites as subscribed to a number of uncomplimentary stereotypes such as those associating Blacks with violence. Research further posited that at times Blacks believe some of the negative stereotypes to which they are associated. Implicit biases favoring the outgroup may stem from a motivation to legitimize the hierarchy observed within society. That is, Blacks sense negativity from Whites and subsequently can internalize negative stereotypes about themselves and develop a negative bias toward their ingroup. In tasks related to areas where Whites have stereotypically outperformed Blacks, research has indicated that Blacks show an implicit outgroup preference. That said, Blacks are aware of negative stereotypes about Blacks but do not necessarily endorse these stereotypes. In fact, Blacks are concerned about being viewed negatively and generally fear inadvertently reinforcing stereotypes through their behavior. Of note, available research has suggested that Blacks are less likely than Whites to endorse negative stereotypes associating Blacks with aggression.

Although much has been learned from studies looking at stereotyping, research has thus far focused on general perceptions or more traditional media evaluations. The dynamic relationship among race, racial identity, video games, and aggressive outcomes was recently assessed within Eastin's research. His study with Appiah and Cicchirillo (2009) indicated that after controlling for demographics such as gender and video game experience, an interaction for participant race by character race existed for character identification. As predicted by the literature, Eastin and Appiah found that Blacks were significantly more likely to identify with a character when they played as Black characters than when they played as White characters. However, not as predicted, Whites' identification was greater when playing as White characters than when playing as Black characters. Much of the identification literature has suggested that Whites have very little identification with racial attributes. Additionally, this study found that after controlling for gender and game play experience, there was a significant interaction for participant race by character race for aggressive thoughts. The data indicated that White participants displayed greater hostile thoughts after game play when playing as Black characters than when playing as White characters. However, when turning to Black participants, hostile thoughts did not differ between Black and White characters. Looking further into game play, data from this study also indicated a significant interaction effect for the participant race by opponent race—that is, interracial game play. Black participants displayed greater hostile thoughts (i.e., this difference only approached significance) after playing against White opponents than after playing against Black opponents. Data on White participants indicated no significant difference in hostile thoughts based on whether they played against Black or White opponents.

Although research on video games within the context of race and violent outcomes is beginning to be understood, behavioral research still needs empirical research, meaning, if stereotyping is taking place through game play, then how people play the game should also differ (i.e., display greater aggression). Additionally, pre–game play effects should also be explored. For example, in Eastin and Appiah's research, participants were assigned racial characters to play. What happens if the participants are able to select their own characters rather than having the characters assigned to them? Moreover, if stereotypical attributes such as clothing are attached to the race of a character, are additional stereotyping cognitions activated during game play?

As media, including games, become more realistic and engaging, outcomes of exposure should heighten, and thus societal concerns should be considered and researched. This entry only begins to explore the various connections that can be made through game play within the framework of race and identification effects.

Osei Appiah and Matthew S. Eastin

See also Aggression and Anger; Audience Interpretation of Media Violence, Effects of; Cultivation Theory; Demographic Effects; Effects From Violent Media, Short- and Long-Term; Gender Stereotypes, Societal Influence on; General Aggression Model; Media Effects Perspectives of Violence

Further Readings

Anderson, C. A., & Bushman, B. J. (2002). Human aggression. *Annual Review of Psychology, 53,* 27–51.

Appiah, O., Knobloch-Westerwick, S., & Alter, S. (2013). Ingroup favoritism and outgroup derogation: Effects of news valence, character race, and recipient race on selective news reading. *Journal of Communication, 63*(3), 517–534.

Berkowitz, L. (1984). Some effects of thoughts on anti- and prosocial influence of media events: A cognitive-neoassociation analysis. *Psychological Bulletin, 95,* 410–427.

Berkowitz, L. (1990). On the formation of regulation of anger and aggression. *American Psychologist, 45,* 494–503.

Cohen, J. (2001). Defining identification: A theoretical look at the identification of audiences with media characters. *Mass Communication and Society, 4*(3), 245–264.

Devine, P. G. (1989). Stereotypes and prejudice: Their automatic and controlled components. *Journal of Personality and Social Psychology, 56*(1), 5–18.

Devine, P. G., & Baker, S. M. (1991).Measurement of racial stereotype subtyping. *Personality and Social Psychology Bulletin, 17,* 44–50.

Devine, P. G., & Elliot, A. J. (1995). Are racial stereotypes really fading? The Princeton trilogy revisited. *Personality and Social Psychology Bulletin, 21,* 1139–1150.

Dixon, T. L., & Maddox, K. B. (2005). Skin tone, crime news, and social reality judgments: Priming the stereotype of the dangerous Black criminal. *Journal of Applied Social Psychology, 35*(8), 1555–1570.

Eastin, M. S., Appiah, O., & Cicchirillo, V. (2009). Identification and the influence of cultural stereotyping on post video game play hostility. *Human Communication Research, 3,* 337–356.

Madon, S., Guyll, M., Aboufadel, K., Montiel, E., Smith, A., Palumbo, P., & Jussim, L. (2001). Ethnic and national stereotypes: The Princeton trilogy revisited and revised. *Personality and Social Psychology Bulletin, 27*(8), 996–1010.

Mastro, D. E., & Tropp, L. R. (2004). The effects of interracial contact, attitudes, and stereotypical portrayals on evaluations of black television sitcom characters. *Communication Research Reports, 21*(2), 119–129.

McGlothlin, H., & Killen, M. (2006). Intergroup attitudes of European American children attending ethnically homogeneous schools. *Child Development, 77*(5), 1375–1386.

Payne, B. K. (2001). Prejudice and perception: The role of automatic and controlled processes in misperceiving a weapon. *Journal of Personality and Social Psychology, 81*(2), 181–192.

Sassenberg, K., & Moskowitz, G. B. (2005). Don't stereotype, think different! Overcoming automatic stereotype activation by mindset priming. *Journal of Experimental Social Psychology, 41,* 506–514.

Tajfel, H., & Turner, J. C. (1986). The social identity theory of intergroup behavior. In S. Worchel & W. G. Austin (Eds.), *Psychology of intergroup relations* (pp. 7–24). Chicago, IL: Nelson-Hall.

Tajfel, H., & Wilkes, A. (1963). Classification and quantitative judgments. *British Journal of Psychology, 54,* 101–114.

RAP LYRICS, EFFECTS OF VIOLENT CONTENT IN

The evidence linking violent content in music and music videos has demonstrated a significant relationship between lyric content and subsequent aggressive thoughts. Recent analyses have shown an increase between 1979 and 1997 in the percentage of rap songs with violent lyric content, with a marked increase in the early 1990s, coinciding with the advent of the "gangsta rap" subgenre. However, increases in violent content in rap music have coincided with decreases in recorded rates of violent crime, troubling the notion that violent content in

rap has a direct and measurable increase on violent behavior. Thus, the question of whether the violence in rap lyrics has resulted in heightened levels of violence merits additional critical inquiry. During the period of time between the first appearance of hip-hop (a term connoting a broader cultural phenomenon) in the 1970s and current rap (a musical form within the broader hip-hop culture), the topic of violent content has generated a significant level of discussion and debate in public and political spheres. It has to a lesser extent generated scientific research that has examined the relationship between violent content in lyrics and videos and aggressive thoughts and behaviors.

Background and History

Even a cursory study of the origins and development of rap music and the attendant critical analysis it engendered would show that as the popularity of the music increased so did concerns about its relationship with crime, delinquency, aggression and violence, sexual risk behaviors, and other problem behaviors. Much of the public discourse that has criticized this musical genre and the artists who perform it reflects discomfort with the identities of its performers more than any real or demonstrable problems that resulted from exposure to the music. In this way, rap shares a similarity with jazz, which was initially and rather widely branded as "problem" music that fostered an overwhelming subculture of drug use along with other forms of social deviance. With jazz, over time the stereotype-fueled concerns about the threat posed by the music's performers and broader subculture subsided. However, the parallels between the critiques leveled at jazz as a musical form and those that have been leveled at rap music and videos are important to acknowledge when considering the factors that motivated much of the research and inquiry in this domain.

Originally, many artists who embraced rap and hip-hop viewed it as an effective means of creative self-expression that could be used to portray life details and to describe hopes, fears, social identities, and aspirations. It was part of a new subculture that built on previous musical genres and styles, but one that moved toward a very direct portrayal of social issues in an unvarnished and "raw" manner. Over a relatively short period of time, the style rapidly evolved and branched out to include distinct musical and stylistic elements that varied based on performer identity and geographic location. Also, over the course of rap's development, several artists drew close critical scrutiny because of the images that they projected and the lyric content that they delivered. Some of the most controversial artists from the late 1980s and early 1990s include NWA, 2 Live Crew, Dr. Dre, Ice Cube, and Ice-T (as well as his rock band Body Count, which fused elements of hip-hop and rock and caused an unprecedented level of attention resulting from the release of the song "Cop Killer"). In the early 2000s, Eminem became a successful rapper, noted for his controversial lyrics. These lyrics contained significant amounts of violent content, with a number of songs containing references to murder and violence against women.

As hip-hop reached a critical mass in terms of its popularity, it became a part of American and the broader global cultures. Gangsta rap artists placed highly on the *Billboard* charts. Their videos were shown on MTV, and pop artists started to collaborate with rappers, incorporating rap verses into a wide range of songs. As a result of high rates of album sales, in 1989 *Billboard* gave the genre its own chart, no longer mixing rap hits in with dance and pop music. Rap's audience expanded rapidly and began to reach a wide range of socioeconomic, racial, and ethnic groups far beyond its initial boundaries. Some sources indicate that that up to 70% of rap music from this era was sold to middle-class teenagers, many of whom were White, who lived in the suburbs. The level of concern about the violent content increased commensurately with rap's level of popularity, particularly as it spread widely among youth populations.

In the popular press, the music was routinely depicted as embracing criminality and deviance, and those performers whose lyrics stressed prosocial messages and positive themes of empowerment and integrity were less frequently cited as representative of the genre than were those who created sensational images of assaults, violence, and system-threatening imagery. Supporters, fans, and advocates of rap music have posited that the emphasis on violence was overstated. To some scholars and industry professionals, this level of criticism has served as an indicator of underlying prejudices in the mainstream media and elsewhere because the vast majority of rap's artists have been young African American males. The public perception of the relationship between rap and its extolling of violence as the primary means of addressing even the most trivial forms of interpersonal or intergroup conflict were sown. Much like that of heavy metal music, this conceptualization of rap as inherently threatening and violent fueled the level of scrutiny and research that ultimately sought to address the question of whether violent content in music—particularly in lyric content—was able to influence the acting out of violent behaviors.

Prevalence of Violent Themes in Lyrics

Several studies have attempted to measure the violent content in rap lyrics over time. However, such studies have struggled to do so reliably, at least partly because of the rich lyrics of hip-hop and the multiple meanings that various lyric passages may convey. The genre makes use of puns, metaphor, and slang—the natures of which are often regional and fluid. Measuring violent content becomes particularly difficult when a violent word is used as slang to convey a positive meaning. For example, *killing* can mean homicide, but it can also mean being highly successful at something—during rap "battles" the winner is often described as killing the beat. Thus, on the basis of words alone, without a careful consideration of the context in which these words are situated, it is difficult to categorize lyrics as violent. Although lyrics can present distinct challenges in terms of classification, the repurposing of previously violent words to take on positive meanings is an interesting element within the genre.

An overarching feature of rap is that it is typically in first-person. This perspective can make the violent lyrics seem particularly jarring. In many instances, the artist is the narrative creator of violence portrayed in the lyrics. The songs can sound like historical accounts of the artist's personal experiences, and indeed many rappers adamantly claim that they are. Some rappers have claimed that their songs are autobiographical and represent the violence that they have experienced over the course of their lives. Other rappers may admit to purposefully making their songs shocking in order to boost sales. However, it is clear that some rap lyrics have been based in fantasy. One example of this can be seen in the earlier work of Eminem, in which he describes graphic violence directed toward an ex-wife. It is important to note that these musings do not reflect reality. When considering the potential impact of violent lyrics, researchers can reasonably question the extent to which lyrics that are a clear expression of fantasy can influence the advent of aggressive behaviors in the same way that lyrics that are meant to reflect reality may (thus implying a higher level of normative support).

Another complication that an analysis of rap lyrics has presented is the heavy use of rhyming and other vocal plays on the pronunciation of words. This artistic and performance dimension introduces a significant amount of room for interpretation, potentially obfuscating the exact content or precise meaning of the lyrics as intended by the performer. This may present an especially acute challenge for parsing and analyzing the impact of the broader influence of lyrics among those who deemphasize the importance of lyrics or among populations that are not native speakers of the performance language.

Evaluating the reach and distribution of music has also shifted with the advent of new technologies and distribution channels that have moved toward more online distribution, along with music listening that has become increasingly portable. Thus, it becomes more difficult to establish clear metrics for the influence of music in real-world settings. In the early 2000s, record sales became a much less effective way of judging a song's distribution as a result of the rapid increase in illicit distribution channels to access music. Accurately measuring a song's "hit" level in the absence of clear metrics is a challenge.

Link Between Violent Content and Behavioral Manifestations of Violence and Aggression

The research examining the influence of music on behavior has largely focused on addressing the potential impact of lyrics with violent and/or sexual imagery. As such, there has been a handful of well-designed and rigorously conducted and evaluated studies that have demonstrated the ability of music to influence behaviors and, most important, have addressed some of the parameters and limiting conditions that are important determinants of the extent to which violent lyrics can influence behavior. In addition, literature has identified which factors can augment or diminish the likelihood of violent lyric content from effectively influencing violent thoughts and behaviors. However, it is clear that music plays an important role in the socialization process of children and adolescents. The extent to which a given individual identifies with or admires a performer has been posited to be an important link in the chain between violent lyrics and the development of violent thoughts, the justification of violence, and the acting out of violent behaviors. The rise of rappers as fashion designers and actors points to their greater influence on both hip-hop and mainstream cultures more broadly.

The admiration of rappers has led to the discussion of a "street code," or set of laws governing behavior. These are rules about how to contextualize violence in everyday life. Supporters of this theory have claimed that although rap may not cause its listeners to be more violent, it gives them a set of instructions for how to use violence as a tool. It also defines the subject of the violence and a set of times that the use of violence is called for. In this way, if a listener encounters a similar situation, he or she has a guide that suggests how to handle it. Violence may be positioned as an appropriate defense of the artist's honor or property. This can be seen in instances of a rapper using violence as a means of responding to an affront caused by another—for example, a police officer or a rival gang member. Violence is also used as a threat to someone who damaged the artist's social standing, economic prosperity, or material possessions.

Causal Link Between Rap and Violence

Music preferences have been linked to criminality in several studies that have focused on rap and heavy metal in particular, although these studies examined the association between preference for these styles and subsequent levels of delinquency without explicitly focusing on the violent content in specific lyrics. For those studies that have attempted to examine the direct influence of violent lyric content on subsequent behaviors, there have been serious challenges—most notably the ability to present a sufficient level of exposure to the music and lyrics in order to approximate the real-world amounts of exposure to music that would better approximate real-world conditions.

Several types of data can be used to estimate the effects of rap music on violent behavior and violent thoughts and ideations. To establish causality in this relationship, there have been several lines of carefully controlled and conducted experimental research that have struggled to demonstrate a distinct and causal effect of listening to music with violent lyrics. These studies typically involve randomly assigning research participants to a condition (i.e., listening to rap with violent lyrics versus listening to rap without violent lyrics) and then examining whether there are statistically significant differences in level of violent thoughts and behaviors as a direct result of listening. Although these forms of research give a more precise view of the causal pathways between violent and/or misogynistic content in rap music and violent behavior, they do not provide a broader context or macro-level view of related phenomena that can plausibly influence this relationship.

Studies have examined broader trends and rates in violent crime juxtaposed with increases in sales and listening to rap with violent themes (specifically, gangsta rap); the findings have challenged the notion of causal links between violent lyric themes and content and recorded rates of violent crime. Careful examination of these levels of data revealed a pattern of increasing levels of violent content in rap music that coincided with decreasing levels of violent crime and homicide—particularly among African American adolescents and young adults, who were purported to be a significant market for this musical form and at whom the concern about the deleterious effects of music was directed.

The Lasting Impact

The perception that rap lyrics can influence aggressive thoughts and violent behavior has been somewhat tempered since the early 2000s. Although there is some empirical evidence to support the claim that music and lyrics can influence behavior, any policy that seeks to limit freedom of artistic expression for even the most violent of content has been met with significant resistance because of the implications that any efforts to censor such music would have serious implications and repercussions on freedom of expression.

One of the most prominent efforts to address violent content in music lyrics more generally (although the genres of music that were of most concern included rock, heavy metal, rap, and hip-hop) was the creation of the Parents Music Resource Council (PMRC), which held high-profile public hearings in which a wide range of musicians were subject to questioning about the lyric content of their music as well as its potential deleterious effects. Although this effort failed to create guidelines that would be acceptable to the industry, the PMRC was successful in persuading the industry to voluntarily place parental advisory labels on album covers. In light of the negative attention and publicity associated with violent and explicit lyric content, record companies have adapted as well. To create the perception of some distance between major record labels and the violent and controversial content in rap (as well as other forms), some have created multiple layers of affiliated labels that are not ostensibly linked to the parent company. Despite all of these efforts, one of the primary factors that seems to have led to the reduced public dialogue around the harmful effects of rap music is a decline in sales.

In conclusion, there is a burgeoning body of research that has examined the impact of music lyrics and music videos on violent behaviors. Overall, the research has documented the potential for violent content to influence violent thoughts and behaviors and to make violence appear to be a more normative means of conflict resolution. However, there are a significant number of factors that can benefit from additional research to better ascertain the limits of this relationship and to develop a more precise understanding not only of the relationship between violent content in music and violent behaviors, but also of those mechanisms that underlie this relationship.

Anthony F. Lemieux and Lisa LaViers

See also Exposure to Violent Content, Effects on Child Development; First-Person Perspective, Violent Content From; Media Rating Systems; Music Videos and Lyrics, Violent Content in; Sexualized Aggression; Stereotyping in Violent Media Content

Further Readings

Alcorn, L. M., & Lemieux, A. F. (2010). The effect of sexually explicit rap music on sexual attitudes, norms, and behaviors. In *Music: Composition, interpretation, and effects* (pp. 1–29). Hauppauge, NY: Nova Science Publishers.

Anderson, C. A., Berkowitz, L., Donnerstein, E., Huesmann, L. R., Johnson, J. D., Linz, D., et al. (2003). The influence of media violence on youth. *Psychological Science in the Public Interest, 4,* 81–110.

Armstrong, E. G. (2001). Gangsta misogyny: A content analysis of the portrayals of violence against women in rap music, 1987–1993. *Journal of Criminal Justice and Popular Culture, 8,* 96–126.

Beaver, W. (2010). Rap and the recording industry. *Business and Society Review, 115,* 107–120.

Council on Communications and Media. (2009). Impact of music, music lyrics, and music videos on children and youth. *Pediatrics, 124,* 1488–1494.

Fried, C. B. (1999). Who's afraid of rap: Differential reactions to music lyrics. *Journal of Applied Social Psychology, 29,* 705–721.

Herd, D. (2009). Changing images of violence in rap music lyrics: 1979–1997. *Journal of Public Health Policy, 30,* 395–406.

Hunnicutt, G., & Andrews, K. H. (2009). Tragic narratives in popular culture: Depictions of homicide in rap music. *Sociological Forum, 24,* 611–630.

Johnson, J. D., Jackson, L. A., & Gatto, L. (1995). Violent attitudes and deferred academic aspirations: Deleterious effects of exposure to rap music. *Basic and Applied Social Psychology, 16,* 27–41.

Kubrin, C. E. (2005). Gangstas, thugs, and hustlas: Identity and the code of the street in rap music. *Social Problems, 52,* 360–378.

Lena, J. C. (2006). Social context and musical content of rap music, 1979–1995. *Social Forces, 85,* 479–495.

Martinez, T. A. (1997). Popular culture as oppositional culture: Rap as resistance. *Sociological Perspectives, 40,* 265–286.

North, A., & Hargreaves, D. (2008). *The social and applied psychology of music.* New York, NY: Oxford University Press.

Richardson, J. W., & Scott, K. A. (2002). Rap music and its violent progeny: America's culture of violence in context. *Journal of Negro Education, 71,* 175–192.

Rudman, L. A., & Lee, M. R. (2002). Implicit and explicit consequences of exposure to violent and misogynous rap music. *Group Processes and Intergroup Relations, 5,* 133–150.

RAPE PERCEPTIONS

Some 40 years have passed since the initial groundbreaking research conducted by Neil Malamuth and colleagues that cast a spotlight on the effects of sexually violent media (see Malamuth, Addison, & Koss, 2001, for a review of the literature). Those early studies, many of them experimental, focused on the effects of exposure to printed rape depictions, audiotaped rape depictions, and depictions of rape in mainstream films. Findings pointed to significant positive relationships between exposure to sexually violent content and (a) acceptance of violence against women and (b) males' self-reported likelihood of raping. Survey research also emerged at this time indicating a positive relationship between exposure to sexually explicit (relative to mainstream) magazines such as *Penthouse* and *Playboy* and men's and women's acceptance of rape myths.

As striking as these studies were (and still are), there has been a relative dearth of recent research on this phenomenon. For example, there has been little understanding of potential audience effects from viewing sexual violence on mainstream television. Although some progress had been made in the study of sex-related and sexual assault–related content in mainstream television programming, these studies have focused primarily on documenting the ubiquity

of such content (Cuklanz, 2006). More recently, researchers have begun to examine the relationship between this pervasive content and audience beliefs about rape—specifically rape myths—and sexual assault, drawing from the cultivation framework and a feminist ecological perspective (Kahlor & Eastin, 2011). The *cultivation framework* refers to the study of long-term television effects that result from heavy television viewing, whereby heavy viewers cultivate beliefs that are more reflective of television's depictions of reality compared with more objective assessments of reality such as crime statistics. Feminist theory suggests that societal-level variables affect men and women differently. The feminist ecological perspective suggests that violence toward women should be studied across the microsystem of the family, the exosystem in which the family resides, and the macrosystem of society that inflicts dominant cultural norms. This entry discusses depictions of rape in the media and summarizes research into the effects of these depictions.

Rape myths refers to false but persistent beliefs and stereotypes regarding forced or coerced sexual intercourse and the victims and perpetrators of such acts. Rape myths include the idea that women frequently allege rape when they regret consensual sex after the fact and that women who claim rape are promiscuous women with bad reputations who dress provocatively and behave wantonly. Such myths are still believed to be prevalent among the general public, despite the sobering reality that 1 in 6 women in the United States has been the victim of a completed or attempted rape at some time in her life (Tjaden & Thoennes, 2006), and only about 5% of the rape complaints received by law enforcement agencies are deemed unfounded.

Although men are significantly more accepting of rape myths, mythical rape perceptions are held by both men and women, and some research has suggested that these myths are more prevalent among minority populations such as Hispanics and African Americans, although the latter links are still considered tentative. Research has indicated mixed results as to whether age or education plays a role in rape myth acceptance; however, it does appear that rape myth acceptance can be lowered through rape-related educational interventions such as conversations with counselors, lectures, and visual programming (movies, videos, etc.).

The persistence of rape myths may in part be facilitated by the prevalence of these myths in television programming. That is, research has suggested that primetime and daytime depictions of rape have become more frequent and, over the course of the 1990s and 2000s, have consistently perpetuated rape myths. The increased frequency of rape-related storylines may be reflective of an increase in coverage of sexual violence in the news media; it is not uncommon for dramatic programming to draw plot lines from national news headlines.

However, despite the relative persistence of rape myths on television, there does appear to be a shift in primetime content toward plots that portray rape with more complexity, including proactive female characters and more ambiguous rape situations (e.g., more references to spousal, date, and acquaintance rape than to stranger rape). For example, in 2013 NBC entered its 14th season of *Law & Order: Special Victims Unit*, a primetime crime drama dedicated to the topic of rape and sexual assault. Typical storylines in the series involve serial rapists, date rape, stranger rape, gang rape, incest, and/or pedophilia. Lisa Cuklanz reported that the show has integrated feminist insights into its episodes; however, its portrayal of women and feminine qualities remains problematic, as does its periodic emphasis on false rape claims.

Areas beckoning for future research include an exploration of the continuum of sexual aggression on television (extending from verbal sexual harassment to sexual assault and rape), analysis of headline news stories related to sexual assault across conservative and liberal news networks and affiliates, analysis of primetime dramas airing on premium cable networks, and an exploration of sex and gender tropes across sports entertainment programming aimed at young male audiences.

LeeAnn Kahlor

See also Aggression and Anger; Cognitive Psychology of Violence; Cultivating Content and the Social Representation of Violence; Culture of Violence; Sexualized Aggression; Social Learning From Media

Further Readings

Cuklanz, L. M. (2006). Gendered violence and mass media representation. In B. Dow & J. T. Wood (Eds.), *The Sage handbook of gender and communication* (pp. 335–354). Thousand Oaks, CA: Sage.

Kahlor, L., & Eastin, M. (2011). Television's role in the culture of violence towards women: A study of television viewing and the cultivation of rape myth acceptance in the U.S. *Journal of Broadcast and Electronic Media, 55,* 215–231.

Malamuth, N. M., Addison, T., & Koss, M. (2001). Pornography and sexual aggression: Are there reliable effects? *Annual Review of Sex Research, 11,* 26–91.

Tjaden, P., & Thoennes, N. (2000). *Full report of the prevalence, incidence, and consequences of violence against women: Findings from the National Violence Against Women Survey* (DOJ Publication No. NCJ183781). Washington, DC: U.S. Department of Justice. Retrieved from http://www.ncjrs.org/txtfiles1/nij/183781.tx

RATING SYSTEMS, FILM

Film rating systems provide information regarding a film's content and suitability for particular audiences. Although various countries use film rating systems, this entry focuses on the film rating system in the United States and includes discussions of its history, ratings and movie content, effects of movie content, and criticisms of the rating system.

History

The film rating system in existence in the United States today was instituted in 1968 in response to what many in the film industry viewed as an overly restrictive set of rules known as the Hays Code. Jack Valenti, then chair of the Motion Picture Association of America (MPAA), worked with theater owners to establish an independent ratings board known as the Classification and Ratings Administration (CARA). CARA was created to introduce film ratings as a guide for parents and is made up of anonymous parent reviewers who are paid by fees charged to producers and distributors for having a film reviewed.

The original rating system consisted of four categories for films: G for general audiences; M for adults and mature audiences; R for restricted, those under 16 years of age require an accompanying adult; X, no one under 16 years of age admitted. With the exception of X, the symbols were trademarked so that film producers could not apply the ratings themselves. The M designation became GP in 1969 and was then changed to PG for parental guidance suggested around 1972. The PG-13 rating, for parents strongly cautioned, was added to the ratings system in the mid-1980s. In 1990 the non-trademarked X became NC-17, for no one 17 years and under admitted. Beginning in the early 2000s, content descriptors were added to the age-based ratings. Today, the X rating is used exclusively by producers of sexually explicit programming (pornography) and is not part of the MPAA system.

Early reports suggested that some moviegoers perceived the ratings as a form of censorship; however, on its face the ratings system makes no judgments on the quality of a film. Valenti has often stated the ratings system was simply designed to serve as a guide for parents as to the suitability of the film for children. Many parents, at least initially, were skeptical of the ratings system, and early reports suggested that teens were more likely to use the ratings system than parents. By the mid-1970s, though, reports published by the MPAA suggested that a majority of parents found the rating system at least somewhat helpful.

As noted earlier, parents are hired to serve on the anonymous ratings board. According to CARA, the only qualification beyond parent status is an ability to judge movies in a manner suitable to most parents. Members of the ratings board decide a movie's rating by majority vote, based on how they think most American parents would evaluate the movie. Filmmakers who disagree with a rating can release the film unrated, edit and resubmit the film, or appeal a rating to a special board. According to a *Lancet* editorial, the U.S. system is the only one with an anonymous board made up of parents. Most other countries use public service employees who hold public deliberations of ratings.

Ratings and Movie Content

CARA maintains that ratings are based on community standards for violence, criminal behavior, drug content, sexual content, and profanity. Media scholar Joanne Cantor (2000) has criticized the ratings, however, for being "vague and uninformative." Cantor has found that parents believe the ratings do not differentiate among different types of content and would prefer ratings about content rather than age recommendations.

Researchers Kimberly M. Thompson and Fumie Yokota (2004) found that nearly half of all G-rated animated films showed alcohol use, and more than 40% showed tobacco use. In response to criticism and changing community standards, the MPAA announced in 2007 that it would also consider smoking as a factor in the movie ratings. Even after smoking was to be considered a factor in a movie's rating, in a multi-year study, researchers Jonathan R. Polansky, Kori Titus, and Stanton A. Glantz (2007,

2008, 2009) found that two-thirds of movies of all ratings included smoking, and nearly 40% of G/PG movies featured tobacco.

Recent research by Jennifer J. Tickle and colleagues (2009) found that tobacco use increased in higher ratings categories. Nearly 90% of films contained some form of alcohol use, and more than one-third of films showed at least one character who was intoxicated by alcohol. Alcohol use increased as ratings category increased. Furthermore, tobacco and alcohol use in movies has decreased from 1996 through 2004. Tickle and colleagues also found that drug use appeared in about 22% of films, but the great majority of these cases were in PG-13 or R-rated movies. Furthermore, very few films showed adolescent drug use. More than 90% of films, however, showed some kind of violence. R-rated movies contained the most violence; however, there was no difference in the amount of violence depicted in movies with the less restrictive ratings of PG-13, PG, or G.

Importantly, Tickle and colleagues found that three-quarters of films contained sexual content. Nearly half of G-rated films and nearly 60% of PG-rated films contained some kind of sexual content. Furthermore, the amount of sexual content increased as the rating category increased.

One study of movies geared toward adults (with either an R, X, or XXX rating) found that sexual behavior was far more prevalent in X- and XXX-rated movies than in R-rated movies. However, Ni Yang and Daniel Linz (1990) found that violence was most prevalent in R-rated movies, accounting for about 35% of all behavior. Sexual violence, although infrequent, was equally distributed across the three categories of movies. Furthermore, nonsexual violence against women was more common in R-rated movies than in sexually oriented movies.

Researchers Yokota and Thompson (2001) found at least one act of violence in every G-rated animated film they analyzed. In subsequent work, they found that animated G-rated films had significantly more violence than non-animated G-rated films. The majority of the violence occurred in scenes in which good characters were fighting bad characters.

Effects

Meghan R. Longacre and colleagues (2009) found that significant exposure to smoking in movies increases the likelihood that young people will begin smoking. Similarly, increased exposure to alcohol use in movies may initiate drinking by younger audiences. Furthermore, according to Meghan R. Longacre and colleagues (2009), parents believe cigarette and alcohol use should be used as movie ratings criteria, and many parents support an R rating for movies with smoking and alcohol use.

However, Cantor and colleagues found that more restrictive ratings might encourage children to choose movies designated as inappropriate for their age. Critics of the ratings system also have noted that more than two "sexually oriented" words will earn a film an R rating while graphic depictions of violence against women fall into the same category as films that contain no sex.

Priya G. Nalkur and colleagues (2010) found that exposure to explicit sexual content by adolescents has been associated with teen pregnancy, early sexual initiation, and unhealthy sexual attitudes. As noted earlier, film producers and distributers can voluntarily submit a movie to be reviewed by the MPAA. If they choose not to submit a film for rating, they cannot use any MPAA rating. Producers of pornography skip the MPAA rating system and simply attach an X, or even XXX, rating to their films, often as an advertising strategy.

Critics have argued that the current ratings system ignores substantial child development research in its considerations of violence. Although researchers have not pointed to media violence as the sole factor contributing to youth aggression, most have agreed that children who are exposed to high levels of media violence become desensitized to real violence and exhibit violent and aggressive behaviors later in life. Exposure to extreme violence shapes a young person's worldview, potentially normalizing graphic violence.

Furthermore, studies have shown that children who are exposed to high levels of media violence feel that the world is a violent and dangerous place and view violence as an effective way to settle conflict. Other researchers have argued that the context of violence is as important as the quantity of violence. The current ratings structure does not consider rewards, punishments, justifications, or consequences of violent activity in children's understanding of violence. Furthermore, the current system makes somewhat arbitrary distinctions related to age and child development, because a child's emotional growth does not fit into neat categories of 13 and under, 13–17, and over 17.

Criticisms of the Ratings System

The MPAA ratings system has been widely criticized for treating sexual content and violence differently, particularly by the NC-17 rating. The NC-17 rating was designed for films that were "patently adult." Although the rating was supposed to indicate material suitable for an adult-only audience, critics have noted that the ratings board often focuses on sexual rather than violent content, despite the board's assertion that the two are treated equally.

Furthermore, critics, including the Federal Trade Commission (FTC), have argued that the ratings system fails because theaters don't enforce the age restrictions, allowing minors to sneak into R and NC-17 movies. Also, critics have asserted that there has been a "ratings creep" whereby behavior or language that once received an R rating now slips into PG-13 movies. Ratings creep has been apparent for violence in R and PG-13 movies. Nalkur and colleagues found that although the amount of violence increased in both PG-13 and R-rated movies over time, the number of R-rated films has declined and PG-13 has increased.

Interestingly, ratings creep has not occurred for sexual content, suggesting that CARA has not changed its criteria for assessing sexual content in films. More than half of U.S. films since 1968 have earned R ratings; however, the top-grossing films have been in the lesser restrictive categories. Many parents argue that ratings creep is driven by bottom-line economics because movie audiences are largely made up of young people.

Jennifer L. Gregg

See also Developmental Effects; Films, Representation of Violence and Its Effects in; Media Ratings; Media Violence, Definitions and Context of; Rating Systems, Television; Rating Systems, Video Games; Social Cognitive Theory; Social Learning From Media

Further Readings

Cantor, J. (2000). Media violence. *Journal of Adolescent Health, 275S,* 30–34.

Hansen, B. (2003). Movie ratings: Is Hollywood's ratings system too lenient? *CQ Researcher, 13*(12), 273–296.

The Lancet. (1994). Reel violence. In C. Wekesser (Ed.), *Violence in the media.* San Diego, CA: Greenhaven Press.

Longacre, M. R., Adachi-Mejia, A. M., Titus-Ernstoff, L., Gibson, J. J., Beach, M. L., & Dalton, M. A. (2009). Parental attitudes about cigarette smoking and alcohol use in the Motion Picture Association of America rating system. *Archives of Pediatric Adolescent Medicine, 163*(3), 218–224.

Nalkur, P. G., Jamieson, P. E., & Romer, D. (2010). The effectiveness of the Motion Picture Association of

America's rating system in screening explicit violence and sex in top-ranked movies from 1950–2006. *Journal of Adolescent Health, 47,* 440–447.

Polansky, J. R., Titus, K., & Glantz, S. A. (2007). *Six months later: Are MPAA's tobacco ratings protecting movie audiences?* San Francisco: Tobacco Control Policy Making: Center for Tobacco Control Research and Education, University of California, San Francisco.

Polansky, J. R., Titus, K., & Glantz, S. A. (2008). *One year later: Are MPAA's tobacco ratings protecting movie audiences?* San Francisco: Tobacco Control Policy Making: Center for Tobacco Control Research and Education, University of California, San Francisco.

Polansky, J. R., Titus, K., & Glantz, S. A. (2009). *Two years later: Are MPAA's tobacco ratings protecting movie audiences?* San Francisco: Tobacco Control Policy Making: Center for Tobacco Control Research and Education, University of California, San Francisco.

Thompson, K. M., & Yokota, F. (2004). Violence, sex, and profanity in films: Correlation of movie ratings with content. *Medscape General Medicine, 6*(3), 3.

Tickle, J. J., Beach, M. L., & Dalton, M. A. (2009). Tobacco, alcohol, and other risk behaviors in film: How well do MPAA ratings distinguish content? *Journal of Health Communication, 14,* 756–767.

Yang, N., & Linz, D. (1990). Movie ratings and the content of adult videos: The sex–violence ratio. *Journal of Communication, 40*(2), 28–42.

Yokota, F., & Thompson, K. M. (2001). Violence in G-rated animated films. *Journal of the American Medical Association, 283,* 2716–2720.

RATING SYSTEMS, TELEVISION

It has long been lamented that television is an information and entertainment technology less easily controlled by parents than other modes of storytelling. The ubiquitous nature of television, as well as its variety, vivacity, and popularity, has made it particularly difficult to limit children's access to ideas and images with which their caregivers might disagree. Early research on the parental mediation of television consistently found that fewer than half of all parents forbade exposure to certain "adult" or "offensive" shows or set limits on viewing, despite their concerns about the nature and quantity of the content being viewed by their children. As television set saturation, cable access, and broadcast network options increased between the 1960s and 2000s and as the entertainment industry's promotion of inappropriate content to an underage audience became increasingly routine, parental control over television dramatically decreased. This entry briefly discusses the television rating system that was introduced by the commercial television networks in response to years of pressure by parents' groups, child activist organizations, and the government.

Government Intervention

In 1954 a Senate Judiciary Subcommittee on Juvenile Delinquency examined the potential impact of viewing aggressive television content on children's behavior. Findings suggested that there could be harmful results, and this idea has since been supported by decades of social scientific research. Efforts to federally regulate inappropriate content available through television have raised concerns about U.S. Constitution First Amendment violation and claims of censorship. In 1975, for example, the Federal Communications Commission (FCC) suggested a voluntary time period that confined the airing of indecent material to after 9 p.m. (ET), but this "family viewing" policy was ruled unconstitutional. In the mid-1980s, Senator Paul Simon (D-Ill.) sponsored legislation that attempted to decrease the amount of violence on television by allowing the television industry to develop its own guidelines, but this was largely ignored by the industry and enforcement proved futile. Six other bills were introduced in the early 1990s to address this issue—including the Children's Television Violence Protection Act and the Parents Television Empowerment Act—but Congress did not pass any of them. Still, all this activity got the attention of the television industry and, rather than face possible legislation in the future, it devised its own form of self-regulation.

A First Warning

In 1993 the commercial television networks agreed to present a warning at the beginning of selected programs in the primetime lineup to facilitate parental mediation. It stated, "Due to some violent content, parental discretion is advised" and was met with general dissatisfaction by the public. The warning, it seems, tended to attract rather than deter young viewers.

In January 1996, the first major rewrite of communications regulation in 50 years—the Telecommunications Act of 1996—was approved by the 104th Congress and, among many other things, encouraged the television industry to develop and deploy a more robust and informative television rating system. The ratings would give parents the ability to block offensive programming through informed program selection and by activating the V-chip—a half-inch square computer chip to be installed in all television sets 13 inches or larger sold in the United States—that can block programs based on ratings criteria.

An Age-Based Rating System

In January 1997, the television industry introduced an on-screen system that separated general entertainment programs on broadcast and cable television into four age-based categories and children's programming into two: TV-MA (mature audiences only); TV-14 (parents strongly cautioned); TV-PG (parental guidance suggested); TV-G (suitable for all audiences); TV-Y7 (suitable for children 7 years and older); and TV-Y (suitable for children of all ages).

This rating system was implemented one month later and shortly thereafter came under intense criticism. Even Representative Edward Markey (D-Mass.), sponsor of the legislation that prompted the ratings, noted that the industry system didn't give parents the information they needed to make appropriate decisions for their children or give them the choices they needed to be able to block programming. The Parents Television Council—the entertainment-monitoring arm of the conservative media watchdog Media Research Center—pronounced the ratings "hopelessly vague" and "inconsistent." Data confirming the age-based rating system's ineffectiveness were reported by the Annenberg Public Policy Center of the University of Pennsylvania, which found that nearly two-thirds of parents were not using the ratings to guide their children's viewing. Other scholars found that parents' attention to the ratings was low, their attitudes only marginally positive, and they seldom used the ratings. Also, those parents who needed mediation assistance the most—that is, those whose children were low-to-average academic achievers and heavy, indiscriminant consumers of television—were least likely to use the ratings.

A Content-Based Rating System

In July 1997, most television programmers agreed to modify the age-based rating system by adding symbols to alert viewers about potentially objectionable content: violent content (V); sexual content (S); coarse language (L); suggestive dialogue (D); and fantasy violence (FV). However, this effort also fell short of expectations. Follow-up research reported an inconsistent application of the content ratings to programming by the industry, particularly in the areas of violence, sex, and adult language. The Kaiser Family Foundation found that nearly one-fifth of parents were unaware of the content-based TV ratings and only half of those parents who were aware of the ratings reported using the system to guide their children's television viewing. Those who did used the ratings as a guideline to establish restrictive viewing hours and forbid the viewing of specific programs rather than programming the V-chip. Other research found that the age-based ratings with content information were more confusing to parents than were the age-based ratings without content. Nielsen ratings data verified their ineffectiveness; prior to the content-based advisories, approximately 630,000 children under the age of 12 watched ABC's TV-14–rated cop show *NYPD Blue*. After the program was assigned V, S, L, and D symbols, under-12 viewership remained intact.

In 2008 Congress passed the Child Safe Viewing Act, which directed the FCC to examine current blocking technologies and ratings systems used in connection with a variety of electronic media, including broadcast television, cable and satellite, wireless devices, and the Internet. In 2009 the FCC concluded that the available technologies vary greatly with respect to level of consumer awareness and adoption rate and noted the general need to provide more effective ways to provide information about these tools to parents. In 2011 the administration of President Barack Obama announced a possible overhaul of the nation's television ratings, potentially enabling the use of alternatives from religious, parental, and other groups that utilize more rigorous standards and adopting more uniform standards for the rating of television shows.

Robert Abelman

See also Aggressive Behavior; Federal Communications Commission; Media Effects Perspectives of Violence; Television Violence

Further Readings

Abelman, R. (2001). Parents' use of content-based TV advisories. *Parenting: Science and Practice, 1*(3), 237–265.

Greenberg, B. S., Rampoldi-Hnilo, L., & Mastro, D. (Eds.). (2001). *The alphabet soup of television program ratings.* Cresskill, NJ: Hampton.

Harris, R. J. (1999). *A cognitive psychology of mass communication* (3rd ed.). Mahwah, NJ: Erlbaum.

Price, M. E. (Ed.). (1998). *The V-chip debate: Content filtering from television to the Internet.* Mahwah, NJ: Erlbaum.

Rating Systems, Video Games

Rating systems are intended to provide consumers with information about the offensive content found in video games. There are a variety of rating systems used around the world; often the ratings are conducted by the government (e.g., Finland, Iran, Australia), but in some countries (e.g., United States, Germany, Japan) the ratings are overseen by the game industry. Still others (e.g., Great Britain) have a hybrid system that is statutory but supported by the gaming industry. Game rating systems are modeled after the film rating systems in many places. In all cases, the ratings provide information in a format that provides recommendations about the appropriateness of the game for children of various ages.

Game rating systems serve multiple purposes. Ostensibly, they have been designed to provide information to consumers about the offensiveness of game content. However, in the United States, ratings also protect game companies from content censorship by the government, just as film ratings did earlier in the 20th century. The concern is primarily minors' access to violent and sexual content; if content is labeled, it is the parents' responsibility to prevent their child from playing the game. Ratings are also used as a public relations tool by the industry. The Entertainment Software Association (ESA) website states that it is "working to help parents make sure that children are safe online and playing video games their parents consider appropriate" by providing ratings information.

Industry rating systems are overseen by the major gaming professional organization. In the United States, the ESA oversees the Entertainment Software Review Board, which is tasked with rating games according to the industry-designed rating scheme. Because of the enormous amount of content in a commercial video game, raters see only short films depicting the gist of the game and any scenes the developer feels may be controversial. The system is voluntary on the part of developers and retail outlets. In addition, the ESRB regulates the manner in which ratings are advertised and the display of the ratings on packaging.

The ESRB rating system was developed in 1994 and consists of a three-part system: ratings in the form of letters, content descriptors, and notification of certain interactive elements. More detailed information about rated games is provided on the ESRB website. The ratings provide a quick, age-based heuristic for identifying appropriate content. The ratings are E for everyone, eC for young children, E 10+ for ages over 10 years, T for teens ages 13 years and up, M for those at least 17 years old, AO for adults over 18 only, and RP for games in which the ratings are pending. Content descriptors consist of a set of 30 brief terms indicating potentially offensive content, such as *blood, crude humor, intense violence, nudity, strong language, tobacco reference,* and *use of drugs.* Interactive elements refer to notification that the game allows sharing of personal information (e.g., e-mail address, credit card number), the game displays the player's physical location, or the game allows users to interact with one another, including through social media.

Other countries have developed government rating systems. For example, Great Britain uses an age-based scheme that delineates appropriate video games for those under the ages of 3, 7, 12, 16, and 18 years. Furthermore, according to the Pan-European Game Information (PEGI), the UK ratings are now the same as those used by countries in most of Europe. Unlike the voluntary American system, it is illegal for retailers to sell a game with a rating of 12, 16, or 18 to someone younger than that age. The British system also contains a set of content indicators consisting of "bad language," "discrimination," "drugs," "fear," "gambling," "online," "sex," and "violence." Although all national rating systems include descriptors about sex, violence, and drugs, other content descriptors are specific to a particular country. For example, Great Britain has a category for "discrimination," and Iran has categories for "religious values violation" and "hopelessness," although the U.S. system includes none of these. However, the U.S. system has a greater variety of content descriptors than the rating schemes of either of the other two countries.

Enforcement of ratings varies by country as well. In many countries, enforcement is by voluntary agreement between the game industry and retailers. Many other countries use statutes that provide for punishment of retail sales of certain games to restricted populations (e.g., to children). More rare is the use of prior restraint censorship mechanisms requiring the game to be approved by the government before it is offered for sale. Germany is an example of a country that uses prior restraint through its *Bundesprüfstelle für jugendgefährdende Medien* (Federal Department for Media Harmful to Young Persons). Games that violate German law are placed on a list (indexed) identifying them as illegal to sell. The most visible case of indexing was the case of the game *Wolfenstiend 3D*, which was indexed because of portrayals that glorified Nazism.

The focus and quality of rating systems remain controversial in academia. One content analysis of popular games found that individuals playing games rated for children were still likely to encounter 1.17 acts of violence per minute of play time. However, these acts of violence were most often conducted by nonhuman characters that didn't use weapons.

John L. Sherry and Matthew Grizzard

See also Censorship of Violent Content; First Amendment Protections and Freedom of Expression; Rating Systems, Film; Rating Systems, Television

Further Readings

Bundesprüfstelle für jugendgefährdende Medien (Federal Department for Media Harmful to Young Persons). (2003). *General information.* Retrieved from http://bundespruefstelle.de/bpjm/information-in-english.html

Entertainment Software Ratings Board. (1998). *ESRB ratings guide.* Retrieved from http://www.esrb.org/ratings/ratings_guide.jsp

Smith, S. L., Lachlan, K., & Tamborini, R. (2003). Quantifying the presentation of violence and its context. *Journal of Broadcasting & Electronic Media, 47,* 58–76.

Thompson, K. M., & Haninger, K. (2001). Violence in E-rated video games. *Journal of the American Medical Association, 286*(5), 591–598.

REALISM OF VIOLENT CONTENT, REAL-WORLD VIOLENCE ON TELEVISION, AND THEIR EFFECTS

Multiple conceptualizations and definitions of realism are used in the media effects field. First, realism can be seen as a characteristic of a genre. Factual media, such as news and documentaries, are more realistic than fictional media such as soap operas and cartoons. Second, *realism* refers to the degree to which the media content is presented in a compelling manner. Convincing acting, sophisticated visual effects, and advanced graphics make a movie or a video game world appear more like the real world. Finally, *perceived realism* can be viewed as a psychological characteristic of the viewer rather than a property of the message. Audience members interpret media messages in multiple ways, and it has been suggested that the subjective perceptions of realism rather than objective accuracy of media representations play a vital role in mediating effects of media exposure. Thus, even unrealistic television representations of violence might lead to negative consequences, particularly in younger viewers who possess limited ability to discriminate between fact and fiction.

This entry first reviews findings of content analyses examining the extent to which television representations of violence are realistic. A discussion of various conceptualizations of perceived realism follows. Then, theory and research in the realm of media effects on violence and realism and perceived realism on postviewing violence are explored. Finally, the entry concludes with a discussion of effects of realism on fear and desensitization.

Realism of Violence Representations in the Media

From the 1950s until the end of the 20th century, numerous content analyses comparing media reality to the real world repeatedly found that media representations of violence are exaggerated. Television overwhelmingly over-represents the prevalence of death from injuries compared with death from illness and natural causes. Furthermore, media portray disproportionately high rates of violent crime, such as homicide and rape, compared with property crimes, which are more prevalent in reality. This discrepancy occurs systematically across genres, including fictional programming, reality-based television shows (e.g., *Cops, America's Most Wanted*), and news. Excess violence is also widespread in children's programming, including cartoons. Reality television shows (i.e., unscripted programs featuring everyday people) depict less physical violence but commonly feature relational aggression. Although most of the research in this area has concerned U.S. television, studies in other countries (e.g., the United Kingdom) replicated these findings.

Apart from the sheer prevalence of violence, several studies examined the extent to which violent depictions are realistic. The National Television Violence Study (NTVS) examined an unusually large sample of cable, broadcasting, primetime, and daytime shows across a three-year period from 1994 to 1997. The results indicate that about half (51%–55%) of the television violence occurs in a realistic setting, but more than a third (34%–40%) of the violent actions result in unrealistically little harm.

Perceived Realism and Media Effects on Learning and Accepting Violence

Perceived realism is a multidimensional phenomenon, and scholars have offered many classifications of these dimensions. One focal component of perceived realism is the perception of the television as a "magic window" that features specific people and objects that exist in the real world. The second central component of realism is the extent to which media fit social expectations. Audience members compare the media world with their knowledge of the real world. Media content that is perceived to be typical of or consistent with the real world is regarded as realistic. Another component of perceived realism includes the likelihood (plausibility rather than merely possibility) of an occurrence of the media events in the real world. Other definitions of perceived realism encompass additional dimensions, such as the utility and applicability of media information to media consumers' real life; internal consistency and coherence of the storyline; and emotional involvement with the characters.

Despite the multiplicity of definitions of this concept, scholars have agreed that perceived realism serves as an important facilitator of media effects in general and media effects on violence and aggression in particular.

Theoretical Mechanisms Linking Perceived Realism With Media Effects

Several theories suggest that realistic media portrayals are likely to be more influential than unrealistic ones.

Realism, Fear, and Desensitization

Studies have found that, overall, realistic media violence is generally more fear provoking than unrealistic media violence. Conversely, viewers tend to trivialize unrealistic media violence. Consequently, whereas the emotional distress resulting from exposure to realistic violence can hinder viewers' approval of violence in real life, exposure to unrealistic and fantasy violence might amplify viewers' desensitization to real-life violence.

Social Cognitive Theory

Albert Bandura's social cognitive theory maintains that media provide audiences with opportunities to learn about social reality, acquire new behaviors, or become motivated to execute already learned behaviors. This learning process occurs through observation of models, with some stimuli having better instructional potential than others. The theory specifies a number of psychological, contextual, and message-related factors that are likely to enhance attention to media and facilitate retention of the learned message. Among those factors are relevancy of the message and similarity between the observer and the model. Because realistic messages can be perceived as more personally relevant and more similar, they are likely to foster social learning. For example, if the viewer detects similarities between the media world and the real world, it will be easier for him or her to relate to the violent character, and he or she will be more inclined to imitate the character's violent behavior. However, if the viewer finds the narrative to be unrealistic, he or she will not transfer the rewards associated with media violence to the real world and thus will be less likely to reenact the modeled violence.

Realism and Transportation

Transportation theory suggests that media consumers can become absorbed in narratives to the extent that they forget the fictional status of the story. When mentally transported into the narrative world, viewers' ability to think about the message critically and resist its persuasive power is compromised. Accordingly, transportation enhances learning and persuasion. Perceived realism plays an important role in enabling and promoting transportation. By making the content more personally relevant, perceived realism can foster transportation. The opposite is also true—transportation can be impeded by disruption of internal realism (contradictions within the story) or by faulty external realism (i.e., gross inconsistencies between the real-world schema and the narrative world).

Realism and Cultivation

Cultivation theory maintains that, over time, repeated exposure to media promotes social judgments consistent with media representations of reality. One psychological explanation of this effect suggests that television viewers use media-based information as a heuristic to estimate the prevalence of social phenomena. Thus, to the extent that media-based information is cognitively accessible, viewers are more likely to rely on it in their opinion formation. It was hypothesized that cognitive management of messages differs depending on the degree of realism of this information. Messages that appear to be highly realistic are more accessible for future retrieval and are therefore more likely to be incorporated in making subsequent social judgments. From this perspective, realistic television messages should play a more prominent role in cultivation of fear and estimation of violence in society.

Developmental Differences in Judgments of Media Realism

The ability to differentiate between television and reality slowly evolves through childhood with cognitive development and experience. Toddlers tend to believe that objects that appear on the television screen are physically present inside the television set. By early childhood (about 4 years of age), children comprehend the difference between the objects and their referents, but many of them continue to uphold a magical window perception of television as a true representation of the world. Only by middle childhood (around the age of 7 years) do children have a good understanding of the difference between reality and fiction.

These stages of development are gradual and variable. A 6-year-old girl watching a scary movie may know it is unreal, but she has to remind herself that it is "make believe" in order to control her fright reactions. A 7-year-old might understand that some fantastic creatures (e.g., witches) are fictional but may continue to believe in the existence of other fantastic entities (e.g., trolls). Given the complexity of developmental changes in children's ability to comprehend fictional media, even extremely unrealistic representations, such as cartoons and fantasy movies, can have a profound impact on young viewers.

This is especially troublesome given that many media contents targeting children understate the consequences of violence. For instance, cartoon characters routinely engage in extreme violence, yet the victims appear unharmed in the following scene. Viewers who lack the ability to comprehend how unrealistic these depictions are might be less aware of the severity of such actions. Additionally, developmental differences in comprehension of fiction and reality have implications for fright reactions of children in different age groups. Younger

children tend to be more scared by fictional violence, whereas adolescents are more frightened by news and realistic media violence.

Empirical Findings of the Effect of Realism on Learning and Acceptance of Violence

Overall, research has provided support for the notion that the various aspects of realism facilitate media effects on viewers' aggression.

Realistic Versus Fictional Genres

A meta-analysis synthesizing more than 1,000 media effects on aggression and prosocial behaviors found that, on average, studies that examined realistic media violence reported substantially greater effects than did studies on fictional media violence. Several experiments have directly compared the effects of exposure to fictional versus factual media violence. Although for the most part these experiments found that factual violence had greater effects on the viewers, a few experiments failed to replicate these results.

To reconcile the inconsistent findings, it was suggested that perhaps the effects are particularly pronounced when it is salient for the viewers that a given message is factual. Salience could have been induced in experiments when the researchers explicitly told viewers what type of media content was being presented to them. For instance, participants in one such experiment were more likely to imitate violent behaviors they saw in what they believed to be a news segment than were viewers who were told that the same clip was a television commercial.

Social Reality of Fiction

Regardless of the factual status of media content, the perceived realism of the message is an important predictor of media effects. Even when media consumers are fully aware of the fact that the media content is fictional, to the extent that it appears to be an accurate representation of the social world, viewers are more likely to be influenced by it.

Studies that considered perceived realism as a trait found that media consumers who tend to view media as true to life are more susceptible to media violence effects. Paul Haridakis examined the relationship between trait-perceived reality (i.e., propensity to perceive media as realistic) and television viewers' aggression. This line of research revealed that when controlling for other variables (personality characteristics, experience with crime, exposure to violent television, and television viewing motivations), trait-perceived reality had no impact on verbal aggression, anger, or hostility. However, perceived realism was a significant predictor of physical aggression. In fact, in this sample, even after including demographic, personality, exposure, and motivation variables, perceived realism explained an additional 1.5% of variance of physical aggression.

Graphic Realism

Visual and technical qualities of audiovisual media and video games enhance the realism of the message. For example, studies on video and computer games have compared the effects of different versions of the same violent game. When the content of the game is held adequately consistent across the experimental conditions, newer games that employ more advanced and compelling visual design are perceived to be more realistic compared with older games. Consequently, such visually realistic games enhance attention to the violence, amplify identification with the violence perpetrator, increase enjoyment from the game, and ultimately have greater impact on gamers' aggression.

Criticism, Limitations, and Future Directions

Despite the compelling evidence of the contribution of realism to media effects, some methodological limitations call for further research. First, although perceived realism has commonly been conceptualized as a multidimensional construct, many studies have employed a one-dimensional measure of perceived reality or treated multidimensional measures as a single construct. To address these concerns, a number of recent research projects have focused on clarifying the contribution of specific subcomponents of realism to media exposure outcomes.

Second, concerns about the validity of retrospective self-report of realism have been raised. Some have argued that realism judgments are made during the media exposure, and thus a proper measurement of realism should capture online realism perceptions. In this view, retrospective realism judgments can constitute a media exposure outcome in and of itself rather than a mediator of exposure effects. In somewhat similar fashion, other scholars have noted that some of the earlier perceived realism measures capture an enduring trait-like characteristic of the viewer (e.g., the magic window belief), whereas perception of realism of specific media content is more appropriate.

Assessment of online realism judgments occurring during media exposure poses many challenges, not the least of which is interruption of the normal pace of message processing and judgment formation. Thus, instead of requesting study participants to report their realism judgments during the media consumption process, attempts have been made to develop retrospective measures that address perceptions of specific components of the message (e.g., characters, events) rather than assessing global postviewing evaluations of the message as a whole.

Riva Tukachinsky

See also Cultivating Content and the Social Representation of Violence; Cultivation Theory; Developmental Effects; Social Cognitive Theory; Social Learning From Media; User Involvement in Violent Content, Effects of;

Further Readings

Busselle, R. W. (2001). The role of exemplar accessibility in social reality judgments. *Media Psychology, 3*, 43–67.

Potter, W. J. (1988). Perceived reality in television effects research. *Journal of Broadcasting & Electronic Media, 32*, 23–41.

Shapiro, M. A., (2005). Perceived reality and media entertainment. In D. Marinelli (Ed.), *ICEC conference proceedings 2003: Essays on the future of interactive entertainment*. Pittsburgh, PA: Carnegie Mellon University Press. Retrieved from http://dl.acm.org/citation.cfm?id=958733

Wright, J. C., Huston, A. C., Reitz, A. L., & Piemyat, S. (1994). Young children's perceptions of television reality: Determinants and developmental differences. *Developmental Psychology, 30*, 229–239.

REASONS FOR CONSUMING VIOLENT ENTERTAINMENT

For many years, researchers have wondered what people find attractive in violent entertainment. Why do people watch movies like *Saw* or play first-person-shooter games like *Call of Duty*? The answer to this question is highly relevant because there is convincing evidence that individuals who are more *attracted* to violent entertainment are also more likely to be *affected* by it—that is, become more aggressive. It is therefore remarkable that research into the appeal of such entertainment has received far less attention than research into its effects. This entry discusses the most common reasons for consuming violent entertainment. Although these reasons are to a certain extent intertwined, three broad categories can be distinguished: person based, social, and experiential explanations.

Person-Based Explanations

Although the answer to the question of why people consume violent entertainment may seem straightforward ("because they like it"), such preferences often result from specific personality characteristics. Two characteristics that are typically associated with violent entertainment consumption are sensation seeking and trait aggression. *Sensation seeking* is a tendency to seek out varied, new, complex, and intense sensations and experiences and a willingness to take risks in order to have such experiences. Sensation seekers are individuals with a high need for arousal, and consuming violent entertainment is a way to satisfy that need. Males and adolescents typically score higher than females on sensation seeking, and it is therefore no surprise that violent entertainment is most popular among male adolescents.

Trait aggression—the tendency to react in a hostile and aggressive way—is also related to a preference for violent entertainment. Researchers have proposed that individuals with more aggressive tendencies find such entertainment more meaningful than do individuals with less aggressive tendencies because violent entertainment can help them to understand and justify their own behavior. Furthermore, more aggressive individuals may feel more familiar with violent characters and scenarios, making violent entertainment more relevant and attractive.

Social Explanations

Media use is typically not an individual activity; it is often embedded within a larger social environment. Peers, parents, and society can have a strong direct or indirect influence on which entertainment individuals are exposed to, resulting in three social explanations for why people consume violent entertainment. The first is a "me too effect"—that is, people consume violent entertainment because their peers do so. This effect is most common in adolescence, when conformity to peers is vital. Violent entertainment consumption is an important way of being part of the group. It also offers adolescents opportunities

for social interaction and for showing off their skills in competition with others.

A second social explanation is the "forbidden fruit effect." Parents often intentionally or unintentionally try to protect their children from exposure to violent entertainment by restricting access to it. However, such restrictions often result in the opposite effect. Especially in adolescence, restriction of violent entertainment often makes such entertainment more appealing.

A third social explanation is rooted within gender roles. Society influences violent entertainment use through processes of gender role socialization. Generally, boys and men are expected and accepted to be more aggressive than girls and women. From an early age, boys learn that violent entertainment is their domain and a way to distinguish themselves from girls. Thus, by choosing violent entertainment, boys and men are offered a way to discover and reinforce their masculinity.

Experiential Explanations

Individuals may also seek out violent entertainment because they like the experience. Violent entertainment offers two types of experience that can be pleasurable and rewarding: excitation transfer and vicarious aggression. Dolf Zillmann's *excitation-transfer theory* proposes that violent entertainment can evoke strong emotions in viewers or players. These emotions are accompanied by arousal that can carry over onto and strengthen subsequent emotions. For example, people may feel fear for characters in threatening situations in a movie or game, and this fear is accompanied by arousal. When the threatening situation is overcome, the viewer or player experiences relief. The feeling of relief is intensified by the arousal that accompanied the feeling of fear. This intensified relief is what makes violent entertainment especially appealing.

The *vicarious aggression* explanation suggests that violent entertainment is appealing because it offers viewers and players a way of experiencing, through a character's eyes, situations that cannot happen or are not allowed in real life. Because violence and aggression are disapproved of by society, the only opportunity for people to engage in these behaviors, albeit vicariously, is via violent entertainment. Especially for children and adolescents, it is a way of dealing with the real-life restrictions they encounter daily, such as rules imposed by their parents or schools. Watching characters that rebel against such restrictions offers children an opportunity to escape from their everyday limitations.

The Attraction of Violent Entertainment: An Alternative Explanation

Although there are multiple explanations for why individuals consume violent entertainment, the question remains whether it is the violent content that accounts for its attractiveness. Violent movies and games are typically fast paced, action packed, and set within adventurous contexts, which could also explain why they are so popular. Indeed, a study among Dutch and American children has suggested that children who like action in entertainment do not necessarily also like violence. This means that future research should disentangle the liking of violence, action, and adventure in entertainment. Only then can we decisively understand why people consume violent entertainment.

Karin M. Fikkers and Patti M. Valkenburg

See also Aggression and Enjoyment; Arousal and Aggressive Content, Theory and Psychology of; Competition, Sports, and Video Games; Excitation-Transfer Theory; Forbidden Fruit Hypothesis; Uses and Gratifications Perspective of Media Effects; Video Games, User Motivations

Further Readings

Cantor, J. (1998). Children's attraction to violent television programming. In J. Goldstein (Ed.), *Why we watch: The attractions of violent entertainment* (pp. 88–115). New York, NY: Oxford University Press.

Krcmar, M. (2009). Individual differences in media effects. In R. L. Nabi & M. B. Oliver (Eds.), *The Sage handbook of media processes and effects* (pp. 237–250). Thousand Oaks, CA: Sage.

Przybylski, A. K., Ryan, R. M., & Rigby, C. S. (2009). The motivating role of violence in video games. *Personality and Social Psychology Bulletin*, 243–259.

Valkenburg, P. M., & Janssen, S. C. (1999). What do children value in entertainment programs? A cross-cultural investigation. *Journal of Communication, 26*, 3–21.

REGULATING SYSTEMS, INTERNET

As regulating systems, mediation strategies have been applied to both newer and older media. Although more traditional media, such as television, have been the subject of much research from the early 1990s through the 2000s, there has been a dearth of information on newer media such as the Internet. Because of its ever-changing and interactive nature, the Internet becomes more complex and challenging to regulate by governmental policies, and parents bear more responsibility to monitor online activities at home.

The strategies employed by parents to manage their children's media use are called "parental mediation." Up to the mid-2000s, with the exception of a few projects led by Matthew Eastin at The University of Texas at Austin, research on parental mediation had mostly focused on mediation strategies related to television content. This line of research had identified three main strategies: co-viewing, active, and restrictive. *Co-viewing* (or *co-using*) refers to consumption when a parent is present while the child is engaged with the media. This shared experience, however, does not include comments or discussions about the content. This strategy has been criticized by scholars because the lack of communication by parents functions as a silent endorsement of experienced material. *Active mediation* consists of discussing, interpreting, and making value judgments with the child about media content (e.g., "The characters in this show are too violent"). *Restrictive techniques* include the implementation of rules that restrict the content, location, and time of use. For example, complete restriction of a show or allowing only one hour of media consumption per day represent restrictive methods employed by parents.

The Internet, however, operates differently from television. Although the aforementioned broad mediation strategies are still used, the regulating systems employed by parents have evolved to meet the challenges posed by the web. For example, co-using the computer implies a more active parental role than co-viewing television because sitting in front of the computer screen leads to more parent–child discussions. In addition, the Internet has allowed the implementation of two types of restrictive strategies: social and technical. *Social rules* include restrictions of activities, location, and time of use (e.g., parents control the amount of time the child is online; parents require password information or that they and their children be Facebook friends), while *technical restrictions* include the use of more sophisticated software programs that filter out unwanted content. Finally, parents can also track their children's online activities after they use the Internet.

Despite these techniques available to regulate Internet content, the web poses new challenges to parental mediation. First, parents have to continually balance between protecting their children from media-related risks and maximizing the benefits provided by new technologies such as the Internet. Second, families increasingly have more media devices in the household, particularly in bedrooms, limiting the opportunities of parents to monitor (i.e., co-use) their children's online activities. Third, children need to use the Internet for schoolwork; thus, it is harder to implement restrictions to online activities and time of use. Finally, children generally have greater digital skills and are more knowledgeable about the Internet than their parents. Therefore, often the lack of digital skills prevents parents from implementing mediation strategies. For example, parents have asserted that the electronic tracking of their children's online activities is hard to follow and that the implementation of filter programs is burdensome. At the same time, children find ways to circumvent parental control efforts.

Factors Related to Internet Regulation

Despite these new challenges for parental mediation, research has consistently found that sociodemographic characteristics are related to Internet regulation. In particular, parents are more likely to implement Internet regulations for younger children. Parental mediation strategies are also more likely to be employed among middle- to upper-income parents than lower-income parents. In addition, tech-savvy parents are more prone to regulate the Internet. Finally, scholars have also found that mediation of the web is associated with parenting styles. Authoritative parents who combine discipline with flexibility and support—the parenting style many child development experts recommend—are more likely to regulate their children's Internet activities than authoritarian or neglectful parents.

Effectiveness of Parental Mediation

Evidence on the effectiveness of parental Internet regulation has been mixed. Some scholars have found that parental control does not lead to less exposure to sexual content on the web. Other investigations, however, suggest a more nuanced scenario. For instance, active co-use and restrictive mediation strategies are not associated with a reduction of online risky behaviors, but parental restrictions to peer-to-peer interactions decreased unwanted Internet behaviors. That is, by reducing the freedom of teenagers to interact with other teens, risky behaviors become

less likely. Similarly, restrictive strategies such as time limits and filtering software programs were successful in reducing unwanted behaviors only if the teens were aware of the restrictions and rules.

Some work has suggested a more optimistic outcome. Scholars have found that parents who maintained a more open communication with their children and greater discussion about the Internet perceived that their children were less likely to be involved in unwanted behaviors. In the same line, their children also reported being less involved in those behaviors.

Teresa Correa

See also Cyberbullying, Definition and Effects of; Internet Blocking; Internet Content, Effects of Violent

Further Readings

Eastin, M. S., Greenberg, B. S., & Hofschire, L. (2006). Parenting the Internet. *Journal of Communication, 56,* 486–504.
Livingstone, S., & Helsper, E. (2008). Parental mediation of children's Internet use. *Journal of Broadcasting and Electronic Media, 52*(4), 581–599.
Livingstone, S. (2009). *Kids online: Opportunities and risks for children.* Bristol, UK: Policy Press.
Shin, W., Huh, J., & Faber, R. J. (2012). Tweens' online privacy risks and the role of parental mediation. *Journal of Broadcasting and Electronic Media, 56*(4), 632–649.

RELATIONAL AGGRESSION

Most research on aggression in the media has focused on physical aggression. However, recent research has focused on relational aggression (also termed *indirect* and *social aggression*), behavior that aims to harm or manipulate an individual's relationships or social standing. Examples include gossiping, spreading rumors, and social exclusion. Compared with the problems that violence in communities can create, relational aggression may not seem as important because victims are not physically harmed. However, relational aggression among children, adolescents, and adults has attracted considerable attention because such behavior can cause considerable psychological harm to victims in ways that are often difficult to identify and prevent. Recent research has shown that relational aggression is commonly portrayed in the media and can influence aggressive behavior in viewers.

Relational Aggression in the Media

Relational aggression in the media has existed for centuries. In Shakespeare's *Othello,* Iago plants ideas and spreads rumors to manipulate Othello to doubt his wife's fidelity, eventually leading to her strangulation and Othello's suicide. Modern-day examples of relational aggression in the media are also rife, such as in television shows *Desperate Housewives,* where housewives manipulate and fight their way through the jungles of suburbia, and *Gossip Girl,* where privileged prep school teens from Manhattan's Upper East Side sabotage one another's relationships to get ahead.

A number of recent content analyses have shown that relational aggression is commonly portrayed on television, films, and in books. For example, one study of British television found that relational aggression was shown in 90% of programs popular among adolescents. Another study found that 100% of animated Disney films contained relational aggression, at around 11 acts per hour on average. Relational aggression is often portrayed as justified, with few negative consequences. Furthermore, such aggression is often portrayed by female characters who are attractive, rich, and popular. Such messages are problematic when examining aggression in the media from a social learning perspective, which holds that viewers learn that relational aggression is common, effective, leads to few negative consequences, and is portrayed in characters with desirable traits. Interestingly, some research has shown that although some programs contain almost no physical aggression, they have extremely high levels of relational aggression. From a ratings perspective, this is problematic, because such programs would be rated as having little violence, when in fact the program may contain substantial portrayals of nonphysical forms of aggression.

Effects of Viewing Relational Aggression in the Media

There is a small but growing body of literature that has suggested that viewing relational aggression in the media can influence subsequent aggression. For example, a number of cross-sectional studies have shown that individuals who view higher levels of relational aggression on television show heightened relational aggression in their friendships and relationships. Experimental research has shown a similar effect. In one study, British adolescents were assigned to view media clips containing relational aggression, physical aggression, or no aggression. Those who viewed the relational aggression clip were subsequently more relationally aggressive to a confederate of the experiment. Other research has found that viewing relational aggression in the media can influence aggressive thoughts. One study showed that emerging adults who viewed the relational aggression clip were more likely to show heightened script activation of relationally aggressive words, suggesting they were primed to think about and behave in relationally aggressive ways. Of course, such priming does not always lead to aggression, but depending on the situation it can increase the likelihood of such behavior.

Effects of Viewing Physical Aggression in the Media on Relational Aggression

Although viewing violence in the media can influence subsequent physical aggression, a number of studies have found that it can also influence subsequent relational aggression. These findings have used experimental, cross-sectional, and longitudinal methodology and have been replicated in preschoolers, students in middle childhood, adolescents, and adults of various ages. For example, L. Rowell Huesmann and colleagues' (2003) longitudinal study revealed that media violence exposure during childhood was associated with increased relational aggression in adulthood. This has been termed the *crossover effect* in some studies; it refers to the idea that viewing one type of aggression in the media can influence other forms. This makes intuitive sense, because certainly most viewers of media violence are unlikely to imitate the exact form of violence they see in the media. Most people who see a movie about an axe murderer do not go on to be axe murderers. However, according to research, is it more likely that lower-level forms of aggression, such as relational aggression, would be influenced. Instead, viewing a movie about an axe murderer might lead to more gossiping and social exclusion, behaviors that hardly warrant criminal investigation but can be extremely harmful to victims nonetheless.

In sum, current research has suggested that relational aggression is common in the media and is often portrayed in ways that may facilitate imitation. Furthermore, exposure to relational aggression in the media can influence both aggressive cognition and behavior. Finally, exposure to physical aggression in the media can influence subsequent relational aggression, both in the short and long term. Given this research, relational aggression in the media certainly warrants further attention as part of attempts to more fully understand media aggression in all its forms.

Sarah M. Coyne

See also Effects From Violent Media, Short- and Long-Term; Effects of Media Violence on Relational Aggression; General Aggression Model; Rating Systems, Television; Social Cognitive Theory

Further Readings

Coyne, S. M., & Archer, J. (2004). Indirect aggression in the media: A content analysis of British television programs. *Aggressive Behavior, 30,* 254–271.

Coyne, S. M., Linder, J. R., Nelson, D. A., & Gentile, D. A. (2012). "Frenemies, fraitors, and mean-em-aitors": Priming effects of viewing physical and relational aggression in the media on women. *Aggressive Behavior, 38,* 141–149.

Huesmann, L. R., Moise, J., Podolski, C., & Eron, L. (2003). Longitudinal relations between children's exposure to television violence and their later aggressive and violent behavior in young adulthood: 1977–1992. *Developmental Psychology, 39,* 201–221.

S

SCREEN SIZE AND VIOLENT CONTENT, EFFECTS OF

Since the 1930s, media violence has appeared on screens of increasingly varying shapes and sizes. Violent content can now be seen in formats ranging from a gigantic IMAX movie to a tiny mobile smartphone game. Consuming violent content in these diverse forms has the potential to differentially shape audience responses. This entry presents a brief overview of screen size as a media technology variable. It then reviews research findings on the effects of screen size and concludes with theoretical considerations for media violence effects as a function of screen size.

Screen Size as a Media Technology Variable

The early 1930s Payne Fund studies on the content of motion pictures called attention to the amount of violence in big-screen movies. Since that time, screen sizes have gotten both smaller and larger. The wide diffusion of television in the 1950s brought smaller-screen violent content into homes, and the motion picture industry responded by introducing larger-screen formats such as Cinerama and, more recently, IMAX, which has a standard screen size of 72 × 52.8 feet. The increase in movie screen sizes has been paralleled by a steady increase in television screen sizes, with Japanese electronics manufacturer Sharp predicting the average television to be 60 inches by 2015. At the same time, screens are also getting smaller. Violent content is now being consumed on handheld gaming systems and mobile devices such as the Apple iPhone, which has a 3.5-inch screen.

Screen sizes clearly vary more than ever, but a consideration of screen size must also factor in other aspects of screen technology. First, the width of screens has changed over time. The classic movie and television aspect ratio was 4:3 (meaning 4 units wide by 3 units high). Now, most movies have an aspect ratio of either 1.85:1 or 2.35:1, and high-definition television (HDTV) sets have an aspect ratio of 16:9. In both cases, the result is a wider screen than in the past. Second, viewing distance affects how screen size is perceived. A small screen placed directly in front of a viewer's eyes, as it might be when the viewer wears a head-mounted display (HMD), may appear to be enormous, while a large screen viewed from far away may appear small. Viewing distance calculators, accessible online, exist to help determine the optimal viewing distance for various sizes of screens. A third consideration is screen resolution. As screen size increases, image quality may appear worse, especially when viewed at close distance. This has become less of an issue, however, with newer high-definition formats than it was with standard-definition television.

Research on the Effects of Screen Size

Screen size effects have been the subject of numerous investigations. In a review of the literature on television screen size, Cheryl Campanella Bracken and Renee Botta (2010) noted that it is the most commonly studied television form variable, with experiments dating back to the early 1970s and peaking in the 1990s. Generally, larger screen sizes have been shown to intensify reactions to content. Specific outcomes of large-screen viewing identified by Bracken and Botta include increased attention, arousal, dizziness, enjoyment, and telepresence (the sense of "being there" in the media environment). Research also has shown that screen size affects receiver perceptions of objects on the screen, with mixed findings. Larger screens have been shown to lead to both more and less favorable evaluations of people on the screen, for example.

No studies to date have directly examined how screen size affects reactions to violent content. In his book on media violence and youth, Steven Kirsh (2012) discussed how the moderating role of screen size in media violence consumption remains unknown. He speculated that movies viewed in theaters could produce greater effects than those viewed on television screens, consistent with research showing a stronger influence of larger screens.

There is indirect empirical evidence for this relationship. As discussed earlier, studies have demonstrated that larger screens create a greater sense of telepresence, or "being there." And telepresence has been predicted and shown to relate to aggressive outcomes, as summarized by Paul Skalski, James Denny, and Ashleigh Shelton (2010) in a review of the literature on telepresence and violence effects. Although no experiments in this area have manipulated telepresence using screen size, it follows because since screen size relates positively to telepresence, and telepresence relates positively to aggression, screen size may relate positively to aggressive outcomes. But given the wide variety of screen sizes in contemporary use, this statement must be considered tentative until directly tested through research.

Theoretical Considerations for Screen Size and Violent Content Effects

Despite the lack of research, media effects theories have suggested ways in which different sizes of violent screen content might affect audiences. Social cognitive theory posits that attention to modeled events begins the process by which audiences exhibit matching patterns. Larger violent images should be easier to attend to and thus more likely to be imitated. Similarly, exemplification theory suggests that information with greater vividness (such as stimuli on larger screens) will be attended to more, be more cognitively accessible, and exert a greater influence on judgment. Theoretical frameworks such as social

cognitive theory and exemplification might seem to point to large-screen violence having more adverse effects (on responses such as aggression and fear) than small-screen violence. But this may not always be true when contextual features of violence are considered. Very small screens, such as those on mobile phones, may make inhibiting cues like punishments and pain or harm less salient to viewers, making this form of consumption more problematic. Again, more research is needed before firm conclusions can be made about the potentially complex relationship among media violence, screen size, and exposure outcomes.

Paul Skalski

See also Social Cognitive Theory

Further Readings

Bracken, C. C., & Botta, R. (2010). Telepresence and television. In C. C. Bracken & P. Skalski (Eds.), *Immersed in media: Telepresence in everyday life* (pp. 39–62). New York: Routledge.

Kirsh, S. J. (2012). *Children, adolescents, and media violence: A critical look at the research* (2nd ed.). Thousand Oaks, CA: Sage.

Skalski, P., Denny, J., & Shelton, A. (2010). Presence and media effects. In C. C. Bracken & P. Skalski (Eds.), *Immersed in media: Telepresence in everyday life* (pp. 158–180). New York: Routledge.

SEX IN MEDIA, EFFECTS ON SOCIETY

Effects of sex in the media have been studied from many different vantage points and at many different levels. These include the ways sex in the media may affect individuals, interpersonal relationships, and larger societal structures, ideologies, and laws. At individual and societal levels, research on effects of sex in the media has focused predominantly on cognitions (e.g., perceptual, memory, and information-processing systems underlying maladaptive attitudes and behaviors, knowledge about sex, and sexual relations), attitudes (e.g., sexist attitudes, attitudes supporting violence, and sexually permissive attitudes), and behaviors (e.g., manifest sexual behaviors, sexually aggressive or sexually violent behaviors) using a variety of research designs and methodologies.

Research on effects of sex in the media has often been divided into two categories. The first category concerns sex in the media in which sexual stimuli are included within a larger, often nonsexual context (e.g., popular movies, TV series, or music videos). Here, references to or portrayals of sexual interactions may be present but typically do not constitute the majority of the content. Furthermore, the sexual explicitness typically does not contain overt displays of (aroused) genitals or explicit sexual acts, and the primary intention is not that of continued sexual arousal and viewer sexual gratification. In this entry, this type of media is referred to as *sexually nonexplicit media*.

The second category concerns sex in the media in which the sexual stimuli typically are not set within a larger nonsexual context, and the primary intention is that of sexual arousal and viewer sexual gratification. The majority of this content typically contains (aroused) genitals and explicit sexual acts. Commonly, this type of sex in the media is referred to as *erotica, pornography, sexually explicit media,* or *sexually explicit materials*. In this entry this type of material is referred to as *sexually explicit media*.

Effects of Sexually Nonexplicit Media

A study of popular movies from 1950 to 2006 showed that more than 80% included sexual content and that the sexual explicitness of both R- and PG-13–rated movies has increased in recent decades. Furthermore, analyses of sexual content on U.S. television and in movies generally have shown increases since the 1990s, with as much as 70% of U.S. television shows from 2004 to 2005 including sexual content.

Teens and young adults generally indicate that they rank entertainment media as a very powerful source of influence for shaping their knowledge and views about sexuality and sexual health, and that such media play an important role in their lives. For example, 57% of 14- to 16-year-old adolescents in the United States report using entertainment media as a primary source of sexual information. Furthermore, sexually nonexplicit media have been found to be associated with a wide variety of attitudinal, cognitive, and behavioral outcomes. These include greater endorsement of dysfunctional relationship models, stereotypical sexual attitudes, and greater acceptance of sexual harassment. Furthermore, increased exposure to sexually nonexplicit media has been found to be predictive of more permissive sexual attitudes, greater sexual experience, earlier sexual debut, and risky sexual behaviors even after controlling for a variety of covariates.

Importantly, effects of sexually nonexplicit media are often moderated and mediated by individual and contextual differences. Furthermore, the associations found between sexually nonexplicit media contents and investigated outcomes are usually modest in effect size. Thus, effectively, sexually nonexplicit media may best be understood as one among a number of factors that influence sexuality and sexual behaviors to a degree that varies across individuals and contexts.

Effects of Sexually Explicit Media

Sexually explicit media have been found to be used by a significant percentage of people, and although consumption rates vary with age, gender, relationship status, and sexual orientation, consumption rates among men typically fall in the 50%–99% range, while for women consumption rates typically fall in the 30%–80% range. Traditionally, those who want to restrict sexually explicit media claim that it may adversely influence beliefs, morals, values, attitudes, and behaviors with negative implications for marriages, gender roles and perceptions, body images, and individuals' sex lives more generally. In contrast, proponents of sexual media have claimed that little or no such effects of sexual media consumption are evident. Rather, sexual media may benefit the individual by enhancing the sex life, contributing to knowledge about sex, providing a recreational sexual outlet, or helping to cure common sexological dysfunctions.

Using experimental, cross-sectional, and longitudinal research, effects of sexually explicit media on a number of cognitive, attitudinal, and behavioral variables have been consistently demonstrated, although these effects have typically been modest in size. For example, sexually explicit media have been found to influence cognitions, including the perceptual, memory, and information-processing systems. Furthermore, associations have been demonstrated between sexually explicit media consumption or exposure and attitudes supporting violence against women, sexist attitudes, sexually permissive attitudes, and attitudes toward sexually explicit media. Finally, significant associations have been consistently demonstrated between sexually explicit media and increased sexual arousal, a variety of sexual behaviors, and sexual aggression.

Importantly, across-the-board effects of sexually explicit media consumption have been increasingly refuted, and effects, if any, have been considered in relation to individual, cultural, and contextual differences. Thus, numerous studies have demonstrated the ways such differences may moderate the associations found between sexually explicit media consumption and (outcome) variables of interest. For example, in the area of sexually aggressive behaviors, Neil Malamuth and associates have consistently demonstrated that adverse effects of sexually explicit media on sexually aggressive behaviors and attitudes are moderated by individual risk levels of sexual aggression, so that sexually explicit media increase the likelihood of sexually aggressive behaviors and attitudes only among individuals already at the highest risk levels of engaging in these behaviors. Conversely, sexually explicit media may not increase the risk of sexual aggression among individuals who are not at high risk for committing sexual aggression.

Explaining and Integrating Effects of Sex in the Media

Historically, a number of theories have been used to explain or hypothesize effects of sex in the media, in particular, conditioning theories, social learning theory, sexual script theory, excitation-transfer theory, and evolutionary theory. The most influential theories guiding research in this area have been social learning theory, and more recently, sexual script theory.

Based on social learning theory, sex in the media may be thought to influence attitudes and behaviors by creating role models, learning environments, and scenarios in which certain sexual behaviors, gender stereotypes, sex roles, and attitudes are normalized, encouraged, and reinforced. Furthermore, the concept of *reciprocal determinism,* referring to a continuous reciprocal interaction between the person and the social environment, is central to the understanding of possible effects of sex in the media. Thus, media consumers actively seek out the types of (sexual) media most consistent with their personalities, interests, attitudes, values, social interactions, and so on. These media experiences in turn reinforce or influence the individual differences either directly or indirectly through, for example, peer influence or group or societal norms.

Sexual script theory has recently emerged as a theoretical perspective to guide research on sex in the media. Sexual scripts may be compared to scripts used by actors. Accordingly, in sexual interactions, sexual scripts may serve as guides and manuals for sexual behaviors. Sex in the media may influence the scripting process, the sexual scripts, or the evaluation of sexual relations. Sex in the media, through culturally mediated messages and social learning processes, may "write" itself into the sexual scripts, influencing perceptions of sexuality (i.e., what is sex), sexual situations (i.e., when is a situation sexual), sexual behaviors (i.e., what does one do when having sex), and evaluations of sexual relations (i.e., what constitutes good sex). Evidently, sex in media content is not the only existing culturally mediated message about sex and sexual relations, but it continually intermingles with other readily available messages and personal dispositions and motives in a continuous reshaping of sexual scripts.

From the early 1990s, effects of sexually explicit media increasingly began to be analyzed and integrated within "cumulative probability models," the most influential being the Confluence Model of Sexual Aggression and the Three-Path Model of Sexual Aggression. In cumulative probability models each antecedent factor (e.g., sexually explicit media) of the outcome variable may show only small associations with the outcome variable of interest (e.g., sexual behaviors), but the confluence or interactive combination of these antecedent factors may be of strong predictive utility and societal relevance.

Recently, Paul Wright and colleagues (2012) proposed the 3AM model, specifically targeting effects of sex in the media in general. Built on the principles of social learning theory and sexual script theory, the 3AM model follows an acquisition, activation, and application perspective (the 3 As in the model) on mass media effects. According to the 3AM model, sex in the media, through culturally available messages and social learning processes, may be written into the sexual scripts. However, the acquisition, activation, and application of these sexual scripts are subject to a number of content factors (e.g., rewards or punishment), audience factors (e.g., model similarity, moral standards), and situational factors (e.g., time pressure, sexual arousal) as well as to the evaluative and automatic thought processes guiding these factors and behaviors. Consequently, the application of activated sexual scripts, however brought about, does not happen automatically or uniformly across consumers but depends on a number of other intervening factors.

Overall, further development and empirical validation of these and similar future models offer the potential for important and decisive contributions in advancing the understanding of effects of sex in the media on individuals and their implications for society.

Gert Martin Hald

See also Aggressive Behavior; Cognition: Schemas and Scripts; Excitation-Transfer Theory; Methodologies for Assessing Effects of Media; Pornography, Violent Content in: Effects of; Sexualized Aggression; Social Cognitive Theory

Further Readings

Gagnon, J. H., & Simon, W. (1973). *Sexual conduct: The social sources of human sexuality.* Chicago, IL: Aldine.

Hald, G. M., Seaman, C., & Linz, D. (in press). Sexuality and pornography. In D. Tolman, L. Diamond (Eds.-in-Chief), J. Bauermeister, W. George, J. Pfaus, & M. Ward (Assoc. Eds.), *APA handbook of sexuality and psychology: Vol. 1. Person-in-context.* Washington, DC: American Psychological Association.

Jamieson, P. E., & Romer, D. (2008). *The changing portrayal of adolescents in the media since 1950.* New York, NY: Oxford University Press.

Knight, R. A., & Sims-Knight, J. E. (2005). Testing an etiological model for male juvenile sexual offending against females. In R. Geffner, K. C. Franey, T. G. Arnold, & R. Falconer (Eds.), *Identifying and treating youth who sexually offend: Current approaches, technique, and research* (pp. 33–55). New York, NY: Routledge.

Malamuth, N. M., Addison, T., & Koss, M. (2000). Pornography and sexual aggression: Are there reliable effects and can we understand them? *Annual Review of Sex Research, 11,* 26–91.

O'Hara, R. E., Gibbons, F. X., Gerrand, M., Li, Z., & Sargent, J. D. (2013). Greater exposure to sexual content in popular movies predicts earlier sexual debut and increased sexual risk taking. *Psychological Science, 23,* 984–993.

Stulhofer, A., Busko, V., & Landripet, I. (2010). Pornography, sexual socialization, and satisfaction among young men. *Archives of Sexual Behavior, 39,* 168–178.

Wright, P. J. (2013). U.S. males and pornography, 1973–2010: Consumption, predictors, correlates. *Journal of Sex Research, 50,* 60–71.

Wright, P. J., Malamuth, N., & Donnerstein, E. (2012). Research on sex in the media: What do we know about effects on children and adolescents? In D. G. Singer & J. L. Singer (Eds.), *Handbook of children and the media* (pp. 273–302). Thousand Oaks, CA: Sage.

SEXUALIZED AGGRESSION

Most media companies, like any businesses, exist to make profits. Because media producers must generate audiences for advertisers, they must grab attention and get people to tune in, download, or log in. Content and methods that excite basic human emotions and motives—frequently sex and violence—are common attention grabbers. Media that feature both sex and violence seem sure to be profitable.

Psychological research on sexualized aggression has focused on three types of research methods: content analyses, correlational studies, and experiments. Researchers have studied sex and violence in the media across a variety of media genres from print to interactive media, with an emphasis on the study of video entertainment (both pornographic and nonpornographic), video games, and music. This entry discusses studies on the preponderance and effects of sexualized aggression in the media.

Pornography

Content Analyses

Today, pornography is lucrative, graphic, global, accessible, acceptable (legally and culturally), anonymous, interactive, immediate, and violent. Given pornography's widespread and growing use, the question of its effects on individuals and society remains important, yet after 30 years of research many questions remain.

Experiments

Edward Donnerstein and Leonard Berkowitz (1981) found that angered men were more aggressive toward women after viewing aggressive sexual content than were control participants. For nonangered men, only videos showing positive reactions by victims to rape provoked more aggression than the other films.

Mike Allen and colleagues (1995a) conducted a meta-analysis and found exposure to pictorial nudity reduces subsequent aggressive behavior. However, viewing nonviolent sexual activity increases aggressive behavior, and viewing violent sexual activity generates more aggression than viewing nonviolent sexual activity. Another meta-analysis by Allen and colleagues (1995b) analyzed the association between rape myth acceptance and exposure to pornography and found almost no effect in nonexperimental studies and a small increase following pornography exposure in experimental studies. Again, violent pornography had a stronger effect than nonviolent pornography. Other studies show that pre-exposure to rape depictions increases sexual arousal to depictions of forced sex. The Confluence Model of Sexual Aggression by Neil Malamuth and colleagues hypothesizes that individual differences in risk for sexual aggression moderate the association between pornography use and acceptance of violence against women.

Correlational Studies

Berl Kutchinsky found that between 1964 and 1984, when censorship of pornography decreased in four countries, incidents of reported rape did not increase more than reported incidents of nonsexually violent crimes. In the Czech Republic, rape and other sex crimes did not increase with the increased availability of pornography, and the incidence of child sex abuse significantly decreased. Other research found the opposite effect.

At the individual level, studies using retrospective, self-reported data typically find no difference in pornography use between sex offenders and relevant comparison groups.

A study of college men found a strong association between rape and rape proclivity with most forms of pornography. An examination of the relationship between rape myth acceptance and men's and women's preferences for nonpornographic films with love story, suspense, or sex and violence themes found that female film preferences and rape myth acceptance attitudes were moderated by exposure to sexually violent media based on true stories. Men's rape myth acceptance attitudes were unaffected by film preferences.

Nonpornography

Content Analyses

A study of 20 James Bond films—in which female characters are typically framed as objects of sex, violence, or both, and often considered easily dispensable—identified a significant longitudinal link between sexuality and violent behavior. A positive relationship was also identified with harm to women.

A content analysis of MTV music videos found that females were significantly more likely than males to be portrayed as recipients of sex and aggression than as initiators and also were found to appear as if they enjoyed aggressive sex. Another study of music videos found that males are portrayed as aggressive, while females are subordinate and sexually objectified. An analysis of *Billboard*'s Hot 100 music videos revealed greater objectification and less agency by female as compared with male artists. Erica Scharrer has noted that common hypermasculine characters demonstrate that being "manly" means having calloused or belittling attitudes toward romance, sex, and women in general, while hyperfeminine characters show submission and dependency, and characterize sexuality as a woman's currency.

Slasher films are popular morality tales that closely follow sexualized aggression scripts: notably, females are punished for sexual activity with violence and death. A quantitative content analysis of 50 slasher films found that sexualized females were more likely than nonsexualized females to die and took more screen time to die.

Between the 1980s and today, content analyses have shown that female video game characters have changed from being mostly nonexistent or damsels in distress to being regularly depicted as simultaneously sexual and aggressive. For example, Karen Dill and Kathryn Thill (2007) found that a sizable proportion of female game characters were both sexualized and aggressive (39%), while very few (1%) male characters were.

Experimental and Correlational Studies

Some studies have shown that males exposed to images of sexually objectified women are more likely than controls to endorse rape-supportive attitudes and myths. Mike Yao, Chad Mahood, and Daniel Linz (2010) found that males who played games with sexualized female characters and imagery demonstrated quicker reaction times to sexual words compared with controls and were more likely to perceive women as sex objects. Dill, Brian Brown, and Michael Collins (2008) found that men exposed to sexualized female game characters showed greater tolerance for sexual harassment compared with controls. Furthermore, long-term exposure to sexualized game violence was correlated with greater tolerance of sexual harassment and greater rape myth acceptance.

Although more data are needed on the effects of exposure to nonpornographic sexualized aggression, current data tell a consistent story.

Karen E. Dill-Shackleford, Ellen R. Albertson,
and Donald S. Grant

See also Pornography, Violent Content in; Pornography, Violent Content in: Effects of; Rape Perceptions

Further Readings

Allen, M., D'Alessio, D., & Brezgel, K. (1995a). A meta-analysis summarizing the effects of pornography: Aggression after exposure. *Human Communications Research, 22,* 258–283.

Allen, M., Emmers, T., Gebhardt, L., & Giery, M. A. (1995b). Exposure to pornography and acceptance of rape myths. *Journal of Communication, 45,* 5–26.

Aubrey, J. S., & Frisby, C. M. (2011). Sexual objectification in music videos: A content analysis comparing gender and genre. *Mass Communication & Society, 14,* 475–501.

Boeringer, S. B. (1994). Pornography and sexual aggression: Associations of violent and nonviolent depictions with rape and rape proclivity. *Deviant Behavior, 15,* 289–304.

Court, J. H. (1976). Pornography and sex-crimes: A re-evaluation in the light of recent trends around the world. *International Journal of Criminology and Penology, 5,* 129–157.

Dill, K. E. (2009). Violent video games, rape myth acceptance, and negative attitudes towards women. In E. Stark and E. S. Buzawa (Eds.), *Violence against women in families and relationships: Vol. 4, The media and cultural attitudes.* Westport, CT: Praeger.

Dill, K. E., Brown, B. P., & Collins, M. A. (2008). Effects of media stereotypes on sexual harassment judgments and rape supportive attitudes: Popular video game characters, gender, violence and power. *Journal of Experimental Social Psychology, 44,* 1402–1408.

Dill, K. E., & Thill, K. P. (2007). Video game characters and the socialization of gender roles: Young people's perceptions mirror sexist media depictions, *Sex Roles, 57,* 851–865.

Donnerstein, E., & Berkowitz, L. (1981). Victim reactions in aggressive erotic films as a factor in violence against women. *Journal of Personality and Social Psychology, 41,* 710–724.

Jaffee, D., & Straus, M. A. (1987). Sexual climate and reported rape: A state-level analysis. *Archives of Sexual Behavior, 16,* 107–123.

Jenkins, T. (2005). James Bond's "Pussy" and Anglo-American cold war sexuality. *Journal of American Culture, 28,* 309–317.

Lanis, K., & Covell, K. (1995). Images of women in advertisements: Effects on attitudes related to sexual aggression. *Sex Roles, 32,* 639–649.

Malamuth, N. M., & Check, J. V. P. (1980). Penile tumescence and perceptual responses to rape as a function of victim's perceived reactions. *Journal of Applied Social Psychology, 10,* 528–547.

Malamuth, N. M., Hald, G. M., & Koss, M. (2012). Pornography, individual differences in risk and men's acceptance of violence against women in a representative sample. *Sex Roles, 66,* 427–439.

Marshall, W. L. (1988). The use of sexually explicit stimuli by rapists, child molesters, and nonoffenders. *Journal of Sex Research, 25,* 267–288.

Marshall, W. L., Seidman, B. T., & Barbaree, H. E. (1991). The effects of prior exposure to erotic and nonerotic stimuli on the rape index. *Annals of Sex Research, 4,* 209–220.

Neuendorf, K., Gore, T., Dalessadro, A., Janstova, P., & Snyder-Suhy, S. (2009). Shaken and stirred: A content analysis of women's portrayals in James Bond films. *Sex Roles, 62,* 747–761.

Scharrer, E. (2004).Virtual violence: Gender and aggression in video game advertisements. *Mass Communication and Society, 7,* 393–412.

Scharrer, E. (2005). Hypermasculinity, aggression and television violence: An experiment. *Media Psychology, 7,* 353–376.

Yao, M., Mahood, C., & Linz, D. (2010). Sexual priming, gender stereotyping, and likelihood to sexually harass: Examining the cognitive effects of playing a sexually-explicit video game. *Sex Roles, 62*(1–2), 77–88.

SITUATIONAL INFLUENCES ON AGGRESSIVE REACTIONS TO MEDIA VIOLENCE

In explaining why exposure to a violent movie or video game may heighten the relatively short-lived chance that some audience members will act aggressively, many researchers have attributed this enhanced risk largely to the priming of existing aggressive scripts and attitudes in the media users, causing the users to believe that aggression is appropriate and/or rewarding (e.g., Media Violence Commission, 2012). To some extent, though, what the viewers and/or players do for a short time after the media exposure can also be affected by situation, including the characteristics of the persons they happen to encounter. These persons might be regarded by the viewers as either safe or dangerous to attack, so that the media users' restraints against aggression are lowered or raised. In addition, the possible targets' characteristics might also affect the strength of the users' aggressive inclinations automatically, with little part played by the users' controlled cognitive processing (Berkowitz, 1993, 2012).

Automatic Reactions to Situational Features

In keeping with Berkowitz's cognitive neoassociation model of automatically evoked aggression, this section of the entry presents the concept that potential targets are especially likely to be attacked by persons with aggressive inclinations to the extent that the aggressors are linked to aggression-heightening associations—more specifically, that they are associated with decidedly unpleasant occurrences and/or have an aggressive meaning. It should be acknowledged, however, that these association-produced effects have often been relatively weak in laboratory settings, and that the findings reported in the following paragraphs have been based mainly on the actions of previously angered research participants who are then exposed to episodes of media violence. Comparable behavior from nonangered persons in situations outside the laboratory might also be seen if the associations are quite strong and restraints against aggression are low.

Unpleasant Experiences

Aversive occurrences, such as frustrations, unpleasantly hot weather, painful stimulation, and depressive feelings, frequently give rise to anger and aggressive tendencies (Anderson et al., 1995; Berkowitz, 1993). Persons linked in some way to unpleasant events can provoke aggressive reactions from others and are especially apt to be the victims of other people's aggressive inclinations. One consequence is that frustration-engendered hostility is often displaced toward those who are greatly disliked by the aggressor (Berkowitz, 1993). As an example, in an experiment by Leonard Berkowitz and Dennis Knurek, frustrated college students were subsequently especially hostile to a fellow student who was regarded negatively because he had a name they had been conditioned to dislike. Although there is no direct evidence showing that media violence–activated aggressive tendencies are likely to be directed against individuals having such negative associations, there is theoretical reason to believe this kind of displacement occurs.

Personal Characteristics

There is clearer evidence regarding other stimulus qualities that can heighten the chances that a possible target will be victimized by someone who had just been exposed to media violence. Just as an occurrence may have an aggressive meaning to the observer, such

as frequently priming aggression-related thoughts, feelings, and impulses, people associated with an aggressive incident are likely to provoke attacks from those disposed to be aggressive at the time (assuming, of course, that it's not dangerous to attack the provocateurs). In Berkowitz's research, previously angered participants exhibited the greatest hostility to their provocateur if they had just watched a filmed prize fight. The person presenting the study said he was a boxer or film maker; the boxer had a labeled mediated connection. The aggressive inclinations activated by both the prior mistreatment of the victim and the fight movie apparently were directed most strongly toward the person whom the aggressor associated with the film. People who had recently been exposed to violent media might well be especially inclined to be hostile to someone they regard as aggressive in nature. But the hostility won't be shown openly if it might be punished.

The specific nature of this linkage with the observed aggression can matter. For example, a disliked target receiving the strongest punishment had a label-mediated connection with the badly beaten loser in the witnessed fight. Simply put, angry people generally wanted to injure the one who had aroused them, and they typically were gratified and rewarded by indications that this person was hurt or even in pain (Berkowitz, 1993, 2012). They might even be pleased by the sight of someone else being aggressively—and appropriately—injured by another party so that their own aggressive urge is strengthened further.

In additional research, the male participants were first deliberately angered by the experimenter's accomplice, who had previously been given one of three names: the same name as the fight loser in the violent film; the name of the observed fight's victor; or a name not used in the witnessed fight scene. When the viewers then were required to deliver electric shocks to their provocateur, ostensibly as a judgment of his performance on an assigned task, they punished him most severely when his name linked him with the defeated fighter. This person evidently drew the strongest attacks because of his association with the movie victim's pain and suffering.

Final Thoughts

This entry's discussion is very much in accord with one of contemporary social psychology's basic themes: our everyday conduct is often greatly affected by influences in our immediate situations.

But more than this, research throughout psychology has shown that many of these influences can operate automatically, with virtually no cognitive processing (e.g., see Shiffrin & Schneider, 1977). People inclined to be aggressive because they've just been exposed to violent media might consciously decide to be hostile or not because of their beliefs and attitudes at the moment. Still, in keeping with the ideas expressed in this entry, the viewers of violent media might also react impulsively in a hostile manner to features of their surrounding situations, including the characteristics of persons they just happen to encounter.

Leonard Berkowitz

See also Aggression, Definition and Assessment of; Aggression and Anger; Aggressive Behavior; Audience Interpretation of Media Violence, Effects of; Effects From Violent Media, Short- and Long-Term; Television Violence

Further Readings

Anderson, C., Deuser, W., & DeNeve, K. (1995). Hot temperatures, hostile affect, hostile cognition, and arousal: Tests of a general model of affective aggression. *Personality and Social Psychology Bulletin, 21,* 366–376.

Berkowitz, L. (1993). *Aggression: Its causes, consequences, and control.* New York, NY: McGraw-Hill.

Berkowitz, L. (2012). A different view of anger: The cognitive-neoassociation conception of the relation of anger to aggression. *Aggressive Behavior, 38,* 322–333.

Media Violence Commission. (2012, September/October). Report of Media Violence Commission, International Society for Research on Aggression. *Aggressive Behavior.*

Shiffrin, R., & Schneider, W. (1977). Controlled and automatic human information processing: II. Perceptual learning, automatic attending, and a general theory. *Psychological Review, 84,* 127–190.

SOCIAL AGGRESSION

See Relational Aggression

SOCIAL COGNITIVE THEORY

Social cognitive theory is founded on a conception of self-development, adaption, and change based on the idea of human agency. To be an agent is to deliberately influence the course of events by one's actions. People exercise their influence through three different forms of agency. In *personal agency,* exercised individually, people bring their influence to bear on what they can control directly. However, in many spheres of functioning, people do not have direct control over conditions that affect their lives. They exercise *proxy agency.* They do so by influencing others who have the resources, knowledge, and means to act on their behalf to secure the outcomes they desire. People do not live their lives in individual autonomy. Many of the things they seek are achievable only by working together. In the exercise of *collective agency,* people pool their knowledge, skills, and resources and act in concert to shape their futures. The distinctive blend of individual, proxy, and collective agency varies cross-culturally. But individuals need all three forms of agency to make it through the day wherever they live. This entry explains social cognitive theory and the ways it applies to various environments, including digital media.

Broadening the conception of agency to the collective form extends the generalizability of social cognitive theory to collectively oriented societies. In evaluating the cross-cultural generalizability of psychosocial theories, one must distinguish between basic human capacities and the ways that culture shapes these potentialities into diverse forms. For example, humans have evolved an advanced capacity for observational learning through social modeling. It is essential for their self-development and functioning regardless of the culture in which they reside. However, the attitudes, values, and styles of behavior that are modeled, by whom, in what mode, in which social contexts, and for what purpose vary widely cross-culturally.

In short, there is a commonality in basic agentic capacities and the mechanisms through which they operate but also a diversity in how these inherent capacities are cultured. In this dual-level analysis, universality is not incompatible with manifest cultural plurality. Henry Murray and Clyde Kluckhohn summarized eloquently the blend of universality, commonality, and uniqueness of human qualities in noting that every person is, in certain aspects, like all other people, like some other people, and like no other person.

In the social cognitive theory of self and society, personal agency and social structure function interdependently rather than as disjoined entities. Social systems are the product of human activity. They are devised to organize, guide, and regulate human affairs in diverse spheres of life through authorized rules, sanctions, and enabling resources. The societal norms, sanctions, and opportunity structures, in turn, influence the course of human activity. Given this dynamic bidirectionality of influence, social cognitive theory rejects a duality of human agency and social structure as a reified entity disembodied from individuals.

Reciprocal Nature of Behavioral Causes

Theorists have engaged in spirited debates over whether the causes of human behavior reside in the individual, as dispositionalists have claimed, or in the environment, as situationalists have claimed. Social cognitive theory conceptualizes the causal structure as triadic reciprocal causation. In this conception, human functioning is a product of a reciprocal interplay of intrapersonal determinants in the form of cognitive, affective, and biological event; the type of expressed behavior; and nature of the environmental events. Because personal influence is an interacting determinant in the causal structure, human agency is not incompatible with the principle of determinism. Individuals are codeterminants in the causal mix.

The environment is not a monolithic force that impinges on the organism. Social cognitive theory distinguishes among three different types of environments. They are the imposed, selected, and created environments. The *imposed* physical and social environment impinges on individuals whether they like it or not. But they have some leeway in how they construe and react to it. For the most part, the environment is only a potentiality. It does not come into being until it is *selected* and activated by appropriate behavior. This constitutes the selected environment. For example, college students within the same campus milieu experience different lived environments depending on the courses they select, the extracurricular events they engage in, and the circle of friends they cultivate. People also *create* environments that enable them to exercise better control over their lives and make them more satisfying. Gradations of environmental changeability require increasing levels of personal agency.

Among the mechanisms of human agency, none is more central or pervasive than people's beliefs in their efficacy to influence events that affect their lives. This core belief is the foundation of human motivation, performance accomplishments, and

emotional well-being. Unless people believe they can produce desired effects by their actions, they have little incentive to undertake activities or to persevere in the face of difficulties. Whatever other factors serve as guides and motivators, they are rooted in the core belief that one has the power to effect changes by one's actions.

This core belief operates through its impact on cognitive, motivational, affective, and decision-making processes (Bandura, 1997). Efficacy beliefs affect whether individuals think optimistically or pessimistically, in self-enhancing or self-debilitating ways. Such beliefs affect people's goals and aspirations, how well they motivate themselves, and their perseverance in the face of difficulties and adversity. Efficacy beliefs also shape people's outcome expectations—whether they expect their efforts to produce favorable outcomes or adverse ones. In addition, efficacy beliefs determine how opportunities and impediments are viewed. People of low efficacy are easily convinced of the futility of effort in the face of difficulties. They quickly give up trying. Those of high efficacy view impediments as surmountable by development of one's competencies and sustained effort. They stay the course in the face of difficulties and remain resilient to adversity. Moreover, efficacy beliefs affect the quality of emotional life and vulnerability to stress and depression. And last, but not least, efficacy beliefs determine the choices people make at important decision points during their lives. A factor that influences choice behavior can profoundly affect the courses lives take. This is because the social influences operating in the selected environments continue to promote certain competencies, values, and lifestyles.

The traditional psychological theories were formulated long before the advent of the advances in communication technologies such as the Internet. As a result, they focused mainly on direct experience as the primary mode of learning, based on influences operating within one's immediate physical and social environment. With today's revolutionary advances in communication technology, people are spending a major share of their waking life using the Internet and other digital technologies. Life online transcends time, distance, place, and national borders and alters our conceptions of these concepts.

Instant communication worldwide is also transforming the nature, reach, speed, and loci of human influence. It has altered the ways that people communicate, educate, work, relate to one another, and conduct their business and daily affairs. Miniature wireless devices make the vast symbolic environment portable. These evolving realities present new challenges and increased opportunities for people to influence their personal development and to shape their national life.

Wrenching changes that dislocate and restructure lives are not new in history. What is new is the vast scope and accelerated pace of human transactions and the growing globalization of human interconnectedness. These transformative changes have profound implications for a theory of human behavior. There are two basic modes of learning. People learn by experiencing the effects of their actions and through the power of social modeling. Direct experience is a tough teacher. Trial-and-error learning is not only an exceedingly tedious process but also a hazardous one when mistakes have costly or injurious consequences. Moreover, the constraints of time, resources, and mobility impose severe limits on the situations and activities that can be directly explored for the acquisition of new knowledge. Fortunately, this process is shortcut by social modeling. Humans have evolved an advanced capacity for observational learning that enables them to expand their knowledge and competencies rapidly through the information conveyed by the rich variety of social models. Indeed, virtually all types of behavioral, cognitive, and affective learning resulting from direct experience can be achieved vicariously by observing people's behavior and its consequences.

The growing importance of symbolic modeling lies in its tremendous scope and multiplicative power. Unlike learning by doing, which requires shaping the actions of each individual through repeated consequences, in vicarious learning a single model can transmit new ways of thinking and behaving simultaneously to vast populations in widely dispersed locales. The accelerated development of electronic technologies has vastly expanded the range of models to which members of society are exposed day in and day out. These electronic systems have become the dominant vehicle for disseminating symbolic environments. By drawing on these modeled patterns of thought and action, observers transcend the bounds of their immediate environments.

Functions of Social Modeling

Social modeling serves diverse functions in promoting personal and social change. In the *instructive function*, models serve as transmitters of knowledge, competencies, values, cognitive skills, and new styles of behavior. Modeled events not only portray styles of behavior but also their effects that serve as motivators. Seeing others achieve desired outcomes by their actions creates outcome expectancies that function as positive incentives. Conversely, seeing others punished for certain actions creates negative outcome expectancies that function as disincentives. At the normative level, behavioral outcomes inform observers about the reward structures and prohibitions in the social systems in which individuals operate.

People are easily aroused by the emotional expressions of others. This capacity for vicarious emotional arousal plays a key role in emotional learning. Observers can acquire lasting attitudes and emotional reactions toward persons, places, or things that have been associated with modeled emotional experiences. They learn to fear the things that frightened others, to dislike what repulsed them, and to like what gratified them.

The behavior of others also serves as social prompts that activate, channel, and support modeled styles of behavior. The types of models who predominate in a social milieu determine which human qualities are promoted from among many alternatives. The fashion and taste industries rely heavily on vicarious influence to promote their wares.

During the course of their daily lives, people have direct contact with only a small sector of their physical and social environment. Consequently, their conceptions of social reality with which they have little or no contact are greatly influenced by vicarious experiences—by what they see and hear. The more people's conceptions of reality depend upon the media's symbolic environment, the greater is the media's social impact. Much of the preceding discussion has centered on vicarious learning at the individual level. Social modeling is coming to play an increasingly influential role across cultural change. In this broader function of *social diffusion*, modeling through the mass media instructs people in new ideas and social practices. Positive and negative incentives determine which of the modeled innovations will be adopted. People are linked together by networks of social relationships. Social networks provide diffusion paths for the spread of new ideas and behavior.

Albert Bandura

See also Audience Interpretation of Media Violence, Effects of; Bobo Doll Studies; Cognitive Psychology of Violence; Developmental Effects; Social Learning From Media; Stereotyping in Violent Media Content; Televised Violence

Further Readings

Bandura, A. (1997). *Self-efficacy: The exercise of control.* New York, NY: Freeman.

Bandura, A. (2005). The evolution of social cognitive theory. In K. G. Smith & M. A. Hitt (Eds.), *Great minds in management* (pp. 9–35). Oxford, UK: Oxford University Press.

Bandura, A. (2006). Toward a psychology of human agency. *Perspectives on Psychological Science, 1,* 164–180.

Bandura, A. (2009). Social cognitive theory of mass communications. In J. Bryant & M. B. Oliver (Eds.), *Media effects: Advances in theory and research* (2nd ed., pp. 94–124). Mahwah, NJ: Erlbaum.

Giddens, A. (1984). *The constitution of society: Outline of the theory of structuration.* Berkeley: University of California Press.

Schwarzer, R. (1992). *Self-efficacy: Thought control of action.* Washington, DC: Hemisphere.

SOCIAL ISOLATION

Social isolation occurs when a person achieves less social interaction than he or she desires. Social contact is a basic human need, and the hierarchy of needs developed by psychologist Abraham Maslow requires some form of social connection at every level, particularly the "belonging" stage. However, sometimes people cannot connect with others, leading to social isolation. It is important to differentiate between the terms *social isolation* and *social exclusion,* because they are not interchangable. Professor of political science Brian Barry has distinguished these two concepts by stating that social isolation is nonparticipation in the institutions of mainstream society, while social exclusion occurs because of powers beyond an individual's control (e.g., terminal illness). Social exclusion could, in turn, lead to social isolation by greatly reducing the level of achieved social contact, which may drop below levels of desired social contact. For this reason, social exclusion is considered in this entry.

This entry first examines social isolation occurrence in relation to new media technology and video games. It then discusses the relationship between social isolation and media violence.

Social Isolation and New Media Technology

Media researchers have often been concerned with negative effects, and media technology would appear to be a culprit in social isolation, as seen in work such as that by Robert Putnam. More recent studies on new media technologies and social isolation have had mixed findings. Some research suggests that cell phones and the Internet have increased social isolation, while other research shows a decline in social isolation due to such technologies. Given the social nature of new media and its ability to connect individuals, the latter finding makes intuitive sense, although mediated networks may lead to social isolation in the physical sense and less meaningful contact.

Sora Park (2012) has discussed the ways multidimensional digital media literacy (the ability to access, understand, and create online media) is related to social exclusion. It was reported by Park that social exclusion relates mostly to the ability to create and participate in the digital world. Individuals may feel excluded if they are unable to post comments in an online forum or if they are restricted from doing so. If excluded, an individual's desired social contact could go below the achieved social contact and lead to social isolation. This social exclusion could be mitigated, though, through education and other efforts to create greater social connection. It seems that the key to eliminating social isolation in digital settings is for people to have access to technology, understand how it is used, and most important, participate.

Social Isolation and Video Games

A common notion about individuals who are deemed "video gamers" has been that they spend their time playing video games in social isolation. It may come as a surprise to some that many participants in online video games spend a lot of time socializing during play. Researchers Jeroen Jansz and Maarten Grimberg (2005) interviewed gamers who were engaging in a local area network (LAN) party and found that a common motivation to play video games is the social aspect. Participants stated that playing cooperatively or competitively with other people makes the game less predictable and more fun. Massively multiplayer online role-playing games (MMORPGs), in which a large number of players participate in a game set in a virtual world, have become extremely popular. The social interaction among gamers while playing games like *World of Warcraft* is not limited to rudimentary text—by using voice-chat programs (e.g., Teamspeak, Ventrilo, Mumble, Skype), many online gamers can engage in real-time communication while playing games. Gaming consoles such as Xbox and

PlayStation also can take advantage of the Internet, allowing people to play games online with others and communicate via a headset and microphone. Therefore, social isolation may be rarer during current video game play than it was during the early years of these games.

Social Isolation and Media Violence

Research has stated that two major sources of vulnerability to effects of violent media content are personality predispositions and social and developmental factors. In a study conducted by Michael Slater and colleagues (2004), these factors were used as moderating variables between the use of violent media and aggressiveness. For personality predispositions, a measurement for sensation seeking was used. For social and developmental factors, measurements for alienation (school, family, peers) and victimization were used. The sample consisted of 2,550 students from 20 middle schools. The results showed that participants who reported a higher sense of alienation from school also reported higher violent media use and overall aggression. However, alienation from family and peers were not significant predictors. Results also revealed that participants who reported having a higher sensation-seeking personality and were prone to victimization reported higher violent media use and overall aggression. If one feels alienated, there is a good chance that desired social contact is below achieved social contact, leading to isolation. If alienation and isolation are seen as relatively similar concepts, this study showed that alienation and isolation may result in greater violent media usage.

Researchers David Bickham and Michael Rich (2006) found that the more time children between the ages of 6 and 12 spent watching violent television, the less time they spent engaging with friends. The authors proposed that viewing violent television may lead to social isolation, which, in turn, leads to more violent program viewing. The reverse could also be happening: perhaps social isolation encourages viewing of antisocial, violent television viewing. Regardless of directionality, this relationship is clearly problematic. Because of this potential link, Bickham and Rich recommended that children's violent television viewing be limited to optimize social development and health.

Conclusion

The emergence of social media and other interactive technologies offers new opportunities to connect with others. To increase social contact through technology, however, a person must be able to create messages and communicate effectively. Without these skills, it is very possible that one's achieved social contact will plummet below his or her desired social contact, causing a sense of social isolation despite numerous tools to make contact happen. Additionally, the use of technology for communication may still lead to feelings of social isolation if people are not engaging in much in-person, face-to-face interaction. Use of passive media like television should continue to flourish, and this type of media use seems most prone to causing social isolation, given its one-way nature. The potential link between social isolation and violent behavior is worthy of continued attention.

Michael Kurtz and Paul Skalski

See also Media Education and Media Literacy; User Trends Toward Aggressive Games; Uses and Gratifications Perspective of Media Effects

Further Readings

Barry, B. (1998). *Social exclusion, social isolation and the distribution of income.* CASE Paper No. 12. London: Centre for Analysis of Social Exclusion, London School of Economics.

Bickham, D. S., & Rich, M. (2006). Is television viewing associated with social isolation? Roles of exposure time, viewing context, and violent content. *Archives of Pediatrics Adolescent Medicine, 160*(4), 387–392.

Jansz, J., & Grimberg, M. (2005). Among the LAN gamers: Men and women playing video games at a public event. *Conference Papers—International Communication Association,* 1–14.

Park, S. (2012). Dimensions of digital media literacy and the relationship with social exclusion. *Media International Australia.* August 1, 2007–Current (142), 87–100.

Slater, M. D., Henry, K. L., Swaim, R., & Cardador, J. M. (2004). Vulnerable teens, vulnerable times: How sensation seeking, alienation, and victimization moderate the violent media content–aggressiveness relation. *Communication Research, 31*(6), 642–668.

SOCIAL LEARNING FROM MEDIA

Many models showing how preschool and school-age children learn from television have focused on the learning and imitation of violent behaviors. Arousal theory focuses on the physiological response children have to viewing violent content. According to this theory, children get "pumped up" when viewing violent programming. They have to focus that energy somewhere, which results in aggressive behavior or hyperactivity. Script theory suggests that by watching aggressive television children create expectations and scripts about aggressive behaviors that guide their own behaviors over time. According to script theory, children observe and model aggressive behaviors, which then become a part of their repertoire of responses. In contrast to these two theoretical approaches, social learning approaches to children's learning from media have built on social cognitive theory, which predicts that children will imitate aggressive behaviors they see on television, especially when characters are rewarded for their behaviors. This entry explains social learning approaches to the study of how children learn from media and discusses research involving these approaches.

Albert Bandura (1989) proposed a model of imitation and learning in social cognitive theory, which argued that children's ability to learn from their social worlds involves five cognitive capabilities: symbolization, forethought, self-regulation, self-reflection, and vicarious learning. *Symbolization* occurs as children become able to think about social behavior in words and images. Children demonstrate *forethought* when they anticipate the consequences of their actions. *Self-regulation* is a child's ability to regulate his or her behavior, and *self-reflection* is a process of monitoring behavior in the context of the intended goal or action. In addition, children have to be able to *learn vicariously* through observing others being rewarded or punished for their behaviors. This capability frees children from learning only through their own actions or for being directly rewarded or punished for their behavior. According to social cognitive theory, when a child applies these five capabilities to an observation of someone's actions, observational learning is possible. Thus, it is possible to learn from a model that has no intention of teaching; exposure to the model may be sufficient.

Ethical concerns about teaching children aggression in the context of an experimental study have limited the amount of quality empirical research into social learning hypotheses involving violence in media. Much of the research into this theory was conducted in the 1960s and 1970s. In their classic 1961 study of social learning from on-screen portrayals, Bandura, Dorothea Ross, and Sheila A. Ross demonstrated delayed imitation of aggressive actions among children after they observed aggressive media. In this experiment, young children watched a video in which an adult behaved in aggressive ways toward a toy, often a Bobo Doll (e.g., punching the doll, throwing the doll). The children were then put in a playroom with a variety of toys, including the Bobo Doll or other toys from the television show. Young children who watched the aggressive actions in the video imitated the specific aggressive behavior they had observed the on-screen adult enacting on the Bobo Doll. In addition, the children behaved in novel aggressive ways toward the toy. Control groups of children who did not watch the film played less aggressively overall.

This study advanced the understanding of social learning because it demonstrated delayed imitation of aggressive actions after observing a behavior on screen. Other research has supported Bandura's results, finding that immediately after exposure to a violent television show children had higher levels of aggressive free play than children who viewed a nonviolent television program. In a 1991 meta-analysis of research examining children's learning of aggressive actions from television, Wendy Wood, Frank Wong, and Gregory Chachere examined 28 field experiments and laboratory studies in which children observed aggressive behavior and then were measured for aggressive behavior toward a person or object after the media exposure. The researchers found increases in children's and adolescents' aggressive behaviors after viewing violent media.

When considering the social factors in children's learning of violence or aggression from television, past research has suggested the importance of considering content; not all children imitate actions observed on all television shows. In a field experiment, Lynette Friedrich and Aletha Stein (1973) observed preschool children's behavior after four weeks of exposure to prosocial, aggressive, or neutral television content. Children in the aggressive content condition declined in their delay tolerance and rule obedience compared with children in the neutral content condition. In contrast, children in the prosocial content condition increased on measures of self-regulation (i.e., delay tolerance, rule obedience, task persistence) compared with children in the neutral content condition. However, the only children who increased in aggressive play were those who were higher in aggression at baseline.

More recent approaches to social learning from media have focused on children's developing relationships with on-screen characters. One way to describe these meaningful relationships has been as parasocial interactions or parasocial relationships in which children act as if they are in a two-way, personal interaction and relationship with a media character when the reality is that the relationship is only one-way, from viewer to character. Parasocial interactions, which are based on perceptions of social contingency between a character prompt (e.g., asking a question) and a child's actions, are different from parasocial relationships, which are based on meaningful social bonds that a child forms with a character. A growing body of research into young children's learning from educational media suggests that children are more likely to learn educational content from characters they like, feel similar to, and physically and verbally interact with (Calvert, Strong, Jacobs, & Conger, 2007). A prediction based on this approach related to learning aggressive behaviors from on-screen characters is that children would be most likely to imitate the aggressive behaviors of on-screen characters they like or want to be like and with whom they verbally and physically interact.

Rebekah A. Richert and Rachel M. Flynn

See also Bobo Doll Studies; Parasocial Relationships; Social Cognitive Theory

Further Readings

Bandura, A. (1989). Social cognitive theory. In R. Vasta (Ed.), *Annals of child development* (pp. 1–60). Greenwich, CT: JAI.

Bandura, A., Ross, D., & Ross, S. H. (1961). Transmission of aggression through imitation of aggressive models. *Journal of Abnormal and Social Psychology, 63*(3), 575–582.

Calvert, S. L., Strong, B. L., Jacobs, E. L., & Conger, E. E. (2007). Interaction and participation for young Hispanic and Caucasian children's learning of media content. *Media Psychology, 9*(2), 431–445.

Friedrich, L. K., & Stein, A. H. (1973). Aggressive and prosocial programs and the natural behavior of preschool children. *Monographs of the Society for Research in Child Development, 38*(4), 1–64.

Wood, W., Wong, F. Y., & Chachere, J. G. (1991). Effects of media violence on viewers' aggression in unconstrained social interaction. *Psychological Bulletin, 109*(3), 371–83.

SOCIALIZATION OF VIOLENCE IN MEDIA AND ITS EFFECTS

The socialization of media violence pertains to the role that media play in instructing both children and adults about violence in the real world and the ways that instruction normalizes violence in reality. The concern is that media violence both overestimates the amount of violence in the real world and teaches the audience that violence is an appropriate means of settling differences and obtaining goals. The extent of this influence has been under continual debate, given that several other social factors (parenting, peer influence, religious teachings, etc.) also play a part in this socialization process. Several scholars, however, have argued that media do play an important part among various socialization factors that lead to a cumulative normative belief regarding the use of violence in society. Several theories have been used to explain the process.

Cultivation Theory

One of the most discussed and researched theories pertaining to the normalization of media violence is cultivation theory (Gerbner & Gross, 1976). This theory proposes that the media serve as a central relayer of symbols and meaning in everyday life. Cultivation theory and study is at an interesting intersection, recognizing and validating the concerns from both cultural studies and quantitative studies. Specifically, cultivation theory claims that the beliefs and behaviors a person witnesses in the media become instilled within him or her over a long period of time and over repeated viewing, so that they form a basis for the person's own beliefs and behaviors. Concern has existed among researchers that the symbols being offered by mass media are capable of distorting a viewer's assumptions about the real world. George Gerbner, the chief proponent of cultivation theory, believed that violent media did not simply blindly brainwash viewers to act aggressively. Rather, violent depictions in the media planted a seed within viewers that over time and with repeated viewings grew to inform their own beliefs and behaviors. In short, one's beliefs and behaviors are cultivated, like a plant from a seed, over a long time by exposure and reinforcement from the media.

This process of cultivation is achieved through two main factors: mainstreaming and resonance.

Mainstreaming refers to the barrage of symbols that flood heavy consumers of media. For example, imagine a child or adult who watches a lot of television. As children watch more violent cartoons and action-adventure programs, they are continually exposed to violent imagery. Over time the children's personal beliefs about violence meld with the world presented in the media. *Resonance* occurs when children witness agreement between the real world and a mediated one. Perhaps they see an aggressive revenge on a school bully on the playground that matches a similar event they saw on television, or vice versa. This event now resonates within them. The mediated world and the real world have now converged to reinforce the belief that bullies must be treated with aggressive revenge.

To investigate cultivation, Gerbner began the Cultural Indicators Project, a periodic study of both television programming and people's beliefs about the world in which they live. Gerbner argued that a social construction of reality was taking place, with television as the driving force. This type of study was, of course, not without its critics. Using content analysis, survey data, and correlational studies, many critics wondered whether any definitive conclusions could be made that cultivation caused anything, especially when the process was supposed to occur over such a lengthy amount of time. Gerbner was the first to admit that the measurable, observable effect that television might have on culture was probably small, but that even a small difference could have large consequences. One of the more popular findings the Cultural Indicators Project revealed was the "mean world syndrome," an effect in which heavy viewers of violent television were more likely than light viewers to believe the world was a mean place. Even though critics found fault with the work for claiming there were significant though possibly unobservable, immeasurable results, many believed that cultivation theory was important in that it took the study of media violence effects out of the lab environment and into the working world. It is still held as a plausible explanation for the socialization and normalization of media violence.

Social Cognitive Theory

Albert Bandura's theory of social cognitive learning is another important explanation for how children and adults learn about violence in their worlds and to the media's role in that instruction. This theory states that aggression, much like any social behavior, is learned by humans either through direct experience or through observational learning. The theory argues that all behavior cannot be learned only through simple trial and error. Early radical behaviorists had suggested that behavior was learned through conditioning and through direct experience only. Behaviors were acquired because they had either been rewarded or punished. Bandura argued that if this were true, learning would be a slow, inefficient process of acquiring knowledge about the world one lives in and how to behave in that world. Bandura argued instead that, in addition to trial and error, people are able to learn by watching others' behavior and noting whether that behavior is rewarded or punished. In this manner, people can learn how to behave in certain situations even if they have never been in those situations before. If behavior is rewarded or reinforced, the viewer is more likely to perform or engage in that behavior in the future. The opposite is true if the viewer witnesses that the behavior is not effective in attaining a goal or if it is punished.

Because of imitation and reinforcement, people can develop habitually occurring types of behavior. Not only can people learn specific behavioral responses, but they can also acquire a knowledge set or a base of rules to use when interpreting, comprehending, and evaluating situations they encounter, such as conflict.

Bandura was interested in the field of learning aggression through modeling. His classic Bobo Doll studies are among the most famous in the investigation of aggression (Bandura, Ross, & Ross, 1961). These studies consisted of children imitating a film they had seen of one of Bandura's students beating up a Bobo Doll. From these studies came the concern that children imitate what they see on television. Much like Gerbner, Bandura acknowledged the importance of learning from symbols used in everyday society. Bandura believed symbols were used to understand and integrate experiences into cognitive models that helped people make future judgments and base action on those judgments. Because of Bandura's growing acknowledgement that cognitive capabilities played a part in how quickly someone learned from observed models, he would rename his theory, which started out being known as social learning theory, into social cognitive theory.

In Bandura's view, one of the most powerful providers of symbols was the media. Because one of Bandura's chief research areas was the learning of aggression, television caused him immediate concern. He believed that television showed that discord, aggression, and conflict were acceptable, successful, glamorized, and trivialized. As such, these portrayals had a higher likelihood of being learned because of their glamour and appeal. According to social cognitive theory, the probability of a behavior being learned can depend on how similar or attractive the violent character is to the viewer, how the viewer identifies with the model, and how rewarding the violent behavior is to the violent character. This may seem like it puts a heavy cognitive load on the viewer, who must continually evaluate every individual character and the consequences of his or her actions and choosing which characters to imitate; however, much of social learning occurs without the intention to learn and without recognition that learning is occurring. In this sense, the flood of violent imagery in television, video games, and other media provide ample unintentional opportunities to "learn" aggressiveness.

Television as the Forefront of the Concern

With the arrival of each new media technology usually comes the expressed concern about the influence the new technology will have on normative beliefs about violence. Concern was expressed about the impact film would have on children with the Payne Fund studies of 1928 to 1933. Social scientists warned parents about the dangers of comic books during their heyday in the 1950s. The widespread adoption of television and the ease with which one could get programming (with a simple antenna) caused a new level of concern about media violence effects. Research into the effects that television violence had on the audience increased.

In 1975 the first meta-analysis investigating the topic of media violence indicated that media violence was positively related to aggressive behavior and that even short-term exposure to media violence was enough to lead to increases in aggressive behavior. A later meta-analysis found exposure to violent television is significantly correlated with aggressiveness and antisocial behavior. Concern over violence on television spawned two major studies of the topic: the Surgeon General's Scientific Advisory Committee on Television and Social Behavior and the National Television Violence Study (NTVS). The findings of both were similar: viewing violence increases the likelihood that viewers will, under certain conditions, behave aggressively. Both studies stressed that "under certain conditions" was the key

phrase. There was no grand effect, such as a hypodermic needle or magic bullet effect, which had been debated around the time of the Payne studies. This served to bolster the limited effects model that was developed in the late 1950s and early 1960s.

Video Games: The Latest Concern

The debate concerning media violence has recently shifted its focus from television to video games. Many researchers believe that playing violent video games should have an equal if not greater impact on children's aggression than television. This belief is held because of the differing characteristics inherent in both media. Although television has traditionally been considered to be more of a passive medium, the interactive and proactive nature of video games makes them more of a concern regarding the impact of violence. The interactive nature of video games allows the player to be rewarded for his or her aggressive action, fostering pro-violent attitudes and portraying the violence in a justified and entertaining light. In addition, the interactive nature of video games may allow the player to identify more easily with the video game character than television would allow. Past research has shown that identifying with a violent game character increases the effect of media violence (Williams, 2011). Players feel more identification with characters because they are controlling their actions and are responsible for the characters' next moves. Still, the results of video game research are not nearly as compelling as the research on television's effects. In one of the first meta-analyses of research on video games' contribution to violence, Craig Anderson and Brad Bushman (2001) found 35 research reports that included 54 independent samples of participants. These scholars concluded that violent video games do influence a player's aggressive thoughts, emotions, and behavior. Detractors have claimed that these past meta-analyses are not valid because of citation bias, improper analysis techniques, and misleading statistics. With the popularity of home video game systems increasing, even more discussion has arisen regarding harmful effects of video game violence on children.

In conclusion, the impact of the media socializing and normalizing violence in the real world is a hotly contested debate, but there is ample evidence to point to its impact on the short-term learning of aggression. Theories such as cultivation theory and social cognitive theory can give us windows into how this works. Its long-term lasting effects and whether it spurs actual violent behavior in society are not as clear. However, it is hard to imagine that the barrage of violent imagery in the media is not teaching some relevant information to today's audience.

Kevin D. Williams

See also Cultivation Theory; Effects From Violent Media, Short- and Long-Term; Media Effects Perspectives of Violence; Methodologies for Assessing Effects of Media; National Television Violence Study; Social Cognitive Theory; Television Violence; Video Game Player and Opponent Effects

Further Readings

Anderson, C. A., & Bushman, B. J. (2001). Effects of violent video games on aggressive behavior, aggressive cognition, aggressive affect, physiological arousal, and prosocial behavior: A meta-analytic review of the scientific literature. *Psychological Science, 12,* 353–359.

Anderson, C. A., & Dill, K. E. (2000). Video games and aggressive thoughts, feelings, and behavior in the laboratory and in life. *Journal of Personality and Social Psychology, 78,* 772–790.

Bandura, A. (1977). *Social learning theory.* Englewood Cliffs, NJ: Prentice-Hall.

Bandura, A. (2001). Social cognitive theory of mass communication. *Media Psychology, 3,* 265–299.

Bandura, A., Ross, D., & Ross, S. A. (1961). Transmission of aggression through imitation of aggressive models. *Journal of Abnormal and Social Psychology, 63,* 575–582.

Bushman, B. J., & Anderson, C. A. (2002, December). Violent video games and hostile expectations: A test of the general aggression model. *Personality and Social Psychology Bulletin, 28*(12), 1679–1686.

Ferguson, C. J., & Kilburn, J. (2009). The public health risks of media violence: A meta-analytic review. *Journal of Pediatrics, 154,* 759–763.

Gerbner, G., & Gross, L. (1976). Living with television: The violence profile. *Journal of Communication, 26,* 173–199.

Gerbner, G., Gross, L., Morgan, M., & Signorielli, N. (1980). The "mainstreaming" of America: Violence profile no. 11. *Journal of Communication, 30*(3), 10–29.

Kelly, P. T. (Ed.). (1999). *Television violence: A guide to the literature* (2nd ed.) Commack, NY: Nova Science Publishers.

Paik, H., & Comstock, G. (1994). The effects of television violence on antisocial behavior: A meta-analysis. *Communication Research, 21,* 516–546.

Sherry, J. L. (2001, July). The effects of violent video games on aggression: A meta-analysis. *Human Communication Research, 27*(3), 409–431.

Sparks, G. G. (2002). A brief history of media effects research. In *Media effects research: A basic overview* (pp. 39–56). Belmont, CA: Wadsworth/Thomson Learning.

Williams, K. D. (2011). The effects of homophily, identification, and violent video games on players. *Mass Communication and Society, 14,* 3–24.

SPORTS, VIOLENCE AND AGGRESSION IN

Sporting events are both widely available and highly popular contributors to the incidence of violence and aggression in media content. This entry reviews social science research for definitions and prevalence of sports violence and aggression in the media, their relationship to sports media consumption, and their effects on the audience.

Definitions of Sports Media Violence

Sports are defined here as activities labeled as sport by media organizations, including basketball, baseball, golf, tennis, motor sports, and Olympic sports. High-contact sports, including football (American and Australian), hockey, wrestling, boxing, rugby, and soccer, have been singled out in scholarly research on sports media violence. Sports media violence is included in media coverage of sporting events but excludes entertainment content featuring sports stories, such as sports-themed television shows, because the latter are covered in standard accounts of media violence. Although studies of live sports venues have arguably been "unmediated," selected studies of live sports that typically receive media coverage are included in this entry to fill gaps in media violence research.

Definitions of violence and aggression are as controversial within the sports media domain as they are elsewhere in media violence scholarship. *Aggression* can be defined as behavior that is harmful or irritating to another, while *violence* is aggression that involves physical as opposed to merely psychological harm. Aggression is usually not considered problematic in the literature of sport; rather, it is a socially sanctioned, inherent part of competition and a desirable quality for athletes. In the sports literature, *violence* is typically defined as harmful behavior that violates the official, but in some definitions also the informal, rules of the game. The intent to cause harm is often, but not always, included. Levels of sports violence can be categorized to distinguish significant body contact within the rules of the game (such as brutal football tackles) from that which violates the rules but is widely accepted (e.g., hockey fights), from that which is both penalized and unacceptable (e.g., attacking an opponent with a baseball bat), and that which is criminal in nature.

Intent is difficult to infer on the basis of observed behavior alone, a problem for sports officials as well as academic researchers. Differences between two influential content analysis projects (that excluded sports coverage) highlight the issue. The National Television Violence Study defined violence as the use or threat of physical force intended to physically harm another. "Physical aggression" was used interchangeably with "violence" to the exclusion of verbal aggression (aside from threats), although other violence definitions (and also the penalty rules of certain sports, described following) do include verbal aggression. The earlier national violence profile studies by George Gerbner and colleagues made no reference to intent or physical harm, defining violence as an overt expression of physical force or use of same to compel or threaten another. Unlike most sports-related definitions, the legality of the behavior is not found in either definition, although the NTVS identifies justification as a risk factor that overlaps with the concept of legality.

Penalty rules define behaviors that violate the rules of the game. In American-style professional football, penalties are assessed for actions that qualify as violence under most definitions. These include unnecessary roughness and unsportsmanlike conduct, such as forceful contact with opponents after they have moved out of bounds and the exchange of blows between players. Aggressive actions with high risks of harm, such as contact with players while in the acts of throwing or kicking the ball, grasping the opponent's face mask, or "spearing" him with a helmet, are also penalized. Other penalties are awarded for actions that are aggressive without necessarily being violent in that they are unlikely to cause serious physical harm: the use of physical force to restrain an opponent ("holding"), jumping on the legs of an opponent who is not in possession of the football from behind ("clipping"), and verbal and gestural aggression ("taunting"). In professional soccer many of the legal aggressive behaviors of the American gridiron, including tackling, pushing,

charging, or jumping on an opponent, are all fouls, as are kicking, tripping, or striking another player, which both sports penalize. Aggression in the form of offensive language or gesture is also subject to penalty. The National Basketball Association (NBA) assesses personal fouls for offenses similar to those of soccer and also for the use of hands to impede an opponent. Flagrant fouls involve hard contact and a follow-through motion that might signal intent. Technical fouls cover unsportsmanlike conduct. The National Hockey League (NHL) has a major penalty category that includes fighting or forcing opposing players to crash into the barriers that surround the ice, with additional penalties if the actions are judged to intentionally cause injury. The NHL's minor penalty category includes hitting opposing players with one's hockey stick or employing it to block the opponent.

Intent is called out only in NHL rules but is implicit in unsportsmanlike conduct penalties in other sports. Intent may not always be evident to officials, however. The New Orleans Saints NFL team engaged in a "pay for pain" policy, in which players received financial incentives for causing injuries, during the 2011 season. An analysis by the Reuters news service found that another team had more violent defensive penalties (e.g., roughing penalties) than the Saints during that year. Admissions by NFL stars such as Jack "Assassin" Tatum reveal that intentional harm that escapes penalty has long been part of that game. In one infamous incident, Tatum administered a "hit" that paralyzed his opponent. The tackle was legal within the rules of football at the time, although the rules were subsequently changed to prohibit it. So it is possible that referees do not always detect intent to injure opponents when it is present. Direct behavioral observation is gaining acceptance in sport psychology research to resolve the problems of definition and inconsistency among sports when using penalty data to measure aggression. However, sports lack the dramatic context found in entertainment content that might allow observers, including referees and audiences as well as media scholars, to reliably gauge the intent behind overt expressions of physical force.

A further problem with intent is that athletes are trained to respond instantly and spontaneously to behavioral cues of the opposition with reaction times so short that they do not allow for the formation of conscious intentions. Must the harm and intent reside in specific interactions among players? Recent research on the long-term health effects of routine, legal collisions in sport (e.g., chronic traumatic encephalopathy, CTE) suggest that serious harm is associated with behaviors that are permitted within the rules of the game and without reference to any specific aggressive interaction. So-called hostile or noninstrumental aggression leading to impulsive physical aggression might also be performed without specific conscious intentions. Thus, although individual aggressive acts may not be subject to an intent to harm, athletes could be said to tacitly form an intention to engage in them when they subject themselves to the training regimens of their sports.

What constitutes physical harm? Does it include fleeting pain or bruising, or only bleeding and broken bones? Are hockey fights nonviolent because the blows fall on heavily padded bodies? Are professional wrestling matches nonviolent because the mayhem is staged and opponents make no effort to avoid it, a requirement of some definitions of violence? The NTVS coding assesses higher risk levels for physical aggression that does not produce serious harm, and "normal" physical aggression that does not draw a penalty in American football might be assigned higher risk than that which is penalized.

Prevalence of Sports Media Violence

According to Nielsen Media Research, sports account for more than 42,000 hours a year of broadcast television coverage and more than 463 million video streams a month in the United States alone. Broadcasts of major events, such as American football's Super Bowl game and international soccer matches, rank among the most popular in their respective home countries.

The prevalence of violence depends upon the definition used. When defining sports violence in terms of penalties for rules violations, the rates of violence in professional sports are low compared with the NTVS, which found an average of more than six violent incidents per hour in entertainment programs. The median incidence of violent defensive penalties in the NFL is .8 per 100 plays, and there are about 120 plays per game, so two teams each with median levels of violence can be expected to commit between one and two violent acts per game. Even counting all penalties as violent incidents, or at least examples of physical aggression outside the rules, the rate is about four per hour during a 3-hour broadcast. Similar calculations for the NHL yield less than one major penalty and seven minor penalties during the course of games that last

two-and-a-quarter hours. Counting all fouls as violent, NBA basketball is the most violent major sport; there are about 40 personal fouls in each two-and-a-half-hour contest, but flagrant fouls occur in fewer than 1 game out of 20.

Using the NTVS coding, Ron Tamborini and colleagues found that professional wrestling had more than double the rate of violent interactions of entertainment television programs. However, if mandatory violence required by the rules of the sport is excluded, there is about one fewer violent interaction per hour compared with other programs. Professional wrestling is more likely than other genres to include multiple violent acts in each interaction, and the violence depicted is high risk in that attractive role models perform violence that is unpunished, is justified, and does not result in extreme harm. The dramatic context of professional wrestling provides cues about intent and risk factors that are typically not present in other sports, however. If instead the conceptual definition found in the violence profile studies is applied to the NFL, the incidence could rise to dozens per play, with each act of blocking or tackling a separate overt expression of physical force, and mount into the thousands per game. Counting each play as a separate scene of crowd violence yields more than 40 episodes of violence per hour, not including replays, which selectively feature rough action.

Does Violence Cause Media Sports?

The audiences that sports attract are a major source of revenue for the media and for sports leagues. To the extent that violence attracts those audiences, it can be said that violence supports the continued existence of media sports and affects the way they are played and displayed.

There has been substantial evidence that violence enhances audience enjoyment of sports media, although other factors, such as the desire to share in the victory of a favorite team or player, are perhaps more salient. Experimental and correlational studies have found that levels of violence, roughness, and aggression in sports coverage are directly related to audience enjoyment, especially among males. Commentary provided by announcers that enhances the perceived aggressiveness of the action increases enjoyment compared with that experienced in experimental conditions in which aggression is not emphasized, even for a sport not known for violent behavior (e.g., tennis). The unpredictability of the violence and a desirable outcome to the contest enhance enjoyment.

Theoretical explanations of audience enjoyment of sports violence include cathartic purging of hostile feelings, indulging feelings of dominance through sports heroes, and enjoyment of competitive drama. More generally, the appeal of sports depends on identification with teams or players, the desirability of the outcome of the contest relative to team identification, the suspense of the game, and quality of play in terms of its novelty, riskiness, and effectiveness. Other general sports audience motivations may be affected by violent content, including arousal and excitement, the opportunity to elevate self-esteem by basking in the reflected glory of a team's victory, and relief from daily stress. Broader theories of media attendance are also applicable, including uses and gratifications, mood management theory, and selective exposure.

Do Sports Media Cause Violence?

There has been mixed evidence of the effects of sports media violence on aggression. A longitudinal study by Monroe Lefkowitz and colleagues found evidence of a causal relationship between viewing of contact sports and aggression among girls, although not among boys. Gordon Russell and colleagues (1988) conducted the only known controlled experimental study of the effects of sports violence. An experimental condition in which a video depicting hockey action, including fights, was compared with one in which the fights were edited out produced higher aggressive moods in the violent media group, regardless of whether the participants were previously angered, although retaliatory aggression was affected in that way only when participants were angered. Unexpectedly, those viewing the nonviolent film containing aggressive acts that are a normal part of the sport exhibited *less* aggressive mood but *more* retaliatory aggression than those in a no-film control condition in which subjects worked on a jigsaw puzzle. Viewership of professional wrestling is positively related to the frequency of engaging in fights in high school and to dating violence, with women more affected than men. Field experiments in live athletic venues have offered evidence that exposure to aggressive sports spectacles increases aggression and hostility among spectators compared with those who attended engaging, nonviolent events, and that violent behavior has an incremental effect over normally aggressive play. However, those who are naturally aggressive or who are induced to harbor aggressive thoughts also were more likely to select violent sports content than others, so bidirectional causation is likely.

Among groups that might be especially sensitive to exposure to violent sport stimuli, male sports fans stay in bad moods and avoid their families longer after witnessing a loss compared with non-fans. The former is a risk factor for violence, while the latter can be interpreted as an attempt to restore control over one's behavior. Young athletes who have aggressive sports heroes also tend to play aggressively themselves and report learning techniques from media sports coverage that allow them to engage in sports violence undetected. Male participants in highly violent sports such as football and wrestling are more likely to participate in serious fights than nonathletic males or those involved in less violent sports.

At the aggregate level, crime rates climb immediately after a local team loses an important game, and homicides increase in the week following the elimination of the local football team from playoffs and after televised heavyweight boxing matches. There is mixed evidence of impacts on domestic violence, with some studies showing substantial increases in hospital admissions and police reports of domestic violence after football games, and others showing little or none. Contrary to the "sports widow" stereotype, there is little evidence that dedicated sports viewing disrupts relationships, and some that indicates strengthening of relationships. Other positive effects have been found: in a study of 30 U.S. cities, it was found that homicide and suicide rates declined in years in which local major sports teams made the playoffs, although when local teams won championships only suicide rates declined. The extant aggregate studies have not assessed the levels of violence, limiting the inferences about causation that can be drawn from them. However, a study of soccer hooliganism found that aggressiveness, defined by the penalties awarded during live matches, was a significant predictor of fan violence.

Theories of the effects of violent sports media include aggressive cue theory, social learning theory, and other elements that have been integrated into the general aggression model. Catharsis theory has often been discussed in contemporary sports media research but has always been dismissed for lack of supporting evidence.

In summary, sports media violence in high-contact sports such as football, hockey, wrestling, and soccer has been found to be either very rare or highly prevalent, depending very much on how violence is defined. The role of intent, the legality of the behavior within the rules of the game, and the seriousness of harm caused present thorny definitional issues. There is evidence that violence increases the appeal of sporting events covered by the media, although other motivational factors may be more important. Evidence of the effects of sports media violence has come from a handful of controlled studies that have produced conflicting and even puzzling results and from analyses of aggregate violence statistics that have not controlled for the amount of violence present in sports coverage.

Robert LaRose

See also Aggression, Definition and Assessment of; Catharsis Theory; General Aggression Model; Media Effects Perspectives of Violence; National Television Violence Study; Television Violence; Realism of Violent Content, Real-World Violence on Television, and Their Effects; Uses and Gratifications Perspective of Media Effects; Violence, Definition of

Further Readings

Bryant, J., & Raney, A. A. (2000). Sports on the screen. In D. Zillmann & P. Vorderer (Eds.), *Media entertainment* (pp. 153–174). Mahwah, NJ: Erlbaum.

Bryant, J., Zillmann, D., & Raney, A. A. (1998). Violence and the enjoyment of media sports. In L. A. Wenner (Ed.), *MediaSport* (pp. 252–265). New York: Routledge.

Gee, C. J. (2011). Aggression in competitive sports: Using direct observation to evaluate incidence and prevention focused intervention. In J. K. Luiselli & D. D. Reed (Eds.), *Behavioral sport psychology* (pp. 199–210). New York: Springer.

Guttmann, A. (1998). The appeal of violent sports. In J. Goldstein (Ed.), *Why we watch: The attractions of violent entertainment* (pp. 7–26). New York, NY: Oxford University Press.

Nielsen. (2012). *State of the media: 2011 year in sports.* Retrieved from http://nielsen.com/content/dam/corporate/us/en/reports-downloads/2012-Reports/state-of-the-media-year-in-sports-2011.pdf

Raney, A. A. (2006). Why we watch and enjoy mediated sports. In A. A. Raney & J. Bryant (Eds.), *Handbook of sports and media* (pp. 313–329). Mahwah, NJ: Erlbaum

Reuters. (2012). *Most offensive defenses.* Retrieved from http://static.reuters.com/resources/media/global/editorial/interactives/the-nfl-violence/nfl-charts.html

Russell, G. W. (2008). *Aggression in the sports world: A social psychological perspective.* New York, NY: Oxford University Press.

Russell, G., Di Lullo, S., & Di Lullo, D. (1988). Effects of observing competitive and violent versions of a sport. *Current Psychology, 7*(4), 312–321.

See no evil? Fouls, cards, and referees in major league soccer. (2011). Retrieved from http://www.soccerbythenumbers.com/2011/04/refs-in-mls-fouls-cards-and-connection.html

Smith, M. (2003). What is sports violence? In J. Boxill (Ed.), *Sports ethics: An anthology* (pp. 199–216). Malden, MA: Blackwell.

Tamborini, R., Skalski, P., Lachlan, K., Westerman, D., Davis, J., & Smith, S. L. (2005). The raw nature of televised professional wrestling: Is the violence a cause for concern? *Journal of Broadcasting & Electronic Media, 49*(2), 202–220.

Wenner, L. A., & Gantz, W. (1998). Watching sports on television: Audience experience, gender, fanship, and marriage. In L. A. Wenner (Ed.), *MediaSport* (pp. 233–251). New York, NY: Routledge.

Whannel, G. (2000). Sport and the media. In J. Coakley & E. Dunning (Eds.), *Handbook of sports studies* (pp. 292–310). London, UK: Sage.

STEREOTYPING IN VIOLENT MEDIA CONTENT

The prevalence and nature of depictions of race and ethnicity in violent media content have raised questions about both the ethics and impact of these images. The same can be said for media that intersect violence with gender stereotypes. Because media effects are (in part) a reflection of the specific features of media messages, understanding these images is critical. In an effort to determine the existence (or lack thereof) of stereotypes in violent media content, a growing (but limited) number of quantitative content analyses have been conducted.

Portrayals of African Americans

The lion's share of the content analytic research on stereotypes in media has focused on depictions of Blacks. In contemporary primetime television programming, African Americans are portrayed at a rate equivalent to or above their proportion of the U.S. population. In this programming, Blacks are seen in a variety of roles. Thus, most researchers agree that in primetime television, African Americans have achieved parity. The same cannot be said for television news.

In news coverage, African Americans are presented in an altogether more unfavorable light than on primetime television. A number of scholars, most notably Robert Entman and Travis Dixon, have devoted considerable attention to documenting portrayals of Blacks in the news. This body of work indicated that although Whites appear with relatively equal frequency in news stories unrelated to crime, Black Americans are seen at nearly twice the rate as Whites when the topic is crime (also see research by Dan Romer). In these news stories, African Americans are more likely to be depicted as crime perpetrators or suspects. They are often presented in a threatening manner and handcuffed (or restrained). In addition, prejudicial information such as prior arrests is more likely to be reported when the suspect is a Black American versus a White American.

In addition, African Americans' rate of representation as criminals in the news exceeds data from real-world arrest reports. In other words, Blacks are over-represented as criminals on absolute (i.e., compared with Department of Justice statistics) and comparative (i.e., versus Whites in the news) bases. It should be noted that the same pattern of over-representation emerges with images of African American youths in the news. Moreover, when compared with Whites, African Americans are under-represented as victims. However, this rate is in proportion with real-world crime data.

As Franklin Gilliam and colleagues (1996) have observed, today's news coverage of crime can be characterized by its violence and by the non-White nature of the depicted suspects. Crime news accounts for one-fourth of news coverage in local TV news broadcasts. Nearly 80% of this coverage is focused on violent crime, and more than one-fourth is focused on coverage of murder (rates that are grossly disproportionate with Department of Justice statistics). Moreover, Blacks are under-represented as nonviolent criminals and over-represented as violent criminals in these stories.

Portrayals of Latinos

Although research by Dana Mastro has indicated that representations of Latinos on primetime television are not dominated by images of violent crime, her work has also revealed that Latinos are found predominantly on crime dramas, where they are depicted as the most volatile characters on television (and, unsurprisingly, discussing issues associated with crime and criminality). According to Dixon and colleagues, Latinos (like their Black counterparts) are portrayed as crime perpetrators on television news

more frequently than are Whites. However, this rate of representation is below real-world arrest figures. A comparable pattern emerges for depictions of Latino youths on television news. Although Latino youths are seen as perpetrators more frequently than are Whites, this proportion is below real-world crime reports. However, when represented as victims on the news, Latinos are seen at a rate below both their White counterparts and real-world Department of Justice statistics. Dixon's work (along with collaborators) also demonstrated that the content of crime-related news varies depending on the ethnicity of the perpetrator. Consistent with his findings regarding African Americans, prejudicial information (such as an existing arrest record) is more likely to be reported in news coverage with Latino defendants (as opposed to White suspects), particularly when the case involves a White victim.

Little or no attention has been devoted to documenting depictions of other racial/ethnic groups in violent media content. This is likely because so few images of other racial or ethnic groups exist in mass media fare, restricting systematic analyses of these characterizations.

Portrayals of Women

Research exploring stereotypes associated with women in media has indicated that themes of women as (a) victims of violence and (b) objects of sexual aggression and/or rape are two dominant characterizations. As Julia Wood (2011) has noted, these stereotypes serve to normalize violence against women, promote acceptance of violence in one's own relationships, glamorize masculinity, and (more generally) discourage objections to violence against women in society. Not only do these stereotypes persist in traditional media such as film, but they are additionally persistent in new media and new technologies such as video games. In fact, an analysis of violence and gender role portrayals in video games by Tray Dietz (1998) indicated that more than 20% of popular video games depicted violence directed specifically at women.

Why Understanding Stereotypes in Violence Is Important

Most research on the effects of exposure to stereotypes in the media has concluded that viewing such content contributes to (a) the construction of social perceptions about the stereotyped groups and (b) the use of these generalizations in later judgment and behaviors. Accordingly, the importance of such representations should not be trivialized, particularly in light of research by scholars such as Jennifer Eberhardt and Mary Beth Oliver that revealed that people tend to associate stereotypically Black physical traits with criminality and that Whites are more likely to misidentify Blacks (versus Whites) as violent criminal suspects. Similarly, work by Patricia Devine and colleagues revealed that Whites continue to identify aggression, violence, and criminal activity as typical attributes of Blacks. Given evidence from survey and experimental studies of media exposure to race and crime, it is safe to conclude that media use is implicated in such perceptions. And, as research on media and stereotyping (in particular research by Mark Peffley and colleagues) has revealed, these stereotypes become self-perpetuating and self-reinforcing.

Dana Mastro

See also African Americans in Media, Character Depictions and Social Representations of; Gender Stereotypes, Societal Influence on; Latinos in Media, Character Depictions and Social Representations of; Media Effects Perspectives of Violence; National Television Violence Study; News, the Presentation and Effects of Violent Content in; Realism of Violent Content, Real-World Violence on Television, and Their Effects; Social Cognitive Theory; Social Learning From Media; Television Violence

Further Readings

Devine, P. G. (1989). Stereotypes and prejudice: Their automatic and controlled components. *Journal of Personality and Social Psychology, 56*(1), 5–18.

Devine, P. G., & Baker, S. M. (1991). Measurement of racial stereotype subtyping. *Personality and Social Psychology Bulletin, 17,* 44–50.

Devine, P. G., & Elliot, A. J. (1995). Are racial stereotypes really fading? The Princeton trilogy revisited. *Personality and Social Psychology Bulletin, 21,* 1139–1150.

Dietz, T. (1998). An examination of violence and gender role portrayals in video games: Implications for gender socialization and aggressive behavior. *Sex Roles, 38,* 425–442.

Dixon, T., Azocar, C., & Casas, M. (2003). The portrayal of race and crime on television network news. *Journal of Broadcasting & Electronic Media, 47,* 498–523.

Dixon, T., & Linz, D. (2000). Overrepresentation and underrepresentation of African Americans and Latinos as lawbreakers on television news. *Journal of Communication, 50,* 131–154.

Dixon, T., & Linz, D. (2002). Television news, prejudicial pretrial publicity, and the depiction of race. *Journal of Broadcasting & Electronic Media, 46,* 112–136.

Dixon, T., & Maddox, K. (2005). Skin tone, crime news, and social reality judgments: Priming the stereotype of the dark and dangerous Black criminal. *Journal of Applied Social Psychology, 35,* 1555–1570.

Eberhardt, J. L., Davies, P. G., Purdie-Vaughns, V. J., & Johnson, S. (2006). Looking deathworthy: Perceived stereotypicality of Black defendants predicts capital-sentencing outcomes. *Psychological Science, 17*(5), 383–386.

Eberhardt, J. L., Goff, P. A., Purdie, V. J., & Davies, P. G. (2004). Seeing Black: Race, crime, and visual processing. *Journal of Personality and Social Psychology, 87*(6), 876–893.

Entman, R. (1992). Blacks in the news: Television, modern racism and cultural change. *Journalism Quarterly, 69,* 341–361.

Gilliam, F., Iyengar, S., Simon, A., & Wright, O. (1996). Crime in Black and White: The violent scary world of local news. *Harvard International Journal of Press and Politics, 1,* 6–23.

Mastro, D. (2009). Effects of racial and ethnic stereotyping. In J. Bryant & M. B. Oliver (Eds.), *Media effects: Advances in theory and research* (3rd ed., pp. 325–341). Hillsdale, NJ: Erlbaum.

Mastro, D., & Behm-Morawitz, E. (2005). Latino representation on primetime television. *Journalism & Mass Communication Quarterly, 82,* 110–130.

Oliver, M. B., & Fonash, D. (2002). Race and crime in the news: Whites' identification and misidentification of violent and nonviolent criminal suspects. *Media Psychology, 4,* 137–156.

Peffley, M., Shields, T., & Williams, B. (1996). The intersection of race and crime in television news stories: An experimental study. *Political Communication, 13,* 309–327.

Romer, D., Jamieson, K., & DeCoteau, N. (1998). The treatment of persons of color in local television news: Ethnic blame discourse or realistic group conflict. *Communication Research, 25,* 286–305.

Wood, J. (2011).Gendered media. In J. Wood (Ed.), *Gendered lives: Communication, gender, and culture* (pp. 255–284). Boston: Wadsworth.

Television Violence

No matter which media effects theory serves to explain whether and how television viewing affects society, the analysis centers on the nature of the content being consumed. Of all the images made available through television that have caused public outcry, advocacy group activity, government attention, industry self-regulation, and social science investigation, the portrayal of violence has received the lion's share of attention. At issue are the effects of cumulative exposure to these images on young and vulnerable consumers' attitudes, values, and behavior. Potential effects include the instigation of imitative aggressive acts, inspiration for the performance of novel acts of aggression, a decreased sensitivity to violence and a greater willingness to tolerate increasing levels of violence in society, and the effect on perceptions of the world's "meanness" and a resultant fear of violence in one's immediate community. This entry presents a brief overview of the primary issues associated with television violence.

Recognizing the Issue

With the development of each modern means of storytelling, there have been debates about its impact on society. A prominent theme in these debates has been a concern about the adverse influences of specific types of content on a young and vulnerable audience. In ancient Greece, for example, Plato's *Republic* declared that children cannot distinguish between what is allegory and what isn't, and that

it is of the utmost importance that the first stories they hear should produce the right moral effect. It was not until the advent of broadcasting, however, that the amount and intensity of debate and concern reached new heights.

Although network television's nationwide reach and extended broadcast schedule did not begin until the late 1940s, and televised violence was not as graphic as it would become in later years, concerns about the social impact of television violence were raised almost immediately. As early as 1952, the U.S. House of Representatives held hearings in response to television's unprecedented prevalence and popularity and concluded that the television broadcast industry was a "perpetrator and a deliverer" of violent content. This set into motion a sporadic stream of government hearings that at first attempted to determine the effects of the introduction of television into the home and then addressed questions specific to violent content.

The Kefauver Committee on Juvenile Delinquency (1954) questioned the need for violent content in television entertainment. The Dodd Hearings (1961) called for academic and industry research to explore the possible ramifications of excessive consumption of television in general and a steady diet of violent content in particular. The Senate Subcommittee on Juvenile Delinquency (1964) was particularly critical of the television networks and the extent to which violence and crime were portrayed on the nation's airwaves. The National Commission on the Causes and Prevention of Violence (1968) concluded that there was a great deal of violence on television and that such content probably had an adverse effect on children. Many of these hearings recommended federal regulation of the airwaves, but this raised concerns about violations to the First Amendment to the U.S. Constitution. The hearings also recommended that the television industry do self-monitoring research, which went largely ignored, and encouraged independent investigation by the academic community.

Television and the Child: An Empirical Study of the Effect of Television on the Young (1958), by London School of Economics and Political Science scholars Hilde Himmelweit, Abraham Naftali Oppenheim, and Pamela Vince, and *Television in the Lives of Our Children* (1961), by Stanford University scholars Wilbur Schramm, Jack Lyle, and Edwin B. Parker, brought the issue of television's impact to the forefront of the academic community. These studies provided important benchmarks for understanding the potential effects of television, although this generation of children's television-viewing habits and practices were still under development. In particular, the studies examined the possibility that certain types of television content stimulated the formation of negative attitudes or induced antisocial behavior, and set the research agenda for social scientists for the next few decades.

Newly assigned Federal Communications Commission chair Newton Minow put the industry on notice and reinforced this research agenda in his May 9, 1961, address to the National Association of Broadcasters in Washington, D.C. He claimed:

> When television is good, nothing—not the theater, not the magazines or newspaper—nothing is better. But when television is bad, nothing is worse. I invite each of you to sit down in front of your television set when your station goes on the air and stay there, for a day, without a book, without a magazine, without a newspaper, without a profit and loss sheet or a rating book to distract you. Keep your eyes glued to that set until the station signs off. I can assure you that what you will observe is a vast wasteland.

An article in the October 22, 1963, issue of *Look* magazine, entitled "What TV Violence Can Do to Your Child," featured Stanford behavioral psychologist Albert Bandura's groundbreaking work on children's potential for imitation. The article began:

> If parents could buy packaged psychological influences to administer in regular doses to their children, I doubt that many would deliberately select Western gun slingers, hopped-up psychopaths, deranged sadists, slap-stick buffoons and the like, unless they entertained rather peculiar ambitions for their growing offspring. Yet such examples of behavior are delivered in quantity, with no direct charge, to millions of households daily. (p. 46)

This article singlehandedly made the television violence issue a vivid reality for the parents among the magazine's national readership and placed it on the forefront of public discourse.

As the 1960s progressed, concern in the United States about violence in the streets of its cities and the assassinations of President John F. Kennedy, Martin Luther King, Jr., and Senator Robert Kennedy (D-N.Y.) stimulated continuing interest in televised violence. In 1969, the U.S. surgeon general was given the task of exploring evidence of a link between television and subsequent aggression. The conclusions of the final report in 1972 were equivocal, although the report noted that television violence was a contributing factor to increases in violent crime and antisocial behavior. In 1982 the National Institute of Mental Health published a 10-year follow-up of the 1972 surgeon general's study. The two-volume report, collectively titled *Television and Behavior: Ten Years of Scientific Progress and Implications for the Eighties,* stated that the consensus among most of the research community was that violence on television does lead to aggressive behavior by children and teenagers who watch the programs.

Defining the Threat

In 1967, in the immediate aftermath of early government hearings and public outcry about violence on the airwaves, George Gerbner and colleagues at the Annenberg School of Communication at the University of Pennsylvania sought to define and quantify the nature of televised violence. They founded the Cultural Indicators Research Project, which tracked and catalogued the content of television programs and surveyed viewers to record the relationship between this content and viewers' perceptions. *Violence* was defined as the overt expression of physical force against oneself or another, compelling action against one's will of being hurt or killed, or actually hurting or killing. In order to be recorded as a violent act, that act must be plausible and credible—that is, no idle threats, verbal abuse, or comic gestures without credible violent consequences were counted. The violent acts may be intentional or accidental, so violent accidents and acts of nature were included. The content analysis measured "prevalence" (the proportion of television hours or programs that contain violence), "rate" (the proportion of violent episodes per television hour or program), and "roles" (the percentage of victims, of violent characters or killers, and of killed characters in the population of television programming).

Gerbner's annual "violence index" revealed that the percentage of programs containing violence and the rate of violent acts had remained a remarkably consistent staple in network television programming over several decades. On average, one hour of Saturday morning children's programming contained five times as many violent acts as did the equivalent amount of primetime television programming. The average child watching an average amount of television, suggested these reports, will see about 20,000 murders and 80,000 assaults in his or her formative years.

The survey portion of this project suggested that heavy viewers of this content are much more fearful of the world around them than are lighter viewers. When questioned about their perceptions of risk, heavy viewers were much more likely to overestimate the chance that they will be the victims of crime in the ensuing six months, had taken greater precautions by changing the security of their homes or restricting their travels at night, and were generally more fearful of the world than were lighter viewers. Gerbner concluded that long-term exposure to television, in which frequent violence is virtually inescapable, tends to cultivate the image of a relatively mean and dangerous world.

Bradley Greenberg and his team of scholars at Michigan State University conducted their own extensive analysis of violent television content, beginning in the 1975, as part of project CASTLE (Children and Social Television Learning). The initiative was to examine a fuller range of antisocial behaviors associated with televised violence than that of the Gerbner research. *Antisocial behavior* was conceptualized as that which is psychologically or physically injurious to another person or persons whether intended or not, and whether successful or not. This included physical aggression, verbal aggression, theft, and deceit. Findings revealed that the prevalence of verbal aggression on television was consistent with the prevalence of physical aggression, and that Saturday morning programming geared for children was significantly more violent in both regards than that of adult-oriented primetime and late-night

programming. Follow-up research found that heavy television-violence viewers were more likely to choose physical and verbal aggressive responses to solve hypothetical interpersonal conflict situations than were lighter television-violence viewers.

Some Children Under Some Conditions

One of the earliest research summary statements about the possible effects of television on youth—from the previously cited 1961 report by Schramm, Lyle, and Parker—indicated that not all children are similarly affected by television. In fact, the report's opening summary statement suggests that "for some children, under some conditions, some television is harmful. For other children under the same conditions, or for the same children under other conditions, it may be beneficial." This observation underscores the fact that children are a highly diverse group and that television violence, no matter how it is measured and no matter its prevalence, does not have a singular effect on all children. The National Institute of Mental Health's 10-year follow-up of the 1972 surgeon general's study made a similar claim, suggesting that the correlations between violence and aggression are positive, but "not all children become aggressive."

In fact, the history of television effects research can be divided into two distinctive phases. The first, the medium-orientation phase, assumed that television had overwhelming power and that audiences were particularly vulnerable to its influence. During this early stage of scientific inquiry, there was little if any consideration of developmental or individual differences that influence the power of the medium. During the ensuing interactive-orientation phase, the potential of media effects in general and the impact of violent content in particular were treated as an interaction between medium variables, such as content, and child variables, such as age, intelligence, media literacy, and factors associated with upbringing, including parental disciplinary style and household rules regarding television viewing.

Although the body of research on the effects of viewing television violence is extensive and fairly coherent in demonstrating systematic patterns of influence, research is ongoing regarding the processes involved in the production of these effects or potential intervening variables. So, too, are efforts by the Federal Communications Commission to regulate television violence, particularly during times when children are likely to be viewing.

Robert Abelman

See also Aggressive Behavior; Attitude, Effects of Media
   Violence on; Bobo Doll Studies; Catharsis Theory;
   Cultivation Theory; Desensitization Effects on Society;
   Media Effects Perspectives of Violence; Rating
   Systems, Television

Further Readings

Bandura, A. (1973). *Aggression: A social learning analysis.*
   Englewood Cliffs, NJ: Prentice Hall.
Huesmann, L. R., & Eron, L. D. (Eds.). (1986). *Television
   and the aggressive child: A cross-national comparison.*
   Mahwah, NJ: Erlbaum.
Huston, A. C., Donnerstein, E., Fairchild, H., Feshbach,
   N. D., Katz, P. A., Murray, J. P., Rubinstein, E. A.,
   Wilcox, B., & Zuckerman, D. (1992). *Big world, small
   screen: The role of television in American society.*
   Lincoln: University of Nebraska Press.
Liebert, R. M., Sprafkin, J. N., & Davidson, E. S. (1982).
   *The early window: Effects of television on children and
   youth.* New York, NY: Pergamon.
Paik, H., & Comstock, G. (1994). The effects of television
   violence on antisocial behavior: A meta-analysis.
   Communication Research, 21(4), 516–546.
Schulenburg, C. (2007). *Dying to entertain: Violence on
   prime time broadcast TV 1998 to 2006.* Los Angeles,
   CA: Parents Television Council.
Sprafkin, J., Gadow, K. D., & Abelman, R. (1992).
   Television and the exceptional child. Mahwah, NJ:
   Erlbaum.

Trait Aggression

Some people are more aggressive than others. Does nature endow some people with more aggressive personalities than others? Or does nurture, in which factors within one's environment shape aggressive tendencies, also matter? Early psychological research on aggression often focused on situational factors, ignoring the role of trait aggression. Indeed, a massive host of environmental variables that affect aggression have been identified, such as temperature, noxious odors, physical pain, and alcohol intoxication. Despite the profound effects that these external influences can have on an individual's aggressive behavior, other work has suggested that aggression is also reliable over time in the same individuals. In a powerful demonstration of this concept, L. Rowell Huesmann and colleagues (1984) conducted a 22-year longitudinal study, tracking the aggressive tendencies of individuals from 8 years old to 30 years old, their offspring, and their parents. The authors of this study found that childhood aggression predicted antisocial behavior, such as serious criminal behavior and intimate partner violence, in adulthood. Whereas the durability of aggressive tendencies across ages was substantial, it was even more powerful across generations within the same family unit, with a profound degree of similarity among the aggressive tendencies of participants, their parents, and offspring at comparable ages. This intrafamily aggressive similarity suggests that an aggressive disposition may have a strongly heritable aspect, a topic addressed later in this entry. Such research has demonstrated that aggressive tendencies are, in fact, stable enough to be considered a personality *trait*, defined as an enduring and pervasive characteristic that predicts future outcomes and behavior. This now-accepted conceptualization of trait aggression has redefined the way researchers approach the topics of hostility, anger, aggression, and violence. This entry discusses the measurement of aggression, models and theories pertaining to trait aggression, and implications for media violence research.

Measurement

The view that aggression can be measured as a durable construct dates back to the publication of the highly popular Buss and Durkee Hostility Inventory (BDHI) in 1957. The BDHI is an instrument that assesses individual dispositions toward aggressive behavior. It contains subscales measuring tendencies to engage in assault, irritability, negativism, resentment, suspicion, and indirect and verbal aggression. Validating this measure, overall BDHI scores correspond to real-world aggression, such as violent crimes (Gunn & Gristwood, 1975). However, the seven aforementioned subtypes of aggression subsumed within the BDHI were not empirically established or validated through statistical procedures psychologists use to identify subtypes of aggression (i.e., principal-components analysis). To address this problem, an improved measure of trait aggression was developed in the early 1990s. This new measure is the Buss and Perry Aggression Questionnaire (BPAQ), which is a modified version of the BDHI that contains four empirically defined subtypes of aggression: physical aggression, verbal aggression, anger, and hostility. Scores from the BPAQ have been ecologically validated, in that they predict greater amounts of behavioral aggression, such as louder and longer noise blasts ostensibly administered to another person (Giancola & Parrott, 2008).

Other work has focused on measuring attitudes and beliefs about aggression. According to the general aggression model, attitudes and beliefs about violence operate through knowledge structures that people develop over time. These knowledge structures influence cognitive and affective appraisals of situations in terms of what to expect in a current situation and motor responses to that situation. Research has also shown that more positive attitudes toward violence and normative beliefs about aggression relate to higher levels of aggressive behavior.

Four-Factor Model of Trait Aggression

The four-factor structure of the BPAQ sheds light onto the specific manifestations of trait aggression. *Physical aggression* is one of the more straightforward subtypes of trait aggression, exemplified by questionnaire items such as "If somebody hits me, I hit back" and "Once in a while I can't control the urge to hit or strike another person." This dimension refers to what many think of as stereotypical aggression, the act of lashing out bodily with the intent to harm others who are motivated to avoid the harm. *Verbal aggression* is an additional subtype, which is measured through questionnaire items such as "My friends say that I'm somewhat argumentative." Physical and verbal aggression share two key features: harming others and the activation of motor responses. *Anger* is the affective subtype of trait aggression that is central to aggressive behavior, often serving as the motivational precursor to it. This factor is assessed through questionnaire items such as "I have trouble controlling my temper." The fourth factor, *hostility*, is a cognitive subtype of trait aggression that refers to an antagonistic mind-set in which perceptions and attributions are biased toward the assumption that the world is unjust toward you. This factor appears in questionnaire items such as "I am suspicious of overly friendly strangers." Not surprisingly, males scores higher than females on all four types of trait aggression, with the greatest difference on physical aggression.

Taken together, these four subtypes of trait aggression establish what Arnold Buss and Mark Perry refer to as a "tripartite division" (1992, p. 457) of instrumental (physical and verbal aggression), emotional (anger), and cognitive (hostility). Although each of the four factors explained unique variance within overall trait aggression, anger strongly and positively correlated with the other three factors, suggesting that anger may serve as the transitional mechanism through which cognitive

processes (i.e., hostility) become aggressive behavior (i.e., physical and verbal aggression).

Displaced Aggression

A dichotomy between aggressive behaviors is direct versus displaced aggression (see Marcus-Newhall et al., 2000). *Direct aggression* occurs when an individual directs an aggressive act toward a provocateur; *displaced aggression* occurs when a provoked individual takes his or her aggression out on an innocent third party. The concept of displaced aggression is often illustrated with the narrative wherein a man is angered by his boss, and because he cannot aggress against his boss without losing his job, he comes home and kicks his dog. Trait aggression as typically measured via the BDHI and BPAQ focuses on direct aggression. As such, the Displaced Aggression Questionnaire (DAQ) was developed by Thomas Denson, William Pedersen, and Norman Miller to measure an individual's trait-level tendency to engage in displaced aggressive behaviors. Like the BPAQ, the DAQ has several subscales identified through principal-components analysis: displaced behavioral aggression, angry rumination, and revenge planning. The displaced behavioral aggression subscale includes items such as "When feeling bad, I take it out on others" and "I take my anger out on innocent others." The angry rumination subscale includes items such as "Whenever I experience anger, I keep thinking about it for a while." The revenge planning subscale includes items such as "When somebody offends me, sooner or later I retaliate." The DAQ was also behaviorally validated in that scores on this measure predicted displaced aggressive behavior in an experimental setting. Whereas DAQ scores correlate with BPAQ scores, displaced trait aggression and direct trait aggression are two very different phenomena. One crucial distinction between the two is that direct aggression activates approach-oriented behaviors, whereas displaced aggression activates avoidance-oriented behaviors. The development of the DAQ is crucial for understanding how both direct and displaced trait aggression influence human thought and behavior.

Biological Contributors

As alluded to earlier, the intrafamily stability of trait aggression likely indicates there is a genetic component, making trait aggression a heritable condition. Validating this prediction, a polymorphism of the gene that codes for the production of tryptophan hydroxylase (TPH) has been associated with higher levels of trait aggression (Manuck et al., 1999). Because TPH, in part, regulates serotonin levels in the brain, individuals with this polymorphism then had lower levels of endogenous serotonin, a neurotransmitter that predicts lower levels of aggressive behavior. This presents a potential opportunity for the application of selective serotonin reuptake inhibitors, such as Prozac, to combat excessive trait aggression in individuals with this genotype.

Individual differences in trait aggression can also arise from changes in brain functioning, even anatomy. Indeed, Denson and colleges (2009) found that trait aggression positively correlates with activation in a neural region called the dorsal anterior cingulate cortex (dACC) when individuals were confronted with an angering provocation. According to Naomi Eisenberger and Matthew Lieberman (2004), the dACC acts as the brain's "alarm system," detecting conflicts in the external environment; and Ulrike Krämer and colleagues (2007) found that it also predicts greater levels of aggressive retribution toward provocateurs. As such, it appears that individuals who are dispositionally predisposed to aggress have brains that exacerbate angering experiences, a known risk factor for aggression.

Cognitive Neoassociation Theory

Despite the substantive gains the literature has made in measuring, differentiating, and understanding the underpinnings of trait aggression, the question remains: How do such dispositional tendencies to aggress arise in an individual? Indeed, it is necessary to answer this question in order to identify and treat individuals who may be in the higher ranges of trait aggression, individuals who are likely to perpetrate violence on others. In 1993 Leonard Berkowitz put forth his cognitive neoassociation theory (CNT), which readily explains how trait aggression can not only arise but how it is a self-reinforcing positive feedback loop. Cognitive neoassociation theory draws heavily from the literature of cognitive psychology to posit that aversive experiences yield negative affect. An uncomfortable emotional state then leads to an array of cognitive, emotional, and behavioral responses that predispose an individual to aggress. These various aggressive concepts arise by the virtue of being semantically related in a cognitive associative framework in long-term memory. As a direct result of this associative network, the perception of one aggressive concept, such as a disliked outgroup, can

lead to the priming of related concepts, such as physical aggression and hostility. This theoretical approach parsimoniously explains how a single stimulus can lead to a diverse array of aggressive affect, cognition, and behavior. More to the point, this associative framework serves as a self-reinforcing, positive feedback loop through which the repeated association between aggressive concepts strengthens these semantic bonds in memory, which then makes them more readily associable. Brad J. Bushman (1996) validated this theoretical approach by showing that individuals high in trait aggression made stronger associations between aggressive words, and even between aggressive and ambiguous words. These findings demonstrate that high trait aggression leads to a biased perceptual strategy in which identifying and associating aggressive concepts is a prepotent response. For instance, whereas a low-trait-aggressive person might view a broom as an instrument with which to clean a floor, someone who is high in trait aggression might readily perceive the broom as a weapon. Viewing the broom as a device with which one can perform aggressive acts increases the likelihood that one will do so, which in turn would strengthen the cognitive association between *broom* and *weapon*. Using such a cognitive framework to understand this example, it becomes readily apparent how life experiences that associate various experiences with aggression can lead to a self-reinforcing disposition to be hostile, angry, and aggressive. To combat this dangerous positive feedback system, interventions need to weaken the associative network of aggressive concepts that individuals high in trait aggression possess.

Relation to Media Violence

The associative network approach has clear implications for research in violent media and trait aggression. Bushman (1995) found that the ability of violent media exposure to increase aggression was stronger among individuals high in trait aggression. Specifically, highly trait-aggressive individuals administered louder and longer noise blasts after watching a video with violent content compared with their less trait-aggressive counterparts. These results were explained as due to the more elaborate and robust associative networks that highly trait-aggressive individuals have among aggressive and violent concepts, an explanation that supports the general aggression model's emphasis on the importance of knowledge structures. Indeed, repeated exposure to violent media may represent a powerful and ubiquitous avenue through which these associative networks are created and strengthened, routinely displaying harmful actions toward others in a rewarding and socially acceptable context. Although it remains unclear whether repeated violent media exposure leads to higher levels of trait aggressiveness, the aforementioned research indicates that highly trait-aggressive people, compared with low-trait-aggressive people, are more at risk for the deleterious effects that violent media can often have on aggressive tendencies.

Summary

Although aggression has often been thought of as a situationally determined behavior, a wealth of research has established that it can be conceived of as a personality trait. Trait aggression can be measured in valid and reliable ways. The leading measure of trait aggression is the Buss-Perry Aggression Questionnaire, which has established a four-factor model that includes anger, hostility, physical aggression, and verbal aggression. Trait aggression can be direct or displaced. Furthermore, trait aggression is rooted in human biology, as it is associated with genetic markers and differential brain function. The ontogeny of trait aggression is complex, although it appears it is largely due to an elaborate associative network in human cognition, through which highly trait-aggressive individuals react more angrily to even neutral events and readily make associations between aggressive and even ambiguous concepts. Violent media have been known to increase aggression, although this appears to be enhanced for individuals high in trait aggression, perhaps because of their robust associative networks between the violent concepts they view from media and those they perpetrate in the real world. Indeed, violent media may contribute to increased trait aggression because they may strengthen these cognitive associations between violent concepts.

David S. Chester and C. Nathan DeWall

See also Aggression, Definition and Assessment of; Aggression, Risk Factors of; Aggressive Personality; General Aggression Model; Genetics of Aggressive Behavior

Further Readings

Anderson, C. A. (1989). Temperature and aggression: Ubiquitous effects of heat on occurrence of human violence. *Psychological Bulletin, 106*(1), 74–96.

Anderson, C. A., Benjamin, A. J., Wood, P. K., & Bonnaci, A. M. (2006). Development and testing of the Velicer Attitudes Toward Violence Scale: Evidence for a four-factor solution. *Aggressive Behavior, 32,* 122–136.

Anderson, C. A., & Bushman, B. J. (2002). Human aggression. *Annual Review of Psychology, 53,* 27–51.

Berkowitz, L. (1993). *Aggression: Its causes, consequences, and control.* McGraw-Hill Series in Social Psychology. New York, NY: McGraw-Hill.

Berkowitz, L., & Thome, P. R. (1987). Pain expectation, negative affect, and angry aggression. *Motivation and Emotion, 11*(2), 183–193.

Bettencourt, B. A., Talley, A., Benjamin, A. J., & Valentine, J. (2006). Personality and aggressive behavior under provoking and neutral conditions: A meta-analytic review. *Psychological Bulletin, 132*(5), 751–777.

Bushman, B. J. (1995). Moderating role of trait aggressiveness in the effects of violent media on aggression. *Journal of Personality and Social Psychology, 69*(5), 950–960.

Bushman, B. J. (1996). Individual differences in the extent and development of aggressive cognitive-associative networks. *Personality and Social Psychology Bulletin, 22*(8), 811–819.

Bushman, B. J. (1997). Effects of alcohol on human aggression: Validity of proposed explanations. *Recent developments in alcoholism, Vol. 13: Alcohol and violence: Epidemiology, neurobiology, psychology, family issues* (pp. 227–243). New York: Plenum.

Buss, A. H., & Durkee, A. (1957). An inventory for assessing different kinds of hostility. *Journal of Consulting Psychology, 21*(4), 343–349.

Buss, A. H., & Perry, M. (1992). The aggression questionnaire. *Journal of Personality and Social Psychology, 63*(3), 452–459.

Coccaro, E. F. (1989). Central serotonin and impulsive aggression. *British Journal of Psychiatry, 155,* 52–62.

Denson, T. F., Pedersen, W. C., & Miller, N. (2006). The displaced aggression questionnaire. *Journal of Personality and Social Psychology, 90*(6), 1032–1051.

Denson, T. F., Pedersen, W. C., Ronquillo, J., & Nandy, A. S. (2009). The angry brain: Neural correlates of anger, angry rumination, and aggressive personality. *Journal of Cognitive Neuroscience, 21*(4), 734–744.

DeWall, C. N., Anderson, C. A., & Bushman, B. J. (2011). The general aggression model: Theoretical extensions to violence. *Psychology of Violence, 1,* 245–258.

Eisenberger, N. I., & Lieberman, M. D. (2004). Why rejection hurts: A common neural alarm system for physical and social pain. *Trends in Cognitive Sciences, 8*(7), 294–300.

Giancola, P. R., & Parrott, D. J. (2008). Further evidence for the validity of the Taylor Aggression Paradigm. *Aggressive Behavior, 34*(2), 214–229.

Gunn, J., & Gristwood, J. (1975). Use of the Buss-Durkee Hostility Inventory among British prisoners. *Journal of Consulting and Clinical Psychology, 43*(4), 590.

Huesmann, L. R., Eron, L. D., Lefkowitz, M. M., & Walder, L. O. (1984). Stability of aggression over time and generations. *Developmental Psychology, 20*(6), 1120–1134.

Huesmann, L. R., & Guerra, N. G. (1997). Children's normative beliefs about aggression and aggressive behavior. *Journal of Personality and Social Psychology, 72,* 408–419.

Krämer, U. M., Jansma, H., Tempelmann, C., & Münte, T. F. (2007). Tit-for-tat: The neural basis of reactive aggression. *NeuroImage, 38*(1), 203–211.

Manuck, S. B., Flory, J. D., Ferrell, R. E., Dent, K. M., Mann, J. J., & Muldoon, M. F. (1999). Aggression and anger-related traits associated with a polymorphism of the tryptophan hydroxylase gene. *Biological Psychiatry, 45*(5), 603–614.

Marcus-Newhall, A., Pedersen, W. C., Carlson, M., & Miller, N. (2000). Displaced aggression is alive and well: A meta-analytic review. *Journal of Personality and Social Psychology, 78*(4), 670–689.

Norlander, B., & Eckhardt, C. (2005). Anger, hostility, and male perpetrators of intimate partner violence: A meta-analytic review. *Clinical Psychology Review, 25*(2), 119–152.

Peeters, B. WikiQuote. Retrieved from http://en.wikiquote.org/wiki/Brain

Rotton, J., Frey, J., Barry, T., Milligan, M., & Fitzpatrick, M. (1979). The air pollution experience and physical aggression. *Journal of Applied Social Psychology, 9*(5), 397–412.

TRANSPORTATION THEORY

Narrative transportation theory is a framework for understanding how media experiences can influence a viewer. The central idea of transportation theory is that individuals can be "transported" into a narrative world, becoming mentally immersed in the world of the story. When individuals are transported into a narrative, they are more likely to change their real-world beliefs and behaviors to match those suggested by the story. Transportation theory suggests several mechanisms to account for this attitude change: reducing counterarguing, creating connections with characters, heightening perceptions of realism, and emotional engagement. The effects of violent media (e.g., arousal, aggression) may be heightened for individuals who are more deeply transported into a story. This entry defines transportation into narrative worlds, describes research on transportation, and discusses how transportation leads to attitude and behavior change.

Transportation into a narrative world is an integrative combination of attention, imagery, and feelings. All of these mental processes are focused on imagining and reacting to the story. Transportation is evoked by narratives. Narratives require storylines with clear beginnings, middles, and ends, during which some conflict is typically raised and resolved. This definition encompasses most films, novels, television shows, and many video games, making transportation theory relevant across media. Individuals can be equally transported into fictional and nonfictional stories.

Transportation Research

Typical studies of transportation have exposed individuals to a media presentation and manipulated transportation (by creating conditions that make individuals more or less likely to become immersed) and/or measured transportation. Melanie Green and Timothy Brock (2000) developed a self-report scale for measuring transportation. Individuals respond to statements such as "I was emotionally involved in the narrative while I was viewing it." Individuals who experience higher transportation are more influenced by the ideas conveyed in a story across a range of topics (social issues, health, marketing).

There are also individual differences in the extent to which people tend to be transported into narratives (transportability). Some people easily enter story worlds, whereas others do not.

How Narrative Transportation Works

Narratives can convey both explicit beliefs (ones stated directly within the story) and implicit beliefs (ones implied by the plot or themes of the story). For example, in violent media, a well-liked main character might openly declare that violence is the appropriate response to a situation (explicit), or a violent character may be presented as a hero and seen as successful via the use of violence (implicit). Either example may cause a transported viewer to feel more positive toward the use of violence, which may in turn lead to more violent behavior. Transportation theory suggests several mechanisms to account for this attitude change, described following.

Reduced Counterarguing

First, transportation may serve to reduce counterarguing, the active rejection of messages conveyed in a communication, in several ways. Individuals may be unwilling to counterargue because they do not want to disrupt their enjoyment of a film by breaking out of the narrative world to critique points made in the story. Alternatively, individuals may not counterargue because they may not realize they are being persuaded. This lack of knowledge may occur because the persuasive content is subtle or because a viewer may believe that others are vulnerable to persuasion but that they themselves are unlikely to be affected (the third-person effect). This tendency may be exacerbated by the fictional nature of most movies. The average person does not expect to be influenced by entertainment and, ironically, may therefore be more likely to be persuaded because he or she does not engage in active consideration of the messages implied by the story. Thus, a likable character who succeeds through the use of violence sends an implicit message that violence is useful. Because of the effects of transportation, people are less likely to disbelieve or counterargue this message than if it had been presented outside the narrative context.

Liking of Characters

Second, transportation may cause feelings of liking and identification with story characters, which then leads to individuals adopting pro-violence beliefs demonstrated by those characters or even shifting their self-concepts to become more similar to an admired but violent character. Social cognitive theory states that individuals can learn vicariously by seeing the experiences of other people and the way in which other people's decisions or behaviors are rewarded and punished. Such effects are amplified when individuals are transported into a story.

Mirroring Direct Experience

Transported individuals may also perceive a narrative's events as more like direct personal experience (e.g., individuals may feel that they have experienced the story events themselves). Direct experience is a powerful predictor of attitudes, and stories provide vicarious experiences. Furthermore, transportation typically leads to vivid mental images, which can also shape attitudes or beliefs.

Emotional Response

A strong emotional response to a film or character may make the messages of that film more influential and memorable, and affective responses may be especially powerful influences on attitudes. Films or games may create a positive emotional context around violence, such as when a hero delivers punishment to a villain. However, transporting media may also promote the rejection of violence by showing consequences for victims.

Narrative Quality

Not all stories are created equal: some are more transporting than others. Plot development, character development, coherent structure, dramatic tension, and production values all contribute to a highly transporting narrative. These features are also hallmarks of entertainment media that people enjoy (such as feature films, which frequently contain positive portrayals of violence).

In sum, transportation theory helps explain how and when media experiences will affect attitudes and behaviors. Transporting narratives with violent content may create pro-violence attitudes through multiple mechanisms, and in turn possibly promote violent behavior.

Melanie C. Green and Jenna L. Clark

See also Attitude, Effects of Media Violence on; Cultivation Theory; Flow Theory; Media Effects Perspectives of Violence; Narrative, Effects of Violent; Presence Theory; Social Cognitive Theory

Further Readings

Green, M. C., & Brock, T. C. (2000). The role of transportation in the persuasiveness of public narratives. *Journal of Personality and Social Psychology, 79,* 701–721.

Green, M. C., & Donahue, J. (2008). Transportation in narrative processing. In K. Markman, W. Klein, & J. Suhr (Eds.), *The handbook of imagination and mental simulation.* New York, NY: Psychology Press.

Green, M. C., Strange, J. J., & Brock, T. C. (Eds.). (2002). *Narrative impact: Social and cognitive foundations.* Mahwah, NJ: Erlbaum.

User Involvement in Violent Content, Effects of

As video game violence becomes more complex and realistic, parents and politicians press forward to understand its impact on the players and society. Early research in the 1980s found that most games required players to virtually attack other characters to win the game. In early 2000 Stacy Smith and colleagues conducted an analysis of 60 popular games and revealed that 90% of Teen- or Mature-rated games featured violence, and 57% of games rated for all audiences contained violence. To understand the effects on players of such violent games, researchers have begun to examine how individual differences, including trait aggression, and situational variables, such as violent video game play, operate as routes to internal states and ultimately aggressive behavior.

Game researchers have used a variety of theoretical frameworks, including arousal and priming, to explain hypothesized effects. Most recently, using social learning, arousal, priming, and cognitive processing theories, Craig Anderson and his research team empirically developed the general aggression model (GAM) to better understand why exposure to violent media increases human aggression. As a conceptual platform, the GAM is used in this entry to examine the effects of violent video game play on hostile expectation bias by incorporating media-related routes as predictors of aggressive cognition.

The Experience of Game Play

Ron Tamborini of Michigan State University suggested that the attributes of video games associated with a first-person point of view and a user's active role in decisions to aggress are powerful conditional forces that influence aggressive outcomes. First-person games are thought to increase identification with the gaming character through involvement and immersion, which subsequently increase short-term outcomes such as aggression. *Involvement,* defined as a psychological state in which attention and energy are focused on the medium, and *immersion,* defined as the extent to which the player or person perceives being in and interacting with the mediated environment, are considered necessary components to the larger construct of presence (i.e., the experience of being in the environment, even when physically located in another environment) (Witmer & Singer, 1998). The decision to shoot or punch "as" a character in a first-person game rather than "with" a character leads to greater presence—as defined through involvement and immersion. It is the decision to aggress that creates or activates existing aggressive scripts that subsequently result in aggressive outcomes.

Attributes inherent to advanced technologies such as virtual reality (e.g., increased vividness and interactivity) are thought to increase presence beyond traditional console and passive-watching environments. According to this logic, the violent gaming situation eliciting the greatest levels of involvement and presence should have the greatest short-term effect on aggression. Research by Matthew Eastin at The University of Texas at Austin found some support for the connections among presence, interactivity, and aggression; however, because of the participants' lack of experience using virtual reality systems and a potential disengagement between firing a gun during game play and the respondent's existing real-world scripts for aggression, overall levels of presence did not predict aggression and were relatively low among virtual reality participants. Here, Eastin's research hypothesized that a violent behavior resembling more common social violence, such as punching, kicking, and so on, would increase the behavior salience (and potentially aggressive cognition) more than a shooting-type game.

Although concepts such as involvement and immersion have been used to explain presence, since the 1990s no clear definition has emerged across disciplines. Matthew Lombard and Theresa Ditton (1997) defined *presence* as the perceptual illusion of nonmediation that occurs when a person fails to perceive or acknowledge the existence of a medium and thus responds as he or she would if the medium were not there.

Taking a slightly different approach, Michael Slater's early work in 1994 suggested that the immersive quality of technology rests in its ability to make the person believe he or she is "being there" in the environment. Later research further refined this definition to include a psychological state in which objects are experienced as real. Further describing the subjective media engagement, Kwan Min Lee explicated three typologies of presence: physical, social, and self. *Physical presence* represents a psychological state in which virtual objects are experienced as actual. In this regard, presence can occur in any locale because it is a psychological feeling rather than the actuality of being in the environment. *Social presence* is a state in which virtual social actors are experienced as actual. Finally, *self-presence* describes a state in which the virtual self is experienced as actual.

Speaking across definitions, the perception of presence experienced is to some extent based on the media's ability to manipulate the senses into believing the virtual sensory world as reality. To this end, the mediated environment becomes the focus and simulates the sensation of real life. Thus, presence is experienced through the interaction between the individual and technology, where involvement and immersion are important interrelated components (Witmer & Singer, 1998). Presence is dependent not only on whether a sense is manipulated, but rather, how many are activated and the saliency of each sensory channel. Technology that increases sensory engagement should ease a player's mental strain by enabling greater focus on the content and action, subsequently increasing the effects of game content. Based on the tendencies of previous work, more recent researchers used Bob G. Witmer and Michael J. Singer's (1998) conceptual and empirical definition of presence that captures the subjective experience of being in one place while physically located in another.

As stated, in today's mediated environments, presence often is discussed within the capabilities of immersive technologies, or virtual reality. Virtual reality is explicated as a three-dimensional simulation in which a user or player can view, move around in, and experience an artificial world. Virtual reality has the ability to create the illusion that a player is part of the game through character manipulation both before and during game play. In addition to presence, Eastin's research has shown that aggression outcomes were higher for participants of a virtual reality game than for passive observers. The decision to aggress and the engaging nature of the medium interact to increase aggressive cognitions.

The Influence of Content

In addition to interface (media) attributes, it has been shown that the salience of game content (Witmer & Singer, 1998) can influence presence levels as well as hostile outcomes. Most research examining violent versus nonviolent game content has assumed that all violent game play is equivalent in terms of influence. The logic behind cognitive scripting is that when choosing to aggress, the player creates and then reinforces knowledge scripts of reactive behavior. It is plausible that shooter games are not as salient to most game users as "violent reaction scripts," thus levels of immersion and short-term aggression comparatively lessen when playing shooter games because the action of firing a gun is not a salient reaction to provocation in the game player's reality. Based on this logic, using a more salient action such as fistfighting should provide an opportunity for players to more easily develop or activate preexisting knowledge scripts, thus allowing for stronger and potentially transferable behavioral responses outside the game environment. Supporting this proposition, Eastin found that game players performing more salient violent acts such as punching and kicking experienced greater hostile outcome expectations than players playing in a first-person-shooter game. He found that as the virtual environment more resembled real life, greater levels of hostile expectations were detected.

The Context of Game Play

Competitively speaking, research has suggested a positive relationship between competition and aggression. According to the research of Leonard Berkowitz, aggression increases through frustrations, and competition between opponents who seek the same goal is thought to be frustrating. Furthering this idea, research has shown competitive situations, or simply priming participants toward competition, increases aggression. However, not all opponents may generate competition levels equivalently. For instance, when looking at face-to-face stranger interactions versus computer opponents during nonviolent game play (e.g., *Monopoly*), computer opponents increased aggression beyond human opponents (Williams & Clippinger, 2002). However, research focusing on violent game play indicates that human opponents did increase aggressive thoughts compared with computer opponents.

Future Research

The nature of violence would also be salient for furthering research in this area. For example, random violence, defined as violent acts not relevant to the game, and gratuitous violence, defined as acts of violence toward others beyond what is required for game success, should all be investigated. Additionally, if, in fact, the GAM is correct and the decision to aggress or the act of aggressing is partly what activates and reinforces aggressive scripts, then those who aggress more often should experience greater short-term state hostility. Simply put, frequent, repeated activation of aggressive scripts through violent behavior should make the construct of aggression more accessible and permanent.

Although research has demonstrated that game interface and game content in combination do influence aggressive outcomes, most of the current literature can be applied only to male game play. Future research should focus on how female players and children are influenced by violent gaming. The fighting game used for the current study was rated T for Teen, meaning it was deemed acceptable for teenagers. Given that many younger children prefer and use these games (because of what is known as the "forbidden fruit hypothesis"), future research investigating children and gaming should not be limited to predefined age groups as defined by the gaming industry. If younger children are playing games that define behavioral scripts, as suggested by current research, how youth react to violent situations outside the mediated context could be defined through actions or decisions made during the gaming process.

Matthew S. Eastin

See also Aggression and Youth; Cognition: Schemas and Scripts; Cognitive Psychology of Violence; Effects From Violent Media, Short- and Long-Term; General Aggression Model; Presence Theory; Rating Systems, Film; Rating System, Television; Rating Systems, Video Games; Video Game Platforms, Effects of; Virtual Reality, Violent Content in

Further Readings

Anderson, C. A., & Bushman, B. J. (2002). Human aggression. *Annual Review of Psychology, 53*, 27–51.

Anderson, C. A., & Dill, K. E. (2000). Video games and aggressive thoughts, feelings, and behavior in the laboratory and in life. *Journal of Personality and Social Psychology, 78*, 772–790.

Bowman, R. P., & Rotter, J. C. (1983). Computer games: Friend or foe? *Elementary School Guidance and Counseling, 18*, 25–34.

Calvert, S., & Tan, S. L. (1994). Impact of virtual reality on young adults' physiological arousal and aggressive thoughts: Interaction versus observation. *Journal of Applied Developmental Psychology, 15*, 125–139.

Eastin, M. S. (2006). Video game violence and the female game player: Self- and opponent gender effects on presence and aggressive thoughts. *Human Communication Research, 31*(3), 351–372.

Eastin, M. S., & Griffiths, R. P. (2006). Beyond the shooter game: Examining presence and hostile outcomes among male game players. *Communication Research, 33*(6), 448–466.

Gentile, D. A., & Anderson, C. A. (2006). Video games. In N. J. Salkind (Ed.), *Encyclopedia of human development* (Vol. 3, pp. 1303–1307). Thousand Oaks, CA: Sage.

Klimmt, C., & Vorderer, P. (2003). Media psychology "is not yet there": Introducing theories on media entertainment to the presence debate. *Presence: Teleoperators and Virtual Environments, 12*, 246–259.

Lombard, M., & Ditton, T. (1997). At the heart of it all: The concept of presence. *Journal of Mass Communication, 3*(2). http://www.ascusc.org/jcmc

Regenbrecht, H., & Schubert, T. (2002). Real and illusory interactions enhance presence in virtual environments. *Presence, 11*, 425–434.

Slater, M., & Usoh, M. (1994). Body centered interaction in immersive virtual environments. In N. M. Thalmann & D. Thalmann (Eds.), *Artificial life and virtual reality* (pp. 125–147). Chichester, UK: Wiley.

Smith, S. L., Lachlan, K., & Tamborini, R. (2003). Popular video games: Quantifying the presentation of violence and its context. *Journal of Broadcasting & Electronic Media, 47,* 58–76.

Tamborini, R., Eastin, M. S., Skalski, P., Lachlan, K., Fediuk, T. A., & Brady, R. (2004). Violent virtual video games and hostile thoughts. *Journal of Broadcasting & Electronic Media, 48,* 335–357.

Williams, R. B., & Clippinger, C. A. (2002). Aggression, competition, and computer games: Computer and human opponents. *Computers in Human Behavior, 18,* 495–506.

Witmer, B. G., & Singer, M. J. (1998). Measuring presence in virtual environments: A presence questionnaire. *Presence, 7,* 225–240.

User Trends Toward Aggressive Games

Since their introduction in the 1970s, video games have experienced a massive surge in popularity, rivaling the audiences for more traditional forms of media such as television and film. Video game players are a diverse group of individuals with representatives from nearly every demographic category. As the audiences and the presence of the medium expanded, aggressive video games began to garner the attention and concern of politicians, advocates, parents, and researchers. Aggressive games are considered games that include content related to physical altercations between characters and violence committed by characters.

Considerable disagreement still exists in the field regarding causal processes and potential effects associated with exposure to aggressive video game content. Furthermore, there has been a dearth of quality data regarding trends related to aggressive content in video games over time. However, broader trends related to human perception, formal aspects of games (e.g., graphic capabilities), and data regarding sales of games allow for some conclusions to be made.

This entry begins with a discussion of attraction to violence and aggression, which is then followed by a summary of findings from quantitative content analyses of games. The content of games has been shaped by technological advancements, so a discussion of the impact of rapid graphical advancements

of video technology on game depictions of aggressive content is also included. The entry ends with a discussion of current trends in video games that relate to the presence of aggressive content.

Attraction to Violence

The appeal of violence, and conflict in general, seems to be almost inextricably linked to human culture. However, aggression is not a purely human trait. Competition for resources and mates leads to aggressive behavior in numerous animal species. Even organisms that are perceived to be simple, such as fruit flies, have elaborate behavioral repertoires related to intraspecies conflict. Humans possess similar repertoires and incorporate aggressive behaviors into various cultural representations, including sports and art.

Early research on the attraction of humans to violence in media has proposed several potential determinants of this attraction, including morbid curiosity, sensation seeking, and adaptive skill learning. Morbid curiosity and sensation seeking have both been discussed thoroughly in the literature on media violence attraction. *Morbid curiosity* is generally defined in the literature as a curiosity about events related to death, violence, and physical harm. Dolf Zillmann, one of the quintessential researchers of media psychology, has often discussed morbid curiosity as an evolutionarily biased motive for viewing violent and disturbing media that is related to the survival need regarding awareness of potential dangers in one's environment. A small, but prominent, portion of aggressive games contains graphic scenes of death, violence, and harm. The *Doom, Mortal Kombat,* and *Grand Theft Auto* series all prominently feature blood, violence, dismemberments, and death, and have been targets of parental outrage at the content of video games. Notably, these series have also been particularly popular with male youth audiences.

In addition to morbid curiosity, sensation seeking has also been proposed as a motivating force for consuming violent and aggressive games. *Sensation seeking* is typically defined as a personality trait related to the enjoyment of and attraction to novel, physically arousing events. As aggressive games are known to elicit physical arousal, research has examined the possibility that sensation seeking is positively related to aggressive video game play and found that sensation seeking is a significant positive predictor of the use of aggressive games. In a closely related topic, research has demonstrated that the use of violent content labels and age suggestions on games, such as those used by the Entertainment Software Review Board (ESRB), increase the attraction of violent games for younger audiences. Research indicates that makers of video games appeal to their audiences through the presence of aggressive content in video game advertisements. Studies have found that violent content is used in more than half of video game advertisements; video game magazines, another advertising forum for game companies, portray the majority of male and female characters as aggressive.

Adaptive skill learning has also been proposed as a potential motivator for the consumption of aggressive media content, and violent video games in particular. Numerous animals, particularly predatory animals, engage in rough, aggressive play. Play acts as an opportunity to build strength and learn techniques for survival skills related to capturing prey, avoiding predators, and increasing group cohesion. While most individuals in developed countries have little use for hunting skills, play's evolutionary history as an adaptive behavior has given it a preferential place in human society and has created associations between play and physiological reward systems in the brain. Research by Clifford Nass and Byron Reeves on differences between mediated events and real-life events has demonstrated that although there are differences in magnitude, mediated events tend to elicit the same physiological processes as their real-life counterparts. Aggressive video games offer their users an opportunity for adaptive skill learning in a virtual space that is capable of eliciting the same type of physiological rewards as their real-world counterparts.

Evolutionary biases seem to hold an important place in the attraction of humans to aggressive media content. However, user trends toward aggressive games are also shaped by the content produced by game makers. The next section examines trends in game content over time.

Game Content

The history of video games, and more precisely, the history of studying video games and their content, is quite limited in time and scope. This lack of scientific literature is due to the relatively young age of the medium as well as difficulties associated with examining a dynamic medium whose content is often determined by the person using it.

Early video games featured fairly standardized content. For example, the levels in arcade games such as *Pac-Man* and *Donkey Kong* are relatively consistent in their content, and individuals who play these games have relatively consistent exposure experiences. Newer games, however, are far different and diverge considerably from standardized content. Many of these games feature an open-world format in which game content can vary drastically from one player to the next. For example, the play experiences in *World of Warcraft* can be drastically different depending on an individual's motivations when he or she plays. If an individual playing *World of Warcraft* is seeking to cause mayhem and destruction, his or her behaviors in the game are likely to be very different from those of an individual seeking to join a guild. As such, research seeking to quantify the amount of violence in new, open-world games is likely to face considerable difficulties in determining both how to quantify the content and what is considered an average play experience.

Despite these challenges, some research has been conducted examining the content of aggressive games. This research has tended to focus on the prevalence of violence in games marketed to children and teens and measures violence using two distinct indicators. One indicator is based on the rating system of the ESRB. In addition to age-appropriate recommendations, such as E for Everyone and T for Teen, ESRB ratings also include content descriptors such as "Violence" and "Blood and Gore." The other indicator is based on obtaining game footage from playing the game or having others play the game and then coding the number of violent acts observed in the content.

Quantitative content analyses of game footage of games receiving the rating of E for Everyone by the ESRB indicate that more than half of games appropriate for young children (a) contain intentional violence and (b) reward or require the injuring of characters for advancement. Nearly all (> 90%) games featuring the content descriptor of T for Teen are categorized as containing violence by the ESRB and reward or require players to injure other characters. Overall, research indicates that games rated M for Mature and T for Teen are more likely to feature violence than games rated E for Everyone, although violence and aggression are prevalent in games for all age groups. Notably, the presence of violent content is largely dependent upon the technological capabilities of video game hardware and software.

The Relationship of Game Technology and Violent Content

Because of the novelty of the technology, early video games' graphic depictions were limited in scope and accuracy. Basic shapes, such as triangles, circles, and lines, represented complex entities, such as spaceships, asteroids, and missiles. However, as the technological capabilities of games increased, in-game depictions moved closer and closer to those of the real world. Technological advancements allowed for more photorealistic depictions of violence and aggression and also increased societal concern regarding potential negative aspects of video games. The years 1992 and 1993 became critical years for violence in games with the release of three major games: *Mortal Kombat, Wolfenstein 3D,* and *Doom.*

Mortal Kombat and *Wolfenstein 3D* were both released in 1992. *Mortal Kombat* was an arcade game that featured head-to-head martial arts fights with huge amounts of blood and the ability to end a fight with one character killing the other in what was termed a "fatality." It was particularly controversial because the characters in the game were created by digitizing video footage of actors, which gave the characters an almost photorealistic appearance. The inclusion of digitized video footage made *Mortal Kombat* a particularly important exemplar for violent video games. The photorealistic appearance of its characters served as a stark comparison to the majority of other games, which used animated, cartoon-like characters.

Wolfenstein 3D was a first-person shooter released on personal computer; the game players control a U.S. soldier imprisoned by Nazis in a German castle. In attempting to escape his captors, the player must complete each floor of the castle, finding weapons, killing guards, and eventually fighting Adolf Hitler himself. All of the footage takes place as if the player were looking through the eyes of the character. This type of game presentation has particularly interested researchers, because a first-person perspective is thought to increase potential negative effects such as aggressive thoughts and actions. Another prominent first-person-shooter game, *Doom,* was released in 1993 on the personal computer. Although minor graphic improvements had occurred between the release of *Wolfenstein 3D* and *Doom,* the basic play mechanics were identical.

The release of these games had a profound impact on research and the public's views on violence in games for several reasons. First, these games pushed the graphic boundaries of the industry forward. *Wolfenstein 3D* and *Doom* were some of the first mass market games to feature a first-person perspective. Second, they were and still are extremely popular. One potential attribute that increased their popularity was that *Wolfenstein 3D* and *Doom* were both released as shareware, a free trial version of software that contains only a portion of a game. Shareware, as its name indicates, is encouraged to be shared by its users, which, for the games in question, resulted in a massive distribution among gamers. Since their original release, *Wolfenstein 3D* and *Doom* have both had several game sequels, and *Mortal Kombat* has spawned more than a dozen sequels, as well as comic books, action figures, films, and a web series.

The passing of time has led to technological advancements in computing power that have increased the fidelity between game representations and their real-life counterparts. Furthermore, time has also allowed for an increase in the saturation of games in the media landscape. This increased saturation has led to greater variety in games and more users playing them.

Popularity of Aggressive Games

The popularity of video games has been increasing in the United States, with sales figures increasing from $100 million in 1985 to $25 billion in 2011. Although most games contain some form of aggression or violence, the presence of aggressive content in games is associated with the ratings that the games receive, with games classified as appropriate for children containing less violence than games classified for teen and adult audiences. The most current data reported by the Entertainment Software Association indicate that out of all of the games sold in 2011, 39% were rated E for Everyone, 17% were rated E10+ (i.e., suitable for children over the age of 10), 17% were rated T for Teen, and 27% were rated M for Mature. These sales figures seem to indicate that highly aggressive and violent games targeted toward teenage and adult gamers make up a minority of the games sold today. However, this may not have always been the case.

The rise in popularity of games has broadened the audience for video games, leading to more diversity and variety in games and their content. In fact, the lack of diversity in games during the late 1980s and early 1990s can be traced to the video game crash of the early 1980s. From 1983 to 1985, the video game market contracted by nearly 97%. Sales went from $3.2 billion in 1983 to $100 million in 1985. The drop in the market meant that many game makers and developers exited the industry, which left a void filled by independent game manufacturers. Because of the lack of competition in the market, the games produced by these independent companies achieved widespread dominance and saturation. Some industry experts have estimated that *Doom*, which was distributed free of charge as shareware, was installed on more computers in the mid-1990s than was Microsoft Windows. The lack of reliable data makes this claim hard to verify, but it does point to the fact that the game software market of the mid-1990s was dominated by aggressive and violent games targeted toward male gamers.

In the early 2000s, the popularity of violent games appears to have decreased compared with those of the mid-1990s. *Manhunt* and its sequel, *Manhunt 2*, released in 2007, is one of the most violent video game series ever released. Players are rewarded for committing murders in the most gruesome manner possible, which includes suffocation, bludgeoning, blunt force trauma, and decapitation. However, this game has been considerably less popular than its less violent predecessors such as *Doom* and *Doom II*. *Manhunt* and *Manhunt 2* sold a total of 1.7 million units, compared with *Doom* and its sequel, which sold approximately 4 million units. In 2008, the year after *Manhunt 2* was released, the video game industry reached $21 billion in sales; in 1995, the year after *Doom II* was released, the video game industry reached sales of only $3.2 billion. This difference in popularity of the games is particularly noticeable when compared with the size of the industry during the respective years of the games' releases.

Despite the fact that violent games are less popular than they once were, aggressive and violent games are still quite popular. With regard to the current generation of home consoles, 9 out of the 10 best-selling games on Microsoft Xbox 360 contain violence and aggression, and 6 out of the 10 best-selling games on Sony PlayStation 3 contain violence and aggression, with most violence coming in the context of war and one-on-one combat.

Current Trends

Numerous factors influence the appeal of violence and aggression in games, including psychological attributes of the users and attributes of game technology. Recently, first-person-shooter games have seen a surge in popularity. This is partially due to technological advancements that allow individuals to play cooperatively with their friends in real time over the Internet. These technological advancements have allowed for multiplayer modes to usurp the single-player, story-driven mode. This is a welcome change for developers and gamers, because multiplayer modes are cheaper to make than story-driven game play and also increase the replay value of games. Although the content of these multiplayer games generally focuses on violence, such as war or fighting, the cooperative aspects of multiplayer gaming may mitigate antisocial outcomes associated with violent content. However, additional research is needed regarding content of games and the context of game play. Although some researchers have made significant effort in quantifying violence in games, quality data that allow for comparisons to be made over time and for a deeper understanding of the motivations and context in which these games are played are lacking. Future research should continue to examine these difficult questions to improve the conclusions and knowledge regarding aggressive games.

Matthew Grizzard and John L. Sherry

See also First-Person Perspective, Violent Content From; Video Game Player and Opponent Effects; Video Games, User Motivations

Further Readings

Dill, K. E., & Dill, J. C. (1998). Video game violence: A review of the empirical literature. *Aggression and Violent Behavior, 3*, 407–428.

Greenberg, B. S., Sherry, J., Lachlan, K., Lucas, K., & Holmstrom, A. (2010). Orientations to video games among gender and age groups. *Simulation & Gaming, 41*, 238–259.

Haninger, K., & Thompson, K. M. (2004). Content and ratings of teen-rated video games. *Journal of the American Medical Association, 291*, 856–865.

Jansz, J. (2005). The emotional appeal of violent video games for adolescent males. *Communication Theory, 15*, 219–241.

Scharrer, E. (2004). Virtual violence: Gender and aggression in video game advertisements. *Mass Communication and Society, 7*, 393–412.

Smith, S. L., Lachlan, K., & Tamborini, R. (2003). Popular video games: Quantifying the presence of violence and its context. *Journal of Broadcasting & Electronic Media, 47*, 58–76.

Thompson, K. M., & Haninger, K. (2001). Violence in E-rated video games. *Journal of the American Medical Association, 286*, 591–598.

Zillmann, D. (1998). The psychology of the appeal of portrayals of violence. In J. H. Goldstein (Ed.), *Why we watch: The attractions of violent entertainment* (pp. 179–211). New York, NY: Oxford University Press.

Uses and Gratifications Perspective of Media Effects

Uses and gratifications (U&G) perspective has been widely used in research to study media audiences. The perspective is grounded in the idea that consumers are motivated to use media to satisfy certain needs or wants and that they receive certain gratifications from this use. Uses and gratifications is a psychological perspective that positions media consumers as active participants whose choices are goal-directed and purposive. These choices can be affected by personal characteristics, social roles, and interaction. Research on U&G has branched out in many different directions, including links among motives, attitudes, and behaviors; motives associated with different media use; social and psychological variables associated with media use; gratifications sought and obtained; links among personal characteristics, motives, and outcomes; theoretical connections between U&G and other perspectives; and examination of the reliability and validity of methods and measures (see Alan Rubin's chapter in *Media Effects: Advances in Theory and Research* [2009] for a comprehensive review of U&G). Because the U&G perspective seeks to explain why consumers use media, it has been particularly insightful when applied to violent media content, allowing media effects researchers to understand not only why people are drawn to violent media but how those motives may relate to outcomes such as aggression. When focusing on media violence, the areas of U&G that emerge relate to gratifications sought and obtained and motives for viewing of media violence.

Uses and Gratifications Perspective

Media gratifications research dates back to the 1940s, yet the perspective really developed in the 1970s as more detailed explanations of media use, with particular focus on motives, began to emerge. Elihu Katz, Jay G. Blumler, and Michael Gurevitch (1974) helped to frame U&G research by surveying early research in this area. They outlined the basic components of the perspective: people have social and psychological needs for using media, and these needs lead people to develop expectations of media use. Based on these needs and expectations, people engage in various patterns of use and, as a result, experience various levels of need gratifications and other outcomes.

One of the first models of the U&G paradigm was developed by Karl Rosengren in 1974. Rosengren mapped out the foundation of the paradigm in that human needs interact with individual characteristics and the societal structure. This interaction results in individual problems and their accompanying solutions, which combine to form motives for gaining gratifications. Individuals then turn to the media and other avenues of communication to satisfy these motives. Use of these different channels produces satisfied or unsatisfied gratifications and may affect individual characteristics and the societal structure. Other researchers have altered or adapted the model, but the basic components appear to remain unchanged.

Alan Rubin suggested that there are five basic assumptions within the U&G framework. The first assumption focuses on motivation and points to the notion that media use is goal directed and with purpose. The second assumption is that media audiences are active and engage in selective exposure to media content. The third assumption is that social and psychological antecedent variables affect media use and behaviors. The fourth assumption stipulates that there are functional alternatives to media use in that other communication (such as interpersonal) can also satisfy wants and needs. And finally, the fifth assumption is that people make conscious choices when selecting media to consume.

Audience activity is a key concept in U&G research. Audience activity is selective and has typically been examined using four concepts: intentionality, selectivity, attention, and involvement. For instance, Rubin and Elizabeth Perse (1987) examined college student viewing of soap operas and noted that the students experienced more gratification when they were active viewers, which the researchers determined based their planning to watch the show, attention while watching, and distraction during viewing.

Gratifications Sought and Obtained

In 1979 Philip Palmgreen and Jay Rayburn brought to the fore the distinction between gratifications sought and gratifications obtained. They utilized a discrepancy model to examine gratifications sought and obtained from public television. They found that such a model was helpful in examining this discrepancy because it helped to distinguish between viewers and nonviewers of public television. In the years that followed, researchers found strong correlations of .40 to .60 between gratifications sought and obtained.

The examination of gratifications sought shed light on the concept of expectancy as a crucial portion for consideration in U&G research. Researchers have viewed the expectancy portion of U&G in various ways, yet when pooled together research has tended to indicate that behavior, behavioral intentions, and attitudes relate to both expectancy and evaluation of media use. Palmgreen and Rayburn worked to develop an expectancy-value model of U&G. They conceptualized gratifications as a function of beliefs and evaluations and found support for this model. Palmgreen and Rayburn's research has indicated that expectations about media characteristics affect motives for use and actual usage, which in turn influence gratifications obtained. This is a reciprocal process because usage and perceived gratifications obtained then affect expectations.

Motives for Media Use

Researchers have developed and adapted different measures to study motives for media use. Bradley Greenberg (1974) developed an early scale of this type. His scale was constructed by having school-children (ages 9, 12, and 15) in London, England, write essays explaining why they liked to watch television. The essays were used by Greenberg to examine the language used, to find prevalent motives and to locate a form of testing that was agreeable within the English school system. Greenberg evaluated 180 essays and identified several general motives: learning, habit, arousal, companionship, relaxation, forgetting, and passing time. Greenberg then used these motives to construct a 31-item scale assessing motives for television use.

Rubin adapted the Greenberg scale and used it to test the television viewing motivations of American children. In so doing, he decreased the number of statements from 31 to 24. Rubin further adapted the scale to formulate a measurement suitable for adults. These scales have been adapted in several different studies so that respondents in various situations could be studied effectively.

Uses and gratifications has been widely applied to television use. Researchers have identified a generally consistent list of motives for television use. These reoccurring motives are relaxation, companionship, habit, passing time, entertainment, social interaction, information, arousal, escape, voyeurism, and parasocial interaction. Researchers have suggested that television viewing motives are related to one another. Rubin found that ritualized television use (e.g., escape, habit, passing time, and relaxation) is associated with habitual and frequent media use. Ritual media consumption also indicates a high regard for the medium. Instrumental television use (e.g., for information and exciting entertainment) is selective and with purpose, yet is not necessarily frequent; nor is it associated with high regard for the medium. Instrumental use is seen as involving consumption of media content. Ritualistic use is associated with a greater amount of exposure to and affinity with the medium, whereas instrumental use is associated with content selectivity, greater affinity with the content, and more perceived reality of the content.

Researchers have linked motives to program types by focusing on specific program genres instead of general television programming. For instance, Rubin has noted positive correlations of relaxation and passing time motives with watching comedy shows, arousal with watching sports programming, information with watching talk-interview and game shows, and companionship and arousal motives with watching adventure-drama programs. Within the television medium, uses and gratifications has been applied to news, public television, religious television, soap operas, rerun programs, music videos, reality television, television shopping programs, and television crime drama.

Although much U&G research has focused on television use, the perspective can and has been applied to other content, media, and technologies such as talk radio, radio music listening, MP3 players, VCR and DVD players, television remote controls, mobile content, texting, computer-mediated communication (CMC) in learning contexts, and video games.

Also, a great deal of U&G research has focused on the Internet. Research in this area has focused on media alternatives based on consumer needs, such as a comparison of television and the World Wide Web. In some ways, the web is functionally similar to television, especially in terms of diversion. However, use of the web did not prove to be as relaxing an activity as was television use. In general, individuals tend to use the web for entertainment, passing time, relaxation, social information, and general information. When examining the Internet as a whole, very similar motives emerged: interpersonal utility, passing time, information seeking, convenience, and entertainment. The most salient motive of the five was information seeking, which implies a more instrumental use of the medium. Furthermore, individuals with less perceived life satisfaction and feeling of underappreciation in their interpersonal communication were more likely to use the Internet as a functional alternative to face-to-face interactions. In studying different media and technologies, often motives specific to a particular medium will emerge. For instance, a motive for using the Internet is to experience the "sights and sounds" of the Internet. This motive suggests that the nature of the Internet, in terms of its hypermedia form, is itself a motive for use.

In addition to studying media consumer uses and gratifications of the Internet in general, many researchers have focused on specific types of Internet content such as social networking sites Facebook, MySpace, and Twitter; online communities; and YouTube, blogs, and online gaming.

Researchers have also examined U&G from the perspective of specific content on the Internet. In one instance regarding politics, MySpace users who accessed candidate profiles for the 2008 primary did so mainly for social interaction with like-minded supporters and to acquire information and entertainment. In another instance, users of the consumer product and service review website Yelp tended to use the site to seek information and for entertainment, convenience, interpersonal utility, and to pass time.

With its emphasis on gratifications sought and obtained from media, the U&G perspective has added insight into the use of many types of media, from radio, to television, to the Internet (and many other technologies), as well as various types of content presented via these media. Researchers have also applied the perspective to violent media content, where it has been particularly helpful in understanding antecedents to and outcomes of use.

Uses and Gratifications of Violent Media

The U&G perspective has been helpful in understanding media consumers' exposure to and need for violent content. Paul Haridakis and Alan Rubin (2003, 2005) have produced a significant contribution to this line of research. For instance, Haridakis (2002) looked at disinhibition, locus of control, and experience with crime as antecedent conditions to motivation for viewing violent television content. He also examined exposure to and perceived realism of violent content as outcome variables. He found that disinhibited men with no prior direct experience with crime and no specific motives for watching violent television tend to experience physical and verbal behavioral aggression. Furthermore, viewers with an external locus of control who watch violent television to pass time, to unwind, and for entertainment tended to repress aggression (defined as anger and hostility).

Haridakis and Rubin found that watching violent television tends to be more ritualized than instrumental viewing. Viewers indicated that they were motivated to watch violent television for amusement, enjoyment, relaxation, and a restful experience more than to find information, learn concepts, or be with others. The researchers further concluded that ritualized viewing may be a better predictor of aggression than instrumental viewing, citing that, of all of the motivations, entertainment was most frequently associated with aggression. The researchers also noted that one of the most important findings of the study is that personal characteristics were often the most important predictors of aggression. For instance, viewers with an external locus of control indicated more aggression, anger, and hostility than did those with an internal locus of control. Furthermore, violent television viewers with an external locus of control who were motivated to watch to pass time tended to watch violent programs more often and were more aggressive than other viewers. When watching violent news stories, such as those that cover acts of terrorism, viewers tended to be motivated to watch for information, and this motive was related to fear of victimization.

Gender differences are a consideration in the relationship between motivations for watching violent content and aggression. Examining this difference more closely, Haridakis (2006) found that, for men, aggression was related to the habitual entertainment motivation, while social interaction was a negative predictor of aggression. Therefore, men's habitual use of television violence, rather than instrumental use, could be a better predictor of aggression. Haridakis postulated that men motivated to watch violent television for entertainment or relaxation may possess a more sensitized tolerance for aggression. For women, the information motive was negatively associated with hostility, perhaps because they were focused on the information presented and not on the violence. Exposure to media aggression has also been found to relate to engaging in relationship aggression, yet the connection between media portrayals of physical violence and physical aggression toward a romantic partner emerged only for men (see the work of Sarah Coyne and colleagues, 2010).

Gratifications sought from consuming violent media are not necessarily gratifications obtained. Using a survey to collect data from junior high, high school, and college students (ages 11–25 years), Kathryn Greene and Marina Krcmar (2005) found that the personality variables sensation seeking, verbal aggression, argumentativeness, and instrumental androgyny (associated with masculinity) were positively related to violent and horror film exposure and to a lesser extent realistic and fictional violent television. But because these personality variables did not consistently predict affinity for violent media, the researchers concluded that although people may seek violent media fare as a form of gratification, actual obtained gratifications are questionable. Furthermore, they noted that exposure to violent media was related to self-reported violent and risky behaviors. In a similar study that Krcmar conducted with Linda Kean (2005), the researchers concluded that gratifications sought and obtained were not strongly correlated. They examined personality variables including neuroticism, extraversion, openness, and agreeableness and concluded that personality variables were not related to watching particular content (gratifications sought), yet personality was associated with gratifications obtained. In both studies, the researchers examined gratifications sought not as motives but as exposure to violent content.

Sensation seeking has been examined as a personality variable related to media content exposure choices. The role of sensation seeking in violent media use can be better understood as having four dimensions: experience seeking, thrill and adventure seeking, disinhibition, and boredom susceptibility. Disinhibition, as well as to a lesser level thrill and adventure seeking, were found to be positively related to exposure to violent television, while experience seeking was negatively related to such exposure. Furthermore, a connection between sensation seeking and real risk taking emerged in that all four dimensions, but especially disinhibition, were related to real risk taking.

Central to the study of gratifications sought and obtained as well as motives for media use in general

are selective exposure to and enjoyment of media violence. Violent content tends to increase selective exposure to violent media, yet it decreases enjoyment of that exposure. Specifically, research has suggested that when presented with descriptions of violent and nonviolent media fare, viewers were more likely to choose the violent content, but they reported higher levels of enjoyment after watching nonviolent programs. A potential explanation for this is that viewers may use the inclusion of violence as a predictor of other types of content they enjoy, such as action or conflict; or that they may initially prefer to watch violent content but experience an adverse reaction while viewing it, thereby decreasing their enjoyment of the content. Andrew Weaver (2011) conducted a meta-analysis of selective exposure to and enjoyment of violence and suggested that, in addition to violent content possibly increasing selective exposure because of other elements of enjoyment, it may also be seen as "forbidden fruit" because parents may have restricted such viewing when the viewers were children; or voyeuristic appeal may play a role, because most people don't experience violence personally and may be curious. With regard to the negative relationship with enjoyment, if viewers experience an aversion to violent content it may be because they attended to the violence more than to the enjoyable content while viewing.

Andrew Przybylski, Richard Ryan, and C. Scott Rigby (2009) examined motivations that relate to violent video game content. As did earlier studies examining violent media content, they found that violent content in video games was not related to enjoyment, motivation, or need satisfaction (a sense of competence and autonomy during play). Instead, they found that trait aggression was related to the desire for future play and value associated with game play in that players indicated a stronger preference and value for violent video games, but they did not display consistently higher enjoyment of the content.

Summary

Application of the U&G perspective has allowed media effects researchers to understand the viewing of violent content. For instance, viewing of violent television tends to be more ritualized than instrumental in that viewers watch for reasons such as entertainment and relaxation instead of information seeking. Although entertainment motivation was the most frequently occurring motive linked to aggression, personal characteristics such as locus of control can be the most important predictors of aggression. Personal characteristics such as sensation seeking and verbal aggression also emerged as predictors of exposure to violent content. The research has shown gender differences as well, in that men's habitual use of violent content has emerged as a predictor of aggression, and portrayals of physical violence in the media were linked to real-world romantic partner physical aggression for men. Interestingly, though, gratifications sought are not necessarily gratifications obtained. Similarly, although viewers may actively select to view violent media, they don't necessarily enjoy the experience.

Juliann Cortese

See also Aggression and Enjoyment; Attitude, Effects of Media Violence on; Effects of Media Violence on Relational Aggression; Gender, Effects of Violent Content on; Video Games, User Motivations

Further Readings

Cortese, J., & Rubin, A. M. (2010). Uses and gratifications of television home shopping. *Atlantic Journal of Communication, 18*(2), 89–109. doi:10.1080/15456870903554924

Coyne, S. M., Nelson, D. A., Graham-Kevan, N., Keister, E., & Grant, D. M. (2010). Mean on the screen: Psychopathy, relationship aggression, and aggression in the media. *Personality and Individual Differences, 48*(3), 288–293. doi:10.1016/j.paid.2009.10.018

Coyne, S. M., Nelson, D. A., Graham-Kevan, N., Tew, E., Meng, K. N., & Olsen, J. A. (2011). Media depictions of physical and relational aggression: Connections with aggression in young adults' romantic relationships. *Aggressive Behavior, 37*(1), 56–62. doi:10.1002/ab.20372

Greenberg, B. S. (1974). Gratifications of television viewing and their correlates for British children. In J. G. Blumler & E. Katz (Eds.), *The uses of mass communications: Current perspectives on gratifications research* (pp. 71–92). Beverly Hills, CA: Sage.

Greene, K., & Krcmar, M. (2005). Predicting exposure to and liking of media violence: A uses and gratifications approach. *Communication Studies, 56*(1), 71–93. doi:10.1080/0008957042000332250

Haridakis, P. (2002). Viewer characteristics, exposure to television violence, and aggression. *Media Psychology, 4*(4), 323–352. Retrieved from http://www.tandfonline.com/doi/abs/10.1207/S1532785XMEP0404_02

Haridakis, P. M. (2006). Men, women, and televised violence: Predicting viewer aggression in male and female television viewers. *Communication Quarterly, 54*(2), 227–255. doi:10.1080/01463370600650951

Haridakis, P. M., & Rubin, A. M. (2003). Motivation for watching television violence and viewer aggression. *Mass Communication and Society, 6*(1), 29–56.

Haridakis, P. M., & Rubin, A. M. (2005). Third-person effects in the aftermath of terrorism. *Mass Communication and Society, 8*(1), 39–59.

Katz, E., Blumler, J. G., & Gurevitch, M. (1974). Utilization of mass communication by the individual. In J. G. Blumler & E. Katz (Eds.), *The uses of mass communications: Current perspectives on gratifications research* (pp. 19–32). Beverly Hills, CA: Sage.

Krcmar, M., & Greene, K. (1999). Predicting exposure to and uses of television violence. *Journal of Communication, 49*(3), 24–45. Retrieved from http://onlinelibrary.wiley.com/doi/10.1111/j.1460-2466.1999.tb02803.x/abstract

Krcmar, M., & Kean, L. (2005). Uses and gratifications of media violence: Personality correlates of viewing and liking violent genres. *Media Psychology, 7*(4), 399–420. Retrieved from http://www.tandfonline.com/doi/abs/10.1207/S1532785XMEP0704_5

Palmgreen, P., & Rayburn, J. D., II. (1979). Uses and gratifications and exposure to public television: A discrepancy approach. *Communication Research, 6,* 155–180.

Przybylski, A. K., Rigby, C. S., & Ryan, R. M. (2010). A motivational model of video game engagement. *Review of General Psychology, 14*(2), 154–166. doi:10.1037/a0019440

Przybylski, A. K., Ryan, R. M., & Rigby, C. S. (2009). The motivating role of violence in video games. *Personality and Social Psychology Bulletin, 35*(2), 243–59. doi:10.1177/0146167208327216

Rosengren, K. E. (1974). Uses and gratifications: A paradigm outlined. In J. G. Blumler & E. Katz (Eds.), *The uses of mass communications: Current perspectives on gratifications research 1* (pp. 269–286). Beverly Hills, CA: Sage.

Rubin, A. M. (1981). An examination of television viewing motivations. *Communication Research—An International Quarterly, 8*(2), 141–165.

Rubin, A. M. (2009). Uses-and-gratifications perspective on media effects. In J. Bryant & M. B. Oliver (Eds.), *Media effects: Advances in theory and research* (3rd ed., pp. 165–184). New York: Taylor & Francis.

Rubin, A. M., & Perse, E. M. (1987). Audience activity and soap opera involvement: A uses and effects investigation. *Communication Research, 14,* 246–268.

Weaver, A. (2011). A meta-analytical review of selective exposure to and the enjoyment of media violence. *Journal of Broadcasting & Electronic Media, 55*(2), 232–250. doi:doi/abs/10.1080/08838151.2011.570826

Weaver, A. J., & Kobach, M. J. (2012). The relationship between selective exposure and the enjoyment of television violence. *Aggressive Behavior, 38*(2), 175–184. doi:10.1002/ab.21417

VIDEO GAME INDUSTRY, REGULATION WITHIN THE

The growing popularity and sophistication of video games has been paralleled by increased calls for regulation of the medium. Politicians, parents, and other critics of games have been especially concerned about the interactive depictions of violence in particular titles, such as the *Mortal Kombat* and *Grand Theft Auto* series. Solutions proposed by pro-regulation forces include outright bans and legislation targeting retailers, and the industry has countered with self-regulatory responses. This entry discusses regulation within the video game industry, including a historical overview and review of regulatory options.

Early Video Game Regulation

Calls to regulate video games came shortly after their emergence as a popular medium in the 1970s. The primitive arcade game *Death Race* (1976), which involved little more than driving a small blocky car and running over stick figures, was the first violent video game to generate controversy. News outlets such as *60 Minutes* broadcast stories featuring the game, and protests followed. Ronnie Lamm, a mother and Parent Teacher Association (PTA) president, emerged as a crusader against video games during the early 1980s. Although other controversial titles were released during this time, most notably the Atari 2600 game *Custer's Revenge*, in which players raped a Native American

woman, no significant attempts were made to regulate content. This is likely due to the rarity and lack of popularity of titles with offending material and (more important) the poor, abstract graphics of early games themselves. Rather than focusing on content or the industry, the first notable attempts to regulate video games attempted to place restrictions on arcades, out of fear that they encouraged truancy and delinquent behavior among children and teens. These efforts occurred at the local level in the early 1980s.

Senate Hearings on Video Games in the 1990s

By the early 1990s, a more realistic generation of video games had become popular, sparking enormous controversy. *Mortal Kombat,* a highly successful fighting game featuring spurting blood and gruesome finishing maneuvers, delighted players but shocked parents and politicians, who launched a movement against home video games. Beginning in 1993, Senators Joseph Lieberman (D-Conn.) and Herb Kohl (D-Wis.) spearheaded hearings investigating the video game industry. They called representatives from major game manufacturers (chiefly Nintendo and Sega) in front of Congress and demanded action to protect children from exposure to certain types of content. In addition to the grisly violence in *Mortal Kombat,* the sexual portrayals in the full-motion video game *Night Trap* also attracted scrutiny. Under threat of governmental intervention and possible censorship, game producers came up with a self-regulatory response. They created an organization called the Entertainment Software Association (ESA) to represent their interests and through it proposed a game ratings system through the Entertainment Software Rating Board (ESRB).

The Entertainment Software Rating Board and Game Ratings

The ESRB, according to the organization's website, is a "non-profit, self-regulatory body that assigns ratings for video games and apps so parents can make informed choices." ESRB ratings now appear on the boxes (or in the online descriptions) of all major games released in North America, with two parts to each rating. The first part, the *ratings symbols,* suggests the age appropriateness of a game. Common ratings symbols include E for Everyone, T for Teen, and M for Mature. The second part, *content descriptors,* indicates specific types of content in a game. The ESRB has 30 common content descriptors indicating multiple varieties of violent, sexual, language, and drug-related content. In the case of violence, the ESRB rating system distinguishes among cartoon, fantasy, intense, and sexual violence. Senators Lieberman and Kohl responded favorably to the ESRB ratings, a response echoed by many others. However, there have been some criticisms of the ESRB ratings, resulting in modifications to the system, such as the addition of an E10+ rating in 2004 (similar to the PG-13 movie rating).

Although ESRB ratings are now the standard in the United States and Canada, other countries have adopted different systems. The most prominent of these is the Pan-European Game Information (PEGI) age rating system, which replaced the individual systems of several countries across Europe. As of this writing, PEGI represents 30 nations and mirrors the ESRB system in that it has both ratings symbols (with numbers representing appropriate ages) and content descriptors (with pictorial symbols), including violence and a category not in the ESRB ratings—discrimination. In other countries, ratings are determined not through self-regulation but through government-run ratings systems. In Australia, for example, the Australian Classification Board (with help from the attorney general's department) rates video games and other forms of media. Worldwide, ratings appear to be a preferred approach to video game regulation, but other regulatory measures have been proposed or taken.

Anti–Video Game Bills in the 2000s

In the United States, the debate over video game regulation did not end with the creation of the ESRB,

for several reasons. First, highly publicized tragedies such as the 1999 Columbine High School (Littleton, Colorado) and 2012 Sandy Hook Elementary School (Newtown, Connecticut) shootings called attention to video game violence. Some blamed the massacres on violent games because of evidence suggesting that the perpetrators played them. Second, by cementing the idea that games are not just for children but adults too, the ESRB in some ways enabled the game industry to create even more violent titles, particularly the *Grand Theft Auto* series. In these games, which rose to popularity in the early 2000s, a player assumes the role of a carjacking criminal who can be made to perform a host of violent behaviors, ranging from running over pedestrians to beating prostitutes to shooting police officers. The severity and breadth of objectionable content in the *Grand Theft Auto* series focused attention on other areas of potential regulation, such as the marketing of games to children and retailer enforcement of the ratings system.

Enforcement of the ratings system received a great deal of attention in the 2000s. From 2003 on, several U.S. states, including Illinois, Indiana, Louisiana, Michigan, Mississippi, and Utah, introduced legislation against the selling of violent and sexual video games. These laws made the sale of M- and AO-rated games to minors a crime punishable by fines, typically. Interestingly, the target of the laws was retailers rather than the game industry itself. Legislators had already won court battles to regulate the sale of sexually explicit materials and tried to make the case that certain video games are similarly harmful to children. Entertainment trade group representatives such as the ESA countered that these laws were unconstitutional, claiming that video games should enjoy the same First Amendment protections as books and movies. Although the courts struck down the laws in case after case, the battle raged on.

In 2005 California passed the most prominent anti–video game bill of the 2000s. Signed into law by then-governor Arnold Schwarzenegger, it restricted the sale of violent video games to minors. Enforcement of the law was permanently enjoined by a district court ruling, but California argued that games are akin to sexually explicit magazines and had no First Amendment protection regarding sales to minors. Although the Ninth Circuit Court rejected this argument, just as other courts had done to laws restricting video games, California's case, *Brown v. Entertainment Merchants Association,* made history when the U.S. Supreme Court decided to consider it, making it the first video game regulation case to appear before the Court. The Supreme Court's decision to hear this case surprised both proponents and critics of anti–video game legislation, who eagerly awaited a ruling.

2011 Supreme Court Ruling and Implications

On June 27, 2011, the U.S. Supreme Court ruled against California's violent video game law for violating the First Amendment. In his review of the case in *Boston College Law Review,* legal scholar Christopher Clements outlined the Court's reasoning. The majority opinion, authored by Justice Antonin Scalia, said only a very small subset of speech (chiefly obscenity and incitement) lacks First Amendment protection, and violence is *not* within this subset. Scalia pointed to the long history of unrestricted media violence in American society. He also rejected the notion that violent video games are different because they have interactivity by calling attention to the interactive nature of media as ancient as literature. Furthermore, he said the state of California failed to make the case that video games pose an immediate threat to minors, pointing to the shortcomings on scientific research on the subject. Finally, Scalia said the California law was not the least restrictive way to keep violent video games away from children, which instead could be achieved through the ESRB rating system.

The 2011 Supreme Court ruling effectively ended attempts to regulate violent video games by punishing retailers in the United States. In discussing the decision, Clements said that the violent video game laws of the 2000s inundated the courts with expensive, lopsided battles between states and entertainment advocacy groups, costing the industry and taxpayers alike. Given the Supreme Court's ruling, it makes little sense to continue attempting to regulate video games through this method. In his concluding analysis, Clements argued for a more effective and constitutionally defendable means to regulate violent video games.

Other Forms of Video Game Regulation

One alternative approach to anti–video game legislation is increased self-regulation. The Interactive Entertainment Merchants Association (IEMA), which represented almost all major game retailers (until merging with the Video Software Dealers Association in 2006 to form the Entertainment Merchants Association), pledged to restrict the sale of certain games to minors. It voluntarily committed to requiring proof of age for all M-rated game purchases. Although the National Institute on Media and the Family questioned the success of this initiative, it noted improvement in compliance over time. To improve self-regulation, Clements suggested that legislators should endeavor to work with the industry rather than against it. Given the continual defeat of anti–video game legislation in the courts, Clements argued that the best method of accomplishing the goals of these laws would be for legislators to accept and expand the efforts of the ESRB. These largely successful efforts already included rating nearly all games sold in retail stores, providing advertising guidelines, and levying corrective actions against publishers that refuse to comply with ESRB requirements. The ESRB efforts could be further expanded, Clements suggested, by making ratings mandatory.

Although this type of industry self-regulation currently seems to be the preferred direction for video game regulation in the United States, there are other options. Craig Anderson and colleagues have enumerated many of them in their book *Violent Video Game Effects on Children and Adolescents* (2007). One of their suggestions, which could be seen as an extension of the ESRB ratings, is warning labels, similar to the ones that appear on tobacco products. These would take age-appropriateness and content labels a step further by spelling out potential effects of certain types of content. A warning label might say, for example, "This game contains violent content. Violent content may increase short-term hostility and long-term aggressive script development." Warning labels would depend on social scientific research findings showing a link between violent video game play and effects, which some experts on media effects have found unconvincing.

Anderson and colleagues also suggested options for video game regulation that rely on governmental intervention. One is licensing requirements through agencies like the Federal Communications Commission (FCC) that are required for broadcast radio and television stations in the United States and could perhaps be extended to other forms of media. Another option, similar to the one proposed by Clements, is for the government to get more involved in ratings systems, such as through government-run ratings systems and agencies, as have been instituted in Australia. Governments might also make the production of certain types of materials illegal, as they do with child pornography.

In her book *Sex and Video Games,* author Brenda Brathwaite (2007) suggested other forms of government regulation. Many of these could also be forms of industry self-regulation (as some already are). Legislators could attempt to require labels on games (such as ratings), for example, as suggested by Clements and Anderson. They could also require electronic prompts for retailers, which many stores already do through checkout systems that tell the sales clerk to check for identification whenever mature games are scanned. Another idea is to require businesses that sell games to obtain special licenses, similar to liquor licenses. Or game retailers could be classified as adult video stores, especially if they sell AO-rated games (which no major ones currently do). Retailers could also be told to separate M- and AO-rated games from more family-friendly titles.

Although Anderson and Brathwaite outline a variety of ways the government can get involved in video game regulation, it seems unlikely that most of these measures would survive First Amendment challenges in the United States. They might work in other nations, however, or as forms of self-regulation.

The Future of Video Game Regulation

A central issue in the ongoing battle over video game regulation concerns whether or not games are a protected form of free speech or a harmful substance subject to government regulation. In many countries, violent game titles have been censored or outright banned, but this seems unlikely to happen in the United States given the 2011 Supreme Court ruling. Games have come a long way since their early days and now incorporate sophisticated narratives and character development on top of advanced graphics and sounds. The addition of these artistic elements aligns games with protected forms of speech, although two future developments may change this and open the door to more stringent regulation such as government intervention.

One pivotal issue in the 2011 Supreme Court ruling was the lack of convincing social scientific research on video game violence effects. As discussed by Clements, courts in many cases involving video game violence have been critical of the research linking game violence with player aggression. This is not to say, however, that there is no link, and many in the scholarly community believe that video game violence may be harmful. If future studies show a more convincing association between video game violence and harmful effects

(perhaps by incorporating physiological measures such as fMRI or longitudinal designs), then courts may be more willing to allow for legislation against them.

Technological advances of video games are a second important issue that could affect future regulation. In the summer of 2005, hidden sexually explicit scenes were discovered in *Grand Theft Auto: San Andreas,* prompting Senator Hillary Clinton and others to call for more controls on violent and sexually explicit games. The sex scenes were not caught by the ESRB, which likely would have likely given the game an AO- rather than an M-rating if it knew about it. This brought attention to the fact that the highly interactive landscapes of many contemporary games may not be possible to fully and accurately rate using existing techniques.

More recent technological advances of video games have generated even further concern. The violent game *Manhunt 2,* for example, initially received an AO-rating in 2007 even though the first *Manhunt* game was rated M. Some speculated that a reason for this rating jump might be the naturally mapped interactivity in the Nintendo Wii version of the game. Instead of pressing buttons to perform violent behaviors on the Wii, players were able to use the system's motion controllers to mimic violent acts like stabbing and strangulation. To get an M-rating, the content of the game had to be censored somewhat.

Clements pointed to several court opinions that seemingly opened the door for more advanced video game technology to be regulated in the future. He said the Seventh Circuit Court remains open to the idea that video game violence could one day reach a level of cultural disapproval similar to that of sexually explicit material, for example, if the games use real actors who convincingly simulated extreme acts of violence (or if the mode of interaction closely mirrored real-life violent actions, as in *Manhunt 2*). Justice Samuel Alito made a similar point in his concurring opinion with the 2011 Supreme Court ruling. He wrote about ways in which video games differ from older forms of media and said that games may become so immersive someday that it makes little sense to classify them alongside traditionally protected forms of media. As video games continue to evolve, the means by which they are regulated will likely need to evolve as well, making the regulation of video games an ongoing process.

Paul Skalski

See also *Grand Theft Auto;* Interactive Media, Aggressive Outcomes of; Legislating Media Violence: Law and Policy; Rating Systems, Video Games

Further Readings

Anderson, C. A., Gentile, D. A., & Buckley, K. E. (2007). *Violent video game effects on children and adolescents.* New York, NY: Oxford University Press.

Brathwaite, B. (2007). *Sex in video games.* Boston: Charles River Media.

Brown v. Entertainment Merchants Association, 131 S.Ct. 2729 (2011).

Clements, C. (2012). Protecting protected speech: Violent video game legislation post–*Brown v. Entertainment Merchants Ass'n. Boston College Law Review, 53*(2), 661–692.

Donovan, T. (2010). *Replay: The history of video games.* East Sussex, UK: Yellow Ant.

Kent, S. L. (2001). *The ultimate history of video games.* Roseville, CA: Prima.

Website

Entertainment Software Rating Board; http://www.esrb.org

VIDEO GAME PLATFORMS, EFFECTS OF

Digital games are referred to by many names, such as *video games, online games, massively multiplayer online role-playing games (MMORPGs), advergames,* and *mobile games.* Regardless of how individuals refer to these types of games, they can be played across a variety of platforms. Video games can be played on cell phones (mobile games), console systems, and on laptop or desktop computers. Digital games played on these platforms can be of different genres and may contain violent content. Just as people once had to go to movie theaters to see films, in the early days of video games people could play them only in arcades and bars. Developments soon led to home console video game cartridge systems (e.g., Atari). As communication technology advanced, so too did console systems, and soon video game developers were selling games that could be played on laptop computers, cell phones, and tablet computers.

One question that arises from the various gaming genres and platforms is to what extent do platforms affect gaming effects? For instance, does mobile gaming offer different experiences than portable gaming—even if both platforms offer the exact same game? This entry outlines the potential platform effects of gaming technology. First, the overall effects of gaming are discussed, followed by the various effects that can be elicited across platforms.

The Negative and Positive Effects of Video Games

Video games may contain violent content regardless of gaming genre or platform. This violent content has raised concerns from parents, consumer organizations, and even the government. However, not all video game content is deemed to be negative and violent. For instance, the Entertainment Software Association (ESA) states that video games have positive impacts upon artistic design and education, increase interactions between parents and children, benefit the economy, help promote healthy behaviors through motion-sensing technology, and bring awareness to social issues.

There has been much debate about the outcomes of playing video games (see Bushman, Rothstein, & Anderson, 2010; Ferguson & Kilburn, 2010). Numerous research studies have found deleterious effects of playing video games. However, other studies have found that playing video games has had positive effects. For instance, it has been reported that video games can have positive effects on educational outcomes, spatial skills, cognitive abilities, sociability, and therapeutic treatments. However, a 2010 meta-analysis by Craig Anderson and colleagues found that violent video game play was associated with increased aggressive behaviors, aggressive cognition, and aggressive affect, while decreasing empathy and prosocial behaviors. Regardless of whether the effects of video games are positive or negative, they can often be broken down into three primary categories related to cognition (thoughts), affect (emotions), and behavior. To understand potential differences in these effects that depend on the video game platform that is used, one must know some of the differences in the platforms.

The Platforms of Gaming

The gaming industry sometimes distinguishes itself by the type of platform used, such as computer gaming, console gaming, portable console gaming, and mobile gaming. This section discusses each of these platforms in turn.

Computer Gaming

Computer gaming was once commonly referred to as *online gaming,* because most often individuals used personal computers to access the Internet. However, newer console systems can connect to the Internet, so the term is no longer used to differentiate between computer gaming and console gaming. Computer gaming differs from console gaming in that computer games are played on either desktop or laptop computers. Thus, the interface is an individual's computing device (which often may be used for purposes other than gaming), with a keyboard used to operate the game. Gaming software can be downloaded from the Internet or purchased on computer discs. Available games for computer gaming include MMORPGs and advergames (games developed by a company to advertise a brand).

Console Gaming

Console gaming generally involves a device used to play games on a gamer's television with CDs or Internet downloads. The three main hardware systems that dominate the console market are Microsoft Xbox, Sony PlayStation, and Nintendo Wii. Typical genres for console system games include fighting, sports, racing, adventure/fantasy, strategy games, and first-person-shooter games. Games played via a console can either be single player or multiplayer and can be played online against other individuals.

The uniqueness of console systems lies in their motion-sensing capabilities, whereby players interact with the gaming interface through game controllers. Game controllers can be broken down into two different interactive formats: traditional interface and physical interface. The traditional interface involves a gaming controller by which the gamer pushes various buttons to interact with the video game. However, the physical interface can transfer a player's movement (e.g., swinging the controller like a sword) into the gaming environment. Although this feature was originated by Nintendo, other manufacturers soon incorporated this technology into their console systems, allowing for both traditional and physical interface controls.

On the one hand, console gaming is similar to computer gaming in that gaming software can be accessed via CDs or Internet download. On the other hand, console gaming differs from computer gaming in interface access. In console gaming, the console is connected to a television set, and the primary interface control is through a video game controller.

Portable Console Systems

The portable gaming system is a portable device that allows individuals to play video games through its own interface. Nintendo was the first to enter the market of portable gaming systems in the 1980s with its Game and Watch devices, followed by the more successful Game Boy series. It later introduced more sophisticated versions such as Game Boy Advanced, Nintendo DS, and Nintendo 3DS. Not to be left out this competitive market, Sony also developed portable gaming systems such as PSP and PSP2. Most portable gaming systems have the control buttons built into the front of the system, keeping them similar in terms of function to their console controller counterparts. However, Nintendo 3DS (which allows for 3D visualization) comes with a drawing/interface wand that is separate from the actual device. In the early days of portable console systems, players had to buy cartridge games that plugged into the systems. But with advancements in wireless technology, individuals can now download those games as software. Portable gaming systems often draw comparisons to what is popularly referred to as "mobile" gaming. However, there are differences between the portable and mobile gaming experiences.

Mobile Gaming

Mobile gaming uses applications that allow users to play games on cell phones and computer tablets. An application is software that is downloaded onto to a device for entertainment (games, music, television, etc.), function (flashlight, QR scanner, ruler, etc.), direction/information (menus, taxis, maps, etc.), connectivity (social networking), or even economic (mobile banking) purposes. The applications generally can be downloaded for free or for a small fee. The increasing popularity of smartphones with advanced computer capability has led to an increase in mobile games.

Regardless of whether a mobile game is played through a regular cell phone, smartphone, or computer tablet, most often mobile games take the form of casual games. Casual games are video games that have wide appeal, are easy to learn and play, and have shorter time commitments than core gaming experiences. Casual games can be played by those without prior gaming experience. Because mobile games are played on an individual's cell phone or smartphone, they typically will use whatever hardware and platform conventions are built into the design of the phone. For instance, some mobile phones have physical keypads, back buttons, and trackballs to interface with applications. Other mobile phones may interface with applications through touch screens. Regardless of the interface method, most mobile games are simple to play; for instance, most games played on touch screens involve a simple swipe of the finger or touch of the screen to interact with the game.

Effects of Video Game Platforms

In terms of effects, mobile, portable, console- and computer-based gaming all have the potential to affect a person's thoughts, attitudes, and behaviors. Media effects researchers have shown that effects associated with the ways online games affect attitudes toward products or brands featured in advergames (Hernandez & Chapa, 2010). Advergames, which focus on brand integration and promotion as the primary goals of play, can be played through mobile devices, computers, and even through consoles (as was the case in Burger King's *Sneak King* video game developed for Microsoft Xbox). Thus, we can see that one form of video game (the advergame) can affect attitudes, cognitions, and even behaviors, and these effects differ across platforms.

Research has shown that violence in video games can affect aggressive thoughts and attitudes and be associated with aggressive behaviors. However, some research has found evidence to the opposite: there is not a link between violent video game play and aggression (Ferguson & Rueda, 2010). Other researchers have argued that the claims for a link between violent video games and aggression are based on flawed methodologies and assumptions (see Ferguson & Kilburn, 2010). This debate will not likely be resolved anytime soon.

Regardless of the types of outcomes (positive or negative) that are examined across or in relation to different platforms, one difference is in the type of experience that they provide. Most gaming experiences can be broken down into either casual or core gaming experiences. A *casual* gaming experience doesn't require advanced knowledge of video games and is targeted toward a wider audience. This type of gaming is not limited to young adult males ages 18 to 35. Instead, these types of games are easy to play and learn, often focusing on reaching a wide array of individuals across various demographic markers. A *core* gaming experience requires advanced knowledge of video games and thus appeals to individuals who often play those types of games. Furthermore,

they require time commitments beyond 5- to 10-minute increments and are often more complex in their design than are casual games.

Although both can be played anywhere, portable gaming and mobile gaming may be very different in the depth of gaming experience that they provide. According to Christian McCrea (2011), "Portable games embody significant and diverse design histories of their own. . . . These games are sometimes more involved than counterparts on home consoles—and it is their portability, not their mobility, which allows that depth. The word 'portable' cannot be productive confused with 'mobile' without ignoring these deep play experiences" (p. 401). Portable gaming allows for a deeper and more engaging game play experience, whereas mobile gaming is often more focused on quick distractions. This is not to say that mobile gaming cannot offer enjoyable or entertaining experiences; however, portable gaming often requires deeper engagement on the part of the player. Mobile games are quick and responsive games that can be played while waiting in a doctor's waiting room or before boarding a plane, for example. Mobile games typically do not have conclusions and rarely have detailed story narratives, unlike games for portable or home console systems.

Three widely popular mobile games illustrate this point. *Angry Birds*, developed by Rovio Entertainment, and *Fruit Ninja* and *Jetpack Joyride*, developed by Half Brick Studios, all require either one or two buttons at most to control the action; all three have very little story narrative and exclude a final conclusion to that narrative; and all take considerably less time to play than console or online games. Players merely advance levels and can earn upgrades and points used to buy new in-game devices. Although these games may be enjoyable, they do not require the same levels of engagement that portable and console games can offer. Console and portable games offer more core gaming experiences and often involve more intricate or complex storylines. For instance, two popular home console games, the *Halo* series, developed by 343 Industries in conjunction with Microsoft Game Studios, have spawned eight different games connected in the *Halo Universe*. Each game offers a unique narrative or point of view in the history of the game, and each one has a unique ending. *Assassins Creed*, developed by Ubisoft, follows a more historical narrative that crosses centuries.

One of the most engaging genres of gaming is the MMORPG. This genre is popular and more readily available through computer gaming than through other platforms. MMORPGs allows players to interact with a gaming environment in which there is no end to the game—merely new quests, adventures, or puzzles to solve. Individuals create their own avatars and can choose from various occupations and professions depending on the genre of the MMORPG. A significant factor associated with MMORPGs is persistence because the gaming environment and game itself have no ending. Research into online gaming is beginning to study how these types of games affect life satisfaction and enjoyment (Chen, Tu, & Wang, 2008), as well as effects on individuals who take on different personas and lifestyles in virtual environments. MMORPG gamers end up feeling involved in their online world and thus ascribe great significance to that world and its relationships. This finding should be warranted with caution, as not everyone who plays online games is psychologically dependent upon that medium for social interaction or happiness. The fact that addiction has been a topic often researched in conjunction with online gaming shows that this type of gaming offers deeper levels of engagement. It is not to say that other platforms cannot offer this type of experience, but MMORPGs may offer greater amounts because of the depth of environments offered to players.

Conclusion

There are different gaming platforms that offer different interface capabilities as well as hardware options. Video games can be played through smartphones, personal computers, portable gaming devices, or home console systems. It is through these different devices that the platforms offer different gaming experiences. Console, computer, and mobile games can all affect an individual's cognitions, attitudes, and/or behaviors. Although all of the platforms can offer engagement, it is in the level of engagement that differences across platforms are seen. This seems to be particularly true in the case of persistent virtual environments in computer and online gaming. The persistence of virtual environments affords the players the opportunity to enter secondary lives and become involved in alternate realities in which they can be any persons or characters they desire. This persistence can also be derived from multiple sequels that keep the storyline going, as with home console gaming series such as *Halo* or *Assassins Creed*. The gaming world is very diverse and can offer quick diversions as well as more engrossing, never-ending gaming experiences. All have the ability to influence enjoyment, excitement, and aggression, but some have a greater ability to engage players and provide them with a sense of meaning.

Vincent Cicchirillo

See also Fantasy Genre, Violence and Aggression in; First-Person Perspective, Violent Content From; Interactive Media, Aggressive Outcomes of; User Involvement in Violent Content, Effects of; Video Game Industry, Regulation Within the; Video Game Player and Opponent Effects; Video Games, User Motivations; Virtual Reality, Violent Content in

Further Readings

Anderson, C. A., Ihori, N., Bushman, B. J., Rothstein, H. R., Shibuya, A., Swing, E. L., Sakamoto, A., & Saleem, M. (2010). Violent video games effects on aggression, empathy, and prosocial behavior in Eastern and Western countries: A meta-analytic review. *Psychological Bulletin, 36*(2), 151–173.

Bushman, B. J., Rothstein, H. R., & Anderson, C. A. (2010). Much ado about something: Violent video game effects and a school of red herring: Reply to Ferguson and Kilburn. *Psychological Bulletin, 36*(2), 182–187.

Chen, L. S., Tu, H. H., & Wang, E. S. (2008). Personality traits and life satisfaction among online game players. *Cyberpsychology & Behavior, 11*(2), 145–149.

Entertainment Software Association. (2012). *Games: Improving what matters.* Retrieved from http://www.theesa.com/games-improving-what-matters/index.asp

Ferguson, C. J., & Kilburn, J. (2010). Much ado about nothing: The misestimation and overinterpretation of violent video game effects in Eastern and Western nations: Comment on Anderson et al. (2010). *Psychological Bulletin, 36*(2), 174–178.

Ferguson, C. J., & Rueda, S. M. (2010). The hitman study: Violent video game exposure effects on aggressive behavior, hostile feelings, and depression. *European Psychologist, 15*(2), 99–108.

Hernandez, M. D., & Chapa, S. (2010). Adolescents, advergames and snack foods: Effects of positive affect and experience on memory and choice. *Journal of Marketing Communications, 16*, 59–68.

McCrea, C. (2011). We play in public: The nature and context of portable gaming systems. *Convergence, 17*(4), 389–403.

Website

Entertainment Software Association; http://www.theesa.com

VIDEO GAME PLAYER AND OPPONENT EFFECTS

Although media options such as the Internet, television, and radio remain popular, video games quickly are becoming a favored media choice of Americans—so much so that gaming could be considered America's new pastime. As a testament to video games' rapid growth, the gaming industry is a multibillion-dollar-a-year industry. The high sales figures are coming from a large percentage of the population. Recent studies have shown that more than 90% of American youth play computer or video games, and the average U.S. household owns at least one dedicated game console, personal computer, or smartphone. Moreover, the Entertainment Software Association (ESA) estimates the average gamer as 30 years old, with 12 years of gaming experience.

Even greater evidence regarding the impact of gaming derives from the amount of game play. Those who play video games tend to manipulate their controllers daily, with some research indicating play times reaching as much as 50 hours per week. The current entry examines the effects of video games on players and how those effects can differ based on a player's traits and the nature of the player's opponent.

Game Player

Generally speaking, most of the media effects research has suggested a significant positive relationship between violent video game play and short-term aggression. One of the most fundamental viewpoints through which to understand differing media effects is gender effects. Past studies consistently have shown that men play video games more than women, although the disparity has closed more recently. Other gender-based findings have suggested that although males and females react to violent content similarly (Anderson & Bushman, 2001), males prefer violent content more than do females, and males are generally more aggressive. Thus, increasing aggressive tendencies through violent game play tend to result in greater aggression-related outcomes by males. Typically, however, men may increase their punitive behavior and decrease their reward behavior toward others following violent game play (Ballard & Lineberger, 1999). Additionally, research has found differential gender effects on emotional response measures to

video games. For example, Stacey Smith's research has found that male characters are more likely to be the perpetrators and targets of game violence.

Craig Anderson's early 2000 research explicitly addressed violent video game effects on female players. His research veered from traditional gaming research by emphasizing the gender of the game character, one of the first attempts to realize the power of a mediating variable: identification. Here, his research team found that participants who played the violent game reported higher levels of aggressive motivation than those who played the nonviolent game, but the character manipulation was not significant.

A player's traits also play a role in video game effects. For instance, research has shown a positive correlation between a person with aggressive tendencies and his or her exposure to violent media. Moreover, those identified as having aggressive personalities are more inclined to consume violent media content throughout life.

Finally, the game player's skill can play a role in the effects of video game play. Those who play games many hours per week do not need to think about the controller or combinations of buttons to press in order for seamless advancement in the game. These players can intuitively respond to conditions on the screen and do not need to consciously determine what to do. Rebecca Chory-Assad and Dana Mastro (2000) indicated that "as skill level increases, players can 'last' longer in the game, leading to increased frequencies of violence exposure and the increased likelihood of encountering even more difficult and possibly more violent challenges as the game proceeds" (p. 7). Alternatively, a novice player may need to think about the controller and consciously determine a combination of buttons, thus lessening the concentration on and awareness of the gaming content. In this light, heavy gamers may more readily experience functional interactivity, or the visual connection to game play, through simple joystick use, which produces a greater sense of presence. Not only may heavy gamers experience more presence, but they likely will experience greater doses of gaming content by playing the game longer and achieving greater success in the game. Given the positive relationship between game play skill and self-efficacy, defined as a player's ability to perform a behavior given his or her perceived skill, research here should consider self-efficacy as a mediator to content effects.

Game Opponent

In one of the few studies investigating the role of opponent, Russell Williams examined the level of frustration and aggression of a person or a computer opponent (i.e., category of opponent, media or human). In this study, a computer-based *Monopoly* game was used as the competition stimulus. When looking at face-to-face stranger interactions versus computer opponents, Williams found that facing a computer opponent increased aggression beyond that of the face-to-face encounter—despite examining competitive play outside the scope of violent content (e.g., *Monopoly*). To further examine the role of competitor, Matthew Eastin manipulated the opponent type (human, CPU) salience of the competitor, hypothesizing that the greater the saliency, the increased hostile effect of competition. Eastin thought that playing against another person would incite stronger hostile expectation bias than playing against the computer. However, Eastin found competition against a computer or against a person did not significantly differ on measures such as hostile expectations, aggressive thoughts, aggressive behaviors, or aggressive feelings. Furthermore, recent research has indicated that playing against another human generated greater presence, engagement, arousal, and positively valenced emotional responses than did playing against a computer (Ravaja et al., 2006)—and playing against a known human elicited greater presence, engagement, arousal, and positively valenced emotional responses than did playing against a stranger.

Research has suggested that there is a relationship between violent video game play and short-term aggression, but the effect appears to differ based on a player's personality and the nature of the player's opponent. More research is needed into factors that may influence the effect of violent video games on players, including whether players' skill level mediates the effect.

Robert P. Griffiths and Matthew S. Eastin

See also Gender, Effects of Violent Content on; General Aggression Model; Group Aggression; Methodologies for Assessing Effect of Media; User Trends Toward Aggressive Games

Further Readings

Anderson, C. A., & Bushman, B. J. (2001). Effects of violent video games on aggressive behavior, aggressive cognition, aggressive affect, physiological arousal, and prosocial behavior: A meta-analytic review of the scientific literature. *Psychological Science, 12*(5), 353–359.

Ballard, M. E., & Lineberger, R. (1999). Video game violence and confederate gender: Effects on reward and punishment given by college males. *Sex Roles, 41*(7), 541–558.

Chory-Assad, R. M., Goodboy, A., Hixson, N., & Baker, S. (2006, November 17). *Exploring involvement in the violent video game context: Effects of player identification, interest, and presence on aggressive outcomes.* Paper presented at the 92nd Annual Convention of the National Communication Association, San Antonio, TX.

Chory-Assad, R. M., & Mastro, D. E. (2000, November). *Violent videogame use and hostility among high school students and college students.* Paper presented at the Annual Meeting of the National Communication Association, Seattle, WA.

Eastin, M. S. (2006). Video game violence and the female game player: Self- and opponent gender effects on presence and aggressive thoughts. *Human Communication Research, 32*(3), 351–372.

Eastin, M. S., & Griffiths, R. P. (2006a). Beyond the shooter game: Examining presence and hostile outcomes among male game players. *Communication Research, 33*(6), 448–466.

Entertainment Software Association. (2012). *Essential facts about the computer and video game industry.* Washington, DC: Author.

Ravaja, N., Saari, T., Turpeinen, M., Laarni, J., Salminen, M., & Kivikangas, M. (2006). Spatial presence and emotions during video game playing: Does it matter with whom you play? *Presence: Teleoperators and Virtual Environments, 15*(4), 381–392.

Williams, R. B., & Clippinger, C. A. (2002). Aggression, competition and computer games: Computer and human opponents. *Computers in Human Behavior, 18*(5), 495–506.

VIDEO GAMES, USER MOTIVATIONS

The appeal of video games lies in the inherent properties of the experiences they provide. Video games, whether online, offline, console based, or mobile based, can be driven by various motivations and gratifications. Individuals are not passive viewers, but active in what they watch, hear, and play. For this reason, motivations for gaming often differ from those for more passive media, but there are some similarities as well. *Motivation* is the involvement and pursuit of goal-directed behavior and influences the degree to which a person continues performing a particular behavior. However, motivation is not a singular concept that occurs in a vacuum. Individuals may have various motivations for choosing a particular medium. This entry outlines the various reasons that individuals have for playing video games.

The Concept of Motivation in Gaming

Whereas motivations were once considered to be needs, they are now believed to be drivers of the means (action) rather that the anticipated end (need satisfaction). For instance, Bobby Hoffman and Louis Nadelson (2010) have shown that motivations to play games influenced both positive affect and cognition regardless of whether the end goal was achieved. Thus, motivation can produce results as well as have affective consequences and direct cognitive processing. People's motivation to play games not only directs their processing of the information or situation of the game but can also have emotional impact, whether excitement, arousal, fear, or anger.

When considering motivation, outside of any one situation, an intrinsic and extrinsic focus can be applied. *Intrinsic motivation* is the drive to perform a task for one's own inner psychological satisfaction. Thus, the individual gets no reward other than his or her own satisfaction. *Extrinsic motivation* is the drive to perform a task in order to receive some form of external reward. For extrinsic motivation individuals will perform a task if there is an incentive to complete that task. Video and online games can offer opportunities for both intrinsic and extrinsic motivations. Intrinsically, a person may play a video game to explore a new virtual world or experience enjoyment. Extrinsically, an individual may play a video or online game in order to gain financial or social rewards. Understanding what these motivations are allows media effects researchers to identify the differences between individuals and predict their gaming behavior (Yee, 2006).

Motivations for Playing Video Games

Achievement/Competition/Challenge

Individuals can be motivated to play video games in order to achieve. Players can be motivated by personal gain, winning, and overpowering others. According to Nick Yee, players seek changes and problem-solving situations and are driven by the appeal of power and manipulation. Individuals can

also play video games for competitive purposes. Competition can incite a person's desire to achieve a goal while being blocked by another person, object, or entity. In video game contexts that impediment can be created by a user-controlled opponent or a computer-controlled opponent. Video games, unlike more passive media (e.g., television), involve more active participation on the part of the game player. Individuals may choose video games because this type of technology offers more instances of competitive situations due to higher levels of interactivity. Furthermore, an individual competing against another person or entity can experience positive emotions when he or she outperforms the other person or entity. In the early 2000s, Peter Vorderer's research found that higher levels of competition resulted in greater enjoyment after playing a competitive video game. Regardless of the outcome, individuals likely seek out video games to partake in a competitive experience or to be challenged.

Social Interaction

Social interaction is a central experience of gaming. The ability to interact with other players and individuals in the context of a gaming environment is a strong motivating factor for seeking out these types of experiences. According to Yee, people can be motivated to play games to make friends, form supportive networks, spend time with significant others, strategize in groups, and collaborate. These all reflect social motivations. Social interaction can be garnered from online functions that allow players to converse through instant messaging and/or live voice audio. Furthermore, these individuals can seek out new relationships (whether platonic or romantic) and/or maintain existing relationships through online game playing. Overall, the research by Yee (2006) and Vincent Cicchirillo (2011) has shown that individuals seek out and enjoy playing video games because they offer social interaction.

Social Escapism/Immersion

The motivation to explore new things, escape from real-world stress, live out fantasies, and role-play are classified by Yee as escape/immersion motivations. Individuals seek out certain types of media for diversionary purposes. A player seeking a virtual gaming experience with the goal of immersing him- or herself into a fantasy world or shedding his or her lived reality for a new one is a motivational factor. Video games offer individuals an escape from their daily routines. Another aspect of this motivation is the ability to experience something that cannot be offered through real-world environments. Gamers can allow the player to partake in historical events (e.g., World War II), visit fictional planets, or live as an alien species. The ability to vicariously experience a new world or past event, or to live as someone or something else, is a strong motivation for gaming.

Entertainment/Enjoyment

Certain types of individuals seek out video games as a fun and enjoyable activity. Although this motivation can be related to social escapism, it is considered a separate motivation. For instance, a person can choose to play video games because they are fun, even if not for diversionary or escapism purposes. Richard M. Ryan, C. Scott Rigby, and Andrew K. Przybylski (2006) found strong correlational evidence that enjoyment is a motivating factor in participating in video games. Regarding media as entertainment, positive affect is likely to result if the media selection was motivationally relevant and resulted in an intrinsically pleasurable experience. This motivation may be considered a higher-order goal. Individuals who seek out a game for competitive purposes or for social interaction (prior motivations) may experience enjoyment because these needs were met. However, video games may also be sought out for the simple reason that they are an intrinsically pleasing experience.

Interactivity/Control

Some individuals seek out video and online games because games can offer a level of interactivity that more passive media such as television cannot. The user is in charge of the medium and can interact with that media environment as well as choose how goals are reached within the gaming context. Many video and online games allow for an enhanced user experience through personalization and customization. An individual can play a game and manipulate certain events that can lead to different outcomes and endings. Individuals also have the ability to create modifications to the gaming environment. For instance, numerous first-person-shooter games allow for players to create their own gaming environments (called *maps*) and share them with other players. A related motivation, as noted by Yee, is the ability to alter one's physical, social, and mental self. Individuals often choose video games because they want

to control their environments or their identities. Video games allow individuals to take on different occupations or genders in various sorts of contexts.

Economics/Money

In some gaming environments individuals have the ability to build virtual economies within the game, which may also transfer to the real world. For instance, in some online gaming environments individuals can buy or trade for weapons, shields, clothing, furniture, or even reputation. Individuals can buy and sell virtual items with real cash or virtual points that represent prepaid money. Furthermore, an individual can play characters in order to build up skill points and advance to certain levels that give the avatar or character more advantage to the gamer. Then that player can sell that avatar or character to the highest bidder. For instance, there are websites such as *BuyMMOAccounts* that offer individuals the chance to purchase virtual characters for a few hundred dollars. According to Cicchirillo, this aspect adds a motivation related to potential economic opportunities from playing video and online games.

Physiological Arousal/Excitation

Physiological-type motivation is somewhat different from the other motivations in that these motivations rely on individuals experiencing physical arousal from playing video games. Instead of, or possibly in conjunction with, seeking out video games to experience emotions or cognitions, they seek out video games for physiological arousal. Numerous studies show that video games influence physiological measures such as heart rate (Barlett, Harris, & Baldassaro, 2007) and skin conductance (Poels et al., 2012). For instance, a person may play a video game that is scary or suspenseful, resulting in increased heart rate in conjunction with a sense of fear. Other motivations may be related to arousal elicited through physical activities during video game playing. Thanks to motion-sensing technology, most of today's video gaming systems allow for players to interact with the game in ways that were not previously possible. The technology (motion sensors) senses players' movements and mimics them in the gaming environment. Examples include swinging a bat, running, or even rotating a symbol or object. A player can use this gaming technology to exercise and burn calories through increased physical movement. Physical activity and exercise motivations should be considered under the higher-order construct of physiological arousal.

Conclusion

Innovations in technology are enabling the emergence of games that are providing new, increasingly deep and longer-lasting experiences for players. This entry has outlined seven major motivations for playing video games (achievement/competition/challenge, social interaction, social escapism/immersion, entertainment/enjoyment, interactivity/control, economics/money, and physiological arousal/excitation). However, this list is by no means exhaustive; as new technologies are developed, individuals will find new motivations for playing video games. Furthermore, we must consider that both intrinsic and extrinsic motivations can be involved in playing video games. Individuals may get intrinsic fulfillment out of playing games for enjoyment, competition, or immersion in a gaming experience. The experience of playing a video game could bring self-fulfillment. However, players may also garner external rewards such as money or prestige from playing a video game. Players can achieve social capital through experience points or even monetary capital by selling an enchanted wand or avatar that has been advanced a few levels. These motivations may also interact positively with one another. Intrinsic and extrinsic motivations may both be met through playing video games, and thus, motivations don't necessarily occur independently.

Individual differences can affect what motivations people have for playing video games (Cicchirillo, 2011). People differ by age, gender, race, and even gaming experience. This is a fundamental consideration when talking about gaming effects and behavior. Different types of video game players have been categorized in prior literature by their gaming behavior. Richard Bartle (2004) has theorized that there are four types of players—Killers, Achievers, Socializers, and Explorers—and that commercially successful video games must provide gratifications for all four. Different types of players choose games based on multiple motivations. Individual differences such as gender and personality can influence players' motivations, but regardless of their differences, players may share many of the motivations outlined in this entry.

Vincent Cicchirillo and Kristin Stewart

See also Media Effects Perspectives of Violence; Parasocial Relationships; User Involvement in Violent Content, Effects of; Uses and Gratifications Perspective of Media Effects

Further Readings

Bartle, R. (2004). *Designing virtual worlds*. Indianapolis: New Riders.

Barlett, C. P., Harris, R. J., & Baldassaro, R. (2007). Longer you play, the more hostile you feel: Examination of first person shooter video games and aggression during video game play. *Aggressive Behavior, 33*, 486–497.

Cicchirillo, V. (2011). Online gaming: Demographics, motivations, and information processing. In M. S. Eastin, T. Daugherty, & N. M. Burns (Eds.), *Handbook of research on digital media and advertising* (pp. 456–479). Hershey, PA: IGI Global.

Chory, R. M., & Goodboy, A. K. (2011). Is basic personality related to violent and non-violent video game play and preferences? *Cyberpsychology, Behavior, and Social Networking, 14*(4), 191–198.

Cole, H., & Griffiths, M. D. (2007). Social interactions in massively multiplayer online role playing gamers. *CyberPsychology & Behavior, 19*, 575–583.

Hoffman, B., & Nadelson, L. (2010). Motivational engagement and video gaming: A mixed methods study. *Education Technology Research & Development, 58*, 245–270.

Klimmt, C., Hartmann, T., & Frey, A. (2007). Effectance and control as determinants of video game enjoyment. *Cyberpsychology & Behavior, 10*(6), 845–847.

Klug, C. G., & Schell, J. (2006). Why people play games: An industry perspective. In P. Vorderer & J. Bryant (Eds.), *Playing video games: Motives, responses and consequences* (pp. 91–113). Mahwah, NJ: Erlbaum.

Poels, K., van den Hoogen, W., Ijsselsteijn, W., & de Kort, Y. (2012). Pleasure to play, arousal to stay: The effect of player emotions on digital game preferences and playing time. *Cyberpsychology, Behavior, and Social Networking, 15*(1), 1–6.

Raney, A. A., Smith, J. K., & Baker, K. (2006). Adolescents and the appeal of video games. In P. Vorderer & J. Bryant (Eds.), *Playing video games: Motives, responses, and consequences* (pp. 147–163). Mahwah, NJ: Erlbaum.

Ryan, R., Rigby, C., & Przybylski, A. (2006). The motivational pull of videogames: A self determination theory approach. *Motivation and Emotion, 30*, 347–363.

Sherry, J., Greenberg, B., Lucas, S., & Lachlan, K. (2006). Video game uses and gratifications as predictors of use and game preference. In P. Vorderer & J. Bryant (Eds.),

Playing computer games: Motives, responses and consequences (pp. 213–224). Mahwah, NJ: Erlbaum.

Vorderer, P., & Hartmann, T. (2009). Entertainment and enjoyment as media effects. In J. Bryant & M. B. Oliver (Eds.), *Media effects: Advances in theory and research* (pp. 532–550). New York, NY: Routledge.

Vorderer, P., Hartmann, T., & Klimmt, C. (2003). *Explaining the enjoyment of playing video games: The role competition*. Paper presented to the ACM International Conference Proceeding of the Second International Conference on Entertainment Computing.

Yee, N. (2006). Motivations for play in online games. *Cyberpsychology & Behavior, 9*, 772–775.

Website

BuyMMOAccounts.com; http://www.buymmoaccounts.com

VIOLENCE, DEFINITION OF

One of the most comprehensive definitions of violence was offered by the World Health Organization (WHO; Krug, Dahlberg, Mercy, Zwi, & Lozano, 2002). As defined by the World Health Organization, *violence* is "the intentional use of physical force or power, threatened or actual, against oneself, another person, or against a group or community, that either results in or has a high likelihood of resulting in injury, death, psychological harm, maldevelopment or deprivation" (p. 5). The WHO definition is a broad one that is important to consider when studying the global implications of violence in different settings and cultures. This entry discusses the various ways violence can be defined and how violence is related to but distinct from aggression.

The WHO definition of violence includes not only physical force but also power, so that such acts as child deprivation or elderly neglect can be considered violent, just as physical child or elder abuse would. The WHO also places importance on the word *intentional*, such that unintentional acts would not reach the threshold of being acknowledged as violence. For example, if a driver loses control of a car through a mechanical defect and runs over a pedestrian, it would not be considered an act of violence. However, deliberately running over a person would be considered a violent act.

Many typologies are categorized within the broader definitions of violence. Much of the categorization of violence depends on the proximal nature of the perpetrator to the victim. Violence can be self-directed, interpersonal, relational, or community oriented. A person may try to intentionally harm another with acts or threats of physical violence. These can be directed toward a stranger or toward someone who has a relationship with the perpetrator. The violent acts could also be directed toward oneself, such as in the case of self-injurious behavior or suicide. A person or group may direct their violence toward another group, such as through ethnic genocide. Violence can involve physical, sexual, or psychological harm. These typologies are not mutually exclusive, leading therefore to different combinations of violent behavior.

Violence and *aggression* are commonly confused terms. Craig Anderson and Brad Bushman (2002) have defined *aggression* as "any behavior directed toward another individual that is carried out with the proximate (immediate) intent to cause harm. In addition, the perpetrator must believe that the behavior will harm the target, and that the target is motivated to avoid the behavior" (p. 28). This definition contains some of the same elements as the WHO's definition of violence (notably the concepts of harm and intent) but adds a requirement that the target be motivated to avoid the behavior. Therefore, a painful treatment administered by a doctor to treat an illness could not be considered an act of aggression. Anderson and Bushman have provided a definition of violence that differentiates it from aggression. The authors stated that *violence* is "aggression that has extreme harm as its goal (e.g. death)" (p. 29). By this rationale, any act of violence is considered aggression, but not all aggression can be considered violence. For example, the eye poking and foot stomping portrayed by the Three Stooges are acts of aggression but technically not violent acts because their intent is not extreme harm. Indeed, much humor would then fit within Anderson and Bushman's classification of aggression, but not violence. In a more realistic analogy, a child shoving another child down on a playground may be considered an act of aggression, but it does not qualify as an act of violence.

It is important to clear up the confusion in using the terms *aggression* and *violence* interchangeably. Although the popular press often talks about media factors leading to violence, scholars usually talk about the media's role in influencing aggression. Reports incorrectly use these terms interchangeably because much of the scholarly work focuses on how variables produce increases in hostile thoughts and cognitions, increases in negative affect, and physiological reactions rather than physical behaviors.

In the minority of instances when media scholars have measured aggressive behavior, it has typically been done through tricking a participant into believing that he or she is delivering an electrical shock or burst of white noise to a real human target (Anderson & Dill, 2000; Anderson & Murphy, 2003). In some cases, researchers have claimed to be studying aggression by proposing to participants various hypothetical situations that may invoke aggressive responses. The participant was asked hypothetically how he or she would respond (Barlett, Harris, & Baldassaro, 2007). Still, the definition of violence (whether one takes it from the WHO or Anderson and Bushman) restricts one morally and ethically from testing a true manipulation of violence because doing so would result in extreme harm to individuals in the study. This entry looked at how the media's depiction of violent acts influenced an audience's beliefs, thoughts, and behaviors regarding real acts of violence.

In short, various definitions of violence exist, many with different classification schemes and qualifiers. Researchers and scholars looking at a deep investigation of such concepts as violence, aggression, hostility, or anger should be careful to explain how violence is being defined for the purposes of their study, so that readers are clear as to what is being discussed.

Kevin D. Williams

See also Aggression, Definition and Assessment of; Violence in Media, Effects on Aggression and Violent Crime

Further Readings

Anderson, C. A., & Bushman, B. J. (2002). Human aggression. *Annual Review of Psychology, 53,* 27–51.

Anderson, C. A., & Dill, K. E. (2000). Video games and aggressive thoughts, feelings, and behavior in the laboratory and in life. *Journal of Personality and Social Psychology, 78,* 772–790.

Anderson, C. A., & Murphy, C. R. (2003). Violent video games and aggressive behavior in young women. *Aggressive Behavior, 29,* 423–429.

Barlett, C. P., Harris, R. J., & Baldassaro, R. (2007). Longer you play, the more hostile you feel: Examination of first person shooter video games and aggression during video game play. *Aggressive Behavior, 33,* 486–497.

Krug, E. G., Dahlberg, L. L., Mercy, J. A., Zwi, A. B., & Lozano, R. (Eds.). (2002). *World report on violence and health.* Geneva: World Health Organization.

VIOLENCE IN MEDIA, EFFECTS ON AGGRESSION AND VIOLENT CRIME

A great deal of attention has been paid to the effects of violence in the media during the past 50 years. Two areas have received the greatest amount of attention: the effects of violent media on aggression and the effects of violent media on fear and desensitization. This entry presents theories that link exposure to media violence and aggressive or violent behavior and reviews the empirical evidence. Although many reviewers have claimed that the association between media violence and aggression is strong and consistent in empirical studies, and some have argued that media violence causes violent crime, the evidence linking media violence and serious aggressive behavior is not definitive.

The Effects of Violent Media on Aggression: Theory

There are many reasons one might expect exposure to media violence to cause violent behavior. For instance, children are exposed to a great deal of violence in the media, and it is expected that they will imitate it. Children are thought to be more vulnerable to potential harms because of their immature cognitive abilities. For example, small children are less able to understand the difference between what is real and what is fantasy and may not recognize motives of the characters. Young children also attend to action more than dialogue and are unlikely to follow nuances of plot or character development.

Most media effects researchers who believe that exposure to media violence causes aggressive and violent behavior do so because of the opportunity for social learning that television, films, and video games afford. Humans learn how to behave in a variety of ways, and observing how others behave constitutes an important mode of social learning. Through the media, children witness more violence than they are likely to see in real life. The earliest studies related to this issue were those conducted by Albert Bandura in the 1960s. Bandura demonstrated that children do imitate aggressive behavior modeled in films in his famous Bobo Doll experiments.

Normally, reinforcement and punishment play a role in social learning. The effects of media violence are thought to operate through *vicarious* reinforcement and punishment. The narratives of many media portrayals of violence include "heroes" being rewarded for violent acts. The maintenance of aggressive behavior is also subject to the same principles of reinforcement and punishment. Some have argued that vicarious reinforcement is unlikely to affect a child's ongoing behavior as much as *actual* punishment would if the child implemented a violent behavior seen in the media in his or her own world.

Others have pointed out that viewing violent media has an excitatory effect on the central nervous system and may "cause" aggression merely because physical activity of any kind becomes more likely in an excitatory state. Because the presentation of exciting movies is not seen as objectionable, the upshot of findings from this line of research has been that studies control for excitation by presenting control subjects with equally exciting media material.

More recent theoretical advances have incorporated violent cues, priming, and cognitive scripts. In these contemporary models, exposure to media violence operates through its effects on complex cognitive processes. In addition to demonstrating various forms of violent behavior, watching violent interactions has been thought to affect beliefs, attitudes, and values. It may prime aggressive thoughts, some objects may become aggressive cues, and some actions may be interpreted as provocations (resulting in hostile attribution bias). Repeated exposure to television and film depictions of common violent interactions may create behavioral scripts that can be called upon by the subject, even if he or she has never committed the violent act in the script. Scripts associating disrespect with a violent response, for example, become ingrained so strongly that the script is activated easily, even in real life.

Some media effects scholars believe that reciprocal effects between aggressive personality and exposure to media are to be important. Trait-aggressive individuals tend to favor watching violence and playing violent video games. Repeated exposure is thought to reinforce the subject's aggressive thoughts, and some researchers have been concerned that it engenders aggressive fantasy. Numerous studies have found interaction effects in which aggressive individuals are most affected by violent media (including a few in which *only* aggressive individuals were adversely affected), although consensus on this issue remains to be achieved.

Many media effects scholars have reasoned that violent video game play should have large effects than other media because of the interactive nature of the games and the rewards the players receive directly. It is expected that many of the same cognitive processes will be at play: the learning of aggressive scripts, hostile attribution bias, and cues for aggression.

Empirical Findings on Television and Film Violence

Despite compelling theory and strong statements by many reviewers, the empirical effects of media violence on physical aggression have been the topic of contentious debate among scholars. Studies of television and film violence have suggested that subjects who watch violent media in the laboratory have, on average, higher scores on subsequent analog measures of aggression, which include willingness to administer shocks to others in shock box studies. Numerous studies have also reported significant correlations between self-reported exposure to violent media and self-reported aggression.

Most of these studies were published in the 1960s, 1970s, and 1980s and have been criticized for methodological weaknesses. First, experimental studies may be vulnerable to demand effects; subjects who were deliberately shown a violent program and then asked by the experimenter to commit aggression (e.g., apply shocks or noise blasts to another person) may have consciously or unconsciously believed that the experimenter advocated violence and have felt pressure to please the experimenter. Second, studies reporting correlations between subjects' exposure to media violence and aggression frequently have failed to control for trait aggression and other important potential confounds. Of note, many of these studies were published before access to computer software that makes it easy to run multivariate analyses was widely available. Because aggressive children and adults prefer to watch violence, a correlation between exposure to media violence and aggressive behavior is no surprise; aggressive people will choose to watch violent shows. Sound research design is needed to establish that the exposure causes the aggression.

The size of the effect varies a great deal across studies. A major meta-analysis reported an overall average effect of exposure to television and film violence on aggression as $r = .34$. Two reviews have reported that the association between television and film violence and criminal violence is lower, $r = .10$. Another meta-analysis reported an average effect for only those longitudinal, multivariate studies that reported findings on the association between television and film violence and violent aggression, controlling for trait aggression. That estimate was not statistically significant, $r = .038$. That said, researchers have argued that even this small effect is likely to be biased in an upward direction. Results from meta-analyses have suggested that effect sizes for the most reliable, realistic measures of aggressive behavior tend to be smaller than those for less reliable, less realistic measures.

Video Games

Studies of video game playing have proliferated since the 1990s. Like studies of television and film violence, two types of designs are common: experiments in which subjects play video games and then are given opportunities to behave aggressively, express aggressive attitudes, and so on, and correlational studies in which subjects are asked about their video game playing habits (amount of time and type of games) and their aggressive behavior. Although numerous studies have suggested that there are associations between violent video play and attitudes or personality styles, the findings for actual aggressive behavior have been mixed. Experiments have tended not to find immediate effects on aggression, perhaps because most of the male subjects play the games often and are not likely to be greatly influenced by one experimental session. Several meta-analyses have reported average effect sizes that are characterized as "small," but none has subjected the studies to critical review based on outcome measures. As with television and film studies, the outcomes in most of these studies have been criticized as only proximate to aggression. Long-term multivariate studies, with careful measures and designs, are needed before any conclusions can be drawn.

The Effects of Violent Media on Violent Crime

Many criminologists believe that violent behavior can be learned, and it is reasonable to hypothesize that witnessing violent behavior in the media or playing violent video games might cause not just aggression but also violent crime. Although some media effects researchers (not all) believe that the same theories that apply to aggression will predict violent crime, this remains to be established. For example, published correlations between proximate measures of aggression and criminally violent behavior are needed to establish the generalizability of research on aggression to violent outcomes, yet these are exceedingly difficult to find. Therefore, media effects researchers have argued that it is

important to limit a meta-analysis to studies using violent behavior (such as hitting, pushing, or self-reported violent delinquency) as an outcome if one wishes to understand the association between exposure to media violence and violent crime. However, the research on violent behavior has been scant by comparison to that for aggression, with only a few dozen studies employing actual violent outcomes.

The findings from television and film studies have noted little to no link between watching violent movies or television shows and committing violent crime. The research has been almost all correlational, because it would be unethical to cause violent crime through a research study (though a few studies do use outcomes of pushing and shoving among child subjects). The correlational nature of the research makes it vulnerable to many confounding factors. Thus, the few studies that have reported this link have been criticized extensively for methodological biases, such as failing to control for important confounds such as trait aggression, family violence, parent education, child's intelligence or academic achievement, neglect, and so on. Conflicting conclusions from several meta-analytic studies appear to be related to the emphasis the authors placed on study methodological limitations. Researchers have generally agreed that correlations between exposure and violent outcomes are much lower than those for other indicators of aggression. Some researchers have argued that effects may be difficult to detect when other causes of violence (e.g., growing up in a violent family, poverty, living in a violent neighborhood) appear to have very strong effects. Few studies at the aggregate level have been published. Notably, several researchers have found that exposure to media violence at the aggregate level is associated with *lower* violent crime rates.

It has been reasoned that the very low correlations between media violence exposure and violent behavior might be due to many other factors at play when behavior escalates to violence, such as the likelihood of violent retaliation, cultural prohibitions against hurting other people, and the threat of legal sanctions.

Video Games, Music, and Violent Criminal Behavior

Studies have not convincingly demonstrated that violent video game playing causes violent criminal behavior. Numerous media effects researchers have found no effects, and some studies that reported significant effects have serious methodological problems. Studies have not found that playing violent video games predicts violent crime, but few studies with methodological rigor have been undertaken, so it is premature to draw any firm conclusions at this time.

Despite occasional discussions in the media about the effects of music, particularly rap music, and violence, there has been very little rigorous research on this topic.

The Big Picture

In the past 20 years or more, exposure to violent media has been increasing exponentially with access to cable television; the proliferation of devices such as VCRs, DVD players, and now DVRs; the invention of increasingly realistic violent video games; and the popularity of the Internet. Children of the 1960s, 1970s, and much of the 1980s simply had no access to R-rated movies, which were not shown on network television. Electronic gaming was limited to games such as *Pong* and *Tennis*. Violent portrayals used in studies published in those decades were usually limited to shows like *Bonanza* and *The Three Stooges*. In spite of the exponential increase in exposure to media violence across all ages, there has been a decline in violent crime. It would be difficult to make the case that exposure to violent media causes violent crime in light of these facts. Some researchers have suggested that video game playing keeps potential offenders occupied or entertained, thus reducing opportunities to commit violent crime. One might speculate that adolescents have more to do at home, in front of their computers or game consoles, and this keeps them out of "real" trouble, in spite of the fact that they might be committing violent acts in the virtual world.

Fear and Desensitization

Other researchers have focused on the effect of violent media on fear, attitudes, and desensitization. Concerns have been raised that exposure to media violence might cause individuals to have reduced empathy for real persons who are being violently victimized. In turn, reduced empathy might result in a lower inclination to help if faced with a situation in real life. In addition, it has been proposed that desensitization brought about by exposure to media violence might result in pro-violence attitudes, negative attitudes toward victims of violence, and less negative attitudes toward offenders.

However, there has not been a great deal of research on desensitization, and it is unclear what implications the existing findings have. For example, we have no measures of trends in helping behaviors at the aggregate level, so we are not able to ascertain whether or not altruism has been in decline with increased exposure to media violence. Furthermore, although published commentary about associations between desensitization and violent behavior can be found, it has not been satisfactorily established that desensitization to violence causes people to become violent.

Joanne Savage

See also Desensitization Effects on Society; General Aggression Model; Music Videos and Lyrics, Violent Content in; Priming Theory; Social Cognitive Theory; Television Violence; Trait Aggression

Further Readings

Anderson, C. A., & Bushman, B. J. (2002). Human aggression. *Annual Review of Psychology, 53,* 27–51.

Bandura, A., Ross, D., & Ross, S. A. (1963). Vicarious reinforcement and imitative learning. *Journal of Abnormal and Social Psychology, 67*(6), 601–607.

Ferguson, C. J., Rueda, S. M., Cruz, A. M., Ferguson, D. E., Fritz, S., & Smith, S. M. (2008). Violent video games and aggression. *Criminal Justice and Behavior, 35*(3), 311–332.

Savage, J. (2004). Does viewing violent media really cause criminal violence? A methodological review. *Aggression and Violent Behavior, 10*(1), 99–128.

VIOLENT ARTISTIC EXPRESSION

What constitutes "violence" and "art" is a subject of cultural construction, conversation, and even contention. Media researchers generally operationalize violence according to levels of aggression, defined as relational (such as defaming, bullying, or isolating—causing social harm), verbal (such as yelling, ridiculing, or threatening—causing psychological harm), and physical (such as hitting, stabbing, or shooting—causing bodily harm) behavior that may be provoked or unprovoked. Scholars such as Nancy Signorelli and George Gerbner have further limited their study of violence to include only overt speech or behavior that threatens or aims to hurt or kill. Definitions focus on action and intention but not aesthetics. This entry discusses how violence is portrayed in various forms of artistic expression and how new technologies have caused changes in violent artistic expression.

Society has broadly recognized art as the expression of creative skill and imagination that may take varied forms via multiple media. Specifically, though, individual interpretations instruct popular perceptions that legitimate some works as art while others remain ignored. Art forms that gain a critical mass of recognition resonate with some regard to aesthetic archetypes, cultural conventions, and human motivations.

Due to the subjective nature of what is violent and what is art, the collective concept of violent artistic expression seems fluid, shifting and evolving within contexts of both media content production and consumption. However discursive, it invites an intuitive impression that the content be somehow stylized, glamorized, fetishized, and aestheticized. Margaret Bruder (2003), in her work on the aestheticization of violence in film, argued that such media representations must be stylistically excessive, significant, and sustained; not only are the narrative acts relevant, but so are the elements of editing and cinematography. Ultimately effective and provocative, violent artistic expression is reflected in sometimes subtle yet often extreme imagery in music, television, film, gaming, and on the web.

Music

Music is a soundtrack for life and a rich outlet for artistic expression—violent and otherwise. It is the audio imagery that captures and classifies memories of youth, friends, lovers, losses, and life moments. Genres span a wide spectrum, from commercial pop, rock, country, and adult contemporary to the more niche styles of classical, bluegrass, hip-hop, and electronica. In the periphery lie subgenres such as punk, gothic, industrial, extreme metal, and gangsta rap that cater to subcultures that subscribe to the ideology, fashion, and scene associated with the music.

Violent artistic expression presents most often in subgenres that feature aggressive audio that triggers emotional resonance echoed in the lyrics. Exploring creation and death, monogamy and promiscuity, and successes and struggles, music lyrics share universal themes and experiences. Punk rock probes sociopolitical perspectives via chaotic, wanton instrumentation and lyrics that strike against class conformity and societal restrictions. Violence in gothic and industrial music is more fetishized and sexualized, celebrating bondage, discipline, dominance/submission, and sadomasochism (BDSM) behavior and aesthetic codes. Metal explores distorted, dissonant

sounds and lyrics with religious undertones as a backlash to traditional Christian values. Gangsta rap relates harsh experiences of life in the inner-city ghetto with drugs, gangs, stabbings, shootings, vandalism, and domestic violence.

Violent artistic expression has been blended into mainstream music. Stories of misogyny, infidelity, promiscuity, domestic abuse, and sexual sadism appear alongside rhythmic beats that appeal to mass audiences for popular artists. Any negative associations in the lyrics get lost in the stylization of the music, which has the power to transform life tragedies into dance floor hits.

Television

Television is a hub for violent artistic expression that has evolved through the decades. In the 1960s, *Batman* featured narratives that frequently called for fights. The scenes displayed comic book–style speech balloons with onomatopoeia words such as *awkkk!, boff!, crunch!, kapow!,* and *zzzwap!* Blasts from brass band instruments amplified the visuals with audio effects. Aestheticized for added impact, the fistfights contextualized the hostility with comic animation because the good guys were winning.

Cartoons express artistic violence via extreme exaggeration in both narratives and graphics. Since the imagination is infinite in animated worlds, actions extend well beyond the realm of reality. Loose storylines string one violent act after another, focusing on destruction rather than resolution. Characters are killed frequently, sometimes within the same show. Unaware of and immune to the cogency of life and the finality of death, animated bodies appear as crudely stylized hubs of harsh art.

Fetishizing the finer details, television dramas frequently focus on extreme close-ups of violence, especially in crime dramas. Multiframe scenes of misconduct and the ensuing investigations highlight blood splatter, gunshot wounds, and strangulation marks as artistic elements that decorate—and moderate—the violent acts. Shots voyeuristically showcase the most stimulating fragments of the overall image: blood leaking, a hand twisted, a limb severed. As gratuitous as pornography, the result is the refined essence of violence, a detached presentation of parts rather than people.

Film

Violent artistic expression is a commodity, capable of coaxing audiences to the box office for that larger-than-life experience. No other medium is as immersive as film. The darkened theater, the towering screen, and the explosive audio optimize and intensify the impact of artistic violence. There is an allure to being invited into a mediated world of danger, fear, and gore while remaining safely tucked in reality.

The evolution of film technology has ushered in a new era of strikingly stylized content. High definition, computer manipulation, and 3D animation achieve vivid violent visuals that activate the imaginations of viewers via novelty, creativity, and anxiety. The result is what Guy Debord (2000) calls the spectacle: a manufactured illusion that is celebrated by society as more real than reality.

Absorbing audience members into the film fiction, movies hyperaestheticize scenes of violence. Slow-motion sequences extend time to accommodate extreme close-ups of images that defy normality and disturb the psyche. Effects (such as meat slapping on a counter) are recorded, amplified, and applied to shots to create more saturated sounds than would ever be evident in real life, making the violence more appreciable. Chroma keying, or layering images based on color hues, simulates worlds that are hyperstylized in which characters endure exaggerated actions, explosions, and mutilations. Fake blood, liquid latex, and authentic animatronics grotesquely yet artistically distort the human form. With the combination of film's advanced robotics technology and computer graphics processing, science has rendered simulated violent artistic expression hyper-real—and therefore intensely experiential.

Gaming

Video games often depict extreme violence in a precise way and with certain conventions. Protagonists and antagonists alike endure inordinate injuries and prolonged brutality in the game world, resulting in black eyes, bloody noses, missing limbs, and blood splatter. Powerful punches, arrow attacks, sword slashes, gunshot wounds, fireballs, and high falls plague players in any conceivable context. More decadent magic spells curse characters via crushing, electrocution, fire/burning/flamethrowers, and ice/numbing/freeze guns. Heroes must heal or be resurrected repeatedly, demanding that death be endured again and again during play; they slay hundreds (if not thousands) of enemies as they pursue the goal of the game. As higher levels unfold, avatars and players encounter greater amounts of violence infused with timely pop culture currents.

In video games, aestheticized violence may be a reward for skill between levels. Players are treated to savage segments within the story that are artistically engineered to be quick reprieves from fighting. These cinematic cut scenes halt the action, shift the camera angle, and suspend player control, affording a voyeuristic opportunity to detach from yet indulge in the violence on screen. The violent artistic asides allow narrative moments that should be tense to transform into gratuitous releases for players. Controller dexterity—sometimes requiring a long string of key commands and joystick manipulation—is similarly rewarded with attacks that are more directly devastating and visually stimulating.

As graphics technology improves, there exists a tangible trend toward rendering the game characters and environments as realistically as possible. Modeling programs deliberately make it difficult to determine what is actual and what is virtual, blurring the boundary between human and animation. Despite the desire to mimic real life, though, the violent acts and abilities almost always steer toward fantasy, engaging the audience with brutal acrobatics and overpowered, oversized, and overfetishized weaponry. Similar configurations appear via the bodies of characters that are manipulated in anatomically impossible ways, limited only by the imaginations of the game designers. The worlds become more naturalistic, while the actions and avatars become more nihilistic: hyperaestheticized, hyperstylized, hyperviolent—as if greater levels of artistic expression are required to invoke affect, effect, and entertainment value.

Web

The openly participatory and generally unregulated nature of the Internet offers a unique environment for violent artistic expression. Without strong, centralized censorship, users around the world share information and images via websites, forums, message boards, and social networking sites. The content is capricious, yet considerately cataloged to appeal to an array of niche interests, such as accidents, crimes, murders, suicides, executions, mutilations, and medical scenes.

Much of the violent material on the web has occurred in real life, captured by security cameras, police or military cameras, and personal devices that record eyewitness accounts. And not all of this material can be considered artistic expression. It is impossible to gauge the intentions of every person who posts content or the interpretations of everyone who views content. Some material may hold aesthetic value, while some may simply satisfy curiosity or provide novelty or shock value. Online responses to these violent videos range widely, expressing anger about abusive acts, genuine fear and disgust, or dark and desensitized humor.

The more vivid violent artistic expression on the web features memes and Internet animated GIFs. A *meme* is an idea, behavior, style, or usage that spreads from person to person within a culture. Although repetitive elements are standard, group members add their own context so memes evolve and intensify. For instance, users may digitally alter figures or create captions that re-relativize gory images in artistic ways. Animated GIFs are short sequences of animated images that repeat infinitely—or until the user tires of watching the cycle and closes it. Concentrated and refined, GIFs present violence that is gratuitous, context free, and silent. Initial exposure carries great impact, but repeated viewing leads to fatigue and desensitization toward the image.

Theory

Contextual media aesthetics serves as a framework for establishing how violent artistic expression is evolving, considering production techniques such as angle, color, lighting, shot composition, camera movement, transitions, pacing, editing, music, and sound effects. Technological advances afford media creators the ability to be more deliberate with artistic elements, freedoms, and liberties in their production, which can be operationalized, categorized, and analyzed with content analysis methodology. The manipulation of sight, sound, and motion creates artistic elements in the media text that prompt predictable patterns of audience reception.

Research has revealed that audiences react to expressions of violence in media according to consequences of actions and attractiveness of characters. Older audiences focus on consequences, whereas younger ones center on attractiveness. Accordingly, one might argue that violent artistic expression affords additional appeal because it stylizes and/ or sanitizes violent vectors via aesthetic elements, thereby also enhancing the impact of the entertainment experience. Meta-analyses of studies in media violence reveal effects such as fear, imitation, and desensitization.

The uses and gratifications perspective of media effects suggests that audiences who choose violent content seek specific kinds of enjoyment from entertainment. Mood management is a key factor for media use. Audience members may choose media that maintain emotions (such as playing upbeat music when happy), or they may select media that counter negative emotions (such as watching a comedy when sad). Research has revealed that people enjoy vicarious aggression because watching characters commit violent behaviors invites them to experience the release of their own aggressions in a safe and socially acceptable way.

Viewing of violent content also involves individual and social identity formation. Audience members may connect with characters, narratives, or situations that echo their own experiences and then share those thoughts with others to situate themselves in the larger social schema. Users of violent content gain empowerment and social status by proving to peers that they are bold and brave enough to handle even the most stirring scenes without flinching; their confidence and egos are reinforced when their friends are unable to do so. Defiance of restrictions is another appeal that has been studied under uses and gratifications in the context of warning labels placed on packaging. The forbidden fruit theory argues that advisory labels make violence more desirable—especially for males. As the spectacle swells within a more mediated culture than has ever existed before, future research could investigate how artistic expressions of violence invite audiences to reorient the fearful as comfortable, the horrible as beautiful, and the brutal as natural, ultimately elaborating the ethos of media use and gratification, identification, and socialization.

Marjorie Yambor

See also Aggression and Culture; Cultural Voyeurism; Fantasy Genre, Violence and Aggression in; Forbidden Fruit Hypothesis; Media Violence, Definitions and Context of; Realism of Violent Content, Real-World Violence on Television, and Their Effects; Uses and Gratifications Perspective of Media Effects; Violence, Definition of

Further Readings

Berger, A. A. (2012). *Media and society: A critical perspective*. Lanham, MD: Rowman & Littlefield.

Bruder, M. E. (2003). *Aestheticizing violence, or how to do things with style*. Bloomington: Indiana University Press.

Bryant, J., & Oliver, M. B. (2009). *Media effects: Advances in theory and research*. New York, NY: Routledge.

Debord, G. (2000). *Society of the spectacle* (K. Knabb, Trans.). London: Rebel Press. (Original work published 1967).

Kirsh, S. J. (2006). *Children, adolescents, and media violence: A critical look at the research.* Thousand Oaks, CA: Sage.

Miller, F. P., Vandome, A. F., & McBrewster, J. (2010). *Aestheticization of violence.* Saarbruecken, Germany: VDM.

Schneider, S. J., & Shaw, D. (2003). *Dark thoughts: Philosophic reflections on cinematic horror.* Lanham, MD: Scarecrow Press.

Zettl, H. (1999). *Sight, sound, motion: Applied media aesthetics.* Belmont, CA: Wadsworth.

Virtual Reality, Violent Content In

Virtual reality (VR) technologies promise to immerse users in media environments, some of which may include violent content. This entry begins by defining violent content in VR and distinguishing it from other forms of media violence. It then describes the types of content that have been used in research on VR violence effects before shifting to a discussion of applications of VR violent content. The entry concludes by considering the future of violence in virtual reality.

VR Violent Content Versus Other Forms of Media Violence

Virtual reality violent content is defined here as media violence designed for and appearing predominantly in immersive virtual environment technology (IVET). The two most common types of IVET are head-mounted displays, which include head and motion tracking to simulate being in a real environment, and cave automatic virtual environments (CAVEs), which involve surrounding the user with projection screens. By treating VR in terms of IVET, this definition differentiates VR violent content from other forms of media violence. Although violent video game content could be experienced through some forms of IVET, it would not be classified as VR violent content unless it was specifically designed to be played through an immersive virtual reality (IVR) system (VR and IVR are used synonymously in this entry).

IVR systems have several characteristics that distinguish them from other media technologies. According to researchers Aitor Rovira, David

Swapp, Bernhard Spanlang, and Mel Slater (2009), IVR must afford users perception through sensorimotor contingencies similar to those in reality. For example, people who experience VR violent content should be able to turn their heads to look at foes and swing their arms or kick their legs to strike them. Rovira and colleagues have argued that when natural sensorimotor contingencies are in place, participants may experience place illusion. This is similar to what has been called "(tele)presence," but *place illusion* refers to the perception of being "in" an IVR environment specifically, such as a virtual war zone. The authors also identified *plausibility,* or the illusion that real things are happening, as another important aspect of IVR. For example, if a user of an IVR system physically moves to avoid bullets being shot and aims to fire at virtual characters as if holding a gun, these reactions would suggest plausibility. When both place illusion and plausibility are in place, IVR users should respond realistically to violence and other virtual content, according to Rovira and colleagues, even though they may cognitively know that the experience is artificial. The extreme realism of VR violent content, above all other forms of media including video games, seems to be another important distinguishing feature of this manifestation of media violence.

Content Used in Research on Virtual Reality Violence Effects

A handful of experiments have examined the effects of VR violence with varying content. In an effort to establish the validity of using IVR to study human behavior, one stream of research has replicated classic media violence studies in virtual environments. For example, Slater and colleagues (as described in Rovira et al.) conducted a virtual version of the Milgram experiment, Yale psychology professor Stanley Milgram's obedience to authority study. A blended reality, CAVE-type environment was created for the investigation in which the teacher (study participant) sat at a table with a "shock machine" across from a virtual reality learner who appeared to be a person behind a glass partition. In the experimental condition, the learner was visible, responded with pain, and complained after the subject pressed the shock button. The virtual character even intervened when the authority figure told the participant to continue, by uttering responses like "Don't listen to him, I want to stop now." Participants with a visible virtual learner became more aroused and stressed (as assessed through a skin conductance test) than those in a nonvisible learner condition, suggesting that the content was perceived as more real.

In a follow-up study, Rovira and colleagues (2009) used similar IVR technology to examine bystander responses during violent situations. They constructed a VR bar environment in which participants were approached by a life-sized virtual character, "the victim," who would engage in a conversation about football. A second virtual character, "the perpetrator," would approach shortly into the conversation and become verbally aggressive toward the victim, including shouting, swearing, and making aggressive gestures. This would escalate into the perpetrator violently pushing the victim into the wall. One manipulated variable was having the victim glance at the participant in some conditions, which the researches believed would enhance the plausibility illusion. Consistent with expectations, participants who received the gaze were more likely to intervene during initial trials, and overall, a number of subjects attempted to break up the conflict. They became involved in a realistic way, lending further support to the notion that IVR violent content may be perceived as real. This type of interactive violent content is interesting in that it does not involve a game; rather, it attempts to simulate real life or at least real-world experimental situations. Additional research following this paradigm replicated Bandura's social learning study in VR.

Another line of experiments by Susan Persky and Jim Blascovich (2007) adopted more of the video game violence research paradigm, using specially designed violent and nonviolent versions of a VR game as stimuli. The violent version had the player engage in a gunfight in a computer-generated environment against computer-controlled opponents. This combat took place in a virtual room with walls for both the participant and opponents to hide behind. The object of the game was to minimize bullet hits to oneself (by hiding and dodging) and shoot opponents as many times as possible. When hit, the virtual characters exhibited three violent cues: they lurched, groaned, and splattered blood. When the player was hit, there was a bullet wound sound, and a flash of red briefly filled the screen. The nonviolent version of the game had a similar setup, but instead of shooting a gun across the room, participants painted across the space onto a virtual canvas. All VR participants wore a head-mounted display that tracked their head movement and orientation, and they controlled the game with a gun-like controller (modified to look like a paint chamber in the nonviolent condition). In another set of conditions players engaged in the experiences on a computer instead of through VR technology. Persky and Blascovich found that players of the IVR violent game experienced more aggressive feelings than those in the other conditions. Research using commercially available video game content played through VR technology has reported similar results. The Persky and Blascovich studies are especially noteworthy, however, for being one of the only lines of research to test for VR violence effects through violent content designed for IVR technology. Taking this custom approach maximizes the match between the capabilities of VR systems and potential actions of players, providing a more immersive experience and increased validity.

Applications of Virtual Reality Violent Content

Although there are potentially harmful consequences of exposure to VR violent content, it has positive applications as well, particularly for military and therapeutic purposes. For example, the U.S. Department of Defense implemented a $20 million virtual training program called *Urban Resolve* in 2006. As discussed by Jim Blascovich and Jeremy Bailenson in their book *Infinite Reality* (2011), the virtual environment created for *Urban Resolve* provides a highly realistic model of Baghdad, including 3D physical structures comprised of more than 2 million digital objects. It also simulates macro-level political, economic, and sociological forces that would be present in a city, providing trainees with a highly accurate depiction of urban warfare. Users have to cope with such factors as improvised explosive devices and different types of enemies. This type of VR content can help prepare military personnel for combat situations in a way that not only simulates reality but makes it more useful for real-world training situations. For example, soldiers may be exposed to conditions that would be impossible to simulate in reality, such as weather patterns unique to a particular region. These and other variables can also be changed with relative ease, quickly preparing users for different contingencies. Most important, perhaps, training through violent VR content is safer than engaging in risky behaviors such as aerial combat training in the real world. Because of these and other advantages, violent VR content has become a staple of military training.

There are also therapeutic applications of military and other types of VR violent content. Virtual reality exposure therapy involves exposing patients to the subjects of their fears within the confines of a virtual environment. It has been successful at treating a number of anxiety disorders, ranging from fear of bugs to fear of flying. Research by Barbara Rothbaum, Skip Rizzo, and JoAnn Difede (2010) has illustrated how violent VR content may be created for the treatment of posttraumatic stress disorder (PTSD). Following up on the first use of VR to treat PTSD, a "Virtual Vietnam" environment tested on veterans of the Vietnam War, Rothbaum and colleagues discussed the development and implementation of "Virtual Iraq," designed to treat PTSD in veterans of more recent wars. Virtual Iraq includes first-person point of view scenarios in which participants are either in a Middle Eastern city or driving on a desert road in a Humvee. During each experience, they can be subjected to a variety of trigger stimuli (in multi-sensory fashion), including weapons fire and explosions (auditory), wrecked vehicles (static visual), and insurgent attacks (dynamic audiovisual). The reality of this violent content may be enhanced through additional stimuli such as smells of body odor and gunpowder (olfactory) and vibrations from gunfire and explosion (tactile). Other variables that can be manipulated include time of day, weather, and user perspective. These types of controls allow clinicians to offer custom treatment to a patient depending on his or her needs, and Virtual Iraq has been successful at helping a number of veterans overcome PTSD. Among the advantages of this type of treatment (discussed by Rothbaum et al.) is that it has been shown to be particularly appealing to digital natives.

The Future of Virtual Reality Violent Content

The manifestations of VR violent content reviewed in this entry have one key ingredient in common: they all strive to deliver highly realistic experiences of violence, exceeding those of all other media forms. What does the future hold for VR violent content, then? Given how technology continues to advance, it seems likely that these experiences will grow increasingly real over time, perhaps to the point of being indistinguishable from reality. With this in mind, it may be instructive to look to popular science fiction for insight into virtual reality violence in the future. IVR violence has been depicted in narrative fiction for decades, spanning media forms, including literature (e.g., *Neuromancer* [1984], *Snow Crash* [1992], and *Ready Player One* [2011]), television (e.g., *Star Trek: The Next Generation* [1987–1994]), and film (e.g., *Tron* [1982], *Strange Days* [1995], and *The Matrix* [1999]). A common feature of these works is that they depict complete immersion in virtual worlds containing violence. In some cases, such as in *The Matrix*, VR is depicted as part of a dystopian future. In others, such as with the Holodeck in *Star Trek: The Next Generation*, VR offers more of a utopian experience. Whether humanity moves in one direction or the other with this technology remains to be seen. The research and applications reviewed in this entry suggest both positive (training, therapy) and negative (increased aggression) possibilities for VR violent content in the coming years.

Paul Skalski and Mu Wu

See also Interactive Media, Aggressive Outcomes of; User Involvement in Violent Content, Effects of; Video Game Platforms, Effects

Further Readings

Blascovich, J., & Bailenson, J. (2011). *Infinite reality*. New York, NY: Morrow.

Persky, S., & Blascovich, J. (2007). Immersive virtual environments versus traditional platforms: Effects of violent and nonviolent video game play. *Media Psychology, 10,* 135–156.

Rothbaum, B. O., Rizzo, A. S., & Difede, J. (2010). Virtual reality exposure therapy for combat-related posttraumatic stress disorder. *Annals of the New York Academy of Sciences, 1208,* 126–132.

Rovira, A., Swapp, D., Spanlang, B., & Slater, M. (2009). The use of virtual reality in the study of people's responses to violent incidents. *Frontiers in Behavioral Neuroscience, 3*(59). Retrieved from http://www.ncbi.nlm.nih.gov/pmc/articles/PMC2802544

Weapons in Violent Media Content, Use, Policy, and Effects of

Television and video games feature a considerable number of weapon portrayals, ranging from clubs, knives, and machetes to revolvers, pistols, rifles, assault rifles, and machine guns. Perpetrators using weapons are mostly adult humans, male, and White. Weapon portrayals often depict moderate or extreme harm. In video games, gun violence is often repetitive, shows unrealistic harm, features blood and gore, and is portrayed as justified. Exposure to portrayals of weapons increases the accessibility of aggressive and hostile thoughts and can lead to aggressive responses. This entry (a) summarizes the prevalence of weapons in society, television, and video games; (b) discusses the effects of weapons in violent media content; and (c) outlines policy issues regarding weapon portrayals in violent media content.

Prevalence of Weapons in Society, Television, and Video Games

The World Health Organization reported that in 2009 there were at least 875 million firearms in the world, of which roughly 25% were owned by civilians in the United States; 70% of homicides and 61% of suicides involve guns. According to the 2011 National Youth Risk Behavior Survey, 16.6% of high school students in the United States had carried weapons (guns, knives, or clubs) during the 30 days before the survey, and 5.1% had carried guns. The

proportion of students carrying weapons decreased significantly between 1991 and 1999 (from 26.1% to 17.3%) and has remained stable since then. A similar pattern can be observed for high school students carrying guns (1993–1999: 7.9%–4.9%). In 2011, 5.4% of high school students nationwide had carried weapons on school property (1993–2003: 11.8%–6.1%). On school property, 7.4% of high school students had been threatened or injured with weapons (1993–2003: 7.3%–9.2%).

In light of these numbers and recent mass shootings, such as those at a Tucson, Arizona, shopping center in 2011; at a movie theater in Aurora, Colorado; in a Sikh temple in Oak Creek, Wisconsin; and in an elementary school in Newtown, Connecticut in 2012, gun violence and gun control remain controversial issues that divide public opinion: a Pew Research Center survey in February 2013 found that 50% of Americans said it was more important to control gun ownership, while 46% said protecting the right of Americans to own guns was more important. Gun violence policy is also a recurring topic in presidential debates in the United States.

Television

According to the Kaiser Family Foundation, 8- to 18-year-old Americans spend, on average, 4:29 hours a day watching television. A longitudinal meta-analysis conducted by Amir Hetsroni that reviewed 57 content analyses on American prime-time network programming between 1960 and 2002 suggested that the amount of television violence has varied considerably over time: depictions of shooting (using guns, machine guns, pistols, or cannons), murder, and assault first peaked in the late 1970s and early 1980s. Per hour, 1.3 shooting incidents were observed in 1976, 0.67 depictions of murder (1981), and 7.3 assaults (1978). A second peak occurred in the mid-1990s, with 2.3 shooting incidents per hour (1997), 1.8 depictions of murder (1997), and 5.5 assaults (1994). By the early millennium, the frequency of violence on network programming had declined compared with a few years earlier. The National Television Violence Study (NTVS) analyzed programming from 23 networks over three consecutive seasons from 1994 to 1997. It shows that the amount of violence and weapon portrayals varied across television channel types and genres: on average, 92% of premium cable primetime programming featured violence, compared with an average of 61% on broadcast networks, 73% on independent broadcast television, and 60% on basic cable. Violence was more prevalent in children's programming (69%) than in other types of programming (57%). Overall, violence was featured in 61% of all programs on television.

Based on the NTVS, Stacy Smith and colleagues (2004) investigated the amount and context of violent gun interactions during a composite week of television content across all channel types: violent gun interactions were most often initiated by perpetrators who were adult (88%), male (82%), White (68%), and human (90%). They were also likely to feature primary characters (70%) who did not work for the government (72%), did not have hero status in the program (87%), and lacked good motives for violent behavior, such as protecting life (59%). However, protecting life was the major motivator for violent gun interactions themselves (35%), followed by personal gain (32%). Gun interactions were often depicted as unjustified (67%) and repetitive (69%), yielding moderate or extreme physical harm (92%) as well as realistic harm (85%) but no pain (49%). On the level of scenes within programs, violent gun interactions were shown in contexts in which aggression involving guns was rewarded (30%), presented humorously (29%), or accompanied by blood and gore (30%). More than half of all violent gun interactions (58%) were not punished. On the level of programs, violent gun interactions were more likely to be present in settings involving realistic characters and events (76%). Smith and colleagues investigated portrayals of gun violence featuring attributes that have been documented to increase the risk of learning, imitating, or enacting aggression: these were "good" qualities (e.g., generous, kind, helpful, considerate) in the perpetrator, repetitive use of gun violence, and the absence of consequences. Across the whole sample, movies ($n = 637$) and children's shows ($n = 435$) were most likely to feature such high-risk portrayals of violent gun interactions. Comedy ($n = 32$) and reality shows ($n = 22$) were least likely to show gun violence. The density of high-risk portrayals was highest for children's programming (.91 incidents per hour), followed by movies (.67) and dramas (.34). Basic ($n = 633$) and premium cable networks ($n = 402$) were more prone to show high-risk portrayals of violent gun interactions than were independent broadcasts ($n = 144$) and public broadcasts ($n = 4$). Premium cable featured the most incidents per hour (.86), followed by independent broadcasts (.55), basic cable (.46), and public broadcasts (.04).

Video Games

Video games have frequently been associated with aggressive player reactions in press coverage and in the public debate. As reported by the Kaiser Family Foundation, 8- to 18-year-old Americans spent 1:13 hours a day playing video games in 2009. According to the Entertainment Software Association, in 2011 action games such as *Call of Duty: Modern Warfare 3* accounted for 19.0% of all video games sold in the United States. The latest available high-quality content analyses have shown that video games contain a considerable amount of violence. Of the games available in 2001 that were rated E (for Everyone) by the Entertainment Software Rating Board (ESRB), 64% contained violence, accounting for 31% of game play, as a study conducted by Kimberley Thompson and Kevin Haninger (2001) showed. Fifty-eight percent of these games featured weapons other than the body, for example, projectiles (49%), explosives (33%), magic (29%), guns (24%), knives or swords (11%), or toxic substances (4%). For the games rated T for Teen, suitable for ages 13 and up, Haninger and Thompson (2004) reported that 98% contained violence, accounting for 36% of game play.

For video games, Stacy Smith and colleagues found that gun violence was mostly initiated by humans (72%), males (90%), and characters lacking "good motives" (95%). Gun interactions were almost exclusively portrayed as justified (95%), repetitive (89%), and lethal (99%). Consequences were depicted as extremely harmful (61%)

combined with rather realistic portrayals of harm (63%). Violent gun interactions were more likely to be presented in nonhumorous or serious contexts (72%) and in scenes without rewards (73%), but they usually featured blood, gore, or viscera (97%).

Although many games require players to engage in gun violence in order to advance, players can determine their level of engagement in violent gun interactions. For instance, René Weber and colleagues (2009) analyzed violent gun interactions in a first-person-shooter game—a game genre that probably features the most weapon-related content—and showed that players used their guns in only 7% of the total playing time. During game play, weapons were almost always visible on the screen, but players engaged in different gun-related activities such as choosing weapons from an equipment menu or using them to attack opponents. Also, the study showed that the type and amount of violent gun interactions vary considerably across different player types.

Effects of Weapons in Violent Media Content

Cognitive priming is the most prominent theory that explains effects of weapon portrayals in violent media content. In one of the earliest weapon effects studies, Leonard Berkowitz and Anthony LePage (1967) exposed angered and non-angered subjects to either guns or neutral objects and then provided study participants with an opportunity to aggress. Angered subjects exposed to rifles and revolvers aggressed toward others with significantly more electric shocks than did those angered subjects who had been exposed to neutral objects. Michael Carlson, Amy Marcus-Newhagen, and Norman Miller's (1990) meta-analysis of 13 studies involving weapon portrayals revealed that the presence of weapons significantly enhanced aggression. The weapon-as-prime hypothesis is based on the assumption that weapon-related concepts are closely related to aggression- and hostility-related concepts in semantic memory, because these concepts are similar in meaning and closely linked in common experience. Repeated exposure to related concepts also leads to a close link between these concepts in memory. When a concept such as "weapon" has been activated (e.g., a gun portrayal in a television program), closely linked concepts like aggressive and hostile behaviors toward others will also be activated and are thus more accessible than they would be without the weapon trigger stimulus. Once aggressive and hostile concepts become more accessible,

they can facilitate subsequent aggressive behavior in several ways. Highly accessible aggressive or hostile thoughts may lead to misinterpretations of social encounters: for instance, an interaction is more likely to be interpreted as a provocation.

Experimental research supports the notion that the mere representation of a weapon as a written word or picture primes aggression-related thoughts. In a series of three experiments, Bruce Bartholow and colleagues (2005) demonstrated that weapons priming effects depend on individual knowledge structures. In their first experiment, they showed that individuals with prior gun experience (hunters) had more detailed and specific information about guns than did individuals with no direct gun experience (nonhunters). Both hunters and nonhunters described assault guns in negative terms, but nonhunters (as opposed to hunters) described hunting guns in even more negative terms than assault guns. This suggests that among hunters, hunting guns are linked in memory with nonaggressive concepts such as spending time outdoors with friends and family. In their second experiment, the researchers demonstrated that people who have had different experiences with guns have different associations in memory to identical gun stimuli: among hunters, aggressive thoughts were more accessible following assault gun primes than hunting gun primes, whereas among nonhunters, aggressive thoughts were more accessible following hunting gun primes than assault gun primes. In their third and final experiment, Bartholow and colleagues showed that differences in aggressive behavior can be predicted with different gun primes between hunter and nonhunters. The authors concluded that (a) different experiences with guns create different knowledge structures, (b) these specific knowledge structures are primed by gun images, and (c) this priming can produce corresponding aggressive behavior.

Cognitive priming provides the most coherent framework and the most consistent results on the effects of weapon portrayals in violent media content. Albert Bandura's social cognitive theory is another frequently used theoretical frame to explain effects of weapon portrayals. In this context, several factors increase the likelihood that a behavior is observed, learned (i.e., memorized), and executed (i.e., produced and motivated) in the future. Among these factors are the attractiveness of the perpetrator, repetition of the weapon portrayal, and the absence of negative consequences for using weapons. Stacy Smith and colleagues demonstrated that many violent gun interactions in television programs are characterized by these factors. Further research is needed to clarify the effects of such high-risk portrayals of weapons on audiences. For instance, do highly graphic depictions of gun violence that feature blood and gore deter viewers from gun violence, or do those depictions instead lead to desensitization combined with an increasing acceptability of gun violence?

Jodi Whitaker and Brad Bushman (2012) showed that playing violent shooting games can improve firing accuracy and influence players to aim for a target's head: participants played a violent shooting game, a nonviolent shooting game, or a nonviolent nonshooting game. The violent shooting game featured humanoid targets and rewarded headshots, while the nonviolent shooting game featured bull's-eye targets. Those who played a shooting game used either a pistol-shaped controller or a standard controller. Next, participants shot a training pistol with the same weight and recoil as a real 9mm semi-automatic pistol at a mannequin. Participants who played a violent shooting game using a pistol-shaped controller had 99% more headshots and 33% more other shots than did other participants. These results remained significant even after controlling for firearm experience, gun attitudes, habitual exposure to violent shooting games, and trait aggressiveness. Habitual exposure to violent shooting games also predicted shooting accuracy.

Other studies suggest that gun use in video games (as opposed to merely the observation of opponents) is associated with increased physiological arousal. René Weber, Ute Ritterfeld, and Klaus Mathiak (2006) demonstrated that gun use in video games results in neural patterns that are considered characteristic for aggressive cognitions and behaviors.

It has been suggested that violent media content is appealing to audiences because it often contains features like complexity, novelty, uncertainty, and patterning that produce sensory delight. However, it seems that explicit graphic depictions of violence, including portrayals of weapons, do not necessarily contribute to media enjoyment. Andrew Weaver and Barbara Wilson (2009) found that both sanitized and graphic violent content decreased enjoyment of a television drama when perceived action was controlled, even for groups that theoretically should prefer violent media content over nonviolent media content, namely males and individuals with increased trait aggression and/or sensation-seeking tendencies. Although levels of action might contribute to enjoyment, it seems the graphic depiction of violence itself does not.

Limitations

The research on weapon portrayals and their effects has several limitations. First, most research is somewhat outdated, especially for television programming. Second, content analyses of video games face methodological problems: most studies have restricted their analysis to short playing times and disregard interplayer differences in playing skill and in the variability of content over time. Third, research on weapon portrayals in media other than primetime television, children's television, and video games is scarce. A few available studies have suggested that violent weapon portrayals are less prevalent in other genres and media forms. For example, Andrew Weaver, Asta Zelenkauskaite, and Lelia Samson (2012) found that only 13% of videos on YouTube feature violence, including violent weapon portrayals.

Policy Issues

Reducing unauthorized access to weapons such as firearms has been suggested as a viable strategy for reducing the number of deaths arising from youth violence. Similarly, it has been suggested that limiting exposure to weapon portrayals in media can reduce priming effects and their potential negative consequences. In general, (violent) media content in the United States is protected by the First Amendment and is available to all Americans. It is primarily the parents' or caregivers' responsibility to monitor and to limit the amount of media violence children consume. A study by Victoria Rideout (2007) conducted for the Kaiser Family Foundation found that 43% of parents are very concerned that exposure to violent media contributes to violent behavior in children, and 66% favor regulations to limit the amount of sex and violence in TV shows during the early evening hours. Television is the medium that parents are most concerned about (32%), followed by the Internet (21%). A number of measures have enabled parents to identify (and block) violent media content. Since 1996, TV manufacturers must add an electronic V-chip (V for violence) that can block violent content, and the networks must offer appropriate advisories for violent programs. Voluntary participation systems provide information on the amount of violence for television (TV Parental Guidelines Monitoring Board), video games (Entertainment Software Rating Board), films (Motion Picture Association of America), and music (Recording

Industry Association of America). However, a report for the Kaiser Family Foundation conducted by Joel Federman (2002) concluded that television and video game ratings have been criticized for limited accuracy and clarity and for being more lenient with violence than with sexual material. Alternative solutions, such as the creation of a (mandatory) universal media rating system, the creation of an independent committee or agency to oversee media rating systems in the United States, the abolition of media rating systems;,or the requirement of an open standard for the V-chip in digital television sets, have been discussed, but changes to the existing rating systems have not yet been implemented.

Sixty-five percent of parents say they monitor their children's exposure to violent media content closely by using rating systems or by watching television together with their children, as the study by Victoria Rideout showed. Only 18% of parents said they should do more to monitor their children's media use. However, only 16% of parents have used the V-chip. Seventy-one percent of those who had used the V-chip found it very useful, which is a higher proportion than for any of the media ratings or advisory systems. Overall, parents use a variety of tools and methods to check the role media play in their children's lives, such as advisories, the V-chip, checking where their children go on the Internet, reviewing their postings, and monitoring their buddy lists. In sum, parents are concerned about their children's exposure to violent media, but they use different means available to handle the amount of violence their children are exposed to, and most parents feel that they already do enough to monitor their children's media use.

René Weber and Katharina-Maria Behr

See also Aggressive Behavior; Media Effects Perspectives of Violence; Media Violence, Definitions and Context of; Television Violence; Violence, Definition of

Further Readings

Bartholow, B. D., Anderson, C. A., Carnagey, N. L., & Benjamin, A. J. (2005). Interactive effects of life experience and situational cues on aggression: The weapons priming effect in hunters and nonhunters. *Journal of Experimental Social Psychology, 41,* 48–60. doi:10.1016/j.jesp.2004.05.005

Berkowitz, L., & LePage, A. (1967). Weapons as aggression-eliciting stimuli. *Journal of Personality and Social Psychology, 7,* 202–207. doi:10.1037/h0025008

Carlson, M., Marcus-Newhall, A., & Miller, N. (1990). Effects of situational aggression cues: A quantitative review. *Journal of Personality and Social Psychology, 58,* 622–633. doi: 10.1037/0022-3514.58.4.622

Federman, J. (2002). *Rating sex and violence in the media: Media ratings and proposals for reform: A Kaiser Family Foundation report.* Retrieved from http://www.kff.org/entmedia/loader.cfm?url=/commonspot/security/getfile.cfm&pageid=14094

Haninger, K., & Thompson, K. M. (2004). Content and ratings of teen-rated video games. *Journal of the American Medical Association, 291*(7), 856–865. doi:10.1001/jama.291.7.856

Hetsroni, A. (2007). Four decades of violent content on prime-time network programming: A longitudinal meta-analytic review. *Journal of Communication, 57,* 759–784. doi: 10.1111/j.1460–2466.2007.00367.x

National Television Violence Study. (1997–1998). (Vols. 1–3). Thousand Oaks, CA: Sage.

Rideout, V. J. (2007). *Parents, children and media: A Kaiser Family Foundation survey.* Retrieved from http://www.kff.org/entmedia/upload/7638.pdf

Smith, S. L., Lachlan, K., Pieper, K. M., Boyson, A. R., Wilson, B. J., Tamborini, R., & Weber, R. (2004). Brandishing guns in American media: Two studies examining how often and in what context firearms appear on television and in popular video games. *Journal of Broadcasting & Electronic Media, 48*(4), 584–606. doi:10.1207/s15506878jobem 4804_4

Thompson, K. M., & Haninger, K. (2001). Violence in e-rated video games. *Journal of the American Medical Association, 286*(5), 591–598. doi:10.1001/jama.286.5.591

Weaver, A. J., & Wilson, B. J. (2009). Role of graphic and sanitized violence in the enjoyment of television dramas. *Human Communication Research, 35,* 442–463. doi:10.1111/j.1468–2958.2009.01358.x

Weaver, A. J., Zelenkauskaite, A., & Samson, L. (2012). The (non)violent world of YouTube: Content trends in web video. *Journal of Communication.* Advance online publication. doi:10.1111/j.1460–2466.2012.01675.x

Weber, R., Behr, K.-M., Tamborini, R., Ritterfeld, U., & Mathiak, K. (2009). What do we really know about first-person-shooter games? An event-related, high-resolution content analysis. *Journal of Computer-Mediated Communication, 14*(4), 1016–1037. doi:10.1111/j.1083–6101.2009.01479.x

Weber, R., Ritterfeld, U., & Mathiak, K. (2006). Does playing violent video games induce aggression? Empirical evidence of a functional magnetic resonance imaging study. *Media Psychology, 8*(1), 39–60. doi: 10.1207/S1532785XMEP0801_4

Whitaker, J. L., & Bushman, B. D. (2012). "Boom, headshot!": Effect of video game play and controller type on firing aim and accuracy. *Communication Research*. Advance online publication. doi: 10.1177/0093650212446622

World Health Organization. (2009). *Guns, knives and pesticides: Reducing access to lethal means.* Retrieved from http://whqlibdoc.who.int/ publications/2009/9789241597739_ eng.pdf

Resource Guide

Books and Book Chapters

Abeles, R. (1980). Beyond violence and children. In S. B. Withey (Ed.), *Television and social behavior: Beyond violence and children* (pp. 7–8). Hillsdale, NJ: Erlbaum.

Allen, M., D'Alessio, D., & Emmers-Sommer, T. M. (1999). Reactions of criminal sexual offenders to pornography: A meta-analytic summary. In M. Roloff (Ed.), *Communication yearbook 22* (pp. 139–169). Thousand Oaks, CA: Sage.

Anderson, C. A., Gentile, D. A., & Buckley, K. E. (2007). *Violent video game effects on children and adolescents: Theory, research, and public policy.* New York, NY: Oxford University Press.

Barak, A., & Fisher, W. A. (2002). The future of Internet sexuality. In A. Cooper (Ed.), *Sex and the Internet: A guide for clinicians* (pp. 263–280). New York, NY: Bruner-Routledge.

Barlow, B., Dill, K., Anderson, K., & Lindsay, J. (2003). The proliferation of media violence and its economic underpinnings. In D. A. Gentile (Ed.), *Media violence and children* (pp. 1–18). Westport, CT: Praeger.

Bogart, L. (1980). After the Surgeon General's report. In S. B. Withey (Ed.), *Television and social behavior: Beyond violence and children* (pp. 112–120). Hillsdale, NJ: Erlbaum Associates.

Buckingham, D. (1998). Doing them harm? Children's conceptions of the negative effects of television. In K. Swan, C. Meskill, & S. Demaio (Eds.), *Social learning from broadcast television* (pp. 25–44). Cresskill, NJ: Hampton Press.

Bushman, B. J., & Huesmann, L. R. (2001). Effects of televised violence on aggression. In D. Singer & J. Singer (Eds.), *Handbook of children and the media* (pp. 223–254). Thousand Oaks, CA: Sage.

Butler, R. W. (2002). Violence in video games is a serious problem. In J. D. Torr (Ed.), *Is media violence a problem?* (pp. 41–42). San Diego, CA: Greenhaven Press.

Cantor, J. (1994). Fright reactions to mass media. In J. Bryant & D. Zillmann (Eds.), *Media effects: Advances in theory and research* (pp. 213–245). Hillsdale, NJ: Erlbaum.

Cantor, J. (1998). *"Mommy, I'm scared": How TV and movies frighten children and what we can do to protect them.* San Diego, CA: Harvest/Harcourt.

Cantor, J. (2000). Television contributes to violent behavior in children. In B. Grapes (Ed.), *Violent children* (pp. 17–20). San Diego, CA: Greenhaven Press.

Cantor, J. (2001). The media and children's fears, anxieties, and perceptions of danger. In D. Singer & J. Singer (Eds.), *Handbook of children and the media* (pp. 225–268). Thousand Oaks, CA: Sage.

Carll, E. K. (2005). Violence and women: News coverage of victims and perpetrators. In E. Cole & J. Henderson-Daniel (Eds.), *Featuring females: Feminist analysis of media* (pp. 143–153). Washington, DC: American Psychological Association.

Carnagey, N. L., & Anderson, C. A. (2003). Theory in the study of media violence: The general aggression model. In D. A. Gentile (Ed.), *Media violence and children: A complete guide for parents and professionals* (pp. 87–106). Westport, CT: Praeger.

Carter, D., & Strickland, S. (1975). *TV violence and the child.* New York, NY: Russell Sage Foundation.

Check, J. E. R., & Guloien, T. H. (1989). Reported proclivity for coercive sex following repeated exposure to sexually violent pornography, nonviolent dehumanizing pornography, and erotica. In D. Zillmann & J. Bryant (Eds.), *Pornography: Research advances and policy considerations* (pp. 159–184). Hillsdale, NJ: Erlbaum.

Check, J. V., & Malamuth, N. M. (1985). Pornography and sexual aggression: A social learning theory analysis. In M. McLaughlin (Ed.), *Communication yearbook 9* (pp. 181–213). Beverly Hills, CA: Sage.

Cline, V. B., Croft, R. G., & Courrier, S. (1974). The desensitization of children to the television. In V. B. Cline (Ed.), *Where do you draw the line?* (pp. 147–155). Provo, UT: Brigham Young University Press.

Coie, J. D., & Dodge, K. A. (1998). Aggression and antisocial behavior. In W. Damon & N. Eisenberg (Eds.), *Handbook of child psychology* (5th ed., Vol. 3, pp. 779–862). New York, NY: Wiley.

Colorito, R. (2002). Violence on television programs is a serious problem. In J. Torr (Ed.), *Is media violence a serious problem?* (pp. 24–29). San Diego, CA: Greenhaven Press.

Comstock, G. (1980). New emphases in research on the effects of television and film violence. In E. Palmer (Ed.), *Children and the faces of television: Teaching, violence, selling* (pp. 131–132). San Diego, CA: Academic Press.

Comstock, G., & Paik, H. (1991). *Television and the American child.* San Diego, CA: Academic Press.

Comstock, G., & Scharrer, E. (2001). The use of television and other film-related media. In D. G. Singer & J. L. Singer (Eds.), *Handbook of children and the media* (pp. 47–72). Thousand Oaks, CA: Sage.

Comstock, G., & Scharrer, E. (2002). Public opinion on television violence. In J. D. Torr (Ed.), *Violence in film and television* (pp. 70–74). San Diego, CA: Greenhaven Press.

Comstock, G., & Scharrer, E. (2003). Meta-analyzing the controversy over television violence and aggression. In D. A. Gentile (Ed.), *Media violence and children: A complete guide for parents and professionals* (pp. 205–226). Westport, CT: Praeger.

Condon, C. (2002). The entertainment industry markets violent media to children. In J. Torr (Ed.), *Is media violence a problem?* (pp. 77–81). San Diego, CA: Greenhaven Press.

Considine, D. (2002). Teen rebellion films and juvenile delinquency. In J. D. Torr (Ed.), *Violence in film and television* (pp. 33–42). San Diego, CA: Greenhaven Press.

Cooper, A., Scherer, C., & Marcus, I. D. (2002). Harnessing the power of the Internet to improve sexual relationships. In A. Cooper (Ed.), *Sex and the Internet: A guidebook for clinicians* (pp. 209–230). New York, NY: Brunner-Routledge.

Cuklanz, L. M. (2000). *Rape on prime time: Television, masculinity, and sexual violence.* Philadelphia: University of Pennsylvania Press.

Cuklanz, L. M. (2006). Gendered violence and mass media representation. In B. Dow & J. T. Wood (Eds.), *The Sage handbook of gender and communication* (pp. 335–354). Thousand Oaks, CA: Sage.

Cullingford, C. (1984). *Children and television.* New York, NY: St. Martin's.

Disney, A. (1995). Media violence should be treated as a public health problem. In C. Wekesser (Ed.), *Violence in the media* (pp. 130–131). San Diego, CA: Greenhaven Press.

Donnerstein, E. I., Linz, D., & Penrod, S. (1987). *The question of pornography: Research findings and policy implications.* New York, NY: Free Press.

Donnerstein, E., & Malamuth, N. (1997). Pornography: Its consequences on the observer. In L. B. Schlesinger & E. Revitch (Eds.), *Sexual dynamics of anti-social behavior* (2nd ed., pp. 30–49). Springfield, IL: Charles C. Thomas.

Donnerstein, E., Slaby, R. G., & Eron, L. D. (1994). The mass media and youth aggression. In J. Murray, E. Rubinstein, & G. Comstock (Eds.), *Violence and youth: Psychology's response* (Vol. 2, pp. 219–250). Washington, DC: American Psychological Association.

Dorr, A. (1986). *Television and children.* Beverly Hills, CA: Sage.

Dorr, A., & Kovarie, P. (1980). Some of the people some of the time—But which people? Televised violence and its effects. In E. L. Palmer & A. Dorr (Eds.), *Children and the faces of television: Teaching, violence, selling* (pp. 183–196). San Diego, CA: Academic Press.

Easterbrook, G. (2002). Media violence makes people more violent. In J. Torr (Ed.), *Is media violence a problem?* (pp. 69–76). San Diego, CA: Greenhaven Press.

Eastin, M. S. (2001). The television ratings: When public and policy collide. In B. S. Greenberg (Ed.), *The alphabet soup of the television ratings* (pp. 1–18). Cresskill, NJ: Hampton Press.

Eastin, M. S. (2008). Computer games and social perceptions. In W. Donsbach, J. Bryant, & R. Craig (Eds.), *The international encyclopedia of communication.* Hoboken, NJ: Blackwell.

Eysenck, H. J., & Nias, D. K. (1978). *Sex, violence, and the media.* New York, NY: Temple Smith.

Feshback, S., & Singer, R. (1971). *Television and aggression.* San Francisco, CA: Jossey-Bass.

Freedman, J. L. (2002). *Media violence and its effect on aggression: Assessing the scientific evidence.* Toronto: University of Toronto Press.

Gedatus, G. (2000). *Violence in the media: Perspectives on violence.* Mankato, MN: Capstone Press.

Gentile, D. A. (2003). *Media violence and children: A complete guide for parents and professionals* (Vol. 22). Westport, CT: Praeger.

Gentile, D. A., & Sesma, A. (2003). Developmental approaches to understanding media effects on individuals. In D. A. Gentile (Ed.), *Media violence and children* (pp. 19–38). Westport, CT: Praeger.

Gerbner, G., & Gross, L. (1980). The violent face of television and its lessons. In E. Palmer (Ed.), *Children and the faces of television: Teaching, violence, selling* (pp. 153–154). San Diego, CA: Academic Press.

Gerbner, G., Gross, L., Morgan, M., & Signiorelli, N. (1980). Living with television: The dynamics of the cultivation process. In J. Bryant & D. Zillman (Eds.), *Perspectives on media effects* (pp. 17–48). Hillsdale, NJ: Erlbaum.

Goldstein, A. (1996). Violence in America: Lessons on understanding the aggression in our lives. Palo Alto, CA: Davies-Black.

Goldstein, J. H. (1998). *Why we watch: The attractions of violent entertainment.* New York, NY: Oxford University Press on Demand.

Goldstein, M. J., & Kant, H. S. (1973). *Pornography and sexual deviance*. Berkeley: University of California Press.

Greenberg, B. S., Eastin, M. S., & Garramone, G. (2002). Ethical issues in conducting mass communication research. In G. Stemple & B. Westly (Eds.), *Mass communication research and theory* (pp. 229–326). Englewood Cliffs, NJ: Prentice-Hall.

Greenberg, B. S., Eastin, M. S., & Mastro, D. M. (2001). Assessing accuracy of the television ratings. In B. S. Greenberg (Ed.), *The alphabet soup of the television ratings* (pp. 39–50). Cresskill, NJ: Hampton Press.

Greenberg, B. S., Eastin, M. S., & Mastro, D. M. (2001). Reinventing the television ratings system. In B. S. Greenberg (Ed.), *The alphabet soup of the television ratings* (pp. 19–38). Cresskill, NJ: Hampton Press.

Greenberg, B. S., & Hofschire, L. (2000). The content and effects of sex on entertainment television. In D. Zillmann & P. Voderer (Eds.), *Media entertainment: The psychology of its appeal* (pp. 93–112). Mahwah, NJ: Erlbaum.

Groebel, J. (2001). Media violence in cross-cultural perspective. In D. Singer & J. Singer (Eds.), *Handbook of children in the media* (pp. 255–268). Thousand Oaks, CA: Sage.

Grossman, D. (2001). Violent video games teach children to enjoy killing. In J. D. Torr (Ed.), *Violence in the media: Current controversies* (pp. 69–71). San Diego, CA: Greenhaven Press.

Gunter, B. (1985). *Dimensions of television violence*. New York, NY: St. Martin's.

Gunter, B., Harrison, J., & Wykes, M. (2003). *Violence on television: Distribution, form, context, and themes*. Hillsdale, NJ: Erlbaum.

Gunter, B., & McAleer, J. (1990). *Children and television: The one-eyed monster*. London, UK: Routledge.

Gunter, B., & McAleer, J. (1997). *Children and television*. New York, NY: Routledge.

Hamilton, J. (1998). Who will rate the ratings? In M. E. Price (Ed.), *The V-chip debate: Content filtering from television to the Internet* (pp. 133–156). Mahwah, NJ: Erlbaum.

Hamilton, J. (2001). Violence on television is a serious problem. In J. D. Torr (Ed.), *Violence in the media: Current controversies* (pp. 23–56). San Diego, CA: Greenhaven Press.

Heins, M. (1998). Three questions about television. In M. E. Price (Ed.), *The V-chip debate: Content filtering from television to the Internet* (pp. 47–58). Mahwah, NJ: Erlbaum.

Hoberman, J. (1998). A test for the individual viewer: *Bonnie and Clyde*'s violent reception. In J. Goldstein (Ed.), *Why we watch: The attractions of violent entertainment* (pp. 116–143). New York, NY: Oxford University Press.

Huesmann, L. R., Dubow, E. F., & Yang, G. (2012). Why it is hard to believe that media violence causes aggression. In Karen E. Dill (Ed.), *The Oxford handbook of media psychology*. New York, NY: Oxford University Press.

Huesmann, L. R., & Eron, L. D. (1986). The development of aggression in American children as a consequence of television violence viewing. In L. Huesmann (Ed.), *Television and the aggressive child: A cross-national comparison* (pp. 46–78). Hillsdale, NJ: Erlbaum.

Huesmann, L. R., & Miller, L. S. (1994). Long-term effects of repeated exposure to media violence in childhood. In L. R. Huesmann (Ed.). *Aggressive behavior: Current perspectives* (pp. 153–186). New York, NY: Plenum Press.

Huesmann, L. R., & Taylor, L. (2003). The case against the case against media violence. In D. A. Gentile (Ed.), *Media violence and children* (pp. 107–130). Westport, CT: Praeger.

Jipping, T. L. (2001). Popular music contributes to teenage violence. In J. D. Torr (Ed.), *Violence in the media: current controversies* (pp. 61–66). San Diego, CA: Greenhaven Press.

Keegan, P. (2002). Video games: The latest format for screen violence. In J. D. Torr (Ed.), *Violence in film and television* (pp. 93–103). San Diego, CA: Greenhaven Press.

Kirsh, S. J. (2011). *Children, adolescents, and media violence: A critical look at the research*. Thousand Oaks, CA: Sage.

Kolter, J., & Calvert, S. (2003). Children's and adolescents' exposure to different kinds of media violence: Recurring choices and recurring themes. In D. A. Gentile (Ed.), *Media violence and children* (pp. 171–184). Westport, CT: Praeger.

Kunkel, D. (2003). The road to the V-chip: Television violence and public policy. In D. A. Gentile (Ed.), *Media violence and children* (pp. 227–246). Westport, CT: Praeger.

Lefkowitz, M. M., Eron, L. D., Walder, L. O., & Huesmann, L. R. (1997). *Growing up to be violent: A longitudinal study of the development of aggression*. New York, NY: Pergamon.

Lefkowitz, M. M., & Huesmann, L. R. (1980). Concomitants of television viewing in children. In E. Palmer (Ed.), *Children and the faces of television: Teaching, violence, selling* (pp. 177–178). San Diego, CA: Academic Press.

Levine, M. (1996). *Viewing violence: How media violence affects your child's and adolescent's development*. New York, NY: Bantam Doubleday Dell.

Lichter, R., Lichter, L., & Rothman, S. (2002). Examining how violence is presented on television. In J. D. Torr (Ed.), *Violence in film and television* (pp. 83–92). San Diego, CA: Greenhaven Press.

Liebert, R. M., Davidson, E. S., & Neale, J. M. (1974). Aggression in childhood: The impact of television. In V. B. Cline (Ed.), *Where do you draw the line?* (pp. 113–128). Provo, UT: Brigham Young University Press.

Liebert, R. M., Neale, J. M., & Davidson, E. S. (1973). *The early window: Effects of television on children and youth.* New York, NY: Pergamon.

MacBeth, T. M. (2003). Media effects on society and communities. In D. A. Gentile (Ed.), *Media violence and children* (pp. 57–86). Westport, CT: Praeger.

Malamuth, N. M., Addison, T., & Koss, M. (2001). Pornography and sexual aggression: Are there reliable effects and can we understand them? *Annual Review of Sex Research* (Vol. 11). Mason City, IA: Society for the Scientific Study of Sexuality.

Malamuth, N., & Donnerstein, E. (1984). *Pornography and sexual aggression.* Orlando, FL: Academic Press.

McDowell, S. D. (1998). Developing television ratings in Canada and the United States: The perils and promises of self-regulation. In M. E. Price (Ed.), *The V-chip debate: Content filtering from television to the Internet* (pp. 23–46). Mahwah, NJ: Erlbaum.

Melville-Thomas, G. (1985). Television violence and children. In G. Barlow (Ed.), *Video violence and children* (pp. 8–17). New York, NY: St. Martin's.

Mosk, R. M. (1998). Motion picture ratings in the United States. In M. E. Price (Ed.), *The V-chip debate: Content filtering from television to the Internet* (pp. 195–203). Mahwah, NJ: Erlbaum.

Mundorf, N., Allen, M., D'Alessio, D., & Emmers-Sommer, T. (2007). Effects of sexually explicit media. In R. Preiss, B. Gayle, N. Burrell, M. Allen, & J. Bryant (Eds.), *Mass media effects research* (pp. 181–198). Mahwah, NJ: Erlbaum.

Murray, J. (1993). The developing child in a multimedia society. In G. L. Berry & J. K. Asamen (Eds.), *Children and television images in a changing sociocultural world* (pp. 9–22). Newbury Park, CA: Sage.

O'Keefe, G. J. (1984). Public views on crime: Television exposure and media credibility. In R. N. Bostrom (Ed.), *Communication yearbook 8* (pp. 514–535). Beverly Hills, CA: Sage.

Parker, C. (1997). *The joy of cybersex: Confessions of an Internet addict.* Kew, Australia: Reed Books.

Potter, W. J. (1999). *On media violence.* Thousand Oaks, CA: Sage.

Prince, S. (2002). A brief history of film violence. In J. D. Torr (Ed.), *Violence in film and television* (pp. 21–33). San Diego, CA: Greenhaven Press.

Provenzo, E. F. (2002). Violence in video games is a serious problem. In J. Torr (Ed.), *Is media violence a problem?* (pp. 45–46). San Diego, CA: Greenhaven Press.

Rabinovitch, M. S., McLean, M. S., Markham, J. W., & Talbott, A. D. (1972). Children's violence and perception as a function of television violence. In G. A. Comstock, E. A. Rubinstein, and J. P. Murray (Eds.), *Television and social behavior* (pp. 28–187). Washington, DC: U.S. Government Printing Office.

Ramirez, A., Eastin, M. S., & Chakroff, J. (2008). Cyber-bullying: Conceptualizing process and effects. In S. Kelsey & K. St. Amant (Eds.), *Handbook of research on computer mediated communication.* Hershey, PA: IGI Global.

Roth, M. (1985). Introduction: The socio-psychological phenomena of violence. In G. Barlow (Ed.), *Video violence and children* (pp. 3–4). New York, NY: St. Martin's.

Rubinstein, E. A. (1980). Television violence: A historical perspective. In E. Palmer (Ed.), *Children and the faces of television: Teaching, violence, selling* (pp. 120–121). San Diego, CA: Academic Press.

Russell, D. E. H. (1998). *Dangerous relationships: Pornography, misogyny, and rape.* Thousand Oaks, CA: Sage.

Sapolsky, B. S., & Molito, F. (2002). Slasher films and violence against women. In J. D. Torr (Ed.), *Violence in film and television* (pp. 52–60). San Diego, CA: Greenhaven Press.

Siegal, A. (1974). The effects of media violence on social learning. In V. B. Cline (Ed.), *Where do you draw the line?* (pp. 129–146). Provo, UT: Brigham Young University Press.

Simpson, B. (2004). *Children and television.* New York, NY: Continuum International Publishing Group.

Singer, J., & Singer, D. (1981). *Television, imagination, and aggression.* Hillsdale, NJ: Erlbaum.

Singer, S. I., Levine, M., & Jou, S. (2001). Heavy metal music preference, delinquent friends, social control, and delinquency. In C. E. Pope, R. Lovell, & S.G. Brandl (Eds.), *Voices from the field: Readings in criminal justice research* (pp. 109–121). Belmont, CA: Wadsworth.

Smith, S. L., & Donnerstein, E. (1998). Harmful effects of exposure to media violence: Learning of aggression, emotional desensitization, and fear. In R. G. Geen & E. Donnerstein (Eds.), *Human aggression: Theories, research, and implications for social policy* (pp. 167–202). New York, NY: Academic Press.

Sparks, R. (1992). *Television and the drama of crime: Moral tales and the place of crime in public life.* Milton Keyes, UK: Open University Press.

Steingeld, J. L. (1974). Statement of the Surgeon General concerning television and violence. In V. B. Cline (Ed.), *Where do you draw the line?* (pp. 177–178). Provo, UT: Brigham Young University Press.

Steyer, J. P. (2002). *The other parent: The inside story of the media's effect on our children.* New York, NY: Atria.

Strasburger, V., & Wilson, B. J. (2003). Television violence. In D.A. Gentile (Ed.), *Media violence and children* (pp. 57–86). Westport, CT: Praeger.

Van der Voort, T. H. A. (1986). *Television violence: A child's-eye view.* New York, NY: Elsevier Science.

Van Evra, J. (2004). *Television and child development.* Hillsdale, NJ: Erlbaum.

Wertham, F. (1974). School for violence, mayhem in the mass media. In V. B. Cline (Ed.), *Where do you draw the line?* (pp. 157–176). Provo, UT: Brigham Young University Press.

Wheen, F. (2002). The first outcry against television violence. In J. D. Torr (Ed.), *Violence in film and television* (pp. 83–92). San Diego, CA: Greenhaven Press.

Williams, T. M. (1986). *The impact of television: A national experiment in three communities.* New York, NY: Academic Press.

Wilson, B. J., Kunkel, D., Linz, D., Donnerstein, E., Smith, S., Blumenthal, E., et al. (1997). Television violence and its context. In Mediascope (Ed.), *National Television Violence Study* (Vol. 1). Newbury Park, CA: Sage.

Wilson, B. J., Kunkel, D., Linz, D., Potter, J., Donnerstein, E., Smith, S. L., Blumenthal, E., & Gray, T. (1998). Violence in television programming overall: University of California, Santa Barbara Study. In M. Seawall (Ed.), *National Television Violence Study* (Vol. 2). Thousand Oaks, CA: Sage.

Wolpe, J. (1958). *Psychotherapy by reciprocal inhibition.* Stanford, CA: Stanford University Press.

Zillmann, D. (1983). Arousal and aggression. In R. Geen & E. Donnerstein (Eds.), *Aggression: Theoretical and empirical reviews* (Vol. 1, pp. 75–102). New York, NY: Academic Press.

Zillmann, D., & Bryant, J. (1984). Effects of massive exposure to pornography. In N. M. Malamuth & E. Donnerstein (Eds.), *Pornography and sexual aggression* (pp. 115–138). Orlando, FL: Academic Press.

Journal Articles

Adachi, P. C., & Willoughby, T. (2010). The effect of violent video games on aggression: Is it more than just the violence? *Aggression and Violent Behavior, 16,* 55–62.

Allen, M., Emmers, T. M., Gebhardt, L. J., & Giery, M. (1995). Exposure to pornography and acceptance of rape myths: A research summary using meta-analysis. *Journal of Communication, 45,* 5–26.

Anderson, C. A. (1997). Effects of violent movies and trait irritability on hostile feelings and aggressive thoughts. *Aggressive Behavior, 23,* 161–178.

Anderson, C. A. (2004). An update on the effects of violent video games. *Journal of Adolescence, 27,* 113–122.

Anderson, C. A., Berkowitz, L., Donnerstein, E., Huesmann, L. R., Johnson, J. D., Linz, D., & Wartella, E. (2003). The influence of media violence on youth. *Psychological Science in the Public Interest, 4*(3), 81–110.

Anderson, C. A., & Bushman, B. J. (2001). Effects of violent video games on aggressive behavior, aggressive cognition, aggressive affect, physiological arousal, and prosocial behavior: A meta-analytic review of the scientific literature. *Psychological Science, 12,* 353–359.

Anderson, C. A., & Bushman, B. J. (2002a). Human aggression. *Annual Review of Psychology, 53,* 27–51.

Anderson, C. A., & Bushman, B. J. (2002b). The effects of media violence on society. *Science, 295,* 2378–2379.

Anderson, C. A., & Carnagey, N. L. (2009). Causal effects of violent sports video games on aggression: Is it competitiveness or violent content? *Journal of Experimental Social Psychology, 45,* 731–739.

Anderson, C. A., Carnagey, N. L., & Eubanks, J. (2003). Exposure to violent media: The effects of songs with violent lyrics on aggressive thoughts and feelings. *Journal of Personality and Social Psychology, 84,* 960–971.

Anderson, C. A., Carnagey, N. L., Flanagan, M., Benjamin, A. J., Eubanks, J., & Valentine, J. C. (2004). Violent video games: Specific effects of violent content on aggressive thoughts and behavior. *Advances in Experimental Social Psychology, 36,* 199–249.

Anderson, C. A., & Dill, K. E. (2000). Video games and aggressive thoughts, feelings, and behavior in the laboratory and in life. *Journal of Personality and Social Psychology, 78,* 772–790.

Anderson, C. A., Ihori, N., Bushman, B. J., Rothstein, H. R., Shibuya, A., Swing, E. L., . . . Saleem, M. (2010). Video game effects on aggression, empathy, and prosocial behavior and Eastern and Western countries: A meta-analytic review. *Psychological Bulletin, 136,* 151–173.

Anderson, C. A., & Morrow, M. (1995). Competitive aggression without interaction: Effects of competitive versus cooperative instructions on aggressive behavior in video games. *Personality and Social Psychology Bulletin, 21,* 1020–1030.

Anderson, C. A., & Murphy, C. (2003). Violent video games and aggressive behavior in young women. *Aggressive Behavior, 29,* 423–429.

Ballard, M. E., & Wiest, J. R. (1995, March). *Mortal Kombat:* The effects of violent video technology on males' hostility and cardiovascular responding. *Journal of Applied Social Psychology, 26,* 717–730.

Bandura, A., Ross, D. & Ross, S. A. (1963). Imitation of film-mediated aggressive models. *Journal of Abnormal and Social Psychology, 66,* 3–11.

Banks, M. (2005). Spaces of insecurity: Media and fear of crime in a local context. *Crime Media Culture 1*(2), 322–332.

Barak, A., Fisher, W. A., Belfry, S., & Lashambe, D. R. (1999). Sex, guys, and cyberspace: Effects of Internet pornography and individual differences on men's attitudes toward women. *Journal of Psychology and Human Sexuality, 11,* 63–91.

Barlett, C. P., Branch, O., Rodeheffer, C., & Harris, R. (2009). How long do the short-term violent video game effects last? *Aggressive Behavior, 35,* 1–12.

Bartholow, B., & Anderson, C. A. (2002). Effects of violent video games on aggressive behavior: Potential sex differences. *Journal of Experimental Social Psychology, 38,* 283–290.

Berkowitz, L. (1984). Some effects of thoughts on the anti- and prosocial influence of media events: A cognitive neoassociationistic analysis. *Psychological Bulletin, 95,* 410–427.

Berkowitz, L., & Rawlings, E. (1963). Effects of film violence on inhibition against subsequent aggression. *Journal of Abnormal and Social Psychology, 66,* 405–412.

Berry, M., Gray, T., & Donnerstein, E. (1999). Cutting film violence: Effects on perceptions, enjoyment, and arousal. *Journal of Social Psychology, 139,* 567–582.

Bryant, J., Carveth, R. A., & Brown, D. (1981). Television viewing and anxiety: An experimental examination. *Journal of Communication, 31,* 106–119.

Bushman, B. J. (1995). Moderating role of trait aggressiveness in the effects of violent media on aggression. *Journal of Personality and Social Psychology, 69,* 950–960.

Bushman, B. J. (1998). Priming effects of media violence on the accessibility of aggressive constructs in memory. *Personality and Social Psychology Bulletin, 24,* 537–545.

Bushman, B. J., & Anderson, C. A. (2001). Media violence and the American public: Scientific facts versus media misinformation. *American Psychologist, 56*(6/7), 477–489.

Bushman, B. J., & Anderson, C. A. (2002). Violent video games and hostile expectations: A test of the general aggression model. *Personality and Social Psychology Bulletin, 28,* 1679–1686.

Bushman, B. J., & Anderson, C. A. (2009). Comfortably numb: Desensitizing effects of violent media on helping others. *Psychological Science, 20,* 273–277.

Bushman, B. J., & Bonacci, A. M. (2002). Violence and sex impair memory for television ads. *Journal of Applied Psychology, 87,* 557–564.

Bushman, B. J., & Cantor, J. (2003). Media ratings for violence and sex: Implications for policymakers and parents. *American Psychological Association, 52*(2), 130–141.

Bushman, B. J., & Geen, R. G. (1990). Role of cognitive-emotional mediators and individual differences in the effects of media violence on aggression. *Journal of Personality and Social Psychology, 58*(1), 156–163.

Bushman, B. J., & Phillips, C. M. (2001). If the television program bleeds, memory for the advertisement recedes. *Current Directions in Psychological Science, 10,* 44–47.

Bushman, B. J., & Stack, A. D. (1996). Forbidden fruit versus tainted fruit: Effects of warning labels on attraction to television. *Journal of Experimental Psychology: Applied 2*(3), 207–226.

Brinson, S. L. (1992). TV rape: Television's communication of cultural attitudes toward rape. *Women's Studies in Communication, 12*(2), 23–36.

Browne, K. D., & Hamilton-Giachritsis, C. (2005). The influence of violent media on children and adolescents: A public-health approach. *Lancet, 365,* 702–710.

Calvert, S., & Tan, S. L. (1994). Impact of virtual reality on young adults' physiological arousal and aggressive thoughts: Interaction versus observation. *Journal of Applied Developmental Psychology, 15,* 125–139.

Cantor, J., & Sparks, G. G. (1984). Children's fear responses to mass media: Testing some Piagetian predictions. *Journal of Communication, 34,* 90–103.

Cantor, J., & Wilson, B. J. (1984). Modifying responses to mass media in preschool and elementary school children. *Journal of Broadcasting, 28,* 431–443.

Cantor, J., Wilson, B. J., & Hoffner, C. (1986). Emotional responses to a televised nuclear holocaust film. *Communication Research, 13,* 257–277.

Carll, E. K. (2003). News portrayal of violence and women. *American Behavioral Scientist, 46,* 1601–1610.

Carnagey, L. N., & Anderson, C. A. (2005). The effects of reward and punishment in violent video games on aggressive affect, cognition, and behavior. *Psychological Science, 16,* 882–889.

Cecil, D. (2007). Dramatic portrayals of violent women: Female offenders on prime time crime dramas. *Journal of Criminal Justice and Popular Culture, 14*(3), 243–258.

Centerwall, B. S. (1992). Television and violence: The scale of the problem and where to go from here. *Journal of the American Medical Association, 267,* 3059–3063.

Chadee, D., & Ditton, J. (1999). Fear of crime in Trinidad: A preliminary empirical research note. *Caribbean Journal of Criminology and Social Psychology, 4*(1/2), 112–129.

Chiricos, T., & Eschholz, S. (2002). The racial and ethnic typification of crime and the criminal: Typification of race and ethnicity in local television news. *Journal of Research in Crime and Delinquency, 39*(4), 400–420.

Chiricos, T., Eschholz, S., & Gertz, M. (1997). Crime, news, and fear of crime: Toward an identification of audience effects. *Social Problems, 44,* 342–357.

Chiricos, T., Padgett, K., & Gertz, M. (2000). Fear, TV news, and the reality of crime. *Criminology, 38,* 755–785.

Cline, V. B., Croft, R. G., & Courrier, S. (1973). Desensitization of children to television violence. *Journal of Personality and Social Psychology, 27,* 360–365.

Cooper, A. (1998). Sexuality and the Internet: Surfing into the new millennium. *CyberPsychology & Behavior, 1,* 187–193.

Cooper, A. (2000). Cybersex and sexual compulsivity: The dark side of the force. *Sexual Addiction and Compulsivity, 7,* 1–3.

Cooper, A., Delmonico, D. L., & Burg, R. (2000). Cybersex users, abusers, and compulsives: New findings and implications. *Sexual Addiction & Compulsivity, 7,* 5–29.

Cooper, A., Scherer, C. R., Bois, S. C., & Gordon, B. I. (1999). Sexuality on the Internet: From sexual exploration to pathological expression. *Professional Psychology: Research and Practice, 30,* 154–164.

Cooper, J., & Mackie, D. (1986). Video games and aggression in children. *Journal of Applied Social Psychology, 16,* 726–744.

Daneback, K., Ross, M. K., & Mansson, S.-A. (2006). Characteristics and behaviors of sexual compulsives who use the Internet for sexual purposes. *Sexual Addiction & Compulsivity: The Journal of Treatment and Prevention, 13,* 53–67.

DeLisi, M., Vaughn, M. G., Gentile, D. A., Anderson, C. A., & Shook, J. (2013). Violent video games, delinquency, and youth violence. *Youth Violence and Juvenile Justice, 11*(2), 132–142.

Demare, D., Briere, J., & Lips, H. (1988). Violent pornography and self-reported likelihood of raping. *Journal of Research in Personality, 22,* 140–153.

Dennis, P. M. (1998). Chills and thrills: Does radio harm our children? The controversy over program violence during the age of radio. *Journal of the History of Behavioral Sciences, 34*(1), 33–50.

Dexter, H. R., Penrod, S., & Linz, D. (1997). Attributing responsibility to female victims after exposure to sexually violent films. *Journal of Applied Social Psychology, 27,* 2149–2171.

Diamond, M. (2009). Pornography, public acceptance and sex related crime: A review. *International Journal of Law and Psychiatry, 32*(5), 304–314.

Diener, E., & DeFour, D. (1978). Does television violence enhance program popularity? *Journal of Personality and Social Psychology, 36*(3), 333–341.

Dietz, T. L. (1998). An examination of violence and gender role portrayals in video games: Implications for gender socialization and aggressive behavior. *Sex Roles, 38*(5–6), 425–442.

Ditton, J., Chadee, D., Farrall, S., Gilchrist, E., & Bannister, J. (2004). From imitation to intimidation: A note on the curious and changing relationship between the media, crime and fear of crime. *British Journal of Criminology, 44*(4), 595–610.

Dominick, J. R. (1984). Videogames, television violence, and aggression in teenagers. *Journal of Communication, 34*(2), 136–147.

Doob, A., & Macdonald, G. E. (1979). Television viewing and fear of victimization: Is the relationship causal? *Journal of Personality and Social Psychology, 37,* 170–179.

Eastin, M. S. (2006). Video game violence and the female game player: Self- and opponent gender effects on presence and aggressive thoughts. *Human Communication Research, 32*(3), 351–372.

Eastin, M. S. (2007). The influence of competitive and cooperative group game play on state hostility. *Human Communication Research, 33,* 450–466.

Eastin, M. S., Appiah, O., & Cicchirillo, V. (2009). Identification and the influence of cultural stereotyping on post video game play hostility. *Human Communication Research, 3,* 337–356.

Eastin M. S., Greenberg, B. S., & Hofschire, L. (2006). Parenting the Internet. *Journal of Communication, 56,* 486–504.

Eastin, M. S., & Griffiths, R. P. (2006). Beyond the shooter game: Examining presence and hostile outcomes among male game players. *Communication Research, 33*(6), 448–466.

Eastin, M. S., & Griffiths, R. P. (2009). Unreal: Hostile expectations and social game play. *New Media & Society,* 509–531.

Emmers-Sommer, T. M., & Burns, R. J. (2005). The relationship between exposure to Internet pornography and sexual attitudes toward women. *Journal of Online Behavior, 1*(4). Retrieved from http://old.behavior.net/JOB/v1n4/emmers-sommer.html

Emmers-Sommer, T., Pauley, P., & Hanzal, A. (2006). Love, suspense, sex and violence: Men's and women's film predilections, exposure to sexually violent media, and their relationship to rape myth acceptance. *Sex Roles, 55,* 311–320.

Eschholz, S. (1997). The media and fear of crime: A survey of the research. *Journal of Law & Public Policy, 9,* 37–59.

Eschholz, S., Chiricos, T., & Gertz, M. (2003). Television and fear of crime: Program types, audience traits, and the mediating effect of perceived neighborhood racial composition. *Social Problems, 50,* 395–415.

Eschholz, S., Mallard, M., & Flynn, S. (2004). Images of prime time justice: A content analysis of *NYPD Blue* and *Law and Order. Journal of Criminal Justice and Popular Culture, 10,* 161–180.

Ferguson, C. J. (2012). Positive female role models eliminate negative effects of sexually violent media. *Journal of Communication, 62*(5), 888–899.

Ferguson, C. J., & Hartley, R. D. (2009). The pleasure is momentary . . . the expense damnable? The influence of pornography on rape and sexual assault. *Aggression and Violent Behavior, 14*(5), 323–329.

Ferguson, C. J., & Kilburn, J. (2010). Much ado about nothing: The misestimation and overinterpretation of violent video game effects in Eastern and Western nations: Comment on Anderson et al. (2010). *Psychological Bulletin, 136,* 174–178.

Ferguson, C. J., & Rueda, S. M. (2010). The hitman study: Violent video game exposure effects on aggressive behavior, hostile feelings, and depression. *European Psychologist, 15,* 99–108.

Ferguson, C. J., Rueda, S. M., Cruz, A. M., Ferguson, D. E., Fritz, S., & Smith, S. M. (2008). Violent video games and aggression: Byproduct of family violence and intrinsic violence motivation? *Criminal Justice and Behavior, 35,* 311–332.

Ferguson, C. J., San Miguel, C., Garza, A., & Jerabeck, J. M. (2012). A longitudinal test of video game violence influences on dating and aggression: A 3-year longitudinal study of adolescents. *Journal of Psychiatric Research, 46,* 141–146.

Fisher, R. D., Cook, I. J., & Shirkey, E. C. (1994). Correlates of support for censorship of sexual, sexually violent, and violent media. *Journal of Sex Research, 31*(3), 229–240.

Fisher, W. A., & Barak, A. (1991). Pornography, erotica, and behaviour: More questions than answers. *International Journal of Law and Psychiatry, 14,* 65–84.

Fisher, W. A., & Barak, A. (2001). Internet pornography: A social psychological perspective on Internet sexuality. *Journal of Sex Research, 38,* 1–11.

Fisher, W. A., & Byrne, D. (1978). Individual differences in affective, evaluative, and behavioral responses to an erotic film. *Journal of Applied Social Psychology, 8,* 355–365.

Fisher, W., & Grenier, G. (1994). Violent pornography, antiwoman thoughts and antiwoman acts: In search of reliable effects. *Journal of Sex Research, 31,* 23–38.

Freeman-Longo, R. E. (2000). Children, teens, and sex on the Internet. *Sexual Addiction and Compulsivity, 7,* 75–90.

Garcia, L. T. (1986). Exposure to pornography and attitudes toward women and rape: A correlational study. *Journal of Sex Research, 22,* 378–385.

Garos, S., Beggan, J. K., Kluck, A., & Easton, A. (2004). Sexism and pornography use: Toward explaining past (null) results. *Journal of Psychology and Human Sexuality, 16*(1), 69–96.

Gebotys, R., Roberts, J., & DasGupta, B. (1988). News media use and public perceptions of seriousness. *Canadian Journal of Criminology, 30*(1), 3–16.

Gentile, D. A., Lynch, P. J., Linder, J. R., & Walsh, D. A. (2004). The effects of violent video game habits on adolescent hostility, aggressive behaviors, and school performance. *Journal of Adolescence, 27,* 5–22.

Gerbner, G. (1972). Violence in television drama: Trends and symbolic functions. *Television and Social Behavior: Media Content and Control, 28.*

Gerbner, G., & Gross, L. (1976). Living with television: The violence profile. *Journal of Communication, 26*(2), 172–194.

Gerbner, G., Gross, L., Jackson-Beeck, M., Jeffries-Fox, S., & Signorielli, N. (1978). Cultural indicators: Violence profile no. 9. *Journal of Communication, 28,* 176–207.

Gerbner, G., Gross, L., Morgan, M., & Signorielli, N. (1980). The "mainstreaming" of America: Violence profile no. 11. *Journal of Communication, 30,* 10–29.

Gerbner, G., Gross, L., Morgan, M., & Signorielli, N. (1982). Charting the mainstreaming: Television's contributions to political orientations. *Journal of Communication, 32,* 100–127.

Gerbner, G., Gross, L., Signorielli, N., & Morgan, M. (1980). Television violence, victimization, and power. *American Behavioral Scientist, 23,* 705–716.

Goleman, D. (1985). Violence against women in films. *Response to the Victimization of Women and Children, 8,* 21–22.

Grabe, M. E., & Drew, D. (2007). Crime cultivation: Comparisons across media genres and channels. *Journal of Broadcasting & Electronic Media, 51*(1), 147–171.

Greene, K., & Krcmar, M. (2005). Predicting exposure to and liking of media violence: A uses and gratifications approach. *Communication Studies, 56*(1), 71–93.

Gross, K., & Aday, S. (2003). The scary world in your living room and neighborhood: Using local broadcast news, neighborhood crime rates, and personal experience to test agenda setting and cultivation. *Journal of Communication, 53,* 411–426.

Gunter, B., & Furnham, A. (1984). Perceptions of television violence: Effects of programme genre and type of violence on viewers' judgments of violent portrayals. *British Journal of Social Psychology, 23,* 155–164.

Hansen, C. H., & Hansen, R. D. (1990). The influence of sex and violence on the appeal of rock music videos. *Communication Research, 17,* 212–234.

Haridakis, P. M. (2002). Viewer characteristics, exposure to television violence and aggression. *Media Psychology, 4,* 323–352.

Harrison, K., & Cantor, J. (1999). Tales from the screen: Enduring fright reactions to scary media. *Media Psychology, 1*(2), 97–116.

Heath, L. (1984). Impact of newspaper crime reports on fear of crime: Multimethodological investigation, *Journal of Personality and Social Psychology, 47*(2), 263–276.

Hogan, M. J. (2005). Adolescents and media violence: Six crucial issues for practitioners. *Adolescent Medicine Clinics, 16*(2), 249–268.

Huesmann, L. R. (1986). Psychological processes promoting the relation between exposure to media violence and aggressive behavior by the viewer. *Journal of Social Issues, 42*(3), 125–139.

Huesmann, L. R., Eron, L. D., Klein, R., Brice, P., & Fischer, P. (1983). Mitigating the imitation of aggressive behaviors by changing children's attitudes about media violence. *Journal of Personality and Social Psychology, 44*(5), 899–910.

Huesmann, L. R., Lagerspetz, K., & Eron, L. D. (1984). Intervening variables in the TV violence-aggression relation: Evidence from two countries. *Developmental Psychology, 20*, 746–775.

Huesmann, L. R., & Miller, L. S. (1994). Long-term effects of repeated exposure to media violence in childhood. *Aggressive Behavior: Current Perspectives, 153*, 186.

Huesmann, L. R., Moise-Titus, J., Podolski, C., & Eron, L. D. (2003). Longitudinal relations between children's exposure to TV violence and their aggressive and violent behavior in young adulthood: 1977–1992. *Developmental Psychology, 39*, 201–221.

Huston-Stein, A., Fox, S., Greer, D., Watkins, B. A., & Whitaker, J. (1981). The effects of TV violence on children's social behavior. *Journal of Genetic Psychology, 138*, 183–191.

Josephson, W. L. (1987). Television violence and children's aggression: Testing the priming, social script, and disinhibition predictions. *Journal of Personality and Social Psychology, 53*, 882–889.

Kahlor, L., & Eastin, M. S. (2011). Television's role in the culture of violence toward women: A study of television viewing and the cultivation of rape myth acceptance in the United States. *Journal of Broadcasting & Electronic Media, 55*(2), 215–231.

Kahlor, L. A., & Morrison, D. (2007). Television viewing and rape myth acceptance among college women. *Sex Roles, 56*(11/12), 729–739.

Kirsh, S. J. (1998). Seeing the world through *Mortal Kombat*–colored glasses: Violent video games and the development of a short-term hostile attribution bias. *Childhood, 5*, 177–184.

Kohm, S. A., Waid-Lindberg, C. A., Weinrath, M., Shelley, T., & Dobbs, R. R. (2012). The impact of media on fear of crime among university students: A cross-national comparison. *Canadian Journal of Criminology and Criminal Justice, 54*(1), 67–100.

Koomen, W., Visser, M., & Stapel, D. (2000). The credibility of newspapers and fear of crime. *Journal of Applied Social Psychology, 30*, 921–934.

Koukounas, E., & McCabe, M. P. (2001). Emotional responses to filmed violence and the eye blink startle response: A preliminary investigation. *Journal of Interpersonal Violence, 16*, 476–488.

Krcmar, M., & Greene, K. (1999). Predicting exposure to and uses of violent television. *Journal of Communication, 49*, 25–45.

Krcmar, M., & Greene, K. (2000). Violent television exposure as a contributor to adolescent risk taking behavior. *Media Psychology, 2*, 195–217.

Langevin, R., Lang, R. A., Wright, P., Handy, L., Frenzel, R. R., & Black, E. L. (1988). Pornography and sexual offences. *Sexual Abuse: A Journal of Research & Treatment, 1*, 335–362.

Lanis, K., & Covell, K. (1995). Images of women in advertisements: Effects on attitudes related to sexual aggression. *Sex Roles, 32*, 639–649.

Lazar, B. A. (1996). Old battles, new frontiers: A study of television violence and social work with children. *Child and Adolescent Social Work Journal, 13*, 527–540.

Lee, M. J., Hust, S., Zhang, L., & Zhang, Y. (2011). Effects of violence against women in popular crime dramas on viewers' attitudes related to sexual violence. *Mass Communication & Society, 14*(1), 25–44.

Linz, D. G., Donnerstein, E., & Penrod, S. (1988). Effects of long-term exposure to violent and sexually degrading depictions of women. *Journal of Personality and Social Psychology, 55*, 758–768.

Mackenzie, C. (1940, June 23). Movies and the child: The debate rages on. *New York Times Magazine*, 9–10.

Malamuth, N. M., Addison, T., & Koss, M. (2001). Pornography and sexual aggression: Are there reliable effects? *Annual Review of Sex Research, 11*, 26–91.

Malamuth, N. M., & Briere, J. (1986). Sexual violence in the media: Indirect effects on aggression against women. *Journal of Social Issues, 42*, 75–92.

Malamuth, N. M., & Check, J. (1981). The effects of mass media exposure on acceptance of violence against women: A field experiment. *Journal of Research in Personality, 15*, 436–446.

Malamuth, N. M., Haber, S., & Feshbach, S. (1980). Testing hypotheses regarding rape: Exposure to sexual violence, sex differences, and the "normality" of rapists. *Journal of Research in Personality, 14*(1), 121–137.

Mann, J., Sidman, J., & Starr, S. (1973). Evaluating social consequences of erotic films: An experimental approach. *Journal of Social Issues, 29*, 113–131.

McFarlane, M., Bull, S. S., & Rietmeijer, C. A. (2000). The Internet as a newly emerging risk environment for sexually transmitted diseases. *Journal of the American Medical Association, 284*, 443–446.

McIlwraith, R. D., & Schallow, J. R. (1983). Adult fantasy life and patterns of media use. *Journal of Communication, 33*, 78–91.

Murray, J. (1995). Children and television violence. *Kansas Journal of Law and Public Policy, 4*(3), 7–14.

Nabi, R. L., & Sullivan, J. L. (2001). Does television viewing relate to engagement in protective action against crime? A cultivation analysis from a theory of reasoned action perspective. *Communication Research, 28*, 802–825.

Nellis, A. M., & Savage, J. (2012). Does watching the news affect fear of terrorism? The importance of media exposure on terrorism fear. *Crime & Delinquency, 58*(5), 748–768.

O'Keefe, G. J., & Reid-Nash, K. (1987). Crime news and real-world blues: The effects of the media on social reality. *Communication Research, 14*, 147–163.

Osborn, D. K., & Endsley, R. C. (1971). Emotional reactions of young children to TV violence. *Child Development, 42*, 321–331.

Padgett, V., Brislin-Slutz, J., & Neal, J. (1989). Pornography, erotica, and attitudes toward women: The effects of repeated exposure. *Journal of Sex Research, 26*, 470–491.

Paik, H., & Comstock, G. (1994). The effects of television violence on antisocial behavior: A meta-analysis. *Communication Research, 21*, 516–546.

Parker, T. S., & Wampler, K. S. (2003). How bad is it? Perceptions of the relationship impact of different types of Internet sexual activities. *Contemporary Family Therapy, 25*, 415–429.

Perloff, R. M., Quarles, R. C., & Drutz, M. (1983). Loneliness, depression, and the uses of television. *Journalism Quarterly, 60*, 352–356.

Peter, J., & Valkenburg, P. M. (2007). Adolescents' exposure to a sexualized media environment and their notions of women as sex objects. *Sex Roles, 56*(5–6), 381–395.

Phillips, D. P. (1983). The impact of mass media violence on U.S. homicides. *American Sociological Review, 48*, 560–568.

Potter, W. J. (1986). Perceived reality and the cultivation hypothesis. *Journal of Broadcasting & Electronic Media, 30*, 159–174.

Potter, W. J., & Chang, I. C. (1990). Television exposure measures and the cultivation hypothesis. *Journal of Broadcasting & Electronic Media, 34*(3), 313–334.

Potter, W. J., & Warren, R. (1998). Humor as camouflage of television violence. *Journal of Communication, 48*, 40–57.

Rivadeneyra, R., & Lebo, M. J. (2008). The association between television viewing behaviors and adolescent dating role attitudes and behaviors. *Journal of Adolescence, 31*(3), 291–305.

Romer, D., Jamieson, K. H., & Aday, S. (2003). Television news and the cultivation of fear of crime. *Journal of Communication, 53*, 88–104.

Rothenberg, M. B. (1975). Effect of television violence on children and youth. *Journal of the American Medical Association, 234*, 1043–1046.

Rubin, A. M., Haridakis, P., Hullman, G., Sun, S., Chikombero, P. M., & Pornsakulvanich, V. (2003). Television exposure not predictive of terrorism fear. *Newspaper Research Journal, 24*, 128–145.

Rule, B. G., & Ferguson, T. J. (1986). The effects of media violence on attitudes, emotions, and cognitions. *Journal of Social Issues, 42*(3), 29–50.

Sacco, V. (1982). The effects of mass media on perceptions of crime: A reanalysis of the issues. *Pacific Sociological Review, 25*(4), 475–493.

Schmierbach, M. (2010). "Killing spree": Exploring the connection between competitive game play and aggressive cognition. *Communication Research, 37*, 256–274.

Schneider, E. F., Lang, A., Shin, M., & Bradley, S. D. (2004). Death with a story: How story impacts emotional, motivational, and physiological responses to first-person shooter video games. *Human Communication Research, 30*, 361–375.

Schneider, J. P. (2000). Effects of cybersex addiction on the family: Results of a survey. *Sexual Addiction & Compulsivity, 7*, 31–58.

Schutte, N., Malouff, J., Post-Garden, J., & Rodasta, A. (1988). Effects of playing videogames on children's aggressive and other behaviors. *Journal of Applied Social Psychology, 18*, 454–460.

Senn, C. Y., & Desmarais, S. (2004). Impact of interaction with a partner or friend on the exposure effects of pornography and erotica. *Violence and Victims, 19*(6), 645–658.

Sherman, B. L., & Dominick, J. K. (1986). Violence and sex in music videos: TV and rock 'n' roll. *Journal of Communication, 36*(1), 79–93.

Sherry, J. L. (2001). The effects of violent video games on aggression: A meta-analysis. *Human Communication Research, 27*, 409–431.

Singer, M. I., Slovak, K., Frierson, T., & York, P. (1998). Viewing preferences, symptoms of psychological trauma, and violent behaviors among children who watch television. *Journal of the American Academy of Child and Adolescent Psychiatry, 37*(10), 1041–1048.

Slater, M. D. (2003). Alienation, aggression and sensation seeking as predictors of adolescent use of violent film, computer and website content. *Journal of Communication, 53*, 105–121.

Slater, M. D., Henry, K. L., Swaim, R. C., & Anderson, L. L. (2003). Violent media content and aggressiveness in adolescents. *Communication Research, 30*, 713–736.

Slone, M. (2000). Responses to media coverage of terrorism. *Journal of Conflict Resolution, 44,* 508–522.

Slotsve, T., Carmen, A., Sarver, M., & Villareal-Watkins, R. J. (2008). Television violence and aggression: A retrospective study. *Southwest Journal of Criminal Justice, 5*(1), 22–49.

Soulliere, D. M. (2003). Prime-time murder: Presentations of murder on popular television justice programs. *Journal of Criminal Justice and Popular Culture, 10*(1), 12–38.

Sparks, G. G., & Cantor, J. (1984). Developmental differences in fright responses to a television program depicting a character transformation. *Journal of Broadcasting & Electronic Media, 30,* 309–323.

Strasburger, V. C., & Donnerstein, E. (1999). Children, adolescents, and the media: Issues and solutions. *Pediatrics, 103*(1), 129–139.

Surbeck, E. (1975). Young children's emotional reactions to TV violence: The effect of children's perceptions of reality. *Dissertation Abstracts International, 35,* 5139-A.

Tamborini, R., Eastin, M. S., Skalski, P., Lachlan, K., Fediuk, T. A., & Brady, R. (2004). Violent virtual video games and hostile thoughts. *Journal of Broadcasting & Electronic Media, 48,* 335–357.

Thomas, M. H. (1982). Physiological arousal, exposure to a relatively lengthy aggressive film, and aggressive behavior. *Journal of Research in Personality, 16,* 72–81.

Thomas, M. H., Horton, R. W., Lippencott, E. C., & Drabman, R. S. (1977). Desensitization to portrayals of real-life aggression as a function of exposure to television violence. *Journal of Personality and Social Psychology, 35,* 450–458.

Van Mierlo, J., & van den Bulck, J. (2004). Benchmarking the cultivation approach to video game effects: A comparison of the correlates of TV viewing and game play. *Journal of Adolescence, 27*(1), 97–111.

Vega, V., & Malamuth, N. M. (2007). Predicting sexual aggression: The role of pornography in the context of general and specific risk factors. *Aggressive Behavior, 33*(2), 104–117.

Weaver, J. B. (1991). Are "slasher" horror films sexually violent? A content analysis. *Journal of Broadcasting & Electronic Media, 35,* 385–392.

Weisz, M. G., & Earls, C. M. (1995). The effects of exposure to filmed sexual violence on attitudes toward rape. *Journal of Interpersonal Violence, 10,* 71–84.

Williams, D., Martins, N., Consalvo, M., & Ivory, J. D. (2009). The virtual census: Representations of gender, race and age in video games. *New Media & Society, 11*(5), 815–834.

Williams, D., & Skoric, M. (2005). Internet fantasy violence: A test of aggression in an online game. *Communication Monographs, 72,* 217–233.

Williams, R. B., & Clippinger, C. A. (2002). Aggression, competition, and computer games: Computer and human opponents. *Computers in Human Behavior, 18,* 495–506.

Wilson, B. J. (2008). Media and children's aggression, fear, and altruism. *The Future of Children, 18*(1), 87–118.

Yokota, F., & Thompson, K. M. (2000, May 24/31). Violence in G-rated animated films. *Journal of the American Medical Association, 283,* 2716–2720.

Zillmann, D. (1971). Excitation transfer in communication-mediated aggressive behavior. *Journal of Experimental Social Psychology, 7,* 419–434.

Zillmann, D., & Bryant, J. (1982). Pornography, sex callousness, and the trivialization of rape. *Journal of Communication, 32,* 10–21.

Zillmann, D., & Weaver, J. B. (1997). Psychoticism in the effect of prolonged exposure to gratuitous media violence on the acceptance of violence as a preferred means of conflict resolution. *Personality and Individual Differences, 22*(5), 613–627.

Index

Entry titles and their page numbers are in **bold**.